Creating Consumers

Carolyn M. Goldstein

Creating Consumers

HOME ECONOMISTS IN
TWENTIETH-CENTURY AMERICA

THE UNIVERSITY OF NORTH CAROLINA PRESS

CHAPEL HILL

THIS VOLUME WAS PUBLISHED WITH THE ASSISTANCE OF THE GREENSBORO WOMEN'S FUND OF THE UNIVERSITY OF NORTH CAROLINA PRESS. Founding Contributors: Linda Arnold Carlisle, Sally Schindel Cone, Anne Faircloth, Bonnie McElveen Hunter, Linda Bullard Jennings, Janice J. Kerley (in honor of Margaret Supplee Smith), Nancy Rouzer May, and Betty Hughes Nichols.

Set in Arnhem and Glytus by Tseng Information Systems, Inc.

The paper in this book meets the guidelines for permanence and durability of the Committee on Production Guidelines for Book Longevity of the Council on Library Resources.

The University of North Carolina Press has been a member of the Green Press Initiative since 2003.

Library of Congress Cataloging-in-Publication Data
Goldstein, Carolyn M., 1962–
Creating consumers : home economists in twentieth-century America / Carolyn M. Goldstein.
p. cm.
Includes bibliographical references and index.
ISBN 978-0-8078-3553-1 (hardback)
1. Home economics—Vocational guidance—United States—History—20th century.
2. Consumer education—United States—History—20th century. 3. Feminism—United States—History—20th century.
I. Title.
TX654.G65 2012
640.023—dc23   2011044467

Parts of this book have been reprinted in revised form from "From Service to Sales: Home Economics in Light and Power, 1920–1940," *Technology and Culture* 38.1 (1997): 121–52, © 1997 by the Society for the History of Technology, reprinted by permission of The Johns Hopkins University Press; "Part of the Package: Home Economists in the Consumer Products Industries, 1920–1940," in *Rethinking Home Economics: Women and the History of a Profession*, edited by Sarah Stage and Virginia B. Vincenti, © 1997 by Cornell University, reprinted by permission of Cornell University Press; and "Educating Consumers, Representing Consumers: Reforming the Marketplace through Scientific Expertise at the Bureau of Home Economics, United States Department of Agriculture, 1923–1940," in *The Expert Consumer*, edited by Matthew Hilton, Alain Chatriot, and Marie-Emmanuelle Chessel, © 2006, reprinted by permission of Ashgate Publishing Company.

16 15 14 13 12   5 4 3 2 1

Contents

Illustrations

Acknowledgments

As a young girl in New York State in the 1960s, I always looked forward to visiting the State Fair in Syracuse, where my grandmother, Helen Bull Vandervort, directed the women's building. Art displays and cooking demonstrations filled the halls, and I took pride in my grandmother's command of this exciting public event. She had studied home economics at Cornell in the 1920s and raised two children before taking this job. Although I did not quite understand what home economics was, I always knew it was important to her. Helen's passion for her field—and the dynamic role she played building institutions in her community—sparked my curiosity about the early days of home economics. My mother, Phebe Vandervort Goldstein, attended the same college program in the 1950s. She became an elementary school teacher and then a homemaker and mother, who also devoted much of her adult life to advocating for arts and education. While neither woman pursued the type of home economics career I explore in this book, both taught me much about home economics and its place in American culture.

In addition, I owe an immense intellectual debt to a community of colleagues that helped me launch this project and sustain it at various stages. In graduate school at the University of Delaware, I found a group of teachers and fellow students who shared and nurtured my interest in the modern material world. I was extremely privileged to have had Anne Boylan, David Hounshell, and Susan Smulyan as my advisers. I want to thank Joan Jacobs Brumberg and Francille Firebaugh for organizing a conference in 1991 that brought me into dialogue with a number of scholars working on home economics, and Sarah Stage and Virginia Vincenti for editing the resulting publication, *Rethinking Home Economics*. I am equally grateful to Ruth Oldenziel, Arwen Mohun, Nina Lerman, and John Staudenmaier for including my work in the special issue of *Technology and Culture* on gender and technology, and to Marie-Emmanuelle Chessel, Alain Chatriot, and Matthew Hilton for convening the "In the Name of the Consumer" conference in Paris in 2004 and editing two collections of essays, one in French and the other in English. This book benefited from the conversations with scholars brought together in these three venues.

My further thanks go to Jane Becker, Marie-Emmanuelle Chessel, Jacqueline Dirks, Steven Lubar, Elizabeth White Nelson, Shelley Nickles, Mark Rose, Doug Rossinow, Margaret Rossiter, Peggy Shaffer, Susan Smulyan, Susan Strasser, and Mary Yeager for reading drafts at various stages of the project; to Rima Apple, Kathleen Babbitt, Molly Berger, Nancy Berlage, Regina Blaszczyk, Eileen Boris, Gail Cooper, Jacqueline Dirks, Robert Friedel, Laurel Graham, Mark Hamin, Amy Hardin, Jan Jennings, Ronald Kline, Suzanne Kolm, Nina Lerman, Ann McCleary, Charles McGovern, Arwen Mohun, Mary Neth, Ruth Oldenziel, Lisa Mae Robinson, Janice Rutherford, Laura Shapiro, Susan Strasser, Joan Sullivan, Mary Summers, Elizabeth Toon, Peter van Overbeeke, and Bill Yeingst for sharing ideas, citations, or drafts of their own works in progress; and to Monique Bourque, Joseph Corn, Ruth Schwartz Cowan, Deborah Douglas, Kathy Franz, Alison Isenberg, Michael Kucher, Tim LeCain, Peter Liebhold, Julie Nicoletta, Joy Parr, Kathy Peiss, Deborah Shelkrot Permut, Kathy Steen, Joel Tarr, Emily Thompson, Tom Valente, Max van Balgooy, and Susan Williams for general support and encouragement.

For assistance with research, I am grateful to many curators, librarians, and archivists. I would like to thank the staffs of the Hagley Museum and Library; the library and Archives Center at the National Museum of American History; the Schlesinger Library, especially Ellen Shea; the Rockefeller Archives Center; the Chicago History Museum; the Cornell University Division of Rare and Manuscript Collections; Cornell's College of Human Ecology; the National Archives; the National Agricultural Library; the University of Chicago Archives; the Museum of Science and Industry; Teachers College Archive, Columbia University; and the History Factory. I am particularly grateful to Anne Roess at the Peoples Gas, Light, and Coke Company; Ed Rider at Procter & Gamble; and Susan Watson and Gladys Gary Vaughn at the American Home Economics Association (AHEA), now the American Association of Family and Consumer Sciences, in Alexandria, Virginia. I owe special gratitude to Marlissa Bannister at the headquarters of the AHEA's Home Economics in Business Section in Westerville, Ohio, and to Connie Cahill, who hosted me in her home while the group's records were stored there.

I am indebted to a number of institutions that made this book possible. Grants from the Hagley Program, jointly sponsored by the Hagley Museum and Library and the Department of History at the University of Delaware, the University of Delaware's Center for Research on Women, the Smithsonian Institution's National Museum of American History, the Arthur and Elizabeth Schlesinger Library on the History of Women in America, and the Rockefeller Archive Center provided access to research collections and supported my work on the manuscript. A History of Home Economics Fellowship from the Office of the Dean in the College of Human Ecology at Cornell University, a postdoctoral fellowship from the American Council of Learned Societies, and a visiting scholarship at the Schlesinger Library allowed me to conduct additional research and revise the manuscript. A leave of absence from my job at Lowell National Historical Park provided time to complete the revisions.

Several institutions and organizations provided me with opportunities to present my work in its developing stages: the Hagley Museum and Library's Center for the History of Business, Technology, and Society; the Smithsonian Institution's National Museum of American History Tuesday Colloquium; the Ninth Berkshire Conference on the History of Women; the Winterthur Museum, Library, and Gardens; the Social Science History Association; the Philadelphia College of Medicine; the Society for the History of Technology; the American Studies Association; the Schlesinger Library; and the Belle Van Zuylen Institute, University of Amsterdam, in the Netherlands.

At the University of North Carolina Press, Chuck Grench guided this project from an early stage. I am thankful to Chuck for his continued support and especially appreciative of the outside readers, Susan Levine and Nancy Tomes, for providing thoughtful, constructive feedback throughout the revision process. I also acknowledge the assistance of the editorial team.

Finally, my family has supported me with endless patience and faith. I am grateful to my parents, Sidney Goldstein and Phebe Goldstein, and to my brother, David Goldstein, for cheering me on at every stage. Herbert Haber proofread at least one full draft; he and Barbara Haber stepped in to provide meals and childcare when finishing the book took me away from family responsibilities. Through their questions, my sons, Eli and Ben, helped me keep my eye on the big picture. My deepest thanks go to Jon Haber, my husband, who generously brought his wide array of talents and natural curiosity to the many drafts he read.

Introduction

In the late nineteenth century, as the economic function of American homes shifted from producing goods and services to consuming them, a group of middle-class women—and a few men—launched an educational reform movement to guide homemakers in this transition. Widely known as "domestic scientists," they organized a meeting in Lake Placid, New York, in 1899 to propose a new field of study that would promote "the betterment of the home." For almost ten years, a diverse group of educators, writers, and scientists—totaling about 700 in all—gathered annually to outline a curriculum for the nation's schools and universities that would prepare women to perform domestic work more efficiently and manage household budgets more economically. They called their field "home economics." In December 1908, the Lake Placid attendees formed the American Home Economics Association (AHEA), which was dedicated to "the improvement of living conditions in the home, the institutional household, and the community."[1]

For women of my generation, who grew up in the 1960s and 1970s, home economics was about learning to sew aprons and to cook "pigs in a blanket." Our experiences in secondary school home economics classes made it easy for many of us to dismiss the whole field as trivial. Raised in a political era that characterized domesticity as insignificant and consumption as wasteful, we ridiculed home economics as a silly—or sinister—vestige of our mothers' and grandmothers' pasts. For feminist historians seeking to understand the forces and factors that conspired to limit women's opportunities in the public sphere, home economics was an easy target. In blaming home economists for confining women to the domestic sphere, this type of analysis reinforced assumptions that home economics was concerned only with private matters of the home. In addition, scholars of consumer capitalism, influenced by the Frankfurt school, characterized women as passive in relationship to historical change. For several decades, these trends in popular culture and in academic circles combined to render invisible the role that many women, including home economists, played in shaping important aspects of American consumer culture.[2]

For Americans today, experiences with consumption—involving careful or impulsive choices, promises fulfilled or dashed, and, above all, dizzying abundance—make it difficult to unpack the origins of our modern consumer society. Whereas historians in the 1970s and 1980s tended to explain consumer culture as a conspiracy in which advertisers exerted power over passive consumers, most scholars now see American consumer society as the result of complex processes in which consumers, experts, managers, and political leaders all played a role—not equally, but actively nonetheless. A few of the most recent historical studies of consumption in the United States point to the degree of contestation and debate that was in play during the development of American consumer capitalism. Lizabeth Cohen's *A Consumers' Republic* (2003), Charles McGovern's *Sold American* (2006), and Lawrence Glickman's *Buying Power* (2009) all highlight the push and pull among competing visions of American consumer society, and the range of critiques and activist approaches proposed as reforms of or alternatives to the dominant corporate capitalist institutions.[3] *Creating Consumers* contributes to these discussions by examining a group of women who, throughout most of the twentieth century, sought to influence homemakers, products, manufacturers, and retailers alike.

The stereotypical image of home economics belies the reality that home economics was a diverse movement whose members had ambitious goals for themselves not only as teachers, but also as reformers and professionals.[4] Like many Americans today, early home economists grappled with a consumer marketplace that seemed to be overwhelmingly complex and out of control. Keen observers of modern consumer society as it emerged at the turn of the twentieth century, they initially came together to direct and control women's consumption, and to define a place for consumption in modern, middle-class American life. Together with other Progressive Era reformers, home economists embraced the promise of new scientific and technical advancement to improve the lives of homemakers, fueled by concern over the quality of modern goods and fears that women of all classes would not know how to function in the chaos of the burgeoning consumer marketplace. As white, middle-class women, they strove to preserve nineteenth-century ideas about morality that were cast in their own image.

Ellen Swallow Richards and the first generation of home economists were equally committed to fulfilling vocational goals for themselves. At a moment when women's identity was shifting—and the very term *consumer* was being defined—home economists staked a set of professional claims as technical experts about consumer goods and consumer behavior. The opportunities they found as participants in and shapers of American consumer society were based on contemporary ideas about women's and men's identity, the predominance of corporate capitalism, and evolving notions of the role of government, experts, and other players in the changing marketplace. In seeking simultaneously to shape consumer society and establish themselves as experts within it, home economists took on a shifting set of identities. Sometimes they functioned as consumer educators, sometimes as consumer representatives, and often they played both roles. As a result, home economists assumed a range of relationships with private enterprises, government institutions, and homemakers. By exploring these often contradictory relationships—and the conflicts that they sparked—this book invites readers to consider the tensions within a movement dedicated to shaping the consumer marketplace on behalf of consumers, a movement that also played an important role in empowering consumer capitalist institutions.

In contrast to nineteenth-century domestic scientists who emphasized efficient production within the home, the first generation of home economists shaped their movement to address the growing importance of consumption for the nation's homemakers at the turn of the century.[5] Through their initial experiences developing improved housekeeping methods, home economists became aware that industrialization involved social and technological changes that created a world in which decisions about what to buy constituted an increasing portion of the work of household management. As developments in consumer products industries expanded the body of knowledge regarding household goods, home economists transformed their preoccupation with efficient production into a concern for what I call *rational consumption*. Drawing on science to help women solve practical problems, early home economists sought to teach women how to buy as well as how to make household goods, lessons that were part of a larger mission to shape the culture of the emerging middle class through a focus on the standard of living of individual homes and families. Home economists found support for this social and cultural agenda from Progressive educational leaders and reformers looking to modernize agriculture and all aspects of rural life in America. As professors and agricultural extension agents, home economists developed curricula to "train" American women in what they called the principles of "intelligent buying" and "wise consumption." To support their educational program and secure an academic niche within institutions of higher learning, home economists created a research agenda centered on the expanding scope of the scientific and technological content of the home.[6]

In the first two decades of the twentieth century, home economics was centered in the academy. But an influx of federal funds in the mid-1910s had the unintended result of broadening home economics education. The expansion of land-grant institutions and private college programs generated a large supply of home economists, many with graduate degrees, who found a new array of career opportunities in the 1920s.[7] By carrying out teaching and research about consumption in a growing institutional network of schools and agricultural extension offices, home economists attracted the attention of male leaders in government and business institutions who (assuming that most consumers were women) sought to understand the impact of new household goods and services from the perspective of female users. Home economists stood ready to supply access to "the woman's viewpoint," a valuable commodity to many mystified male managers. Home economists' scientific training, especially in the field of nutrition, and their self-professed ability to "train" consumers provided further reassurance to political and business leaders who sought to control production and distribution while simultaneously inventing new ways of communicating with consumers.[8] At a time when the essential elements and practices of the ideal home were in flux and consumer capitalism seemed inherently irrational, home economists' claims that it could and should be rational offered the promise of a roadmap, welcome to producers and consumers alike.[9] The endorsement of home economists' expertise in nutrition and food consumption by U.S. Food Administration director Herbert Hoover during World War I allowed dozens of women in the field to assume prominent roles in the agency's food conservation campaigns, where they earned a reputation for their ability to influence the buying habits of the nation's homemakers.

Soon after the war's end, officials at the U.S. Department of Agriculture (USDA) and managers of consumer products firms took steps to draw more deliberately on home economists' knowledge of consumers and consumer goods, giving women in the field opportunities to move beyond the academy and become not just consumer educators but also consumer representatives within wider institutional frameworks. One such institution was the USDA's Bureau of Home Economics (BHE). Established by agricultural policymakers in 1923 to create markets for farm products in the midst of an agricultural depression and to modernize rural life through the newly established Extension Service, the BHE gave home economists an official platform from which to research consumer products from the user's perspective and to investigate consumer behavior. Under the bureau's first director, Louise Stanley, a pioneering generation of home economists used this government agency as an information clearinghouse to serve consumers and reform the marketplace for consumer goods by advocating for more reliable goods and retail methods.

Industry provided a second institutional niche for home economists during the interwar era, as consumer products manufacturers and utility companies created new kinds of jobs for home economists inside their operations. Corporate home economics and home service departments became standard tools for helping manufacturers and power companies understand consumers, control demand, and comply with or preempt government regulations. As company employees, home economists functioned as mediators who could tell engineers what homemakers wanted and needed, helping to test, evaluate, and improve products in development. They also proved effective instructors in new foods and household equipment, writing recipes and instruction manuals about how to use these new goods in the context of everyday life. By projecting a friendly, human image of utility companies through live demonstrations, home economists assisted private power companies in a massive public relations campaign and technical education initiative. In the process, they helped define new products and technological systems as essential components of modern American middle-class homes.

While the majority of women educated in home economics became homemakers, educators, or extension workers, by the early 1920s mastery in what University of Chicago home economics professor Faith M. McAuley called the "'Science' of Consumption"[10] won a smaller group of home economists jobs as guides to a complex modern world of newly emerging consumer products. This elite corps of home economists in government and business served as the nation's leading authorities about domestic consumption in the interwar period. After 1940, however, home economists' expertise gradually became less important to the continued development of the nation's consumer economy. During World War II, home economists in the Bureau of Home Economics and in industry once again worked to identify consumer goods with patriotic values, linking consumption with citizenship, but in a less singular role than they had played during World War I. After 1945, home economists in government and business faced a series of challenges to their claims to possess knowledge about consumer products and to represent "typical" consumers. With the growth of new consumer and feminist movements in the 1960s, most home economists fell behind the progressive vanguard of social and cultural change, a trend which led to the increasing marginalization of home economics and its once unique collective identity as a source of consumer expertise and advocacy.

By examining home economists' struggles to shape consumers and products as well as to create a vocational niche in modern American consumer society, this book charts the rise and fall of a women's profession from its origins at the turn of the twentieth century to its virtual disappearance by the 1970s. Looking closely at the four decades between World War I and the early 1960s, when home economists' employment in the Bureau of Home Economics and in corporations provided a cohort of women with a relatively protected niche at the center of the marketplace for consumer goods, this study considers how home economists' efforts to reform consumption influenced and reflected the formation of modern consumer society itself. For this historical moment, and from within two key institutional arenas—government and business—home economists served as liminal actors in three interrelated historical processes: (1) technological change in the home and the rise of a new kind of consumer market for household goods; (2) the changing role of the state in relation to consumer capitalism; and (3) the cultural influence of gender ideology and the central role of women in the first two processes.

To investigate home economists' experience with professionalization is to explore their key position in the development of American consumer capitalism. First, the central role of home economists in bringing about technological change in American homes provides important insights into how new products were developed and marketed. With the industrialization of the home, women saw the introduction of mass-produced utensils and packaged foods and the availability of gas and electric utilities in urban areas, and eventually women began to face a new series of practical concerns regarding what to make at home and what to buy. As families increasingly purchased rather than manufactured household goods, including packaged foods and household appliances that had never before existed, they interfaced in new ways with commercial institutions. This complex transformation of both the marketplace and the home took place over several decades and involved many different types of actors. Especially as the elements of the modern American kitchen became defined, home economists helped shape the physical dimension of goods, providing engineers of new packaged foods and appliances with insight into what homemakers wanted. As teachers, researchers, government representatives, and corporate employees, they also helped imbue these new goods with social meanings based on the values of efficiency, economy, sanitation, and healthfulness, establishing new products as necessities of everyday living. In this sense, home economists participated in the "social shaping" of technological artifacts by suggesting stable meanings for consumer goods (and consumption itself) at a moment of social and cultural restructuring. Industrial innovation was also accompanied by new techniques for businesses to understand, communicate, and sell to consumers. As participants in both product development and marketing, home economists served as both "coproducers"[11] and consumer representatives, a dual role that reveals the interplay between how new goods emerged, the terms by which users adopted them, and how consumer society took form in relation to changing technology.

Second, home economists' experiences during World War I and within the Bureau of Home Economics beginning in 1923 shed new light on the role of the state in the development of American consumer society. Cohen's landmark synthesis, *A Consumers' Republic*, describes the development of top-down government reforms in response to consumer activism in the twentieth century. Cohen begins her story in the 1930s, when consumers became understood not just as economic players in the marketplace but also as political actors, or "citizen consumers," needing protection by and representation within government. Charting the rise of a greater regulatory role in the New Deal, Cohen highlights a major shift after World War II, when a "purchaser consumer" paradigm dominated and private market mechanisms prevailed. These purchasers became politicized once more with the rise of a "third-wave consumer movement" in the 1950s and 1960s.[12] *Creating Consumers* complicates this narrative by exploring the interplay of citizenship and consumption through the lens of an earlier period—the first three decades of the twentieth century—when home economists' efforts at consumer education and consumer representation helped shape not only American consumers' experiences but also their cultural and political identities. In what Charles McGovern has characterized as a multifaceted and contested political economy of mass consumption, home economists were early pioneers in the development of state policies and public propaganda regarding consumption.[13] With the majority of the nation's population still residing outside of the growing cities at the beginning of the twentieth century, public officials initially understood the consumer to be a rural woman. While state and federal governments generally favored free enterprise and the growth of large corporations, agricultural policy promoted consumer goods in the name of modernization, with the goal of keeping families on the farm. The expansion of land-grant colleges and the agricultural extension service aimed at disseminating modern methods of farm production. As the home economics field emerged, male political leaders relied on home economics education and home demonstration work to promote a domestic equivalent among rural homemakers. State advocacy for participating in the commercial market and purchasing manufactured household goods—and government endorsement of home economists as consumer experts—took root in this context of a developing modern agricultural establishment.[14]

But even as they promoted mass consumption, home economists also used their government platform to attempt to reform the marketplace on behalf of homemakers, acting as both educators and representatives of consumers and advocating for better, more reliable goods. As participants in World War I home-front activities and in Herbert Hoover's "associative state" from within the Bureau of Home Economics in the 1920s, home economists drew public attention to issues of product quality and value by publishing guides to the selection of goods and urging manufacturers to enhance the utility of their products and to label them more clearly. Many New Deal reformers built on these initiatives and frequently relied on the bureau to educate and speak for women consumers. Home economists' influence on the political economy of mass consumption persisted into the Cold War and beyond. Just as Glickman's *Buying Power* points to the need to examine a range of forms of consumer activism in American history, this book broadens historians' understanding of the multiple ways that consumers were constructed and represented in the public policy of mass consumption by focusing attention on an influential social group that has been acknowledged but relatively unexamined.[15]

Finally, home economists' ability to carve out a niche of expertise within government and business between the realms of production and consumption of household goods highlights the central place of gender and women in the formation of modern American consumer society. Home economists' roles as shapers of both products and consumer behavior stemmed from a specific gender ideology that constructed the new, modern consumer as a white, middle-class woman. The notion that domesticity was a separate sphere for women and that buying products for the home was their special responsibility dated at least as far back as the early Industrial Revolution, but it gained authority in the 1890s and took on new power in the 1920s. Mark Swiencicki has demonstrated that men, too, had distinct identities as consumers in the expanding market culture of this period, primarily purchasing consumer services outside the home. Further, married homemakers were not likely to exercise purchasing decisions without consulting their spouses. Although the common wisdom that women were responsible for 85 percent of purchases in the marketplace seems to have had little or no scientific basis, it did exert a powerful pull on manufacturers and associated "agents" (such as advertisers) trying to understand the characteristics, needs, and desires of "Mrs. Consumer." Sociologist Michael Schudson points to the double meaning of consumers as female at this time: on the one hand, they were emotionally vulnerable; on the other hand, they were capable of being budget-conscious. The identity of the female consumer was highly contested, and "discovering" her became an ongoing challenge for mostly male businesspeople.[16] While Charlotte Perkins Gilman argued that women should shun their identities as consumers altogether, most home economists seized on the dominant ideology of female consumption and found within it opportunities for social reform and professional advancement.[17] On this basis, home economists were some of the first women to help create private corporate mechanisms for internalizing the needs and desires of certain groups of consumers, and shaping market behavior.

The creation of the Women's Bureau and the Children's Bureau in the Progressive Era constituted a "maternalist" welfare state that placed female social workers in leading roles shaping public policy with respect to women's labor and motherhood.[18] This reform spirit, persisting after women won the vote in 1920 and coupled with the equation of "woman" and "consumer," similarly informed home economists' influential role in the creation of the Bureau of Home Economics and in the development of its research agenda. Home economists' public roles in business and government were ridden with ironies stemming from contemporary gender ideologies that carefully circumscribed the basis for women's participation and that were, in turn, reinforced by home economists' work in these spheres. Yet under the guise of domesticity, home economists exerted a powerful influence on the development of consumer products and on modern American consumer society. This book seeks to understand the diverse and often contradictory ways home economists participated in the consumer revolution's sexual division of labor.

WHAT KIND OF HISTORICAL actors were home economists in these major transformations in American life? Although home economists were never autonomous actors in the twentieth-century "culture of consumption," interacting as they did with corporate organizations on subordinate terms, they were active participants in shaping this culture. *Creating Consumers* explores home economists' attempts to shape American homemakers' identities and experiences as consumers, and their efforts to establish themselves as professionals in the expanding consumer marketplace. It seeks to understand the specific set of circumstances that enabled home economists to establish what I call a *mediating role* in the development and marketing of consumer goods. It examines the ideology and material culture that this small but influential group of women brought to their work in the arenas of government and business, and the impact home economists had, as mediators, on the physical form and cultural meanings of everyday household goods. The book argues that home economists—as teachers of rational consumption, as corporate employees, and as self-appointed consumer representatives—played a central role in the development of middle-class consumer culture in twentieth-century America.

Experts of all kinds led the creation of institutions devoted to new ways of making and selling goods around 1900. With a significant restructuring of American society around consumption, manufacturing engineers, advertising agents, salespeople, marketing managers, magazine writers and editors, retail store managers, industrial designers, and reformers all experimented with new ways of producing, selling, and interpreting goods to diverse groups of consumers. These specialists helped create consumer capitalism by linking a myriad of cultural institutions to the aims of business and helping large corporations move into the daily lives of Americans. Historian William Leach calls these individuals "a new group of brokers" who—during "a century of intermediaries"—facilitated "the movement of images, money, and information" in the new consumer culture.[19] These new brokers helped government agencies, business institutions, and consumers create new ways of communicating with one another. Business enterprises relied not only on advertisements in mass-circulation magazines but also on a wide range of publications, including promotional brochures and instructional booklets, to spread their messages. Included in the communication mix were live demonstrations, sales and marketing campaigns, and new retail environments designed to reach consumers. Nothing about this process was straightforward, intuitive, or predestined. Company managers did not know what people wanted to buy or how to generate demand for new products. Consumers did not automatically embrace every new commercial offering. Some products and promotional techniques succeeded, while others failed. Corporate capitalism required a great deal of fine-tuning to determine how to correlate supply with demand, to provide consumers with reasons for buying new goods, and to supply producers with knowledge of what consumers wanted. Exchanges among this new class of brokers facilitated communication among manufacturers, purchasers, and intermediaries and, in the process, helped formulate the modern notion of a consumer as an individual who both purchased and used mass-produced commodities—a new kind of actor in twentieth-century corporate capitalism.[20]

Home economists belonged to this "brokering class," and they shared most of the defining characteristics of the brokers Leach describes. I prefer to call them *mediators*, however, because the latter term conveys the unique relationship that home economists assumed in relation to the market, distinct from other categories of broker. Unlike advertisers and salespeople, home economists had a secondary, rather than a primary, relationship to the market. While some of the home economists working in business shared the goals of their corporate employers, they did not see themselves as mere servants to commercial enterprise. Instead, because they were trained within a culture of reform, they sought to answer a higher calling, to achieve a broader social mission: to educate consumers while reforming the production and distribution of domestic goods on their behalf. Home economists involved themselves in the market not merely to help business turn a profit, but also as a means to achieve their greater social goals. Women who were educated in home economics and then joined corporations in the late 1910s and early 1920s approached their work idealistically and did not identify themselves purely as businesswomen. This view reflected the reality that, even as the first generation of home economists participated in the modern consumer capitalist economy, they were usually at least one step removed from the cash nexus itself, from actually making deals. In this sense, the term *mediation* comes closest to the language with which home economists described their relationship to business and government institutions as well as consumers—a self-image based on being interpreters, translators, diplomats, or ambassadors.[21] *Mediation* further conveys the mutuality of interests that most home economists believed existed among the many actors in the marketplace for consumer goods.

Understanding home economists as mediators allows us to consider not only the commercialization of their work but also the creative role they played in facilitating negotiations among producers, retailers, and consumers.[22] Home economists brought a specific type of gendered expertise to American culture at a time of technological and social transformation. The term *mediation* reflects the reality that home economists did not fit neatly in the category of either production or consumption; rather, they operated as key actors in a dynamic process of bridging these two worlds. Ronald Kline characterizes home economists working in utility companies as "agents of modernity," and Mark Rose calls them "agents of diffusion."[23] While home economists did serve as agents in ushering in new, modern goods and meanings, the term *mediation* helps describe how home economists facilitated exchange of information in multiple directions, not only from corporate organizations to consumers but also among manufacturers, power companies, government agencies, voluntary associations, women's organizations, and consumers themselves—a wide array of individuals, groups, and institutions who came together around 1900, as historian Olivier Zunz has written, "to engineer and manage a new America" centered around consumption.[24] The boundaries between these spheres were in flux as modern consumer society took form in the United States, and home economists performed the important technological and cultural work of both solidifying and connecting these various audiences.[25] At what Ruth Schwartz Cowan calls the "consumption junction," home economists played a leading role generating and exchanging knowledge about the home and knowledge about products and, in the process, helped make way for the introduction of new domestic technologies.[26]

Home economists in government and industry combined their identities as reformers, educators, and researchers in ways that transcended the scope of any single one of these roles. By performing work that defied easy categorization, home economists mediated in two principal ways: first, by generating new knowledge about household goods from a user's perspective, and second, by translating between consumers and producers.

Inside the world of production, home economists developed a distinct "science of consumption" in relation to male designers, engineers, and farmers, a discipline through which they defined the needs of the "ultimate consumer" or "end user" in materialist terms, helping them provide insight into the development of marketable goods that production-oriented engineers did not supply. Within government, primarily at the Bureau of Home Economics, home economists' user-oriented approach to researching both commercial and agricultural goods allowed them not only to instruct homemakers in the selection, use, and maintenance of household products, but also to propose standard specifications, with government imprimatur, for the production and merchandising of such goods. Business organizations similarly relied on home economists to provide a user's perspective on the products they created and sold. Home economists in business used the information they generated about their company's products not only to advise homemakers about how to use them, but also to advise engineers about how to design and improve them. Their contributions led to incremental adjustments to product features that were nonetheless significant to producers and consumers alike. In an era when scientific market research, product testing, and consumer surveys were yet to be fully developed or embraced by manufacturers, home economists played the critical role of providing manufacturers with information regarding the needs of their current and potential customers, the new emerging class of consumers.

In addition, home economists in government and business mediated by facilitating two-way communication between large corporate bureaucracies and the mass of individual homemakers.[27] By serving as professional, "typical" consumers themselves, they enabled government agencies and corporations to imagine "the average female consumer" and to internalize "her" demands inside their operations. When home economists represented the needs of consumers to managers, this communication took on many forms, including reports of consumers' written requests and complaints, informal information gathering, or full-blown, formal social-scientific surveys. While often rigorous and systematic, home economists' interpretations of consumer information had a symbolic, subjective quality as well. Home economists did as much to *construct* ideal consumers as they did to *discover* who consumers actually were and what they needed or desired. Home economists' own assumptions about women's needs were embedded in their representations of "the woman's viewpoint."

As mediators, home economists had a special relationship to the middle class. Robert Wiebe, Marina Moskowitz, and numerous other historians have pointed to the rise of a new middle class in early-twentieth-century America and to the central importance of experts in shaping middle-class culture and aligning it to modern consumer society. Janice Radway argues convincingly that World War I was a pivotal moment when experts on a wide range of topics gained cultural power, reaching middle-class readers largely through the increasingly prevalent mass circulation magazines. In this context, home economists deliberately aimed their prescriptive messages about modern, efficient, and healthy homemaking at this new middle class in formation, which they imagined in their own image. They found a receptive audience among many of its young female members who expressed interest in learning about how to improve their homes, spend their leisure time, and make decisions about what to buy, what to make at home, and even what books to read.[28] This target audience tended to be college-educated, upwardly mobile, and first-time owners of houses as well as the household appliances and food products with which to fill them. While women did not respond uniformly to home economists' messages during this era, a significant segment of the population embraced values of sanitation, health, cleanliness, economy, and efficiency as hallmarks of a new identity, as secure points of reference through which to demonstrate that they belonged to this social group. The high attendance at live demonstrations in the home service departments of utility companies and the large print runs of government and corporate publications generated by home economists suggests that many women found home economists' instructions valuable. Home economists' arrival on the scene around 1900, and their success in establishing a collective niche for themselves in modern consumer society, calls our attention to the cultural role that they played in not only paving the way for new commercial goods but also in shaping a consumer culture that depended on a wide range of experts to educate, represent, and protect average citizens.[29]

Home economists' influence was uneven. While they exerted a broad and powerful impact on consumer culture, they confronted many constraints when working within large commercial and state bureaucracies. Although home economists never achieved what Margaret Justin, dean of Home Economics at Kansas State Agricultural College, called the "distant goal" of transforming American homemakers into rational consumers, they proved influential enough to create a place for their ideas about scientific cookery, cleanliness, wise purchasing, and functional design at the center of American middle-class culture. Through teaching and research, as well as lobbying via the AHEA and other women's clubs and organizations, home economists played a key role in shaping popular expectations of what historian Lizabeth Cohen has termed the "Consumer's Republic, an economy, culture, and politics built around the promises of mass consumption." As such, home economists' influence moved in conflicting directions in the interwar period, generating a current of consumer-consciousness that helped sow the seeds of the consumer movement beginning in the 1930s, while also helping manufacturers and retailers increase profits by aligning their product development strategies and marketing messages with modern, middle-class values. This central tension pointed to the limitations of home economists' notion of rational consumption as well as their power to control the ultimate decisions of players in the marketplace. Like other groups of women who participated in the development of a culture of consumption in the United States, home economists' efforts to shape consumption were fraught with confusion and anxiety, but also with opportunity and empowerment. With all of the contradictions inherent in playing a mediating role in a time of social and technological change, home economists' experiences suggest that women's relationship to the culture of consumption was neither passive nor complicit but rather as complex and contested as the culture itself.[30]

GENDERED NOTIONS OF CONSUMPTION as female opened up avenues for home economists to professionalize even as these notions confined their professional activities to goods associated with the domestic sphere. In this sense, home economists had much in common with other women professionals in the Progressive Era who combined occupational goals with reform agendas derived from socially acceptable "feminine" pursuits. Teachers, librarians, social workers, public health nurses, and other members of feminized service professions all walked a fine line between being "reform-minded" and "professional."[31] Like them, home economists based their professional status partially on their womanhood, yet they also used claims of science and objectivity to transcend this gender identity and establish themselves as consumer experts. Just as a gendered division of labor in medicine and public health placed women trained in bacteriology in charge of health education and other public outreach efforts, home economics provided an important vocational outlet for scientifically trained women who were unable to find employment in conventional male-dominated spheres of activity, such as product engineering.[32] For home economists, reform and professionalism were linked in complex ways, allowing them to carry ideals forged in the Progressive Era into their experiences as consumer experts in the interwar period. As historian Robyn Muncy has argued in the case of child welfare reformers, "women were freer in their attempts to reconcile professional ideals with values from female culture, which produced uniquely female ways of being professional."[33]

Home economists also faced a unique set of obstacles in their attempts to achieve professional status within the institutions of government and business. Like many male professionalizing groups, they sought to prove that their field of expertise—homemaking—was a science, and they strove to articulate the esoteric qualities of their knowledge and skills. Home economists similarly sought to establish and maintain at least a degree of autonomy from the institutions of corporate capitalism.[34] As women, however, home economists participated in these struggles on particularly unequal terms. The professional world was a male world, and this reality posed special challenges for any group of women making professional claims. As with nurses and other women professionals, home economists' status as women significantly limited their sphere of influence. Because it derived so strongly from socially prescribed norms regarding the gendered division of labor, home economists' work in the consumer society, like so many other areas of "women's work," was often devalued.[35]

Mediation was a difficult, ongoing, and always contested professional strategy. To the extent that home economists did succeed in moving home economics from an academic discipline to a position of influence in government and industry, the reform goals that motivated the movement's founders eventually came into irreconcilable conflict with home economists' individual and collective vocational aspirations. The Bureau of Home Economics, manufacturers, and utilities provided home economists with resources, placed them in close relation to points of production, and provided them with opportunities to shape consumer products. At the same time, these positions meant that home economists' specialized knowledge was to a great degree derived from the work they performed within these institutions, rather than from more remote reform activities or educational credentials. In addition, home economists' participation at points of production in corporate America aligned their collective authority as experts more closely to the goals of producers than those of consumers. As their relationships to the agricultural establishment and consumer products firms strengthened, home economists were frequently forced to compromise their reform goals in ways that undercut their authority as professionals, reformers, and consumer advocates in the public eye. Women at the Bureau of Home Economics found that their attempts to realize a rational consumer society conflicted with the USDA's priorities to promote agricultural production. The inability of the AHEA to establish a professional code of ethics or "standards" for home economists working in corporations suggests the difficulty its members had integrating their ideals of rational consumption with the needs of the modern corporations. Finally, the invisible and intangible nature of home economists' contributions to the broader goals of business and government left them vulnerable to economic downturns, competing institutional priorities, and the claims of other experts.

Home economists' mixed success with professionalization should not obscure the significance of the mediating function they collectively performed for almost half a century. Home economists' movement among corporations, government agencies, and homemakers suggests the interconnectedness of the worlds in which processes and products were developed and the worlds in which they were used. By considering home economists as mediators we can begin not only to explore the complexity of their goals and experiences as reformers and professionals, but also to construct a more comprehensive and nuanced picture of how American consumers adapted to new technological systems, how government agencies shaped the commercial marketplace for consumer goods, and how corporations reached out to consumers. It allows us to explore the inner workings of consumption systems, just as industrial historians have done for systems of production, and to see the two types of systems as intricately connected to one another.[36]

CREATING CONSUMERS IS ORGANIZED chronologically, but its bulk is comprised of a series of parallel narratives. The first chapter examines the emergence of the home economics movement in the years before 1920. The subsequent five chapters address home economists' activities in the years between World War I and World War II. These chapters trace the simultaneous establishment of two career paths home economists followed in the interwar period: through the Bureau of Home Economics within the U.S. Department of Agriculture, and within consumer-goods manufacturing firms and utility companies. Two final chapters examine the differing identities and goals, but common decline, of these two paths between 1940 and 1975.

Chapter 1 situates the origins of home economics within the context of Progressive Era reform, the emergence of American higher education, and the development of a modern consumer society. By the 1910s home economists succeeded in carving out a place for themselves in a set of growing educational institutions. Their focus on consumption provided home economists opportunities to develop both teaching and research specialties within higher education, as well as an esoteric body of knowledge on which to base a professional identity. For the women who headed home economics programs at land-grant colleges, private universities, and local agricultural extension agencies, the advent of World War I presented a chance to demonstrate the usefulness of these institutions and the importance of their rational consumption message to American society. By serving as rank-and-file agents in the U.S. Food Administration's food conservation campaigns, home economists established a public identity as patriotic experts in nutrition capable of regulating consumer demand through education. Wartime employment in a wide range of areas encouraged many home economists to develop a new, more occupationally focused vision for the discipline.

With the establishment of the Bureau of Home Economics under the USDA in 1923, the profession obtained a higher degree of authority that allowed women in the field to extend their mediating role. Under the bureau's first director, Louise Stanley, a pioneering generation of home economists initiated the development of a federal information clearinghouse in the service of consumers. Chapters 2 and 3 demonstrate how home economists in this federal agency used scientific research to define the physical qualities of a wide range of consumer goods, thus imbedding them with middle-class values of health, cleanliness, efficiency, and economy. Together, the two chapters examine how the influence of women in the Bureau of Home Economics worked in two directions: to reform consumer behavior and to influence manufacturers. Chapter 2 examines the bureau's origins, its function as a training ground for home economists, and its efforts to develop a research agenda specializing in the user's perspective on consumer products as well as the study of consumers themselves. Intent on converting homemakers into rational consumers, bureau home economists cast practical matters of canning vegetables, sewing clothes, or choosing an appliance in terms of public citizenship and encouraged cost-benefit analyses among a diverse audience comprised primarily of white, middle-class homemakers living on farms and in small towns.

Within the agricultural establishment, home economists also took action as advocates for the consumers they sought to influence. Chapter 3 shows how, to promote rational consumption, the bureau's home economists negotiated with manufacturers and other government officials, providing them input from the perspective of consumers. As part of a growing number of social and scientific experts in an expanding federal bureaucracy influenced by Hoover's vision of an "associative state," home economists participated actively in committees of the National Bureau of Standards charged with the standardization of such diverse products as home refrigerators, brooms, and measuring cups. By standing in as typical consumers on standardization committees, they advocated for more reliable, better quality goods and for more transparent labeling and marketing systems. Two case studies—the bureau's refrigeration investigations and its textiles and clothing research—demonstrate home economists' efforts to exert influence on both production and retail methods.

Cooperation between the Bureau of Home Economics and industry representatives took place in the context of a growing role for home economists within business enterprises. Chapters 4, 5, and 6 explore the origins of corporate home economics and home service departments after 1920 and the consequences of home economists' participation in business. Chapter 4 focuses on the values and aspirations that home economists brought with them to full-time employment with corporate manufacturers of foodstuffs, appliances, textiles, and other consumer products. Within the Home Economics in Business Section of the American Home Economics Association, business home economists developed a set of professional ideals that they used to articulate their relationship to other home economists and to potential employers. By examining home economists' background and educational training, and their assumptions about what they could accomplish within corporations, the chapter reveals the complex relationship that the first generation of business home economists had to the commercial market.

Chapter 5 analyzes the motives that led corporate managers to hire home economists and identifies a range of ways home economists helped food and household equipment manufacturers understand consumers, control demand, and comply with or preempt government regulations. Over the course of the interwar period, home economists demonstrated products to consumers, tested them behind the scenes in laboratories and experimental kitchens, suggested improvements, and provided homemakers with written instructions about how new products could be used. As the real women behind corporate identities such as General Mills' Betty Crocker, home economists served as personal ambassadors for the corporations that employed them. In the process, they helped construct models of "typical consumers" that were used both inside and outside of manufacturing firms.

Chapter 6 examines the analogous mediating role played by home economists in power and light companies, organizations with special reasons for hiring consumer-minded professionals. Private power companies needed not only to ensure a sufficient domestic load on their systems, but also to legitimize their expanding presence in American cities and towns in the face of public criticism that they were greedy, profit-seeking institutions working against the public interest. Home economists were part of a massive public relations campaign by utilities, providing a friendly, human image of otherwise remote organizations. Face-to-face interactions between home economists and the public assumed a primary importance as home economists demonstrated appliances and defined them in ways that made the new technological systems central to modern housekeeping.

After 1940, home economists maintained an active role in manufacturing firms, power companies, and the USDA, but under changing circumstances. Chapter 7 explores how home economists in government and in business collaborated to fight World War II at home by identifying manufactured goods with patriotic values and (as in World War I) by linking prescribed consumption patterns with good citizenship. After the war, however, home economists gradually lost their institutional platform in government, as the USDA shifted away from an agenda of reform and modernization toward concerns with the management of problems associated with overproduction. Inside consumer products companies, home economists' mediating role expanded in the short term, but their importance as consumer experts contracted by the late 1960s as tasks they originally performed became subsumed under expanding marketing and consumer service efforts. Business managers discarded the idea that there was an "average" consumer, embraced new tools for understanding consumers, including modern marketing and public relations, and hired specialists in these new male-dominated fields to develop and test products. Business schools began training men in the emerging management specialties, altering the gendered division of labor in many firms and eroding the niche once occupied by home economists within corporations.

All of these changes within home economists' government and business niches occurred in a larger context of dramatic social and political change in the United States. Chapter 8 explores the impact of the consumer and feminist movements of the 1950s, 1960s, and 1970s on home economists' identity as consumer experts and representatives of the "woman's viewpoint," demonstrating how these broader transformations left women in the field disconnected from mainstream society and unable to continue to serve in capacities they previously enjoyed. It was during this period, when the baby boomer generation's primary exposure to home economists was in school "home ec" classes, that understandings of women in the field as consumer advocates or representatives became all but forgotten.

In this study, home economists emerge as a diverse social group that shaped popular ideas about consumer products, and often the material goods themselves. By unmasking home economists' historical presence in the marketplace, I hope to reveal the critical ways they influenced the discourses and experiences of consumption in twentieth-century America.

1

Envisioning the Rational Consumer, 1900–1920

"The consumer who desires to be economical," Teachers College professor Mary Schenck Woolman and Ellen Beers McGowan advised in *Textiles: A Handbook for the Student and the Consumer*, a textbook they coauthored in 1913, "should not make a practice of wandering about the shops to get ideas, for in that way her desires increase and are apt to become confused in her mind with her needs." A mother should consider her family's needs from all angles "before she does any shopping at all." She should obtain samples of materials and take them home for testing before purchasing them. Only the most informed shoppers should shop for bargains, as "the thoughtless shopper is apt to buy more than she needs."[1] Building on the efforts of Ellen Swallow Richards and other first-generation home economists, who in the 1890s founded their educational movement around principles of wise consumption, Woolman and McGowan's book taught women to be careful consumers of fabrics and ready-made garments. In the first two decades of the twentieth century, home economists developed dozens of textbooks like these, as well as courses and academic programs, to teach female students to appreciate their economic power and use it responsibly.

Because home economics emerged at a moment when women's work in the home was changing from making things to buying them, many women in the field, including Mary Schenck Woolman, began their careers emphasizing household production and gradually shifted to a focus on consumption. Woolman entered home economics with an interest in vocational education and manual work, devoting her early years as a teacher to providing working-class women with skills for their roles as factory workers or domestic servants. Born in 1860, she received a diploma from Teachers College in 1895 and a B.S. degree in 1897. As a member of the Teachers College faculty beginning in 1892, Woolman taught household arts, sewing, and domestic science and introduced the study of textiles in the school's Department of Domestic Arts. In

1902, she helped organize the Manhattan Trade School for Girls, an institution that taught sewing and clothing construction as part of an industrial education program to prepare girls for work in the garment trades.[2]

In 1910, when the trade school was absorbed into the city's public school system, Woolman returned to Teachers College's newly reorganized School of Household Arts. As a textile professor and director of the Domestic Arts Department, she developed courses for the school's growing body of middle-class students, instructing would-be homemakers and teachers in how to make purchasing decisions about ready-to-wear garments and household furnishings. The school's uniquely outfitted textile laboratory enabled students to conduct "chemical and microscopic studies of textile fibers and fabrics" and to carry out experimental work in dyeing.[3] Two years later, Woolman moved to Boston to become the acting head of the Home Economics Department at Simmons College and president of the Women's Educational and Industrial Union, an organization devoted to assisting women workers throughout the city. During World War I, Woolman put all of her teachings into action in her capacity as textile specialist for Massachusetts under the War Emergency Fund of the U.S. Department of Agriculture (USDA). Although most home economists spent the war years promoting food conservation on behalf of the U.S. Food Administration (USFA), Woolman organized a Clothing Information Bureau to encourage homemakers to consider the "economic, social, and industrial connections" involved in choices about textiles and clothing. From a temporary structure located on Boston Common, Woolman worked to "increase intelligence" in the making of new clothing and the renovating of old garments, by emphasizing the selection of textiles and clothing, "clothing economy," and more "efficient" and "healthful" manners of dress. Woolman's Clothing Information Bureau was devoted to "training" the consumer to make "intelligent" choices in the selection of clothing based on such criteria as health and thrift. The ideal trained consumer's civic duty, according to Woolman, was not only to be knowledgeable about the goods she purchased but also to live on a budget and within her family's means.[4]

Woolman's notion of the trained consumer who had a thorough understanding of both commercial goods and the priorities of her family's budget typified home economists' educational initiatives launched between 1900 and 1920. Like many women in the field, Woolman shifted to a new focus. By 1920, she was directing her energies toward educating middle-class women in university programs about their identity as consumers, reflecting the changing thrust of home economics toward the education of the "rational consumer." In the course of these two decades, Woolman and her home economics colleagues transformed a series of disparate ideas and exponents, college programs, and publications into a full-fledged academic discipline and national community of practitioners. Through the formation of a professional association, the development of educational programs for disseminating their messages, and the application of their expertise to domestic food conservation during World War I, these early home economists placed themselves at the center of public discussions about the meaning of consumption in twentieth-century American culture and framed these discussions in terms that compelled would-be modern homemakers to interact with a new group of women experts.

Reforming the Middle-Class Consumer: Lake Placid Conferences, 1899–1907

"The young woman of today is besieged on every side by allurements in the shape of cheap and fantastic ornaments. To steer one's course amid these complicated temptations and purchase wisely and prudently is no easy task." With these words in 1896, Ellen Swallow Richards and a group of women educators in Boston summarized their concerns about women consumers in the United States at the turn of the century. Richards, a pioneering women scientist, had spent more than two decades investigating sanitary science and other public health matters, and advocating for reform of the nation's eating habits. Now in her mid-fifties, she sought to integrate science with social change by helping prepare American homemakers to assume their new responsibilities as consumers. Convinced of "the power of the woman as an economic factor in the home, and the imperative necessity that she be so educated as to understand her task," Richards and her fellow members of the Women's Education Association (WEA) argued for domestic science instruction in Boston's public high schools. This group assumed that the home was "the chief of all factors in the making of the citizen," but Richards and her colleagues proposed to use the city's public education system to encourage women to take control of domestic consumption by teaching them the principles of "wise expenditure."[5]

A series of ongoing economic and technological developments placed the functions of the home and women's domestic work in a state of flux at the turn of the century. To a greater or lesser extent, Americans of all classes witnessed a broad array of changes not only in the way goods were produced but also in how they were bought and sold. These changes altered patterns of daily domestic life, especially for urban middle-class women who saw the production of many household goods move into the factory. For generations, women had made soap in their homes with lye and fats; now homemakers with disposable income could purchase it in mass-produced bars. An expanding array of food-stuffs, such as bread, canned goods, and packaged meats, came into industrial production as well. Ready-made clothing was available for purchase by middle-class women in new retail environments such as department stores. Personal relationships with neighborhood merchants became less common, as women in smaller towns and rural areas relied less on the recommendations of trusted sellers and more on mail-order catalogs, brand-name identification, and ad-vertising in mass-circulation magazines. With food and clothing constituting a large part of most family budgets, the changing structure of the market-place presented uncertainties for American homemakers, who faced not only a steadily rising cost of living but also a real public health crisis that seemed to stem from domestic sanitary practices. As houses and apartment buildings in urban areas became connected to public utility systems, elite and middle-class women were beginning to enjoy modern plumbing as well as gas and electric appliances. Once prized as the source of a family's independence, the home—especially the middle-class home—was now more intertwined than ever be-fore in an expanding national market, a growing network of new technological goods and systems, and an emerging culture of consumption.[6]

The identity of the female consumer was a central theme for Richards as she forged alliances throughout the 1890s with a diverse group of reformers, educators, and scientists to launch their educational reform movement. By 1900, a first generation of home economists commanded an ambitious project to transform American homemakers into rational consumer citizens while at the same time establishing themselves as experts in the developing consumer society.

Ellen Swallow Richards's career, in which she integrated scientific research with social service and reform, served as an important point of reference for how the new academic discipline of home economics would define a standard of living for American families. After graduating from Vassar College in 1870, Richards became the first woman to receive a B.S. degree from the Massachu-setts Institute of Technology (MIT). With support from the WEA, a catalyst for many educational innovations for women beginning in 1873, she established a Women's Laboratory at MIT. For the next two decades, she investigated the adulteration of food products and the contamination of water, as well as the chemical processes involved in cooking and digesting food, while training a co-hort of younger women in methods of chemical analysis. In the 1880s, Richards emerged as a leading expert in the fields of sanitary science and nutritional science, and a vocal advocate for applying scientific solutions to public health conditions in the urban home environment.[7]

Beginning around 1890, Richards's interests became increasingly focused on food and sanitation as avenues of reform. In a major effort to change the eating habits of workers and immigrants, she launched the New England Kitchen, a distribution center for healthy, low-cost meals to families in Boston. At the 1893 Chicago World's Columbian Exposition, a great celebration of European and American technological developments and the consumer durables they generated, Richards received national attention for planning the Rumford Kitchen exhibit, in which she demonstrated principles of "scientific cookery." The following year she contracted with the Boston public schools to provide nutritious school lunches. While many of Richards's early reform initiatives sought to improve the standard of living of working-class families based on middle-class values, by the late 1890s, as urbanization and industrialization disrupted the closing century's understandings of class distinctions, Richards sought as much to influence her socioeconomic peers as to draw on middle-class standards for uplift among the lower classes.[8]

Richards's approach to reform reflected her ambivalence about the social impact of economic and technological changes under way at the turn of the century, and in particular of their effect on American homes. Like many contemporary politicians, social scientists, community activists, and industrial leaders, she worried that the expanding working-class population and the continued influx of immigrants into white Anglo-Saxon culture would result in social fragmentation. Turn-of-the-century reformers were also troubled by the place of the individual citizen in a society where distant market forces and interactions with large, powerful corporations replaced face-to-face relationships. Richards feared that values associated with industry—individualism and personal isolation—would undermine the home as a place of refuge and destabilize it as a cornerstone of civilization, hence threatening the nation's moral order. Lamenting the loss of production in the home, she wrote: "Gone out of it are the industries, gone out of it are ten of the children, gone out of it in large measure is that sense of moral and religious responsibility which was the keystone of the whole."[9]

At the same time, Richards viewed the economic and social transition under way as a moment of great promise, one that presented opportunities to control the emerging urban industrial order. Like many reformers of her day, Richards assumed that physical environments shaped social relationships and conditions, and she embraced surveys and other types of fact-finding endeavors by experts as strategies for shaping domestic consumption in the United States.[10] Specifically, she proposed that women draw on science and engineering to navigate the new world of consumption and create homes that would be "unhampered by the traditions of the past" and modeled instead on business and industry. New technologies and new values of efficiency offered the possibility of liberating women from much drudgery. "All science and engineering stands ready to help [the homemaker] to easier conditions," Richards announced confidently in 1900.[11]

By the end of the nineteenth century, Richards's experience at the School of Housekeeping in Boston led her to envision a professionalized home economics that would apply modern technological advances to the needs of American homes, while at the same time carve out a productive place for scientifically trained women. In 1899, as she formulated a new women's field in public life, Richards organized a meeting of ten other educators at the home of Annie Godfrey Dewey and Melvil Dewey in Lake Placid, New York, to further "the improvement of living conditions in the home, the institutional household and the community." Richards invited professors and instructors from a range of academic fields to attend the first of what became known as the Lake Placid conferences. While made up mostly of women, this group also included two men in addition to Dewey: USDA nutrition researcher Wilbur Olin Atwater and his assistant Alfred C. True. The group met annually for ten years between 1899 and 1908, and eventually expanded to include more than 200 meeting participants and a total membership list of over 350. The group's composition was concentrated in the northeastern and midwestern states. Most attendees were white, middle-class individuals who identified themselves as teachers, writers, scientists, or reformers. The meetings provided a chance to bring under one umbrella the broad array of activities the participants had under way. During this ten-year period, the group forged an ambitious agenda for a new academic discipline that embraced the study of a wide range of issues related to the home, issues which together addressed a larger, central purpose: to shape the material conditions in American households by reforming women's role as consumers in modern industrial society.[12]

Richards and her cohort proposed home economics as a subject of study to guide homemakers through the dramatic transition they identified as taking place in the American home, and the home economists framed domestic consumption in terms characteristic of Progressive Era reformers. As a group, they shared Richards's critiques of urbanization and industrialization, her belief in scientific and technological progress, and her faith in the ability of experts and educators to improve social conditions. These common values shaped the group's understanding of who consumers were, what problems they faced, and how the new field of study would address these problems.

The Lake Placid attendees shared a moral conviction about the centrality of middle-class culture (informed by a white Anglo-Saxon Protestant identity) to American life. At least since the publication of Catherine Beecher's *Treatise on the Domestic Economy* in 1841, domestic advisers had prescribed the norms of middle-class culture in terms of material conditions and women's responsibilities for maintaining them. Now, as industrialization and the rise of a consumer society threatened to disrupt these norms, the reformers, scientists, and educators convened at Lake Placid used the terms "right living" and "standard of living" to articulate concerns that American identity might be at risk. They feared that changes in the economic function of the home would lower women's status—and along with it, the status of the middle-class family—in American society. Like Richards, many attendees had focused their reform efforts on urban low-income families, but by the late 1890s they found that their reform messages (particularly about food) did not resonate with working-class concerns. As other groups such as social workers and settlement-house leaders increasingly addressed the needs of working-class women, the Lake Placid participants focused on a new target audience: young middle-class women in cities, and those in rural areas who wanted to learn about the cosmopolitan ways of their urban sisters. The industrialization of the home presented Richards and her cohort with a chance to redefine middle-class domestic life, and to do so in ways that put their group at its center. As new consumer goods and ways of buying them became available to middle-class families, home economists seized on the opportunity to interpret the meanings of those goods—and of consumption itself—for a social group in formation. For home economists, defining the parameters of "right living" was a way of compensating for the loss of woman's traditional position in American life and reinventing an identity for her as a public citizen in the context of modern consumer capitalism.[13]

Even as the first generation of home economists proposed a new field of study that would prepare homemakers to perform domestic work efficiently and manage household budgets economically, they also sought to characterize middle-class culture as a hallmark of a "comfortable" American standard of living. At the first meeting in 1899, Richards articulated a special concern for middle-class families, those with a total annual income of between $1,500 and $2,500, "whose character and principles demand more than the necessities of life." In spite of their "educated" tastes, Richards observed, "they are rarely skilled in the use of money; the home is not managed on an economical basis and fails in many essentials of comfort." To enable homemakers in these families to realize the values of sanitation, health, economy, and efficiency that she so highly prized, Richards argued that they required a new kind of education to ensure the "rational division of the income."[14] In proposing a new set of standards to address the changing marketplace for women's labor and for household goods, Richards generated discussions about how to derive her "essentials of comfort" in precise, scientific terms. Together, conference attendees proposed a collective research and teaching program that would reorder homemakers' responsibilities within a newer set of duties related to managing the family's spending budget, while simultaneously preserving their role in the more subjective cultural work of maintaining class and gender identity.

Many of the Lake Placid attendees were active participants in a growing women's political culture. In the late nineteenth century, a new generation of white, college-educated, middle-class women in the North brought "autonomous, mass-based women's organizations into the nation's political mainstream," as historian Kathryn Kish Sklar has argued. Claiming the home as their special sphere of authority, women activists such as Jane Addams brought private, home-related issues into the public arena through the social settlement movement and a broader call for "municipal housekeeping."[15] Several women at the meetings were among the first to attend institutions of higher education. Some had degrees from agricultural land-grant colleges or state normal schools with programs designed to train women as teachers as well as homemakers. Others attended eastern women's colleges such as Smith and Vassar. A significant number held membership in a number of other women's organizations, including the General Federation of Women's Clubs, the Boston Women's Educational and Industrial Union, the Women's Trade Union League, the Women's Municipal League of Boston, the Twentieth Century Club, the New England Women's Press Association, and the Association of Collegiate Alumnae. Nearly all of these organizations shared concerns about raising standards of living, alleviating improper diets and poor housing conditions, and improving public health through regulation of the milk supply and other "pure foods."[16]

Informed by their connections to this wide variety of organizations, most Lake Placid participants assumed that women's work began in the home but did not necessarily end there. "Educated women are entering upon public work not as a substitute for that work which is done in the interest of home life, but as a necessary means under present conditions of realizing those ideals for which the home stands," Caroline Hunt, a regular and outspoken attendee who taught domestic science at Lewis Institute in Chicago and the University of Wisconsin, explained to her colleagues at the ninth conference. Women were compelled to demand pure food, clean markets, and sanitary streets, she told the audience, because "they see that under present conditions they cannot without adding public to private work accomplish the tasks which have always been theirs and always will be." Like Hunt, many other conference speakers defined the home broadly and emphasized domestic material conditions as part of a larger project of reform that various women's groups divided into manageable pieces.[17]

Many contemporary women reformers understood social problems largely through their status as consumers. They were influenced by discussions among economists, social critics, and middle-class women's organizations about the place of consumption in the changing social and economic order. In the 1890s, theorists Thorstein Veblen and Charlotte Perkins Gilman were among the leaders in raising concerns about a culture and an economy based on consumption rather than production. Their books, *The Theory of the Leisure Class* (1899) and *Women and Economics* (1898), respectively, criticized consumer culture and, in particular, women's role in it. Both Veblen and Gilman portrayed women as excessively preoccupied with spending, economic parasites who were responsible for the backward movement of civilization. Other social commentators understood consumption more positively, and they opened up women's consumption as an avenue for reform. In the late nineteenth century, as economists began to take an interest in consumption, many rejected the classical view that the value of commodities was derived from their cost in human labor. They argued instead that value came from the utility consumers found in commercial goods. In the place of the labor theory of value, some economists in the 1890s began to substitute the "law of marginal utility," which held that demand and consumption were more important than supply and production. Among these theorists, Simon Nelson Patten believed in the moral potential of consumption, viewing women's household drudgery as unfortunate and unnecessary in the modern industrial order. Patten's student, Edward T. Devine, addressed the topic of women and consumption more directly. In his 1895 article "Economic Function of Woman," he called attention to the importance of the household and argued that women's domestic work—which directed "how the wealth brought into the house shall be used, whether much or little shall be made of it, and what kind of wealth shall be brought"—constituted "production" and had economic value. By identifying the potential for reform in women's economic power, Devine inspired middle-class and elite women to use their purchasing power as consumers to improve working conditions for other women. Beginning in 1891, Florence Kelley and Lucy Randolph Mason organized the National Consumers' Leagues to promote principles of "moral consumption."[18]

The Lake Placid participants, too, took the economic power of women's consumption as their jumping-off point. Like members of the Consumers' Leagues, the first generation of home economists sought to reshape middle-class women's identities as consumers by urging them to make productive use of their economic power. In part to uplift the urban and rural poor, and in part to rescue what they perceived as an erosion of the moral authority of women as producers, home economists worked to reform the consumer's economic role. Caroline Hunt was one of several speakers at the meeting who supported the National Consumers' Leagues. She lived at Addams' Hull House in Chicago in the early 1890s while pursuing graduate studies in chemistry and German at Northwestern University and the University of Chicago and conducting nutritional investigations for the USDA. Hunt published articles in opposition to child labor, sweatshops, and other dangerous working conditions. During the decade the Lake Placid conferences were under way, she brought her vision of consumption and social justice to teaching domestic economy at Lewis Institute in Chicago and as the first professor of home economics at the University of Wisconsin. At Lake Placid, too, Hunt argued for using women's power as consumers to improve the lives of working-class women and found support from fellow participants such as University of Chicago professor Marion Talbot, who was a member of the American Association for Labor Legislation, and Ruby Green Smith, who later became active with the National Housewives' League, an organization based in New York City in the 1910s that blended concerns about labor conditions, municipal housekeeping, pure food, and domestic reform in its programs and publications.[19] At the same time, Hunt was among the most articulate advocates of the larger group's desire to secure better quality goods for homemakers. She envisioned home economics as a way to provide homemakers with the tools to resist the power of the marketplace. "Manufacturers and dealers," Hunt exhorted, "actuated by a desire for profit, are bombarding us with multitudinous articles of the same general character, differing only in name, with appliances which have not stood the test of experience, with fabrics whose wearing-power has not been proved. Before this fusillade of articles the individual housekeeper is powerless. The forces of commerce, by dealing with us separately, conquer us. It is for us to display a solid front by organizing as consumers and by collecting and distributing information."[20] Equipped with a home economics education, Hunt believed, a woman would be a more discriminating, demanding consumer and, in the process, influence the making of superior products. Improving working conditions and the quality of manufactured goods were for Hunt, and many other Lake Placid attendees, intertwined.

Domestic reform led some Lake Placid members into politics, but, like many women's voluntary organizations in the first decade of the twentieth century, they were divided on the issue of women's suffrage. Although Ellen Richards opposed women's suffrage in the 1870s, Lake Placid host Annie Dewey was a vocal proponent of votes for women. Of the fifty-one conference participants included in John Leonard's 1914 biographical directory of women, twenty-seven claimed to "favor woman suffrage." Those supporting the vote for women included Caroline Hunt, Mary Schenck Woolman, Marion Talbot, and Alice Peloubet Norton, also from the University of Chicago, as well as Cornell University home economics professors Flora Rose and Martha Van Rensselaer, and the young Louise Stanley, who attended the conference as a graduate student, began teaching home economics at the University of Missouri in 1907, and later became the first director of the USDA's Bureau of Home Economics. Several of these supporters of women's suffrage also listed membership in the Equal Suffrage League. Twenty-three of the women at Lake Placid chose not to include a stand on the issue, but only one conference attendee listed in Leonard's dictionary put herself on record as against women's suffrage.[21]

Even as the founding members of the home economics movement embraced the idea that women were responsible for "municipal housekeeping," for many Lake Placid participants, the home—not politics—was the most important and promising site for social change. Henrietta Goodrich, who directed the School of Housekeeping in Boston, articulated a shared conviction "that the home is the organic unit of society, that to raise the standard of living and of life in the home is to elevate the whole social system."[22] In approaching reform, home economists focused their attention primarily on material goods—their systematic selection, their physical qualities, their moral meanings, and their value in the microeconomies of private household budgets. Home economists used their power to enlist governmental support to shape these material conditions by educating private, individual homemakers to assume an engaged and active role in the developing consumer society. While many home economists supported legislation benefiting women and children as workers, they formed more active alliances with reformers who shared concerns about the quality of manufactured goods and the manner in which they were distributed to American households. The Lake Placid conferences attracted a number of agricultural reformers who hoped that laborsaving technologies would solve the problem of the "overworked farm woman." Many of these individuals had contributed to the growth of early domestic science programs at land-grant colleges and were looking for ways to enhance the place of home economics in the education of American farm families. Influenced by the thinking of Liberty Hyde Bailey, Theodore Roosevelt, and the country life movement, they were concerned about the drain of population away from rural areas. These men and women hoped that exposure to modern housekeeping methods and improvements in the standard of living on American farms would encourage the white Anglo-Saxon population to remain tied to the land rather than join the masses in the cities.[23]

A number of the women at Lake Placid were scientific investigators who, like Ellen Richards, had built careers studying specific techniques for improving food consumption and home sanitation in support of a modern, middle-class standard of living. New findings in chemistry, physiology, and bacteriology provided not only reassuring solutions to problems of domestic consumption but also opportunities for many of these women to earn a living as scientists and become members of previously all-male scientific societies. The largest cohort of scientifically trained women at Lake Placid had become well-versed in the emerging science of nutrition, which by the 1890s described a coherent vision of how the human body used foods. Mary Hinman Abel studied with pioneering nutritional scientists in Germany in the 1880s and won the 1888 Lomb Prize from the American Public Health Association for her essay "Practical Sanitary and Economic Cooking." She later collaborated with Richards on the establishment of the New England Kitchen and the Rumford Kitchen at the Chicago World's Fair. Isabel Bevier, Marion Talbot, and Caroline Hunt belonged to a younger cohort that trained with Richards at MIT and worked under the direction of the nation's leading male nutritional investigators. Henry Clapp Sherman, Wilbur Olin Atwater, and Charles Ford Langworthy led American studies devoted to separating foods into carbohydrates, proteins, fats, minerals, and water as well as demonstrating the specific physiological functions performed by each nutrient. Each man attended at least one of the Lake Placid meetings. In mapping out the American diet in quantitative terms, Atwater, as professor of chemistry at Wesleyan University, generated a comprehensive set of food composition tables and popularized the calorie as a unit of measurement, both of which became building blocks for home economists' research and teaching. Atwater welcomed women students and researchers into his laboratory, and he enlisted a number of Ellen Richards's protégées in an ambitious survey of the nation's eating habits in 1894. The participation of Bevier, Hunt, Van Rensselaer, and others in these investigations did much to legitimize them as scientists; their role in preparing recipes and government bulletins based on Atwater's findings established them as important interpreters of nutrition to the general public. Other women, such as S. Maria Elliott of Simmons College, had worked with Richards to popularize "useful knowledge about evading microbial harms." Experience with nutrition and bacteriology, and familiarity with their application on behalf of family health and welfare, made these women optimistic about the possibilities of science and technology to promote social change from within the home. Their identity as scientists reinforced the orientation of home economics—as it took form in the first decade of the twentieth century—toward the physical qualities of domestic surroundings and objects within them.[24]

A lesser but significant number of Lake Placid participants shared Richards's interest in the scientific study of social conditions. Like many other women reformers, they were influenced by the emerging social sciences, which relied on the methods of experimental natural science to illuminate the interrelation of social groups and institutions. Several conference attendees, including Abel, listed an affiliation with the Charity Organization Society, which held a social scientific approach to poverty. Susan Kingsbury, a pioneer in the emerging field of social research, conducted a study of child labor in Massachusetts and assumed the helm of the Women's Educational and Industrial Union's Social Research Department while also teaching economics at Simmons College.[25] Kingsbury and others shared with many Progressive reformers a belief in the power of factual information to change society and experience with social research efforts of their day.

Educators were another vocal contingent at the Lake Placid conferences, and their dominant presence explains the program's emphasis on developing a curriculum that would achieve the group's social reform goals. One cohort included self-described "lecturers" and "writers" who spoke regularly before women's clubs, farmer's institutes, chautauquas, and other informal educational channels, or had published articles in popular magazines and newspapers. Members of another group identified themselves as professional teachers and members of the National Education Association; dozens of these women had taught domestic science in high schools, teachers' colleges, or land-grant colleges for as many as ten or twenty years. Since the 1870s, Janet McKenzie Hill and Mary Lincoln had led urban cooking schools for immigrant women in northeastern cities to promote more economical and healthful ways of preparing food—defined in terms of Yankee New England cookery. Others, like Mary Schenck Woolman, of the Manhattan Trade School for Girls, and Abby Marlatt, of the Manual Training High School in Providence, Rhode Island, taught domestic science at trade schools or schools for teacher training.

Martha Van Rensselear of Cornell University and Isabel Bevier of the University of Illinois belonged to a group of attendees who were founding directors of new domestic science or home economics programs at land-grant colleges. A number of women came from Teachers College at Columbia University, a prominent institution for teacher training where Dean James Earl Russell worked to upgrade the status of domestic science education by attracting bright, ambitious young women to the field.[26]

The Lake Placid conferences provided a context for these educators to establish common ground with Russell and other male educational reformers who sought to adjust school curricula to the needs of urban industrial society. Influenced by John Dewey, who argued that schools should be responsible for the development of children's character and serve as a socializing force in a democratic society, these reformers advocated vocational education as a practical solution to the changing conditions of men's and women's work. Although Dewey called for schools to challenge the status quo, advocates for vocational education were primarily concerned with educating and training boys for work within the existing industrial structure. Many argued that separate, specialized schooling for boys and girls was the best way to ensure an effective link between education and the division of labor in the larger society. Through the National Society for the Promotion of Industrial Education, created in 1906, they embraced home economics as something for girls and young women to study while male counterparts were learning to be better industrial workers. The organization's diverse base of support included the National Association of Manufacturers, organized labor, and many home economists. David Snedden, a prominent educational sociologist and vocational education advocate who taught at Teachers College, attended the last two Lake Placid conferences. He called for sexual difference in education as practical training for life after school and special courses for young women in "applied" chemistry and physics to suit women's needs in housework. By forming an alliance with Snedden and his fellow "administrative progressives," home economists committed themselves to upholding the industrial capitalist order and working within the existing gendered division of labor.[27]

Early female home economists and allied male educational reformers believed that schools should not only prepare students for the workplace but also mold citizens to participate in modern industrial democracy. Discussions at Lake Placid explicitly linked educational reformers' ideas about "training for efficient citizenship" with specific, material notions of "right living" and American middle-class identity.[28] Material things could either "enslave" or "emancipate," argued Caroline Hunt in a 1901 speech that became a home economics landmark. They could cripple families, or they could be used to promote "spiritual and bodily growth." Host Annie Dewey warned of "the tyranny of things" and the accumulation of "material impedimentia" that led "only to conspicuous waste," asking, "How shall we free ourselves? How [shall we] cultivate that sense of proportion which enables one to choose essentials, to discard all that does not minister to the highest efficiency? This is the problem."[29] Hunt's and Dewey's concerns about extravagance echoed older, republican ideas about the corrupting influence of luxury, as well as Veblen's and Gilman's more contemporary critiques of women as economic parasites. The new field of home economics would serve as a beacon of "freedom of the home from the dominance of things and their due subordination to ideals," Richards and her collaborators proposed, and technical training by experts would teach women "to understand the use of machines" and place them in command of their homes, just as it put men in charge of industrial factories.[30] At Lake Placid, a first generation of home economists articulated a vision of an ideal woman citizen consumer who, with proper training, would control the new domestic technologies available to her and use the power of discrimination to participate actively in the American economy.[31]

By designing a new academic discipline—"home economics"—in the years between 1899 and 1907, Lake Placid participants launched a broad educational movement that aimed to reform women's roles as consumers and secure the nation's standard of living according to middle-class values. Simultaneously, they began to define a body of knowledge that would provide an avenue for women to pursue scientific and social scientific training and careers. Pointing to the example of librarians who—with the assistance of Lake Placid host Melvil Dewey—organized themselves professionally in 1876 under the aegis of the American Library Association and, more recently, established educational institutions for training its members, Richards and her cohort sought to convince colleges of "the possibility of a new profession commanding adequate compensation."[32] With the implementation of a system of home economics education, Henrietta Goodrich, director of the School of Housekeeping in Boston, anticipated that "professions as yet unthought of would arise from the present undifferentiated mass." After the final conference, the Lake Placid group enlisted 700 individuals to form the American Home Economics Association (AHEA) in 1908, an organization devoted to continuing the development of this new discipline, and to winning state funding for home economics education and research initiatives that would provide the basis for an expanding multitiered curriculum and the emergence of a new set of vocations for women.[33]

Teaching Rational Consumption, 1900–1920

The AHEA's lobbying for government support of home economics education brought swift results. Administrators at private women's colleges did not embrace a developing home economics curriculum, viewing the subject as less elevating than the subjects being taught in most eastern liberal arts institutions for women.[34] However, in the 1910s the AHEA won passage of two crucial pieces of legislation that allowed home economists to establish formal niches for research and teaching within institutions of higher education. The Smith-Lever Act of 1914 and the Smith-Hughes Act of 1917 provided funding to expand demonstration work in rural communities and to develop and teach a home economics curriculum on the campuses of most state land-grant colleges.

The Smith-Lever Act of 1914 fueled the growth of the home economics extension service by authorizing the land-grant colleges in each state to run cooperative extension programs sponsored by the USDA in both agriculture and home economics. Before this new law, many states and private foundations funded home demonstration agents, but the 1914 legislation placed all state and privately funded extension activities under the supervision and control of the USDA. Within three years, 27,000 women attended 450 home economics extension schools throughout the forty-eight states, extending the reach of home economics education to unprecedented numbers of adult homemakers.[35]

Enacted in 1917, the Smith-Hughes Act promoted home economics education at the high-school and college levels by providing the funds to increase the number of home demonstration agents and home economics teachers. Smith-Hughes committed federal monies for teachers' salaries at state-operated vocational education programs teaching home economics and for teacher-training programs in the subject at the college level. This legislation also created a Federal Board for Vocational Education within the Department of the Interior's Office of Education and charged it with developing home economics curricula and providing guidance for teachers and professors throughout the nation. These initiatives quickly spurred an increase in and expansion of home economics departments in colleges and universities. As the emphasis of most of these home economics programs was on teacher training, their growth fueled that of home economics in secondary schools where, by 1920, nearly one of every three young women enrolled in high school in the United States took courses in the subject.[36]

Home economists also succeeded in establishing programs in a few private universities. By the 1910s, two important institutions—Teachers College at Columbia University in New York City and the University of Chicago—offered not only bachelor's degrees but also specialized graduate degrees in home economics and related subjects at both the M.A. and Ph.D. levels.[37] These programs trained women to become college professors and high-school instructors, further increasing the growth of home economics programs and the creation of new opportunities for women in the field.

Originally established in 1887 for the purpose of preparing students to become elementary public school teachers, Teachers College expanded its facilities and curriculum and raised its admissions standards to become one of the primary training grounds for college professors and high-school instructors in home economics in the 1910s. Seeking to upgrade the status of domestic science education by attracting top-quality ambitious women to the field, Dean James Earl Russell created the nation's first academic department of nutrition, hiring faculty members Henry C. Sherman, Hermann Vulte, and Mary Swartz Rose. By 1917, most of the 174 graduate students in the college's School of Practical Arts were enrolled in this department specializing in nutrition, physiological chemistry, household chemistry, while others pursued studies in textiles, household administration, bacteriology, hygiene, and applied arts.[38]

Simultaneously, the new University of Chicago (founded in 1892) became a progressive institution for women students and a leading center of graduate education in home economics. Influenced by ties to Hull House, a dynamic center of urban reform led by Jane Addams, and to women's clubs in the city, as well as by the university's orientation toward "learning by doing," two University of Chicago departments offered courses and graduate degrees to women seeking training in home economics. At the College of Arts, Literature, and Science, the Department of Household Administration grew out of the Department of Social Sciences (later Sociology and Anthropology), where Marion Talbot, a former student of Ellen Richards at MIT, established a program in sanitary science in 1892. Soon Talbot began taking on graduate students, mostly women, in the study of applied nutritional science. Her first doctoral student graduated in 1906. In the same department, Sophonisba Breckinridge taught courses addressing the relationship between the home and the government, planting roots for later courses that explored "the problems of the consumer," before moving on to launch the university's School of Social Service Administration in 1920. In addition, the School of Education inaugurated its Home Economics Department in 1901 with the appointment of Alice Peloubet Norton, another Richards student. Norton's program emphasized technical skills and offered courses on foods, textiles, and home economics education. After Katherine Blunt's arrival at the university in 1913, the faculty developed graduate research courses in food chemistry and nutrition, including a specialty in child nutrition. By 1920, there was a thoroughly established graduate program with tracks in home economics education, food and nutrition, and home or institution management. The development of flagship home economics programs in these two new private institutions of higher learning offered opportunities for graduate training in the field to a growing number of women and elevated the academic status of the field.[39]

Teaching women about their social responsibilities as consumers gradually emerged as the defining framework of home economics instruction in most college programs. Consumption served as a unifying theme that allowed home economists to develop a unique and legitimate academic discipline that combined practical utility with scientific research, striking a balance between the two that was important to early-twentieth-century university administrators, especially those in land-grant colleges.[40] Home economics administrators and professors at these schools placed consumption at the center of their curriculum because they believed it would be useful to their students. Early home economists recognized that all American homes were not changing in lockstep with one another and that working-class families still made many of the goods at home that middle-class and elite women could afford to buy. Understanding that household management at the time encompassed activities related to both production and consumption, early home economics educators adjusted their focus depending on the class of women they intended to instruct.[41] By the 1910s, students in land-grant colleges came from rural areas or small towns, and were members of families with enough flexibility in the family economy to allow at least one young daughter to leave home. Home economics faculty at land-grant colleges directed their attention to an audience of young women who expected to become homemakers and defined themselves as middle class in part by seeking a college education or choosing to learn "modern" household practices at agricultural extension demonstrations. For these students, home economists adjusted their instructional emphasis away from household skills of cooking and sewing toward those of buying ready-made and manufactured goods. College and university home economics professors aimed their lessons at an ideal consumer of middle-class means, a woman who had a limited disposable income with which to make discriminating purchases, rather than targeting the urban or rural poor.[42]

Even as home economics professors sought to be useful, they drew a sharp distinction with respect to trade schools, reducing content related to the manual arts and paying close attention to teaching consumption in scientific terms. Although many early home economists shared the romantic view of the value of handmade objects held by proponents of the arts and crafts movement, most early university home economics instructors sought to distance themselves from teaching "handicraft skills." "Educators are agreed that manual training does not belong in a university course," declared Charlotte M. Gibbs, who taught textiles in the household science program at the University of Illinois, in 1907. Although she recommended that sewing be required of high school girls seeking to enter college home economics programs, Gibbs thought it more important for young women to learn how to dress intelligently. "The study of materials then may be our starting point. The consumer of products should know what the market affords, what the adulterations of materials are, how to tell good material from indifferent, how to tell one kind of material from another and what she should pay."[43] Like many other male and female researchers in the new nutritional and social sciences, home economists struggled to establish secure disciplinary boundaries for themselves within American universities and colleges. Teaching about consumption allowed female professors to claim an esoteric body of knowledge in an area that was already considered women's special sphere. It also provided women trained in the sciences and the social sciences with opportunities to carve out specific areas of expertise within the broad rubrics of disciplines such as nutrition, economics, and chemistry. By shaping research and teaching strategies around consumption, home economists created an applied science devoted to generating new knowledge that would have practical applications in everyday life, a field that University of Chicago's Faith M. McAuley termed the "'science' of consumption."[44]

Drawing on both science and nineteenth-century notions of morality, home economists' lessons about consumption offered young, female members of a new middle class an alternative identity to that of the irrational female consumer so vividly conjured up by contemporary social critics. By articulating an ethic of rational consumption, home economists linked notions of the ideal home with Progressive ideas about science, efficiency, and good citizenship. According to this new ideal, *how* women selected and purchased household goods was at least as important as *what* they purchased. Rational consumption was home economists' prescribed code for homemakers to follow in making choices in the marketplace. To prevent young potential homemakers from being manipulated by emotion, intuition, persuasion, or the surface appearance of goods, home economists' lessons in "intelligent buying" aimed to guide students in making purchases according to such criteria as economy, efficiency, health, sanitation, nutrition, comfort, convenience, durability, and quality.[45] Modern consumers, home economists told their students, should shop for "value" rather than bargains or fads. They used a systematic process of cost-benefit analysis in choosing what to make at home versus what to buy as well as where to purchase household products. Challenging the notion of consumption as a passive, destructive activity, rational consumption cast women in an active, engaged role as nutrition scientists, sanitary investigators, or quality-control inspectors of their homes and, by extension, the world around them. Home economists used producerist language to argue for a consumer economy in which homemakers demanded superior products and merchandising systems. "This department at Ames is not teaching young women to spend money, but to save it," wrote Iowa State College's Mary Sabin in 1901. "And in saving money they simultaneously produce, by scientific practices, more palatable foods and foods that are correctly calculated to sustain." [46] Home economists' lessons thus made purposeful, directed shopping a matter of social responsibility and civic duty for American homemakers. Informed by both the emerging philosophy of home economics and contemporary developments in science and technology as they applied to the household, course material defined specific "standards" for various aspects of domestic life, mapping out in precise detail a set of principles and guidelines for understanding such topics as household economics, food, sanitation, textiles and clothing, household equipment, and good taste.

Home economics teachings in household economics provided students with instruction on what to make at home, what to buy, how to shop, and how to recognize quality products, emphasizing that all decisions should be the result of careful, objective, and thorough analysis. Although they published "typical budgets" in many of these books, home economists encouraged each woman to plan her own budget to suit her family's particular needs and preferences. Bertha Terrill's 1905 textbook, *Household Management*, taught students to judge the quality of goods and to distinguish between shoddy and durable kitchen utensils, fabrics, and ready-made clothing. Rather than defining a "universal standard" for all women to follow, Terrill advocated instead that each student establish a "standard of life" for herself. She further urged middle-class women to be present at the point of consumption, warning against relying on domestic servants or the telephone for placing orders without examining merchandise or posted prices. Home economics instruction outlined a hierarchy of priorities—"necessities" over "superfluous things"—for homemakers to follow in formulating household budgets. Food took precedence over clothing in advice from many instructors. "It is a duty to look well, but it is not necessary, nor does it show good sense, to sacrifice the health, happiness, and higher life of the family by economizing on food and other essentials in order to secure hats, shoes, gowns, and accessories that cater to a mania for show," wrote Teachers

College professors Helen Kinne and Anna Cooley in their textbook *Foods and Household Management* (1918).[47]

Many of the era's courses in household economics aimed to teach economics from the perspective of consumers. While the economic marginalists broadened the study of economics to include the consumption of wealth as well as its production, university economics departments tended to leave "the household use of wealth" and the "economics of consumption" to home economists or to female economists such as Hazel Kyrk, who taught in the home economics program at the University of Chicago. In the university's Department of Household Administration, Sophonisba Breckinridge offered a course titled The Organization of the Retail Market, in which students learned about the development of various trading systems and the characteristics of contemporary retail organizations such as department stores and mail-order houses. Breckinridge taught her students about retailers' efforts to control consumers through advertising and brand names, and about consumers' attempts to control merchants through cooperative buying, consumers' leagues, trade unions, social legislation, and education. With her colleague Marion Talbot, Breckinridge also offered courses including The Consumption of Wealth, The Economic Basis of the Family, and Public Aspects of the Family, which together became the basis for their widely taught textbook, *The Modern Household*, published in 1912. On the West Coast, home economists at the University of California relied on this publication as well as on works by Thorstein Veblen and Scott Nearing to teach a course titled The Household as Economic Agent.[48]

The selection, purchase, and storage of foodstuffs, as well as the preparation and serving of meals, received special emphasis in home economists' quest for "right living" based on rationality. Ellen Richards had trained a cohort of younger women to study food in scientific terms and to prepare healthy and economical meals under sanitary and efficient conditions. As Richards's students took on leading roles in home economics departments at land-grant colleges around the country, they found support from the agricultural establishment for the continued study of food and nutrition. To explicitly distance their subject from "cookery," many home economics administrators abandoned the term *cooking* in course titles, offering courses instead in such topics as "selection and preparation of food," which taught the composition of foods and the body's nutritional requirements, and the "economical use of food," which taught how to tailor family budgets to maximize the nutritional value of family diets. Although the specific instruction varied according to the individual teacher and the audience she sought to address, the quantifiable aspects of foods and their constituent parts took precedence over taste and pleasure for most home economists. Efficiency in fueling the human body, economy in purchasing ingredients, and sanitation in preservation were thus the main tenets of home economists' lessons about food.[49] By incorporating these modern values into a new understanding of a homemaker's responsibility for her family's food consumption, home economists expanded the technical terrain of meal planning and preparation and taught ordinary women a new language with which to navigate it.

Home sanitation, or "household bacteriology," constituted another science-based area of home economists' instruction. In the 1870s and 1880s, concerns for the spread of infectious disease had informed domestic science teachings about the proper design and planning of domestic dwellings. Drawing on both the chemist's understanding of health and disease and the experimental science of bacteriology, Ellen Richards's work in the field of sanitary science helped give precise definition to the issue.[50] By 1900, the germ theory of disease and bacteriology had been incorporated into the older discipline of sanitary science as the basis for a widespread public health campaign. Scientific findings about the spread of "house diseases" provided home economists with an opportunity for action. "Domestic disease prevention," writes historian Nancy Tomes, "served as a perfect illustration of how science applied to the home could promote individual, familial, and social uplift." S. Maria Elliott, a professor of home economics at Simmons College in Boston, taught women to understand the domestic environment through lessons about germ life. Her textbook, *Household Bacteriology* (1907), described a world full of invisible microbes and told homemakers how to distinguish good ones from bad ones. Prescribing a set of habits for the "intelligent management of human wastes" and other organic matter, Elliott stressed the importance of sanitary toilets and their maintenance, as well as the dangers of dust. College professors and extension agents relied on texts such as Elliott's to teach these guidelines and their scientific rationale. To convey the vitality of bacterial life in the household, teachers had students conduct simple experiments such as growing "dust gardens" in petri dishes. At Cornell, Martha Van Rensselaer instructed women to ward off infectious disease by paying extra for safe milk, buying packaged goods, and patronizing markets where groceries were kept under cover. Together, these lessons provided homemakers with scientific knowledge and practical tips about links between modern home life and the outside world.[51]

While early teachings on the topic of textiles and clothing emphasized the making and sewing of clothes, in the 1910s university home economics programs began to focus on teaching students to make purchasing decisions about ready-to-wear garments and household furnishings. Kate Heintz Watson's *Textiles and Clothing* (1907) reflected the reality that most women at the turn-of-the-century still produced or oversaw the production of their clothing. This textbook offered technical instruction in fiber and fabric identification, weaving, basic sewing techniques, dressmaking, and clothing repair, but it contained little in the way of explicit instruction to women as consumers.[52] Appearing six years later, Woolman and McGowan's far more comprehensive text, *Textiles: A Handbook for the Student and the Consumer* (1913), provided readers with a thorough technical basis on which to evaluate the quality of fabric and ready-made clothing.

The authors took their cue from home economists' scientific and health-oriented approach to cooking and household sanitation, teaching readers to dress "according to good sense rather than fashion." Extending the call of late-nineteenth-century dress reformers who encouraged women to think of clothing in terms of the needs of the body, the authors proposed a set of criteria for what they called "rational clothing" to prevent disease and promote "the desired state of perfect health." The body's ideal condition should be clean, well-ventilated, and unrestricted. Fiber and fabric choices should be made with consideration for keeping the body dry and at a constant temperature. The book urged readers to avoid tight clothing such as pointed-toed shoes, poorly fitted corsets, and heavy skirts, all of which were "worn at a sacrifice not only of comfort but of health." *Textiles*, which was reprinted several times before a revised edition was published in 1926, further encouraged students to consider their purchasing decisions in the context of both individual household budgets and national market conditions. Woolman and McGowan warned that "extravagance in clothing" not only was a bad investment but also carried additional dangers: it led to corrupt selfish spending; it encouraged women of lesser means to emulate the rich by buying "flimsy, showy fabrics" that were shoddy and often also had "a degrading moral effect on the wearers"; and it led young wage earners to sacrifice money needed for food and shelter. To help students purchase clothing in line with their income levels, the authors offered budget guidelines and instruction in laundering and repair. At the same time, *Textiles* argued that women's buying habits were only partially to blame for a poor situation. The book devoted an entire chapter to the "economic and social aspects of textile purchase," advocating the standardization of textiles and a labeling system for consumers to use in making purchasing decisions. Although McGowan and Woolman welcomed new materials and new processes, they urged individual consumers and organized women's clubs to demand "pure textiles" "honestly standardized and labeled," just as they called for "pure foods."[53]

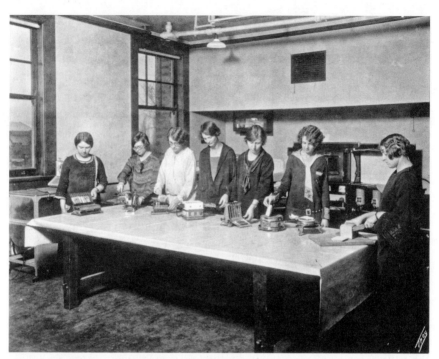

*Home economics students at Cornell University testing toasters, 1924.
(Division of Rare and Manuscript Collections, Cornell University)*

In teaching about household equipment, home economists assumed that their students needed to know less about doing work by hand and more about how to select, operate, and maintain new laborsaving devices of the household.[54] Household appliances and utensils became a part of the curriculum, which at Teachers College included coverage of gas stoves in cooking classes and courses such as The Technology of Cookery.[55] Seeking to keep up with the latest products, professors at many schools assembled collections of readily available commercial goods. Teachers College established an Educational Museum where lantern slides, illustrations, and a range of household utensils were on display.[56] Collections like these helped introduce young students to the new gas and electrical systems and their possibilities for the home. They further allowed home economics professors to provide object lessons in the tools' inner workings and teach their students to distinguish between a practical, laborsaving item and a more frivolous, wasteful one. By the 1920s, most land-grant schools had built "practice" or "home management" houses to provide students with laboratory environments in which to experience consumer goods in the context of simulated and idealized domestic spaces.[57]

Instruction in "good taste" constituted another important element of home economists' teachings. Courses in the history of art and home decoration became standard components of the home economics curricula on college campuses. "Everyone recognizes the desirability of educating women to be intelligent consumers of the commodities that form so large a part of their own possessions and are so important in furnishing their homes," announced Isabel Bevier when she established a course in household art at the University of Illinois in 1905.[58] By 1920, many schools had initiated courses in applied art that linked lessons in art history with guidance in the aesthetics of interior decoration. At the Garland School of Homemaking in Boston, Amelia Muir Baldwin lectured students on the history of Western art and took them to museums, with the aim of providing them with a set of guidelines with which to plan and decorate a house in good taste. Her final exam asked students to compare medieval Christian art with the art of ancient Greece and also to explain how to use aesthetic principles to select a gift for a friend: "If you wanted to buy a piece of pottery for a wedding present, from what points of view would you criticize it?"[59] Educators such as Baldwin sought to provide their students with a systematic method of relating art to everyday living. Informed by a larger set of concerns about refinement and gentility as hallmarks of middle-class identity, home economists' lessons in good taste were often also included as part of general instruction in budget planning and household management.

Together, home economists' lessons in the years prior to 1920 aimed to prepare women to be ideal, rational consumers and, by extension, productive homemakers and good citizens. By teaching women to think about consumer products in scientific and technical terms, and by framing a set of principles for evaluating household consumer goods according to values of health, economy, sanitation, and good taste, home economics professors and extension agents gave a generation of homemakers a roadmap for achieving middle-class identity through consumption. Home economists' tight focus on material conditions in the home reinforced the idea that consumption was a matter of private, individual decisions, and it tied women's social responsibility to their work in the home. At the same time, by emphasizing women's roles in consumption over their roles in production, home economists' instruction in rational consumption also elevated the status of that role by maintaining that women's work as consumers had social and economic value. Although they also argued that other actors in the marketplace—namely, manufacturers and distributors—had a responsibility to make the world of consumption more efficient and less wasteful, home economists taught women that their private decisions in the marketplace had a special public significance.

"A Wonderful Opportunity":
Directing Household Consumption during World War I

In the summer of 1917, Cornell University home economics professors Flora Rose and Martha Van Rensselaer campaigned tirelessly in New York State for the U.S. Food Administration (USFA). Like other home economists throughout the country, they responded to the nation's entry into World War I by leading local efforts encouraging homemakers to conserve food for the American military and its allies in Europe. "[We] have been like two bumble bees all summer and we buzz early and late," Rose wrote to a student in late August. "I think never before have we spent so many hours a day in the office, nor have we traveled around the country, north, south, east and west at so vigorous a rate trying to get the necessary interest in food conservation aroused and stimulated. It has been a great summer, however, in spite of all its work, for we both feel that it is really a wonderful opportunity to be able to share in this big new movement and to feel that we have something to contribute that is really needed and of value."[60] With these words, Rose captured the importance of World War I food conservation campaigns for herself, Van Rensselaer, and their fellow home economists.

World War I was a watershed moment for home economists' reform and professional struggles. When the war began in 1914, home economists had already carved out a sizeable niche for their field in the nation's educational system. But the field's leaders sought additional channels through which to influence American homemakers and to increase their professional status, which remained unproven in the eyes of male counterparts. Rallying behind the newly appointed U.S. food administrator, Herbert Hoover, to spread "the gospel of the clean plate" gave Rose, Van Rensselaer, and their colleagues an unprecedented chance to demonstrate their knowledge about the efficient consumption of household goods, particularly foodstuffs, and to prove their effectiveness as educators. "Suddenly this stepchild of modern education, Home Economics, was discovered to be an extremely valuable ally," Flora Rose reflected after the war. Food policy was a vital part of the Allied war strategy, and participation in the food conservation campaigns gave home economists an official context in which to join with other organizations of men and women to promote a patriotic common cause and to prove that they had a unique set of useful skills to bring to bear on the national crisis. By helping to frame the welfare of the nation and its allies in terms of how Americans chose and prepared their food and spent their money, home economists won federal endorsement of their cause to promote a scientific diet and the ideal of rational consumption, and, in the process, gained public recognition as consumer experts.[61]

Spreading the food conservation message was a key component of the USFA's mission to send food to the American military and to the Allied civilian population in Europe. Just months after the United States joined the war effort and even before Congress passed the enabling legislation to control the food supply, President Woodrow Wilson appointed mining engineer and business manager Herbert Hoover to direct the new temporary agency and help compensate for the food shortage in Europe. Since the war's onset, Hoover had directed the Commission for the Relief of Belgium (CRB), a federally sanctioned volunteer effort to feed millions of people in Belgium and German-occupied northern France. For assistance in his new role at the USFA, Hoover assembled an inner circle that included male administrators, friends, and former CRB colleagues, as well as his contacts in mining engineering, the food industry, and at Stanford University. Hoover and his fellow food administrators belonged to a group of managerial liberals who advocated a new governing system that relied on corporate self-regulation through welfare capitalism, scientific management, and philanthropy. While coordinating the efficient production and consumption of foodstuffs, the agency sought not only to supply relief food to Europe but also to demonstrate that industrial leaders, in cooperation with government, could manage public policy at a time of crisis through the application of technical expertise. Although these managerial liberals used temporary executive powers to direct and regulate the domestic production and distribution of foodstuffs with the goal of sending as much as possible to Europe and fighting inflation at home, they were also committed to "intense decentralization" of their programs through a system of state food administrators.[62]

To meet the Allies' demands for food, the domestic consumption of certain foods—wheat, meat, sugar, and fats—would also have to be curtailed, but Hoover was determined not to implement a system of home-front rationing. Intent on defying the German example of an autocratic state, Hoover preferred to rely on experts to encourage voluntary conservation through publicity and persuasion. Toward this end, Hoover appointed his close friend, Stanford University president Ray Lyman Wilbur, as director of the USFA's Food Conservation Division, which was later renamed the Home Conservation Division. Wilbur assembled a sizable apparatus to promote conservation at all sites of food consumption throughout the country, including bakeries, restaurants, hotels, and other retail outlets. Although Wilbur's team operated outside the propaganda machine at the Office of War Information, it employed many techniques pioneered there by war information director George Creel. Through press releases, bulletins, recipes, exhibits, films, posters, billboards, and a speaker's bureau, the division disseminated the food conservation message to magazines, newspapers, schoolteachers, university professors, and public libraries. The division also relied heavily on other government agencies and existing voluntary organizations to enlist American citizens in support of what Hoover called an "unprecedented adventure in democracy."[63]

"Food will win the war!" was the USFA's rallying slogan, and Hoover and Wilbur looked to women to implement this strategy. The Food Conservation Division focused much of its attention on the home, where Hoover and Wilbur assumed that decisions about how food was consumed rested primarily with women. In a major campaign to enlist American homemakers in a "great army drafted by conscience," the division asked volunteers to send pledge cards to Washington, D.C., promising to "carry out the direction and advice of the Food Administrator in the conduct of my household in so far as my circumstances permit." In return, each woman received a "home card" with the organization's insignia—a shield with the national flag surrounded by heads of wheat—to hang in the front window of her home. On the reverse side, the card gave instructions for adhering to "the gospel of the clean plate" in the name of patriotism. The card was available in multiple languages. For a small fee, women could purchase a copy of a pattern for sewing the USFA uniform and an insignia badge.[64]

Hoover and Wilbur soon recognized that theirs was an ambitious undertaking. Wheat, meat, sugar, and fats were staples of the American diet, after all. Even for those homemakers committed to adjusting the management of their households in conformity with the demands of war, it was not immediately obvious how to select groceries and prepare meals according to the USFA guidelines while still ensuring a healthy, palatable, and economical diet. Besides, food conservation faced potential opposition from industrial workers who were eager to spend increased wartime wages on food for their families and who had little interest in or were suspicious of lessons from the government about how to prepare their meals. A large segment of the working population was comprised of European immigrants who depended on bread as a staple as much as did the European allies. Demonstrations by Jewish women in New York City in the winter of 1917 protesting high food prices and the substitution of rice for chicken suggested that the nation's political leaders had reason to fear popular rejection of food conservation measures. In addition, families in many rural communities were skeptical of a call for reduced consumption of the agricultural goods they produced.[65] Thus Wilbur made education—as well as publicity and propaganda—integral to his approach. "The American people can be led, but they cannot be driven and they can only be led by understanding," Wilbur wrote to Hoover. "Your greatest achievement will be recorded as your service to democracy in standing for the intelligent will of the people guided and controlled by a common consent and common understanding, instead of autocratic methods." For Wilbur, education was "absolutely vital" to the success of the USFA's voluntary approach and to the maintenance of "the proper public attitude toward the Food Administration." He further envisioned that public exposure to guidance by experts would be important to "the conduct of the nation after the war."[66] Although many state food administrators dismissed this educational initiative as "the work of women and teachers," Wilbur and Hoover shared a commitment to their chosen direction. They were far less familiar with how to influence homemakers' consumption patterns, however, than with how to control commodity production and prices. Convincing homemakers to voluntarily adjust their purchasing and cooking habits to conserve foodstuffs required familiarity with tasks Wilbur and Hoover associated with women's responsibilities in the home. "The guiding hand of women in the home can alone control this matter," they announced in an early press release. Lacking a ready apparatus of their own, they turned to women's organizations to help mobilize the home front.[67]

To reach the nation's homemakers, Hoover relied heavily at first on the Women's Committee of the Council of National Defense (CND), which was charged in April 1917 with coordinating all types of women's war-related work. The Women's Committee helped cultivate support from women's organizations to recruit individual volunteers to sign pledges. But Hoover had difficulties working with this group, and by the summer he confronted a "thorny problem" with its members. Led by the outspoken women's suffragist Anna Howard Shaw, the Women's Committee sought to use women's war work to gain political authority and equality with men. Specifically, in exchange for their contributions to the war effort, Shaw and most of her cohort sought to win the support of male political leaders for women's suffrage. Toward this end, Shaw wanted the Women's Committee members to serve "not as adjuncts, not as a by-product, but as an integral part of the national citizen power." Committee members bristled at Hoover's being in charge of the USFA in the first place. They disliked his use of the pledge card and were frustrated by his rejection of their call for a subtler, more personal approach to food conservation. Shaw's group was committed to furthering a broader range of social causes, including

Assembled in Washington, D.C., at the U.S. Food Administration headquarters, staff home economists with the Food Conservation Division proudly wear the uniform designed by colleague Sarah Field Splint (back row center). Featuring the USFA insignia on the cap and on the left sleeve, the uniform soon became known as the Hoover apron. (U.S. Food Administration Records, Env B, Hoover Institution Archives)

labor reform, than was implied by the requirement to "don an-apron-and-cap-uniform"—an essentially domestic guise—to meet substantial responsibilities with only minimal authority.[68]

Home economists' priorities were less overtly political than those of the Women's Committee, and unlike Shaw and her colleagues they embraced the uniform apron and the official, scientific identity that it conveyed. Most of the home economists who took leading roles at the USFA favored women's suffrage. However, while Shaw and her fellow Women's Committee members resented Wilson's failure to select a woman to head the USFA, home economists were willing to accept gender segregation, a strategy that ironically gained the movement's leaders significant levels of prestige.[69] A prominent role in a successful wartime campaign promised home economists a chance to consolidate their recent gains in education and to legitimize their special knowledge about domestic consumption in general and food in particular. In this context, Sarah

ENVISIONING THE RATIONAL CONSUMER

Field Splint, editor of *Today's Housewife*, not only went on record in support of votes for women but also designed the very uniform that Anna Howard Shaw and her cohort rejected. Because home economists located the source of their power in expertise rather than politics per se, they took pride in the uniform that others found to be in conflict with a changing political role of women during this period.[70]

In home economists, Hoover found a group of women that staked its professional identity on teaching the very messages he sought to deliver. The U.S. food administrator believed it was "particularly necessary to receive assistance from skilled women," and that home economists' training and experience in household management were ideally suited to disseminating information about food and integrating this knowledge into the realities of homemakers' lives. To ensure that food conservation messages were presented in the context of the latest developments in nutritional science, Hoover enlisted leading experts in the field to serve on his Advisory Committee on Nutrition. In addition, Hoover took pains to win home economists' "allegiance" by giving them "their proper position" in the USFA's food conservation work. Seeking their advice in early June 1917, he convened a group of leading women in the field and appointed them to the Advisory Committee on Home Economics. Hoover's committee included many veteran participants of the Lake Placid conferences, among them Henrietta Calvin, Caroline Hunt, Helen Louise Johnson, Mary Hinman Abel, Isabel Ely Lord (Pratt Institute), and Abby Marlatt (University of Wisconsin), who served as its first chair. In spite of opposition from some food administrators who doubted the value of home economics training, Hoover insisted that a home economics director be appointed to work with the food administrator in each state. In most cases the state directors for home economics extension work were appointed to these positions. Although he continued to rely on a range of women's organizations, including the Women's Committee of the CND and the General Federation of Women's Clubs, Hoover created a special leadership position in the USFA for home economists.[71]

Hoover placed home economists in this leadership role on the basis of their expertise, their values, and their organizational networks. Because home economists had their fingers on the pulse of the latest developments in nutritional science, they were perfectly placed to translate these scientific findings to American homemakers. Several leading women in the field had studied or worked with members of the Advisory Committee on Nutrition. Some had pioneered in the development of food preservation methods such as canning and drying. A much larger group of home economists had incorporated recent findings in these areas into a vast body of instructional literature.[72] As a group, home economists were thus well-qualified to determine appropriate food substitutions and to incorporate them into conservation messages.

Home economists further identified with the larger reform vision that Hoover brought to his leadership of the USFA. As an engineer and a progressive politician who believed in technical solutions to the nation's social problems, Hoover framed food conservation as a social engineering project and an experiment in the role of experts in modern democracy. His food conservation strategy combined expert advice and voluntary cooperation in a manner he hoped would be a model for the new industrial order that would emerge after the war. In addition, Hoover and most home economists held similar convictions about the moral importance of regulating household consumption for its own sake, not just for the war effort. Home economists' calls for "rational living," and their emphasis on ideals of health, sanitation, and economy, dovetailed nicely with Hoover's critique of American society as wasteful and inefficient, and with his goal to achieve the "moral consolidation of our people" by persuading 30 percent of the American population to become "disciplined . . . in simple living."[73]

Finally, home economists had the additional advantage of being tied into an established institutional structure through which to communicate with the nation's homemakers. Especially in the early months of World War I, before the USFA had obtained congressional authorization, Hoover needed to work through existing channels as much as possible. Home economists were at the center of the newly created extension service—a complex nationwide bureaucracy for modernizing agriculture supported by federal, state, and local funds. Headquartered at land-grant colleges in most states, this network enabled home economists to tap into the energies of not only extension agents but also university professors and their students. The number of recruits was still small—in 1916, only 480 counties had home demonstration agents—but the extension service nonetheless provided home economists, and Hoover, with an organizational infrastructure to mobilize for the cause of food conservation in rural areas. Organized by state and by county, it was an ideal structure through which to realize Hoover's commitment to decentralized methods of operating.[74]

For all these reasons, Hoover and Wilbur viewed this group of new female professionals as an ideal resource for combining education and persuasion to engineer consumer behavior to meet wartime needs. With the appointment of Sarah Field Splint to direct the national program and the naming of prominent home economics professors to lead the effort in each state, home economists converged on Washington and state headquarters beginning in the summer of 1917. Martha Van Rensselaer took a leave from Cornell University's Home Economics Department to replace Splint in the spring of 1918. Splint and Van Rensselaer recruited several members of the Advisory Committee on Home Economics and other colleagues to join them in Washington for short periods on a rotating basis. Flora Rose, Katherine Blunt (University of Chicago), Isabel Bevier (University of Illinois), and Mary Swartz Rose (Teachers College) were among the most active collaborators: mature, educated women between the ages of thirty and fifty who had each spent up to twenty years researching, writing, and teaching various aspects of food, nutrition, and household management. Together they enlisted not only their peers but also younger home economists, including their junior colleagues as well as students.[75]

Home economists in the USFA's Food Conservation Division served as the official advisers on the selection, preparation, and preservation of household foods during the war. These women drew on their network of contacts at the AHEA, the USDA, the Bureau of Education, women's magazines, and land-grant colleges across the country to prepare instructions for homemakers about how to maintain a healthy diet while also honoring patriotic food conservation pledges. From a central experimental kitchen in the USFA's Washington headquarters, they conducted and coordinated research into substitutes for wheat, meat, sugar, and fats. To make diet restrictions possible, palatable, and healthy, they developed recipes that gave precise instructions for wheatless breads, meatless meals, and sugarless sweets. In addition, they refined food preservation methods such as canning and drying. Dozens of home economists wrote, edited, and reviewed hundreds of pamphlets and cookbooks, lesson plans, books, recipes, magazine and newspaper articles, and press releases offering guidance on food conservation, many of which were locally or commercially published. They sent guidelines in the form of press releases to newspaper and magazine editors, or packaged them into instructional materials and lesson plans aimed at target audiences.[76] In addition, home economists within the USFA coordinated cooking and canning demonstrations and organized canning kitchens and clubs in local communities.

In these publications and demonstrations, home economists promoted the gospel of scientific cookery. The concept of substituting one food for another was based on the idea that certain foods had analogous "food values" and therefore could be exchanged. The nation's leading nutritional scientists had developed food charts identifying the calories contained in each food, as well as quantifying protein, carbohydrates, and fats within different foods. Wartime cookbooks and pamphlets synthesized these findings and presented them to homemakers in an accessible, colloquial manner. By emphasizing each food's contribution to an individual's diet, home economists provided homemakers with a conceptual framework for understanding that substitutes were not only possible but also healthy and nutritious. At the same time, they encouraged homemakers to think about meal preparation and dining according to the bodily requirements that food fulfilled. In *Everyday Foods in War Time* (1917), Mary Swartz Rose urged readers to consider potatoes "not in terms of their hot mealiness and spicy mildness, but in terms of that elusive thing called 'DIET.'" Rose explained that, when evaluated on the basis of its fats, proteins, carbohydrates, and mineral salts, the potato could be considered a "staff of life" in the place of wheat bread.[77]

Recipes for wheatless and meatless meals followed from these principles of food value. Janet McKenzie Hill's *Economical War-Time Cook Book* (1918), written privately but "in accordance with the rules and regulations of the USFA, and with its requests," included a typical array of dishes. Recipes for "Victory Breads," made with at least a 20 percent substitution of alternate grains rather than wheat, aimed to achieve the lightness of the wheat loaf without its gluten. Like most wartime cookbooks, Hill's compilation offered suggestions for quick breads and muffins made with baking powder or soda, allowing for even less wheat. "War Time Boston Brown Bread," made with equal parts of oatmeal, rye, and cornmeal and a bit of molasses and leavened with both baking soda and baking powder, was a recipe that appeared in Hill's and several other cookbooks. The *Economical War-Time Cook Book* emphasized main dishes that were rich in protein but used cheese, nuts, beans, fish, and little, if any, beef. "Baked Bean Loaf," "Peanut Butter Loaf," and "Pecan Nut-meat Sausage with Bananas" tried to simulate the textures of meat, while other dishes—such as "Scalloped Rice and Cheese" and "Fresh Fish Smothered in Tomato Sauce"—encouraged cooks to appreciate the qualities of less commonly consumed foods.[78]

New knowledge about vitamins came to light just before the war, and to a limited extent home economists used the food conservation drive to spread the word about this latest nutritional research to American homemakers. Although researchers still had only a vague understanding of how vitamins functioned in the diet, home economists heralded the healthful effects of fruits and vegetables, declaring them no longer a luxury but a nutritional necessity. "Any vegetable," the USFA's *Food Guide for War Service at Home* (1918) pointed out, "can be used as a 'meat extender.'" The authors recommended French-style stews, with a little bit of meat and lots of vegetables. "[But] the more America eats of almost any kind of vegetable or fruit, the less of the more durable, concentrated food she will require. The products are so varied in kinds and composition that they can be used to save almost any purpose—beans and peas to save meat; potatoes and others to save wheat; sweet fruits to save sugar; jams, even, when spread on bread, to save fat. All will improve the health and therefore increase human energies for winning the war."[79]

To ensure the availability of fruits and vegetables for household consumption year-round, home economists at the USFA devoted much attention to refining canning methods and disseminating them throughout the country. Home canning techniques were developed in the early nineteenth century, becoming common after John Mason's 1858 invention of a glass jar and zinc lid for "putting up" fresh produce. Although fruits could be preserved in sugar without much trouble, poor seals on canned vegetables tended to result in significant spoilage. After the 1890s, when bacteriological studies revealed the causes of contamination and the mechanical production of glass jars provided consumers with more consistent, high-quality storage, canning became less expensive and significantly safer. By the early 1910s, many modern cookbook authors urged homemakers to can at home and incorporated lessons about anaerobic and aerobic bacteria in their instructions on food preservation. The USDA's Office of Home Economics developed a "cold pack method" in 1915 that involved blanching vegetables before putting them in jars, where they were cooked and processed simultaneously. Although differences of opinion remained on the best techniques, this new method made canning vegetables easier than ever before. Due in part to promotion by extension agents, canning clubs were gaining popularity in many communities by 1917. Still, canning was a difficult, time-consuming process that often led to large amounts of spoilage and waste. Because of the potential health dangers involved, Hoover was determined to teach proper canning methods "by personal instruction and demonstration, and not a printed propaganda," so as to ensure clear instruction and to prevent poisoning.[80] Home economics demonstrations about food preservation provided face-to-face guidance on sanitary, bacteria-free techniques, combining instruction and hands-on practice with friendly encouragement. The state- and county-based organizational structure of the extension service was well-suited to providing live demonstrations in communities, where instructions could be adjusted to the needs of local residents.[81]

While teaching scientific cookery and sanitary food preservation, home economists used wartime publications and demonstrations to promote a broader message about rational consumption. Hoover's calls for all Americans—including homemakers—to "eliminate waste" provided an ideal context for home economists' lessons about "wise expenditure."[82] Teachers College professor Mary Swartz Rose used the wartime emergency to encourage home-

U.S. Food Administration home economists shared their expertise in canning methods by offering a series of live demonstrations and by establishing model community canning kitchens where women could preserve fruits and vegetables for household use or commercial sale, such as this one in Asheville, North Carolina. (Division of Rare and Manuscript Collections, Cornell University)

makers to eat not only more healthily but also more economically. "There are few diets which cannot be so rearranged as to give a better nutritive return on the money spent than is usually secured by our haphazard methods of planning meals," she told her readers, arguing that increased spending of "money, time and thought on food" would benefit society in the long run. In its Food Thrift series, the USDA's Office of Home Economics provided similar instruction in "how women can avoid waste of food in the household," including the use of leftovers and the "economical use of meat." The leaflets were the result of collaboration with Alice Peloubet Norton at the Treasury Department's Division of Savings. Norton, a student of Ellen Swallow Richards and professor at the University of Chicago, also was the editor of the *Journal of Home Economics* and a member of the editorial staff at the Food Conservation Division in these years. Like her contemporary in Boston, the Clothing Information Bureau's Mary Schenck Woolman, who organized efforts to promote the "economical use" of a wide range of household items, Norton used her position at the Department of Treasury to promote rational consumption in the context of war-time patriotism.[83]

Many communities responded enthusiastically to the USFA's campaigns, but not all homemakers greeted the food conservation drive with open arms. As early as late July 1917, the USFA reported that more than 2 million homemakers had signed pledge cards.[84] Communities in the South and West proved particularly supportive, and Wilbur found communities in Iowa and Indiana well organized and effective. However, rural women in these and other states were already overworked, and few had time or energy for canning or drying fruits and vegetables. Many viewed home economics extension agents as intrusive. Other homemakers were suspicious of signing a pledge card that resembled all too closely the documents their husbands and sons had signed before being called to military service. In urban areas, many industrial workers resented being told how to spend their wages; German sympathizers, numerous in the midwestern cities, were certainly not interested in supporting Uncle Sam. Although many farming communities benefited from the increase in prices brought about by the food crisis, others resented the government controls that Hoover's agency put in place to keep inflation in check. Some farmers were disappointed when they did not earn prices as high as they anticipated or were hit with losses when consumer demand failed to follow increased production.[85] Food conservation agents were often most effective when they could meet with women one on one, but there simply were not enough women in their ranks to ensure this level of contact with all of the nation's homemakers or to overcome these sources of resistance.

Still, in the political climate of the era, home economists' work in promoting food conservation became all the more important as the war progressed, and as Hoover and the USFA implemented more stringent conservation measures. A renewed pledge campaign drive in the fall of 1917 enlisted 13 million members of the nation's 20 million households. The introduction of one "meatless day" and "one wheatless" day per week had helped achieve the campaign's goal. In December of that year Hoover increased his commitment of wheat to Europe and sparked an even more ambitious food conservation crusade. But the nation's supply of wheat was down from the year before, and Hoover failed to pass legislation to increase his control on food manufacturers and distributors. To meet the daunting challenge of Hoover's promise, the USFA called for Americans to observe "wheatless days" on Mondays and Wednesdays and "meatless days" on Tuesdays, and to consume at least one wheatless meal and one meatless meal on all other days. As Wilbur and Hoover sought ways to convince Americans to conserve more wheat, resistance to their efforts made them concerned about the USFA's image. By the winter of 1918, the USFA discontinued the use of the "home cards" and home economists adjusted their message to a general call for "no waste."[86]

Hoover declared the USFA's food conservation efforts a success, however: by mid-May 1918 he announced that Americans had reduced wheat consumption to 60 percent of the usual rate. The USFA claimed to have received pledge cards from more than half of U.S. households; a USDA survey indicated that middle-class Americans were eating less meat and consuming more fruits, vegetables, and milk than before the war. Home economists took credit for reducing food consumption overall by 10 percent in 1918. Despite these various claims, the precise results of campaigns to reduce the consumption of wheat, meat, and sugar in American households are unclear. All accounts show that the United States sent increased amounts of wheat to Europe during the war, but it is difficult to know how much of this wheat was saved through conservation of individual households rather than other controls that the USFA put in place at the time, notably stricter rules for food usage placed on hotels, restaurants, and commercial bakeries.[87]

Yet the food conservation campaigns had results beyond any statistical measures of changed consumer behavior, and for home economists they were an unquestionable triumph. Deep involvement with wartime government conservation initiatives provided home economics with the official sanction of a legitimate, patriotic cause. "World War I meant excitement and activity and feeling of participation in a great movement," wrote home economist Lita Bane in an early history of the field.[88] A single busy week of organizing a team of demonstrators at a New York City food conservation exhibit represented "the high water mark of our career," Mary Swartz Rose later recalled.[89] The USFA elevated the nation's diet and consumption habits to the level of public policy, and it established a connection between daily patterns of living and a greater national purpose. These circumstances placed home economists in the limelight and allowed them to demonstrate that their knowledge of consumers and consumer products could make an important contribution to public life. By helping legitimize the USFA conservation campaigns, home economists' expert status was in turn reinforced in the public eye.

Patriotic endorsement further gave home economists the resources to disseminate their messages about scientific cookery and rational consumption nationwide, allowing them to reach their largest audience to date. The food conservation efforts raised a new kind of awareness about nutrition and household consumption, and positioned home economists, in the words of Flora Rose, to further "direct that consciousness into educational channels." Isabel

Bevier recalled that the war sparked "an awakening of interest—people were asking many questions about food. The war experience had taught the layman the close relationship between food and health."[90] The food conservation campaigns' emphasis on a balanced diet and their celebration of economy over wastefulness was a dream come true for many home economists. Certainly not everyone was inclined to think about food scientifically, but home economists' wartime efforts did much to bring messages about wise, scientifically informed consumption—and the value of expert advice itself—into the mainstream of white, middle-class culture. Members of the USFA's Advisory Committee on Home Economics noted with pride during the war that a step "toward the control of courses of information" had taken place in that women's magazine editors and the reading public became accustomed to "turning to experts, instead of faddists, for information." By stimulating the "demand for authentic information," the food campaigns confirmed a central place for home economics among middle-class women who looked to experts for advice about healthy eating, household management, and consumption, and who derived their class identity in part through following the standards they prescribed.[91]

In addition, the wartime food conservation efforts provided a context for home economists to strengthen their own networks. Rather than building a separate organization for food conservation, Hoover contributed significant portions of the USFA budget to expanding the agricultural extension service, transforming it, in the words of historian Wayne Rasmussen, from an educational organ to a "service agency for individuals and organizations and for the federal government." The war emergency introduced home economists into many communities for the first time; New York State alone saw the placement of new home demonstration agents in thirty-three counties during the war years. Despite the protests and resistance of some individuals, wartime food conservation efforts legitimized home economists and the extension service in the eyes of many rural people.[92] In their university posts, home economics professors gained status by championing the war effort and leading state food conservation efforts.

Finally, the war created new kinds of opportunities for home economists, just as it did for women in other fields. "Hotels and hospitals asked for dietitians, banks and other commercial enterprises looked for women trained in the study of the problems of the home to help in teaching thrift," recalled Isabel Bevier, director of home economics at the University of Illinois. "The Children's Bureau, the Red Cross, the Public Health Service—all called persistently for home economists." In celebrating home economists as professionals, Bevier claimed, the war experience gave them "growing respect from the public" as well as "a wider vision of the world's needs."[93] The nation's male leaders looked to home economists to communicate with women consumers. As corporations joined in the food conservation campaigns, seeking to align themselves and their products with the patriotic cause, they relied on home economists to construct their image. With the assistance of home economists, food manufacturers such as Pillsbury and Armour & Company issued cookbooks and magazine advertisements articulating the value of their products in light of the national emergency. Her experience during World War I made at least one home economist, Mary Schenck Woolman, "a firm believer in the cooperation between business and education."[94]

World War I was a turning point for the home economics movement. Through the war effort, home economists consolidated their identity as both reformers and professionals with particular expertise in the area of household consumption. In the name of patriotism, home economists seized the opportunity to promote their ideas about nutrition and rational consumption. The food conservation campaigns allowed them to show that their expertise in food preparation and preservation could be useful to American society. Hoover's celebration of home economists as ideal homemakers and as experts in the fast-developing science of nutrition legitimized their collective identity in the public eye. With his endorsement, home economists emerged triumphant after 1918 in a newly sanctioned role as expert interpreters and regulators of consumer demand. Throughout the next decade, as Hoover became U.S. secretary of commerce and then president, home economists' alliance with him also helped launch the women in important new, and more complex, directions.

Conclusion

By bringing together intersecting groups of professors, researchers, teachers, extension agents, popular writers, and college-educated homemakers, the Lake Placid conferences—and later the American Home Economics Association—drew on the multiple legacies of the Progressive Era to embrace this growing educational movement. The AHEA's success in winning government support allowed home economists to carve out institutional niches in secondary and higher education and to firmly establish their discipline as a professionally grounded, reform-oriented movement focused on promoting a broad public understanding and acceptance of rational consumption. World War I solidified the centrality of consumption as a focus for home economists' teachings, legitimized home economists as experts about consumption, and confirmed that middle-class women could be receptive to the lessons of this new women's profession. As undergraduate and graduate university programs in home economics continued to grow in number and in size throughout the 1920s, a younger generation of home economists would continue to pursue this agenda while finding new and unexpected roles and opportunities outside of the classroom and the home, notably in government and business.[95]

2

Creating a Science of Consumption
at the Bureau of Home Economics, 1920–1940

When Secretary of Agriculture Henry C. Wallace decided to create a Bureau of Home Economics (BHE) in 1923, he chose as its director Louise Stanley, a prominent home economist at midcareer with a broad vision of the field's potential and a commitment to using research into the quality of household goods to serve consumers. Born in 1883, Stanley had attended the Lake Placid conferences as a young graduate student and shared Ellen Swallow Richards's commitment to education as the basis of reform and to scientific expertise as a means of creating opportunities for professional women. Raised on a Tennessee farm, Stanley received a B.S. in home economics from Peabody College at the University of Nashville as well as additional degrees from such institutions as the University of Chicago and Teachers College Columbia University. As one of several female students of Lafayette B. Mendel at Yale University, Stanley earned a Ph.D. in biochemistry in 1911. Acutely aware of the limited employment avenues for women scientists, Stanley belonged to a cohort of scientifically trained women who found opportunities in home economics. Beginning with her first teaching position in the Department of Home Economics at the University of Missouri in 1907, Stanley soon became prominent in the field. She was appointed head of the department at Missouri in 1917 and served as coordinator of World War I food conservation campaigns for the state of Missouri. In the process, Stanley emerged as a leader in the American Home Economics Association (AHEA), playing a principal role in winning increased federal expenditures for home economics education. As chair of its Legislative Committee in 1920, she advocated for a public role for home economics beyond the home and classroom.

During her two decades of leadership at the bureau, Stanley developed a vision for home economics that included "practically everything from the problems of production to those of distribution and consumption," with a particular interest in women's new roles as consumers: "The homemaker's value is too likely to be estimated in terms of pies, cakes, jellies, jams—the garments she makes or the vigor and frequency of her housecleaning," she told the press soon after her appointment as bureau chief. "There has been a failure to appreciate the corresponding importance of good judgment in deciding what to buy in order to secure health and the major satisfactions in life for her family."[1] Stanley's emphasis on "deciding what to buy" was characteristic of a new generation of home economists who worked after World War I to create a women's profession based on scientific expertise in consumption-related matters. In the early 1920s, they began to leverage their experience and reputation in research and teaching to secure a place for home economists as consumer experts inside institutions of government and business.

The increased visibility of home economics research and teaching contributed to Secretary Wallace's decision to create the bureau, an institution that provided a succeeding generation of women in the field with new, heightened political authority to confirm their status as experts not only in food and nutrition but also in a broad array of household goods. Congress charged this new bureau with a dual mission: helping to create markets for agricultural products (through research into their "utilization") and supplying home demonstration agents with ways to improve rural home life.[2] This dual mission gave home economists room to target a wide audience and study a wide range of products. Every household, after all, consumed agricultural goods. Likewise, most families faced choices about purchasing industrial products such as refrigerators, kitchen utensils, and ready-made clothing. The mandate of the U.S. Department of Agriculture (USDA) favored modernization in broad terms, but Secretary Wallace left it to home economists to determine what constituted "improvements" in the domestic lives of America's families. By enlisting a group of top university home economics professors to advise him on plans for the bureau, and by placing at its head a young woman with a broad vision for the field, Wallace gave home economists a chance to secure the identity of their discipline as a women's profession based on scientific expertise about consumption.

As bureau chief from 1923 to 1943, Stanley used the Bureau of Home Economics as a strategic institutional platform to strengthen home economics as a research field for women committed to generating new knowledge about the rapidly expanding scientific and technological content of the home. She hired the largest staff of women scientists in the federal government—indeed, in any U.S. institution—and put them to work analyzing a variety of agricultural and manufactured goods. Their approach to the home would prove to be wide ranging, covering issues of production, distribution, and consumption of foods, clothing, and household equipment. By integrating their findings with research results generated by industrial engineers, university professors, and social survey investigators, Stanley and her staff established the bureau as an information clearinghouse about consumer goods and (to a lesser extent) consumer behavior. Together with similar research programs conducted at colleges and universities, this clearinghouse elevated home economics as a gender-based applied science of "the user," an applied science that both gave a cohort of scientifically trained women opportunities to develop new, unique areas of expertise and reinforced contemporary understandings of consumption as a feminine activity.

Creating the Bureau

"Many women get so discouraged wasting hardly saved money on things that are more bother than helps and have to be thrown aside that when something real[l]y good is brought to their attention they refuse to risk any more experimenting," wrote H. E. Brennan, a young woman from rural Virginia, in 1921. Brennan was having trouble obtaining the product information she needed to make a sound purchase of an oil stove. For assistance, she contacted Minna C. Denton, assistant chief of the USDA's Office of Home Economics (OHE). Brennan lived six and a half miles from Manassas, a distance too far for her to travel to shop for the stove that best suited her needs. Expressing frustration at being "dependent on mail order houses" for information, she pleaded for Denton's assistance: "Housekeepers all around us are half sick from over work. A few real conveniences would stop much of this, take off last straws at any rate. . . . The farmer's wife seldom know[s] just what to get, where to get it and what it costs. . . . If you can help us perhaps you will be helping our neighbors too."[3] Through this inquiry, Brennan summarized a dilemma faced by many rural women in 1920s America. The availability of new consumer durables for the home carried both the promise of relief from household drudgery and the risk of wasting limited household income. In search of satisfactory information for making choices in a changing technological and commercial landscape, many women turned for help to government home economists, whose visibility had increased with the growth of the extension service in the 1910s.

Beginning in the late nineteenth century, a first generation of home economists played an important role in establishing the USDA as a center for research about food and nutrition on behalf of consumers. As far back as Wilbur O. Atwater's USDA-sponsored human nutrition investigations in the mid-1890s, a group of home economists studied the impact of various cooking processes on the nutritional value of foods and shared these findings with homemakers through the publication of dozens of government bulletins. This group included Atwater's daughter, Helen, who served as editorial assistant to her father after graduating from Smith College, and Lake Placid conference veteran Caroline L. Hunt, who earned a B.A. from Northwestern University and pursued graduate studies in chemistry at Northwestern and the University of Chicago. Both women were members of the National Consumers' Leagues. Atwater and Hunt assumed permanent positions in the USDA after Charles Ford Langworthy took over nutrition research in 1909, and together they created an experimental kitchen in which they studied the chemical and physical processes of cooking and canning.[4] With the establishment of the OHE in 1915, this kitchen became a hub of research activity during the World War I food conservation campaigns. After receiving one of the nation's first doctoral degrees in household management from the University of Chicago in 1918, Minna C. Denton joined the OHE as assistant chief. Denton's dissertation concerned the nutritional effects on food of various cooking methods, and she continued investigations along these lines at the OHE. Soon after her arrival, however, the agency broadened its work to include studies of household equipment, clothing, and consumer behavior. It also published a series of Thrift Leaflets instructing homemakers to spend wisely in the immediate aftermath of World War I.[5]

Secretary Wallace's decision to elevate home economics to the status of a bureau in 1923 stemmed from his assumptions that living conditions on American farms would improve if women like H. E. Brennan had a reliable source of scientific information to support their new roles as consumers, and that home economists were the experts to provide that help. In the summer of 1922, he sent Assistant Secretary Charles W. Pugsley to the AHEA meeting in Corvallis, Oregon, to announce his plans to "greatly strengthen the scientific work of the Department as it may be related to home economics" by creating an independent bureau for such work, and to place at its head "a woman of executive ability, thorough scientific training, and a broad and sympathetic understanding of what is needed to make such a bureau most helpful to the women of the land." Responding to a deepening depression in the sales of agricultural products and the growing importance of rural women's organizations, Wallace sought to remedy the agricultural crisis by enhancing the USDA's existing programs to modernize agricultural production and family farm life. In reorganizing the USDA to increase the efficiency of its operations, Wallace looked for ways to strengthen the place of home economics within the modern agricultural establishment that his agency commanded. The Smith-Lever Act of

1914 had fueled the growth of the extension service and enlarged its capacity to reach American homemakers. Now Wallace saw a need to devote more resources to supply home demonstration agents with up-to-date facts about the nutritional value of various crops and the utility of manufactured goods. Through the establishment of the Bureau of Agricultural Economics and the consolidation of the department's previously dispersed economics work, he encouraged the application of modern management techniques to not only the production but also the distribution and marketing of agricultural crops. A new Bureau of Home Economics would supplement the USDA's agricultural economics research program, generating information useful to American women who were, on the one hand, consumers of agricultural goods and, on the other hand, farmers' wives and business partners.[6]

A bureau run by women and charged with addressing women's concerns in the home promised to be an effective instrument for tapping the new political constituency that had emerged after women won the right to vote in 1920. Through the Women's Joint Congressional Committee, a strong and growing group of women's voluntary organizations lobbied successfully for federal funds for maternal and infant health protection (realized by the Sheppard-Towner Act of 1921) and for independent citizenship for married women (realized partially by the Cable Act of 1922). The American Home Economics Association and the General Federation of Women's Clubs participated in these efforts while pressuring the USDA to expand its home economics extension and research program.[7]

The decision to represent women in the federal government through a Bureau of Home Economics directed by a woman stemmed from (and reinforced) an ambiguous relationship between domesticity and feminism after suffrage had been won. USDA officials assumed that women's work on the farm primarily involved consumption, whereas men's duties were those of production. Although some leading home economists such as Isabel Bevier argued for a coeducational approach to the developing field, the segregated structure of the extension service gave institutional form to the notion that modern feminine and masculine roles in farming were and should be divided along these lines.[8] Plans for a separate Bureau of Home Economics run by women and for women drew on this existing framework as well as on the precedent established in the Progressive Era with the creation of the Children's Bureau (1912) and the Women's Bureau (1920) within the Department of Labor. These two agencies reinforced women's special claim to influence industrial conditions as they affected constituencies traditionally under the care of women, giving women reformers significant control over a governmental infrastructure devoted to guaranteeing the social welfare of working mothers and their children. In a similar manner, the Bureau of Home Economics would provide an institutional structure for a more explicit politicization of the domestic sphere. Just as the Labor Department bureaus made women's work a matter of public policy, the Bureau of Home Economics cast home management and household consumption as public concerns. This new bureau would also address the needs of women, but it would differ from the Labor Department bureaus in its primary constituency: agricultural families. Rural populations at a range of socioeconomic levels were the main intended audience, rather than the industrial working poor. Government officials categorized these audiences as "normal," meaning not ill or impoverished, but average or middle class. USDA officials sought to reach individual homemakers who, they assumed, held a special, social responsibility for the material and moral conditions of their homes and families. By elevating home economics to the status of a government research bureau while also establishing that bureau's domain and constituency very specifically, USDA officials embraced a set of contradictory assumptions about both consumer identities and women's proper place in American society.[9]

Home economics leaders had proposed the establishment of a Bureau of Domestic Science as early as the late 1890s.[10] Twenty-five years later, USDA administrators' determination to serve the nation's rural population through scientific research opened the door for a succeeding generation of home economists to shape the new women's bureau according to a vision for the field developed over the previous two and a half decades. Wallace, Pugsley, and their colleagues at the USDA sought to define a research agenda for the Bureau of Home Economics as rigorous as the scientific work of the department's other bureaus, with the goal of achieving practical results to improve living conditions in American homes.[11] Wallace put Elmer W. Ball, director of scientific work at the USDA, in charge of soliciting advice from home economists on how to organize the bureau to develop new knowledge useful to consumers. In preparation for a spring conference devoted to that purpose, Ball asked ten prominent home economics professors to consider their field "from the standpoint of the discovery of new facts."[12]

Collectively the women Ball surveyed recognized the establishment of the bureau as an unprecedented opportunity to develop a comprehensive plan for their field, but they were not in complete agreement on how this new department should prioritize its work. Most of the women were in their forties and fifties and had spent recent decades building university home economics programs throughout the country. Each professor had developed her own research specialty within the broad rubric of home economics. Mary Matthews, head of home economics at Purdue University, feared that the Bureau of Home Economics would be too exclusively weighted toward research at the expense of enhancing the "correlation" of research, teaching, and extension. She suggested that a new director have significant teaching experience, and that a careful plan for the bureau be *developed by those who understand conditions as they exist in the field.*" Isabel Bevier, the director of home economics at the University of Illinois, who was in her sixties and the oldest professor surveyed, expressed similar resistance to specialization within the field of home economics. "I want a woman who will use home economics not for food, clothing, health, or shelter, valuable as these separate units are, but for the *home*," she later wrote Ball. Reflecting an ongoing tension between the competing priorities of research and education among home economists, however, the majority of home economists who advised Ball shared his proposed research orientation and counseled him to choose someone who had excelled in home economics research to lead the bureau.[13]

This majority (consisting of the most vocal and influential home economists) called for the bureau to become a research center that would serve homemakers as consumers, a mission they felt would also bolster the status of home economics profession by enabling its practitioners to generate new scientific knowledge. "We are at a standstill unless we have some new material in the research field," explained Edna White, director of the Merrill-Palmer School in Detroit. Jessie Whitacre, dean of home economics at the Agricultural College of Utah, suggested using a recent article on graduate work in home economics by Katherine Blunt as a roadmap for organizing the bureau's research. Blunt, who directed home economics at the University of Chicago, called for more consideration of financial problems of the home and family, the economic value of women's work in the home, and household equipment. "Why have we not studies of advertising, not from the point of view of the producer, but of the consumer—the real victim of the system?" asked Blunt. "Why do we not know more of the relative ultimate cost to the household of domestic and commercial laundering?"[14]

Sharing Blunt's critique of modern merchandising and household consumption practices, Ball's advisers called for the new bureau to supplement the OHE's research in food and nutrition with increased attention to other areas. Many mentioned the need to study textiles and clothing, particularly "the economic aspects which will serve the consumer as a guide to buying." As White explained, the "chemistry of textiles has been studied from the manufacturer's viewpoint, but that surely is not the viewpoint of the consumer nor is it translatable." In addition, a number of home economists signaled the need for more information about household equipment of all kinds. "The individual household cannot afford to try out the relative merits of different types of equipment and at the present time we have only the tests suggested by commercial concerns and commercial interests," alerted Ruth Wardall, Bevier's successor at the University of Illinois.[15]

Denton, the OHE assistant chief, agreed. Arguing for improved consumer service through government testing, she invoked the letter she had received from H. E. Brennan requesting guidance in choosing an oil stove. Five years' experience at the USDA had led Denton to envision a new bureau charged with developing "accurate and reliable methods" of testing household products and equipment. Denton had worked with researchers at the Bureau of Standards on such projects as the standardization of household measuring cups and the deterioration of rubber seals for glass jars, and she hoped the new bureau would give home economists more opportunities to test household consumer goods in collaboration with male investigators in other departments. Denton's recent compilation of a list of government research projects relevant to home economists was one of many projects that reflected her ambition for home economics to embrace the entire array of household consumer goods. Yet her own attempts to study kitchen appliances and utensils had been discouraged by manufacturers, trade associations, and the USDA itself, which "feared antagonism of commercial interests." Denton asked, "Might it not be well to consider as soon as may be convenient both the problem of developing and applying satisfactory tests for a number of articles of household equipment, and also the problem of means of publishing the results of expert tests on such manufactured products for the benefit of the consumer?" Denton called for Wallace to outline a broad research agenda for the new bureau, and to find a way around existing government policies that prevented the mention of commercial trade names in public reports of government tests.[16]

Many of Ball's advisers wanted a director who shared their ambitions for expanding the profession through the development of scientific research programs about consumption, programs that would have as broad a social impact on the home as the Children's Bureau and the Women's Bureau had on the world of work. Alice Blood, director of the School of Household Economics at Simmons College and then president of the AHEA, recommended that the person appointed to head the bureau be someone "who will understand modes of attack on the social and economic problems which affect family life even though her training may have been in the physical sciences. Most of us inevitably think of the work which Julia Lathrop did in the Children's Bureau, and grope for an analogy in regard to the development of the Home Economics Bureau." Many home economists echoed Blood's wishes for a technically trained woman to direct a scientific research program devoted broadly to the problems of the home and linked to larger social and economic trends. Ruth Wardall recommended that the new bureau seek "information in the order of importance to the consumer who is expending the family income for things material and immaterial." Noting that cost-of-living and economic studies had been limited to production and marketing, Anna Richardson suggested: "These problems should be further considered from the standpoint of the homemaker's viewpoint as a consumer." The scope of research, she argued, should be "as broad as is the homemaking vocation." Reflecting changes in home economics over the last thirty years, Blood, Richardson, and White listed the "economics of consumption" among the topics most in need of investigation.[17]

Louise Stanley's response to Ball outlined the ambitions of her home economics colleagues most comprehensively, foreshadowing the vision and leadership she would later exercise as bureau chief. Her letter stressed the need to orient the bureau's agenda toward improving home economics education. Although Stanley held a doctoral degree in a scientific field from an Ivy League institution, she believed that home economics should focus primarily on social and economic issues, not purely technical ones. Home economists were divided along generational lines in terms of their hopes and expectations for the bureau, and Stanley firmly allied herself with the newer generation of home economists. Inclusion of "at least some young blood" on an advisory committee would help direct the field out of and away from its "traditional ruts," notably, its focus on home cooking and sewing. Instead, she advocated moving the study of food from its earlier focus on empirical "recipe preparation" to the scientific study of the "principles underlying food preparation." Investigating "the effect of manufacturing processes, and the methods of preparation on the nutritive value of foods," Stanley argued, represented "a fundamental step in the proper and economic nutrition of our people."[18]

The voice of Stanley and her cohort of midcareer home economists dominated the meeting Ball convened in June 1923 to determine the bureau's mission. Of the eight home economics leaders he invited to Washington, four were among the younger (between forty and fifty years old) university home economics professors who had responded to his April query. These included Louise Stanley, Ruth Wardall, Helen Thompson, and Edna White. Mary Sweeney, former head of home economics at Kentucky and Michigan and now the executive secretary of the AHEA, also attended the meeting. Three older and more senior women also sat on the committee: Ruby Green Smith, a home demonstration leader from New York State; Mary Hinman Abel, home economics pioneer and the first editor of the *Journal of Home Economics*; and Office of Home Economics veteran Minna Denton. The group recommended organizing the bureau into six divisions: Food and Nutrition; Textiles and Clothing; Economics and Sociology (including household management and the economics of consumption); Eugenics (covering "heredity and environment, including child care" or "social relationships" in the home); Housing and Equipment; and Art in the Home. These six divisions amounted to a broad set of long-term plans for the bureau, so broad that it generated considerable discussion over the term *home economics* itself, as well as enthusiasm regarding what the new bureau meant for the future of the field. Meeting attendees returned to their campuses and home states excited about the potential of the new bureau to shape a research program embracing all of the sciences related to the home. "I feel a great sense of encouragement for the entire field of home economics," wrote Ruby Green Smith to Ball, "in that at last there is to be developed a national source of scientific truth as a foundation for the resident and extension teaching of Home Economics, and for the practice of home science and art by homemakers."[19]

Following the meeting, Ball offered the position of bureau chief to Ruth Wardall for one year. But Wardall turned down the offer and insisted that Isabel Bevier, her mentor, was the woman for the job. Bevier, she argued, understood home economics "as a whole" and would not "line up with the older crowd,"[20] reflecting ongoing concern that a broad, forward-looking mission be the priority of the new bureau's leadership. Rather than offering the position to Bevier, Ball turned to Louise Stanley. She was hired at a salary of $5,000, with a promise of $6,000 after one year, the highest pay of any woman in the USDA and an enormous salary by both university and industry standards. Age may have played a role in this decision. Bevier was sixty-three and nearing the end of her career. Moreover, Bevier had sparked controversy in her first decade as director of the Home Economics Department at the University of Illinois by refusing to offer short courses in home economics to older homemakers, a move that alienated many rural women of Illinois. Bevier's opposition to the specialization that Ball intended to bring about with the expansion of home economics research was another likely reason that she was not chosen. Stanley, in her forties, was in the middle of her career and her background reflected more of the balance that USDA administrators and most leading home economics professors in the 1920s sought for the new bureau. In addition to her training in physiological chemistry, Stanley had demonstrated a commitment to home economics education, working as a special agent for the Federal Board for Vocational Education to develop a high-school curriculum for southern agri-

Louise Stanley, chief of the Bureau of Home Economics, 1923.
(Library of Congress, Prints and Photographs Division, LC-DIG-npcc-24560)

cultural schools during a leave from Missouri. Furthermore, Stanley's personal friendship with members of the Wallace family made her a familiar quantity to the key decision maker building the new bureau.[21]

In hiring Stanley, Wallace and Ball staked the new bureau's future on an emerging group of home economists who were almost a generation younger than those of Bevier's generation, and they committed the USDA to developing a scientific research program at a considerable remove (geographically and culturally) from the rural women they were charged with serving. Stanley and her cohort represented the scientific, professionalizing side of home economics as reflected in many university programs, more so than the outreach mission represented by extension programs working on the ground in rural areas.

To anchor the bureau's research mission in the reality of women's daily lives, Stanley convened an advisory committee that included members of several women's organizations to whom home economists already had strong ties. These included the League of Women Voters, the General Federation of Women's Clubs, the National Congress of Mothers and Parent-Teachers Association, the American Association of University Women, the American Home Economics Association, the Woman's Christian Temperance Union, and the National Council of Women (an umbrella group that included representatives from the General Federation of Women's Clubs, the Daughters of the American Revolution, the League of Women Voters, and other white, middle-class groups). Despite the bureau's mission to focus on the needs of rural women, most of these organizations had largely white, middle-class, urban-oriented memberships. Only one advisory board member, Mrs. Charles Schuttler—who had served as an officer of both the American Country Life Association and the American Farm Bureau Association—was chosen to represent the perspective of "the rural women." And even she joined the group as an individual, rather than an official representative of either organization, reflecting Stanley's desire to not "start the precedent" of having representatives from "organizations in which men and women are combined." In drawing up this list of advisers, Stanley not only placed "the rural women" in a minority position but also excluded such rural organizations as the Grange, the Farmers' Alliance, and the American Farm Bureau Federation (AFBF), where in at least some cases men and women shared a political culture. The AFBF, for example, had recently rejected the idea of creating a "women's" in favor of a "home and community" department in which both men and women participated.[22] By turning to university home economists and the leaders of middle-class women's clubs for advice at this early stage in the creation of the Bureau of Home Economics, USDA officials oriented the new government agency toward issues of consumption, driven largely by white, middle-class, urban professionals. The perspective of this group would become the priority of a bureau whose major constituency was more rural, less educated, and with less disposable income but who, like H. E. Brennan, looked to state and federal officials for advice about how to buy "intelligently."

A Women's Profession and a Feminized Culture of Expertise

Louise Stanley was an astute institution builder and strategist. She led the development of the Bureau of Home Economics with a keen eye toward shaping the bureau while enhancing the status of home economics as a women's profession, much as Julia Lathrop had directed the Children's Bureau as what historian Robyn Muncy calls a "female dominion."[23] Like Lathrop, who had created an environment to train a cadre of women social workers and reformers to extend women's maternal role into government programs, Stanley built the bureau as a training ground for women to develop expertise on behalf of public service. As bureau chief from 1923 to 1943, she used the government agency to strengthen home economics as a research field that generated new scientific and social scientific knowledge about the selection and use of household goods. Reflecting the educational curriculum that university home economists and extension agents had developed since 1900, the bureau's focus on consumption and consumer products grounded home economists in a reform agenda; at the same time it provided an esoteric body of knowledge that served as the basis for a distinct professional identity for the field's practitioners. Stanley fostered a "culture of expertise" in matters of consumption akin to what other professional groups—including road engineers, landscape engineers, mining engineers, food chemists, and social workers—achieved through institutionalization in government bureaus. The creation of a fact-finding government bureau dedicated to disseminating expert information was a common way that many of these specialists carried Progressive Era ideals and objectives into the 1920s.[24] Using science to serve social and economic ends had a long tradition in the USDA, where agricultural scientists had generated knowledge to optimize crop production since the Civil War. In recent decades, the department had supported the regulation of public health through the study of pure foods and drugs, the control of pests, and practices such as meat inspection. While food inspectors used their expertise to enforce regulations safeguarding the nation's food supply, USDA home economists investigated the marketplace for household goods and offered guidelines for their design, distribution, selection, and maintenance.

Soon after her arrival, Stanley put women in charge of reorienting the bureau's research into food around the latest thinking in nutritional science. Illustrating the importance of this aspect of the bureau's work, Stanley herself replaced Charles Ford Langworthy—the former dean of the USDA's human nutrition investigations—as chief of the Division of Food and Nutrition and charted a research agenda that reached beyond Langworthy's long-standing focus on respiration calorimetry. Langworthy's work had continued the research of Wilbur O. Atwater into the energy supplied by different foods and its consumption by the human body. As director of the Office of Home Economics and a supporter of the field, Langworthy had enlisted a first generation of home economists in pioneering efforts to popularize nutritional science. Yet by 1923, he was approaching sixty years old, and respiration calorimetry had lost much of its importance to the "newer nutrition" and the study of vitamins. Stanley, in her new role as BHE director, judged this respiration work too costly to remain a priority. To make room in the budget for other activities, Stanley changed Langworthy's title to "Specialist in Home Economics" and put him to work on "more definitely home economics projects"—including energy studies of housework—until his retirement in 1929.[25] While Stanley kept Assistant Food Chemist Samuel C. Clark on along with many of the women from the OHE staff, she filled the top new food and nutrition research positions with scientifically trained women holding doctoral degrees and specializing in the "newer nutrition" centered around vitamins, including nutrition chemists Hazel E. Munsell and Laura Ida McLaughlin and, later in the 1930s, biochemist Florence B. King.[26]

Although food and nutrition remained the backbone of the bureau's research program, Stanley balanced this part of the bureau's mission with a commitment to initiate "other lines of work."[27] She hired two dynamic women—Hildegarde Kneeland in economics and Ruth O'Brien in textiles and clothing—to carve out new research areas. Both women were in their thirties and had, as graduate students and young professors, developed new technical specialties within home economics. Because of Kneeland's training in both nutrition and statistics, her name had been mentioned several times in the preliminary discussions of who should lead the new bureau. She was one of a small but growing group of women educated in economics who found a niche in home economics in the early twentieth century. After receiving a B.A. from Vassar College in 1911, Kneeland pursued graduate work in nutrition and household administration at Teachers College. This training won her a position as a nutrition instructor at the University of Missouri in 1914. After three years, she resumed graduate study in sociology, statistics, and the economics of consumption under Hazel

Kyrk at the University of Chicago and later at Columbia, where she was enrolled as a doctoral student. Immediately prior to coming to the Bureau of Home Economics, Kneeland had directed the Department of Household Economics at Kansas State Agricultural College.[28] Although another home economist, Ilena Bailey, had begun studies of time use in the home under the original OHE, Stanley placed Bailey under the better-educated Kneeland and charged this new research group with directing a more comprehensive attack on "the economic problems of the home."[29]

Ruth O'Brien came to the bureau with extensive experience in textile science and consumer activism. The daughter of a midwestern foods commission merchant, she earned a bachelor's and a master's degree in chemistry at the University of Nebraska in 1914 and 1915. After a year of continued graduate study in chemistry at the University of Chicago, O'Brien moved to Iowa State College where, as an assistant professor in the Department of Chemistry from 1917 to 1924, she developed a Division of Textile Chemistry. While at Iowa State, she acquired practical experience in textiles through summer employment in a dry cleaning plant and a textile mill. As "one of the few women in colleges known as textile chemists," O'Brien pioneered research into the effects of bleaching and laundering on cotton fabrics. She was a vocal advocate for training women in science and an equally outspoken proponent of using science to help women "formulate an intelligent opinion on modern textile problems" and to support the standardization of textile fabrics. O'Brien's commitment to both endeavors shaped her work at the bureau, where she took on a leadership role second only to Stanley's. Because O'Brien assumed many of the bureau's administrative duties and also engaged in negotiations with manufacturers, retailers, and other government agencies, she obtained a law degree from George Washington University in 1931 and joined the District of Columbia bar two years later.[30] With this background, O'Brien directed a division that aimed to derive experiment-based criteria by which consumers could judge fabric quality "on a rational basis," while also providing suggestions for "suitable and logical uses" for American-produced natural fibers.[31]

By 1925, Stanley expanded the bureau's staff threefold to a total of twenty-two scientific workers. Almost all of these employees were women, including many of the best educated home economists in the country. Stanley, Kneeland, and O'Brien recruited the bureau's professional workers from the professors and students at leading university programs and from the group of well-known home economists who frequently published articles in the *Journal of Home Economics* and related publications. Many staff members at the bureau had received undergraduate training at private women's colleges such as Vassar and Smith and had obtained second bachelor's degrees or graduate degrees in home economics or related fields at such institutions as Teachers College or the University of Chicago. Like Stanley, several had earned doctorates in scientific fields and later obtained teaching or administrative jobs in university home economics schools. Of the nineteen women employees on staff in 1925, five had earned doctorates, five had master's of arts degrees, three had master's of science degrees, three had bachelor's of science degrees, and two had bachelor's of arts degrees. Only two women—the library assistant and a "subprofessional in foods"—did not have any college degree.[32] Although most of the women transferred from the OHE were older than the director, the majority of those Stanley hired were in their thirties.[33]

Although Stanley established the Division of Economics and the Division of Textiles and Clothing in only two years, budgetary constraints forced her to move cautiously in expanding the bureau. The initial appropriation of $71,760 was insufficient to pursue all the lines of work proposed by the June 1923 planning conference. Resources did not become available for a Division of Housing and Household Equipment until the mid-1930s. Divisions for "social relationships" and "art in the home" never materialized at all.[34] Still, through Stanley's efforts the bureau's annual operating budget more than doubled to $148,937 by 1929, allowing her to enlarge the staff and initiate projects that expanded the bureau's mission beyond the boundaries of its existing divisions.[35] After six years as chief, Stanley reported that the bureau had assembled a staff of sixty employees, thirty "of whom are specialists in professional service." By 1930, the staff totaled seventy-two workers. The Great Depression hit the bureau relatively hard: the bureau's operating budget was reduced by one-third in 1934, and it remained the least funded of the USDA's bureaus throughout the Depression. On the eve of World War II, however, the BHE employed nearly seventy scientists, including forty home economists, thirteen chemists, seven physicists, two physiologists, and one bacteriologist. Stanley's success in establishing and maintaining these positions and filling most of them with women made the Bureau of Home Economics the single-largest employer of women scientists in not only the federal government but also the United States.[36]

Throughout the 1920s and 1930s, Stanley used the bureau as a platform to move the professional training of home economists beyond what she described as its "chaotic condition."[37] She took every opportunity to publicize what she saw as the "double function" of home economics: to train homemakers, but also to prepare women "for various professional applications" outside the home. She worked to overcome the prejudice against home economics in women's liberal arts colleges and to see that her definition of home economics—which minimized "handicraft skills" in favor of "scientific train-ing"—prevailed in Office of Education publications as well as in those of other government agencies.[38] Most important, she built an institution that provided young women educated in the sciences and social sciences with opportuni-ties to gain research experience and become successful investigators. While Stanley oriented the bureau's operations to support the advancement of these younger women, her own scientific research took a back seat to writing that popularized the bureau and home economics. These priorities were similar to those of other female scientists and educators, notably deans and school ad-ministrators, who put aside their own investigations to promote the scientific careers of other women.[39]

During these years, Stanley oversaw the development of a specialized re-search niche around consumption, an esoteric body of knowledge through which she and her fellow home economists sought to make a unique contribu-tion to American social reform. Within the USDA, as Stanley pointed out in a 1929 speech, the bureau had "two quite different, yet overlapping, functions." For farmers, staff home economists explored "the relative utility and economy of agricultural products for food, clothing, and other uses in the home." For extension workers, they also studied "practical, everyday, home problems" to modernize rural home life by promoting scientific housekeeping and sanita-tion.[40] The user's perspective on consumer goods provided a focus for home economists to draw these goals together and develop a body of knowledge unique to their discipline. Toward this end, Stanley proceeded with an am-bitious research agenda that pushed beyond the primary focus on food and nutrition in the OHE to shape a broadly conceived applied science of the home, an applied science that embraced the study of a wide array of agricultural and manufactured goods that families made or purchased.

Investigating the User's Perspective

The Bureau of Home Economics combined professional development with consumer service in a collective project to systematically gather facts about the quality of goods, their use and care in the home, optimal design principles and standards, and the behavior of consumers. Other government agencies had investigated consumer products and issues of relevance to homemakers. In the 1910s, for example, government scientists and engineers in the Com-merce Department's National Bureau of Standards produced publications such as *Measurements for the Household* (1915), *Materials for the Household* (1917), and *Safety in the Household* (1918). However, these publications were aimed at industrial and commercial managers, not homemakers.[41] As Stanley positioned the new bureau as the first place for women to turn for practical advice about household consumption, she and her staff not only continued collaborations with the Bureau of Standards (building on initiatives begun earlier by Minna Denton and the Office of Home Economics staff) but also commanded an independent research program in which homemakers' needs and priorities—as seen through the eyes of Stanley and her staff—were primary. Under Stanley's direction, the Bureau of Home Economics emerged in the 1920s as the federal government's clearinghouse for information about household consumer goods.

In carving out a specialized niche around consumption, bureau home economists used technical, scientific, and social scientific inquiry to raise questions about the value of domestic goods, specifically regarding the utility of such products to homemakers and their place in family budgets. This scientific approach to defining domestic material life—and evaluating consumer products and behavior—in measurable terms united the bureau's various research projects. While agricultural goods continued to be a priority, home economists strove to embrace the expanding cornucopia of mass-produced goods available to middle-class Americans. "New developments in home economics," wrote Stanley in 1932, "are not due so much to changing conditions in family life as changing industrial conditions which affect family life."[42] Throughout the interwar period, bureau home economists investigated cooking methods, sewing techniques, fiber and fabric properties, consumption habits, nutrition guidelines, measuring cup tolerances, meat palatability, child-rearing practices, and family accounting systems. Homemakers, Stanley claimed, were "asking the help of science" on these types of home problems. When considered as a whole, rather than as a set of individual and separate studies, she intended the bureau's many projects to contribute collectively to improving the American standard of living. "Satisfactory solution of these questions, trivial as some may seem," she argued, "makes its contribution to national welfare, and when these small contributions are multiplied by the millions of homes to be reached, the boundless possibilities of such studies are seen."[43] Bureau staff united seemingly diverse projects by framing the "woman's viewpoint" about consumption in quantitative terms and using science to enhance the status of the home economics profession.

In response to the growing influence of the corporation over the private, domestic lives of Americans, Stanley and her staff designed a research program aimed at tempering the power of manufacturers and retailers to manipulate consumers against their best interests.[44] Bureau home economists purposefully aimed their research at both consumers and producers. By uncovering the "secrets" of a chaotic marketplace and sharing this information with homemakers, home economists constructed the bureau as a resource center for an envisioned, ideal American female consumer who desired to "buy intelligently." This imagined consumer was the same rational consumer that home economists in universities and in the extension service sought to create through their teaching and outreach efforts. While home economics educators framed the problem of consumption as a lack of information, bureau researchers worked to generate and communicate that information, conducting systematic analyses of consumer goods and family budgets that would help homemakers save time, energy, and money. Just as the bureau home economists hoped consumers would use their findings to make rational purchasing decisions, they also guided producers to design products according to criteria home economists believed would benefit consumers and encouraged producers to label these products with information that would be useful to the ideal consumer. In placing responsibility on producers, Stanley and her colleagues posited an ideal producer who was committed to satisfying the needs and demands of rational consumers. Rather than manipulating homemakers, ideal producers would educate them, providing them all of the information needed to facilitate rational purchasing decisions. Such producers competed on quality as well as price, and they communicated honestly, directly, and thoroughly with consumers about the value of their wares and how to use them most effectively. Farmers needed to know how the agricultural commodities they grew or raised would be used in the home and how to produce them in ways that would appeal to and benefit "ultimate consumers." Manufacturers of appliances, utensils, processed foods, cloth, and ready-to-wear garments also needed to understand their products from the perspective of those who selected and used them.

By aiming the bureau's research program at both producers and consumers, Stanley and her staff generated information that allowed home economists to facilitate a two-way process of translation between the languages of producers (notably farmers and manufacturers) and of female consumers. Home economists at the bureau understood consumption as part of an integrated system, and they used their research program to correlate supply and demand. Influenced by Herbert Hoover, with whom they had allied in World War I, home economists tended to perceive a mutuality of interests among these players and to have faith in "good" or "progressive" companies.[45] The USDA context reinforced home economists' assumptions that products, merchandising systems, and consumer behavior could all be fine-tuned and improved to yield a more smoothly running market that met the needs of all. Home economists believed that their role in this process was to provide consumers with needed technical information that was summarized in plain language, accessible, and easy to apply. At the same time, they supplied producers with information about homemakers' requirements for various goods. Bureau home economists used scientific research to facilitate an ongoing conversation between those who produced and those who purchased a rapidly expanding set of goods in the marketplace.

In creating a science of consumption that home economists could claim as their own, bureau employees drew on work taking place in mainstream scientific, technical, and social scientific circles, but they usually chose projects that did not duplicate research under way in other arenas. For example, home economists did not concern themselves with the internal workings of a refrigerator or other appliances if such details seemed irrelevant to efficient and economical home management. Because they valued service, healthfulness, quality, and economy above aesthetics and promotional gimmicks, home economists evaluated goods they studied in light of these priorities. Often they built on the research of male scientists, engineers, and social scientists, either by expanding on projects begun by these other experts or by applying methods developed by researchers in more traditional areas to new topics. In some cases, bureau home economists simply translated knowledge generated in other fields, while in other cases they developed new techniques and equipment to explore subjects specifically from a user's perspective. In the process of establishing user-oriented rather than producer-oriented priorities, bureau home economists developed a research program that contested received notions of science and technology. While male engineers defined technology in terms of production and advertisers made claims that anything "scientific" was worth buying, the bureau's home economists used their scientific and technical training to analyze the relative merits of one product over another from the user's perspective.

Studying Products

Home economists generated, gathered, and synthesized information about the precise physical properties of foods, textile fabrics, clothing, and household equipment that they thought consumers wanted to know about to make "wise selections." By extension, these were properties that home economists encouraged producers to enhance in their products. This approach of assessing the physical properties of goods from a user's perspective stemmed largely from the research of the Division of Food and Nutrition, which aimed at determining the value of foods in terms of bodily needs. Building on the pioneering food composition studies begun by Wilbur O. Atwater in the 1890s, Caroline Hunt developed a new version of Atwater's 1906 wall chart showing 100-calorie portions of twenty different foods. Under the leadership of Charlotte Chatfield in the 1920s, the division collected analyses of meats, fruits, and vegetables conducted by other government agencies, university laboratories, state experiment stations, and commercial enterprises. This effort resulted in the publication of information regarding the calorie, protein, carbohydrate, fat, water, and total ash composition of more than one thousand food items by the late 1930s.[46] The bureau's study of the importance of specific vitamins to an "adequate diet" was similarly ambitious in scope. While male nutrition researchers conducted cutting-edge investigations to identify and isolate new vitamins and understand their effects on the human body, the bureau's nutritional chemist, Hazel Munsell, collaborated with Sybil Smith at the USDA's Office of Experiment Stations in the labor-intensive laboratory bench work required to determine the precise vitamin content of individual food items. These studies revealed how vitamin content varied based on the conditions of food production and handling. By playing a coordinating role among home economists, nutrition scientists, and vitamin researchers, Munsell and Smith consolidated the findings of diverse investigators and synthesized them in illustrational charts for use by teachers in home economics and other subjects.[47]

Just as the Division of Food and Nutrition investigated the composition of foods, the Division of Textiles and Clothing aimed at deriving definitions and "landmarks" by which consumers could judge fabric quality. Home economists working with textiles had fewer precedents to follow than those working in nutrition, as criteria analogous to calories or vitamin content had not been created for quantifying the characteristics of cloth. Textile science was a relatively new field, and in the early 1920s few people—women or men—had devoted much attention to the study of fabrics and garments from the perspective of the consumer. But because textiles and clothing constituted major purchases in American households and their selection posed numerous challenges to consumers, the bureau determined that the quality and cost of textiles merited serious investigation. Most immediately, staff home economists sought to address issues stemming from the emergence, after World War I, of new manufactured cellulosic fibers such as rayon and acetate alongside the usual naturally grown fibers of cotton, wool, silk, and linen. The poor quality of many of the rayon fibers, the lack of a standard nomenclature for them, and their resemblance to natural fabrics created a confusion among consumers about how to distinguish one fiber or finish from another, how to decide which type of fabric was preferable for what purpose, and how to care for and maintain fabrics once purchased. The number and variety of new dyes and finishes was on the rise as well, and the wartime deprivation of synthetic dyes from Europe had undermined consumers' confidence in the ability of industrially produced cloth to hold its color.[48]

Ruth O'Brien, chief of the Division of Textiles and Clothing, put her knowledge of textile chemistry to work helping consumers make sense of the mind-boggling array of fabrics available on the market. "A large percentage of the income of every family in the country is being spent on textiles," O'Brien announced in 1930, "and the fact that these must be purchased almost entirely by guess is becoming a serious menace to the economic well-being of every home." As a member of the American Chemical Society, the American Society for Testing Materials, and the American Association of Textile Chemists and Colorists, O'Brien maintained contacts with scientists in industrial laboratories, state experiment stations, and other government agencies. With her knowledge of the work of outside researchers, she used her scientific training to cover uncharted territory in the consumer-oriented niche staked out by home economists. Her division synthesized a wide range of findings that would ultimately, via home economists' lessons or specifications home economists encouraged manufacturers to provide, give consumers information necessary to make wise textile-related purchasing decisions. Topics of investigation addressed either "the textile problems the consumer is meeting or those confronting the producers who are trying to meet consumer needs."[49]

O'Brien hired a staff of women who had the scientific training to study the chemical and physical properties of fabric, and she stocked her laboratories with state-of-the-art equipment enabling them to pursue a broad, user-oriented research agenda. Well aware that the bureau was one of the few places where women could work as scientists, O'Brien brought on women such as A. Elizabeth Hill, who held a master's degree from the University of Pennsylvania with an emphasis on organic chemistry and who worked as a chemist in the Henry Phipps Institute of Chemical Research in Philadelphia before joining the bureau in 1925. By 1930, the division had eight full-time staff members, including four textile chemists, two textile physicists, and two home economics specialists in clothing, as well as two part-time seamstresses and a part-time secretary.[50] The division's laboratory, constructed in 1930 when the bureau moved into a new building, enabled bureau home economists to conduct tests of tensile strength, weight, thickness, and air permeability as well as the chemical composition of fibers. It included a controlled-humidity room modeled on the ones used by other chemists and physicists engaged in textile research and testing, often on behalf of textile producers. With this equipment, O'Brien and her staff practiced the standard methods of these scientific disciplines and shared them with other home economists at colleges and universities who also pursued consumer-oriented textile research.[51] Bureau staff members directed their investigations into textile fibers, fabrics, and clothing in ways that supported the qualities—such as durability, or "serviceability," and colorfastness—they believed were ultimately desirable to and needed by consumers. In addition, O'Brien's team studied clothing from the standpoint of both physical and mental health.[52]

The bureau's research into both nutrition and textiles often led to investigations of new household technologies. Questions about kitchen equipment—ranging from meat thermometers to measuring cups to gas and electric stoves and refrigerators—arose from the bureau's food and nutrition work, leading Stanley to initiate a number of projects concerned with evaluating the quality of domestic utensils and appliances. In the mid-1920s, she hired Greta Gray and cooperative housing advocate Edith Elmer Wood—"two of the foremost women on the housing question"—to research housing and equipment matters on a temporary basis. Gray had studied at MIT and Teachers College and authored *House and Home* (1923), a textbook on the construction, decoration, and economics of housing for home economics students. A critic of installment credit at the turn of the century, Wood used her seat on the American Association of University Women's Housing Committee to advocate for government ownership and funding of low-cost housing based on European models, and she later joined Ethel Puffer Howes at the Institute for the Coordination of Womens' Interests.[53] Stanley's choice of these two women signaled her commitment to seeking innovative solutions to the nation's housing problems even as she and most of her colleagues assumed the single-family dwelling as the norm. Although she failed to garner the resources needed to continue their work for more than a few years, the growing centrality of consumer durables in the lives of homemakers led her to seize every opportunity to fold the study of household equipment into the bureau's research agenda. On an ad hoc basis, bureau home economists compiled lists of market offerings and conducted comparative "experimental studies" of refrigerators and a number of other appliances. Finally, in the mid-1930s, when Stanley succeeded in establishing the Division of Housing and Household Equipment, staff members conducted tests of "insulated coal ranges" and gas stoves for low-income families, studied the comparative costs of fuels, and developed guidelines for the "efficient use and care" of gas and electrical appliances to help farm families fit these items, described by a bureau report as "long-desired conveniences," into household budgets.[54]

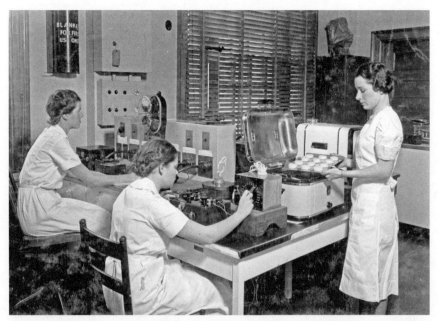

Bureau of Home Economics employees testing electric ovens in the household equipment lab, South Building, Department of Agriculture, October 1939. (National Archives)

The use, care, and maintenance of various products in the home represented another major research focus at the Bureau of Home Economics. Staff home economists applied their knowledge about the design and physical properties of household goods to establish methods of use, care, and maintenance to optimize beneficial characteristics. The bureau staff's investigations into the "use" of raw foodstuffs essentially amounted to developing methods of preparation and preservation to maximize and maintain nutritional value. Home economists developed recipes featuring vitamin-rich foods as well as cooking techniques—"waterless cookery"—for vegetables to maximize the preservation of mineral and vitamin content.[55] Food preservation, an important research topic at the OHE before and during World War I, remained a subject of investigation at the bureau throughout the 1920s and 1930s. The bureau's canning bulletins underwent constant revision in response to changes in cooking equipment and established the bureau as the nation's authority on canning among women's magazine editors, homemakers, and home economists.[56] The bureau's thorough work in this area laid the groundwork for the division's parallel studies of the use of ice and mechanical refrigeration, in which staff members investigated optimal temperatures and storage locations to ensure the safe preservation of perishable foods.

In response to a demand for up-to-date information on both home laundering and stain removal throughout the 1920s and 1930s, the bureau continued
studies begun by the Office of Home Economics in the late 1910s on "the problem of prolonging wear and lengthening the period of usefulness." During this
period, the Textiles and Clothing Division used an experimental washing machine to evaluate the impact of various temperatures and washing agents on
the efficiency of the laundering process and on fabrics of different composition
and construction. Staff home economists assembled a group of washing machines in the Washington headquarters and ran comparative tests on them.
Women trained in organic chemistry analyzed changes in physical and chemical properties of fabrics due to washing. Staff members also developed an artificial technique of soiling to simulate home conditions and a photometric
method to determine the amount of soil removed with each process.[57] Like
the bureau's recommended methods of preparing and preserving foods, these
guidelines were intended to optimize efficiency and economy in the use of materials (in this case, textiles) in the home.

As home economists at the bureau studied the qualities of products, developed suggestions for how to use them, and researched the impact of new equipment on standard products such as food and clothing, they frequently worked
to establish optimum design principles and standards for various goods. The
bureau's systematic analysis of consumer goods aimed to encourage and assist
manufacturers in designing products according to criteria home economists
believed would most benefit consumers. Because designing products was not
the primary responsibility of bureau home economists, their involvement in
this activity was usually more inadvertent than purposeful. The presence of
Stanley and O'Brien as consumer representatives on committees set up by the
American Standards Association and other industrial trade organizations provided channels to collaborate with agricultural producers and manufacturers
and to encourage them to consider user perspectives. Typically the focus of
these committees was more on setting standards for specific product features
rather than comprehensive product design. Yet home economists' roles as consumer experts in these settings allowed them to make substantial contributions to the ultimate design, appearance, and function of many manufactured
goods, ranging from clothing for women and children to kitchen appliances.

Studying Consumers

Whereas the bureau's divisions dedicated to food and nutrition, textiles and
clothing, and household equipment each focused on consumer products, the
organization's Division of Economics made consumers themselves objects of

study. Division chief Hildegarde Kneeland sought to carve out a niche for home economics in the study of the economics of consumption in the context of contemporary social sciences. In the Progressive Era, social surveying became a standard method by which reformers, influenced by positivist sociology, investigated the living conditions of the urban working poor.[58] Kneeland's graduate training in the economics of consumption tied her to a new academic specialty forged by Hazel Kyrk and others, as well as to a reform tradition oriented toward improving the American standard of living. Her doctoral studies in economics at the Robert Brookings Graduate School of Economics and Government, completed in 1930, provided her expertise in statistical analysis. At the bureau, Kneeland used these tools to analyze rural Americans in relation to middle-class standards. An outspoken advocate for using home economics to investigate the home in relation to the larger society or "why family expenditures are as they are," she dismissed the field's early focus on family budgets as a mere technique of household management. "We cannot restrict ourselves to those phases of consumption with which the individual homemaker deals directly," Kneeland wrote in the *Journal of Home Economics* in 1925. "For no other group of workers is more concerned with these problems than we, and no other groups and but few individuals are working on them. We must overcome our tendency to stay within the four walls of the home in our research. We must go out into the complexities and difficulties of the economics world to find the answers to our problems."[59] In using the bureau's Economics Division to understand the realities of household production and consumption in the context of broad social and economic trends, Kneeland tapped into many of the assumptions and techniques of women's Progressive Era reform movements to investigate the interwar period's consumer economy from the perspective of American homemakers.

The division's charge—to investigate "the economic problems of the home"—was divided into two general categories: "household production" and "consumption economics." Under Kneeland's direction bureau staff members aimed to capture an accurate and comprehensive picture of the daily lives of American homemakers, a picture that would provide the basis for improving those lives. By studying family expenditures, the Division of Economics also aimed to achieve a closer correlation between market supply and demand, especially for products grown on the nation's farms. The division emphasized rural areas, but staff investigators collected data on city dwellers as well, primarily for comparative purposes. To gather data, Kneeland used a network of other home economists, including home demonstration agents, university professors, women's club members, and editors of women's magazines—women who tended to be "well acquainted with both the home economics and the extension work of the department" and "sympathetic toward its undertakings."[60]

The "household production" studies of the Division of Economics aimed to address one of Kneeland's primary concerns, shared by most contemporary agricultural reformers: that rural homemakers were overworked. The division's household production studies, concerned with time use, sought to understand this problem in a detailed, quantified manner. Bureau staff members designed studies to determine the variety of tasks constituting "housework," the efficiency with which these tasks were accomplished, and the economic value of this work. Homemakers kept weekly records of the time they spent performing housework. "In spite of the importance of the work of the household," reported one observer in 1930, "little information is available in regard to this phase of economic life." The goal of the bureau's housework studies was to determine how much time and energy homemakers devoted to household duties and how much leisure time they had. As much as possible, the bureau's investigators aimed to illuminate the relationship between ownership of "laborsaving devices" and the time spent doing various household tasks such as preparing meals and washing dishes. With these investigations, the division sought to determine the most efficient methods of performing these tasks and to establish a baseline from which to gauge improvements to the household economy.[61]

Bureau researchers and their home economics colleagues across the country were surprised to find evidence that ownership of appliances did not reduce—and often increased—the time women spent performing household tasks. In the late 1920s, a bureau survey of "a superior group" of women who owned laborsaving devices in New York, the Midwest, and the Far West revealed that farm women surveyed worked an average of fifty-two hours a week at household tasks and an additional eleven hours doing jobs on the farm. "This is a very different picture indeed from the one which is usually painted concerning the modern home maker," concluded Kneeland, who maintained that any workweek over fifty hours was excessive. Like most home economists, Kneeland's ideological faith in the promise of technological progress led her to play down results that questioned the effectiveness of laborsaving devices.[62]

Yet Kneeland publicly advocated two additional solutions to the problem of the "overworked" homemaker: increased employment of paid domestic workers and increased use of "large-scale, outside agencies" such as commercial laundries, housecleaning services, and meal providers. In calling for women to transfer housework out of the home, Kneeland echoed the cries of material feminist Charlotte Perkins Gilman as well as those of Ethel Puffer Howes, who waged a 1923 campaign for women's cooperative home service clubs in the *Woman's Home Companion* and served as an early adviser to the bureau, representing the American Association of University Women. Support for experiments in cooperative living dwindled throughout the decade, but even as late as 1929 the bureau announced plans to study "multiple housing," "the grouping of the individual homes around some centralized agencies for taking care of certain necessary parts of housekeeping," and "apartments which can combine some of the advantages of the separated home with those of a multiple dwelling." An annual report listed "centralized heating, centralized service for cleaning, some centralized food preparation, even extending so far as the central dining room," among the possible shared services. Even as many home economists at women's magazines, who depended on appliance advertisements for their operations, had abandoned interest in these approaches, the BHE remained one of the few places where such experiments were considered, analyzed, and in some cases, recommended. In addition, Kneeland's efforts to establish "the economic value of the work of the housewife" (by using as indices the wages of paid domestic workers and the cost of commercial agencies outside of it) represented a similarly progressive stance with regard to not only nineteenth-century ideas about women's work but also reformers of the interwar period.[63]

Over time, family consumption habits, rather than work patterns, increasingly became the focus of the Division of Economics. These studies sought to illuminate the living conditions of farm families just as standard-of-living studies were designed to reveal details about working-class families in urban industrial cities. The Office of Home Economics had ventured into this realm of investigation in the late 1910s with county-based surveys of farm families in Michigan, New York, Vermont, Maryland, Kentucky, and Alabama.[64] Kneeland continued these studies, collaborating with the Bureau of Agricultural Economics and Cornell's New York State College of Agriculture to analyze the general findings with regard to clothing and food expenditures. Her division's consumption studies expanded considerably and evolved to adopt the techniques of positivist sociology. Faith Williams, who received a Ph.D. in economics from Columbia University in 1924 and wrote her thesis on the food manufacturing industries in New York City (published as part of the Regional Plan of New York), joined the bureau in 1929. Before coming to the bureau, she assisted Robert Lynd with his famous social survey of Muncie, Indiana, taught for a few years at Cornell, and worked on behalf of the American Home Economics Association to promote the standardization of consumer products. Her professional experience with these high-profile projects led Williams to change the way the bureau performed its survey research, replacing earlier subjective techniques of the survey method that placed the burden of interpretation on the investigator with studies based on a "schedule method" that relied on the subject of the study to provide information.[65]

The bureau added a social scientific element to its research program in food and nutrition when Edith Hawley joined the staff in 1924 as a food economist and initiated a new set of surveys assessing national trends in food consumption to help establish standards for diets that were both healthy and economical. Trained as a biochemist under Henry Sherman at Columbia, Hawley worked for two years under Alonzo Taylor and Carl Arlsberg at the Food Research Institute at Stanford University before joining the bureau. In California she conducted research on the "food fraction of the cost of living, together with an analysis of the index number of this fraction," investigations she published in her doctoral dissertation. Arlsberg regarded Hawley as a "very competent woman" and a serious independent researcher, and recommended her for work at the bureau only if she would find worthwhile opportunities there rather than "the ordinary sort of extension or hack work." The bureau's serious approach to scientific investigation made it a good fit for Hawley, who drew on her dual background in nutrition and economics to develop methods for researching the relationship between a family's budget and the nutritional health of its members. By developing techniques to establish "scales of relative food requirements" with which to compare existing nationwide food studies, as well as a "short-cut method" for assessing the nutritive value of individual diets, she led the creation of the new field of food economics.[66] Hazel K. Stiebeling, who had studied under Henry Sherman and Mary Swartz Rose at Teachers College and obtained a doctoral degree in chemistry there in 1928, replaced Hawley as senior food economist in 1930 and continued the work of analyzing standardized information on both the economic and the nutritional value of various foods, developing diet plans at different income levels, and studying nutritive values of diets around the world.[67] The division added Day Monroe, another woman trained in family economics by Kyrk at the University of Chicago, as its new chief in 1935. Before joining the bureau, she taught in a number of leading university home economics programs and coauthored, with Kyrk and Ursula Stone, *Food Buying and Our Markets* (1925).[68] Together, Hawley, Stiebeling, and Monroe led the way in establishing food economics as a home economics specialty.

The work of the Division of Economics went beyond the study of food consumption, however. In addition to determining the best diet homemakers could expect for their budget, Kneeland's staff worked with home economists in other bureau divisions to determine how specific goods or categories of goods fit into family budgets and how families made decisions about what to buy and what to make at home. Kneeland and her colleagues aimed to develop model budgets that would define the standard of living for an "average" American household. They sought to establish a systematic and scientific method for quantifying such optimized budgets and offering advice to homemakers on how to achieve this goal. The division received many requests from home economists around the country for access to their model budgets, but it resisted supplying them until systematic research backing up its recommendations was completed, or until an emergency such as the Great Depression demanded guidance of this sort. In spite of its official focus on "average" rural families, the Economics Division also developed "family measurement scales" with which to compare family expenditures across the economic spectrum.[69]

The bureau used its consumption studies to facilitate the "adjustment of production to meet consumption."[70] After 1932, as New Deal economic planners began building assumptions regarding consumption into national policies and initiatives, they turned to the bureau's Division of Economics for information about the nation's consumption habits. Following the salary reductions of federal employees in 1933, the bureau worked with the Bureau of Labor Statistics (BLS) to study the cost of living of government workers at various salary levels, family sizes, and living arrangements. Also with the BLS, Kneeland's team began planning for a large-scale study "of the consumption of farm and industrial products at different income levels in different types of communities and regions." These plans culminated in the Consumer Purchases Study (CPS), the most comprehensive study to date on this subject, which was launched in 1936. Cosponsored by a number of federal agencies which saw the need for a better understanding of how Americans spent their money, the CPS was funded by the Works Progress Administration and coordinated by the bureau's own Hildegarde Kneeland, who soon left the bureau to continue this work under the auspices of the National Resources Planning Board. Faith Williams contributed to the project from her new seat as chief of the Cost-of-Living Division at the BLS. From inside the Bureau of Home Economics, new Division of Economics chief Day Monroe and senior food economist Hazel Stiebeling investigated food expenditures as part of the larger study, with their home economics colleagues contributing analyses of trends in the consumption of other items and how these related to family budgets.[71]

By the late 1930s the CPS was the bureau's most important and most visible project. It represented a major triumph for home economists' investigations of the nation's consumption habits, particularly the specialized knowledge of food economics they brought to this important work. At the same time, the promotion of Kneeland and Williams out of the bureau and into other government agencies—by the early 1940s Kneeland moved to the Bureau of Agricultural Economics and then the Office of Price Administration—removed the social scientific study of consumer behavior from the bureau and placed it in the hands of male civil servants with other professional interests. While the significance of home economics research on consumer behavior was affirmed by experiences in the 1930s, success in establishing the importance of consumption as an area of government research eventually undermined the bureau's status as the primary source of such information.

Correlating Production and Consumption

Home economists at the bureau integrated all of these research areas—product quality, methods of use, design standards, and the study of consumers themselves—in efforts to facilitate what Louise Stanley called a "closer fit between consumption and production," particularly with regard to agricultural goods.[72] Initiated as part of the USDA's solution to the 1920s agricultural depression, many investigations aimed to encourage the "utilization" of surplus farm-raised products. These types of projects provided Stanley and her colleagues with opportunities to integrate diverse elements of the bureau's research program and make connections between how foods and fibers were grown, how they were processed, and how they were used in the context of daily domestic life. In the bureau's food utilization studies, home economists studied the nutritional value of various foods—such as rice polishings, native-grown lentils, soybeans, or honey—and developed recipes to encourage women to increase their use of these ingredients.[73] Other studies aimed to determine the effect of growing techniques on the quality of foodstuffs and to provide suggestions for cooking with these products.[74] Investigations into meat cookery, a cooperative project with the Bureau of Animal Industry and the Bureau of Agricultural Economics that began around 1926 and continued through 1940, constituted one of the bureau's most extensive projects of this type. To establish the ideal quality and "palatability" of meat produced and cooked by various methods, division staff members roasted beef, lamb, mutton, and pork of different grades and from different states. Bureau home economists also determined ideal roasting times and temperatures for these meats to maximize flavor and tenderness, minimize shrinkage, and economize on fuel, drawing on the results of this research to develop standard "techniques of meat cookery."[75] In the 1930s, under the direction of former Iowa State College professor Florence B. King, the bureau's work with food utilization expanded to

*Bureau of Home Economics food and nutrition specialist Lucy Alexander;
retired University of Illinois professor Isabel Bevier, credited with originating "modern
meat cookery" using a thermometer; Bureau of Animal Industry chief John R. Mohler;
and Bureau of Home Economics chief Louise Stanley prepare for a lamb-roasting
experiment in the bureau's meat lab, May 1935. (National Archives)*

include subjects such as bread flavor and the comparative food value of home-made versus commercially prepared foods.[76]

The bureau's cotton studies similarly sought to correlate the production and consumption of another agricultural commodity. To address a depression in the cotton textile industry in the 1920s, Ruth O'Brien and the bureau's Division of Textiles and Clothing took on a range of interrelated projects that together connected the USDA's investigations in the production and marketing of these fibers with their "ultimate purpose"—their use by consumers. These initiatives aimed not simply to promote the use of cotton but to understand this commodity from the consumer's perspective, to recommend improvements in fabric quality to enhance the value of cotton to homemakers, and to assist the cotton industry in the development of cotton fabrics and clothing designs that women would want to buy. Together, the bureau's cotton textile studies demonstrated the comprehensive approach to research that bureau home economists sought to achieve for all major agricultural and manufactured household goods. "Our ambition is to establish in the Department of Agriculture the idea that no production problem is being adequately studied until all the utilization aspects are being considered and properly evaluated," assistant textile chemist Margaret S. Furry explained in 1930.[77]

One of the first steps of the cotton utilization initiative involved assessing the nature of consumer demand. When cotton growers and textile manufacturers complained of a decline in demand for cotton, bureau home economists surveyed farm women to determine why they seemed to prefer silk and rayon. They learned that families and individuals with higher incomes frequently chose silk or rayon over cotton because they found it more attractive and easier to handle.[78] In response, home economists at the bureau produced a series of bulletins suggesting uses for cotton and encouraging women to consider it for summer clothing and to choose osnaburg, a fabric made of low-grade cotton, for curtains and upholstering furniture. Bureau home economists also developed designed specifications for a durable fabric of short-staple cotton that could replace imported jute burlap as a foundation for hooked rugs.[79]

In addition, bureau home economists studied cotton fibers and fabrics "with a view to suggesting ways in which they could be modified so as to meet better the needs of the consumer." Division chief Ruth O'Brien and her staff investigated the relationship between fiber properties and the durability of finished cotton sheets. They designed and commissioned sample sheets made of different kinds of cotton and compared them with ready-made sheets by testing their durability in the laboratory and under "typical conditions of wear and laundering." A physicist at the bureau "devised an apparatus for measuring the heat and pressure of home irons" to simulate their effects on the cotton sheets.[80] Cotton fibers "of known grade and character" were woven into sheets at Clemson College and distributed to the Grace Dodge Hotel, where the impact of regular use by sleeping guests and various washing temperatures was assessed. Managed by home economist Mary Lindsley and located on Capitol Hill in Washington, D.C., this hotel for professional women had served as the headquarters of the American Home Economics Association until 1924, and on this occasion bureau home economists used it as an improvised laboratory—located within the boundaries of women's sphere—to study the actual conditions of use. Using data collected from these studies, bureau staff provided suggestions to manufacturers about what types of cotton were most suitable for making sheets and where to reinforce fabrics after weaving.

Home economists further held conferences to urge pattern companies, advertising agencies, commission merchants, and textile industry representatives to find ways to make cotton clothing more attractive to consumers. One of the many challenges cotton producers faced in the mid-1920s was a decline in demand due to the shortening of dress lengths and competition from manufacturers of cellulosic fibers and silk, especially in the undergarment, summer dress, and hosiery markets. In response, bureau home economists urged manufacturers to pay more attention to design and to make cotton fabrics and patterns "according to the present vogue." To help show off the "inherent qualities of cotton," the Textiles and Clothing Division also developed "appropriate dress designs for various types of figures" and worked with the Cotton Textile Institute, a trade association, to publicize these designs.[81] Finally, when a bureau survey revealed that many women were dissatisfied with cotton's tendency to lose its "crisp new appearance" in laundering, the agency's home economists conducted studies—and developed special devices for these investigations—that ultimately allowed them to determine that dasheen starch produced a desirable finish for cotton to help it compete with the other fabrics, especially in ready-made garments for "the professional woman."[82]

The cotton studies suggest that the bureau's focus on the science of consumption could be quite comprehensive when the USDA's mission and sufficient financial resources aligned with home economists' research and reform objectives. More typically, however, the combination of home economists' broad, ambitious goals, the USDA's narrower emphasis on assisting agricultural producers, and limited funding made for an uneven, piecemeal program. Bureau home economists had more resources available for food research than for any other area, but they only rarely were able to extend their work beyond farm products to thoroughly investigate other areas, such as commercially canned or processed foods. In spite of Ruth O'Brien's encompassing vision for the Division of Textiles and Clothing, her ongoing struggle for funding and skilled workers led by 1941 to what one journalist described as "a confusingly diverse program."[83] The Division of Economics similarly lacked the resources to pursue as thorough a strategy for studying homemakers' production and consumption trends as Hildegarde Kneeland intended. Although Louise Stanley aspired to satisfy requests for guidance on choosing appliances from women like H. E. Brennan, she was not able to set up a wide-ranging program to study household equipment. Rapid change in the scientific and technical content of domestic consumption required ever increasing levels of specialization to fully understand these emerging technologies. Bureau home economists attempted to map out and order the array of products and services available to consumers, but the enormity of the task made it beyond their power to complete. While work at the bureau represented some of the most rigorous science under way on behalf of a newly emerging class of consumers, the breadth of change in the marketplace and bureau home economists' need to generate new knowledge in a field they were at the same time creating limited the organization's ability to achieve many of its ambitious goals.

Nonetheless, in the interwar period, the bureau emerged as the nation's foremost center for home economics research and a leading resource for information about domestic consumer goods, servicing not only consumers but also a wide array of other experts and educators. By compiling and publishing bibliographies synthesizing the results of home economics studies as well as the work of others in related fields, bureau home economists influenced the research carried out far beyond their Washington offices — in land-grant and private universities, state extension services, and commercial organizations. Many of the bureau's leaflets and technical bulletins were specifically aimed at university home economics professors who relied on the bureau for up-to-date information about agricultural and commercial goods and their use in the home.[84] At the same time, for agricultural officials, industrial managers, and reformers searching for ways to understand consumers or consumer products, bureau home economists filled a void between consumers and producers. Operating in the liminal space between the nation's fields and factories and the homes of its citizens, bureau home economists brought the user's perspective to the attention of both agricultural and industrial producers and a diverse array of other professionals in related disciplines. Nutrition scientists, textile chemists, appliance engineers, and social science researchers were among the many experts who turned to Louise Stanley and her colleagues for an enhanced understanding of such matters as product quality, household uses, design specifications, consumer behavior, and the utilization of agricultural goods. By creating and communicating a body of information about consumer goods in a language different than that used by male farmers, engineers, and business managers, the bureau's research program played an important role in facilitating communication about products and consumers in the developing consumer economy.

Conclusion

Officially established in the early 1920s to promote the use of agricultural products and improve living conditions in rural America, the Bureau of Home Economics emerged as a national headquarters from which home economists advanced their professional agenda by carving out a niche of expertise within the culturally prescribed boundaries of a female sphere, the realm of consumption. Director Louise Stanley channeled the bureau's resources to create opportunities for women scientists and to realize the vision that her generation of home economists shared of a "science of consumption," one that was oriented toward the needs what they perceived to be the ideal, rational (and generally white and middle-class) homemaker. Throughout the interwar period, the bureau served as a primary training ground for home economics researchers and a strategic location from which dozens of leading home economists expanded the boundaries of their field and enhanced their authority as consumer experts.

Stanley and her colleagues used the bureau's research program to position themselves at the center of the American consumer economy in the interwar period. From the 1890s through World War I, home economists in the USDA translated male expert knowledge to homemakers; in the Bureau of Home Economics they generated new knowledge about agricultural and industrial goods from the perspective of users and translated that information to multiple audiences. Whereas the Office of Home Economics, established before the bureau, had identified the home primarily as a place for food consumption and devoted most of its research efforts to nutrition, the Bureau of Home Economics, led by Stanley, embraced textiles and clothing, household equipment, and furnishings in an ambitious project to study the full array of market offerings for the home. Although resource limitations of this government agency prevented bureau home economists from fully achieving all of their goals, Stanley and her staff drew on their investigations to promote rational consumption among American homemakers and to influence the production and distribution of consumer goods on their behalf.

3

Reforming the Marketplace at the Bureau of Home Economics, 1923–1940

In late 1927, Frederick J. Schlink, consumer activist and assistant secretary of the American Engineering Standards Committee, wrote to Ruth O'Brien, who directed the Division of Textiles and Clothing in the Bureau of Home Economics (BHE), inquiring about the existence of the old-time "thrifty buyer." He wanted to know if a recent study had determined "to what extent the individual housewife is buying for value rather than for ephemeral appeals of vogue or sales pressure." Earlier that year, Schlink had coauthored the bestselling *Your Money's Worth*, a polemical critique of consumer capitalism, and participated, with O'Brien and many other home economists, in a conference, "Problems of the Household Buyer," held at the University of Chicago. Schlink and O'Brien corresponded regularly about their shared commitment to consumers. On this occasion, the home economist informed Schlink that the study of thrifty buying was never completed, but she agreed that such an investigation was worthwhile. Sharing Schlink's interest, O'Brien contacted leading colleagues in her field to inquire about launching such a study. Hazel Kyrk, associate professor of home economics at the University of Chicago, Helen Canon, professor of home economics at Cornell University, and Benjamin Andrews, professor of household economics at Teachers College, all acknowledged the topic's importance, but none of the three scholars knew how to approach the subject. Kyrk, the nation's reigning expert in the economics of consumption, admitted that she did not know "the extent to which homemakers 'buy for value.'" She wrote, "Of course we would all be tremendously interested in any information on that point." Kyrk regarded "with utmost suspicion questionnaires that try to reach motives for buying directly" and suggested that the best approach might be "through the salespeople." Canon questioned whether funding would be available to carry out such a "large study."[1] Home economists and other reformers disagreed about how to use social scientific methods to understand consumers' motivations; the "thrifty buyer," or rational consumer, was an abstraction for them.

Despite a lack of concrete information on what constituted this "thrifty buyer" in the 1920s and 1930s, O'Brien, bureau chief Louise Stanley, and their coworkers struggled to reform the marketplace on behalf of an "average" consumer who had many of the characteristics of this abstract figure. Officials at the U.S. Department of Agriculture (USDA) sought to improve living standards in rural homes, especially among "poor white folks," but they also intended the bureau to be helpful to "the women of the land," serving a broad population of rural and urban families. "I draw no distinction between city and rural houses," explained Stanley.[2] Toward this end, bureau home economists directed their attention to an individual, female consumer who was responsible for managing a household budget, a woman consumer they characterized as "normal" and "average." Whereas other government agencies such as the Women's Bureau and the Children's Bureau aimed their services at working-class Americans, Stanley and her colleagues understood the BHE to be "responsible for the normal child."[3] To home economists, "normal" meant an urban, white, middle-class woman—not particularly needy in terms of income or health—who was already becoming entangled in the growing consumer society. This consumer, they imagined, welcomed the idea of scientific buying and rational consumption.

Framing problems of consumption as a lack of information, home economists used the bureau both to educate and to advocate for this "average" consumer who wanted to "buy for value." Bureau home economists collaborated closely with university home economics professors and the American Home Economics Association (AHEA)—with its headquarters located on Capitol Hill, and later in the Mills Building one block from the White House—to create a marketplace where the information required to make cost-benefit analyses of purchasing choices was readily accessible. Work on behalf of an ideal, informed consumer also led home economists to build relationships with producers and distributors. In informal exchanges and formal negotiations with commercial growers and manufacturers who wanted to understand "the woman's viewpoint," bureau home economists served as professional, "typical" representatives of the very consumers they sought to create and influence. When social science data regarding the attitudes of buyers was not available, home economists used their own scientifically derived standards to stand in for the preferences and needs of "average" consumers, and to argue for useable, dependable goods and merchandising practices that helped to educate, rather than confuse, potential buyers.

Home economists' dual identity as experts about consumer products and as representatives or stand-ins for the consumers for whom they advocated was forged in the political economy of the 1920s and continued into the 1930s, when New Deal reformers articulated a more explicit political understanding of consumers in a planned economy. Throughout the interwar period, home economists' confidence that consumers and products could be more precisely understood and controlled appealed to a wide range of government officials, politicians, social critics, and reformers concerned about the problem of mass consumption. The feminized, fact-finding approach of home economics, committed to fine-tuning consumer capitalism, flourished in the dominant political economy of associationalism in the 1920s. As secretary of commerce and then as president, Herbert Hoover advocated efficiencies of all kinds and encouraged cooperation among business and political leaders, creating a climate that celebrated bureau home economists' vision of rational consumption and provided opportunities for them to assert themselves as mediators in the marketplace for consumer products. In the 1930s, when correlating production with consumption became an imperative of economic policy in President Franklin Delano Roosevelt's New Deal, home economists also found support for the "more effective consumption" they had long sought to promote. Although home economists lost much of the political clout they had in Hoover's Republican administration, Democratic political leaders and policy makers relied on the BHE to both educate consumers and represent consumers on technical committees and other forums that were part of the New Deal reform agenda.[4]

For bureau home economists, reforming the marketplace for consumer goods was an investigative and educational project that promised to bring about social, economic, and cultural change. Although they saw themselves primarily as professional—rather than political—actors, the technical work that home economists performed as civilian government employees of the bureau often took on a political significance. In spite of limited resources, the absence of a clearly articulated federal policy concerning matters of consumption gave this elite group of home economists considerable room to maneuver. Without any binding regulatory authority, home economists in the bureau operated as some of the first official government advisers to, and representatives of, citizens as consumers. Consumer education quite often blurred into consumer advocacy, and bureau home economists' mediating position placed them in a confused and contradictory relationship with American homemakers. Still, home economists at the bureau used their government position to infuse consumer goods—and consumption itself—with the values of economy, efficiency, sanitation, and health, and to construct these values as hallmarks of American middle-class identity.

Consumption and Citizenship

Conducted on behalf of the public interest, the bureau's user-oriented research elevated the significance of women's roles as consumers to the level of public policy and provided an institutional means to address the needs of a constituency of homemakers. Research on household goods at the bureau sent a message to women and men that consumption was an important economic activity, significant enough to merit attention from a government science program. While framing consumption as women's special responsibility, the Bureau of Home Economics also taught that being a consumer in modern America involved being in communication with, and guided by, a new group of experts. In effect, the federal government told Americans that consumption was a matter of scientific facts and research, a message delivered by the government's official spokespeople on the subject: scientifically trained home economists.

Institutionalization in Washington endowed home economists' messages about consumption—based on wise purchasing and rational living by trained consumers—with official governmental status. Through the scientific and systematic study of fibers, foods, and household appliances, bureau home economists aimed to establish a rational basis for consumption. Although the bureau was a key player in the USDA's overall strategy to modernize the lives of American farm families, it did not merely promote consumption per se.[5] Rather, the bureau's research program sought to redirect the homemaker's attention away from commercial advertising that appealed to "her primitive instincts" and toward a more utilitarian, practical framework with which to evaluate the offerings of the commercial marketplace.[6]

Using the language of science, home economists in the BHE spoke in an alternative voice about the meaning of consumption in interwar America. They used the bureau to challenge the cultural constructions of female consumers as vain, emotional, and irrational and to combat the manipulative aspects of the growing consumer economy. The fact-finding research and communication used by Louise Stanley and her staff aimed to compensate for the paucity of information about goods available through modern merchandising practices. At the same time, bureau home economists used science to cast the kinds of qualitative changes they wanted to bring about in American domestic life in quantitative, measurable terms. Under their command, "the woman's viewpoint" was not just a matter of a single individual's subjective opinion but a set of "standards" imbued with the values of health, nutrition, quality, economy, sanitation, and durability. The bureau's research program generated a technical discourse about consumption that bolstered the cultural authority of these values, aligned them with the identity of white, middle-class women, and linked them to an array of manufactured commercial goods. In the booming economy of the 1920s, home economists proposed value-laden standards as a guide for homemakers to manage their families' disposable income in the context of abundance. "National prosperity and lack of unemployment alone do not guarantee a higher standard of living to the people of any nation," explained Stanley just months before the stock market crash in 1929. "Better wages must be directed into wise channels of expenditure if they are to be reflected in family and individual well-being. Standards are essential for the education of the consumer in the wise use of the goods available. The wider the opportunity for choice the greater the necessity for this education."[7] By constructing the bureau as an information clearinghouse devoted to defining such "standards," home economists promoted these material conditions as hallmarks of white, urban, middle-class identity, and they projected them as the goal for all of the nation's families.

By providing a platform for home economists' scientific and cultural agenda, the federal government also sent the message that rational consumption was a matter of civic duty. The nation's political economy in the 1920s provided fertile ground for home economists to solidify the equation between their vision of rational consumption, middle-class identity, and citizenship. During the World War I food conservation campaigns, Herbert Hoover's embrace of home economists' expertise had allowed women in the field to use the state's wartime propaganda machine to deliver messages that aligned nutritional diets with patriotism in a very explicit manner. As secretary of commerce and then as president, Hoover continued his campaigns against waste and relied on alliances with home economists and other middle-class women's organizations to promote improvements in the American standard of living. The bureau's information about consumer products and consumers was an important resource for Hoover as he organized conferences to address issues of child welfare, housing, and domestic life.[8] Many New Deal reformers challenged the assumptions about the mutuality of interests held by Hoover's fellow managerial liberals and many home economists, but they, too, relied on the bureau's expertise as they worked to cast consumption in political terms. In the process, Democratic reformers infused bureau home economists' educational agenda with a new sense of legitimacy and kept the bureau in the public eye throughout the 1930s.[9]

Throughout the interwar period, home economists used their location at the center of an extensive communication network to disseminate practical domestic advice to a large segment of the American population. Even as Stanley worked to bolster the bureau's standing as a research center, she tended to downplay her identity as a scientist and emphasize her rural roots while promoting the bureau as "really a sort of clearing house for the needs of housewives."[10] The bureau's research formed the basis for published bulletins on dozens of topics such as stain removal, laundry methods, canning techniques, and the selection of manufactured goods for use in classrooms and demonstrations. Offered to individual households free of charge or for a small fee, these bulletins were in wide circulation throughout the interwar period and reached an enormous audience. In the 1927 fiscal year alone, the bureau distributed copies of its twenty-seven bulletins to more than 2 million people.[11] In addition, bureau home economists shared the results of their investigations through live radio programs and exhibits. At the bureau's Washington, D.C., headquarters, displays of sewing machines, washing machines, and children's clothing designs allowed homemakers to "see and compare all types of such devices."[12]

Home economics faculty at agricultural land-grant colleges in each state, home demonstration extension agents in most rural counties, and high-school home economics teachers all recognized the bureau as the nation's authority on practical matters regarding domestic consumption—particularly food and nutrition, and they were an important audience for its bulletins and unpublished research findings. In addition, editors of women's magazines similarly came to rely on the bureau for advice on a variety of household matters during the interwar period. Home economists at the bureau offered an easily accessible source of authority with which to impress and inform readers of these mass-circulation publications. Building on the collaborative relationships forged in the food conservation campaigns during World War I, bureau home economists took pains early on to strengthen their alliances with editors of magazines targeting American homemakers. While some editors resisted publishing information by government scientists, overall the bureau's efforts to cultivate this important channel were effective. Throughout the 1920s and 1930s, many writers for women's magazines, who tended to be trained in home economics themselves, regularly turned to the bureau for information about cooking, canning, and the selection of industrially produced household goods. Manufacturers, too, depended on the bureau to verify proper methods of food preparation and preservation.[13] Dissemination of information through women's magazines and corporate trade literature ensured bureau home economists a wider audience than they ever could have commanded through government publications and home demonstrations alone.

Home economists at the bureau used this complex communications net-work to campaign for making rational cost-benefit analyses a part of home-makers' daily lives and decision making. By uncovering the "secrets" of a chaotic marketplace and sharing them with homemakers, home economists constructed the bureau as a resource center for an imagined, "average" Ameri-can consumer who needed and wanted technical information about products synthesized and summarized in plain language that was easy to apply. Although bureau staff assumed that most homemakers lived in single-family homes, they emphasized the message about rational consumption far more than they promoted this particular living arrangement.[14] Bureau publications and out-reach were aimed at a wide group of homemakers, including women who made things in the home as well as those that did not. Decisions on whether to en-courage home production or purchase of the latest product were based on how these choices fit into the bureau's framework of efficient, economic living, and these decisions varied according to the staff's assumptions about the intended audience.

Although Ruth O'Brien, head of the Division of Textiles and Clothing, as-sumed that the ascendance of ready-made clothing was an unstoppable trend, she worked to meet the practical needs of rural women who did not have ac-cess to such garments. Because the "average woman" purchased an increasing percentage of her clothes ready-made as "merely a part of the great and inevi-table transfer of home industry onto a commercial basis," O'Brien considered it "rather futile to make any large-scale attempts to turn the tide." Still, home economics surveys in the 1920s, including one she directed, indicated that "an enormous number" of women—principally those "on the farm and in the small city"—still sewed garments at home and needed "assistance in doing it more satisfactorily."[15] To meet the needs of these women in the 1920s, O'Brien devoted the majority of her division's bulletins to clothing decisions, fitting, and fabric selection. Two focused on laundering, while others dealt with fit-ting women's garments, making window curtains, and constructing children's clothes. Bulletins on how to choose cloth for home sewing—such as "Selection of Cotton Fabrics" (1926)—aimed at taking the guesswork out of purchasing, teaching women about the details of fabric composition and construction and how these qualities related to the durability and use of cloth. "There are today buried back behind the scenes in the manufacturing and distributing world many quality standards which the consumer never hears about and which would be very useful to her," O'Brien told the attendees of the Kansas Farm and Home Week in 1930. "There is also in connection with many commodities a more or less technical language which describes the various qualities accurately and are essential to the setting up of any quality specifications for those articles. I believe very thoroughly that one of the best helps the consumer can give herself today is to ferret out these terms, learn their meaning and be able to talk the language of every commodity."[16] Despite the growing market for manufactured clothing, the popularity of these bulletins—the bureau's 1930 publication on stain removal was described as a "best seller," with a distribution of almost 1 million copies—demonstrated the continued importance of home production and maintenance of textiles.[17]

As New Deal political and economic leaders directed political attention to consumers, they encouraged bureau home economists' consumer education initiatives. At the request of President Roosevelt's National Emergency Council, Ruth O'Brien wrote "Present Guides for Household Buying," which synthesized and summarized, for the first time, the consumer guides to quality grades developed by the USDA and other government agencies. When the Consumer Advisory Board (CAB) of the National Recovery Administration (NRA) organized county consumer councils to make consumers' voices heard at the local level, the councils distributed copies so widely that O'Brien and her colleagues revised the bulletin two years later and printed another popular edition. Soon O'Brien's team developed a series of "quality guides" to buying ready-made items such as blankets, towels, dresses, coats, and hosiery, translating technical terms into plain language to assist homemakers in the selection of such manufactured goods.[18]

From inside the USDA, the Consumers' Counsel Division of the Agricultural Adjustment Administration (AAA), led by Frederick Howe and his successors, relied on the BHE to supply articles on food values, household purchasing, and other topics for the AAA's *Consumers' Guide*. Intended to explain to consumers why food prices were increasing as a result of government production controls, this semimonthly publication also listed retail prices of various goods and provided information about various grades and standards. According to historian Lizabeth Cohen, the *Guide* became by the mid-1930s "almost a service organ of the consumer movement." The bureau also worked with the Consumers' Counsel on a number of related projects, including a study of the nutritional value of dried skim milk and a campaign to promote the acceptance of this new food product among low-income families as well as a general effort to promote the compulsory grading of certain canned foods.[19]

The Great Depression led the bureau to shift its attention to assisting individuals and families enduring serious economic hardship. Food and nutrition became a public issue with the food shortages of World War I, and it emerged again with the crash of the stock market in 1929. During Hoover's presidency the bureau launched the "Market Basket," a weekly press release (which became a regular feature in many newspapers) containing suggestions for canning and low-cost recipes. Throughout the economic crisis, the bureau's popular canning bulletins were directed at "women who are canning as a necessity to save surplus products and make the garden last throughout the year" as well as to those who could not afford to purchase either canned or fresh fruits and vegetables. To support New Deal relief programs, the bureau's food economists developed "Diets at Four Levels of Nutritive Content and Cost" as a guide to making nutritious dietary choices in hard times. Publicized by First Lady Eleanor Roosevelt and distributed widely throughout the 1930s, these diets served as the primary standards for social service and relief agencies in urban and rural communities.[20]

Communication between home economists and homemakers went in both directions, with the bureau receiving 15,000 letters annually in the late 1920s.[21] Home economists in all divisions devoted significant time to answering the myriad requests they received from the nation's homemakers. Women sent questions regarding a range of household matters, especially food and cooking. "When I am tangled up in some culinary difficulty, I say 'Write to the Bureau of Home Economics,'" penned M. L. Manning, who operated "a little Kitchen-Shop" in the basement of her Baltimore apartment. "Disgusted" with a recipe for gingersnaps she had heard described on the commercial radio by home economist Ida Bailey Allen, she wrote to junior specialist in foods Fanny Walker Yeatman: "The dough wont [sic] roll out without so much flour that the consistency and flavor are somewhat spoilt. Can you give me a really good recipe?" Manning and Yeatman corresponded regularly about canning and jelly making over a four-year period.[22] Other homemakers sought instructions on how to make gelatin, whether canning destroyed the vitamin C content of fruit and tomato juice, and how to cook with new appliances. In gratitude for advice she received on the bureau's *Farm and Home Hour* radio show about baking bread as well as for some written suggestions about safe methods of canning asparagus, Edna McCulley of Belle Vernon, Pennsylvania, sent a handmade doily to her "radio friend."[23]

Women also turned to the bureau as an objective source of information about making purchasing decisions. In the 1930s, Mary Maloney of Pittsfield, Massachusetts, was one of many women who requested information about "how to run a house, food and otherwise on a small budget. Possibly your information contains lists of best values in various products, so one will be safeguarded against alluring advertising." Radio listener Mrs. Harold B. Rex of Lynn, Massachusetts, thanked local extension agents for teaching her "many things I have never given a thought to before. The day you talked about the labels on canned fish foods I took mine all from the closet and examined them. I will surely be more careful in buying in the future." Others asked the bureau to compensate for the shortcomings of manufacturers' instructions about new appliances such as pressure cookers. "I have a 21-quart cooker," wrote Mrs. Joe Malano from Rural Route 1 in New Castle, Colorado, "and wish to use it for most of my home cooking. I have a small booklet given with the cooker but it does not give complete information. Does it require longer cooking in a larger cooker than a smaller one?" One woman sent a sample of pongee silk to the bureau inquiring how to prevent the discoloration caused by washing the material.[24]

By providing answers to these kinds of practical questions about consumer products, bureau home economists served homemakers who had the time and inclination to make carefully calculated purchasing choices. Educated women, women with daughters in college, or women who had been exposed to home economics, perhaps through the work of the extension service, were among those most likely to seek advice from the bureau. Through this type of communication, home economists supported both Hooverist and New Deal initiatives, contributing to the work of other professionals who shared their assumptions that consumption could and should be rationalized. By the mid-1930s, the bureau's role in supplying this type of practical information earned it a reputation among many Americans as a "consumers' bureau."[25] The bureau proved a more neutral alternative to the Good Housekeeping Institute and other "institutes" operated by newspapers and women's magazines that were firmly allied to commercial advertisers. At the same time, the bureau's work was part of a more ambitious agenda to promote a cultural language about consumption based on efficiency, economy, sanitation, and health that would give women a set of technical criteria and quantitative measures by which to exercise their buying power. This broad mission made bureau home economists influential contributors to critiques of consumer capitalism. Stuart Chase and Frederick J. Schlink's bestselling *Your Money's Worth* (1927) drew on a discourse of consumption and rationality, reaching a wide audience in the 1930s as New Deal reformers argued for consumers' political interest and launched initiatives like the AAA's *Consumers' Guide*. Thus home economists supported the reform of consumer capitalism while simultaneously supporting the underlying assumptions of that system as they related to the roles of producers and consumers (especially women).[26]

At the same time, the political and economic ideas that informed the New Deal revealed the limitations of locating within the USDA a bureau in the service of consumers. They also raised questions about the identities and needs of consumers and how the bureau's research program served them. For young women like H. E. Brennan from rural Virginia who sought specific advice about which oil stove to buy, bureau home economists had no legal means of publicizing the complete results of the comparative tests they conducted. As USDA officials, they were legally barred from mentioning specific brands and could report only general results of their studies. Many of the bureau's bulletins therefore emphasized principles of household management on such matters as the care of food in the home or efficient kitchen arrangements, rather than comparative product analysis. When Anita Newcomb McGee, of Southern Pines, North Carolina, wrote to the bureau in 1936 to ask what was "the best and most complete cookbook now on the market," Lela E. Booher, head of the Food and Nutrition Division, responded that she "cannot recommend any one cookbook." Bureau home economists made repeated, public calls for a change in this government policy. Speaking "off the record" to a Cornell University audience in 1935, Ruth Van Deman, who directed the bureau's publications program, lamented that when consumers requested advice from the bureau on certain brands of goods, it sent back only "a lot of general patter about this type and that principle of operation that doesn't help that taxpayer a nickel's worth in making his choice in the store." She proposed modeling a revised policy on that of the Connecticut Agricultural Experiment Station—a state agency that analyzed branded food products and published their chemical composition—but the USDA maintained its strict policy, leaving home economists in the bureau to rely on more indirect and general ways of communicating with both manufacturers and consumers.[27]

In addition, the bureau's alliance to the agricultural establishment often kept staff members focused on farm products at the expense of manufactured goods, and it sometimes prevented Stanley and her colleagues from making objective statements about even standard agricultural goods. Occasionally home economists' emphasis on the needs of consumers led them into conflict with agricultural producers, who complained about the content of some of the bureau's bulletins. In 1935 wheat producers took senior home economist Hazel Stiebeling to task for her bulletin "Diets at Four Levels of Nutritive Content and Cost." In this publication, Stiebeling recommended that families who could afford the most expensive diet reduce their consumption of wheat. Milling industry representatives protested that the bulletin was "directed against the wheat producer." Although Stanley and Stiebeling insisted that they only aimed, through the bulletin, to encourage a balanced diet and did not intend to discriminate against cereals, a group of senators representing wheat-belt states tried to attach a rider to the USDA appropriations bill mandating that any Agriculture Department employee who suggested reducing the consumption of any "wholesome agricultural food commodity" be fired. Wallace and Stanley helped get the rider defeated by calling in experts to demonstrate that Stiebeling's recommended menus actually would require American farmers to produce more, not less, overall (and that surplus of any particular grain could be consumed by livestock). In this struggle, home economists benefited significantly from the vocal support of a coalition of women's groups—including the League of Women Voters, the National Congress of Parents and Teachers, the American Association of University Women, the AHEA, and the Women's Trade Union League—which all spoke in favor of the bureau and its importance to consumers.[28]

Over time, the limitations on the bureau's ability to share its research findings and its ties to agricultural producers led many reformers to give up hope that the BHE would ever become a full-fledged consumers' bureau. As assistant secretary of the American Engineering Standards Committee (AESC), and later the American Standards Association (ASA), Frederick Schlink worked closely with bureau home economists on standardization efforts through the 1920s. But in the following decade he relied on his own organization, Consumers' Research, to provide consumers with comparative information about brand-name goods based on product testing, and to advocate for consumers in ways that the BHE and other government agencies could not. Although Schlink encouraged home economists to bolster their technical expertise and specialize more in subfields of economics and engineering that pertained to the home, he and his colleagues eventually became vocal critics of the bureau. Consumers' Research staff member Eleanor Loeb argued that the bureau's published information was too general, and that its operation was "too much hampered by traditional restraints and taboos," while Schlink dismissed the bureau for being "too academic" and not practical enough to be of assistance to women in making purchasing decisions. He called for the bureau to take a more critical position in evaluating commercial goods, and he ultimately rejected the idea of a bureau devoted to consumers' needs inside the government altogether.[29]

Critiquing the bureau from another angle, University of Chicago economist Hazel Kyrk questioned the value of a bureau research program centered on consumer products. Writing in the AHEA's journal in 1933, Kyrk argued that home economics should focus instead on "the problems of the family" rather than conduct studies of mass-produced goods such as those undertaken at the Bureau of Home Economics. "Home economics research is not anything or everything pertaining to food or to textiles or clothing, to equipment, or to any other commodity the family uses," Kyrk argued. "I can see nothing uni-fied or integrated in a plan of research that proceeds along commodity lines." For Kyrk, home economics was a methodology for approaching those already established fields. "Home economics is the concept, the organization, that integrates and focuses," she explained—not a distinct specialized research discipline. "Home economics represents rather the plan or the direction be-hind the research that gives it point and meaning, that makes the whole greater than the sum of its parts."[30] Kyrk pinpointed one of the main weaknesses of the kind of consumer advocacy research carried out by Louise Stanley and Ruth O'Brien at the BHE. The idealism and ambition of bureau staff members and the political climate of the times led them to seek cooperative solutions to re-forming consumer capitalism. As they worked to understand "the problems of the family" in the context of the marketplace, bureau home economists be-came drawn into a product-oriented research program in which manufacturers ultimately had the final word. Once they entered into joint projects with indus-try, it was hard for them to maintain a focus on the greater "home" to which Kyrk referred. Home economists' power within such cooperative relationships would always be limited and circumscribed by consumer capitalism.

Additional obstacles kept Louise Stanley and her staff from using the bu-reau's educational program to create a population of ideal, rational consumers. Although the BHE became an established source of information for nutrition and food preparation in the interwar period, it fell short of being a comprehen-sive clearinghouse for information on all consumer products. Staff members had trouble transcending the "cooking and sewing" image of home economics, often encountering resistance within the USDA when they tried to broaden the field's scope. Limited funding, home economists' struggle to professionalize—get jobs, conduct new research, and defend their intellectual turf—as well as competition with Consumers' Research, all presented additional challenges to the bureau's becoming a center for practical information in the service of consumers. As a result, the bureau's publication program was uneven and fragmented, failing to embrace the full range of household products. The gov-ernment's publicity operations, with its use of blurry, black-and-white photo-graphs and line-drawn illustrations, could not compete with the enormous advertising apparatus that private corporations had at their command to pro-duce professionally designed and color-filled promotional literature. Finally, as discussion and debate over the identity of the "thrifty buyer" revealed, it was not at all clear, even to home economists and other reformers, that American homemakers either were or wanted to become the rational consumers whom home economists sought to serve with all of this information. Not all homemakers had the time, energy, or desire to select commercial goods systematically, or to master the technology behind an ever expanding array of products on the market. By the late 1920s, at least one home economics professor reported a "great lack of interest in the scientific approach to home problems." Ruth O'Brien admitted that she had difficulty convincing consumers to learn the meaning of technical textile terms like *tensile strength* in which she and her colleagues were so well versed.[31] As new types of goods and new models of existing products proliferated, acquiring a high degree of knowledge about all of them was fast becoming impossible—for homemakers and home economists alike. Further, Stanley and her staff eventually came up against the practical reality that the needs and priorities of American consumers—even within the middle class, their main target audience—were more diverse than any single research or educational program could support. Even so, bureau home economists found unique opportunities to speak on behalf of a population of imagined homemakers as they took on an equally difficult challenge, that of influencing manufacturers and retailers.

Representing Consumers

For bureau home economists, educating consumers and representing consumers were inextricably linked. To create a marketplace where the information required to make cost-benefit analyses of purchasing choices was readily accessible, home economists used the bureau's research program to change the attitudes of not only consumers but also manufacturers and retailers. Bureau home economists forged cooperative relationships with industrial producers and distributors, interpreting the perspective of women users to designers, engineers, and marketing representatives of a wide array of commercial goods. In this role, they participated in the market as professional representatives of the very consumers they sought to educate.

In the interwar period, home economists' science of consumption attracted the attention of manufacturers, and provided employees at the Bureau of Home Economics with opportunities to collaborate with engineers and sales managers in shaping the production and distribution of a wide range of household goods. Although the agricultural extension service was not officially allowed to "engage in commercial activities," female home demonstration agents and male extension agents alike blurred the lines between government service and the promotion of privately produced goods. Throughout the agricultural establishment, ties to industry fundamentally informed scientific agendas. When the BHE was created in 1923, the enabling legislation explicitly allowed it to collaborate with outside "public and private agencies" and set the stage for staff home economists to contribute to a larger project of fostering cooperation between government and industry, a project central to the political philosophy of Herbert Hoover.[32] While USDA policies prohibited bureau home economists from making public, official endorsements of specific products, department staff members were allowed to consult privately with manufacturers. Bureau home economists provided informal advice to manufacturers and advertising agents who turned to the bureau for opinions on new products and insights into the current thinking of women consumers when writing publications and magazine articles for potential customers. Behind the scenes and in a manner invisible to consumers, bureau home economists made suggestions for improving foods, textiles, and household equipment, as well as writing instructions about how these products could be used in the home. Sometimes this input to manufacturers was based on research. For example, in preparing copy for a cookbook in the early 1930s, the General Foods Consumer Service Department requested up-to-date information about proper procedures for cooking meat from bureau home economist Lucy Alexander and incorporated the standard roasting temperatures she developed into the *General Foods Cook Book*.[33] In other cases, however, bureau input was based on the subjective opinion of individual home economists. When a representative of the Pompeian Corporation asked the bureau to evaluate samples of its new olive oils and salad dressings, staff home economists were eager to make "suggestions as to improvement in flavor and consistency." Fanny Walker Yeatman, junior specialist in foods at the bureau, responded that she would "prefer a little more salt and acid." But because consumers could add those ingredients to suit their individual tastes, she wrote: "I would not think it necessary for you to change your formula."[34] Although in this case Yeatman had no investigations on which to base her claims, the bureau's ongoing practice of surveying and corresponding informally with homemakers provided staff home economists with the confidence to speak for their preferences in this type of casual manner.

Bureau home economists took on more formal roles as consumer representatives in a number of organized initiatives aimed at standardizing household goods. *Standardization* became a buzzword among the growing number of politicians, industry leaders, and government agency experts at work in Hoover's "associative state" in the 1920s. Having witnessed the success of uniform standards in facilitating efficient production during World War I (as president of the Federated American Engineering Societies in the late 1910s), Hoover called for not just the standardization of many product features but also the "simplification" of products, or the elimination of unnecessary variations (such as sizes) for specific product categories. Public support for this agenda led to Hoover to continue the standardization projects as secretary of commerce from 1921 to 1929, encouraging producers to cooperate voluntarily with government initiatives in order to enhance the efficiency of the nation's economic system. Hoover relied on the department's Bureau of Standards to coordinate this endeavor, and he established a separate division—the Division of Simplified Practice (DSP)—to facilitate the voluntary simplification of goods within various communities of producers. Committees consisting of representatives from relevant industries established specifications for goods and then left it to manufacturers to decide whether they were "willing-to-certify" that their products met the committee's specifications. The DSP worked closely with the American Engineering Standards Committee (known after 1928 as the American Standards Association) which was revitalized in 1919 as an affiliate of the Bureau of Standards.[35] The DSP and the ASA were primarily oriented toward the needs of producers, but as the leadership showed an increasing interest in coordinating the supply and demand of household articles they turned to the American Home Economics Association and the Bureau of Home Economics to identify the perspective of women consumers in relation to manufactured goods.

For home economists, standardization promised to simplify the marketplace and enhance consumers' ability to make rational purchasing decisions. Just as they relied on scientifically derived "standards" to guide homemakers along a path of "right living," home economists embraced the idea of standard products and product qualities that would solve practical household problems and make informed shopping by comparison possible. To influence the marketplace for fabric and ready-made clothing, the AHEA established its Central Committee on the Standardization of Textile Fabrics in 1919. Within a few years, the organization created the General Committee on Standardization to work with Hoover's DSP and submitted a list of products in need of standardization or simplification based on a national survey of directors of university home economics departments and home demonstration leaders. By the late 1920s, the ASA emerged as the leading organization for standardization, with the AHEA serving as an official member and placing representatives on committees concerned with commodities "of interest to the homemaker."[36] To participate in these committees, the AHEA relied on technical expertise from home economists in the BHE, who were among the first and most vocal advocates of standardization within the organization. Even before the bureau was established, Minna C. Denton, assistant chief of the Office of Home Economics, served as chair of the AHEA's Committee on Standardization of Measuring

Cups and collaborated with engineers at the Bureau of Standards to eliminate excessive deviation in cup sizes and adopt a code of specifications and tolerances that at least one manufacturer agreed to follow.[37]

Under Louise Stanley's leadership, standardization became even more of a priority in the bureau as the inability to fully share the information they gathered about product qualities led the bureau chief and her staff to pursue alternative ways to influence producers to improve and label their goods. Bureau home economists believed an excess array of goods overwhelmed consumers and reduced purchasing choices to whims motivated by manipulative advertising techniques. While they judged some machines on the market to be truly laborsaving and economical, they found other devices to be inefficient and not worth the expense. "There is nowhere that the housewife, either rural or urban, has been exploited more than in the sale of labor-saving equipment," Stanley lamented in 1926. She blamed the problem on "too many designs."[38] Standardization, she hoped, would limit unnecessary choices and help make distinctions between specific brands clear for consumers, marking a first step in the labeling of various kinds of goods. Time and again, staff home economists asserted that homemakers both wanted and needed standards to guide them in the selection of foods, clothing, and household appliances. Bureau employees published articles in technical and trade journals encouraging manufacturing firms and trade associations to incorporate recommended standards and features in products, to grade their products according to the results of scientific tests, and to label their products with this information. By the late 1920s the bureau had official representation alongside the AHEA on most of the major standardization committees. In this capacity, staff home economists worked closely with the DSP and the ASA to target products to be standardized, simplified, and documented with technical specifications.[39]

The New Deal brought a new level of attention to consumption and sparked public debate over the identity of the American consumer. President Roosevelt's aggressive, multipronged approach to helping the nation survive the Great Depression and trigger economic recovery—particularly his reliance on economic planning—included a range of policies aimed at increasing consumer purchasing power, and it brought consumer representatives into government decision-making in unprecedented ways. The increased politicization of consumption in the 1930s also introduced competing actors who, like home economists, claimed to know and represent consumers. During this decade, home economists (with their strong ties to Hoover and the Republican Party) were kept on the margins as new organizations came to the fore in discussions regarding what government bureaus would focus on the needs of consumers. For example, the director of the National Recovery Administration, Hugh Johnson, appointed academic men such as Robert Lynd and Progressive Era female labor reformers such as Mary Harriman Rumsey and Emily Newell Blair to its Consumer Advisory Board but did not include home economists in the organization. "The N.R.A. has its Consumers' Committee without any home economists," lamented Louise Stanley to a colleague in the summer of 1933. "Mrs. Rumsey is chairman and there are one or two other representatives of the Consumer's League, which as we all know is a labor rather than a consumer's organization." Stanley took some consolation that Grace Morrison Poole, president of the General Federation of Women's Clubs, was "finally put on." Still, she resented the exclusion of her profession: "In spite of the fact that Mrs. Rumsey had promised Miss Edwards that the AHEA would have a representative none was appointed."[40]

Even as these political setbacks undermined home economists' status as consumer representatives, bureau home economists and the AHEA were still supported by New Deal economic planners in their efforts to standardize and label goods, and many agencies continued to rely on the bureau as a source of information about consumer goods and consumers themselves.[41] As technical advisers and educators, Stanley, O'Brien, and their colleagues from the AHEA played important roles within the CAB and other New Deal agencies, serving as consultants and providing testimony at hearings to formulate quality standards for specific consumer goods. Although the CAB did little to set up NRA codes to safeguard consumers and the Supreme Court disbanded the NRA within two years, this group's reliance on bureau home economists demonstrated the importance of their research and reinforced their authority as consumer experts.[42] Many home economists were appointed to the CAB's nonpolitical county councils and made significant contributions to New Deal efforts to educate consumers. Throughout the decade, the AHEA organized state and local club programs—among home economists and women's clubs—to teach women about product specifications and generate consumer demand for standards and "informative labeling."[43] In these ways, home economists served as a critical resource for information about consumers' perspectives on the American economy that New Deal political leaders sought to understand and control.

By working to define standards for consumer goods throughout the 1920s and 1930s, bureau home economists used their scientific expertise to shape the marketplace for household goods for the benefit of American homemakers. Two case studies—the work of the bureau's Division of Textiles and Clothing and the refrigeration investigations led by Stanley—provide a window on the terms in which bureau staff members spoke on behalf of consumers, and the strategies they used to realize their vision of a rational marketplace for household goods. Together, the examples illuminate how the drives for standardization and labeling in two different industries provided Stanley, O'Brien, and their colleagues with opportunities to draw on user-oriented research to promote the design and production of useable, dependable goods as well as merchandising practices that would allow homemakers to make rational selections. In each case, home economists used their positions as scientific experts in consumer goods and representatives of (mostly female) consumers to directly impact a fast-changing market for manufactured products. At the same time, these examples illustrate how limitations faced by the bureau, notably lack of resources and regulatory authority, as well as the inability to discuss brands when communicating to consumers, bounded home economists' capacities to maneuver when working with powerful forces in production, government, and public opinion.

Textiles and Clothing

At the 1927 conference "Problems of the Household Buyer," Ruth O'Brien, chief of the Division of Textiles and Clothing at the Bureau of Home Economics, painted a picture of an urban homemaker lost in a consumer society out of control: "The dilemma with which she is faced in attempting to choose wisely from the mass of products of unknown quality not only offered but forced upon her by the salesmen who follow to her very doorstep, is of vital economic concern. Blind sailing with no lights to mark the channel is bad enough but when the rocks become animated and flock around the ship, disaster is sure to follow." To be knowledgeable about the expanding array of products, O'Brien argued, consumers needed government assistance just as commercial ships required state intervention in navigating waterways. Pure-food laws and meat inspection practices represented landmarks of progress by enhancing the federal government's role in helping household buyers. O'Brien called for the government to assume a similar strong, deliberate role in consumer affairs to make government laboratories "more directly focused on the problems of the consumer." If women of the nation were asked, O'Brien speculated, they would call for "a grading system of every commodity based on impartial testing and research and maintained by the combined efforts of manufacturers, producers, and distributors." Grading systems were in effect for many agricultural and industrial goods, but most were voluntary and there was no standard nomenclature across product lines. Laboratories in the Departments of Commerce and Agriculture were equipped to streamline these systems, but whether they should be so employed, she asserted, "depends on the desires of the public." O'Brien called for a change in government policy to allow federally employed engineers such as herself not only to study the properties of fabrics and garments but also to conduct comparative studies of products that would serve consumers.[44]

O'Brien believed that the guesswork in buying textiles was a "menace" to every family. As head of the bureau's Division of Textiles and Clothing from 1923 to 1954, she drew on her background in textile chemistry, her experience with consumer activism, and her legal education (completed in 1931) to wage a battle against what she perceived as the sources of this confusion. While the USDA maintained its policy against the mention of company names, O'Brien pursued alternative strategies for guiding consumers through a chaotic marketplace where quality goods were often indistinguishable from shoddy, impractical ones. In addition to teaching consumers how to evaluate cloth and clothing, O'Brien combined scientific research and consumer advocacy to create a new set of standards and specifications for fabric quality that would enhance consumers' abilities to make "intelligent selections" without having to master so many technical terms. "Fabric standards and specifications are the only solution to the problem," O'Brien declared in 1930, "and the demand for those on the part of the consumer is becoming more insistent each year. The bureau, organized as it was in the interest of homemakers, has a definite responsibility in assisting in the determination of what such specifications should be and cooperating with manufacturers and retailers in getting these in usable form for the consumer." To this end, O'Brien studied staple textile commodities, analyzed the specifications of those on the market, correlated these specifications with performance under actual use, and conducted other investigations that would assist her in encouraging manufacturers to guarantee minimum standards of quality.[45] O'Brien organized her investigations into the qualities of textile fibers, fabrics, and clothing in a way that supported values such as durability and colorfastness which she believed consumers wanted and needed.

While O'Brien deployed her laboratory's resources to pursue a research agenda designed to support a more comprehensive system of product specifications and labeling, she worked through the AHEA and various other organizations to encourage fiber and textile producers to establish a system of grading fabric quality and labeling fiber content. Before joining the bureau, O'Brien was a founding member of the AHEA's Central Committee on the Standardization of Textile Fabrics, which began in 1919 to pressure manufacturers to adopt specifications for labeling fabric quality. The committee also promoted the passage of protective legislation such as the Barkley Misbranding Bill, which penalized the misrepresentation of merchandise of all kinds.[46] O'Brien continued to play a role on this committee after she joined the bureau, serving several terms as chair of the AHEA's General Committee on Standardization, which concerned itself with a wide range of industrially produced household items. Her activities in this realm led to O'Brien's appointment to President Hoover's 1931 Conference on Home Building and Home Ownership, where she coauthored, with bureau colleague Olive Hartley, the paper "Selection: An Analysis of Consumers' Facilities for Judging Merchandise," summarizing resources available to guide homemakers in the marketplace.[47]

In one major initiative, O'Brien investigated the durability of a variety of cotton bedsheets on the market and provided suggestions to manufacturers about what types of cotton were most suitable for this use and where to reinforce fabrics after weaving. Cotton sheets were among the priorities for standardization recommended by the AHEA in 1926. After a home economics survey indicated that buyers and salespeople alike had difficulty comparing sheets in the store, the AHEA requested that the ASA establish a committee to determine specifications to serve as the basis for product labeling. At a first meeting in 1927, representatives from cotton manufacturing, retail, and the laundry industry agreed that there was a need for standardizing sheets, but that adequate research on the performance of sheeting of various construction and composition needed to be completed before any specifications could be developed.[48] As part of the bureau's work on cotton utilization, O'Brien and her staff soon took up the investigation of the relationship between cotton fiber properties to the durability of finished cotton sheets. O'Brien used her findings to shape the ASA's recommendations that sheets be labeled with information about the size, thread count, tensile strength, weight, and percent of finishing material.[49]

The AHEA's campaign for sheet labeling resulted in the inclusion of construction details in mail-order catalog descriptions, and a few companies introduced "specification sheets" in the mid-1930s. However, most manufacturers resisted the ASA's specifications, arguing that it would undermine the branding of their products and the technical information would be too confusing for most consumers.[50] This resistance typified the challenges O'Brien confronted as she worked toward the long-term goal of establishing quality specifications for textile products and attempted to convince manufacturers and retailers to adopt her specifications and labeling schemes. Her vision for fabric identification labels was only partially realized with the passage of the Textile Fiber Products Identification Act in 1960, which required labels to identify fiber content but not any other information about fiber quality.

O'Brien's efforts to standardize garment sizes were similarly ambitious yet frustrated. As garment producers brought women's and children's ready-to-wear clothing onto the market in the early twentieth century, they lacked a clear standard of measurements for establishing sizes. Men's sizes had been relatively standardized based on military priorities since the Civil War, but as ready-to-wear garments became available for women and children several decades later, consumers discovered a chaotic array of clothing sizes and shapes that bore little resemblance to actual bodies.[51] Two dresses that were marked the same size rarely actually measured or fit similarly. Retailers faced dissatisfied customers as well as great expenses in returns and exchanges and, by the mid-1920s, some of them began to look to standardization to solve the problem. Encouraged by fellow home economist and textile chemist Elizabeth Weirick, who directed the testing laboratory at Sears, Roebuck & Company, as well as other retailers, O'Brien prepared to conduct body measurements with which to establish standard sizes for women's and children's ready-to-wear clothing and patterns.[52] O'Brien studied all of the various precedents for such a project and compiled an extensive bibliography. After thorough networking with anthropologists and anthropometrists, she outlined a project to measure and analyze "500,000 people of both sexes between the ages of two and twenty-one years."[53] Despite her vision and careful planning, O'Brien had trouble getting funding for this large-scale project. The Bureau of Standards endorsed the proposed study in 1929, but USDA officials declined to bear the full cost because they viewed the project as more valuable to commercial interests than to consumers. Garment producers and retailers expressed support for the study, but none came forward with the necessary funds.[54]

In the late 1930s O'Brien won enough financial support from Roosevelt's New Deal programs to complete the body measurement studies and recommend a set of size standards, but she was unable to convince the women's garment trade to adopt these measurements. In 1937, the Works Progress Administration (WPA) supplied funds and surveyors to take thirty-six measurements of almost 150,000 children, aged four to seventeen, in more than a dozen states. In another WPA-funded project, O'Brien oversaw the measurement of 15,000 women. The ASA organized a procedure to establish size standards on the basis of the data collected by the bureau, and mail-order companies adopted some of these standards. But overall, O'Brien's work had little impact on women's clothing sizes, which still are not standardized today.[55] Standardizing garment and pattern sizes required reforming a large number of small and medium-sized producers who operated in a relatively disorganized, decentralized industry over which the BHE had little influence and ultimately no control.

In contrast to the limited effectiveness of O'Brien's efforts to promote the

Eleanor Hunt, an associate anthropometrist at the Bureau of Home Economics, trains a group of colleagues to conduct scientific measurements of the body, July 1937. Under the direction of Ruth O'Brien, the bureau spearheaded an ambitious cooperative project to allow for the standardization of children's garment sizes. (Library of Congress, Prints and Photographs Division, Theodor Horydczak Collection, LC-DIG-hec-23082)

standardization of fabric quality and clothing sizes, her division's research into clothing construction resulted in direct influences on the development of important marketable products: children's clothing. O'Brien took up clothing designs in response to her division's survey of homemakers' needs, the cotton utilization program, as well as her interest in the relationship between clothing and health. Further influenced by the growing "child study" movement, which sought to apply scientific and social scientific methods to the study of children, O'Brien and her team looked for ways to design garments that children could put on independently and wear comfortably. In 1927, they began to issue publications featuring guidelines for making "hygienic" children's clothing such as rompers and sunsuits they believed would permit children's "greatest possible physical and mental development."[56]

The publications sparked immediate interest from homemakers who wrote requesting patterns, as well as from a number of pattern manufacturers.

Grace Dimelow, who held a degree in home economics from Cornell University, contacted the bureau in 1928 soon after she assumed charge of the Butterick Publishing Company's Educational Department and the Home Institute of its *Delineator* magazine. The company had a history of associations with home economists, including Cornell's Martha Van Rensselaer, and had established the new position out of appreciation for the "tremendous growth of the Home Economics movement" and hoping that an in-house home economist would help foster a close rapport with sewing teachers. Dimelow wrote to Ruth O'Brien to inquire about the demand for the bureau's children's rompers and sunsuits. O'Brien reported having received sixty-six requests for sunsuit patterns in the first six months since publication of the bureau's bulletin, and she offered to draw on the USDA's extension service to promote any patterns the company would produce. Soon, after an intense collaboration with the bureau, Butterick issued the bureau-designed pattern, and O'Brien's team worked on additional designs with the pattern manufacturer and several other firms to bring a number of patterns to market, including girls' dresses that buttoned in the front "so that the wearer can manipulate the buttons without assistance"; boys' trousers with "fastenings easy to manipulate," encouraging "good toilet habits"; and a "self-help" bib for nursery school children. By 1932, twenty-nine patterns designed by the bureau had been adopted by eight pattern manufacturers.[57]

The designs proved popular with American consumers. Homemaker Kathleen Paul Jones, from Huntsville, Alabama, praised the bureau for its leaflet "Suits for the Small Boy," which contained guidelines for making boys clothes with a minimum of buttons. She found it unfair that her daughter did not have any buttons on her clothing whereas her son, "poor soul, has buttons on his union suit, both fore and aft—no elastic bloomers for the poor little boys! And then a waist which buttons before and pants which button all around—nineteen button holes to be conquered! So if there is any way to make the path easier for my little boy, just about to graduate into pants, I surely want to know it."[58] Retailers responded quickly. A number of stores throughout the country invited O'Brien to develop a traveling exhibit about children's self-help clothing. Consumers flocked to these exhibits, generating such a demand that the bureau ultimately developed four separate versions and installed another in its lobby in Washington. At Sears, Leone Anne Heuer, a home economist in the company's Educational Division, used the success of this exhibit to convince her employer to sell similar garments.[59]

The children's clothing project enabled bureau home economists to infuse a set of products with their values about childrearing and child develop-

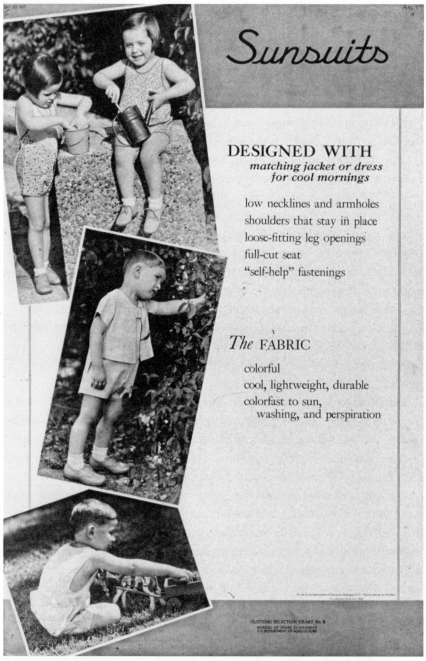

Sunsuits

DESIGNED WITH
matching jacket or dress for cool mornings

low necklines and armholes
shoulders that stay in place
loose-fitting leg openings
full-cut seat
"self-help" fastenings

The FABRIC

colorful
cool, lightweight, durable
colorfast to sun,
    washing, and perspiration

CLOTHING SELECTION CHART No. 9
BUREAU OF HOME ECONOMICS
U.S. DEPARTMENT OF AGRICULTURE

The Bureau of Home Economics Division of Clothing and Textiles designed sunsuits for children featuring loose-fitting openings and "self-help" fasteners to promote ease of movement and independence, which proved popular with young mothers in the late 1920s and early 1930s. (National Archives)

ment. With their "self-help" clothing patterns, O'Brien and her staff struck a chord with middle-class mothers trained in the latest "child study" methods, mothers who perceived their relationship with their children as an issue to be resolved and managed. Clothing that children could put on themselves and move around in freely promised to relieve daily conflicts between parents and children in one very specific arena. It also seemed to promote values of freedom and comfort to enable a child "to become an independent and considerate adult." By working closely with pattern producers and clothing retailers, O'Brien facilitated the diffusion of these garments and set off a minirevolution in clothing styles for children.[60]

The bureau's success in influencing the marketplace for textiles and clothing was highly contingent on the support of industry leaders. Because manufacturers wanted the bureau's help to develop and market a new product, O'Brien was able to exert a significant impact on the design of children's clothing in this period. Yet their resistance to O'Brien's vision for standardizing fabric quality and clothing sizes for women and children prevented her from realizing it.

Refrigeration

Bureau home economists' intersection with the refrigeration industry represented a second significant opportunity to influence the marketplace for consumer goods to meet the practical needs of American homemakers. Through studies organized in the mid-1920s, the BHE played a leading role in shaping public understandings of a new domestic technology, establishing refrigeration as a public health necessity. Louise Stanley and her colleagues developed guidelines for homemakers' use of both ice and mechanical refrigerators, and worked with industry representatives to define a set of "healthful" and "efficient" specifications for refrigerator design and labeling. Stanley's ability to obtain direct financial support from private industry for this project made it unique among bureau endeavors. By forging a more lasting alliance with producers through its refrigeration investigations, bureau staff proved able to combine consumer representation and education to influence the development, marketing, and cultural meaning of this domestic technology.

Mechanical household refrigerators, powered by gas or electricity, were relatively new in the early 1920s. Developments in absorption and compression techniques were widely adopted for commercial cold-storage purposes in the late nineteenth century, but the first mechanical refrigerators designed for domestic use were not sold until close to World War I. At the same time, commercial mechanical refrigeration—as well as technical improvements in harvesting and storing ice—increased the supply of ice, allowing for expanded use of iceboxes beginning in the 1880s. By the mid-1920s, about half of American families had refrigeration of some kind, and the majority of those households used ice. Middle-class families in small towns and cities typically owned a $150 or $200 cabinet insulated with cork and supplied with twenty-five to fifty pounds of ice at the cost of fifteen to thirty cents a day. The other half of the population, however, did not use ice or mechanical refrigeration of any kind. On the West Coast, the use of built-in "coolers," placed away from direct sun to take advantage of cool nights, was a common alternative; cool cellars and spring houses were still widely used in rural areas in other regions.[61] Although, as historian David Nye argues, "it was not economically rational to purchase one before 1930," mechanical refrigerators were becoming affordable to increasing numbers of Americans owing to falling prices, the availability of consumer credit, and the expansion of gas and electrical systems.[62]

Home economists understood cooling as a matter of public health, and in the bureau's early years Stanley saw in the changing marketplace a chance to define both old and new technologies in terms of this priority. Since the early twentieth century, health experts and bacteriologists had established a link between food contamination and improper storage methods, and in the 1910s home economists worked with public health officials to encourage ice refrigeration as a solution to the dangers of spoiled foods. The U.S. Public Health Service offered guidelines for families to make small "refrigerators" to keep milk cold for babies, and the USDA's Office of Home Economics produced bulletins instructing homemakers in safe methods of food storage.[63] "Farm Home Conveniences," published in 1918, emphasized the importance of adequate cold storage space, urging rural homemakers to pay attention to the quality of box construction and insulation. Although it mentioned the possibility that homemakers might have a "motor" to cool their cabinets, the 1926 Bureau of Home Economics bulletin "Convenient Kitchens" was written with ice-box owners primarily in mind. "Care of Food in the Home," first published by the bureau in 1923 and revised in 1926 (before the bureau's refrigeration studies had gained momentum), ignored the advent of mechanical refrigeration.[64] The expanding market for mechanical refrigerators pressured bureau staff to update these publications.

In discussing the issue with a colleague, Stanley made clear her preference for both ice and mechanical refrigeration over the older built-in cooler technologies that she found too dependent on outside temperature and humidity, and thus subject to seasonal variations. Yet because she and her staff were aware that most Americans could not afford to buy newer (as well as larger and more expensive) mechanical refrigerators, they focused their attention on the more affordable ice refrigeration with a goal of guiding middle-class owners of iceboxes to select the appropriate unit and optimize its use for the benefit of household economy and welfare. How much ice to buy, how often to replace it, what kind of a cabinet to buy, what kind of insulation, where to place the ice in the box, where to place the refrigerator in the house—these were among the practical issues Stanley and her staff considered as they sought to define proper and safe food storage.[65]

Even as manufacturers of gas, electric, and ice cabinets worked to sell their products in the competitive and shifting market for domestic refrigeration of the 1920s, all had an interest in promoting the idea that refrigeration was modern and healthy. To expand the market for refrigerators beyond the luxury niche, large corporations in the gas and electrical industries enlisted advertisers to depict refrigerators as a source of clean, healthful living and an expansive cornucopia of foods. Magazine advertisements of the 1920s presented electric refrigerators as icons surrounded by small groups of family members. In these "tableaux," printed ads personalized the product and triggered what historian Roland Marchand called "moments of secular epiphany." Beginning in 1923, the *Ladies' Home Journal* contained at least one refrigerator advertisement per issue; between 1927 and 1931 the magazine regularly featured two or three.[66] While industry leaders used these advertisements to convey the promises of the new cooling technologies, they also looked to home economists to solve a common problem: to determine and communicate the health effects of refrigeration. "The great majority of the public has only a vague idea of what refrigeration means," declared an electrical industry representative in 1925. "If the butter does not soften, they are usually satisfied."[67] At the same time, the National Association for Ice Industries (NAII), placed on the defensive by the emergence of mechanical refrigeration, established a Household Refrigeration Bureau in 1923 under the direction of chemist Mary Engle Pennington to promote ice refrigeration among homemakers. Pennington drew on almost ten years' experience investigating ways to create a "cold chain" of foods from farmer to consumer—including research on the effects of cold storage on poultry, eggs, and other foods at the USDA's Bureau of Chemistry and designing refrigerated boxcars for the American Balsa Wood Company—to help sell ice refrigeration through a campaign to educate consumers about ice-box care and maintenance. Pennington collaborated closely with home economics professors at Cornell University and Teachers College to conduct tests on ice refrigerators, tests that served as the basis for ice industry bulletins including "Where to Place Food in the Household Refrigerator," "The Care of the Home Refrigerator," and "Why We Refrigerate Foods."[68]

Manufacturers in both the electrical and ice industries wrote to the bureau seeking information about what health and nutrition experts recommended and what consumers desired in a cold storage unit. "We are very anxious to get information concerning data on the proper temperatures to keep perishable foods, such as meats, milk, butter and vegetables, in a refrigerator in a home," explained W. D. McElhinny, a representative of the Frigidaire Corporation in 1926. He also wanted to know the length of time food products could be safely maintained at different temperatures. Sales managers in the electrical industry hoped home economists would help them establish "high-grade" approaches to salesmanship that educated consumers about the importance of refrigeration to food preservation and health.[69]

Requests such as McElhinny's opened the door for Stanley to form an alliance with Pennington and establish a collaborative relationship with leaders in competing sectors of the refrigeration industry. Lacking a division of household equipment or a full-time staff to pursue the scientific research necessary to determine the health effects of refrigeration, Stanley literally banked the bureau's refrigeration studies on what she called a "friendly rivalry between the ice industries and the manufacturers of electric units for cooling refrigerators."[70] She obtained grants in 1927 from both the NAII and the Society for Electrical Development for a research project that would merge investigations in food preservation, household equipment, and home management and budgeting in the exploration of this new technology.[71] The bureau's studies would determine real answers to "the home questions" and provide women, through a new refrigeration bulletin, with criteria for selecting the right box and instructions on how to store foods in it.[72]

Simultaneously, by working closely with industry leaders, Stanley and Pennington hoped to encourage manufacturers and sales managers to incorporate better instructions about food storage requirements into an educational strategy for promoting refrigeration, and to guide refrigerator producers in improving and labeling their machines to meet the practical needs of American homemakers. "Our desire [is] to educate the public to what they really are getting in a refrigerator," Stanley explained to a cabinet manufacturer. "I am hoping that we may be able to show them that the investment is justified." Representatives from the ice industry, the electrical industry, and the bureau agreed that better information about refrigeration in general would help consumers weigh the comparative advantages and disadvantages of new and old technologies; the publication and distribution of this data would promote refrigeration of all kinds without favoring one technology or company. These studies served as the basis for a "cooperative advertising campaign" that would demonstrate the benefits of all types of household refrigeration while also supporting home economists' larger goal of supplying homemakers with the information required to make a rational selection and operate their refrigerators with optimal effectiveness.[73]

Stanley used grants from the ice and electrical industry to hire two women "trained in household management"—Lucile W. Reynolds and Mildred B. Porter—to expand the bureau's investigations. While assistant food chemist Samuel Clark continued earlier studies on the "physical" or "engineering" side of refrigeration, Stanley directed home economists to consider refrigeration in the context of family buying and cooking practices. With experience as a home demonstration agent in Montana and Massachusetts, a B.S. in home economics from the University of Minnesota, and a master's degree in family economics from the University of Chicago, Reynolds conducted a survey of the refrigeration methods in use in a range of homes in rural, urban, and suburban communities throughout the country.[74] Reynolds discovered that while homemakers in many rural communities (especially in the western and midwestern states) used built-in "coolers" to chill food, women in cities preferred mechanical refrigeration to daily interactions with the ice men and also expressed a desire for higher-quality machines.[75] The survey results revealed that women chose refrigerators that were the "best for [the] money," confirming Stanley's conviction that women sought guidance in making rational purchasing decisions.[76] To complement this survey, Stanley brought on Mildred B. Porter, a former faculty member of Carleton College and Smith College who had studied physics at the graduate level at the University of Chicago, to investigate the temperature and humidity levels in various box arrangements and the effects of these factors on food preservation.[77] Stanley also hired Anna Pabst, a graduate student at George Washington University, to conduct bacteriological studies in conjunction with Porter's tests.[78]

By framing refrigeration as a matter of food preservation and articulating a set of scientific principles and measurable guidelines about the relationship between the two, the bureau's refrigeration studies resulted in joint publicity campaigns that helped broaden the appeal of refrigeration. One result was the publication of six "Household Refrigeration Charts" offering guidelines for the cold storage of food, which the bureau made available to the public in late 1928 at the cost of fifty cents. One chart, featuring bar graphs of the relationship between temperatures and bacterial growth in milk, made a striking graphic

BE SURE
MILK AND MEAT
ARE PLACED IN
COLDEST SECTION
This will vary with design of box

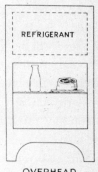
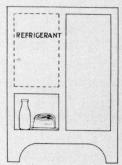

OVERHEAD
REFRIGERATING UNIT
OR ICE COMPARTMENT

REFRIGERATING UNIT OR
ICE COMPARTMENT
BAFFLED

REFRIGERATING UNIT
WITHOUT
BAFFLE

TEST YOUR OWN BOX
DIFFERENCE IN DESIGN MAY CHANGE LOCATION OF COLD PORTION

BUREAU OF HOME ECONOMICS·UNITED STATES DEPARTMENT OF AGRICULTURE

Household Refrigeration Charts 2 and 6, 1929. Refrigeration studies at the Bureau of Home Economics resulted in the publication of a series of instructional charts guiding homemakers in using refrigerators, whether cooled by ice or electricity, to maximize safety and economy in food preservation. (National Archives)

SAVE FOOD ~ NOT ICE
DO NOT WRAP YOUR ICE

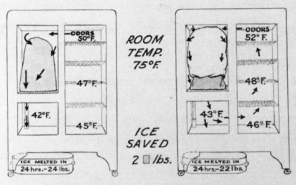

ICE UNWRAPPED   ICE WRAPPED

Wrapping may save ice, (a cent a day), but it does not save food Unwrapped ice melts slightly faster, therefore gives lower temperatures and furnishes surfaces for condensation of odors

BUREAU OF HOME ECONOMICS–UNITED STATES DEPARTMENT OF AGRICULTURE

impression that milk must be maintained at fifty degrees Fahrenheit. Three other charts indicated where to place certain foods inside boxes to ensure that they were stored at the most desirable temperature. For owners of iceboxes, two charts told how much ice to use and how to use it.[79] The bureau placed the "Household Refrigeration Charts" on display at a General Federation of Women's Clubs meeting, and industry leaders immediately began distributing these charts to salespeople, home service workers, and consumers.[80] Although home economists and engineers alike understood that optimal cooling temperatures varied according to the food being stored, the campaign called attention to the "50 degree danger line" for the sake of delivering a consistent—if oversimplified—message about refrigeration to consumers.[81] Within five years, Stanley claimed victory. "The housewife now looks upon refrigeration as a necessity," she declared, indicating the success of the bureau and its allies in convincing homemakers that the health of their families depended on refrigeration. Demonstrating how much this method food preservation had become a standard of modernity, the Electric Home and Farm Authority (EHFA), a New Deal program launched in 1933, declared the streamlined, electric kitchen a right for all citizens and offered government loans for major appliances, including refrigerators.[82]

By promoting the *idea* of refrigeration, the BHE deflected direct conflict between the ice and electrical industries and appealed to the broader cause of healthy food preservation. The government's policy against discussing trade names in its publications further kept home economists from answering consumers' requests for information about which refrigerator type was best or which brand to buy.[83] Yet, like many other early-twentieth-century scientists who tried to pursue neutral investigations, bureau home economists had difficulty controlling the way manufacturers and trade associations used the information and materials they generated. Incidents occurred where one industry or manufacturer used government-sponsored research to its advantage at the expense of another party. When the NAII complained that the Frigidaire Corporation used statements from government bulletins about "improper refrigeration" to argue for the superiority of electric over ice refrigeration, Stanley could only reiterate the bureau's official position: "We have constantly made the statement that the desirable temperature can be maintained by an iced refrigerator provided it is properly constructed and properly handled."[84]

The bureau's refrigeration studies bolstered staff home economists' claims that they represented "the woman's viewpoint" and brought them into informal dialogue with industry members. Stanley and Pennington seized every opportunity to suggest improvements to refrigerator units as well as their distribution and servicing, constantly arguing that homemakers valued function and utility over style.[85] Making frequent appearances at industry meetings, the two women called for producers to make "good boxes" with high-quality insulation and price them affordably, within reach of not only the very wealthy. Homemakers cared more about insulation than the look of the machine, Pennington told her fellow members of the American Society of Refrigeration Engineers, urging engineers to build equipment according to "the best refrigerating engineering standards" and to guarantee quality insulation rather than be "hampered by the endeavor of stores trying to sell to the purchaser a box with fancy nickel trimmings and glossy paint." With proper insulation, Stanley claimed that optimal temperatures could be achieved with both ice and electricity.[86] Although mechanical units could reach even lower temperatures, Stanley doubted whether this was desirable for normal home needs. "The household refrigerator is not a cold storage plant," she declared. "A normal housewife wants cold from her refrigerator more than anything else," Stanley told manufacturers and distributors of electrical goods. A supply of ice, she added, was almost as important.[87] Maintaining that homemakers valued "convenience" above all, bureau home economists further urged industry leaders to provide better service to potential buyers and owners of refrigeration units.

In addition, the bureau's refrigeration studies positioned Stanley and her colleagues to participate in a more formal set of negotiations aimed at standardizing and labeling refrigerators. Building on collaborations between Office of Home Economics staff, Bureau of Standards officials, and industry representatives to establish standard specifications for ice refrigerator cabinets in the early 1920s, Stanley and Pennington envisioned a "refrigerator card" that told consumers what to expect from a refrigerator in terms of performance. Such a card would contain instructions about the handling of food, the care of the machine, and measurement along a yet-to-be-defined "standard" by which to judge and select the quality of its insulation. Refrigerators were included on the list of products that the AHEA recommended for standardization, and in 1928 the Bureau of Standards' Division of Simplified Practice and the American Standards Association convinced manufacturers of iceboxes to form a committee on household refrigeration cabinets to determine standard features that could serve as the basis for a system of grading refrigerator cabinets. Facing the threat of mechanical refrigeration, the ice industry agreed to work with the ASA, which invited bureau home economists Louise Stanley and Mildred Porter and a number of women from the AHEA to stand in as representative "users" at the initial meetings.[88]

For several years, bureau home economists worked with cabinet manufacturers, ice distributors, and refrigerator users to determine "how ice-cooled refrigerators should be labeled so that the housewife will know what she is getting." Home economists made specific recommendations for a product label to help the homemaker "select the ice box best adapted to her needs."[89] In 1933, a grading system was established for refrigerator cabinets—"further . . . than any other piece of household equipment"—to "tell the homemaker what she is buying." Together, Stanley and Pennington convinced the ice industry to create a grading system for icebox designs that limited the number of different sizes on the market and required quality insulation to allow for a high ratio of space for food storage in relation to ice storage. Classes A, B, and C all provided for uniform minimum temperatures in the internal compartments, and minimum standards for size, construction materials, and insulation materials were established for each class.[90]

The use of these ASA-endorsed standards and the grading system was voluntary, however, and Pennington and Stanley struggled to convince cabinet manufacturers to produce ice refrigeration cabinets according to the new grading system and send their machines in to be graded. In the face of the threat from rivals who sold mechanical refrigerators, the "ice men" tended to compete with one another on the basis of price rather than quality. Few, if any, manufacturers adopted the labels Stanley and Pennington labored so fiercely to promote.[91] Bureau staff later advised the EHFA on the development of standard specifications for low-grade refrigerators and other appliances to be installed in Tennessee Valley Authority homes. That agency, however, did not follow bureau recommendations that consumers buy a unit of six cubic feet or more, instead pushing a small, three-to-four-cubic-foot, chest-style refrigerator onto the market, a model that proved unpopular with consumers.[92] Despite bureau home economists' continued efforts to press for standard labeling of the "size, performance, and durability" of both ice and mechanical refrigerators,[93] the bureau's 1940 mimeographed pamphlet about buying refrigerators essentially admitted defeat, telling consumers there was no way to judge the effectiveness of insulation "except through the performance of the refrigerator." Its conclusion read, "At present there are no labels to give the purchasers of a refrigerator the desired definite facts about construction and possible performance. Perhaps the day will come when all refrigerators will carry an information label."[94]

Ultimately, the bureau's refrigeration studies were more influential in shaping the meaning of "constant cold" in a newly emerging marketplace than they were in shaping actual appliances. Home economists succeeded in promoting the idea of refrigeration as a healthy, safe requirement of food storage, establishing a scientific and rational criteria for thinking about this new household technology, and spreading the word about it as a way of serving consumers. Bureau home economists defined ways for consumers to see beyond the merely aesthetic design features of refrigerators and to articulate preferences regarding these appliances in terms of functional utility. By working with manufacturers to develop an educational advertising campaign, home economists extended their influence to an even larger audience than they could reach through the USDA's communication network. In this way, they educated consumers about the science of food preservation and defined a cultural framework for understanding refrigeration in terms of health and sanitation. For an urban or urban-oriented homemaker who had access to electricity or gas, or who at least needed to preserve purchased milk or meat products because she could not get them from her own farm, bureau home economists helped establish health, food safety, and "constant cold" itself as hallmarks of middle-class identity. While the promotional campaign gave homemakers a language with which to understand refrigeration as a modern necessity, it simultaneously aided refrigerator manufacturers and utility companies by helping expand their markets. Through the 1930s and beyond, refrigerator manufacturers and advertisers continued to draw on home economists' framework for understanding refrigeration—which emphasized a unit's consistent, low temperature and its public health benefits—as they worked to shape consumers' expectations and expand markets for this domestic technology.[95]

Conclusion

Emerging in the 1920s in the context of an economy based on business and government cooperation, and a state agricultural policy that endorsed home economists' special expertise in consumption, the Bureau of Home Economics pioneered in the federal government's discovery of consumers and their place in the national economy. Home economists used state authority not only to develop a science of consumption from within the bureau but also to launch an ambitious set of initiatives to reform the marketplace for consumer goods. By providing practical information about domestic production and consumption through a complex communication network, home economists publicized their vision of rational consumption as the basis for good citizenship. In the process, they served a wide range of consumers, particularly those who looked to government experts for guidance in making "intelligent" selections of agricultural and manufactured goods. But not all consumers wanted to consume rationally, and the bureau ultimately missed the mark as a fully comprehensive, objective information clearinghouse for those who did. Many factors—including the limitations on the bureau's budget, a rule against publishing information against trade names, and the constraints of operating inside an agency charged primarily with assisting agricultural producers—prevented Louise Stanley and her team from fully realizing their vision of using science to form a nation of consumers who used cost-benefit analyses to transcend the mere appearance of household technologies. Still, bureau home economists' efforts to focus homemakers' attention on the utilitarian, scientific value of consumer goods challenged prevailing ideas about women and consumption in the interwar period.

Simultaneously, bureau home economists were pioneering consumer advocates. They used state authority to represent consumers and to shape products and distribution methods on their behalf. By forging alliances and winning endorsement as consumer representatives with utility companies, manufacturing firms, retail outlets, and women's magazines, home economists seized informal and formal opportunities to argue that American homemakers wanted useable, dependable goods. However, home economists met with only limited success in their efforts to standardize commercial goods or improve their quality; manufacturers resisted standardization efforts that threatened to undermine brand-name identities. Ultimately, bureau home economists had little authority to force desired improvements in the design or distribution of consumer goods, or to counteract the proliferation of new products and models that was such a fundamental logic of consumer capitalism.

Although American free enterprise found little room for the standardized, grade-labeled ordering of goods on the consumer-oriented terms that bureau home economists envisioned, consumer-product manufacturers of the interwar period invited these government scientists to map out a set of cultural criteria by which goods would be promoted and evaluated. Home economists' participation in negotiations around clothing and refrigeration indicate some of the ways that they helped business managers to legitimize products even as they promoted rational consumption. Bureau home economists proved far more successful in shaping the social construction of household technologies than in influencing the nuts-and-bolts qualities of the goods themselves. In their relations with industry, home economists at the Bureau of Home Economics were most effective when they had an idea to promote, a broad cultural concept that established meaning and value for a product or a set of products. Most manufacturers—especially the family-owned businesses that dominated among the clothing and textile trades and refrigerator cabinet manufacturers—lacked the ability to address consumers in the kind of ideologically powerful language in which home economists were so well versed. Advertising offered one avenue through which to attract potential customers, but government home economists provided producers with an occasion for dialogue with "typical" consumers as constructed by home economists. By supplying technical definitions of healthy clothing design and safe, sanitary food storage, bureau home economists helped to define middle-class identity in precise, material terms that helped both to legitimize products and to shape consumers' expectations. In these ways, bureau home economists drew on government authority and resources to perform the technical and cultural work of making commercial consumer goods into necessities.

4

Selling Home Economics: The Professional Ideals of Businesswomen, 1920–1940

In June 1936, a group of home economists performed a play at an afternoon meeting during the convention week of the American Home Economics Association (AHEA). Representatives of the AHEA's Business Department and Student Club Department took time from a busy annual meeting to attend a dramatic work titled *Experiment 63*. Commissioned by these two departments, written by journalist Charles Dillon, and directed by Marye Dahnke (the home economics director for the Kraft Cheese Company), the play was intended to instruct home economics students about opportunities for employment in the corporate world. Since the early 1920s, this vocational path had been expanding for home economists, and by 1935 the section counted a total of 360 members working as permanent employees in more than 400 private enterprises, including utilities, manufacturers of processed foods and branded goods, producers of electrical appliances, women's magazines, and retail firms.[1] Business home economics had developed a glamorous—and controversial—reputation, and women in the field wanted to demonstrate dramatically (and entertainingly) to potential newcomers the realities behind the image. The success of the play at the convention led to repeated performances at student club meetings in many of the nation's home economics colleges and at local gatherings of business home economists the following year.[2]

Experiment 63 follows the "trials and tribulations" of a home economist named Miss Welldone during her first day on the job in the experimental kitchen of the Bigger and Batter Advertising Agency. She arrives early in the morning only to discover that her predecessor, Miss Regulator, has quit after having a nervous breakdown in the kitchen. Miss Welldone's assignment for the day is to create six "new," "fancy," and "inspiring" promotional recipes for the agency's Bingo Beans account. Before the day ends she produces a soup, a salad, a soufflé, baked beans, beans with pork chops *en casserole*, and a bean loaf. Miss Welldone also drafts eloquent descriptions of these dishes for the ad

136

copywriter and helps a photographer shoot her creations. To top off this well-rounded performance, she gives health advice to Mr. Gastro, a man in the office suffering from stomach distress.

Maintaining her composure throughout a busy day's schedule, Miss Well-done also deftly handles an unannounced visit from the "Man from Research Revelation," a consumer group investigating Bingo Beans' labeling practices. "We've made an examination of your labels and we find that you do not mention the all-important fact that Bingo Beans make premature babies ill if more than one pound per day is fed," he reports. This omission threatens the "unsuspecting consumer who is already ground under the relentless heels of the industrial monarchs of America," he explains, and his organization is determined "to wipe out this evil" by exposing it to the public. Miss Welldone handles his aggressive accusations, presented in the script as extreme and irrational, with patience. Refusing to make a statement under pressure, she cooperatively invites him back in the morning to receive answers to his questions.

At the end of the day, Mr. Bingo, owner of the canned bean company, drops in to see and taste the dishes Miss Welldone has prepared. He readily compliments her on her recipes. Thanking him, Miss Welldone offers a suggestion about how to improve his product. "Have you ever thought of developing some fast cooking beans that wouldn't have to soak before being used?" she asks. He is thrilled with this "million dollar scheme" and determined to make it a reality. The play ends at the conclusion of the workday, when the president of Bigger and Batter (Mr. Batter) congratulates his employee, then asks an exhausted Miss Welldone to "go out to the suburbs tonight and talk to the girl scouts."

Experiment 63 dramatizes (and satirizes through slight exaggeration) the role home economists in business had been playing in America for close to fifteen years: communicating between business and the public and arbitrating consumer relations in the marketplace. Although an outsider wrote the play, home economists commissioned it and used it to represent themselves and their jobs at a professional annual meeting. Underlying this dramatic representation was the assumption that home economists were objective professionals, dispensing with critiques from the growing consumer movement by negotiating diplomatically and effectively with various parties involved in production and consumption. The play portrays home economists as diligent, proud, and loyal employees who work hard to serve their employers while helping to create and market high-quality products and services for consumers. The play also suggests that women in these jobs make up for the incompetence of men in the corporate world, acting as the true brains behind lucrative company decisions.

In sum, the business home economists who commissioned and performed this play argued that their profession made important contributions to both consumer products and consumer satisfaction.

A closer look at the dramatic choices in the play suggests that business home economists operated in a world full of tensions, a world in which they engaged both their employers and consumers in daily struggles over the development of industrially produced household goods and the cultural construction of their meanings in modern America. *Experiment 63* hints at some of the constituencies in this less-than-harmonious picture. The fate of Miss Welldone's predecessor suggested that jobs in business could be frustrating and that home economists exercised influence over producer-consumer relations only within closely circumscribed boundaries. The demands and imperatives of corporate employers, focused as they were on the bottom line, meant that home economists were never autonomous actors. Nor were they the sole spokespersons for American consumers. The intrusion of the "Man from Research Revelation" signals the growing influence of consumer advocacy groups such as Consumers' Research that by the early 1930s began challenging home economists' claims to represent consumers. Finally, the choice of characters and situations encountered by Miss Welldone demonstrates a telling absence of actual consumers, highlighting the limited contact of home economists in corporate jobs with the consumers they claimed to speak for and represent. With the exception of a reference to the Girl Scouts, consumers are markedly absent from *Experiment 63*, making the play yet another example of a recurring theme in home economists' rhetoric: the implied assumption that home economists could speak for consumers, regardless of how much or how little they were actually involved with them.

The play provides a glimpse into the status of home economists working in corporate America in the interwar period, including insights into the professional ideals that home economists carried into the business world as well as the struggles they waged for legitimacy within both corporations and the larger community of home economists. Like dozens of other professional groups that emerged after 1900, home economists in business struggled to define a professional identity that promised to win them respect and approval from their peers and other women, as well as jobs and a degree of autonomy within capitalist managerial bureaucracies.[3] From within the Home Economics in Business (HEIB) Section, established in 1924, business home economists formulated a set of professional ideals that bound them to one another and to other home economists, on the one hand, and distinguished them from other women in advertising and business, on the other. Reconciling their identity in

PROFESSIONAL IDEALS OF BUSINESSWOMEN

relation to both their fellow home economists and employers was, however, a contested process for the home economists who charted new occupational ground in industry.

Just as the Bureau of Home Economics (BHE) gave home economists an institutional platform from within government to develop expertise about consumption and to use this knowledge to reform the marketplace, jobs in business—and the opportunity to create and direct home economics departments there—provided home economists with another important arena in which to influence the development and distribution of consumer products. Home economists' identity as consumer experts took a new turn, however, when they began to join industrial corporations on a full-time basis. In government-sponsored extension work and, to a lesser extent, in the research-oriented federal BHE, the role of home economists followed more or less directly from women's inherited nineteenth-century duties as domestic educators and reformers. The first generation of business home economists also drew on experiences in teaching and extension work to foster a set of assumptions about the potential of home economics to bring about social change. However, home economists' limited power with respect to their employers undercut these ideals and forced the larger community of home economists to confront the field's relationship to the commercial market, especially the inherent conflicts between home economists' vision of rational consumption and the imperatives of product promotion. The rise of corporate power in American life, the critique from groups like Consumers' Research, and experiences on the job eventually exposed fundamental contradictions in business home economists' professional ideals, forcing them to make a complicated series of adjustments and compromises within the demands and priorities of corporate capitalism, and often placing them in tension, if not open conflict, with the larger body of home economists.[4]

Christine Frederick

"Is Christine playing to the Gallery? Is she interested in Education or Exploitation?" Anna Burdick asked in the margins of a newspaper clipping she sent to Louise Stanley, chief of the Bureau of Home Economics at the U.S. Department of Agriculture (USDA), in 1930. In an attached letter she exclaimed, "I get quite wrought up over having women exploit their own kind." Burdick, a home economist at the Federal Board for Vocational Education, was reacting to Christine Frederick, the nationally known authority on "Mrs. Consumer." Reiterating many of the opinions she had outlined in her 1929 book, *Selling*

Mrs. Consumer, Frederick had shared with department store managers, merchants, and other participants at the annual meeting of the National Retail Institute her intimate, firsthand knowledge of women's buying psychology. She had urged them to capitalize on women's natural "eye-appeal and instinct" and their "emotional desire for change," phrases that Burdick underscored to indicate her disapproval. Cornell University home economics professor Day Monroe similarly disagreed with Frederick's portrayal of women consumers as volatile and suggestible. "We can only hope," wrote Monroe, "she is wrong in her diagnosis of Mrs. Consumer's characteristics."[5]

In characterizing the relationship between home economists and the rise of consumer capitalism in the early twentieth century, historians have relied heavily on Frederick's writings and her career as an early spokeswoman for scientific management in the home. Raised under the doctrine of separate spheres in the late nineteenth century, Frederick became one of the nation's most prominent advocates of household efficiency in the 1910s. In her articles for the *Ladies' Home Journal* and her books *The New Housekeeping* (1912) and *Household Engineering* (1919), Frederick advised women to exercise their moral authority as homemakers by adopting business methods to housekeeping. In the 1920s, she shifted her lessons to teaching women to apply standards of efficiency to budgeting and purchasing manufactured consumer goods. Frederick used expertise about women consumers developed throughout her career to write *Selling Mrs. Consumer*, a guide for manufacturers selling to female consumers, a move that historian Glenna Matthews has characterized as an indication of "the ease with which corporate America would be able to 'buy' home economists as spokeswomen." For historian Dolores Hayden, Frederick's publication of *Selling Mrs. Consumer* represented "the final corruption of home economics, representing not women's interests but businesses' interests in manipulating women, their homes, and their families." Many other scholars have used Frederick to portray home economists as sellouts who became willing instruments of corporate control or who were duped into manipulating American consumers against their better interest. To buttress their arguments, they point to Frederick's rather abrupt transition from homemaker's advocate and teacher to agent of consumer exploitation. Sarah Stage has argued, for example, that by adopting male standards of business professionalism, Frederick and business home economists immediately relinquished their female claims to moral authority.[6]

That historians have devoted a great deal of attention to Christine Frederick is not surprising. She was not only an expert on household matters but also a champion self-promoter who achieved wide public visibility in the interwar period. Her career was similar to those of home economists in business, and in some respects Frederick paved the way for the work home economists would perform for private enterprise in the years following World War I. Like Frederick, who wrote for several women's magazines, including a regular column in the *Ladies' Home Journal* from 1912 to 1920, business home economists found opportunities in the publishing industry. Frederick's product testing under home conditions at her Applecroft Experimental Station and her production of promotional literature as a consultant to businesses were also important precedents for home economists. A talented speaker and writer (and possibly the originator of the phrase "the woman's viewpoint") and the era's most vocal exponent of the notion that women had a special relationship to consumption, Frederick developed a rhetorical language about women and consumption on which all home economists could draw selectively.[7] Like Frederick, home economists in business also embraced the irony of advocating for the home, having made career choices that involved specializing in domesticity yet placed them in the public realm. Both Frederick and business home economists also had complex and ambiguous relationships with the consumers they claimed to represent and advise. Ultimately, both had to contend with similar realities and dualities as they tried to sell their female expertise in the marketplace.

Despite these shared experiences, however, closer examination reveals that Frederick operated entirely outside the context of the professional circles of AHEA members who worked in business. In fact, she was not a home economist at all. Although Frederick often called herself a "home economist" and sometimes a "household engineer," she was not a representative home economist of her generation. After high school, she followed the "scientific course" in the College of Liberal Arts at Northwestern University, which did not offer a single course in home economics when she received her degree in 1906. Having studied advertising with Walter Dill Scott, Frederick associated herself more closely with the advertising business than with home economics associations. A year after graduating from college she married J. George Frederick, a business writer and editor who founded the Business Bourse publishing firm and edited the advertising trade journal *Printer's Ink* from 1909 to 1911. Together they founded the Advertising Women of New York in 1912, an organization that Christine Frederick energetically spearheaded for decades. Her consulting for manufacturers in the 1910s grew out of these ties to the business world cemented during the Progressive Era. If Frederick identified her professional interests with any group it was with women working in the advertising field, not with the AHEA and not even with home economists in business, a group that perceived itself as distinct from women in advertising.[8]

Although Frederick chose to specialize in an area that clearly overlapped with the developing home economics field, her career does not serve well as a stand-in for home economists' aspirations, assumptions, and experiences. Her successful, publicly visible career was distinct from the years of conflict and tension business home economists experienced trying to justify their place in both industry and the AHEA. To see Frederick's career as representative of the home economics field obscures these struggles and oversimplifies a very different history experienced by women entering the business world through the field of home economics. Anna Burdick's critique of Frederick's stereotyping of female consumers as essentially emotional, intuitive, and hence malleable, suggests that she and her fellow home economists in government and industry viewed Frederick as an outsider rather than as one of their own. Women's rationality regarding consumption was a contested concept during this period, and not everyone in business and industry accepted the stereotype that Frederick promoted. Lillian Gilbreth, who worked for manufacturers, retailers, and advertisers in the 1920s, also opposed Frederick's characterization of women consumers as susceptible to manipulation.[9] To understand how home economists developed a relationship with corporations and reconciled that relationship with their traditional role as domestic educators, it is important to see how Burdick's notions of domesticity and the market differed from those of Christine Frederick.

By juxtaposing education, on the one hand, and exploitation, on the other, Burdick framed a complex context in which home economists transported the tradition of nineteenth-century domestic reform into the burgeoning twentieth-century consumer society. The transition they experienced entailed the messy process of sorting out the fluid categories of public and private, production and consumption, and what Warren Susman has termed the cultures of "character" and "personality."[10] For home economists who entered business in the 1920s, navigating among these categories became a matter of professional identity. At the beginning of the decade, a small but growing group of AHEA members made it their project to invent roles for themselves both in the women's organization and in the corporate world. In New York City, not far from Frederick's Applecroft Experiment Station on Long Island, and in a network connecting other urban industrial centers such as Boston, Chicago, Cleveland, and San Francisco, home economists in business struggled to define a set of standards and values with which to distinguish themselves as a professional group in the eyes of both their peers and corporate employers.

Struggle for Legitimacy

At the 1921 annual meeting of the AHEA in Swampscott, Massachusetts, twenty women, who worked in "some commercial capacity" and feared resistance from an "old guard," met behind the scenes—in secrecy and by invitation only—to lobby for the creation of a separate section within the organization. "Our meeting was really clandestine, and every one invited was warned to keep it a deep dark secret," Marie Sellers, an editor at *Pictorial Review*, later recalled. "We held it in a room at the back of the hotel way off from other activities of the general meeting." Employment in business was controversial for home economists in the early 1920s, and a secret meeting allowed the women to discuss common concerns in a supportive environment. By restricting attendance, the women sought to exclude the "untrained" women working in publicity and promotion who posed a threat to the group's distinct identity. Mary E. Keown, of the American Washing Machine Manufacturers Association, and Bess Rowe, field editor at the *Farmer's Wife* magazine, had circulated a proposal to the AHEA's officers the previous year. Keown, "a good looking woman with a soft Southern accent" and a former home demonstration agent in Florida, had recently been hired by the trade association to establish "a kind of non-partisan education advertising bureau." In a letter to AHEA president Edna White, she explained her cohort's dilemma: "I have met a good many representatives of various commercial concerns who have been so-called home economics specialists and I found, as I know you have, that some of these women who have been much in the public eye, have no home economics training and no real standards by which to measure themselves or their work."[11] Although White agreed that these "so-called" home economists posed a risk to the status of the entire organization, she took no action on the proposal. Now, with the women assembled, Keown and Rowe tried again to form a separate business subgroup of the AHEA and appointed a committee of five to draw up a petition. In addition to Sellers, Keown, and Rowe, the committee included Harriet Cole Emmons, field editor at *Modern Priscilla*; Virginia Kraft Barnes of the *Ladies' Home Journal*; and Sarah MacLeod of the Society for Savings Banks in Cleveland, Ohio. The three magazine editors "seemed to give respectability to the project, since editors at that time were not as suspect of commercialism as those in other business fields," Sellers remembered.[12]

In proposing to carve out a distinct, official niche for business home economists within the AHEA, the petitioners sought to achieve two major goals: first, to use their connection to the larger group of home economists to distinguish themselves from other women in business in the eyes of employers and, sec-

Mary Keown, a home economist employed with the American Washing Machine Manufacturers Association, initiated the creation of a special Home Economics in Business Section in the American Home Economics Association in 1924. (Home Economics in Business Section Records, Schlesinger Library)

ond, to win the approval of other AHEA members.[13] Vocational opportunities for home economists outside of teaching were growing each year, and AHEA membership already included women who were pioneers in business, the petition explained. Its authors proposed that the AHEA work with the new section to create a set of "home economics standards" with which business home economists could mark themselves off from other women in business.[14] Official affiliation with the larger organization, business home economists hoped, would help to expand professional opportunities for home economists by educating business organizations "about the great possibilities in this work and help them get the right conception of it." Endorsement by the AHEA promised to bolster the status of these jobs by helping to create high standards for membership that would "prevent uninformed or unethical people from misusing the Home Economics Association."[15]

To gain the official sanction of their colleagues, business home economists had to convince the AHEA's leadership of the validity of carrying the field's mission into the business world. The bulk of the organization's membership, comprised primarily of professors, teachers, and extension agents, looked askance at home economists' entry into the world of commerce and distrusted the idea of cooperating with institutions of consumer capitalism. Many of the organization's leaders had joined Progressive Era reformers in critiques of big business less than a decade earlier; they tended to see the world of commerce as a threat to their mission to promote rational consumption. In the late 1910s and the early 1920s, college home economics professors customarily wrapped manufactured foodstuffs under study in plain containers, covering any brand names in paper. They "frowned upon publicity as not quite 'refined,'" a group of business home economists later recalled.[16] "The home economics woman [in business] was a pariah among her professional associates. She was considered unethical, a backslider from the ideals of her Alma Mater," remembered Mary Reed Hartson, who began a career in the food industry in the mid-1910s. When Elsie Stark left work as a home demonstration agent a few years after World War I to join the R. B. Davis Company, a manufacturer of baking powder, she found it difficult to talk to her university colleagues. "The men, and especially the women, felt I was selling my birthright and name by going into commercial work; they seemed to feel that I was going out into the dark unknown to meet disaster," Stark recalled. When Mary Barber, Ruth Watson, and Margaret Sawyer joined Kellogg's, Royal Baking Powder, and Postum, respectively, Marie Sellers recollected: "It was pretty generally felt in high professional circles that these girls had sold their profession down the river."[17] Disapproval of business employment faded over the course of the 1920s but lingered in some home economics circles for much longer, reflecting ambivalence among educators about becoming dependent on corporate resources.

Winning approval from home economists working in the agricultural extension service was of practical significance to many home economists in business seeking to market products through the extension service in these years. They learned that this entailed convincing extension agents of the educational value of a commercial presentation. Ina Lindman worked as a demonstrator for the Boston Woven Hose and Rubber Company, makers of Good Luck Jar Rubber for home canning in the early 1920s. Based for almost three years in the states west of the Mississippi River, Lindman traveled extensively from state to state via railroad. To secure audiences, she turned to the U.S. Extension Service as the "only logical agency." When, by Lindman's own account, she "bravely" requested permission to give canning demonstrations "under the auspices of" county agents in Ohio, extension service officials told her the agency was "not interested in having anyone from the *Business Field* advertising the use of a *product*, under their jurisdiction." Only after she passed an "examination" about "the authenticity of my canning information and methods of demonstration procedure" did the University of Ohio faculty allow her to schedule canning demonstrations throughout the state. Lindman later characterized this event as a "'landmark' which helped to open the doors to future cooperation with Home Economists In Business." After cultivating these ties, Lindman often relied on county agricultural agents to transport her by automobile from county to county within a state and occasionally brought state home demonstration agents or girls' club leaders along with her to a demonstration. Recalling the early 1920s, Mary Barber at Kellogg's similarly pointed to the uneven pattern by which educators came to accept commercially produced material and "the inconsistency of some school systems that refused to allow home economics teachers to show labels on certain food products, but shut their eyes to labels on soaps, spices and glass jars." The collective efforts of Lindman, Barber, and their fellow business home economists helped to pave the way for lessons about commercial goods to be incorporated into educational institutions, even as they sparked controversy among home economists about the educational value of corporate publicity materials—largely produced by home economists—and highlighted the divide between home economics teachers and their counterparts in business.[18]

By the mid-1920s, however, there were signs that these attitudes were gradually changing, as Herbert Hoover's ideas about the mutuality of interests between producers and consumers permeated the larger culture. An emerging younger generation of home economists identified with the nation's increasing orientation toward business values and understood commercial growth as a sign of progress and modernity.[19] AHEA leaders began to consider whether to allow commercial exhibitors at their annual meetings, a practice they officially endorsed in 1926.[20] In this context, business home economists and extension workers managed to work out terms by which commercialism would be accepted. A 1925 *Printer's Ink* article advised manufacturers and advertisers to ensure that their demonstrations conformed to the extension service's guidelines and to approach home demonstration agents through the proper channels, beginning with the national and then the state offices. "While they do not wish to encourage general correspondence, they will welcome ideas and commercial material which reinforce or parallel the extension teaching and demonstrations of the State agricultural colleges," the article further emphasized. Advertisers should not expect to "use the Extension Service merely as a means of distributing samples or advertising material," however, and instead should offer them something of instructional value that "facilitates the work of the agents and that does not carry an obvious advertising appeal."[21]

In the meantime, the new AHEA president, Mary Sweeny, gave tacit support to business home economists, acknowledging in her 1921 presidential address that commercial work constituted a significant vocational path for the organization's members.[22] The AHEA leadership turned down the Swampscott petition but granted permission to the committee of five businesswomen to prepare a program for the following year's gathering at the Oregon Agricultural College in Corvallis. Business home economists used their inclusion in the 1922 annual meeting program to argue that home economists' work in industry furthered the educational goals of all members of the organization. A panel of four speakers showcased the range of home economics jobs in business. Marie Sellers, of *Pictorial Review*, spoke about home economics and women's magazines; S. Agnes Donham, of the Society for the Promotion and Protection of Savings in Boston, discussed the work of home economists in financial institutions; Louise Fitzgerald, of the National Dairy Council, addressed home economics work in the food industry; and Martha Jane Phillips, of the North American Dye Corporation, represented home economics work in textiles.[23] In addition, Bess Rowe delivered a speech to a general session in which she encouraged all home economists to use business as a channel through which to teach and serve homemakers. "Home economics cannot hope to counteract false or misleading information unless it functions through this tremendous organized educational force," she claimed. "The business world today offers us our most effective means of making standard home economics information really function in the homes of today." Rowe argued that, although home economists had had reason to fear becoming exploited by corporations in the past, "the up-to-date businessman has a real idea of service."[24]

Whether Rowe's audience of AHEA members was persuaded by her argument and those of her fellow businesswomen is unclear. However, having achieved inclusion in the annual meeting program, the business home economists still needed to convince many of their colleagues that the Home Economics in Business Section would not corrupt the field. In 1920, the AHEA included three special sections—Education, Institutional Economics, and Textiles. The sections focused on a narrower set of concerns than the general AHEA but were required to identify the broader mission of the AHEA in their constitutions. The young association had yet to establish criteria for membership qualification, however, placing the organization's leadership in a quandary as to what it should do about this request for a separate business section. As AHEA president Edna White explained, a separate business section "might easily enough have a considerable majority of untrained people and the Association has, therefore, been somewhat in doubt as to the best policy to pursue."[25] After careful consideration, the organization's executive council agreed to approve a business section if sufficient membership qualifications could be established to ensure that the section would not be undermined through the infiltration of women lacking education, and socialization, in home economics. Bess Rowe chaired the appointed Standards Committee, composed of the four panelists at Corvallis; Helen Louise Johnson, a participant in the Lake Placid conferences and a veteran consultant to commercial enterprises since the turn of the century; as well as two women from outside the business world: Grace Frysinger, representing home economics extension, and Katherine Blunt, representing home economics education.[26]

The Standards Committee outlined requirements for voting membership and a procedure for gaining acceptance into the section. The permanent Membership Committee, with seven members, would regulate the composition of the section. To ensure that professional standards would not be compromised by affiliation with commercial organizations, three of the seven committee members were required to represent home economics outside the business world. Extension work, education, and the organization at large would each have one representative on the committee. The other four members would speak for different facets of business work—textiles, foods, home equipment, and home management. Membership required approval from at least five members of the committee. Although the Standards Committee preferred members to have a degree in home economics from a well-established college program, it granted eligibility to applicants without home economics degrees if they had "academic training with substantial special training in home economics superimposed" or with at least five years of business experience of a kind "which has made a constructive effort to raise home standards and has made a real contribution to home economics as a whole." Legitimate substitutions for a college degree in home economics were left to the discretion of the committee members on the basis of an applicant's references, résumé of education and work experience, and a statement from a supervisor regarding the policies of the firm in which she was employed. With the approval of the Standards Committee's proposal in 1924, and a change in the AHEA constitution allowing special requirements for voting membership in a section, the path was cleared for the HEIB to become an official association section.[27]

By establishing a separate Home Economics in Business Section of the AHEA with clear rules for membership, home economists specializing in corporate work created a legitimate, although minority and contested, place in the organization. It was achieved, in the words of Marie Sellers, "only with great deliberation and considerable tact."[28] When Mary Keown stepped down as chair of the HEIB Section, she warned her colleagues to pursue a "conservative policy" and proceed cautiously in developing the section, and throughout the 1920s the new section's members remained focused on promoting a positive image in their colleagues' eyes. "The old idea was that one lost caste when one 'commercialized' the profession, but now some of our best known pedagogues have at least one finger in the commercial pie," declared Jean K. Rich, of the Educational Department at Royal Baking Powder Company. Likewise, Winifred Stuart Gibbs, home economics editor of the *American Food Journal*, applauded her cohort for making progress toward overcoming resistance from within their "own ranks" and from the larger public realm where many contended that "business is no place for a woman." But, Gibbs signaled in 1926, "They are not, let me hasten to add, however, entirely overcome."[29] Gradually, throughout the 1920s, home economists' acceptance of commercial work shifted to reflect the era's probusiness attitudes as well as an understanding that business jobs represented professional opportunities for women in the field. By the end of the decade, the AHEA leadership celebrated business home economists for fostering cooperation between producers and consumers. Margaret Justin, who served as AHEA president in 1929, characterized the businesswomen as "'liaison officers' between the producers and distributors on one hand, and the women who do 'the world's shopping' on the other." Home economists in business were in a "strategic position to render unusual service," she proclaimed, advising both producers and consumers in a way that promoted "that better day for America."[30] But the change in sentiment was gradual and not straightforward for home economists as a group. Even in the early 1930s, Cornell University's New York State College of Home Economics took little initiative to expose its students to the HEIB group and job opportunities in business—despite Dean Martha Van Rensselear's engagement as editor of the *Delineator*, a commercial woman's magazine, and her founding membership in the HEIB group.[31] Distrust of business among home economists lasted throughout the interwar period and was fueled again in the political economy of the New Deal. As the membership of both the HEIB Section and the AHEA grew, business home economists continued to struggle, through a focus on membership standards and other issues, to justify their career choices in terms of both the reform and occupational goals of the larger group.

A Profile of Members

Once formed, the Home Economics in Business Section grew rapidly in the 1920s and continued to expand in the following decade despite the economic depression. From a few dozen participants at the founding meetings, the membership increased to include more than 600 home economists by 1940. This growth paralleled that of the AHEA as a whole (which by 1940 had almost 17,000 members), with the result that the HEIB Section remained a small, minority segment of the larger group of home economists.[32]

The earliest official membership list of the HEIB Section, compiled in February 1925, included ninety-one women.[33] Of these, the largest group (thirty-eight, or 42 percent) worked for food companies such as Washburn Crosby (later General Mills), Kellogg's, and Swift, or trade associations charged with promoting particular foods, such as the Institute of American Meat Packers and the National Dairy Council. Fourteen members (15 percent) worked as journalists for women's magazines such as the *Delineator*, the *Ladies' Home Journal*, and *The Farmer's Wife*, or for the women's or home departments of city newspapers. Ten members (11 percent) worked for utility companies, including one woman employed by the ice industry.

Although their career track was different than what was expected by university administrators and professors, early members of the HEIB Section shared many assumptions with home economics educators regarding women's special responsibility to serve society. The founding members included some long-standing AHEA members, such as Alice Bradley, Helen Louise Johnson, and S. Agnes Donham, who were born in the early 1870s and studied in the northeastern urban cooking schools founded in that decade. Donham earned her early reputation as an author of books on managing household incomes, while Bradley and Johnson had a history of commercial work well before the HEIB Section was founded.[34] Most members, however, were born in the 1880s and 1890s, attended college in the 1910s, and belonged to the same generation of home economists who extended Progressive Era reform into the 1920s and 1930s as teachers, extension workers, or government researchers. They were in the early stages of their careers when the HEIB Section was formed. Educated in the home economics programs of four-year colleges—primarily land-grant institutions that emphasized science—they came at subjects such as textiles and nutrition with backgrounds in chemistry, physics, and biological science.[35] Six of nineteen members on the 1925 list for whom data on educational background are available had master's degrees in home economics, nutrition, or chemistry.[36] Information about previous work experience is available for twenty-two, or slightly more than 20 percent, of the total members. Of these twenty-two, all but three worked in education, extension work, or some kind of social service before taking commercial jobs. Hannah Louise Wessling studied chemistry before becoming a food analyst at the USDA, where she worked for close to fifteen years before taking a position as director of home service at the Northwestern Yeast Company in Chicago. Having started out in the extension service in 1916, Mary Keown, the section's founder, worked for the American Washing Machine Manufacturers Association for four years in the early 1920s. By the end of the decade she resumed what the *Extension Service Review* called "a long and distinguished career" in extension work. Margaret Sawyer left her job as nutrition director of the American Red Cross to develop a home economics department at the Postum Cereal Company (later General Foods) in 1924. In this position she remained an outspoken advocate for curriculum reform to train home economists to be leaders in public health and nutrition.[37]

Although the majority of the members in 1925 were single women, at least fourteen, or 15 percent, of the group were married. In some cases, being married and an experienced housekeeper was an asset. In other cases, the challenge of balancing a career with a commitment to a husband, family, and household created the same difficulties confronted by the growing number of married women in the professional labor force, many of whom were forced to give up their jobs if they chose to have children. After three successful years in the Home Service Department of the Binghamton Gas Works, Marian Burts explained to her college adviser that her potential marriage would put her career in jeopardy. "I can't keep my present position if I marry and besides I feel that homemaking is a full time job. So does he," she wrote. Many HEIB members resigned from their jobs when they married, but some managed to work as part-time consultants while filling their roles as wives and mothers. Dorothy Knight worked at Libby, McNeill and Libby in Chicago until she married and moved to the Detroit area in 1926. After giving birth to a son the following year, she reported to her colleagues: "In my spare moments when I am not pouring doses of cod liver oil, or pushing vegetables through a sieve, or other numerous and necessary things that one does for a nine-month-old son, I am still editing the weekly Homemaker's Page in the *Detroit Times*, and keeping in touch with one or two business contacts and prospects. Anyone seeking advice on babies and careers may write me."[38] Women who did not remain actively employed as consultants, however, usually lost eligibility for membership in the HEIB group.

As the HEIB Section expanded, its membership continued to reflect this range of educational backgrounds, industry affiliations, and personal profiles, although as time went on younger members joined who had been children, not reformers or educators, during World War I. Most programs in home economics remained oriented toward preparing students for teaching and extension work, although a few colleges gradually adapted their curricula to the needs of the small group of students interested in business jobs. In 1934, a survey found that 292 of the 350 active members (84 percent) had bachelor's degrees, seventy-five (25 percent) had master's degrees, two held doctorates, and fifteen (4 percent) had dietitian's certificates. A significantly large group— fifty-eight (15 percent)—had no degrees at all but instead had a combination of academic and professional experience of up to four years or more.[39]

By 1940, the section's 612 members represented various industries in more equal proportions than when the HEIB Section was founded. Food companies continued to employ the largest proportion, 24 percent, of the membership. The number of women employed by utility companies grew to 103 (17 percent). Twelve percent managed restaurants or tearooms or worked for hotels, and another 12 percent held positions as journalists with national magazines or local newspapers. Seven percent listed themselves as independent consultants. Retail establishments such as department stores and grocery chains employed 4 percent, whereas manufacturers of household equipment employed 3 percent. Smaller proportions of members also worked for banks, insurance companies, retail distributors, and as independent consultants.[40]

Because of the predominance of HEIB members working in the food industry, the geographical distribution of the membership closely mapped to urban areas with large concentrations of food processors. The largest majority lived and worked in New York City or Chicago, with significantly smaller numbers based in Philadelphia, Boston, Cleveland, and San Francisco. In addition to professional links via membership in the HEIB Section, home economists in business maintained relationships with one another as members of profes-

Home Economics in Business Section, Employment of Members, 1925–1940

Employer	1925			1930			1935			1940		
	#	%	Rank	#	%	Rank	#	%	Rank	#	%	Rank
Food industry	38	41.8	1	107	27.1	1	96	26.7	1	154	25.2	1
Newspapers & magazines	19	20.9	2	55	13.9	2	55	15.3	2	88	14.4	3
Utility companies	9	9.9	3	52	13.2	3	48	13.3	4	106	17.3	2
Restaurants & tearooms	0	0		34	8.6	5	27	7.5	6	73	11.9	4
Banking & insurance	5	5.5	4	7	1.8	10	4	1.1	10	5	0.8	12
Retail	4	4.4	5	15	3.8	8	15	4.2	7	31	5.1	7
Equipment manufacturers	1	1.1	7	16	4.1	7	11	3.1	8	24	3.9	8
Hotels	1	1.1	7	2	0.5	12	3	0.8	11	12	2.0	10
Advertising agencies	2	2.2	6	3	0.8	11	5	1.4	9	12	2.0	10
Textile products industries	1	1.1	7	11	2.8	9	4	1.1	10	6	1.0	11
Radio	0			0			4	1.1	10	6	1.0	11
Consultants	5	5.5	4	16	4.1	7	4	1.1	10	41	6.7	5
Other	4	4.4	5	26	6.6	6	32	8.9	5	20	3.2	9
Government	0	1	0.3	13	3	0.8	11	1	0.2	13		
No stated employment	2	2.2	6	50	12.7	4	49	13.6	3	33	5.4	6
TOTAL	91			395			360			612		

Sources: "Membership List: Home Economics in Business Section, 1925"; and "Our Membership List," *Timely Topics* (July 1930), both in HEIB Records; *Yearbook: Home Economics Women in Business* (June 1935); and *Directory of Home Economics in Business* (1940), both in AAFCS Records.

sional associations with overlapping concerns, such as the Electrical Women's Round Table, the American Grocery Manufacturer's Association, and the American Dietetic Association.[41]

Many home economists moved freely from business to government and back again. Myrtle Floyd moved from her position as a field representative of the Soft Wheat Millers Association to the extension service of North Carolina. Eloise Davison started out in university teaching and moved to the electrical industry. For a time in the 1930s she directed the Home Economics Department of the Electric Home and Farm Authority. At the end of that decade she changed jobs again, this time joining the *New York Herald Tribune* Institute. Having worked as an educator for ten years, Marjorie Heseltine spent only a few years in commercial work at Hills Brothers Foods and then turned to an extended career as a government nutritionist, first for the Federal Emergency Relief Administration and later as the director of the Children's Bureau.[42]

Many of those who remained in business found opportunities for mobility from company to company, while other individuals built an entire career inside a single firm. Ina S. Lindman worked for at least four commercial employers in the course of her career. Like many of her peers, Lindman started out as a secondary school teacher, later becoming a Girls' Club Leader in rural Minnesota. During college she worked summers operating a small canning establishment on a Pennsylvania farm, where she learned home canning procedures from the local extension service. In 1921 she began to apply her canning expertise in the commercial world when she took a job with Boston Woven Hose Company, makers of Good Luck Rubber Rings used to seal containers during the canning process. In 1926, she transferred to the Ball Brothers Company in Muncie, Indiana, and later became the head of educational field service for Postum (later General Foods) in the fall of 1928. Five years after that she moved again to become director of home economics at the United Fruit Company, a position she held until her retirement in the 1950s.[43] During this same period, Eleanor Ahern at Procter & Gamble, Elizabeth Weirick at Sears, Marye Dahnke at Kraft, Mary Barber at Kellogg's, Lucy Maltby at Corning Glass Works, and Marjorie Child Husted at General Mills were among a group of women who established, and then directed, corporate home economics departments for decades. Because most of them started by running one-woman shows, their names became synonymous with the firms they served, continuing to personify the departments they created and directed even as they built staffs of home economists underneath them.

Many business home economics jobs were distinguished by relatively high salaries, and some of those who directed corporate home economics departments earned impressive amounts compared to salaries earned by the average extension agent or classroom home economics instructor. But these latter cases were more exceptions than a rule. While there is little evidence regarding pay of individual women in specific firms, vocational guides written during this era describe a market in which most home economists earned salaries comparable to or just slightly more than teaching or extension work. For the years 1929–30, vocational adviser Ruth Yeomans Schiffman reported that home economists in "outstanding positions" with newspapers and magazines received "$10,000 or more," while women in charge of home economics departments in corporations could earn "up to $15,000." Genevieve Callahan's *Preparation for the Business Field of Home Economics* (1934), published at the height of the Depression, noted that there was "theoretically no upper limit" to the salaries business home economists could earn. However, she situated the median salary between $2,500 and $5,000, with starting salaries ranging from only $840 to $1,800 per year. "There are a great many more $1800 salaries than $18,000 ones!," she explained. In a 1942 edition of her guide, Callahan declared home economics work in business "no gold mine." Remuneration in business nevertheless either matched or exceeded that in teaching, but as Laura Clark, another student of home economics occupations, put it, "when one considers that the business year is fifty-two weeks instead of thirty-six, the larger salary does not seem so attractive." While high salary was an important factor in attracting and retaining home economists to commercial positions, affiliation with large corporations also afforded these women a measure of status that helped make industrial home economics jobs "the prizes of the field."[44]

United through their status as employees of business organizations, HEIB members during the interwar period were also members of a generation that came of age around 1910, when they could take advantage of the recent establishment of the AHEA and the expanding array of opportunities in home economics. With shared educational backgrounds and work experiences, HEIB members had a sound social basis for forging a group identity and professional ideology that justified their legitimacy to home economics educators and their expertise to employers.

Service, Science, and the "Super Statesmen"

The first generation of business home economists entered the corporate sphere with a strong sense of service to consumers derived from the educational and occupational context in which they had been educated. Home economists in business drew on this notion of consumer service as they worked to make sense of their roles in industry. To prove their legitimacy to fellow home econo-mists and distinguish themselves from other emerging groups of consumer ex-perts, they developed a professional identity in which service and sales comple-mented, rather than contradicted, one another. This framework incorporated four basic assumptions: first, that their work was educational; second, that as women they represented "the woman's viewpoint"; third, that their work was scientific and objective; and fourth, that they were "interpreters" and "diplo-mats" in the consumer marketplace. All these elements of business home economists' professional ethics rested on and reinforced a deep-seated belief in progress through corporate capitalism and a far-reaching optimism—which they shared with their colleagues at the BHE as well as other aspiring women professionals—regarding the potential of feminine professional participation in that system.[45]

Early home economists in business argued that their work would enhance the educational goals and reputation of the AHEA and all its members. From inside the corporation, they could broaden the audience for home economics messages about the "art of right living" and rational consumption in Ameri-can homes. With home economists contributing to "the best kind of educa-tional advertising," consumers could learn from the experts about proper dietary habits and the safe, economical use of products. Mary Reed Hartson argued that home economists specializing in business actually created "new standards" for the home economics profession at large. Describing her move to Borden's, Mary O'Leary explained, "I left the classroom, but not teaching." She claimed to reach an audience of "nearly ten thousand" in her first year on the job.[46] Marie Meloney, editor of the *Delineator* and a strong advocate for home economics education, similarly equated women's magazines with "ser-vice magazines" and used her position to promote various causes, from child welfare to better housing.[47] The notion that selling could be educational paral-leled claims by women and men in advertising that promotional material was of instructional value to consumers. But the idea had a special resonance for home economists who had been teachers before joining the business world. These women argued that the financial resources available to large, private cor-porations had the potential to support a more comprehensive program than home economists had been able to develop with public funds: industry-funded literature, often printed in color, could be important resources to the teacher and the home demonstration agent, who were often limited to poorly produced government pamphlets or mimeographed materials. "The state, county, or city worker cannot do all the work, both from lack of time and lack of funds," explained Jean Rich of the Royal Baking Powder Company. "The manufacturer on the other hand has the money."[48]

Home economists' teachings could enlighten the business community as well as consumers, the women in business also argued. By showing manufacturers how to elevate the standards of product quality and helping to orient banks and utilities toward a more service-minded approach, some women went so far as to say that home economists' presence in the workaday world would improve products and lessen women's dependence on male producers. "We take pleasure in culture and all that makes for culture," asserted Martha Phillips, "but we are also aware that we are members of a Nation of Producers, and if we are to give our best to the community in which we live, we cannot hide our candle of usefulness under the bushel of culture." A business home economist "uses her knowledge to better the products upon which the application of the new methods and theories depend," she argued. "We are more dependent than we sometimes realize on the manufacturing and business worlds for the products which make possible modern home making." The home economist's presence as a "wedge" in the corporation, Phillips envisioned, would be a "powerful force for betterment and uplift" and, she implied, temper corporations' hold on American domestic life.[49]

Phillips' notion of home economists' "candle of usefulness" suggested that she and her colleagues charged themselves not only with instructing women, but also with representing them as official, "typical" consumers. Insight into the "woman's point of view" constituted a second integral part of the professional ethic that bound the businesswomen together. As several business home economists agreed at a 1931 meeting, a home economist was valuable to her employer only "in so far as she understood the viewpoint of the housewife." By "housewife" they meant a specific formulation, home economists' carefully constructed vision of a middle-class white woman who had high and rigorous demands for product quality. Interest in health and dietary issues, Mary Keown suggested, was "a direct result of the work of home economics forces" in schools, colleges, extension agencies, and women's magazines. Because home economists taught homemakers to be more discriminating, rational consumers, Martha Phillips assumed that they were best suited to interpret products to those women. "Where better can the manufacturer . . . turn for an interpretation into the language of the housewife, of his answers to these questions which are being put to him every day, than to the same school which is teaching the home maker to ask the question?" she asked. While working to construct and disseminate an ethic of well-informed, health-minded consumption, home economists viewed their representation of this particular group of consumers to business managers as a logical extension of their mission. On the basis of this rather specific identity, however, home economists in business claimed to be the "voice of the public" much more generally.[50]

Business home economists' reliance on the established networks of state extension agencies and school systems to maintain close contact with home economics teachers and other women reinforced their identification with the white middle-class woman's point of view. But the women in business situated themselves in a contradictory relationship with consumers, professing, on the one hand, to represent them and claiming, on the other hand, to be able to second-guess and uplift them. As one 1931 observer commented of the home economist in business, "She does not scorn the homemaker. She does not, however, depend blindly upon the homemaker's reactions. She senses that the homemaker is frequently inarticulate and does not know what she really wants. This cannot be done if she puts the company above a woman's needs. Her job is to correlate the two."[51] The effectiveness of such correlation, in the eyes of home economists, depended on contact with consumers on an "individual" rather than a "standardized" basis.[52] Complex attitudes of both empathy and condescension toward homemakers were embedded in the professional identity of business home economists as they assumed responsibilities for translating between their employers and what was, in reality, a diverse group of American consumers.

In their struggle to obtain professional legitimacy and to distinguish themselves from women in the advertising industry, the business home economist pioneers of the early 1920s constantly argued that their job could not be accomplished by just "any sensible woman." Manufacturers, Mary Keown explained, needed "not alone a woman's point of view . . . but the point of view of a woman thoroughly trained to know the housewife's problems and to understand the effective appeal to her."[53] Likewise, Jessie Hoover, a newly appointed home economist at Montgomery Ward in 1929, requested a letter of endorsement from the USDA's Bureau of Home Economics to impress on the mail-order firm the relative value of home economics over advertising training.[54] The boundaries between the work of home economists in business and that of women in advertising could be rather fluid, but Hoover and her fellow business home economists had much at stake in marking themselves off from other categories of professional women. Although the HEIB Section included women employed by advertising firms and the organization associated professionally with groups of advertising women, business home economists generally kept these women at arm's length, often criticizing advertisers. In 1928, HEIB chair

Marjorie Heseltine characterized the League of Advertising Women as "very likely to make misleading statements. Perhaps," she added, "it is in line with their profession." The New York City Home Economics Association held dinners with the league earlier in the decade, but the HEIB Section now recommended ending this practice. "Frankly, we don't like this group and we are eager to reduce our contacts with them to a minimum." HEIB members had a different relationship to the market than did advertising women, but throughout the interwar period they also often faced real competition for home economics positions from advertising women who were not trained in the field.[55]

The term *home economics training* conveyed not only an education in home economics at a four-year college but also a third element of the business home economists' ideology: a scientific and objective approach to understanding consumer products. Whereas home economists' ability to represent "the woman's viewpoint" seemed to make them naturally suited to projecting a human, friendly image of the corporation to the public, their college training in the sciences—and their mastery of the scientific and technical aspects of manufactured goods—qualified them to test and evaluate products as well as to educate consumers about them. Martha Phillips's job with the North American Dye Corporation helped homemakers understand "why colors are, what colors are, and how and where best to use them," she explained. In fact, being positioned so close to the point of production, she argued, helped home economists learn more about textiles: "In the business world we are brought so much more closely into contact with the conditions surrounding the manufacture of clothing and house furnishings that it is here that we gain our working information on colors, technique of garment construction, and so on. It is because of this closer contact to the Textile Industry as presented on the large plane, that we feel that we know the why's and wherefore's of the textile field."[56] Just as Mary Schenck Woolman and other home economics educators had argued for incorporating information gleaned from industry into their textbooks and college courses in the 1910s, HEIB members used a similar rationale a decade later to explain their entry into business as a logical extension of home economists' established role as educators and researchers.

Business home economists' service to consumers came from a conviction they shared with many corporate scientists that their academic background qualified them to operate on a plane above that of profit-making employers.[57] For S. Agnes Donham, of the Society for the Promotion and Protection of Savings in Boston, home economists' experience with systematic fact-finding ensured that the company brochures they wrote met standards of truthfulness and clarity. "Definite instruction as to use," "clear, honest statements of results," and "few claims made without supporting fact" characterized the work of a trained home economist. Misleading advertising copy would be eliminated, Winifred Stuart Gibbs predicted, "if the home economics woman [was] given free rein and instructed to keep the company straight in the path of scientific truth in its every endeavor."[58]

Home economists' technical training further distinguished them from other product demonstrators. "The trained mind of the Home Economics Woman would put the demonstration of any article upon a higher and more intelligent plane" than that of the "so-called professional demonstrator," Phillips contended. "Is this manufacturer to select a person to handle the publicity of this article who has merely a pleasing appearance, ingratiating manner and glib tongue?" Such a woman would "look upon it as something that just had to be sold, whose main advertising points had to be run over parrot-like, omitting perhaps those of most vital importance to the Consumer and making possibly unconsciously, false statements, and advancing the price of the article as its main consideration." The home economist, in contrast, would hold the consumer foremost in her mind and analyze a product's "degree of usefulness and the particular field for which it is intended and is most suited." Phillips added that "the very same principles apply to the relationship between the Home Economics Woman and the Advertising profession." Faith in factually based information about products was precisely what enabled Mary O'Leary at Borden to describe advertising as an educational "means of communicating information about products."[59] Being inside industry brought home economists closer to the technical details behind products and thus reinforced their definition of themselves as technical experts. Exposure to the inside story on this level also gave home economists an investment in the technical processes they helped to popularize, while further reinforcing their faith and confidence in technological progress.

The synthesis of the female viewpoint with scientific training, home economists argued, qualified them for their unique role in the corporation as interpreter between the firm and its customers. Designating themselves as translators in this respect constituted a final dimension of business home economists' ideal of service. These women believed they occupied a strategic link between manufacturers of goods and women who used them. The HEIB Section credited itself with helping consumers understand what to expect from new products. Early members observed, for example, that manufacturers, dealers, and customers had been often dissatisfied because products were "misinterpreted."[60] Katharine Fisher, the director of the Good Housekeeping Institute, elaborated on this notion in a 1928 speech to a group of home service workers

PROFESSIONAL IDEALS OF BUSINESSWOMEN

affiliated with the National Electric Light Association. For Fisher, if engineers were "statesmen," then women in the appliance field were "super statesmen." She characterized the woman who ran a utility home service department as a "partner" and "balance wheel" to the industrial (mostly male) engineer, a woman who brought to the engineer's "attention the need for certain refinements which will mean added convenience to the user." Whereas an engineer developed a device, the home economist instructed women about the proper way to "use it to advantage."[61]

Often, home economists in business expressed their interpretive role through the same metaphor of diplomacy that Fisher employed. Marye Dahnke highlighted the duality of her function in a 1937 autobiographical account of her tenure at Kraft: "Like the two-faced Janus, I must in my job look two ways at once. First of all, I must represent my company to the consumer. Second, I must represent the consumer's point of view to my company. Only in this way can I fulfill my function, both as a business woman and a home economist." Home economists experienced a daily challenge of forging consensus and compromise. As one woman put it at a 1931 gathering of her peers, home economists in business understood "the value of cooperation and the dangers of 'high-hatting' any phase of her concern's work." Rarely did they use oppositional terms to express their relationship to their corporate employers, although Dahnke admitted she preferred "the conflict of business" to the "rewards of teaching." Many women were drawn to the thrill and excitement of the commercial world and derived a sense of professional satisfaction from their ability to negotiate within it. One occupational adviser stipulated in 1938 that a home economist in business must not only "be able to see both the business point of view of the employer and the home needs of the consumer, but also bring the two into harmony. She must be a happy medium between the professional and the commercial worker." Understanding their role as a matter of "correlating" consumers' desires with corporate goals, business home economists put a feminine twist on managerial liberals' faith in corporations by arguing that the home economist's gentle diplomacy would foster and maintain the inherent mutuality of interests between producers and consumers.[62] This interpretive role, however, embodied a paradox and professional dilemma for home economists in business, because consumers' interests and corporate goals did not always coincide. The translating function they assumed depended not only on manufacturers' goodwill and consumers' desire for the guidance of experts, but also on gendered notions of how women should negotiate.

Achieving "harmony" from within the corporation often involved channeling charm and grace toward interactions with consumers, whether speaking with them on the telephone or addressing them publicly. Career advisers made the social skills required for the home economist in business seem merely a matter of etiquette, and they explained home economists' diplomatic successes in terms of their individual abilities to negotiate potential conflicts. Within this framework, forging the common interests of manufacturers and consumers seemed as natural as the women's role as hostess and entertainer. Vocational literature advised women interested in careers in business to cultivate interpersonal skills and to perfect their personal appearance in ways expected of them in more traditional contexts. "Don't enter business unless you are interested in people," Mary O'Leary warned. Poise, grace, and the ability to relate to and handle "a cross-section of humanity" were also on her list of necessary qualities. Because communicating with different ethnic groups could result in "difficult situations," she stressed the need for "a sense of humor and tact." By the 1940s, experienced women also recommended that newcomers ground themselves in the new twentieth-century fields of psychology and sociology. A burgeoning literature about how to find and qualify for a home economics job in business stressed the importance of dress and composure, suggesting that part of what home economists had to offer was the culture and the refinement of their upbringing and class. Exposure to art, for instance, enabled "a complete development of self and the social graces," according to O'Leary. Women's vocational guides made these types of required social skills seem like a matter of etiquette rather than work.[63]

Thus, on an individual level, home economists' translating role between consumers and corporations constituted a kind of interpersonal, "emotional labor," to use sociologist Arlie Hochschild's term, or what historian Suzanne Kolm has called "personality work."[64] Home economists usually used the term *personality* to describe qualities of appearance and social interaction necessary to a successful career. Public lecture demonstrations, a basic component of many home economics jobs in business, demanded charm and charisma on the part of the presenter. In celebrating Ina Lindman's move from the Ball Brothers Company to Postum in 1928, the *Timely Topics* editor attributed her success to her personality. "Ina . . . is a living exemplification of 'A merry heart goeth a long distance,'" she wrote. "Add to this happy trait, real ability plus personality, and the reason is found why Ina always has her audience 'with her' from start to finish during a demonstration." Louise Fitzgerald similarly listed "personality" alongside knowledge about health and organizational skills as a factor critical to the success of the National Dairy Council's home economics program.[65]

This emphasis on an engaging, positive, and outwardly directed personality was the glue that held business home economists' particularly feminine notion of service together. "Any woman with training in home economics and a bent for business must be prepared to be as busy as a one-armed paper hanger, once she is launched on her career. She must be an executive and a cook, an explorer and an inventor, a scientist and a publicist, an indefatigable worker who performs her business activities with all the composure of a hostess at tea-time," explained Marye Dahnke.[66] "Personality" thus contributed a female cast to business home economists' gendered professional identity as mediators of consumption. And it gave some home economists the impression that, through their diverse jobs, they held significant power at the center of the corporate milieu.

Yet home economists were also rooted in a culture of "character"—of self-control, duty, and honor—that stemmed from the reformist orientation of their field. Trained in college programs where morality, etiquette, and propriety were part of the curriculum, home economists came, as young women, out of a world that stressed the social virtues associated with "character." In the new occupational environment of the corporation, home economists experienced first-hand the shift in emphasis to "personality." In this sense, members of the first generation of business home economists were liminal figures between the culture of character (represented by educational and reform goals of the general home economics movement) and the culture of personality (stressed particularly with home economists who operated in the world of advertising, marketing, and product promotion). The location of early business home economists between these two cultures does much to explain how and why they perceived themselves simultaneously as educators and as saleswomen, as objective scientific investigators and as loyal corporate employees. Business home economists' ability and willingness to embrace and exploit these contradictions amid the cultural changes of the interwar period made them valuable to employers and convinced other home economists of the legitimacy of their place in the larger group. With one foot in the world of character and another in the world of personality, home economists in business managed to blur company and community, not just in the eyes of consumers, but also to peers and themselves.

A Women's Club and Professional Organization

The structure and activities of the Home Economics in Business Section reflected the worldview of its members and the contradictions contained within a group of women constructing a new professional identity. The section resembled something between a male professional organization and a women's club. In the pages of the group's quarterly newsletter, at local and national meetings, or on visits to the sites of members' offices and laboratories, shop talk intersected with socializing. *Timely Topics* reported news of business home economists' personal lives as well as their activities at work. Reports of engagements, weddings, and births appeared alongside notices of changes in employment, notable developments on the job, and occasional reprints of important articles. Accounts of new purchases of automobiles and trips to Europe called attention to the high standard of living afforded by members' careers, a reality that set them apart from many other home economists as well as from most of the consumers they interacted with on the job.[67] Yet members also spent significant amounts of time discussing professional matters, defining the purpose of their organization, and negotiating their relationship with the AHEA. Both in the full group and in smaller committees, they addressed such issues as publicizing their work among manufacturers and other home economists, training high school and college students for home economics business careers, coordinating the supply and demand of home economists in business, making contact with consumers, and maintaining membership standards that guaranteed the group's reputation.

Just as the issue of membership standards plagued engineering societies and other professionalizing groups, it generated passionate discussions— described by one AHEA president as "orgies"—among home economists in business throughout the interwar period.[68] Controlling membership was the basic mechanism by which business home economists defined and maintained the boundaries between themselves and other experts. Having established basic requirements for joining the group in 1924, the HEIB Section continued to refine these rules to maintain a set of clear standards while still allowing for group's expansion. The initial standards gave the Membership Committee wide latitude to determine who was a legitimate business home economist, but in 1926 the section sought to make the requirements more precise. While some members objected to admitting women who were merely "interested in home economics in business," the HEIB leadership found the standards too stringent and proposed liberalizing the requirements, pointing out that membership in the AHEA was open to "almost everyone."[69] In the end, a telling a lack of consensus within the HEIB Section prevented revision of the membership standards until 1932, when the membership agreed to require all members to hold degrees in home economics.[70] Later in the 1930s, in response to fluctuations in the job market caused by the Depression, the section developed a policy allowing special membership status for consultants. In this decade, the HEIB group gradually became increasingly independent of and autonomous from its parent organization by taking more control over its own membership, reducing outside representation in its Membership Committee to a single individual, and convening separate meetings and conferences.[71]

With respect to their employers, members of the HEIB organization also tried to create a degree of autonomy for members by addressing the issue of ethical standards of behavior in the workplace. HEIB members worked to maintain the section's "high standards of service" and looked for ways to solve problems "that may confront individual members in their relations with their own organization and the consumer."[72] The HEIB membership application process, for example, required home economists to submit their employer's policies and procedures, but there was no mechanism to assess whether these policies remained the same over time in a given firm. In 1926, a committee argued for the formulation of a code of ethics aiming "to set up standards of work, which would help to guide public opinion regarding the work of home economics people in business." It suggested a series of "approved practices" in contacting consumers: home economists should "learn the policies of the group with which you expect to work" and obtain permission from those in charge before approaching the group. A principal should be consulted before dealing with a teacher, and state extension heads should clear all invitations from home demonstration agents. Women should also be "up and above board" about disclosing their business "connections." In addition, they should provide "sound"—not simply "technically correct"—information and avoid "statements which may be misleading to a gullible person."[73] Although the 1926 committee agreed on these general guidelines, it did not come up with an actual "code" in support of what section chair Marjorie Heseltine later called "courageous members of our group."[74] Despite continued discussions about a code of ethics guiding home economists' work in commercial enterprises, the section never formulated such a code or wrote a manual of recommended business practices, reflecting a lack of consensus in this fast changing field.[75]

Business home economists' failure to establish a manual of standard practice in business also reveals the limitations of the organization's power to bolster its members' status inside corporations. The numbers of home economists in business were too small, and their significance to their firms too marginal, for the HEIB group to wield much authority over the large corporations that employed its members. Employers had the upper hand, and many insisted on keeping their policies and practices secret. The lack of a standard code of practice left individual home economists to struggle on the job without a consistent set of guidelines and in isolation from their colleagues working both inside and outside business. It also left the HEIB Section vulnerable to censure from within the AHEA as changed political and economic circumstances led many critics to question the educational value of home economists' work for corporations.

On the Defensive

In the 1930s, as part of a growing consumer movement, the AHEA joined with other women's groups to voice opposition to corporate power and to bring the needs of consumers to the forefront of public discourse. The national organization of home economists took steps to expand and publicize its consumer education efforts, to advocate for product grading and information labeling, and to work toward improved retailing methods through participation in the National Consumer-Retailer Council and the American Standards Association.[76] In this climate, the HEIB Section came under considerable attack from within the educator-dominated organization. After having spent the previous decade establishing a professional identity that bridged the worlds of education and commerce, business home economists began to feel uncomfortable around their teaching colleagues again. "In company with our fellow Home Economists in the educational field we may not be walking quite as gaily or lightly as we have done in the past," announced business section chair Florence LaGanke Harris in 1932. Aubyn Chinn, who also chaired the section in the early 1930s, later described the era as "stormy times, times when private enterprise was under constant criticism."[77] The increased politicization of consumption in the United States raised the question of where the AHEA stood in relation to the consumer, and where the HEIB Section figured in that program.

The issue of the AHEA's relationship to consumer capitalism came to a head when outside critics at Consumers' Research, an organization that allied with the AHEA in standardization efforts in the 1920s, began pressuring home economists to adopt Frederick Schlink's strategies for reform on behalf of consumers. In 1932, Schlink's associate Dewey H. Palmer submitted a manuscript to the *Journal of Home Economics* titled "Are Home Economists Helping the Ultimate Consumer?," criticizing home economists for using advertising materials in the classroom and heightening "brand consciousness" among students rather than educating them to evaluate products objectively.[78] The question of whether to publish Palmer's article generated much discussion within the AHEA leadership, revealing considerable divisions about the relationship some members had established with the business community by the early 1930s.

AHEA president Frances Zuill, a professor of home economics at the University of Iowa, told *Journal of Home Economics* editor Helen Atwater that she found it difficult to "accept responsibility for either approving or vetoing printing it." In a long letter, she recalled her early days as a teacher in the 1920s when commercial promotional material by home economists became commonly disseminated in many schools. In the Baltimore public school system, a rule against the use of all commercial material had provided a "real protection" against material that "seemed to be purely advertising," but also had prevented the use of illustrative material "which would have been extremely valuable." A decade later, Zuill found "the advertising racket" much more problematic. Only reluctantly had she approved the list of exhibitors at the 1932 national AHEA meeting, noting the mediocrity of many of the products to be displayed. "Down in my heart I sincerely wish that we could curtail this activity in our Association," she wrote the journal editor. As long as the organization received support from commercial firms in return for advertising and exhibits, however, Zuill could not see how the group could simultaneously publish a warning or prohibition against advertising material. "I do not think there is a shadow of a doubt that we would get into trouble with the business section," she added. Unable to see a way out of the contradiction of receiving funds from the business community while at the same time criticizing it, Zuill suggested holding a symposium on advertising material using Palmer's piece, an essay by "some reliable member of the business women's section," and other perspectives to generate discussion. In the meantime, she turned the question of publication over to the Executive Council.[79]

The Executive Council members were similarly divided. Several home economists wanted to publish Palmer's article. Cora Winchell, a professor at Teachers College, considered Palmer's argument useful "from the point of view of the curriculum maker who is seeking an accurate, honest picture of the 'current American scene.' Personally," she added, "I bank upon the Consumers' Research information very confidently." She concluded her letter with a strong statement of idealism: "I should like to believe that we were a *free* body of women—free to publish *facts*. Curriculum makers in most localities find so many handicaps in the matter of 'controls' that it would surely be gratifying to sense every emancipation possible." Marie Dye, secretary of the association and dean of home economics at Michigan State College, echoed Winchell's recommendation, calling for a journal "free from the influence of advertising." In contrast, Lucy Gillett, of the New York Association for Improving the Condition of the Poor and chair of the AHEA's Social Service Department, believed that publishing Palmer's article would attract more advertisements from manufacturers committed to honest advertising as well as enlighten home economics teachers.[80]

Many of the women who supported publishing the article expressed dissatisfaction with Palmer's confrontational tone and style, however, suggesting ways to make the article "less offensive." Other Executive Council members objected strongly to the article's message, contending that it was not appropriate for the association's journal. "While I realize that there is danger in ultra conservatism which prevents the possibility of desirable and justifiable information being given to the consumer," wrote Margaret Whittemore, chair of the AHEA's Department of Research and a professor of home economics at Rhode Island State College. "I also feel that a bald statement of the facts of the case may, under certain conditions, work an injustice to the producer." Whittemore spoke for a large number of home economists not working in business who nonetheless looked favorably on "good" manufacturers and who approved of the practice of buying products by brand name that Palmer critiqued so harshly.[81]

In the end, the AHEA decided not to print Palmer's article but offered to use it as the basis for a symposium discussion. Palmer ignored the suggestion and responded with a plea to the AHEA as a "professional society . . . to take a position in favor of the ultimate interests of the society and of its membership, rather than what appears to [its] immediate and narrow interest of avoidance of controversy or commercial pressure." After the AHEA proved unwilling to join the consumer crusade on the terms proposed by Consumers' Research, Palmer and Schlink broke with the association and found other venues to publish critiques of home economists and their connections to business.[82]

The influence of Consumers' Research and the New Deal's politicization of consumption led the AHEA to emphasize and expand its consumer education initiatives. The organization's vocal embrace of "the consumer"—reflected in the association's choice of theme for its 1934 annual meeting, "The Consumer and the New Economic Order"—sparked complaints from at least one business home economist who perceived herself to be under attack. "Entirely too often our organization has seemed to take the attitude of putting all commercial concerns in the same class regardless of their ethics," complained Edith Tolton Raye, a HEIB member employed with the McCann-Erickson advertising agency in Cleveland, Ohio, to AHEA president Frances Zuill. "I am weary and disgusted with reading constantly in our Journal and hearing speakers at our meetings characterize all advertisers as 'advertising vultures' preying on 'the consumer.' I hope this year we will see an intelligent approach and an open-minded recognition of the fact that just as all lawyers are not shysters and all doctors are not quacks, so all business organizations are not 'vultures.'"[83] Raye expressed the frustration of many business home economists with the scornful attitude the organization took toward them in these years.

In spite of Raye's lament and continued attacks on business home economists from Schlink and his cohort, the AHEA leadership continued to promote the organization as a consumer advocate while maintaining support for this minority contingent that had powerful ties to commercial funding sources. Although many members may have tried to ignore the contradiction, at least one woman found it unacceptable. Mathilde C. Hader, one of Schlink's colleagues at Consumers' Research who attended AHEA meetings and contributed to the association's journal, wrote to AHEA executive secretary Alice Edwards in 1934. Hader taught home economics in Norway, her country of origin, before marrying an American and moving to New York City, where she became affiliated with New York University and took at least one course at Teachers College. In Hader's view, the more home economists became involved in consumer issues, "the more anomalous is the membership in the Association of the Home Economics in Business Women—and the more dangerous. By no stretch of the imagination can they be called *home* economists, unless home economists are to include everyone who once happened to take courses in home economics in college." To her, the home economists' loyalties to "the home and family" inherently conflicted with the "firms and trade associations by which they are employed." She believed it was "obvious that in the great majority of cases the position of these women in their respective concerns is not one of power and influence," so that "the issue for these women is to conform or quit." Hader's concern was over the influence of the business home economists on the AHEA as a whole and the entire home economics profession. "To let the present condition continue is, therefore, like ignoring a cancerous growth: it may grow beyond repair. As a group within, these women are powerful—in regard to training, ability, and energy they are among the best of the Association's members."[84] Hader called for the complete elimination of the HEIB Section, but believing this change unfeasible, she suggested amending the constitution and by-laws to prohibit the participation of the business home economists in the association's Division of Family Economics, the Committee on the Standardization of Consumers' Goods, or in "any subgroup of the Association engaged in work and study of economic problems of the home."[85]

Whether Edwards or any members of the Executive Council took Hader's advice seriously is unclear, but no indication exists that any AHEA leaders attempted to abolish the HEIB Section. Some home economists looked for ways to "keep the business group in control." Others, such as Marion Breck, Delaware state supervisor of home economics, defended business home economists because they were in a "strategic position . . . to render invaluable assistance given to us as a group of consumers. I would much rather have them working with us than against us, and I question whether excluding them entirely from our group will accomplish this purpose." The businesswomen were among the best trained and energetic home economists, argued Breck, and they were further strengthened by "money to back them far beyond anything that we, who are in the other group, can have." Still, by continuing to stay in touch with consumers as well as the businesswomen, home economists could slowly "build up a resistance which will in time be effective." Breck urged Hader to be patient with the process, admitting that the AHEA "needs to clean house on advertising done by commercial firms at its annual meeting." After another Dewey Palmer article attacked the use of advertising in the classroom, Breck reiterated her faith that home economics teachers would use promotional material critically and selectively. "I do not agree," she wrote, "with Mr. Palmer's tendency toward assumption of complete lack of intelligence among teachers, nor do I feel that his sardonic and sarcastic approach always brings the results he hopes for." [86]

Palmer's and Hader's critiques prompted the AHEA Executive Committee to survey its members' opinions about the utility of advertising in the home economics teaching in 1934. The results of the questionnaire, "Use of Commercial Helps in Home Economics Classes," revealed a wide range of opinions about the educational value of the home economics materials generated in ever larger quantities by home economists in consumer products firms.[87] Perhaps because of the diversity of attitudes regarding commercial home economics publications in educational settings, the organization did not take any serious action against commercially produced materials in home economics teaching. The AHEA leadership ultimately upheld Breck's position that advertising in the classroom was not generally offensive and that its selective use by individual home economics teachers could be valuable to students. Meanwhile, the organization's leaders refrained from publicly endorsing the HEIB Section's activities and took steps to distance themselves from the section's members. "The AHEA is in no way responsible for the policies and practices of the business firms with whom our members are associated," explained President Kathryn Van Aken Burns in 1936. "I think, however, that it is the professional minded and progressive home economists in the business field who are affiliated with their national, professional organization." [88]

For its part, the HEIB Section made little of these challenges to its legitimacy, and its members were reluctant to admit any conflict of interest until the end of the decade. At the 1938 midyear meeting, HEIB member Mary Barber, who worked at Kellogg's, characterized the section as the AHEA's "adolescent child" in need of "careful, tactful guidance." The ability of HEIB members to persuade their employers to advertise in the association's journal and annual meeting exhibitions brought the AHEA substantial income, she argued. However, Barber conveyed a degree of discomfort with the HEIB Section's relationship to the AHEA:

> I feel that we confuse the *Home Economics Woman* in business with the home economics woman in *Business*. As the latter, we have every right to demand from the American Home Economics Association good exhibit space at conventions, good position for our ads in the Journal, certain printed cooperation in the Journal and possibly in the bulletins, lists of registrants at the conventions. . . . But we must ask for these as employees of commercial firms—not as members of the association. The editor and business manager of the Journal should accept comments and suggestions from us in our business positions as impersonally as they accept them from a printer in regard to the make-up of the magazine.[89]

Acknowledging confusion and misunderstanding about business home economists' professional identity, Barber urged the AHEA and the HEIB Section to work more cooperatively together.

To improve their reputation and respond to the decade's criticisms, HEIB members took a number of steps to demonstrate their service to consumers. Marietta Eichelberger, home economist at the Evaporated Milk Association, conducted a survey in 1937 to show that a significant amount of home economics research was accomplished in commercial home economics departments.[90] Emulating the AHEA's earlier consumer initiatives, the group readily adopted the contemporary language of "consumer service" and "consumer education," and even considered publishing a magazine similar to that of Consumers' Research "which would tell the truth about products." When business home economists failed to receive approval for such a publication from managers in their firms, the HEIB group dropped the matter.[91] Vocational guides continued to represent home economics commercial work as an educational service for consumers, as exemplified by Chase Going Woodhouse's choice to introduce her 1938 manual on business home economists with a chapter titled "Consumer Service: The Place of the Home Economist in Business." The perceived threat of a lasting consumer movement promised a new need for business home economists' translating role, explained consultant Harriet Howe in a speech to a HEIB gathering in 1940. With home economists helping "make advertising serve a social purpose," she argued, "the producers and the consumers of goods can work together effectively." Howe and her colleagues maintained a faith in the mutuality of interests between producers and consumers in spite of the changed political and economic context of the 1930s. Although many home economists remained distrustful of the "facts" as presented to them by the "business women," the association as a whole continued to endorse their activities, albeit with caution.[92]

In the meantime, both the AHEA and the HEIB Section continued to struggle to prove themselves as female professionals in a man's world. "Perhaps women are not yet ready to form professional organizations as strong as those men make," reflected Janette Kelley, home economist at Lever Brothers, in a 1938 speech. "Then, too, Home Economics is almost exclusively for women, and we all know the popular belief of how women stick together. And then, just because men have done something that has been successful for them is no guarantee that it will be the thing women want. . . . Home Economics as a profession is still a child, and the business section is in its infancy." Kelley was less than optimistic that the HEIB Section could look forward to "healthy vigorous growth." After two decades of expansion of home economics jobs in business, she and her colleagues continued to struggle with the challenges of projecting a distinct identity and selling their services to employers.[93]

Conclusion

After World War I, business home economists developed a set of professional ideals that aimed to reconcile their membership in an educational reform organization with their employment in the corporate sphere. With the creation of the Home Economics in Business Section within the AHEA in 1924, this small group of home economists won a measure of legitimacy within the larger group of home economists. As many members of the first generation of home economists in business maintained their positions into World War II and beyond, they used this organization to formulate a professional identity that blended service, science, diplomacy, and femininity. Through regular meetings and presentations such as *Experiment 63*, home economists in business transmitted these ideals to a younger generation, so that women who graduated from college in the 1930s inherited a professional culture based at least tacitly on the same principles as the HEIB founders. Yet as the AHEA's business section came under fire from social critics and other home economists, the tensions and contradictions in business home economists' claims to serve both consumers and producers became clear. When economic depression required home economists in business to defend their unique value to corporations (while also defending their identity as authentic consumer representatives), HEIB members struggled to hold on to ideals forged in an earlier era when a growing economy and values of business and science prevailed in the dominant culture.

In spite of the challenges and contradictions they embodied, the professional ideals of home economists' shaped their accomplishments in the industrial and business sectors in the interwar period. Home economists' assumptions about their role in the marketplace intersected in complex ways with their actual experience in commercial jobs. The rhetoric of diplomacy that home economists used to describe their jobs in business often conflicted with the reality that they negotiated between two unequal parties. In practice, those who worked in business ultimately served corporations more immediately than they did consumers or their own professional goals. But because business home economists cast themselves as ambassadors in the marketplace for consumer goods and because they assumed there was a mutuality of interests between producers and consumers, home economists' identity dovetailed with corporate needs. Home economists' professional investment in promoting consumer goods enabled them to assume a comfortable position accommodating the profit-seeking aims of their employers. Their faith in "progressive" big business, as well as their belief that they had something at stake in the process of producing foods and appliances suitable to American consumers, predisposed them to take cues from the emerging corporate culture, to participate in it, and even to shape it.

5

Product Testing, Development, and Promotion: Corporate Investment in Home Economics, 1920–1940

As a girl growing up in Tennessee in the 1910s, Marye Dahnke aspired to a career that would combine her interest in food and nutrition with her attraction to the world of business. "I decided that I wanted to be, first and foremost, a business woman," she later recalled. "And secondly, to be a factor, however small, in the food business, so that I could use the knowledge I had of foods in selling goods. This was a most worthy ambition, but the job which might fulfill my desire was still to be made." When Dahnke's father discouraged her from pursuing a career in business, she chose to enter a college home economics program as a way of appeasing him while still working toward her personal goal. "They thought my interests were all those of the well-trained southern lady, with no sinister desire to apply the knowledge to the bold bad world of business. I kept my ambitions to myself and went dutifully about the matters of the moment, namely, to secure all the academic knowledge of home economics as possible."[1]

Dahnke succeeded in leveraging her home economics education into a new kind of job being created in the food manufacturing business in the 1920s, and her narrative of her career in home economics suggests the strategies that she and her peers used to win jobs for themselves in the expanding consumer products industries. After graduating from Teachers College in 1921, she worked for a few years as an instructor of home economics at the University of Tennessee. By 1924, Dahnke moved with "conviction" to Chicago, in search of work at the heart of the nation's burgeoning food industry. Experience gained through "several little secret sorties" into institutional home economics work in hospitals and hotels helped her convince managers at the Kraft Cheese Company to hire her as a consultant: "Strictly on a trial basis I was given a desk and a package of cheese, and told to make my own job." Within a year, the company

Marye Dahnke, director of the Home Economics Department, Kraft Cheese Company, 1920s. (Home Economics in Business Section Records, Schlesinger Library)

offered Dahnke a full-time position as director of the new Home Economics Department, which would report to both the Advertising and Sales Divisions of the company. Kraft charged Dahnke with developing educational material about the firm's new, processed cheese products that would encourage home cooks to use them as ingredients in meal preparation. "Miss Dahnke determined that the fear could be taken out of cheese cookery—and that her department could help to do it," the company's house organ later explained. Within three years she credited herself with success, claiming cheese was no longer "something to joke about."[2] Dahnke remained at Kraft for more than thirty years, and as director of home economics she oversaw a team of women who helped introduce an array of cheeses, cheese spreads, and salad dressings to homemakers and home economics teachers throughout the country.[3]

Like Marye Dahnke, dozens of home economists carved out spaces for themselves in the consumer products industries in the early 1920s. While home economists in business struggled to win legitimacy within the American Home Economics Association (AHEA), they also faced challenges convincing corporate executives and managers that their expertise was necessary to effective consumer-oriented production and marketing. Many producers of consumer goods in the interwar years needed to be sold on the very idea of placing women in salaried positions within their managerial hierarchy. Even when managers took the initiative to invite home economists into their firms, they were often uncertain about what the function of a home economist should be and how to categorize or organize her work. Although no business home economist could create a job for herself without the support of male management, women like Dahnke found significant room to maneuver inside these firms. With "no cut-and-dried pattern" to follow, a pioneering generation of business home economists drew on their self-styled professional identity to invent roles for themselves in the service of consumer capitalism.[4]

Business investment in home economics in the early 1920s was part of a series of steps by modern corporations to move closer to consumers, internalizing the market forces of demand within the firm. The publicly celebrated accomplishments of the U.S. Food Administration's domestic conservation campaigns during World War I reinforced the construct of the female consumer and suggested to corporate managers that home economists' expertise about food could be useful in communicating with—and influencing the behavior of—women homemakers. Business enterprises such as Kraft also saw home economics as a means of self-regulation in an era of increased government oversight of business, akin to welfare capitalism in labor management. By relying on home economists to add a dimension of integrity to advertising and marketing initiatives, producers sought to create a reputation for good corporate citizenship in the eyes of both consumers and government officials.

Together, home economists and business managers created a new corporate institution: the home economics department. During the 1920s and 1930s, they made a place for home economists' science of consumption inside modern consumer products manufacturing firms and established a mediating role for home economists in the production and marketing of a wide range of household goods. The corporate embrace of home economics was most significant in the food industry, but manufacturers and retailers of household equipment such as glassware, aluminum cooking utensils, gas and electrical appliances, and textiles also brought home economists on board. By 1940, the membership of the AHEA's Home Economics in Business (HEIB) Section included more than 600 leaders in the field, about half the total number of home economists working in business.[5] Commercial work situated home economists directly inside the realm of production, and the open-ended nature of their jobs provided many women with opportunities to influence both the development of new consumer products and their cultural interpretation. Cooking was "in a transitional state" characterized by "the almost daily appearance of some new food or some new method which is a substitute for something now in use," reported the authors of the Good Housekeeping Institute's *Cooking by Temperature* in 1923. Often home economists' corporate cookbooks and other types of instructional materials outlined wholly new systems of food preparation. Managers looked to home economists to both serve as their company's public face to homemakers and represent the "average" consumer inside the firm. Home economists' participation in product design and testing on "her" behalf helped to solidify managers' assumptions that this average consumer was a white, middle-class woman.

Marye Dahnke and her cohort of home economists assumed varied and contested roles in the nation's consumer products firms. In the process, they transformed their professional identities from educators, reformers, and scientists to corporate employees and spokeswomen. Like their colleagues in teaching and research, home economists working in business drew on the ideals of rational consumption to carve out and secure places for a new array of manufactured food products and other household goods in middle-class American domestic life. By helping to characterize processed foods and appliances as efficient, scientific, nutritious, or tested, home economists reinforced general messages that consumption was at the center of domesticity, and that being a modern consumer required managing a household based on these principles. The focus and resources of commercial institutions gave business home economists as much if not more influence than the federal Bureau of Home Economics to deliver these messages. At the same time, by lending their authority as educators and researchers to achieve corporate goals, business home economists also collapsed distinctions between education and sales in American consumer culture, casting instructional messages in commercial terms. This activity drew protests from colleagues in education and government, for whom the work of business home economists undermined the ideals of rational consumption that the first generation of home economists espoused so ardently. As many homemakers became accustomed to receiving practical advice about the mysteries of modern domestic life from commercial home economists, they heard confused and contradictory messages from them about what was educational and what was promotional.

Homing in on the Consumer: The Demand for Home Economics in the Food Industry

Food manufacturers had good reasons to be receptive to hiring ambitious young home economists like Marye Dahnke. Government regulation, a push for "truth in advertising," and advances in nutritional sciences all created pressures for food companies to ensure that their products were considered healthy by the standards of the day, and to communicate to consumers through fact-based advertising. As they innovated to create new foods and other domestic goods, company managers were not sure what homemakers wanted. A cadre of women trained in scientific approaches to products used in the home was an ideal resource for manufacturers to draw on when facing these challenges.[6] But there were few precedents for incorporating women into a firm, and food manufacturers did not have fully developed expectations or strategies for bringing professional women into an organization. Lacking clear models, but desperate to keep up with competitors by investing in "progressive" activities, company managers turned to home economists—and kept a close eye on one another—as they invented new business practices and institutions.

The decision of manufacturers to bring home economists into their firms had roots in the late nineteenth century, when a number of companies turned to the growing community of women experts on household matters to bridge the gap between production engineers and their customers. Trade catalogs for patent medicines and other chemical household products such as bicarbonate of soda commonly featured recipes or "receipts" by well-known domestic scientists.[7] Sarah Tyson Rorer, director of the Philadelphia Cooking School from 1883 to 1903, regularly lent her name to the promotion of various commercial goods, offering free testimonials for such food products as Niagara Corn Starch, Butcher's Dutch Cocoa, and Cleveland's Superior Baking Powder. In addition, as a writer for *Table Talk* magazine, Rorer was paid to develop recipes and cookbooks featuring items ranging from Washington Butcher's Sons' "olive butter" to the Keystone Culinary Beater. Rorer's popular cooking lessons at Philadelphia's Pure Food Convention, held annually beginning in 1889, similarly promoted commercial foods and utensils. Rorer was a "show-woman" concerned as much with entertainment as education. Dressed in a silken gown, she cultivated a dramatic "platform style" while demonstrating the advantage of such novelties as gas cooking and the chafing dish. Rorer also took credit for suggesting eventual improvements to Knox gelatin and, in 1910, developed her own blend of coffee. Her success as a nationally prominent domestic scientist was intricately bound up in her active commercial career.[8]

Around 1900, manufacturers and trade associations developed a standard practice of hiring well-known domestic scientists and "cookery" specialists of Rorer's generation as consultants to write recipes for trade catalogs and promotional cookbooks featuring their products. Authors included Helen Louise Johnson, Mary J. Lincoln, and Janet MacKenzie Hill, all of whom had attended the Lake Placid conferences that launched the home economics movement. Like Rorer, these women were caught up in the enthusiasm of the pure-food movement and, especially in the years preceding the passage of the Pure Food and Drug Act of 1906, heartily endorsed "standards of purity" in food processing. Mary Virginia Hawes Terhune, who wrote under the pseudonym Marion Harland, provided official advice on canning for the National Canners Association, and the Rumford Company hired cooking school directors Fannie Farmer and Mary Wilson to develop recipes and instructions for the use of its baking powder. With the drive to save wheat during World War I, leavening agents took on new importance for homemakers who chose to make quick breads using heavier, less refined flours. In this context, the baking powder companies were among the most visible food producers who turned to home economists to align their organizations with patriotic food conservation campaigns and to new ideas about nutrition and diet.[9]

By 1917, thirty-five food enterprises, most of which had been founded around 1900 and each of which controlled assets of $20 million or more, took pioneering steps to modernize their industrial operations. Through the application of continuous-process machinery, many of these firms implemented cost-effective mass production. Control of sources for raw materials, transportation, and distribution networks also contributed to production and sales efficiencies. By investing in advertising with an emphasis on brand-name identification, these companies were able to compete based on brand-name recognition, rather than price. In the 1920s, a wave of mergers in the food industry increased competitive pressure to further control not just production but also demand.[10]

The decision to establish corporate home economics departments grew out of a marketing revolution under way at the time in which managers in food companies and other consumer products firms sought to establish two-way communication between themselves and consumers. The products that many of these firms produced—such as processed cheese, lard substitutes, or manufactured leavening agents—were new, and it was far from certain that people were interested in buying them. Many company leaders discovered that advertising alone could not create a desire for unfamiliar goods. Looking beyond promotion, they turned to what sociologist Michael Schudson calls a "marketing mix" of activities that involved "reading" potential markets and "listening" to consumers.[11] Although it was expanding in the 1920s, the field of marketing remained a rudimentary science. Business school professors began to investigate the institutional structures of marketing processes after 1900, but the discipline had few standard principles or procedures until the 1930s, when institutions for training business managers established marketing departments staffed by academics with an interest in the comprehensive, complex "channels" that began with the acquisition of raw materials and finished with produced goods being purchased by consumers. A number of large manufacturing firms, advertising agencies, and publishing companies stepped up their efforts to collect information about potential consumers, their preferences, and their behavior. While leading consumer durable companies like General Motors conducted hundreds of market research investigations through the 1930s, such efforts were not widespread or institutionalized in terms of method or as standard practice. As historian Steven Sass explains, there was "no stable occupational structure in marketing" before World War II.[12]

During the interwar period, when understanding consumers was valued, but techniques for learning about and communicating with customers were not yet well understood, manufacturers of food products and household goods assumed that the vast majority of their customers were women. For firms in this era trying to reach out to a primarily female clientele, home economics was a tangible way to connect with the homemaker's perspective. Advertisers attempting to rise above crass strategies that relied on "knocking" competitors had begun hiring women to write copy that was sensitive to "the woman's viewpoint." But while advertising professionals in the 1920s still thought of consumers as "nonrational" actors, managers of food companies and other consumer products firms looked for ways to transform consumers into more consistent and predictable actors in the marketplace.[13]

Home economists were uniquely positioned to play a role in shaping a changing set of relationships between producers and consumers. Home economists came with ties to communities of women, especially rural homemakers and young female high school and college students. Their expertise in the new science of nutrition positioned them to educate (rather than just sell) consumers and potential consumers on uses for manufactured food products. In many cases food industry managers established home economics departments at the same time they invested in research and development laboratories to control the creation, improvement, and testing of their products. Drawing increasingly on the expertise of chemists, biochemists, bacteriologists, and dietitians, the food industry created more than sixty research facilities by 1921.[14] Several firms and trade associations concerned with food and other consumer products also endowed fellowships in graduate programs akin to the industrial fellowships sponsored by DuPont and other chemical firms.[15] By 1928, William A. Hamor, assistant director of the Mellon Institute of Industrial Research, estimated that about twenty of his institution's seventy-one fellowships for that year were concerned with investigating consumer products and other subjects that overlapped with the interests of home economists. Although home economists themselves held very few of these fellowships, the support for research around consumer products signaled the growing importance of systematic product improvement and development. This ultimately led manufacturers to draw on the resources of home economists, who offered corporations both the knowledge of the "newer nutrition" and the practical experience with household management that appealed to corporate leaders' desires to control the invention process.[16] Home economics departments or "laboratories," as they were sometimes called, operated as parallel sites for experimentation and testing that offered food company managers a strategy for involving homemakers and other potential end users in corporate research and development efforts.

Firms also valued the willingness of home economists to serve as translators and diplomats to consumers and other audiences. Consumer products manufacturers hired home economists precisely because they tended to come with a network of contacts among schoolteachers and home demonstration agents in the agricultural extension service, contacts that promised to smooth the way for educational advertising campaigns. Popular criticism regarding the extent of economic concentration in these industries, and especially charges of misleading advertising, pressured leaders in the consumer products industries to go out of their way to construct and disseminate positive images of their organizations and the goods and services they sold. Facing new and expanding challenges in fostering public goodwill, company managers welcomed home economists' image as friendly, objective standard-bearers who represented themselves as "missionaries at heart."[17] Home economists' identity as educators could also help corporations expand markets for their products in a manner that seemed to foster the public interest. It especially appealed to manufacturers looking to usher in strategies of modern consumer service akin to those employed by retail organizations at the turn of the century. Just as department store managers developed new kinds of spaces, workers, and credit systems to create an atmosphere of "commercial hospitality," managers in consumer products firms turned to home economists in the 1920s to help play down the profit-seeking nature of their enterprises and create an image of manufacturers as good corporate citizens, providing education and service to consumers and the community.[18]

Home economists' technical expertise and their professional image also suited corporate managers' search for strategies to cope with increasing government regulation. Progressive Era antitrust, pure-food, and fair-trade legislation encouraged industries to regulate themselves to minimize conflict with state and federal officials. One way to emulate this "good trust" was to embrace home economics as a mechanism to ensure "truth in advertising."[19] Likewise, as they demonstrated through their work in the Bureau of Home Economics, home economists could help facilitate the kind of cooperation between business enterprises and government agencies that characterized the political economy of the 1920s.

Closely related to these tactics to preempt government regulation was many firms' shift to a system of welfare capitalism as a strategy for labor management. Assuming that promoting workers' happiness and physical well-being could enhance a company's productivity, managers of large corporations employed female social workers as official company matriarchs to nurture and educate their employees. "Housemothers" of corporate welfare departments advised workers on health, physical fitness, and thrift, while a new coterie of dietitians—often also trained in home economics—directed new lunchrooms and cafeterias. Business home economists' instruction of consumers paralleled these labor management strategies, and in some firms all of these functions came under the direction of a single home economist.[20] The notion that the success of modern industrial labor processes required control through uplift and enlightenment paralleled similar attitudes that marketing was a matter of education, with the firm serving Americans as citizens by serving them as consumers.[21]

As women, as scientists, and as educators, home economists had the skills needed to fulfill these complex roles within the firm. They offered expertise about consumer products and the behavior of consumers that management needed in many areas: research and development, advertising and marketing, public relations, and even welfare-capitalism strategies of labor management. By the early 1920s, a consensus had emerged that having a full-time home economist on board was the hallmark of the progressive company, especially for food manufacturers and other producers of household consumer goods.[22]

Home Economics at Procter & Gamble

The experience of Procter & Gamble (P&G) reveals how the drive for various kinds of corporate control led manufacturers to establish home economics departments in the early 1920s. Having pioneered the use of advertising and brand identification with Ivory Soap in the 1880s, P&G relied on the marketing and promotion of products with low unit cost as its strategy for success.[23] Soon after its incorporation in 1890, P&G moved into cottonseed oil production. From Germany, it imported technological know-how in the emerging field of hydrogenation, a chemical engineering process that transformed liquid oil into a solid and eventually led to the production of Crisco shortening. At a time when butter was expensive and lard considered malodorous, P&G promoted manufactured shortening as a "pure food" that was produced under controlled, predictable, and advanced technological conditions.

In the 1920s, a new set of managerial attempts to control demand coincided with efforts to control the supply of raw materials and to develop new products, production methods, and labor-management strategies. As the firm diversified its product range to include other soaps and oils, it expanded its production facilities to include four North American locations in addition to the original Ivorydale, Ohio, plant near its Cincinnati headquarters. In addition, the firm established a research laboratory in Ivorydale staffed with twelve chemists devoted to the "improvement of plant processes and products" and the Economic Research Department, which kept track of fluctuations in commodity markets. In an attempt to increase demand for its products, the company sought to reinvigorate the national campaign for Ivory by removing it from Allen C. Collier, the Cincinnati printer who had been responsible for Ivory advertisements since 1900, and giving it to the Blackman Company, a New York City advertising firm. Simultaneously, P&G took steps to reduce demand fluctuation by shifting from wholesalers, who tended to stockpile product, to a distribution system based on direct sales to retail stores. By maintaining an even flow of business, P&G's managers hoped to guarantee not only predictable revenue but also steady year-round employment at its main plants. In 1923, the company adopted an employment plan promising forty-eight weeks' work to all hourly workers in its main factories.[24]

P&G's decision to hire home economists and establish a home economics department occurred in the context of these new business strategies. The company also had a history of working with home economists in the development and promotion of Crisco before World War I. Beginning in 1911, P&G hired J. Walter Thompson, a major New York City advertising firm, to develop a pioneering campaign for the new shortening. The agency assigned the job to a female copywriter who provided "the women's point of view" in defining the product and developing a promotional campaign. As part of this campaign, the company consulted with university-based scientists and home economists, and it sent a group of women demonstrators to conduct free week-long cooking schools throughout the United States. P&G also commissioned well-known cookery specialists such as Marion Harris Neil and Janet McKenzie Hill to develop cookbooks with recipes highlighting the ways to cook with Crisco. Neil's *The Story of Crisco* (1913) and Hill's *The Whys of Cooking* (1916) were elegantly produced publications containing many color illustrations and recipes for dishes that reflected the Anglo-American backgrounds of these women authors and their main target audience.[25]

While women's expertise continued to prove helpful in promoting the company's products during World War I, concerns regarding product testing led Benjamin B. George, sales manager of the Food Oils Department, to initiate a discussion among his colleagues that ultimately resulted in the creation of a home economics department within P&G. In March 1922 he suggested to the new sales manager, Richard Redwood Deupree, and the advertising manager, Ralph Rogan, "that this Company should have some sort of experimental bakery or kitchen, where cooking and baking tests of various kinds could be made by a man or woman thoroughly competent to do the work."[26] Such a facility would reduce Procter & Gamble's reliance on outside bakeries, which could only accommodate testing requests on an irregular basis. Soon John P. Darnall, a clerk under Rogan, began investigating the possibility of building such a test kitchen. His first step was to turn for advice to the Blackman advertising firm, which had opened an office in the same building as the P&G headquarters and now handled the Crisco account. Blackman, like several other national advertising firms, had established an experimental kitchen staffed with home economists at its New York City office.[27] Corinne Tetedoux, a domestic science graduate employed with Blackman who had been handling P&G's consumer correspondence for about six months, estimated that it would cost about $1,500 to outfit a facility within P&G similar to the one at her agency.[28]

Darnall was prepared to give a woman considerable responsibility and freedom when he decided to launch P&G's experimental kitchen. He proposed to hire Tetedoux away from Blackman to staff the new kitchen, and he recommended giving her "a month to get her bearings, find out what she wants to do and how she wants to do it, make investigating trips to other Plants where there are such kitchens, . . . and then propose to us the equipment and the arrangement she thinks we need and proceed to buy and install it." Six months' experience at Blackman seemed "sufficient training to get the advertising point of view," and Darnall offered to supervise her in what he felt would be "a very interesting and progressive job." Ralph Rogan was less convinced. In May, even as he announced a plan to establish a test kitchen and laundry, he still wondered whether the firm would have enough work "to keep a woman completely occupied." Rogan was uncertain about what to do with such a woman and was at least slightly unnerved about having a home economist in his midst. He was reluctant to hire anyone until he had established "some means of having her controlled as it were, by somebody else and myself." Rogan claimed he was too busy to supervise her alone, and his concern for control suggests that he did not know where a home economist would fit in the business organization. Benjamin George estimated more optimistically that his sales department for food oils could make use of a home economist two days a week and strongly favored the idea "as a very useful adjunct to our work." A well-equipped experimental bakery, he argued, would "make it possible for us to conduct a more thorough line of experiments and in the same way and in the same proportions as would ordinarily be used by a baker," thus ensuring the success of the firm's products.[29]

Before making any final decisions about what sort of a kitchen to create and with whom to staff it, Rogan and Darnall sought advice from other firms in the industry that had established test kitchens. Their interest in these companies suggests an important reason why the men at P&G wanted to create an experimental kitchen: to keep up with current trends in the food industry. Darnall's letters of inquiry also reveal some of the issues at stake for P&G in deciding whether or not to invest in a home economics laboratory. He asked managers at Calumet Baking Powder, Armour, Igleheart, Swift, Royal Baking Powder, and Merrell-Soule Sales Corporation how their kitchens functioned and how they contributed to the development of brand identification and advertisement.

He also asked how many people were employed and whether they worked full time. Finally, he wanted to know the bottom line: What was the value of the test kitchens relative to their cost?[30]

Responses from these leading companies suggested that the industry as a whole was moving forward with the establishment of home economics departments. By 1922, Calumet had installed a test kitchen and a chemical laboratory for evaluating all of its baking powder ingredients, as well as finished product. In a separate home economics department, an "expert" and an assistant conducted "cooking and experimental bakery work." Both individuals were "kept busy practically all the time" answering consumers' questions and testing all of the recipes used in the firm's *Reliable Recipes* cookbook. In addition, Calumet maintained a complete model bakery for experimenting with larger mixes for institutional uses. Regarding the relative expense of "kitchen work," Calumet's sales manager mentioned no method that he had employed to determine the value of Calumet's experimental bakery. Rather, he reported, "we consider that it is self sustaining due to the fact that this satisfies customers and brings new customers. The actual expense of maintaining such departments is largely up to your own judgment as to the equipment, number of people employed and the class of work which they do."[31]

Austin S. Igleheart of Igleheart Brothers, makers of Swans Down Cake Flour and an instant cake batter mix, responded that the company had a "Laboratory and a Kitchen" and "a competent cake baker" to advise the firm's managers and its customers "in regard to their cake baking problems and to try out recipes for us." In his correspondence, Igleheart did not indicate whether the cake baker was a home economist. By the following year, however, Igleheart hired home economist Mary Irene Hart to organize a home economics department after she wrote to company managers suggesting that they could sell more cake flour if they provided women with reliable instructions for making cakes.[32]

One enthusiastic reply came directly from a working business home economist. Since 1915, Ruth Watson had directed the Royal Baking Powder Company's Educational Department, a "household experiment establishment" in charge of recipe testing for advertising. At the firm's New York City headquarters, Watson supervised two or three full-time home economists as well as some part-time workers. "It is indispensable," she wrote, "to an advertiser to have such a department for this work." In addition, she reported that Royal had operated a "Demonstration Kitchen" for homemakers, domestic science teachers, and students in Milwaukee since 1920. Watson described the test kitchen, directed by home economist Mildred Brooks, as "quite novel with manufacturers and with us it is an experiment." The kitchen, she claimed, was "a most effective and convincing way of reaching people in all stations of life in any locality and a wonderful opportunity to emphasize the quality of any product for general home consumption. While it is expensive it is effective advertising and if it could be carried out systematically in all sections of the country it would be a thorough method of reaching the consumer. On the other hand the cost is excessive for the number reached and in our opinion anything which cannot be made national in scope is not a profitable activity for a national advertiser." Despite this qualification of the importance of such a department's scope, Watson boasted the success of seven years' home economics work at Royal Baking Powder.[33]

The Merrell-Soule Sales Corporation of Syracuse, New York, reported that it had recently hired Mary Reed Hartson, "a graduate dietitian as well as an expert in cookery," with several years of experience at the Royal Baking Powder Company, to develop "the uses of our product for the housewife and in the hospitals and institutions." According to Vice President and General Sales Manager Robert G. Soule, Hartson's Department of Dietetics and Cookery helped his firm make close contact with consumers. Hartson devoted most of her time working at the firm's experimental kitchen in Syracuse. The rest of her schedule was spent traveling throughout the country to consult with dietitians and to address women's organizations. Soule claimed that Hartson's "expert advice" was integral to the company's latest distribution plan for KLIM, Merrell-Soule's powdered milk product. "We consider that the expense incurred is an excellent investment, considering the value of such work," he concluded. Soule's satisfaction echoed the sentiments of a company colleague who reported in an industry trade journal that Merrell-Soule had "found greater stability in the increased business that is stimulated through this co-operative link between [this firm] and the teaching profession—and I say unhesitatingly, that our department of dietetics and cookery is a large factor in helping our industry."[34]

Although none of these respondents to Darnall's inquiry used hard cost-benefit figures to assess the value of home economics, together they suggested that incorporating home economists into business practices was a growing trend in the food industry. In fact, by this date, several other manufacturers of food products had hired staffs of home economists and were beginning to establish a place for them in their institutional structure. An early list of fifteen home economists employed by business institutions, compiled in the fall of 1922, included an additional five women working in the food industry: Hannah Wessling at the Northwestern Yeast Company, Louise Fitzgerald at the National Dairy Council, Gudrun Carlson at the Institute of American Meat Packers, and

Janette Kelley at Washburn-Crosby.[35] In addition, Darnall and his colleagues at P&G were likely aware of the *American Food Journal*'s new Food Service Bureau, where notable food reformer and home economist Winifred Stuart Gibbs assisted manufacturers with such matters as investigating the nutritional value of products, developing recipe suggestions for them, preparing publicity materials and educational campaigns, and promoting foods that were "proven in nutritional value and quality" in institutions such as hospitals or charitable organizations, where they could be accepted "in large quantities." By offering the "scientific research and investigation that few manufacturers are equipped or able to make before determining the ideal method of producing or marketing their product," Gibbs's work at the trade journal demonstrated the potential of home economics to help food manufacturers understand their products from the perspective of American homemakers.[36]

With an eye to industry trends and encouragement from peers in the trade, P&G's executives decided in late 1922 to build a test kitchen and a laundry that would be shared by the company's Advertising and Manufacturing Departments. Rogan initially intended to locate the test kitchen and laundry at the P&G's headquarters, close to the Advertising Department. However, an overall strategy to link manufacturing more closely with marketing led company managers to place the home economics group in the Chemical Division of the Manufacturing Department at its Ivorydale plant. A new Product Service Section of the Chemical Division, headed by Wes Blair, was launched in 1923 to study customers' use of P&G products, and the establishment of a Home Economics Department the following year represented a similar effort to tie the experimental and research work of the Chemical Division to consumers' needs and desires. In his April 1924 statement of the policy and purpose of this department, Renton K. Brodie, the Chemical Division's superintendent, noted that home economics work at P&G had begun with the introduction of Crisco and since then had been most closely connected to advertising. The inclusion of the test kitchen and laundry within the Chemical Division, however, meant that the kitchen's operations would also contribute to research and development, "rather than [serving] the Advertising Department alone." Brodie declared: "It is our policy to permit the Head of our Domestic Science laboratory to select a certain portion of the problems, the remainder being the outgrowth of our contact with the Advertising and Sales Departments."[37] Brodie's staff would play a large role in organizing and directing the test kitchen's work "as a part of the general field of investigations pertaining to the use of our products," and he positioned the Home Economics Department to enhance the Chemical Division's activities, particularly in product service. Blair's staff in the Product

Service Section had "unrestricted contact with those branches of the Sales or Advertising Departments for which their services are available," and Brodie fit the test kitchen into this structure.[38] At the facility, staff would study "food problems" such as fat absorption, the use of oil in salad dressings and mayonnaise, and rancidity, and they would develop standard formulas, frying and baking temperatures, and cooking processes. P&G's executives required the Chemical Division to report monthly to the Advertising Department on the results of the new lab.[39]

Managers' personnel choices stemmed from their decision to locate the laboratory in Ivorydale and to create a home economics position that would be as useful to manufacturing as it would be to advertising. Rather than hiring Tetedoux, P&G brought on Eleanor Ahern, a seasoned home economist with ten years' experience in a variety of positions, to lead this pioneering enterprise. Her first job after graduating with a home economics degree from the University of Chicago in 1913 had been as a high-school home economics teacher in West Chicago. Remaining in Chicago, she became the director of home economics for Wilson & Company meatpackers and then spent three years employed as a dietitian at Michael Reese Hospital. Most recently, as a member of the American Dietetic Association, Ahern had helped compile the organization's publication, *Recipes for Institutions*. While Ahern's background specifically qualified her to oversee P&G's test kitchen, the company's managers also put her in charge of the test laundry. Ahern remained with P&G until her retirement in 1958.[40]

Coordinating the instructional aspects of promotional campaigns for Crisco was one of Eleanor Ahern's major contributions to the Advertising Department. In 1924 one manager estimated that Ahern devoted about a quarter of her time working with advertising agents on conceptual ideas, photography, layout, and review of recipes and cookbooks produced by consultants under the supervision of P&G's advertising firm.[41] One of her first moves was to introduce a "modern," scientific style of writing for P&G's published recipes, featuring level measurements and (purportedly) fool-proof, step-by-step guidelines. First popularized by Fannie Farmer in the 1890s, "scientific cookery" was aggressively promoted by Ahern's second generation of home economists to distinguish themselves from other women in the food business. Before Ahern's arrival at P&G, Olive Allen, a copywriter and director of the test kitchen at the Blackman (later Compton) Company, had cultivated a public image as a "home cook." Ahern objected that Allen "wasn't a Home Economist" and that she failed to adhere to the profession's principles of scientific cookery. Allen used "heaping teaspoons" and other rule-of-thumb measurements in her cookbook, *200 Tested Recipes*, written for P&G. Although Blackman's advertising agent criticized Ahern for her "scientific attitude of mind," the home economics director convinced managers at P&G to hire a "more modern" consultant to compile another collection of Crisco recipes in 1926. Sarah Field Splint, an editor for *Woman's Home Companion* and a former home economics leader in the U.S. Food Administration, drew on the magazine's "know-how" and its practice of level measurements in compiling *The Art of Cooking and Serving* (1927). The company asked customers for twenty-five cents and a product label for each copy of the book, a lavishly illustrated publication which became a classic. Eventually, the advertising firm determined that Allen was "pretty out of date" and hired Dorothy Constantine, a trained home economist, to replace her.[42]

Ahern convinced P&G's managers that the success of Crisco hinged on its proper use by consumers, as defined by company employees—home economists. She ultimately took over the work of developing recipes and cookbooks using Crisco, overseeing the expansion of a home economics department to perform this work. Collaborating with Constantine on recipe development, by the late 1920s she created a new corporate entity for P&G: Winifred S. Carter. General Mills' "Betty Crocker" had recently emerged as a popular icon, and home economists at P&G began signing some of the company's advertisements with the initials "W.S.C." Ahern resisted using her own name, so they decided to designate the fictitious Winifred S. Carter as the author of future cookbooks, with company home economists assuming the role of anonymous (and invisible) ghostwriters. Ahern's team prepared other cookbooks—including a series of twelve short manuals with titles such as *Pastries*, *Vegetable Cookery*, and *Frying Facts*—which credited "the home economics department" as author.[43]

Whereas celebrity authors received acknowledgment on the title pages of many pre–World War I publications and a number of companies continued this practice in the interwar period, P&G's decision to draw on the professional identity of home economists as a group was also a common way that manufacturers sought to legitimize the scientific and technological authority of their firms and their products. Developing recipes and cookbooks emerged as a key communication strategy about specific manufactured foodstuffs and appliances that placed Ahern and her cohort of business home economists at the center of a dialogue with consumers. Commercial recipe booklets proliferated throughout the 1920s: the list published by the *American Food Journal* included dozens of new titles every month.[44] Companies reprinted as many a dozen editions of some cookbooks, distributing them to consumers at no cost or selling them for as much as two dollars apiece. Manufacturers and advertising agencies continued to invest in the production and distribution of cookbooks and recipe booklets in enormous quantities well into the Depression years. By the 1940s, the genre included hundreds of titles, and commercial cookbooks could be found on the kitchen shelves of most American homemakers.[45] By making the scientific and technical developments in corporations relevant to consumers in a specific set of ways, these books brought the home economics laboratory into the public realm, and in particular into the homes and kitchens of middle-class homemakers.[46] In writing corporate recipe booklets, home economists created technical manuals for the use of food products such as leavening agents and flavored gelatin and kitchen appliances such as gas stoves and electric roasters, products new to many consumers. The production of these texts gave home economists opportunities to define elements of the modern kitchen in terms of the values of health and efficiency, and to package these components into hallmarks of middle-class identity. Through a vast how-to literature, home economists made their specialized knowledge and value system central to the use of a whole new realm of commercial products, much as contemporary writers of other types of technical guides—such as automobile repair and maintenance manuals—worked to popularize the ideas of the experts who wrote them.[47] In telling "the story of Crisco," Ahern constructed narratives to make an unfamiliar food familiar and to place common foods in new contexts, much as her fellow home economists in other food companies helped to establish a place in the American diet for specific foods ranging from salad dressings to processed meats to cheese spreads.

Although managers initially expected that the Advertising Department would use the majority of Eleanor Ahern's time, her primary role at P&G was to help the company's engineers and managers understand consumers and how they used P&G's products. Ahern assisted with early market research efforts, which the P&G's economist in charge of monitoring commodity price fluctuations, D. Paul Smelser, was getting off the ground at this time.[48] As she tested food products and developed recipes for them, Ahern also sought to improve the company's products. In the mid-1930s, when Crisco faced competition from Spry, a Lever Brothers shortening, Ahern contributed to the reformulation of Crisco. When Crisco sales dropped, Ahern's department reported that homemakers thought Spry creamed more easily than the P&G product. The Chemical Division in Ivorydale argued that its test, which consisted of dropping a plunger into cans of both products, showed no difference between the two. Ahern's team tested the actual behavior of the two products by timing women stirring them both with sugar. Under these conditions, Spry indeed turned out to be the easier product to use. Based on the results of work in the test kitchen, engineers changed the manufacturing process to make Crisco a more competitive product. Ahern recalled that this incident was "really the only time the Home Economics kitchen won a full scale argument . . . over the scientific boys of the Chemical Division."[49]

Many of Ahern's activities centered on "washability" with regard to the use of the company's soap products. Before Ahern arrived, Blair installed equipment to duplicate actual conditions under which commercial laundries used P&G's products. Now Ahern operated a test laundry, which served as the domestic equivalent to this commercial workshop. The Home Economics Department collaborated with chemists in the firm's product service operations to perform "home laundry tests" on Ivory and new products such as Chipso, an improved version of Ivory Soap Flakes introduced in 1921; Oxydol, a detergent made of hollow granules; and later Dreft, an early synthetic household detergent developed in 1933.[50] To share with consumers knowledge gained by analyzing the performance of laundry products under controlled conditions, Ahern also developed promotional brochures often termed "cleanliness manuals" for the company's soap products such as *Approved Methods for Home Laundering* and *Housecleaning*, which the company made available for ten and five cents, respectively.[51]

By virtue of her placement between the Advertising and Manufacturing Departments, Ahern acted as a conduit between these two groups. Her value to P&G derived from her ability to make connections among the company's many activities rather than controlling or directing any single one of them. As a result of the shared status between these two departments, Ahern performed a wide range of duties that made her work difficult to categorize. Managers relied on her to keep in touch with consumers, and she helped generate new knowledge about homemakers' preferences and about the performance of P&G's products in the context of daily domestic routines. Ahern often helped translate the work of the Chemical Division in terms that the Advertising Department, and by extension homemakers, could understand. She combined her knowledge of food preparation in the home with that of company production processes to support more than just advertising. In her own opinion, which was shared by the company, she performed a series of functions critical to the commercial success of P&G and its products. By World War II, the company had established a series of household testing laboratories in addition to the test kitchen and laundry. Dental and skin-research laboratories, a complete experimental beauty parlor, a commercial kitchen, and a bakery were some of the more specialized strategies the company used to internalize the opinions of various categories of customers into its operations.[52]

Ahern's responsibilities at P&G encompassed the spectrum of duties between manufacturing and advertising that business home economists typically performed in the interwar period. Some women worked directly on product development; others devoted their energies along more promotional lines. Collectively, commercial home economists explained consumers' needs to corporate managers, helped develop or improve products, tested them for quality, and interpreted them to consumers. In these ways, and primarily behind the scenes, home economists such as Ahern mediated the relationship between consumers and manufacturers of not only processed foods but also a wide variety of household goods.

Product Development and Testing: Sears, Roebuck & Company

In a 1927 full-page advertisement, a manufacturer of domestic appliances sought a "Domestic Science Leader" to conduct "field research" into homemakers' preferences. The candidate was expected to supply the firm's Engineering Department with "specifications that are written from the standpoint of the users of these appliances" and to design and perform tests and "supply accurate, expert information . . . that can be embodied in the design of new or improved products."[53] Like the managers of this firm, producers and retailers of a wide array of consumer goods in the 1920s—including kitchen appliances and utensils as well as ready-made clothing—followed the food industry in turning to home economists for assistance in investigating their products from the viewpoint of consumers. Many manufacturers hired home economists as consultants and full-time employees to advise them on the development and improvement of their products. Retailers, too, brought home economists on board to help select and evaluate merchandise for sale.

Much of this testing was intended to form the basis for explaining new products to American homemakers. At the research kitchen of the American Stove Company in Cleveland, home economists performed regular tests on the six stove models the company produced. In the process, they developed recipes and instruction booklets to promote the "intelligent use" of the Lorain oven heat regulators that were controlled by a "red wheel" on each model. Because these regulators allowed for unprecedented control of baking temperatures, the work of the research kitchen centered on determining optimal baking temperatures for various dishes as well as the ideal cooking duration "in order that women can always have uniform baking temperatures." The staff assisted individual homemakers in determining the proper cooking time and temperature for their favorite recipes. In addition to producing a cookbook for its customers, company home economists worked out methods of canning inside ovens and comparisons with the water bath method of canning.[54]

However, a good deal of home economists' work for equipment manufacturers was aimed at designing or improving goods to meet the needs and desires of homemakers. Aluminum Goods Manufacturing Company salesman Gene Chloupek took an interest in the work of Mary Irene Hart, home economist at the Igleheart Milling Company, while working on a program that allowed purchasers of Ingleheart flour to redeem premiums and receive cake pans, measuring cups, and measuring spoons. Within a few years he convinced his superiors at the firm to hire Hart to launch the firm's own home economics test kitchen. By 1927, Hart had brought on two other home economists—Ruth Heath and Beatrice Smith—to assist her. In cooperation with the company's Research Department, Hart and her team suggested ideas for new utensils and evaluated models of utensils before they were approved for production. "We try out these models thoroughly first," she explained, "and determine whether or not they are correct as to gauge of material, durability, and cooking properties."[55]

As director of a similar operation at the Wear-Ever Test Kitchen, Margaret Mitchell contributed to the development of new baking pans. In 1933, at the suggestion and encouragement of an electric range manufacturer, the company began developing utensils suitable for use in an electric range. Utility companies had found that homemakers complained about the amount of their first electric bill after they had had a range installed. When a home service agent visited the utility's customers to determine out what the problem was, "nine times out of ten she would find the trouble was due to improper utensils." In the hopes that more appropriate cooking tools and baking pans would "simplify" the utility company's work by requiring fewer service calls (as well as help sell ranges), sales managers and home service agents offered suggestions for redesigning this equipment.[56]

With this input, Mitchell studied the sizes, shapes, and capacities of what the electric range manufacturers thought would be "efficient utensils." She also surveyed editors of women's magazines and visited department stores as a "typical" consumer to find the optimal pans for electric stoves. After testing recipes in a spectrum of different pans, Mitchell concluded that utensils for the electric range should have straight sides and perfectly flat bottoms, that they should fit the range elements precisely, that they should be of two-, three-, and four-quart capacity, and that they should be suitable for both surface and oven cookery. Mitchell worked with Wear-Ever product development engineers to make sample products, and then she and her team checked these samples "from every possible angle and gave what would be equal to approximately six months use in a home." Mitchell and the engineers made alterations to the designs and "worked out styles and designs that gave them eye appeal and watched closely to make certain that any changes incorporated increased the practicability and beauty without changing the actual cost." After this trial period, Mitchell made the case for investing in "several thousand dollars of machinery" to build and sell the newly reconfigured products. Placed on the market in June 1935, the products proved tremendously successful. Within a year sales increased fivefold and utilities soon included the utensils with ranges in promotions. "The day is not too far off when they will be just as much a part of the equipment of the range as the oven heat regulator is today," Mitchell predicted in 1937 about the utensils she had helped develop.[57]

At Corning Glass Works, home economist Lucy Maltby made similar contributions in the 1930s to the development of Pyrex-brand glassware for baking. Hired by the glass manufacturer in 1929 at a moment when sales of its consumer housewares were stagnating, Maltby advised the company's engineers on the design of one of Pyrex's range-top glassware products. Based on the knowledge she gained from consumer correspondence and practical experimentation with Corning's products in her test kitchen, Maltby also collaborated with research scientists on improving Pyrex cake dishes. Sales of Pyrex soon began to increase rapidly.[58] Although only 3 to 4 percent of business home economists in the interwar period (or 24 women by 1940) were employed by equipment manufacturers, many others found ways to include providing suggestions for the development and improvement of products in their list of responsibilities.[59]

In addition to assisting manufacturers with product design, several home economists took positions with retailers where they tested the quality of goods to be sold in department stores and other distribution outlets. At Sears, Roebuck & Company, Elizabeth Sophia Weirick emerged as a leader of the mail-order firm's testing laboratories in the 1920s and 1930s. Trained in chemistry at the University of Chicago, Weirick allied herself to the home economics profession soon after her graduation in 1903, taking a job teaching chemistry at the Pratt Institute School of Household Science and Arts in Brooklyn, New York. At Pratt, Weirick developed a course in textile and dye chemistry to train women for industrial positions. In preparing the course, she spent a summer studying bleaching, dyeing, and finishing processes in a New Jersey bleachery, apprenticed under silk expert James Chittick, and later trained with J. Merritt Matthews, chair of the Chemical and Dyeing Department at the Philadelphia Textile School and one of the nation's foremost textile chemists.[60]

In 1919, A. V. H. Mory invited Weirick to head the Textile Division of the product testing laboratories he had recently established at the Sears headquarters in Chicago. The mail-order firm created the labs in 1911 to enable the retailer to back its "satisfaction guaranteed" promise to its customers, and to ensure that the grocery products and patent medicines it sold complied with the recently passed Pure Food and Drug Act. Drawing on his experience as a food chemist for Armour & Company meat processors and as director of the U.S. Laboratory of Food Inspection in Kansas City under Harvey Wiley, Mory developed the labs with an eye toward bringing Sears's whole line of merchandise "into harmony with the spirit of the Food and Drugs [*sic*] Act." By the time Mory arrived, Sears had largely removed patent medicines from its catalog, and he shifted the labs' investigations to a broader program of chemical and textile analysis.[61]

Weirick was ultimately placed "in charge of the laboratories" and guided them through more than a decade of growth and expansion. Although Mory used the labs to groom company executives, he hired Weirick to build up the laboratories' Textile Division with the intention that she would continue in a technical role. When Mory resigned in 1920, a year after Weirick's arrival, the laboratories were temporarily disbanded. Weirick and her assistant remained on board, with Weirick earning an exceptionally high salary for a woman working in a commercial textile chemistry position. The laboratories were revived in 1928, a few years after Sears began opening retail stores and establishing its own brand of merchandise. Weirick was chosen to head the laboratories and, with the go-ahead from Technical Director General W. I. Westervelt, she soon reestablished the Chemical Division and expanded the laboratories to include four new divisions: Mechanical, Electrical, Home Economics, and the Scientific and Technical Library. Weirick oversaw another major expansion of the laboratories in 1933, and by the time she retired in 1940, Weirick had built her staff from just a few people to more than eighty chemists, physicists, engineers, and home economists working in three main divisions: Chemical, Engineering (including home economics), and Textile.[62]

Many members of the laboratories' staff were women, attesting to Weirick's ability and commitment to use her authority to promote the careers of home economists and other women scientists. Her assistant, Lucille Crissey, held a degree in chemistry, as did the two librarians Weirick hired in the late 1920s. One of them, Virginia Pearson, recalled that Weirick was "a true Victorian lady" who commanded great respect from both the men and women in the labs. "She ran a very tight ship": women were not allowed to smoke in the offices, and all employees were required to change from their uniforms to street clothes when they left the labs.[63] Although Weirick's original job title at Sears was "Textile Chemist," she was one of the first members of the AHEA's Home Economics in Business Section and maintained her loyalty to the group throughout her tenure at Sears, frequently arguing to her employer that home economists could "act as interpreters between the distributor and the consumer." In addition, Weirick forged ties with textile specialist Ruth O'Brien at the Bureau of Home Economics, providing collegial support to her efforts to establish standard sizes for women's and children's garments.[64]

The labs at Sears provided factual and analytical information about the merchandise sold by the company, a goal tied to the overall corporate objective of increasing sales.[65] Laboratory workers performed tests to uphold the company's guarantee that its catalog contained honest descriptions of featured goods. In this way, they collectively functioned as a service bureau to Sears's Advertising and Purchasing Departments. By testing products under household conditions, the labs helped Sears select which merchandise to carry and made suggestions to manufacturers about how to improve their products. As the company expanded its merchandise lines and distribution channels, the labs assisted Sears's work with smaller producers. Supervising quality control of stock merchandise, writing instructions for care and use, and investigating customers' complaints were other responsibilities of the laboratories.

Following Mory's legacy, Weirick understood Sears's technical laboratories to be central to the company policy of science-based retail service to consumers. Speaking to a joint meeting of the American Chemical Society and the American Institute of Chemical Engineers in 1932, she pointed to the "clever manufacturing processes" that scientists and engineers had developed to disguise inferior production methods, and she claimed that "the only way [for a retail buyer] to know merchandise accurately and to protect his customers is by having it analyzed or tested in his laboratories or by having its manufacture supervised by his own scientists." Weirick argued that the laboratories' service to Sears's buyers was "most valuable" during the Depression, when competition was most keen, and when manufacturers, retailers, and advertisers tended to cut corners and lower quality standards. By determining the utility, safety, and overall quality of new products through both "practical" and "scientific" tests, the laboratories helped buyers decide whether to accept, reject, or advocate improvements to products ranging from wire fences to automobile tires to lubricating oils.[66]

Textiles and apparel represented 35 to 40 percent of Sears's business by the early 1930s, and Weirick's expertise in textile chemistry suited the company's goal of maintaining a reputation for reliable merchandise in these categories. Because prices for raw silk imported from Japan dropped with the onset of the Depression, standards for silk grading lowered along with the price of silk hosiery. To allow Sears to control its standards of quality for this product, an entire department analyzed the yarns, fabrics, and stitching of hosiery samples. Other textile-related tasks in the Sears laboratories, performed by home economists as well as other scientists and engineers, included inspecting sheeting to see that it met specifications for Sears's labeled brands; assisting manufacturers with the development of preshrunk shirting and denim fabrics; identifying fibers in all fabrics, brushes, and furs; and analyzing the chemical content of fabrics, weightings, and sizings.[67]

In addition, at least one home economist with a master's degree in physics worked in the Electrical and Mechanical Division, testing household appliances and "criticizing them from a housewife's point of view." As Weirick explained, "Engineers are likely to miss some important features they have never had occasion to use." By the early 1930s, percolators, waffle irons, toasters, flat irons, ranges, and heating pads were among the long list of electrical goods this division inspected for construction and operating efficiency on a regular basis. When tests on a range of coffee percolators demonstrated that metal percolators made bitter-tasting coffee, buyers tried substituting glass and pottery types and teaching consumers about the advantages of these materials. Laboratory staff likewise studied the heat distribution and temperature maintenance of electric irons, the construction of electric heating pads to guarantee safety, and the thermal efficiency and consistent performance of gas ranges.[68]

The laboratories were fundamental to Sears's strategy as a retail company to regulate itself in the face of government guidelines and the growing consumer movement. To support Sears's "truth in advertising" policy, laboratory staff read and checked proof sheets for all catalog copy, making sure that descriptions were accurate and complied with Federal Trade Commission regulations. Reviewing the work of advertising copywriters and retail agents and urging them "to give more and more definite facts that will help the customer to evaluate merchandise" was, in Weirick's words, "no small task."[69] In related efforts, the laboratories advised on the consumer education campaigns Sears initiated in the 1920s and expanded in the early 1930s. Beginning in 1924, Weirick assisted the company's new Home Advisory Division in the development of the company radio station WLS and presented some of its early programs on the *Woman's Hour*. After 1931, in response to President Herbert Hoover's 1931 Conference on Home Building and Home Ownership, when the company launched the Educational Division and hired home economist Leone Anne Heuer to direct it, Weirick collaborated with her on a number of "better buy-manship" programs. Enlisting home economists to develop consumer education programs was one way that many manufacturing and retail firms sought to foster public goodwill—and even co-opt the more radical fringes of the consumer movement—in the face of critiques from Frederick J. Schlink at Consumers' Research and other reformers in the 1930s.[70]

Together, Weirick and Heuer launched new initiatives that brought the testing laboratories' principles to the consuming public, and they invited consumers themselves to become technical evaluators of product quality. The Sears Clinic of Household Science opened in late 1932 at Sears's large State Street store with an enthusiastic speech by Mary King Sherman, chair of the American Home Department of the General Federation of Women's Clubs. Intended as a "purely educational" venture to "aid in intelligent buying," the facility featured changing exhibits of household articles along with laboratory test findings to teach consumers how to shop by comparison. The clinic was staffed with home economics students who gave visitors midafternoon lectures on how to determine the quality of merchandise, as well as ongoing demonstrations in areas such as cooking, home finance, interior decoration, styling, and child welfare. Women's clubs, study groups, church organizations, and school home economics classes frequently visited the clinic. Backed significantly by the Sears testing laboratories, the clinic's activities and displays were designed to encourage buying according to the rational principles home economists had advocated since the turn of the century.

To broaden the audience for this message, Heuer's division developed additional traveling exhibits throughout the early 1930s. Weirick worked with her on many of these, as well as on Sears's *Consumers' Shopping Guide* (1936), which encouraged women consumers to make quality comparisons of fabric and clothing based on scientific investigation. This "tabloid laboratory and library" was tailored to allow homemakers to inspect fabric and clothing closely and systematically on their own. The guide consisted of a box file kit containing forty cards mounted with different fabric samples, a magnifying glass, and a *Handbook of Facts*. Each card included information about a particular fabric's special characteristics. The magnifying glass allowed consumers to examine quality variations among the fabrics. The handbook provided general information about textile production and care as well as the selection of ready-made clothing. Sears sold the kit for one dollar to teachers, extension workers, and individual homemakers.[71]

Weirick's leadership of the labs was dependent on specific relationships with male superiors in Sears's corporate hierarchy. Although she had a great deal of support from Mory and other managers such as Donald Nelson, other male managers were less comfortable with her prominent role. Eventually, these men forced her to retire early. Virginia Pearson recalled that T. V. Houser, who took over as vice president in charge of merchandising in 1939, "did not like the idea of a woman being in charge of the laboratory." Houser appointed a male assistant for Weirick and charged him with reporting on the laboratories' management. Less than a year later Weirick, then in her late fifties, left the company.[72]

Despite this unfortunate ending, Weirick's tenure at the testing labs included diverse activities held together by an ethic of objective, scientific knowledge and training to promote the welfare of both the retailer and its customers. Weirick's 1936 policy statement specified that the laboratories' purpose was to generate "scientific information concerning merchandise or scientific facts." It promised "independent, unbiased results, free from prejudiced influence of any department or person."[73] Success in the retail business depended on effective correlation of the supply and demand for goods, and at Sears the testing laboratories operated as a mechanism for the firm's ongoing internal adjustment. Critic F. J. Schlink at Consumers' Research dismissed Sears's laboratories as a "kind of window dressing, . . . a form of pseudo-sincerity, designed to disarm the consumer's normal and critical doubting attitude," and the efforts certainly had a public relations value in addition to a technical one.[74] But both the promotional and technical dimensions of the labs' operations were important parts of doing business for the mail-order firm since their creation in 1911, and the two aspects became increasingly intertwined by the early 1930s. In the meantime, Weirick and her labs established a precedent for other retailers and offered a model for women's magazine editors to emulate as they, too, developed testing facilities to evaluate the expanding range of consumer goods that the market afforded.[75]

Good Housekeeping Institute

"The magazines are fast becoming scientific research stations," reported home economist Marie Sellers in 1927.[76] The 1920s saw the explosion of "bureaus" or "institutes" at women's magazines and newspapers, in which many home economists found employment testing household products. The Priscilla Proving Plant at *Modern Priscilla*, the New York Tribune Institute, and the Delineator Home Institute were among the testing bureaus allied to commercial publications and the companies that advertised in them. Home economists in these testing bureaus had a great deal more visibility among American home-makers than did those who worked in laboratories run by manufacturers and retailers. All of these "household experiment stations" were modeled on the Good Housekeeping Institute (GHI), which began operating at the turn of the century as a confidential testing lab for merchandise advertised in *Good House-keeping* magazine and for other goods that manufacturers submitted in hopes of receiving its highly sought "Seal of Approval."[77] In the interwar period, as *Good Housekeeping*'s circulation doubled from 1 to 2 million and became the nation's most popular monthly, the institute became an especially important feature of the publication.[78]

The founders of *Good Housekeeping*'s "Experiment Station," as the institute was first named, intended to serve readers by recommending, in the tradition of nineteenth-century domestic advisers, efficient methods of household management. Named to trade on the official status of government-sponsored centers for agricultural research, the scientific laboratory supported the magazine's fact-finding approach to creating editorial content, a feature of many Progressive Era endeavors. The lab began with investigations of various labor-saving devices, and by 1902 the Household Engineering Department was testing products and providing instruction to readers about the use of a wide range of household equipment advertised in the magazine. *Good Housekeeping* established a policy of selling advertising only to manufacturers whose specific product claims the magazine's lab could substantiate through its tests. On the basis of this "ironclad contract," *Good Housekeeping* guaranteed the reliability of all goods advertised in its pages and promised to reimburse dissatisfied consumers. By 1905, in response to the pure-food movement, the publication's Department of Food and Cookery issued its "Roll of Honor for Pure Food Products."[79]

Magazine publishers had long relied on well-known domestic advisers to write and edit their copy, but in the early twentieth century they turned to a new generation of university-trained home economists to enhance the scientific authority and credibility of their publications. Reflecting the growing importance of home economics in the eyes of magazine publishers, *Good Housekeeping* publisher Richard H. Waldo renamed the laboratory the Good Housekeeping Institute in 1909 and hired home economist Helen Louise Johnson to direct the expansion of its testing operations. A graduate of Sarah Tyson Rorer's Philadelphia Cooking School, Johnson had edited Rorer's *Table Talk* magazines and participated in the Lake Placid conferences that launched the home economics movement. After receiving a B.S. from Teachers College in 1904, she taught at the University of Illinois, James Milliken University, and

Rhode Island State Agricultural College before heading the institute. Under Johnson, the institute began performing tests to generate the magazine's list of "Tested and Approved" products and to help inform editorial content. Johnson remained at the GHI until 1911, when William Randolph Hearst purchased the publication, moved its headquarters to New York City, and brought William Frederick Bigelow on board to raise the magazine's profile. Ethel Rose Peyser and Cecelia K. Bradt each directed the GHI for brief periods, but in the early 1910s the institute took a back seat to the more newsworthy arrival at the magazine of famed health and pure-food crusader Harvey Wiley.[80]

Bigelow invited Wiley, formerly of the Bureau of Chemistry at the U.S. Department of Agriculture, to found a Bureau of Foods, Sanitation, and Health at *Good Housekeeping*. Wiley's presence on the staff from 1912 until his death in 1930 increased the visibility and the scientific credibility of both the magazine and the institute. In this lab, Wiley created the Good Housekeeping Seal of Approval for foods, drugs, and cosmetics. Once a manufacturer demonstrated that a product was nationally distributed and, therefore, available to all *Good Housekeeping* readers, Wiley tested it at no cost. He analyzed the content and checked it against claims made on its package and labels. Wiley's lab then put food products up to a "performance" test for satisfactory taste. The manufacturer was allowed to use the seal for two years after signing a contract promising to maintain the quality as tested.[81]

The institute did not achieve a profile to rival Wiley's "bureau" until Bigelow hired Katharine Fisher to lead it in 1924. Like her predecessors, Fisher was a prominent home economist, but her university teaching position and background made her a member of a newer generation of women in the field. Born in Canada, Fisher directed the School of Household Science at McGill University in Montreal before moving to the United States in 1917. Three years later she earned a master's degree from Teachers College, where she taught for a few years prior to joining the GHI. Fisher used her ties to university home economics programs, magazines, businesses, and government agencies to position the institute's technocratic program for product evaluation at the center of a system for the production and marketing of household goods, a system aimed directly at the middle-class American homemakers who made up the readership of *Good Housekeeping*. Staff members tested the performance of hundreds of machines and devices, ranging from washing machines and dishwashers to egg beaters and can openers. At one time in the early 1920s, the laboratories stocked as many as 200 products waiting to be tested. Under Fisher's guidance, the institute expanded rapidly and moved into new and larger quarters in the Hearst International Magazine building in 1928.[82] In this period, the GHI became a major source of information about manufactured household goods for American homemakers and an important vehicle for manufacturers—many of whom sought ways to honor truth-in-advertising standards established in the Progressive Era—to demonstrate that they were committed to product quality and customer satisfaction. In addition, the GHI emerged as an important platform from which home economists represented homemakers' needs to manufacturers and influenced product development. Under Fisher's direction until 1953, the institute drew on home economists' science of consumption to provide legitimacy to a wide array of new household products and to a middle-class consumer culture guided by women experts.

In the institute's technical work, home economists' expertise constituted one-half of a two-tiered system. Evaluation of the quality of workmanship and the efficiency of gas and electrical appliances fell "within the province of the engineers," the men in the GHI's engineering and research laboratory. Special equipment enabled engineers to take apart a spectrum of devices and study their inner workings. "Every gear, lever, bearing—in fact, each part, is carefully examined so that we may determine if it is designed and constructed to insure service," a 1923 brochure claimed. In addition, men used electrical instruments to measure both alternating and direct electrical current at a range of voltages found in American households, and meters to determine flow of water, air, and gas.[83] To supplement the work of male engineers, home economists evaluated products in practical settings intended to replicate life in "typical" American households. According to the GHI's official literature, home economists represented the woman's point of view by testing products as they would be used in the home "*by women*." To test mechanical refrigerators in the late 1920s, male engineers measured the efficiency of these large consumer durables, while home economists conducted an "operating test," which assessed the refrigerators' "ease of cleaning, suitability of rack spacing, and general serviceability." After about two months of "daily use," home economists recorded temperatures, changes in the finish, and other signs of wear. The GHI's promotional material emphasized the systematic nature of all these tests, which determined whether a manufacturer's claims were either proved or disproved.[84]

Officially organized to verify manufacturers' advertising claims, these tests also allowed the GHI and its staff of home economists to interpret "the needs of the housekeeper" to manufacturers. Staff home economists, a 1923 pamphlet explained, "have studied the problems of the manufacturer and are in a position to tell him what women want and need." Said the brochure: "This unusual perspective which the Institute has gained in the household appliance field makes it possible to offer definite constructive criticism on a manufacturer's appliance that often puts him on the right track in the development of his machine." Disapproval reports contained suggestions for "constructive changes." Fisher claimed the tests enabled home economists at the GHI to make recommendations to manufacturers "who are coming to us in increasing numbers for advice and counsel in developing new equipment, or in improving their present models." When staff members discovered that a gas oven failed to reach the temperature of 550 degrees Fahrenheit when the regulator was at that setting, the institute did not grant approval to the manufacturer, but "after the results of our tests were discussed with the manufacturer he re-designed the oven burner so as to give it greater heating capacity." In a retest, the oven temperature reached that of the regulator setting and institute staff approved it "in view of the fact that the range was well made and satisfactory in all other respects." Likewise, the Cookery Department boasted close cooperation with food manufacturers and their advertising agencies, claiming that staff members assisted firms "in perfecting new products and working out directions for the use of these before they attempt to market them."[85]

The political economy of the 1920s set the stage for the GHI to maintain that it promoted the overall improvement of household goods to the advantage of both discerning consumers and well-intentioned producers. "Good Housekeeping firmly believes," a 1923 publicity piece read, "that the manufacturer desires to produce the kinds of products that housewives are anxious to buy." In cases of consumer dissatisfaction, the GHI channeled complaints to the manufacturer. If the manufacturer refused to "meet his obligation to the consumer," the magazine guaranteed a refund. Although it insisted complaints were rare, institute publicity concluded that the "result is wholesome. The manufacturer is given an opportunity to demonstrate his interest in the user of his machine. The housewife, in response receives a distinct impression of service. Something of mutual benefit to both purchaser and manufacturer is gained through the increasing vigilance of Good Housekeeping Institute." By positioning themselves as objective arbiters in the marketplace, Fisher and her colleagues used science to normalize cooperative relationships among producers, magazine publishers, and consumers. "Our testing service is an entirely unbiased one," claimed one brochure.[86]

In spite of the GHI's official rhetoric, however, its operation offered more benefit and more access to information to manufacturers and advertisers than to consumers. The Seal of Approval allowed manufacturers to claim that the products they made were generally of high quality, although GHI staff tested goods only for specific features claimed in the advertisements. The tests were free of charge to manufacturers, who received the added benefit of knowing that the GHI would not share consumer complaints with other consumers.[87] Aside from the magazine's list of "tested and approved" products, most of the GHI's operations were shrouded in secrecy. Unlike many of the studies conducted by Consumers' Research, which emerged with a more specific criteria-oriented approach in the late 1920s, the GHI's tests provided few opportunities for consumers to compare products.[88] The institute had no objective criteria for evaluating products or stipulating ideal product features but rather relied on subjective standards to react to producers, rating appliances according to whether they were "the best the market affords." Although the home economists, engineers, and other experts at the GHI were paid by advertising dollars, they expected the buying public to trust the criteria they selected and the testing processes they employed, and to accept the results of its tests. Staff members received a regular stream of letters from consumers, but they had no systematic means of determining what consumers actually thought about the products they tested.[89] The Good Housekeeping Institute's credibility was publicly thrown into doubt in 1939, when an investigation by the Federal Trade Commission found that its claims were exaggerated and fraudulent. Only a small percentage of the products advertised were actually tested, and the Hearst company management admitted that 40 percent of its tests were in error. After a prolonged battle between the magazine publisher and consumer activists, the GHI was forced to change its testing and accountability procedures.[90] Even with these challenges, the Good Housekeeping Institute, like similar institutions affiliated with many other women's magazines, continued to draw on home economists' female identity to claim that it represented consumers' needs and to rely on the scientific authority of the laboratory to mute distinctions between sales and service for manufacturers and consumers alike.

Conclusion

By the late 1930s, home economists had acquired a legitimate yet contested place in a great number of major consumer products firms, retail organizations, and women's magazines. By testing products behind the scenes in laboratories, suggesting ways to improve those products, and providing homemakers with instructions about how to use them, women such as Eleanor Ahern, Elizabeth Weirick, and Katharine Fisher occupied central places in the complex networks among producers, distributors, and the mass media. In this capacity, they facilitated the buying and selling of a whole new array of products. Whether labeled "science" or "sales" or "publicity," home economists' work became part of doing business, part of the technical and cultural work of making a product and marketing it successfully. In their jobs as food specialists, recipe writers, textile scientists, or product testers, home economists helped to establish and maintain a set of technological and cultural systems geared not only to producing consumer goods but also to conveying their significance to American homemakers in terms of middle-class values. The knowledge, ideology, and aspirations of home economists became part of the package.

Convincing employers of the value of their contributions remained an ongoing project for home economists employed in business. Support for home economics inside the firm was always contingent on business cycles and trends pursued by male managers. Initially, managers did not expect that hiring home economists would directly increase sales. For the most part these managers heeded Winifred Gibbs's 1926 warning: "All that can be looked for is an indirect effect and that only after a year or more of effort. It is seldom that any direct and immediately traceable results flow from the endeavors of the home economics woman. To any business sincerely interested in this subject I would say: 'Do not expect any immediate sales result.'"[91] While many firms found that the activities of their home economics departments helped move their products or improve relations with customers, especially in the expanding consumer marketplace of the 1920s, company managers did little to measure home economists' contributions in hard figures.

The fate of corporate home economics departments varied with the onset of the Great Depression. Some manufacturers, retailers, and magazines expanded these operations or related "institutes" as a part of more aggressive marketing campaigns or, in the case of Sears, to help them confront the growing consumer movement. But many large corporations reduced their expenditures on home economics during this same period.[92] As the HEIB Section launched initiatives to encourage firms to hire its members, home economists in corporate positions looked for ways to make themselves indispensable and to articulate their worth and accomplishments to male supervisors. In the mid-1930s, when hundreds of home economists held jobs in business, one woman claimed that many businessmen "know little if anything of home economics—literally, they don't know what it is supposed to be or do."[93] A home economics director remarked that her male colleagues still did not approve of women's presence in the firm. "However well a man may like women as women," she said, "I never knew one who did not prefer infinitely to work with men in business hours. They admit the value of women in this type of work but they are fundamentally opposed to women in an office." When women were tolerated, it was due not to their "sex appeal" but to their "business usefulness." The writer felt obliged to let men take credit for her ideas "in order to get them over." When home economists persuaded company managers to adopt their suggestions, they tended to accept that "the main object must be to put [their ideas] to work and to find satisfaction in seeing them succeed, even if they are changed beyond recognition."[94]

Like that of all corporate employees, male or female, business home economists' professional status depended entirely on the operation and priorities of the larger enterprise. As women who spent most of their time dealing with women, however, home economists were particularly vulnerable to changes wrought by the business cycle. At first, because home economists in corporations did not replace or compete with men, they did not confront the same difficulties as women professionals in such fields as medicine and law. Like female nurses, social workers, and child welfare workers, business home economists pursued a strategy to establish an area of female expertise within a male domain. While this strategy provided home economists with an important influence over product development and marketing, it also relegated the women to marginal positions within the firm. Because their authority derived from establishing connections between divisions more than from a specific responsibility allied to a male profession, their translating contribution often remained hidden from upper management. Unlike company product managers who could take credit for the success of the product they were in charge of promoting, the "product" of home economists' work was harder to discern. "Is there any way in which we can show more definite results," asked Cora Irene Leiby, a home economist with the W. W. Gossard Company, a Chicago advertising firm, summarizing a chronic problem, "or does the value of this work rest in its very intangibility?"[95] The "very intangibility" of home economists' activities in consumer products firms proved a constant challenge for home economists as they worked to maintain a clear domain of expertise inside the firm. At the same time, the continuing contradictions between the promotional messages that business home economists delivered from inside large corporations and their colleagues' classroom teachings about rational consumption sent confused messages about home economists' identity to consumers.

6

From Service to Sales: Utility Home
Service Departments, 1920–1940

In 1917 the Public Service Electric and Gas Company of New Jersey hired Ada Bessie Swann to develop an ambitious program to educate homemakers about the benefits of gas and electricity. In less than a decade, Swann—playing a dramatic translating role between utility companies and consumers—transformed a set of simple cooking demonstrations into a full-blown "home service department" offering instruction in all aspects of modern housekeeping. Aimed primarily at adult homemakers who did not have the opportunity to learn home economics in high school or college, Swann's program covered topics ranging from cooking and canning to laundry, lighting, and cleaning. Lecture demonstrations in department stores and before organized women's groups, classes at the utility company facilities, and calls to customers' homes were among the many ways that her team of home service agents communicated directly with homemakers. In addition, through radio programs and individual correspondence, Swann established the New Jersey utility company as a constant presence in its community of power customers. By the early 1930s, she assembled a large staff of hundreds of home economists who together ensured regular contact with homemakers—including a radio audience of 18,000—throughout an extensive metropolitan area centered in Newark.[1] While Swann's operation was extraordinary in scope, her leading role in the Electrical Women's Round Table, an organization of women employed in the electrical industry founded in 1923, and in planning utility home economics departments nationwide gave her considerable influence in the two decades before she became director of the Home Service Center at *Woman's Home Companion*. Furthermore, her activities typify the work of college graduates in home economics who found jobs in gas and electric utility companies in the interwar period, a population that constituted a growing proportion of home economists working in business. In 1940, the gas and electrical industries each employed more than 1,500 home economists in 650 home service departments.[2]

While manufacturers and retailers of packaged food, clothing, and house-hold equipment employed home economists in a range of capacities be-tween product development and promotion, utility companies brought home economists into their operations primarily to demonstrate new technologies powered by electricity and gas, and to encourage women consumers to buy products that used these new sources of energy. This difference stemmed from a set of business conditions unique to the power and light industries in the interwar period. First, managers of electric power and light systems under-stood as early as the 1890s that balancing energy load through domestic con-sumption was critical to the success of central generating systems.[3] Although gas industry managers did not face the same load issues as did their counter-parts in electricity, they confronted analogous pressures to align consumption with massive investments to build an infrastructure for delivering power to industrial and residential users. In the 1920s, as utility companies sought to en-large the market for power and light to include the homes of a growing middle class in their networks, they hired home economists to help establish and re-inforce the idea that gas and electricity were fundamental to a whole range of household tasks, ensuring that consumers made regular use of the new sys-tems. Second, utilities relied on home economists to assist with massive pro-grams of self-regulation and public relations. During the 1920s and 1930s, pri-vate utility companies faced charges by reformers who argued that the rates of profit-making utilities were too high and that these companies lacked con-cern for their customers' interests. To challenge the critiques of David Lilien-thal, Morris Cooke, and other reformers who called for the public ownership of utilities, private electric utility owners and managers waged an aggressive, multipronged campaign to convince the American public of the superiority of private ownership in the power industry. Through the National Electric Light Association (NELA, renamed the Edison Electric Institute after 1933), private power companies launched one of the most ambitious and elaborate public relations campaigns of the period after World War I.[4] In this context, NELA, as well as trade associations in the gas and ice industries, embraced "home ser-vice" as a way to help construct and uphold positive identities for their member firms among customers and potential customers. Thus, at the same time that food manufacturers shifted from demonstrations to radio, print advertising, and written correspondence as ways to reach homemakers, utility companies moved in the other direction, supplementing advertising with significant in-vestment in live, personal interaction with the public.

In the years after World War I, as gas and electrical service became avail-able in most American cities and small towns, homemakers faced a series of

Demonstration of electric stoves, Electric Institute of Washington, D.C.,
Potomac Electric Power Company building, late 1930s. (Library of Congress, Prints
and Photographs Division, Theodor Horydczak Collection, LC-H814-T-1979-052)

choices about how to live with these new power systems and the domestic appliances they made possible. Dreams of an "all-electric kitchen" had been promoted since the 1893 Chicago World's Fair, but it was not until the early 1920s, more than two decades later, that the electrification of the domestic market took off in earnest. By the end of that decade, most homes were wired, used electric lighting, and contained at least a few small appliances. Many families still did their cooking on wood and coal stoves, but by 1930 gas cooking emerged as the prevailing cooking method in American households. Throughout the interwar period, as electrical and gas companies expanded their systems they competed vigorously with one another to displace older methods of cooking. With electrical service available in 79 percent of homes by 1940, increasing numbers of homemakers had a choice between the two power sources. The transition toward adopting gas and electricity for cooking and heating was neither automatic nor uniform, varying by region, city, and even neighborhood. As consumers became connected to these new systems, many were still afraid of the dangers of electricity and had to decide for which household tasks they would use new appliances based on these new power sources.[5] Families and homemakers faced decisions such as which power source to use for a specific purpose, which fixtures or appliances to buy, and how to make the transition to a new way of performing traditional household tasks. For many middle-class urban homemakers, gas and electricity held promise of saving labor in a servantless household or allowing for a higher standard of living. For those women eager to embrace the promise of gas or electric systems, a new cooking range, heating system, or refrigerator constituted a significant investment both in money and in the time needed to sort out an increasing array of bewildering choices. Particularly in the kitchen, appliances based on gas or electricity also meant major changes in how tasks related to cooking and storing food were accomplished. The generation of women who experienced the introduction of these new systems in their communities and their homes had few cultural reference points for making these decisions and little technical know-how for incorporating the new sources of power and light into their lives.

For gas and electric company managers working to expand their systems in most North American cities, homemakers' lack of familiarity with—and to some extent resistance to—the new power sources constituted what one electrical merchandiser called a "social problem" in the way of creating a domestic market for their services.[6] As manufacturers launched ambitious design innovations and advertising campaigns, they found that these strategies alone could not convince homemakers to embrace an overwhelming array of new products.[7] To help control and direct the demand for power and manage consumers' expectations in a marketplace where buying and selling appliances was not a straightforward matter of a simple cash transaction, male utility executives enlisted home economists such as Ada Bessie Swann. By separating home service departments from direct sales responsibility, utility company managers and home economists created a system of complimentary labor between the work of women and men managing service and sales, respectively. The name *Home Service Department*, rather than *Home Economics Department*, reflected the intentions of utility companies (now presenting themselves as "public service corporations") to rely on home economists for assistance in emphasizing company commitment to the good of consumers over profit-seeking motives. The utilities' rhetoric of "service" appealed to the Progressive Era sensibilities of many home economists, who approached utility work as an opportunity to enhance the efficiency of household consumption and American living standards.[8] By working to project a human, "caring" dimension for utility companies, they allied with male utility company managers to build institutional networks that bound utilities, women's clubs, universities, and the wider community of home economists to one another. It took the economic crisis of the early 1930s to challenge and upset this balance, transforming the role of utility home economists into one more clearly defined as sales than education. Debates about this shift, and home economists' resistance to it, call attention to the multiple dimensions of the work they performed in ushering in these new technological systems.

Home economists' central presence in utility companies in the interwar period established them as key players in the complex world of power and appliance retail merchandising.[9] As utility company home service agents, they became such ubiquitous public figures in urban and small-town communities that they provided the first introduction to gas and electricity for most homemakers. Through demonstrations initially of gas and electrical cookery and later of electric home lighting and laundry, home economists performed an important educational role in interpreting the new power sources for American consumers. From inside utility companies, home economists helped spread a technical as well as a cultural understanding of the new power sources and their potential use in the home. Home economists' ability and willingness to deploy their personalities as well as their technical knowledge of domestic goods and homemaking made them important "servants of power" for utility companies, especially influential in creating and shaping a place for gas and electricity in twentieth-century American domestic life.[10]

Women in the Electrical Business

Prior to 1920, electrical appliances were used by only the wealthiest members of urban communities served by relatively small power grids. Potential customers lived in urban areas, where lighting was first introduced in public buildings and private homes. The expense and novelty of the new power sources placed the appliances they fueled in a luxury market. Electricity tended to be perceived as expensive and dangerous and used only by elite, scientifically minded persons. As power companies expanded their distribution networks after 1900, they sought to establish these new power sources as accessible to more than just the wealthiest Americans. Utility companies supplemented printed newspaper advertising with sizeable sales forces and a broad array of what historian Mark Rose calls "agents of diffusion" to promote the use of gas and electricity through a series of house-to-house promotions, demonstrations, and cooking schools.[11] Early home economists and other women were important members of this contingent, serving as "home service agents" who in the first two decades of the twentieth century pioneered utility-sponsored cooking demonstrations to convince homemakers to adopt gas stoves. Employment opportunities for women in utilities expanded during World War I, when many salesmen were drafted into the armed services. But utility home service was still relatively "new and untried enough to make a big splash," according to one observer.[12]

Following World War I, home economists became part of a bolder, more deliberate corporate strategy to sell power and light to middle-class American homemakers. As the electrical industry continued to expand and joined the ranks of the nation's most capital-intensive big businesses, corporate giants General Electric and Westinghouse channeled resources into extensive research and marketing organizations that enabled them to maintain monopolistic control of the industry.[13] Local divisions of these utility giants emerged as leading retailers of electrical appliances by the mid-1920s, establishing entire home service departments to cultivate and maintain a female clientele for gas and electricity. The merchandising of electrical goods shifted among a diverse array of retail settings (including small specialty shops, hardware stores, furniture stores, and drugstores) with department stores eventually emerging as the source for the majority of electrical merchandising in large urban areas by the late 1930s. Antitrust legislation during the New Deal limited direct appliance sales by utilities, but utilities continued to rely on home service to stimulate the sale of electrical goods, enhancing demand for power from their expanding systems.[14]

Utility investment in home economics in the early 1920s reflected a consensus within the industry that fitting electricity to the home required fitting women to the electrical business. A close look at the electrical industry's discussions about selling appliances in the interwar period illuminates the gendered terms with which electrical merchandisers expressed their business challenges and shows why home economists' training and status as professional women ideally qualified them for a set of overlapping responsibilities being defined by industry leaders. In the pages of *Electrical Merchandising*, a trade journal devoted to marketing electricity and electrical appliances, utility managers, local storeowners, and appliance manufacturers articulated the problem of creating and controlling domestic demand for power. Although this trade journal reveals more about the ideal that electrical dealers and utility company managers were striving for than it does about the reality of their experiences, it nonetheless contains clues about how concepts of gender informed their assumptions about consumers, their efforts to expand the domestic market for power, and their ideas about how women and home economists could fit into the larger retail landscape.[15] The case of the electrical industry further demonstrates how, by hiring home economists on a systematic basis, utility company managers sought to achieve three interrelated goals: to demonstrate how gas and electric appliances worked in practical terms, to increase demand for these products among women consumers, and to create a positive public image for the industry.

As electrical dealers shifted their marketing focus away from novelty and toward more practical benefits of new appliances, instructing consumers about how to use and maintain electrical appliances became a major priority after World War I. Promotional photographs featuring images of women in kitchen settings using the new electrical gadgets replaced earlier depictions of the products in abstraction, while advertisements emphasized the laborsaving qualities of appliances.[16] Selling through demonstrations not only increased initial sales but also ensured that appliances would remain in use. Proper instruction could eliminate costly problems of servicing and repairs for dealers, who typically offered free repairs within an initial one-year guarantee period.[17] *Electrical Merchandising* editor Frank Rae Jr. described the dangerous misuse of appliances that could occur when their correct operation and care was not fully explained:

> Some women who buy electric cleaners are not even told that it is necessary to empty the dust bag; few are given any idea as to when, how or with what an appliance should be oiled. Because of sketchy, slovenly salesmanship, too many clothes are put into a washing machine and too many fed into the wringer. Flatirons are set into a pan of water to cool because the salesman didn't do his job right; washing machine connector cords are allowed to be scuffed about on concrete cellar floors or to lie in the wet; half a dozen appliances are tapped on a single circuit with consequences ruinous to fuses, and women expect dishwashers not only to clean off, but to consume and wholly obliterate all table scraps, including meat bones.[18]

As merchandisers worked to manage consumers' expectations of these new technologies, they came to agree that selling "rightly and completely" required teaching a customer how to use a product. Demonstrating became a central part of the merchandising process and, by the early 1920s, customers would typically encounter a demonstration when they went to the utility company to pay their light bills.[19]

Increased attention to "the wants of the customer" paralleled the electrical industry's emphasis on demonstration, but merchandisers expressed confusion about the gender identity of this customer, whom one commentator described in 1917 as "the least understood man in the electrical business." Strongly suspecting that the consumer was not a man at all, electrical merchandisers shared with other manufacturers and retailers in the domestic products industries the assumption that the consumer was a woman and that the consumer's "language" was a woman's language.[20] Influenced by the era's oft-touted truism that women purchased about 85 percent of American household products, merchandisers grasped after "the women's viewpoint." While this statistic may have been accurate for many other household purchases, it did not necessarily apply to higher-priced electrical appliances during this era. One observer estimated in 1920 that women, shopping on their own, bought only 10 percent of electrical goods. The other 90 percent of purchases were made by "husbands and wives together or by men alone."[21] Electrical merchandisers lacked a clear consensus about how to increase the proportion of women customers for their goods. They debated such questions as whether a major appliance purchase usually required the approval of the woman's husband and whether homemakers appreciated door-to-door salesmen. But, perceiving middle-class women as the gateway to a larger place for electricity in the home, the community of male dealers developed a series of strategies to cultivate a female clientele.

To make their shops attractive to women buyers, electrical specialty shop managers sought to add a "feminine touch" to their otherwise utilitarian supply outlets. Accustomed to selling electrical hardware such as sockets, wiring, and plugs, the electrical contractor-dealer or specialty shop manager normally had a no-nonsense approach to decor and store arrangement. Many stores, outfitted primarily for repair and technical service, displayed electrical goods in a state of disarray and discouraged customers from browsing. For assistance, many other electrical specialty shop managers turned to their wives or to local women's organizations in their communities. When Jack Carrigan organized a temporary model electrical home exhibit for Westinghouse in Boston in 1923, he enlisted members of women's clubs to help him make it attractive to potential women customers. "After the men had finished assembling the mere house and electrical equipment," he explained, "it was the women who added the touches that really made it attractive. Looking back, we all now agree that before the women took hold, we merely had an electrical *house*. It was they who converted it into a *home*." F. M. Mosley made a similar attempt to domesticate his Montgomery, Alabama, store, locating it in a residential district to establish it as "a neighborhood affair where women would drop in as casually as they do in a drugstore" and naming it "Electrabode."[22]

The overall effect in many shops was to foster a welcoming ambiance that made women customers feel comfortable, much as they did in the lounges and reading rooms in department stores where they could relax and socialize during a day of shopping. Locating this lounge space so close to the merchandise itself, however, marked a departure from the department store and its explicit compartmentalization and specialization of space according to function. Dealers placed plants and wicker furniture in the new electrical shops to create a charming atmosphere free of hard selling and to demonstrate how to establish a place in the domestic environment for new, technical equipment that seemed to belong to a more male-centered domain. In particular, these shops geared themselves toward middle-class women rather than the narrower luxury market targeted in the industry's earliest retailing efforts.[23]

By the early 1920s, as demonstrations became standard to sales strategies and informal, women-friendly sales environments became more common, merchandisers found that model or demonstration electric homes offered pressure-free settings for exposing women to new products in a flexible, inviting manner. But such homes required a certain amount of explanation, dealers thought. A 1922 *Electrical Merchandising* article explained that a demonstration home, which received 1,000 visitors per day, "cannot be left to shift for itself under such circumstances. It must be explained and interpreted, so that the whole story will not only be well told, but told completely to each individual who passes through this demonstration house." As demonstration houses became standard to the industry, managers relied increasingly on women to serve as "hostesses" and to interpret the contents of these "Homes Electric" to potential consumers in a personal way, creating narratives that placed new products and services in familiar contexts.[24]

Face-to-face interaction—especially with women—allowed merchandisers to push the sale of electric ranges while also fostering positive public relations. As increasing numbers of homes became wired with electricity in the 1920s and electric ranges became more affordable for middle-class families, electrical industry managers adopted cooking demonstrations to compete with the gas industry, which had successfully used cooking instruction to win consumers in the previous decade. To persuade homemakers of the advantages of switching from wood or coal to electricity rather than gas, demonstrators of electric ranges not only explained the technical workings of the new machines but also provided guidance in a whole new way of cooking. Showing how to use an electric range required not only knowing how to take advantage of temperature controls that the range featured but also a degree of diplomacy and ability to empathize with potential buyers who did not always have a reason to value the new products over their older ways of doing things. "The tactful salesman-demonstrator will do his instructing by leading her to draw her own conclusions, rather than by forcing ready-made ideas upon her," advised one commentator.[25] Electric ranges were expensive to purchase and operate, and sales remained slow throughout the 1920s. "Electric range cooking is slowly but surely winning its way in the favor of housewives," one industry commentator reported in 1923, "but it is undeniably true that much still remains to be done in *teaching* them this new method of cookery."[26] While some individuals recommended that appliance salesman keep up-to-date with methods of housework by reading women's magazines, company managers viewed instruction in "electric cookery" as women's work.[27] To local dealers, who assumed that women held important insight into sensitive matters of customer relations, women also seemed naturally suited to projecting a human, friendly image of a business enterprise. The Spurr electrical jobbing house in Paterson, New Jersey, for example, initiated an "investment in good-will" in 1919 when it hired four women to serve as "missionaries" and "business developers."[28]

By the mid-1920s, the importance of women in the electrical industry was clear. "Once upon a time the electrical field was looked upon as man's peculiar province," noted an *Electrical Merchandising* editorial. Since then, "a few women did find a loophole that could be widened into an unlimited circle. From a few pioneers the number of women now engaged in the electrical industry has grown unbelievably."[29] Electrical merchandisers moved from informally seeking advice from their wives and members of local women's clubs on an ad hoc basis to making women a permanent part of the business. Dealers hired middle-class women to assist in window displays, store arrangements, and sales techniques. Increasing numbers of women managed and owned their own shops. Women assumed a range of duties in the electrical industry, including demonstration, sales, and advising on the choice and design of retail sites. *Electrical Merchandising* enlisted Florence Clauss to report routinely on the industry from a woman's viewpoint. A few individuals, such as Sarah Sheridan, vice president and sales manager at Detroit Edison, and Clara Zillessen, advertising manager at the Philadelphia Electric Company, even obtained high-level executive positions.[30] Carving out niches for women in the industry was closely intertwined with the industry's efforts to cultivate a female clientele, and to establish women's identity as consumers of electrical goods (and vice versa). By 1924, one trade journal editorial estimated that women were the primary decision makers for 50 percent of appliance purchases (up from 10 percent in 1920), further encouraging the industry to press on toward the 85 percent believed to be the general percentage of household purchases controlled by women.[31]

Ongoing efforts to enlist women in the project of selling electrical appliances to women gave home economists in particular an expanding array of employment opportunities in the power industry. As a group, home economists seemed best able to meet the needs of electrical merchandisers to demonstrate appliances and appeal to women consumers while also promoting positive public relations. With a home economist, "you have more than a simple sales clerk," explained dealer W. A. Bayard. "You have someone who has been trained not only to understand and talk about modern cooking methods, but sweeping, washing, ventilation and sanitation as well, and she will have dabbled a bit into the chemistry and physics of the household." In addition, as a woman, she can explain appliances "in women's words."[32] Home economists filled a need in the electrical business at this moment in time because they were able and willing to draw on their expertise in domestic matters, their feminine identity, and—perhaps most important—their faith that new electrical ranges and other appliances represented both technological and social progress to convince homemakers to buy these goods while simultaneously fostering an image of industry goodwill.[33] Utility companies across the country aggressively invested in the creation of home service departments, relying on home economists to pioneer a new form of customer service work. By 1926, one insider declared: "That home service work among electrical consumers is a vital factor in promoting the use of more electricity in the home and that it is one of the best-known methods of achieving ideal public relations, has all been admitted long ago. . . . In fact, almost all companies are seeking to work with their consumers in home-service work of some kind—whether on a large or small scale."[34] Numbers rose from only 16 home service departments in utility companies in the United States and Canada in 1923 to 240 companies in the two countries with such departments by 1928.[35]

The rapid establishment and growth of utility home service programs was due in large part to the purposeful efforts of the leading trade associations in both the electrical and the gas industries. Facing public outcries of overcapitalization, rate-fixing, and calls for municipal ownership in the early 1920s, the National Electric Light Association organized a public relations initiative and designated women as key players in its strategy. Under the leadership of Chicago utility magnate Martin Insull, NELA began by setting up a speakers' bureau and put the new Women's Public Information Committee in charge of an educational program to teach women employees "the fundamental principles of the electric light and power business and the interdependence of the public and the industry." With this move, Insull recognized that the industry already had a large proportion of women employed as office clerks, stenographers, telephone operators, and stock "salesmen" and that these women often were a company's front line of contact with consumers. Although many of the women remained on staff for only a short while, Insull foresaw that if they left their jobs to become homemakers they would still be consumers of domestic electrical goods. At the same time, Insull and other industry executives understood women (who had just won the vote) as a growing and important political force. Believing that women had natural abilities to disseminate information (especially to other women) with exceptional "patience, tact, and courtesy," industry leaders recruited a leading cohort of women to spread the gospel of private power to women workers with the expectation that they, in turn, would speak positively about the company to customers and potential customers. The Women's Public Information Committee organized lectures and published informational booklets aimed at "selling" women employees of private utilities on the industry's perspective regarding the political economy of power distribution. Topics included explanations of rate structures, how to read a meter and a bill, and how the utility business operated. This committee's work functioned as a feminized public relations avenue running parallel to male-oriented industrial public relations that emphasized government and labor relations. The committee took on a number of other initiatives with the aim of organizing women in the industry to promote appliance and power sales to women consumers.[36] Ada Bessie Swann of the Public Service Electric and Gas Company of New Jersey and Jessie McQueen, who joined the American Gas Association (AGA) in 1929—two younger members of the Home Economics in Business Section of the American Home Economics Association—emerged as outspoken leaders within NELA and the AGA, respectively. The two women spearheaded the establishment and growth of utility home service departments, working together to coordinate the first National Home Service Conference in Chicago cosponsored by the Home Service Committees of the AGA and NELA in 1930.[37] This conference culminated in the publication of a thirty-five-page manual that outlined standard goals and techniques for operating home service departments in electric utilities throughout the country. NELA's *Home Service* outlined the purpose of home service departments in utility company management and provided guidelines for their operation. The manual, as well as a similar one published by the AGA, also provided explicit instructions for designing facilities for public outreach, as well as sample programs and presentations for specific types of audiences.[38]

Home economists and other women serving on the trade association home service committees worked to forge ties with universities, women's clubs, women's magazines, food companies, and government agencies. NELA established a partnership with Mary Sherman, president of the General Federation of Women's Clubs, to conduct a survey of the use of electrical appliances in American homes.[39] Swann and others created an institutional network for recruiting graduates of college home economics programs and training them to be representatives in utility home service programs. They served as liaisons to university home economics professors and worked with them to develop courses about new household appliances, drawing on the technical education programs that a number of women had established on the campuses of the nation's home economics colleges. One important player in this effort was Eloise Davison, who pioneered one of the earliest courses on household equipment in 1923 while a graduate student at Iowa State. By 1927, Davison had become an associate professor of home economics at Iowa State, and her household equipment course was required of all 1,200 sophomore home economics students. Her research on the comparative study of electrical equipment—and her determination not to let new household devices "become a major menace instead of a boon"—led to the creation of "a laboratory of household engineering, a laboratory that would be devoted to finding out how to use newly-invented mechanical devices in order to simplify women's household tasks."[40] Davison's course and laboratory—one of the most "electrically equipped" in the country—attracted the attention of NELA, which hired her in 1927 to initiate a free week-long course on electrical equipment for women interested in utility company employment. The course drew 100 women's magazine editors, home economics instructors, women's club leaders, and utility home economists from fifteen states. The success of this course led NELA to hire Davison as a "home economics advisor" to its New York office.[41] In this capacity, Davison helped to inaugurate similar NELA-sponsored short courses in home service and equipment studies at Teachers College as well as other universities around the country. In 1935, she moved on to become head home economist at the Tennessee Valley Authority's Electric Home and Farm Authority, continuing her electrical education program on behalf of government-sponsored electrification.[42]

While preparing women to work in home service, these types of courses reinforced the identity of Davison and other home economists as experts in the use of electricity in the home. At the same time, collaboration between utility companies, universities, and extension agencies facilitated the integration of home service demonstration repertoires into college curricula, exposing increasing numbers of students to the perspective of utilities and encouraging them to seek employment in utility home service after graduation. As many home service directors lectured at colleges and assisted home economics departments with planning their laboratories, these courses did much over time to collapse the boundaries between education and utility home service work for professors and students.[43]

In less than a decade, home service departments became the basis of utility companies' relationship with their domestic consumers. Trade association activities solidified the broad commitment of the gas and electrical industries to a community service program based on home economics teachings. "Whether or not a home service department should be installed is no longer the question among central station executives," noted *Electrical Merchandising*'s Florence Clauss in 1930. "The present problem, if a problem exists, is that of providing still larger quarters for a rapidly growing home service department." Although home economists continued to cultivate more "active support" for home service programs, at least one utility company executive reported: "Should we be obliged to cut down company expenses at any time, the home service department would be the last to feel the pruning knife."[44] Having carved out a place for their profession within utility company operations, home economists were positioned to play a dynamic translating role between company managers and their expanding clientele. Home economists drew on their female gender identity to help foster positive social relations between power companies and their local communities, while at the same time using their technical expertise to interpret both the operational features of domestic appliances and a cultural framework for these goods in the lives of American homemakers.

Blending Company and Community

Initially, home service departments focused primarily on education and public relations rather than sales. As new roles for home economists inside utility companies proliferated in the 1920s, members of the profession became part of a gendered division of labor in which women gave instruction about appliances while men sold them. By no means natural, this division of labor reflected late-nineteenth-century notions of men's and women's separate spheres and represented utility company managers' attempts to replicate boundaries between public and private, market and home, within the framework of gas and electrical merchandising operations. Teaching had long been established as an acceptable activity for women, and the focus of home economists' work on "educational selling" made sense in the utility industry. For home economists, not dirtying their hands or corrupting themselves through over-the-counter exchanges of money provided an important context for understanding utility work as an extension of their reform mission. As home service representatives who instructed, advised, and even cultivated prospective buyers but refrained from "closing a sale," home economists work in utilities reinforced stereotypical images of women as clean, moral, and respectable, providing support to a male culture of salesmanship that had been in the making since the late nineteenth century.[45] Although home economists did a great deal to help train dealers, they rarely received commissions in addition to their salaries. By drawing a line at the actual point of sale, managers reinforced the cash nexus as a male domain, preserving sales as a male activity rewarded for competition and aggressiveness. Such a structure also justified paying home economists lower wages than salesmen. As in the industrial workforce, where male managers segregated men's and women's work based on the sexual stereotyping of jobs to preserve male autonomy and authority, utility company home economists worked alongside salesmen on a separate and unequal basis that also mirrored the division of labor between married men and women characteristically established at home.[46]

NELA's 1930 home service manual codified this division of labor just as it codified other aspects of home service program operations. Although the manual called for more efficient and streamlined home service programs, it nonetheless stressed the importance of the "human element" and generally described home service work as distinct from, but complementary to, sales. Similarly, in her speeches to new home service representatives and utility company managers, Ada Bessie Swann promoted home service departments on the basis of both sales and service: "It is seldom that ideals and commercialism are seen as harmonious teammates in the performance of any job, but home service in a utility, rightly administered, effects this happy fusion. The returns which follow the activities of a well administered department are both moral and material." With these words, Swann finessed what was in reality an ambiguous relationship between sales and service in utility home service work.[47]

As cornerstones of this "happy fusion," home service departments facilitated a division of labor in which men and women were in charge of the hard and the soft sell, respectively. A general educational briefing by a home economist often preceded more direct sales pitches from door-to-door salesmen. "Home service takes hold before advertising and merchandising begin," one woman in the industry explained, "and it's right there to continue functioning after they stop. Home Service tills the field for appliance sales because it reaches the older women who don't read advertising and the younger women who don't believe all they read. Home Service is a *service*. . . . It goes the salesman one better because it is not primarily interested in individual sales, and so increases customer-confidence."[48] Home service classes or "parties" created a comforting cushion around male sales campaigns by introducing women to appliances in a pressure-free context. These demonstrations paved the way for visits from door-to-door salesmen and often helped close a "doubtful" sale afterward.[49] Home service representatives typically accompanied salesmen to a home when a major new appliance such as a refrigerator, a washer, or a range was installed to give an initial demonstration of its maximum possible efficiency. Home service agents also paid "courtesy calls" to new residents and visited homemakers in the event of a complaint. When sales and service men had difficulty getting customers to talk openly about problems they had with new equipment, they often found that homemakers felt more comfortable talking "frankly" with members of their own sex. Claiming that a home economist had the capacity for "trouble shooting" and for "soothing over distraught feelings" experienced by dissatisfied customers, one commentator called her the "the Dorothy Dix of the appliance business," likening her to the twentieth-century advice columnist.[50]

While many home economists served as confidential advisers to individual homemakers, they also performed as "hostesses" at public events, couching instruction in a warm, welcoming context. "The work of a home service department is 'mass' education to create a greater demand for a product, so subtly done that it creates 'mass' friendship along with the demand," one utility executive explained.[51] Utility home economists gave lectures and demonstrations at the invitation of church groups or women's clubs and also held forth to high school and college classes and extension meetings. In effect, many home service departments formed "clubs" around their operations. This practice formalized the more casual alliances dealers had forged with local women's clubs in earlier decades. The Dallas Power and Light Company extended a free membership in the Dallas Electrical Arts Club to all of its customers. Regular classes on weekday afternoons and a weekly radio program offered lectures on subjects ranging from scientific cooking, budgeting, child feeding, interior decoration, and party ideas. At no cost, various groups could reserve demonstration halls, equipped with all-electric kitchens, for bridge parties, dinners, teas, and club meetings. The Tampa Electric Company provided similar services at its Leisure House, an electric model kitchen and party room, and declared it the "headquarters for the modern women of the Company's territory."[52] By drawing on home economists' identities as participants in women's culture to help fashion the utility company as a community center, home service programs extended the presence of private firms into local social structures, in some cases serving as the basis for forming new groups around domestic topics.

Finessing consumer relations in utilities demanded the emotional, interpersonal labor of surrounding new products and services with an atmosphere of friendliness. Home economists in utilities pioneered an early form of "personality work" or "emotional labor" that historians and sociologists associate with late-twentieth-century service industries. Like the jobs later performed by female airline flight attendants, home service work in utilities required interacting with consumers in a way that involved channeling emotional energy into making the company appear human and responsive to their needs. The language of "hostesses" and "parties" used by utility home economists presaged the central place these terms would have in post–World War II marketing strategies for such products as Tupperware.[53] Business home economists, as I have noted in previous chapters, developed a professional identity compatible with the new culture of "personality" that emerged in the early twentieth century. As relations between large corporations and "great masses" replaced face-to-face relations between individuals, the culture of "personality" put a premium on a definition of the self that stressed performance and presentation.[54] While male leaders in the gas and electrical industries pointed to public relations as an important component of their business, utility home economists carried the burden of projecting a feminized version of the ideal for service-oriented corporations.[55]

Home service personality work helped utilities creatively blur the line between company and community. The home service representative, explained Swann, was "a friend to everyone."[56] The example of the Peoples Gas, Light, and Coke Company of Chicago illustrates how utility home economists blended traditional social activities and modes of women's culture with corporate operations to provide a form of community outreach that simultaneously enhanced customers' understanding of gas appliances and fostered loyalty to the company among the city's homemakers.

When Peoples Gas launched its Home Service Department in 1922, the house organ explained the company president's intentions to promote public relations by offering the women of the city "a service that will make housework easier, show them how to feed their families for less money and tickle 'hubby's' palate so that he will never be late for dinner. Yes, all this without a cent of charge."[57] To direct the program, Peoples hired Anna J. Peterson, an experienced homemaker, mother, and commercial home economist already well known in the city. Born in New England as Anna Josephine Murphy, Peterson was the oldest of nine children and had helped manage a household since the age of seventeen. After marrying, she studied with Fannie Farmer at the Boston Cooking School. As a member of the early generation of home economists, Peterson first taught in the public schools and, after divorcing, worked to support her children for more than a decade in the commercial field. She conducted food demonstrations for the Corn Products Refining Company for almost ten years and developed recipes for the Rumford Baking Powder Company for a short time. The *Peoples Gas Club News* described Peterson as "a woman who needs no introduction to the housewives of Chicago, since for many years she has been giving lectures and demonstrations before clubs and groups of women all over Chicago." In addition to touting her experience as a homemaker and home economics instructor, the company organ cast Peterson as a warm and caring maternal figure with a warm personality suited to providing friendly advice. "She's just the sort of woman you'd like to have as a neighbor," the company announced, "and she's here to be a good neighbor to all the women of Chicago." The company publication further invited homemakers to "ask Mrs. Peterson" about "all sorts of housekeeping and housekeeping problems." Until her retirement in 1936, Peterson oversaw the growth and development of the Home Service Department at Peoples Gas in which an expanding cadre of home service agents facilitated regular contact with consumers throughout the Chicago metropolitan area.[58]

As in most home service departments, Peterson's operation concentrated on cooking. She and her team gave lessons in two rooms located in the basement of the company's downtown headquarters. Like many utility companies in the 1920s, Peoples Gas hired prominent domestic adviser Christine Frederick to consult on the design of the department, an operation that consisted of an efficiency kitchen for lectures and demonstrations, a model home laundry, and a dining room for displaying "the latest ideas in table decoration and entertaining." In a separate room "furnished in restful grays," women could sit and rest, read, or write while waiting for a lecture to begin.[59]

Peterson's department aimed its programs at a broad cross-section of women customers in the greater metropolitan area, including ethnic, working-class, and middle-class white Anglo-Saxon women. Her team began its work by offering a short Better Home cooking class for the more than 500 women employees of Peoples Gas. About 250 of them expressed interest in a weekly course taught for an hour and a half after work on Thursday evenings. Six lessons were offered: Bread and Sandwiches, Meats and Vegetables, Cakes and Cookies, Pies, Salads, and Desserts. After this initial educational project, Peterson's team offered similar classes for the city's homemakers, including a complete twelve-part cooking course on Tuesdays and regular classes in canning, which culminated in a canning exhibit and competition each summer. For children, the Home Service Department offered Saturday morning courses in candy making.[60]

Radio broadcasts emerged early on as an integral part of a wider campaign that the Peoples Gas Home Service Department presented to its public. Using the new communication medium of radio, home economists' programs extended corporate messages into domestic spaces, paralleling the way live demonstrations brought community groups into direct contact with the corporation. Historian Susan Smulyan has written that radio broadcasting, like the instructional formats that home economists were already developing, "allowed advertisers to sell and at the same time present their product in a warm and friendly atmosphere; radio provided the private experience of public messages." Peoples Gas began its radio program in December 1922 as a daily fifteen-minute spot at 11:30 in the morning on KYW. Soon Peterson began offering a twelve-lesson cooking class on the air, a program that drew about 1,000 registered listeners. Women who sent in written reports on at least nine of the twelve lessons earned certificates and were invited to have them presented in person at a radio tea. More than one-third of those registered—416 of 1,136—received certificates at the end of this first radio cooking class. Two hundred and eighty-eight lived in Chicago; 128 resided outside the city, mostly in the suburbs but some in Indiana, Michigan, Wisconsin, and Iowa.[61] Peterson and her assistants rapidly expanded the Home Service Department's radio programming to embrace a larger and broader audience. Ruth Chambers began broadcasting for Peoples Gas at ten in the morning daily on WBCN, complementing Peterson's later morning show, and on KYW at nine o'clock Wednesday evenings; Vivette Gorman launched an additional home service talk "for women busy during the day and the girls who are employed." Peterson added a *Woman's Hour* program every Friday afternoon on KYW from four to five o'clock. In 1925 Nena Badenoch offered enrollment in a Radio Home Service Club for Girls and Boys once a week on summer weekday mornings and enrolled 660 children. For individuals not able to listen at these times, Peoples arranged to have these radio programs printed in the local newspapers.[62]

Along with regular newsletters and phone campaigns, the radio programs' success in stimulating the interest of growing numbers of individuals led the Home Service Department to expand its main demonstration hall at the downtown headquarters on Michigan Avenue and to open branch locations throughout the city. "Radio parties" drew whole families of listeners to visit the company for live lectures and demonstrations, but the main auditorium's initial capacity of 500 could not accommodate the crowds. "Within a month eager housewives were sitting on the stairs," wrote one historian of the company. An estimated 1,500 women showed up for a cake-frosting demonstration by cake specialist Helen P. Farquhar. Within a year, Peoples Gas enlarged

The Peoples Gas building in Irving Park, pictured here in 1926, was one of several neighborhood branches constructed by the utility company in the 1920s. Most branches included lobbies to display appliances and large auditorium spaces to accommodate audiences attending the home service demonstrations conducted by Anna Peterson and her staff. (Peoples Gas, Light, and Coke Company Library)

this main auditorium to double its capacity for home service programs and to provide a "most attractive background for the lecture-demonstrations." Between 1923 and 1926, the utility built nine branches of its Peoples Gas Stores throughout the Chicago metropolitan area, allowing the gas utility to reach not only middle-class neighborhoods but also some of the industrial city's growing and diverse ethnic and working-class communities. The locations included the fashionable suburb of Irving Park on the northwest side but also West Town (an East European immigrant neighborhood), the commercial retail district of Englewood, and another shopping area in a growing German and Polish neighborhood along Commercial Avenue in South Chicago, as well as two communities on the South Side: Roseland (home to workers employed at the nearby Pullman railcar factory) and Cottage Grove (a relatively poor neighborhood south of the lakefront). Daily classes were offered at many of these branch stores, which were designed specifically for the purpose of presenting home service lectures and demonstrations. The Irving Park facility featured a ground-floor showroom and grand staircase leading to a large, high-ceilinged home service auditorium on the second floor.[63]

Additional home service initiatives and programs extended the reach of

*Peoples Gas deployed Kitchens on Wheels featuring home service
agents who provided free gas-cooking demonstrations throughout Chicago.
(Peoples Gas, Light, and Coke Company Library)*

Peoples Gas into an even wider range of Chicago neighborhoods. In specially equipped vehicles—Kitchens on Wheels—home service representatives took their act on the road to more remote ends of the metropolitan area. Advertisements trumpeted that these white-and-gold painted trucks, which visited parks, playgrounds, settlement houses, and other public places, were available to organized groups on request.[64] Women's clubs and church groups also invited Peterson's team to offer cooking classes for their members. The Home Service Department routinely sent recipe cards in gas bills to increase women's interest in cooking, and within two years it published *Simplified Cooking*, which provided "basic or standard" recipes for a wide range of dishes. Coauthored by Peterson and Nena Badenoch, the cookbook saw multiple editions and became a staple in Chicago households for several decades.[65] By 1926, Bernard J. Mullaney, vice president of Peoples Gas and a leader in the public relations campaign to promote private utilities, estimated that the Home Service Department had put the utility company in contact with more than 200,000 customers in the previous year by phone, mail, or demonstrations.[66]

Through this diverse array of communication modes, home service representatives at Peoples Gas fused instruction about gas cooking with friendly public relations. A woman employed in this capacity was expected not only to understand how to cook but also to have a pleasing and charming disposition. "The personality which you create is the amount of YOU which you give to the other fellow," explained Peterson in a lecture to her staff. "It is demonstrating yourself in an unselfish manner. It is giving service; giving of yourself." A woman with personality "puts herself into whatever she does"; a homemaker with personality "puts so much of herself into her home—so much personality—that [her husband] is always interested in getting home."[67] Peterson made it a point to publicly express her pride in "the lovely womanliness of my girls," who also incorporated "how to be a married woman" into home economists' lessons.[68] Entwined as it was with cooking instruction, home service representatives' personality work was a prime technique for making the acts of homemaking and patronizing Peoples Gas both seem like matters of civic duty. Speaking before a group of city businessmen in 1923, Peterson portrayed her department as integral to the economic and social well-being of the city and its residents: "Home Service means healthy, sturdy children, happy wives and mothers, and contented husbands and fathers. It means more money, more energy, more happiness for you and the families about you."[69] In the Peoples Gas and other utility company home service departments throughout the country, cooking demonstrations that merged presentation and personality with demonstration and instruction in modern techniques of food preparation became a standard strategy for blending company and community.[70]

Balancing Technics and Aesthetics

The dual identity of utility home service demonstrators as technical advisers and friendly neighbors allowed them to bridge and obscure another cultural dichotomy between the utilitarian and the aesthetic dimensions of gas and electric appliances. "They avoid approaching the situation from the expert angle," noted one electrical industry observer in the 1930s, "but come at it as one woman friend would talk with another in giving her a new receipt or a novel serving stunt."[71] Food preparation involved not only the practical know-how of appliance operation and nutrition but also taste and style in meal planning and presentation. As home service departments expanded the scope of their activities in the late 1920s, they drew on their experience with cooking lessons to develop instructional presentations that similarly merged the technical and the stylistic aspects of a wide range of household goods.

For home economists, utility company cooking lessons were not just promotional events but also opportunities for teaching and instruction. "Scientific cookery is not only possible but necessary with electric ranges," explained

Electrical Merchandising's Florence Clauss. By developing recipes that specified exact temperatures, utility home economists taught homemakers how to take advantage of new control mechanisms on gas and electric stoves. Utility cooking lessons made the latest ideas about nutrition integral to these new systems, reinforcing the larger messages about modern, healthy living that home economics educators promoted in schools and in the agricultural extension service. Home service demonstrators pointed out that the relative slowness of electric stoves in boiling water encouraged the more healthful practice of "waterless cookery," in which a minimum of water was used to steam vegetables in order to preserve vitamins.[72] At the same time, home economists highlighted the new opportunities for cake baking made possible by new oven temperature controls. Whether attracted to home economists' messages about nutrition, interested in learning how to bake attractive and tasty cakes, or simply curious about food preparation, homemakers were drawn by the thousands to these cooking demonstrations. A 1924 survey of electric company cooking schools on the West Coast found an especially strong interest in small town communities, where many reported that as much as one-tenth of a town's population attended such schools that year.[73] As Ruth Schwartz Cowan has argued, home economists' efforts to introduce science into housekeeping, raise standards of nutrition and cleanliness, and promote modern cooking methods had the cumulative effect of creating "more work for mother" in the twentieth century. The popularity of utility cooking demonstrations suggests that many American women warmed to home economists' instruction and, in the process, bought into their ideas about food preparation, even as these new methods also contributed to making housework more complex and time-consuming.[74]

By 1930, as the expansion of gas and electrical systems promised to change methods and standards of sanitation, health, and lighting in the home, utility companies broadened home service programs to include topics such as kitchen planning, laundry, and home lighting. While gas companies branched into heating systems and refrigeration, electric companies relied on home service departments to communicate the message of "all-electric living." Home economists were eager to move beyond "cookery problems" and to expand the scope of their offerings to parallel the range of topics in their field.[75] "Demands made on the company woman have grown so insistently that home service now includes everything from the handling of the family laundry to bringing up the baby," announced an *Electrical Merchandising* editorial in 1929. "Gradually, the home service woman has made of her department an educational institution for the women of the community, a housekeeping school and an advisory bureau to which the housewife can turn for guidance on any household problem."[76] Soon home service departments offered instruction in "correct and scientific laundry methods," including not only the operation of washing machines but also techniques for removing stains from various fabrics. They stressed the importance of weighing load volumes and identified criteria for sorting separate loads, "feeling" different temperatures, and selecting soaps.[77] Home service agents found their female clientele was less interested in laundry and textile-related educational programming, noting difficulty getting "them to attend laundering demonstrations in anywhere near the numbers turning out for food demonstrations." A 1931 survey of 360 homemakers attending home service classes in Brooklyn, New York, revealed that cooking was the most popular subject, with cleaning and laundering ranking second and third. Three hundred and twenty women expressed interest in "electrical cooking," 227 in "electrical house cleaning," but just half (180) showed interest in "washing problems." To overcome this relative lack of interest, many home service departments included a short presentation of laundry equipment during a cooking demonstration.[78]

Through all of these programs, utility company managers relied on home service agents to determine the appropriate amount and type of technical detail to suit the audience. As industry leaders worried about the characteristics of "the female consumer," they wondered how technically inclined she was. Some believed that reducing the amount of mechanical jargon was the way to keep women interested. They invoked the perspective of homemakers such as Dorothy Blake, who claimed to be attracted to the "charm and dignity" of electrical appliances first and foremost: "Without an electric toaster, [the homemaker] must leave the table, provided she has no maid, watch the toast in the kitchen range, and return to the table hot and flushed. Her mind is on the toast and not the guests. She can't possibly appear, as she would like to appear, calm and interested. But place her behind an electric toaster and the conversation goes smoothly on, while her charm as a hostess is increased a hundred times!"[79] To reach homemakers such as Blake, home economists were mindful not to become a "too-expert expert" who spoke more about "the miracles of the research laboratory" than those of the kitchen. "The housewife knows what a skillet is and what it is for, but a technical explanation of a calroid unit leaves her dazed—and unsold." Other industry members recognized that many homemakers wanted more access to the internal workings of appliances. "There actually are some women today who have a fair knowledge of mechanics and whose choice of an electric washer is based on something more than the color of the enameled finish," one editorial pointed out. "It's up to the salesmen to see that that kind of woman is supplied with the facts." Another dealer put it more succinctly: "The buyer is not dumb."[80]

Seeking to achieve the appropriate balance of discussion on technical detail versus practical function, utility home service departments directed many of their programs at homemakers who were, in the words of one woman, "interested in details of mechanism and like[d] to know, like their husbands and sons, 'how it works.'"[81] Convinced that a new generation of progressive women demanded higher standards of quality and specifics about the features of new products, home economists eagerly pitched their instruction to this critical clientele. Vera B. Ellwood, the home service director at the Milwaukee Electric Railway and Light Company, offered a course on the care and use of electrical equipment. Designed to help women think "concretely" about electricity and "to remove some of the mystery from it," the course taught women the basics of electricity as well as the construction, function, and repair of various appliances. Ellwood also covered such topics as how to read a meter, repair an iron, and replace a plug on a cord. Homework assignments required students to determine the numbers of amperes, volts, and watts used by the appliances they owned as well as to draw diagrams of the circuits and fuses in their homes. A lesson on the electric iron, Ellwood reported, had "one of the women go home and take apart three discarded irons which she had put into the attic, put them together again, and find that all three were perfectly good irons with only minor adjustments necessary." Programs such as Ellwood's suggest that home economists working in utilities provided technical education for homemakers who were interested in learning basic information about the operation of household appliances.[82]

The example of electric lighting demonstrates how utility company home economists helped negotiate the conflicting meanings of a particular product, and, in the process, defined ideals of middle-class consumption. From the beginning, the electrical industry emphasized both the technical merits and aesthetic qualities of this new source of lighting but continued to oscillate between these two marketing perspectives well into the twentieth century. In the decades before World War I, General Electric's advertising downplayed the technical aspects of the company's Mazda lamps by portraying them as luxurious and magical. By 1920, industry promotions stressed the laborsaving aspects of electric lights. But selling lighting on the basis of work reduction had its limitations. It required electric dealers to stock and sell lighting fixtures, which had been understood as decorative items long before the era of electricity. In the early 1920s many merchandisers of electrical goods found this meant discussing aesthetic details with which they were either unfamiliar or uncomfortable. They believed that, in the words of one dealer, "a woman buys a lamp more for its decorative than for its utilitarian value. . . . And she reasons about it even less than a man would. The difference is that her feeling and sense of harmony are more highly developed both because of her experience in handling fabrics and because she usually has done the actual furnishing and decorating of a home." Assuming women consumers possessed an inherent and exclusive ability to discern "graceful forms" and "good workmanship," salesmen felt particularly at a loss in the area of lampshades. "It's when she comes to consider the shades for her lamps and fixtures that the lighting salesman stands helpless," explained one salesman.[83]

Home service representatives such as Helen A. Smith at the Rochester Gas and Electric Corporation rescued salesmen from this kind of predicament by providing advice about the decorative as well as the technical aspects of lighting. Among the most technically trained home service directors in the country and the first woman to receive a B.S. in electrical engineering from the University of Michigan, Smith joined Rochester Gas and Electric in 1920 soon after graduation and a brief stint designing electric lamps for an electrical equipment manufacturer. Her earliest title at the utility was "illuminating engineer," and, for reasons that are unclear, she became the company's home service director by 1927. Most likely she found, like many scientific women of her day, that heading a home service department was the most effective strategy for career advancement. Smith's technical background was an asset on the job, and certainly helped establish her expertise with male colleagues. "Just the mere fact that I have an engineering degree counts, I think," she wrote, "as much with the men I meet in business as does the work that I do—at least it is a good introduction." Smith drew on her experience to establish a department that taught the utility's customers "that there is something about lighting other than buying the fixtures and turning on the current," helping clients develop illumination plans that included wiring, fixtures, and lamps.[84]

Although the utility did not sell fixtures, the Rochester Gas and Electric Home Service Department devoted much attention to heightening consumers' interest in products with decorative elements. Smith herself designed a living room fixture for local dealers to sell. Under her guidance, the department also took advantage of popular interest in paper and parchment lampshades and offered classes in lampshade making. First offered as a free service in 1927, these sessions grew so rapidly that the utility, in an effort to make them self-supporting, charged students for instruction and materials, a cost comparable to that of a hand-painted, imported silk shade readily available at Sears. Two years later, the utility added a Saturday morning class for children. Lamp customers were

Nineteen home-lighting specialists, working for the Dallas Power & Light Company, prepare to make house calls to instruct customers in properly lighting their homes as part of a Better Light for Better Sight campaign, 1936. (Electrical Merchandising)

motivated by varying degrees of interest in style, taste, pleasure, and economy, forcing utility home economists to be sensitive to the diverse ways Americans experienced the era's burgeoning culture of consumption. For, even as home economists promoted a consumer culture centered on new, mass-produced domestic goods, they also tapped into aspects of that culture that valued the handcrafted and homemade.[85]

In home service departments like Smith's at Rochester Gas and Electric, home economists also helped launch campaigns based on the technical merits of electricity. While the lampshade classes were based on the assumption that "interest in lighting must be created through the appeal of beauty," a Better Light–Better Sight campaign in the early 1930s attempted to avoid style discussions altogether.[86] After all, even the lampshade, which became the principal means of distinguishing domestic lighting from that in public spaces, had a distinct utilitarian function: to diffuse the brightness of electric light.[87] This campaign promoted "The New Science of Seeing," which stemmed from work begun in 1930 by Matthew Luckiesh and Frank Moss at General Electric's Lighting Research Laboratory. During the 1920s, illumination engineers had begun to direct their investigations, originally aimed at promoting industrial efficiency and controlling lighting conditions in large outdoor spaces, toward problems of domestic lighting. These leaders in the industry established lighting "institutes" to teach home service representatives, other home economists, and homemakers about the solutions they found for manipulating the quantity, quality, deflection, diffusion, and distribution of light in the home. Lucki-

*A home-lighting specialist teaches a homemaker how to measure the light provided by the fixtures in her living room and to determine whether it is sufficient for healthy eyesight, 1933. (*Electrical Merchandising*)*

esh and Moss provided these institutes with a focus when they established "artificial sunlight" as the standard for proper and healthy vision. In connecting lighting with vision, the two engineers sought to make seeing easier by reducing glare and reflection and, most important, increasing the intensity of illumination. After engineers at Weston developed the "sightmeter," a device that made Luckiesh's concepts measurable and demonstrable, the industry kicked off its Better Light–Better Sight campaign based around a sentiment best expressed by one sales manager that "artificial lighting is now in competition with daylight, [and] it is no longer in competition with darkness." [88]

In the campaign to sell "seeing instead of fixtures," teams of home lighting specialists interpreted this new definition of light for American homemakers. Equipped with a sightmeter and an array of lamps, shades, reflectors, and extension cords, the lighting adviser compared the amount of light used for seeing in daylight with that usually used in the consumer's artificial light. Focusing on improving the lighting conditions of living rooms and children's study areas, the adviser would then recommend changes in lamp wattage, arrangement of portable lamps, and the addition of new fixtures to help the homemaker "protect the eyesight of her family." In Utica, New York, a campaign of this type added an average of 220 watts and eight dollars of merchandise to each home visited.[89]

Like the home economists' demonstrations of electric cookery, the Better Light–Better Sight campaigns equated motherhood with science even as home lighting advisers also explained the new lamps in terms of interior decorating principles.[90] Likewise, in their interpretations of other electrical appliances, such as washing machines, vacuum cleaners, and refrigerators, home economists mixed product technicality with middle-class values of health, efficiency, sanitation, and taste. Whether focused on practical or aesthetic issues, utility company home economists used their authority as experts to construct an ideal consumer, defining her as a woman who promoted her family's standard of living on the basis of these values. This modern homemaker was not only receptive to but also savvy about new domestic technologies. She cooked "scientifically" with gas or electricity, maintained a budget, knew how to remove stains, protected the well-being of her family members, presented attractive meals, and entertained with personal flair. For women who attended home service demonstrations in the 1920s and 1930s, these lessons about how to be a modern, middle-class homemaker and consumer were embedded in instruction about gas and electricity. Home economists' key place in the expanding gas and electricity networks made utility work one of the most influential arenas for women in the field. In the process, utility home economists contributed to changing expectations about housework that continued to keep many women busy cooking and cleaning in spite of the widespread adoption of "labor-saving devices."

Service versus Sales

The establishment and growth of home service departments within central station utility operations in the 1920s was based on a common understanding among utility company managers and home economists about how sales and service complemented one another. Different companies arranged the division of labor in different ways, but by 1930, industry members had agreed on some basic guidelines. "At present the consensus of opinion is that the home service woman should do all she possibly can to promote the sale of any piece of equipment but that the actual closing of the sale be turned over to the sales department," Florence Clauss reported, adding that most electrical industry leaders opposed paying commissions to home service representatives.[91]

Yet in this same 1930 issue of *Electrical Merchandising*, an editorial advocated "a more definite tie-up between the home service and sales organizations within the industry."[92] Indeed, just as the place for home economists in utilities became clearly defined and standardized, structural change in the gas and electrical industries in the 1930s led utility company managers to reconfigure the parameters of their work. Domestic appliances, as opposed to heavy industrial goods, constituted a growing proportion of overall sales in the electrical industry, and price competition for these goods was fierce. In response, industry leaders pursued more aggressive sales and marketing strategies that included streamlining industrial design, planned obsolescence, and dramatic displays at world's fairs and other public events. In the refrigerator market, whereas old-line producers such as General Electric had promoted these large appliances as specialty goods, new manufacturers such as Sears and Norge used mass-market techniques to gain market share in the early 1930s. With the rise of mechanical refrigeration, leaders in the ice industry faced similar pressure to attend to the bottom line in all of their activities.[93]

In the wake of these transformations, conflicts brewed as early as 1928 over the extent to which home economists should be involved with the "commercial" side of the business. Within the National Electric Light Association's Home Service Subcommittee, a "public relations" contingent argued that goodwill was the primary purpose of home service departments; "commercial" people, in contrast, maintained that home service was "a sales activity, no matter how its functions [are] disguised." While one woman who favored home service as public relations pointed out that her staff was "purposely uninformed" about prices so as to guarantee the educational content of its demonstrations, a "commercial" woman made the case that she could serve customers best by helping with actual sales transactions. Subcommittee chair Ada Bessie Swann argued that the line between the two kinds of activities was too fine to be drawn. Although the distinction between sales and service was important to home economists, where the line fell had never been clear, and it became even more muddied in the late 1920s and early 1930s. Although in the past "many Home Service Departments have been quite divorced from Sales Departments," one woman in the field reported in 1930, "the closer connection between these two has become quite evident." In utility companies where home service and sales were more closely intertwined, some home economists demonstrated on sales floors, while others worked as saleswomen once a week.[94]

Economic crisis further fueled the controversy over how much to commercialize home service. By 1931, contingents of utility home economists involved with "public relations" versus "sales" were at loggerheads. More than ever before, the Depression put pressure on home economists to justify the worth of the home service departments in measurable economic terms. Prior to the 1929 stock market crash, utilities had been content to assume that the investment in home economics paid for itself. After the downturn, some companies cut back on home service, considering it nonessential. By the late 1930s, many power companies, such as the Central Hudson Gas and Electric Corporation in New York State, decided to discontinue their home economics activities altogether.[95]

Most power companies, however, maintained or augmented their home service departments but realigned them more closely with sales. Efforts to measure the dollars-and-cents value of home service became commonplace. At the Georgia Power Company in Atlanta, Home Service Director Fern Snyder demonstrated that her staff of fifty-five women had increased annual power consumption by 5 million kilowatt-hours in a six-month period in late 1934. A commercial manager of the Idaho Power Company estimated that home service was worth the expense. At a cost of $40,000, his staff of twenty-two home economists called on 18,000 different customers in a year, resulting in an average increase of four kilowatt hours per month in each home. He credited home service representatives with demonstrations to 16,000 customers, sales of $36,000 worth of lamps and small appliances, and various "intangible accomplishments," emphasizing that these responsibilities were "not, however, the major purpose of their work." The message "Home service pays!" replaced an earlier broader notion of service that had allowed utilities and home economists room to conduct their mutual endeavors with different, but overlapping, assumptions and goals.[96]

Home service representatives in the gas and ice industries experienced a similar shift toward increased sales roles by the mid-1930s. Reporting for the gas industry in 1938, Jessie McQueen noted that more companies were opening home service departments than closing them, but that a sales orientation had overcome the service orientation of these departments. "Home service work, particularly in the last three years," McQueen explained, "has become very sales slanted—not selling on the dotted line, but giving information that will lead to more sales. We entitle it 'Subtle Selling.'" In the ice industry, the National Association of Ice Industries hired Eleanor Howe as a consultant to replace permanent employees Mary Pennington and Margaret Kingsley in the middle of the decade. Whereas Pennington and Kingsley had been charged with "educational selling," Howe promised to recruit home service workers "who can really go out and sell our product to Mrs. Consumer."[97]

This shift to a narrower sales function came slowly and with resistance from many home economists. Despite the exigencies of the 1930s, some held out against becoming mere saleswomen. Ada Bessie Swann continued to argue that home service increased consumption of gas and electricity, but that these results could not be measured. Criticizing those who, like Swann, were reluctant to embrace the profit-making aspects of home service, Valentine Thorson, director of home service for the Northern States Power Company, urged her colleagues in 1936 to "come off the pedestal" and do more to sell small appliances.[98]

Echoing Thorson, other home economists willingly embraced the sales imperative and argued that it represented a new professional standard. The home service director of a New York gas company expressed her frustration with home economists' resistance to sales when she responded anonymously to a survey in 1935. "Utilities are past the stage of vague general good will campaigns," she explained. "Many companies in the past have spent too much public money on free entertainment for the idle, putting on shows and overplaying the service angle." Despite the rapprochement of manufacturers and educators during this period, the home service director blamed university home economics departments for not going far enough to prepare students for the business world. She found students too academic, too technically trained, and, she implied, too suspicious of sales: "In utilities work we could do with less of the technical home economics training if we could get more of the professional idea across—that promotion is necessary education of the general public in the use of available civilized equipment. The fact that it sells—is not a sin, any more than health education is a sin because it sells antiseptics, soap, toothbrushes etc. Instructors need to recognize promotion as a legitimate field of work and prepare students for it in a spirit of realism." To "develop the practical sales mind" in home economics students and graduates, this home service director advocated training them to write recipes and cookbooks in a clear, direct manner "without resorting to new fangled and fancy, expensive dishes." Utility home service work "absolutely requires professional-minded applicants," she said, "not the academic-minded student type the colleges are turning out almost without exception."[99] Her juxtaposition of "professional" versus "academic" home economists signaled not only that business employers valued home economists' promotional assistance more than their technical skills, but also that university home economics programs resisted commercial culture to a great degree as late as the mid-1930s. Throughout the decade, however, increasing numbers of utility home economists came to define "professional" in terms of merging ethical standards with sales goals, rather than upholding the one against the other. These disputes about the proper scope of home service work suggest that the newer, sales-oriented identity formed slowly. Rather than molding themselves automatically to corporate goals, home economists continued to contend with differing aims almost two decades after their initial entry into the business world.

Nevertheless, by 1940, the circumstances and content of utility home service work had clearly changed. The public relations and educational aspects of home service were still important, but the sales dimension dominated. Beatrice C. Jackson expressed the significance of this shift in a 1941 letter to Flora Rose, director of the College of Home Economics at Cornell University. Having worked at Brooklyn Edison Company since her graduation from Cornell in 1929, Jackson wrote for advice from the college's Placement Bureau about making a career change. "We had a change of organization some four years ago and as time goes on our work becomes less and less of Home Economics and more and more of selling and so I feel I would do better elsewhere." She reported that Florence Freer, Brooklyn Edison's former home service director, had left the utility to manage an inn in Connecticut. "I mention Florence so that you can see that I am not the only one, who had found conditions, for a home economics person, so disagreeable."[100]

Utilities maintained home service departments long after they aligned home economists' work more deliberately and directly with sales. By 1940, within the Home Economics in Business Section of the AHEA, utility home economists comprised a growing proportion and formed the second-largest group—106 or 17 percent—of business home economists. Representing a younger generation of business home economists who did not graduate from college until after World War I, they tended to be trained in more practical ways to serve utilities and other business operations on new, more sales-oriented terms. These changes in utility work had implications for business home economists more generally. The professional ideals of service, education, and interpretation that had preoccupied their predecessors continued to influence younger home economists' ideas about their work. But because their college coursework and on-the-job training was increasingly geared toward the newer emphasis on sales, they gradually embraced standards of professionalism that were more closely allied to business goals of profit and promotion.

Conclusion

In the end, like all corporate employees, home economists served the interests of business more than their own reform causes. Through their demonstrations, radio programs, and college courses, utility home economists contributed to the enormous public relations campaigns of NELA and the AGA, and to the efforts of gas and electric companies to sell power even in the Depression, when home economists might have more reasonably encouraged consumers to reduce their reliance on it. For about a decade, home economists were able to promote their educational agenda while supporting power company goals. When the agendas of employees and employers came into conflict, however, home economists' vision of rational consumption lost out to profit-making priorities. In their efforts to extend values of reform into the new environment of the private corporation, utility home economists experienced this larger shift haltingly over the course of the interwar period. Yet the story of home economists in utilities sheds light on the ways business home economists experienced the broader social and economic transition from the Progressive Era to an age of corporate capitalism. Gradually, as they helped establish courses in electrical equipment and the Home Service Division of NELA, business home economists reshaped the relationship between education, reform, and capitalism in ways that ultimately blurred distinctions between instruction and sales. This conflation proved powerful for companies and consumers alike, and it played a pioneering role in shaping "noncommercial" components that became standard in corporate capitalist marketing systems.

Whether as educators or as saleswomen, home economists functioned as critical mediators between utility companies and their customers in the interwar period, and thus became active agents in the process of technological change. By connecting private homes with the managers of centralized power systems, they bridged boundaries between company and community, technology and culture, and the public and private spheres. In this manner, through live demonstrations and radio broadcasts, utility home economists enabled firms to humanize and animate products while also legitimizing them in terms of science and efficiency. Home economists' success in facilitating communication between producers and consumers involved a careful balancing act between their technical expertise and their social ability to interact with domestic consumers of gas and electricity, especially middle-class women. By constructing and disseminating new principles of nutrition, cleanliness, and proper lighting that linked the practical and the aesthetic dimensions of electrical goods, home service demonstrations helped utility companies construct a typical female consumer based on home economists' ideas about modern homemaking. Through these programs, they made power companies and their products (as well as their own expert advice) integral to that definition and solidified a place for home economists and the values they celebrated at the center of American consumer culture.

7

Mediation Marginalized: Home Economics in Government and Business, 1940–1970

"What [home economists] are called on to do today is what they have been doing for years, but now they have a flag to carry," declared Jessie McQueen, home economist at the American Gas Association, in 1942. With the entry of the United States into World War II, concern for the strength of the defense industries and the morale of the civilian population boosted the importance of nutrition in the public eye. As government agencies sought to make information about healthy eating available through every possible channel, they relied on home economists—established experts working in relatively secure positions in many government agencies and corporations—to devise strategies for developing "physically sound individuals" and building morale among American homemakers. In addition, through canning kitchens, scrap drives, and victory gardens, home economists helped bring public attention to the importance of "making do" on the home front. Home economists had supported voluntary conservation measures during World War I, but during World War II organized state bureaucracies relied on them to help keep American families clothed and nourished during mandatory rationing. With leadership and encouragement from the American Home Economics Association (AHEA)—whose members totaled 15,000 in 1942—home economists served on local nutrition committees, taught nutrition classes for the American Red Cross, and helped establish factory canteen services and child care centers for families in which both parents were working in the defense industries.[1] By rallying to help government regulate the nation's dietary and consumption habits at a time of shortages, home economists solidified the reputation they had established as consumer experts working in government and business in the 1920s and 1930s. However, unlike World War I (where home economists had been singled out as important leaders in Herbert Hoover's voluntary food conservation campaign), in World War II home economists wore no special uniforms and collectively served as only one of many professional groups enlisted to help American families cope with wartime limitations.

Economic prosperity after the war, fueled in large part by the growth and expansion of consumer products industries, presented American homemakers with the contrasting challenges of managing unprecedented abundance and choice. More consumer goods on the market meant more work for an expanded Bureau of Home Economics (BHE; renamed the Bureau of Human Nutrition and Home Economics in 1943), which continued its mission of researching consumer products from the user's perspective until the 1950s, albeit with a narrower agenda focusing primarily on food and nutrition. The boom in the consumer products industries also created new opportunities for home economists in business, as manufacturers and retailers continued to rely on them to facilitate communication with homemakers as companies sought to create markets for new foods and household goods. The rise in home ownership and suburban living brought increasing numbers of families into the middle class, creating new social groups for corporations to cultivate. By continuing to serve as liaisons between producers and consumers, business home economists fulfilled the drive of many firms to fit and refit new products to newly discovered or defined consumer groups, with more and larger departments of home economics established in food companies, utility companies, and women's magazines.

At the same time, the political economy and ideology of Cold War America had a powerful influence on these institutions, on home economists' professional place within them, and on cultural discussions about domestic consumption. Private corporations and government agencies alike embraced "big science" and basic research that tended to be led by male-dominated hard scientific fields. With the rise of systems theory, many of the softer disciplines were pushed aside. Still, although the space program and the military-industrial complex occupied center stage, kitchen technologies received significant attention in the late 1950s as American political leaders worked to compete with the Soviet Union on the basis of consumer goods. These heightened stakes raised the profile of many corporate home economics departments, enlisting them in the struggle for international security. An analogous quest for domestic security revived "traditional" values centered on the home. While government leaders pursued strategies for "containment of communism abroad," women experienced what historian Elaine Tyler May has described as "gender containment." Whereas large numbers of women joined the workforce and contributed to industrial productivity during World War II, most of them returned to the domestic sphere as homemakers in its aftermath. Rosie the Riveter reemerged as a homemaker, and public images and stereotypes about women's separate spheres became solidified, making home economists' public roles in government and business seem less compatible with cultural stereotypes than before—even as public agencies and corporations continued to rely on them as consumer experts and representatives.[2]

In this context, as a result of changes inside the U.S. Department of Agriculture (USDA) and within consumer product firms beginning in the 1950s, home economists in both government and business confronted a series of simultaneous challenges to their professional identities as mediators of consumption. While the war brought increased resources to the Bureau of Home Economics, in peacetime government home economists had difficulty holding on to the bureau as a major platform for a broad program of consumer research. The bureau's location within the federal government's agricultural bureaucracy made it vulnerable to changes in agricultural policy, especially as that policy changed from improving the standard of living on American farms and promoting the "utilization" of agricultural goods to managing postwar abundant agricultural production in an era of a diminishing national farming population. Home economists in business also faced a professional landscape transformed by the emergence of male-dominated business and technical specialties such as food technology and engineering, market research, marketing, and television advertising, fields that undermined home economists' special feminine connection to food preparation and the "average" homemaker—whose identity seemed less clear to male managers than ever before.

Expansion and Disintegration at the USDA, 1940–1968

World War II gave an immediate boost to research at the Bureau of Home Economics, which adjusted its program to meet wartime emergency needs of both homemakers and government policymakers. Women on the home front confronted high prices, variable quality and quantity of available goods, and eventually rationing. To help homemakers face these challenges, bureau home economists updated buying guides for ready-made clothing and household equipment in light of changed market conditions. Instructions for extending the life of domestic appliances, sewing slipcovers for furniture, and remaking men's suits—discarded as fathers and sons joined military service and put on uniforms—into garments that could be worn by other family members were representative of the "practical, tested information" that bureau home economists supplied to assist wartime homemakers in coping with the limited availability of many consumer goods. "Be a Victory Planner in Your Home," urged one of the bureau's publications.[3] With silk for stockings in short supply, Ruth O'Brien and her team in the Textiles and Clothing Division studied ways to use surplus cotton for producing hosiery. With the help of a newly installed power-knitting machine, the bureau's textile specialists developed and tested hosiery designs, which they supplied to private manufacturers for commercial distribution. They further pioneered mildew resistance methods for household fabrics and defense equipment such as military uniforms and tents, and designed work garments, or "functional clothing," to prevent accidents and conserve human energy for women in factories and on the farm.[4]

At the same time, the bureau supplied information about consumer behavior, product qualities, and nutritional needs to the leaders of wartime government agencies. The beginning of the war saw the publication of the *Consumer Purchases Study*, initiated in 1936 as a coordinated effort between the BHE and a number of other agencies. Bureau staff and an array of government planners used this data to track spending and saving patterns as well as follow changes brought about by wartime circumstances. The bureau received special funds in late 1941 to conduct a new study of income, spending, and saving by rural families in parallel with an investigation of urban families at the Bureau of Labor Statistics. For the War Production Board, the bureau prepared estimates of American families' needs for canning in 1942, "as an indicator of the extent to which rubber and metal should be allocated for jar rings and tops for home use." The Office of Price Administration (OPA) similarly relied on bureau research to understand the nation's sugar consumption patterns prior to establishing rations for sugar and other food commodities. To assist the OPA in making decisions about the use of strategic industrial materials, the bureau also compiled specifications regarding household appliances and the use of these devices by consumers. When the OPA established price ceilings for the household equipment still available on the market, bureau home economists found support for their long-sought goal to develop appliance performance standards and worked with the National Bureau of Standards to create "simplified testing methods" for refrigerators and electric ranges.[5]

The bureau's food and nutrition research was particularly important to the war effort. Political and economic leaders relied heavily on bureau research to assess the quality of American health, define requirements for a nutritious diet, and popularize ways to improve the eating habits of families showing deficiencies. Food and nutrition subjects had always received the largest pool of resources at the bureau, a focus that only became stronger during the emergency needs of the Great Depression. As the United States entered World War II, government planners found new uses for bureau data compiled during the inter-war period on the dietary habits of Americans, and they supported continued studies throughout the war to help keep track of the nation's nutritional condition. In addition, bureau leaders and other home economists assumed important positions on new federal food-related committees that aimed to improve the nation's cooking and eating habits.

In late 1940 the wartime emergency prompted the National Research Council (NRC) to establish the Committee on Food and Nutrition to provide a scientific basis for determining dietary needs of Americans and the Committee on Food Habits to take a more social scientific (specifically anthropological) approach to adjusting the nation's approach to eating in light of these findings. Hazel K. Stiebeling, the bureau's senior food economist, served on the Committee on Food and Nutrition and became a governmental liaison to the Committee on Food Habits. These committees were strongly supported by President Roosevelt and Federal Security Administrator Paul McNutt, who also created a special advisory committee of eighteen experts, which included seven AHEA members, to take charge of organizing state nutrition councils throughout the country. At the National Nutrition Conference held in May 1941, nutrition experts presented a report titled "Are We Well Fed?," which drew on the bureau's data to make the case that American dietary habits needed improvement. Also at this meeting, the NRC's Committee on Food and Nutrition announced recommended daily allowances (soon known as "RDAS") of vitamins, calories, and carbohydrates needed for a healthy diet. Stiebeling played a leading role in establishing RDAS, and soon bureau staff translated them into suggested serving sizes and revised the BHE's guidance on food budgets accordingly. Henry Clapp Sherman's 1944 brief on the state of nutritional knowledge and the booklet *Eat the Right Food to Help Keep You Fit*, published by the BHE in cooperation with the Children's Bureau, U.S. Public Health Service, and U.S. Office of Education, made home economists even more central to efforts to solve the nation's wartime nutrition crisis. The success of Stanley, Stiebeling, and other bureau home economists in translating nutritional scientific information into practical recommendations for American homemakers reinforced their expertise, leading to new opportunities during and after the war consulting with the Foreign Agricultural Service and later the new United Nations on how to encourage similar improvements in the eating habits of populations around the world.[6]

The bureau's close association with the hot topic of nutrition, and its contributions to the big wartime nutrition effort, brought the agency and its staff

Olive Allen, a bacteriologist with the Bureau of Home Economics, studies heat resistance of organisms likely to cause food spoilage, c. 1945. Canning experimentation remained a staple of research at the bureau during and after World War II. (National Archives)

great clout and fueled its expansion during the war. The BHE's renaming in 1943 as the Bureau of Human Nutrition and Home Economics (BHNHE) reflected a shift in the agency's emphasis from general consumption (covering topics such as textiles, appliances, and domestic budgets) to food and nutrition. Placed under the USDA's Agricultural Research Administration (ARA), the BHNHE consolidated the old BHE with the Bureau of Agricultural Chemistry and Engineering's Division of Protein and Nutrition Research. "This change of name should announce to the world our conviction that human nutrition and home economics are one and indivisible," ARA head Eugene C. Auchter explained. Auchter's decisions to transfer Louise Stanley out of her position as bureau chief to serve as his special assistant for food problems overseas and to replace her with prominent nutrition scientist Henry Clapp Sherman further solidified the equation of home economics with human nutrition at the USDA. In the short term, the bureau's focus on food brought funding that allowed the agency to expand research its laboratory facilities at the new Agricultural Research Center in Beltsville, Maryland, and bolster its publication program, which reached an all-time distribution high of 28 million bulletins in 1943.[7] And as long as there was an increase in the bureau's overall budget, home economists had resources and opportunities to conduct research on topics beyond food and nutrition and to disseminate "wise buying" messages.

Yet even as Auchter assured home economists that the work of the renamed bureau's other divisions—Family Economics, Textiles and Clothing, and Equipment—would remain important after the wartime emergency, women in the field who were committed to a comprehensive federal research program centered on consumption expressed fears that the equation of home economics with nutrition would mean that the full scope of home economics research would be "lost in the shuffle."[8] Responding to these concerns from members, the AHEA soon called for a change in the bureau's authorization to allow it to expand its scope of research to include topics relevant to urban as well as rural homes such as home management, family relations, child growth, and economic issues. In 1944, the organization helped win congressional approval of an additional appropriation of $275,000 for the BHNHE, which represented a 62 percent budget increase from the previous year.[9] Despite this brief victory, the continued emphasis on foods and nutrition marked the beginning of a decline in the USDA's support for the broad program of scientific research in the service of consumers embodied in all of the bureau's divisions. As more resources were directed toward an exclusive focus on food, Louise Stanley and her cohort's broader vision for the bureau and the field during the interwar period began to lose ground.

Whereas Stanley devoted her tenure to building the bureau and expanding its mission, bureau leaders in the late 1940s and 1950s faced the challenge of holding the organization together at a time of waning support from Congress and USDA administrators. Home economist Hazel K. Stiebeling (who joined the bureau as senior food economist in 1930) replaced Henry Sherman as bureau chief in 1944. Like Stanley, Stiebeling held a doctoral degree in a scientific field (chemistry) from an Ivy League university (Columbia) and had studied with the nation's nutrition experts, Sherman among them. Through her studies of the nation's food habits and food-related expenditures, as well as her development of diet plans for four different income levels during the Depression, Stiebeling had further proven herself as a leader in home economics. Forty-eight years old at the time of her appointment, Stiebeling shared Stanley's vision for a bureau in the service of a broad-based, consumer-oriented profession, but she also had staked out her own expertise in the area of food and dietary study that the bureau now emphasized.[10] During her tenure, however, appropriations to the bureau failed to keep pace with what they had been under Stanley.

In 1947 Congress dealt the BHNHE a "staggering blow" when it cut $245,000 from its budget of $1,045,000. By bringing the bureau's annual budget down to 1944 levels, this reduction effectively erased the progress AHEA made during World War II and forced the bureau to eliminate many publications and curtail numerous research projects. Although the bureau benefited from funding for cooperative home economics research projects with the state experiment stations, this support was not sufficient to secure the guaranteed, long-term financial support necessary to maintain and develop the bureau's activities. In spite of the AHEA's advocacy, the BHNHE experienced continued cuts to its budget into the early 1950s. From a staff of more than 300 people in 1948, the BHNHE was reduced to just 240 staff members in 1952.[11]

Diminishing resources made it increasingly difficult for Stiebeling to maintain Stanley's legacy of a government agency dedicated to a broad research program serving domestic consumers. Food composition charts were updated to include the nutrient content of more foods. The bureau established a quantity cookery laboratory to develop recipes for surplus foods sent in support of the USDA's school lunch program. Outside of food work, however, BHNHE staff members struggled to continue investigations in the other original research areas. The bureau's economics division was renamed "family economics," but its staff suffered from a general shift away from social survey work that accompanied congressional decisions in the late 1940s to dismantle the Bureau of Agricultural Economics.[12] The scope of the group's economic surveys never again approached the level of ambition of the Consumer Purchases Study conducted in the mid-1930s. Instead, many of the division's staff members turned to interpreting food composition data that had earlier been the province of the Foods Division. In textiles, Ruth O'Brien, one of two assistant chiefs under Stiebeling, continued to spearhead an ambitious research program to support minimum fabric standards and consumer education until her retirement in 1956.[13] From her position in the bureau's Housing and Equipment Division, Lenore Sater Thye coauthored and revised several editions of the definitive textbook *Household Equipment*, which she first wrote as a professor at Iowa State University. Thye's division conducted a national farm housing survey, using the results as the basis for creating ideal plans for building and furnishing rural farmhouses, including a "step-saving kitchen" and other improvements to domestic spaces. Through a cooperative project with USDA researchers in agricultural engineering, experimental houses were built in Beltsville, Maryland, and the bureau published bulletins making these plans available to the general public.[14] Yet the overall number of publications the bureau generated declined in the postwar years, and the scope of the bureau's activities never fully recovered from its focus on food and nutrition that resulted from the wartime effort.

In addition to shrinking budgets and the narrowing of research programs, the existence of the BHNHE as a separate "female dominion" came to an end with the consolidation of many of the USDA research bureaus into the Agricultural Research Service (ARS) in 1953. President Dwight Eisenhower's election the previous year prompted a reexamination of the previous decade's expansion of federal agencies and, at the USDA, triggered a reining in of the bureaus that many Republican leaders found to be too independent, too powerful, and too meddlesome in private enterprise. Home economists lost their status as leaders of a separate government bureau, reversing the success that had been so critical to their quest to professionalize thirty years earlier. As home economics historian Helen Pundt put it, home economics became "submerged" in the ARS. The BHNHE no longer received a specific appropriation from Congress but rather received a portion of the allocation made to the ARS. The group was split into two units, Human Nutrition Research (headed by Callie Mae Coons) and Home Economics Research (headed by Ruth O'Brien). Although no functions or research areas were officially eliminated with this reorganization, just two years later, in early 1955, ARS administrator Byron T. Shaw announced that the work of the Home Economics Research unit would be curtailed. Eighty-seven percent of the funds for the whole group would now go to foods and nutrition, with the remainder divided across all other subject areas. The study of food economics, family economics, and home management would be brought into Human Nutrition Research, leaving only work on farm housing and the "serviceability" of clothing and textiles to be maintained in Home Economics Research. The study of new uses for agricultural products would be moved to a different part of the department altogether. Shaw discontinued the study of commercially produced household equipment and appliances, as well as most research into the selection, construction, and maintenance of textiles and clothing. The administrator further proposed to eliminate all publication of bulletins about the selection, care, and use of such goods, and he suggested that homemakers could rely instead on manufacturers for that type of information. Taken by surprise by Shaw's announcement, the AHEA formed the Committee on Federal Research Related to Home Economics. This committee's protests and its efforts to "develop a broad and well-balanced research service to home economics" forced the ARS administrator to back off from drastic changes that would have all but eliminated broad home economics work from the department. Within six months, Shaw established branches for "clothing and housing" and "household economics" in addition to the one for "human nutrition."[15]

Although the AHEA proved influential enough to reverse the blows of 1955, its efforts over the next decade to press for what its members called a "well-balanced" program of home economics research within the USDA proved unable to prevent department administrators from reducing funding for research in areas such as family economics, textiles and clothing, or housing. In the meantime, as it became clear that the USDA could no longer be considered an institutional platform for the profession at large, home economics leaders turned their attention to creating a new federal agency altogether, one devoted to the welfare of the American home and family. The concept for the new agency, first discussed in 1956, stemmed from the shifting orientation of home economics in the postwar years toward sociological and psychological issues and away from a focus on material goods and consumption. Rather than conduct its own research, a proposed Institute for the American Home (changed in 1957 to Research Foundation for the American Home) would promote and coordinate all research that was under way in state and federal agencies across many disciplines related to "family well-being." Although research on subjects relating to family welfare was being conducted in dozens of federal agencies, AHEA members argued that the lack of a single agency caused gaps and hindered the government's ability to serve the true needs of American families. This vision failed to gain enough support to make the proposed agency a reality, however, and after nearly six years of lobbying political leaders, AHEA members ended their advocacy for it.[16]

The AHEA's lobbying may have had the effect of forcing yet another name change at the USDA, however. In 1957, Shaw announced that the home economics research unit would now be called the Institute of Home Economics, and he appointed Hazel Stiebeling to head its three divisions.[17] Within three years, however, the ARS administrator tried to switch the name back again, arguing that a bureau title that emphasized human nutrition would attract more funds. Although he failed to persuade the AHEA to approve this change, Shaw eventually had his way in 1962, when the ARS eliminated the Institute for Home Economics and dropped "home economics" from the title of the remaining organization, arguing that the general public no longer associated nutrition with the women's discipline. The three divisions remained, but Hazel Stiebeling was appointed deputy administrator for "nutrition and consumer-use research" in the Agricultural Research Service.[18] In late 1964, Secretary of Agriculture Orville L. Freeman called once again for the elimination of the ARS's Division of Clothing and Housing Research. The AHEA succeeded in convincing

Freeman to retain the clothing portion of the threatened division, but funding for research on housing and household equipment was eliminated altogether. By this time, however, most key staff members were gone. O'Brien had retired in 1956, Stiebeling in 1963, and Thye in 1964, leaving few successors who had any connection to the legacy of the early days of the original BHE.[19]

Gradually, the BHNHE was, in the words of historian Margaret Rossiter, "reorganized out of existence."[20] Vestiges of the old program remained within the USDA, and a significant number of jobs in nutrition and food economics continued to be filled with female (and, increasingly, male) graduates of home economics programs. But home economics no longer functioned as an organizing rubric for a broad, consumer-oriented program of research at the USDA. In the interwar period, the BHE had served as a woman's domain of scientific expertise devoted to serving rural homemakers and encouraging them to be modern, middle-class consumers. Home economists had found the space for this project because agricultural policymakers looked to them for assistance with improving rural living conditions and promoting the use of agricultural goods. By the 1960s, however, this rationale for state sponsorship of home economics no longer held sway. Except for some significant pockets of rural poverty, family farms had largely modernized in the period after World War II, and the USDA's home economics programs and other efforts had not been able to keep young Americans in rural areas from migrating to towns and cities. The bureau's function of guiding modern consumption in United States household lost its significance in a larger male-dominated agricultural bureaucracy that was increasingly oriented toward contending with the problems of overproduction. As the department sought other, more aggressive and large-scale strategies for absorbing surplus farm products, politicians intent on creating a Great Society launched a series of growing national and international welfare programs aimed at improving food distribution to poor families in American cities and in underdeveloped countries around the world. With consumer issues increasingly framed as problems of distribution rather than education—and consumers defined as "the needy" rather than as middle-class homemakers—home economists' approach to mediating consumption was no longer seen by political leaders as the obvious pathway to serving consumers.[21]

With the erosion of the bureau, home economists lost not just the official governmental information clearinghouse they had developed, however unevenly, to serve consumers, but also one of the field's most important institutional bases from which to train young women in the scientific study of consumer goods from the user's perspective. Before it disbanded in 1965, the

AHEA's Committee on Federal Research turned its attention to areas of the federal government outside of the USDA, and eventually the *Journal of Home Economics* suspended its regular column devoted to home economics research at the USDA. With the end of the bureau, state-based land-grant colleges and private universities became the only remaining, albeit also weakened, source of support for noncommercial home economics research.[22]

The timing could not have been worse for home economists, for the dismantling of their niche within the federal government occurred just as consumer issues began to rise again in the nation's political consciousness. When liberal politicians looked for a place within the federal government to advocate for consumer needs in the late 1950s, little of the consumer-oriented home economics bureau was left at the USDA. By the time President John Fitzgerald Kennedy appointed the twelve-member Consumers' Advisory Council in 1962, there were few women in the USDA even vaguely connected to home economics work who were in a position to support the council. Although these home economists contributed articles about nutrition and "consumer use" to the 1966 USDA yearbook titled *Consumers All*, their collective efforts were a far cry from having a government bureau to themselves from which to mediate among public officials, producers, and consumers.[23]

At the same time, the demise of home economics at the USDA freed the women's profession from constraints on its work that stemmed from operating within the framework of the agricultural establishment. Historian Harvey Levenstein has argued that the USDA was the "kiss of death" for nutrition programs. Earl J. McGrath and Jack T. Johnson made the same case in their 1968 study *The Changing Mission of Home Economics*, asserting that home economics should be disengaged from agriculture. Still, in spite of the limitations that home economists confronted within the USDA, they never found another institutional platform with equivalent status and power through which to influence the marketplace for household goods.[24]

"The Future Is Bright": Home Economics in Business, 1940–1970

Business home economists found considerable demand for their services during World War II. Home economists' reputation as authorities in health and food made them important resources for corporations eager to support nutrition and conservation programs connected with national defense. Pressured not to push sales at a time of rationing and limited production, corporations used their advertising and marketing apparatus to maintain their presence in American life and to associate themselves with goodwill and patriotism. The public relations value of home economics work gained renewed importance at many firms that, during wartime shortages, had little or nothing to sell.

Major food manufacturing firms relied on home economics departments to help keep their corporate identities in the limelight, focusing their wartime efforts on promoting the government's nutrition program and helping families cope with shortages and rations. Company home economists adjusted recipes and revised cookbooks to emphasize ways to adapt to the limited availability of many ingredients. General Mills launched a "Nutrition Study Kit" for teachers that included booklets on daily nutritional requirements, balanced meals, enriched flours, and a "Personal Nutrition Record Sheet" for keeping track of food consumption. While this kit resembled a government publication, its creators pointed out that the company's Gold Medal flour and its Wheaties cereal were "enriched" according to the National Research Council's recommendations. *War-Time Services for the Home-Front*, a companion publication authored by General Mills' signature home economist, "Betty Crocker," provided homemakers with "ten easy steps" for optimizing nutritious and economical meals within the ration points they were allocated. A "point stretcher recipe" for "Emergency Steak" called for one cup of Wheaties cereal (!). Home economists at General Foods touted the qualities of the company's Swans Down Cake Flour in a booklet titled *How to Bake by the Ration Book* (1943), declaring that Swans Down "works wartime miracles" by allowing home cooks to cut down on shortening "and still get proud, patriotic results!"[25] By lending their voice and authority to these types of publications—which had the appearance of noncommercial instructional manuals—home economists helped businesses merge their identities with those of federal agencies during the wartime emergency.

Although some utility companies temporarily discontinued their home service departments during the war, most reshaped them to meet emergency conditions. Because military needs for many metals took priority, the manufacture of domestic appliances was restricted or discontinued. Home service work became an important element of utilities' strategy to keep homemakers' attention. In a temporary reversal of the 1930s emphasis on sales, many utilities recast their home service programs to stress education about nutrition and the care and conservation of equipment. At the Union Gas Company in Brooklyn, New York, Home Service Director Ruth Soule changed her program almost overnight from sales-slanted to educational demonstrations. The new programs generated unprecedented attendance from crowds eager to learn about "dollar stretcher" recipes. While many home service departments spearheaded local war programs handling nutrition and canteen-feeding classes, others opened their auditoriums to community groups promoting the same agenda.[26]

As most manufacturers of household equipment shifted their operations to war production and ceased producing goods for domestic use, they similarly emphasized the proper care and maintenance of appliances already sold as well as nutrition. The lack of availability of metals forced the Wear-Ever Aluminum Company to suspend product development, making equipment conservation critical for maintaining a connection to existing customers. "Our advertising can keep our name before the consumers until the war is over," reported Margaret Mitchell, Wear-Ever's home economist in 1942, "but our Home Economics department can help to keep homemakers using our equipment—something straight advertising cannot do." At the Westinghouse Electric and Manufacturing Company, Home Economics Director Julia Kiene led an ambitious Health-for-Victory campaign. She and her staff authored *The ABC's of Eating for Health* (1942) based on the national nutrition program's guidelines and launched hundreds of public demonstrations throughout the country. The company presented an exhibition at the Museum of Science and Industry in Chicago titled *The Homemaker and the War* that highlighted lessons about nutrition and featured a fully operational electrical laundry and a demonstration kitchen stocked with a range, refrigerator, dishwasher, and roaster. The exhibition's eight "wartime assignments" for the American homemaker aimed to help her with the selection, care, and preservation of foods to "meet the added demands on her time" brought about by the emergency. Additional displays explained how to conserve fats and metals for government scrap drives, follow air-raid precautions, and care for and use electrical appliances. Two motion pictures—*V Men* about vitamins and "protective cooking" and *40 Billion Enemies* about food bacteria and refrigeration—further supported the exhibition's didactic goals while also elevating homemaking to the status of a patriotic duty.[27]

A number of home economists in business—thirty-four members of the American Home Economics Association's Home Economics in Business (HEIB) Section—took leaves of absence to participate more directly in military mobilization. Mary I. Barber, director of home economics at the Kellogg Company, became the first "dollar-a-year woman" when she joined the Army in 1941 as an "expert food consultant" in charge of menu planning for soldiers. Since the early 1930s, Barber and her staff had furnished guidelines for meal planning to a number of government institutions, both civilian and military. During the war, she drew on these experiences as well as the new federal nutrition

Kathryn Jameson, a home economist at the Westinghouse exhibit, Museum of Science and Industry, Chicago, demonstrates how to steam vegetables quickly using a pie tin for a cover to maximize nutritive value, 1941. (Archives, Museum of Science and Industry, Chicago)

program to prepare a "Master Menu" that served as the basis for field rations of Army soldiers stationed at home and abroad.[28] Ina S. Lindman, director of home economics at the United Fruit Company, served for two years as consultant for the Navy, where she edited a new edition of the *Cookbook of the United States Navy.* The book incorporated the latest nutritional knowledge into its instructions for quantity cooking and earned Lindman a Distinguished Civilian Service Award.[29] Grace Dimelow, who worked for five years as director of educational services and sales promotion at the Butterick Publishing Company, then for eight years as president of Diamond Dee Brassiere Incorporated, also served in the Navy as liaison officer for the women's reserve and was ultimately promoted to lieutenant commander. Numerous other home economists remained in their business jobs but served in voluntary positions on state and county nutrition councils, taught American Red Cross nutrition classes, gave demonstrations in war plants, and helped to organize "industrial feeding."[30]

Postwar reconversion and the expansion of the consumer products industries after 1945 continued to generate opportunities for business home economists, especially as manufacturers introduced new products for the civilian market and stepped up their promotional efforts in the face of rising per capita income. Product innovations touched on almost every conceivable area of domestic life and included packaged and convenience foods; fabrics and ready-made clothing made of synthetic fibers; remodeling and decorative materials; carpets and furnishings; and new types of appliances such as garbage disposers, home freezing units, and air conditioners.[31] Increased competition in these industries rested on a company's ability to market these types of new products successfully, a process that required ongoing instruction about why and how to use them. Business home economists, already established as the professionals to hire for preparing how-to materials for consumers and for facilitating other types of communication between producers and consumers, prospered in this climate. They further benefited from a larger trend in women's corporate employment, where the number and proportion of women scientists and engineers employed in business and industry rose in the 1950s and 1960s, particularly in the area of customer service. World War II proved to be an important turning point for many of these women and for home economists in business who now reported that they were widely viewed with "high regard" and that there was increased demand for their services. "The future is bright," Frances Maule announced in her *Executive Careers for Women* (1957), for young home economics graduates seeking entry-level positions as "advisers to industry."[32] Between 1940 and 1945, membership in the Home Economics in Business Section of the AHEA increased rapidly from a total of about 680 members to more than 900; in the next decade, membership more than doubled, reaching over 2,000 by 1955. A survey that year found 3,400 home economists employed by industry, or about the same number that worked as professors, researchers, and administrators in higher education. The expansion of jobs for home economists in business continued through the 1960s, reaching about 5,000 positions by 1967.[33] Although a 1950s culture of domesticity encouraged women to stay at home, the demand for business home economists exceeded supply in the immediate postwar period.

To ensure that corporations filled vacancies with only those women trained in home economics, HEIB members devoted significant energy in these years to recruitment, vocational counseling, and curriculum reform. Attracting high-quality, well-trained students to their field was an important means by which business home economists sought to maintain their professional identity and uphold their reputation inside corporations. Good Housekeeping Institute director Katharine Fisher, an outspoken leader in business home economics in the interwar period, articulated the stakes in 1947:

> Although the future of home economics in business is rosy, it has its dark aspects, too. Unless our profession attracts more recruits to the ranks of home economists, sets itself to the task of adapting and expanding college curricula to better equip the young home economists to fill a wide variety of business jobs, and makes apprenticeships and in-service training more available in business, we may see these jobs taken over by ill-trained or untrained people. When demand exceeds supply, substitutes for the real thing often become acceptable. This is a problem our profession must face and solve if it is to discharge its responsibilities to the consumer and retain its high standards of professional qualification, ethics, and service to society.[34]

To preserve their legacy and to guide the preparation of a younger cohort, Fisher and the pioneering generation of business home economists (who had defined their positions and careers on the job) worked closely with university administrators to design specialized courses to train young home economists for corporate work. During World War II, a number of university home economics programs (including the School of Home Economics at Kansas State College and Teachers College, Columbia University) offered courses in utility home service and commercial demonstration. Soon Cornell University started a vocational guidance program for home economics students interested in business work.[35] Business home economists collaborated with university administrators and faculty to further organize full-blown majors and specially tailored programs allowing home economics students to put together courses of study in preparation for future work in business. By the late 1960s, Pennsylvania State University introduced a new major called Commercial Consumer Services, and Margaret Morrison Carnegie College at Carnegie Mellon University merged its home economics program with the Business and Social Studies

Departments, creating a Department of Business and Resource Management.[36] To supplement these changes in the home economics curriculum, local HEIB groups hosted career days and sponsored scholarships for the purpose of recruiting home economics students into these courses and programs and, eventually, into business careers. While these initiatives convinced some home economics graduates to seek employment with corporations, most young women in the field continued to choose careers in teaching, dietetics, or extension work; college administrators, who faced difficulty attracting enough students to fill positions in these priority areas, also admitted to giving little encouragement to students to go into business.[37] The issue of how to attract smart young women to enter the business world remained a constant preoccupation of the HEIB Section through the mid-1960s.[38]

Recognizing that part of the problem stemmed from the difficulty of generating interest among young women in home economics careers in the first place, business home economists led efforts in the late 1940s and early 1950s to promote home economics generally and to boost the profession's overall image. In spite of a general rise in female college enrollment and much discussion among administrators about reforming curricula to provide a "feminine" education for women in keeping with the era's dominant gender ideology, enrollment in home economics college programs was in decline in the 1940s. By the 1967–68 academic year, college home economics graduates constituted less than 5 percent of all women college graduates in the United States. Women who were serious about education found more opportunities in liberal arts institutions, or even new coed programs offered at land-grant colleges; women interested in studying science and business found other options outside of home economics. "Many high school counselors [were] still unconvinced that home economics could challenge the 'bright girl,'" explains home economics historian Helen Pundt. The general trend of high drop-out rates among women students and early marriage rates among female graduates posed additional challenges for home economists who sought to attract smart young women to lifelong leadership careers in the field.[39] Whereas in the 1920s home economists' association with science and efficiency had helped make them the very model of the "modern woman," the field's leaders found the need to update their image after the war. Katharine Fisher recommended "depicting more vividly to the young, imaginative girl . . . the varied, interest-absorbing, creative, and constructive jobs open to her as a home economist in business. We must show her that the drab, standing-over-a-hot-range picture many modern girls believe they see in a home economics career is only an illusory image." Perhaps because HEIB members perceived they had the most to lose from this stereotype, General Mills home economics director Marjorie Child Husted initiated the formation of a Public Relations Council within the AHEA, served as its first chairwoman, and used her corporate ties to "glamorize the home economics courses and teachers" in print and on radio and television.[40]

Although business home economists' recruiting persisted, their efforts succeeded in attracting enough women to oversee the growth of the corporate departments that the pioneering generation had established in the 1920s and 1930s. Eleanor Ahern at Procter & Gamble, Mary Barber at Kellogg's, Elsie Stark at Best Foods, and Marye Dahnke at Kraft were members of a generation who had started out as one-woman operations within large food corporations. Many hired assistants before the war, but in the 1940s they expanded their home economics departments to include dozens of home economists. By 1950, Marjorie Child Husted supervised forty-eight women in the Home Service Department at General Mills, one of the largest departments of its kind. Helen Wolcott at Pillsbury reported forty home economists and supporting personnel working in seven kitchens in 1964. Utility companies also enlarged their home service departments. In the late 1940s and 1950s, the Philadelphia Electric Company had about thirty-five home economists on staff. The larger national appliance manufacturers employed almost twenty home economists each to test, demonstrate, and write instruction booklets. These women served as important role models in training a next generation, and in the 1950s and early 1960s, many of them passed the baton to their successors: Willie Mae Rogers succeeded Katharine Fisher at the Good Housekeeping Institute in 1953, Jeanne Paris took over for Beth Bailey McLean at Swift in 1955, and Dorothy Holland replaced Marye Dahnke at Kraft in 1962.[41]

Rapid change and innovation in the chemical fibers, textile, and apparel industries in the immediate postwar period prompted many firms to expand existing home economics work or to hire home economists for the first time.[42] After the debut of nylon at the 1939 New York World's Fair, DuPont and other manufacturers introduced dozens of synthetic fabrics in the 1940s and 1950s. While the early promotion of nylon as a "miracle fiber" raised consumers' expectations for the performance of synthetics, wartime problems with poor, inconsistent quality textiles and limited availability of some fibers made it important for manufacturers to explain the properties and benefits of substitute fabrics to skeptical consumers. Homemakers expressed confusion about the large number of new fibers and finishes that appeared so quickly on the market, and many complained about their performance. The ability to control the properties of fibers and fabrics through chemical engineering further raised the issue of what characteristics homemakers needed or wanted. In this context, many producers turned to home economists to help them bridge the gap between the staff engineers and customers. Knowing how these fabrics performed when laid out on a pattern, cut, basted, sewn, draped to the figure, and pressed was a critical factor in marketing these modern fabrics successfully. In addition, experimentation on end use was required to determine the proper care and cleaning procedures for various fabrics. By the early 1950s, DuPont added home economists to its Textile Fibers Department and put them to work developing instructions for the care of the new widely varying fabrics and cultivating the support of home economics teachers. As they relied on home economists to help establish performance standards for new products, textile companies became some of the biggest employers of women in the field.[43] Home economists' role in helping firms communicate with consumers became especially important after the passage of the Textile Fiber Products Identification Act in 1960, which required identification of the fiber composition of all garments and created a new context for manufacturers to share product information with consumers.

New fabrics and finishes were only one facet of a larger pattern of rapid technological change in the "consumption system" of laundry during this period. Changes in soap and detergents as well as in gas and electrical appliances further transformed laundering into a household task that required knowledge about an array of new technologies. Innovations in different industries built on one another: new textiles could require special temperature settings on washing machines for optimal wear in laundering, while new laundering equipment might work best with specially developed cleaning agents.[44] Through their work for manufacturers of detergents and appliances, home economists helped pave the way for the acceptance of this new system. When Procter & Gamble introduced Dash, a detergent designed for automatic washers, the firm set up a Dash Home Laundry Institute. Anne Lyng joined the company in 1953 to take charge of a special home economics division devoted to the company's soaps and detergents. Having specialized in laundry equipment and procedures as a home service representative at the Rochester Gas and Electric Company in New York State, Lyng used her position at P&G to collaborate with home economists in related industries and firms to work out the "interrelationship of textiles, equipment, and laundry products." Home economists at Maytag similarly helped with the planning, testing, and marketing of new products and product features that allowed for machine washing of woolens and synthetic fabrics, eliminating ironing with wash-and-wear fabrics, and using automatic controls to dispense bleaches, water softeners, and detergents as well as to regulate temperature.[45] At the National Institute of Cleaning and Drying, staff home economist Dorothy Siegert Lyle, who held a Ph.D. from Pennsylvania State University, played a leading role in this area.[46] As important participants supporting each of the new products and technologies that transformed the use of textiles by American consumers, home economists in these industries collaborated to construct and publicize whole new systems for the selection and care of fabrics and clothing.

As appliance manufacturers' and utility companies' home service departments worked to meet the pent-up postwar demand for washers and other appliances such as refrigerators, freezers, and dishwashers, they relied on home economists to extend their reach into America's homes. In a competitive market, home economists helped brand-name manufacturers and dealers establish corporate reputations as producers of high-quality merchandise with a service-oriented ethic. Home economists at gas and electric utilities targeted customers who had only recently been connected to power systems and could now afford to purchase the consumer durable goods powered by gas and electricity. Home economics work in power companies saw exceptional growth in the postwar years, by 1957 overtaking foods as the field employing the largest number of HEIB members.[47]

Within the broad base of industries maintaining and expanding home economics departments, the food industry, however, remained the major employer of home economists in business in the 1940s and 1950s. "Convenience foods"—aimed at the increasing numbers of women homemakers who also worked outside of the home—provided a primary focus for home economists' work in these decades.[48] A look at the Consumer Service Department at General Foods—one of the food industry's largest—reveals the major food producers' reliance on their expanding home economics departments and test kitchens to facilitate the introduction of a flurry of "instant" or value-added packaged foods and to define new ways of cooking and eating that placed them at the center of the American diet in the two decades after World War II. Under the direction of Ellen-Ann Dunham, a growing staff of home economists participated in product development tests, the preparation of package directions, recipe development and testing, publicity campaigns, and consumer correspondence for the dozens of product lines owned by General Foods. Adding to the early Jell-O gelatin products, Jell-O puddings, Minute Rice, Instant Swans Down cake mixes, and an array of instant beverages were among the new products introduced by the company soon after the war's end.

Having introduced frozen foods and mixes for some baked goods before the World War II, General Foods, like many producers, spent the war years developing new products for the anticipated peacetime boom. "War meant less food and more problems for us," recalled Maria Sellers, a home economist at General Foods. "It was a hectic time here, not only changing recipes to suit shortages but working with the laboratories on changes in products. New General Foods products were being developed looking toward new 'end of the war' markets. These were planned to interest women who wanted quick and easy food preparation."[49] Frozen foods, which had been part of the company's product lines since the acquisition of Bird's Eye in 1929, began to show a profit in 1941, and took off in the postwar period. Frozen orange juice concentrate was a big seller and the Bird's Eye product line soon included prepared meals such as potpies, turkey, and pot roast dinners.[50]

As the Consumer Service Department expanded to mirror the company's range of products, it became an established part of the company's operations. By the mid-1950s, General Foods manufactured a total of about 120 products and the Consumer Service Department consisted of 140 staff members, including sixty women, primarily home economists. The department's goal was to represent the consumer inside the company, "to anticipate Mrs. America's problems as they concern General Foods products, and then help the company solve those problems." After products were developed at the firm's Central Research Laboratories, they were sent to a team of twenty women in six different kitchens to be tested "from the consumer's viewpoint." One kitchen was maintained for Certo and Sure-Jell, the company's pectin products. Others included a baking kitchen, a recipe kitchen, and an "institution" kitchen for testing and developing quantity recipes. Another separate kitchen was reserved for food photography. Products in development typically moved back and forth between the laboratories and product kitchens where home economists organized taste tests of new products, tested competitors' products, explored ideas for new products, and developed recipes for the research laboratory to duplicate. In this capacity, home economists served as "product representatives" who applied their understanding of homemakers' needs to assist with marketing, advertising, sales, research, and production. In 1954, General Foods constructed a new facility to house these functions and serve as a showcase for consumer relations. A 1958 brochure invited the public to tour the company's test kitchens in White Plains, New York, and introduced its staff home economists as "your ambassadors," explaining: "We relay your dreams of revolutionary convenience foods of the future to the production engineers who must sometimes develop completely new manufacturing processes if those dreams are to become realities."[51]

Recipe writing was a mainstay of home economists' work at General Foods. Recipes could have a huge impact on sales, company research showed. In 1958,

Ellen-Ann Dunham (to left of woman standing), director of General Foods Consumer Service Department, with five of her thirty-five staff members in the company's New York City branch, 1951. A portrait of Frances Barton, General Foods' trademark home economist, hangs on the wall above them.
(Journal of Home Economics/*Kraft Foods Archives*)

a recipe for cheesecake almost doubled sales of Jell-O Lemon Instant pudding. By creating such recipes, and by inviting homemakers to participate in the recipe-writing process itself, home economists provided homemakers with a chance to be "creative" and assert their individuality with ready-made foods. Although some home economists' comparative studies of manufactured and homemade foods revealed the superiority of the latter, most home economists bought into the laborsaving ideology behind these products, believing that they were helping women homemakers who also worked outside the home. Marie Sellers and her colleagues were responsible for saving "the housewife time and effort without losing the quality she expects. We must be able to gauge how long to use traditional recipes and when to switch to 'quick and

easy,'" she explained in 1950. To test consumer responses to package directions and recipes, the Consumer Service Department also drew on its Homemaker Testing Service. An outgrowth of General Foods' 1930s radio program,
this service built up a group of 25,000 "consumer testers" from a list of radio
listeners gathered when the radio program went off the air in 1935. Within a
decade, home economist Eugenia Hatcher had set up the company's Homemaker Testing Service in Washington, D.C. (a location company managers felt
represented all regions of the country), to coordinate testing by select groups
of homemakers in their own kitchens. Hatcher's operation maintained correspondence with consumers, gave rewards for home-generated product recipes,
responded to complaints, and developed materials for teachers, advertising,
and packaging.[52]

Corporate strategies for introducing and expanding markets for new products—such as synthetic fibers, electrical appliances, and value-added processed foods—defined an explicit role for home economists in the 1950s. In
their work for manufacturers of consumer goods, home economists continued
to understand themselves as consumer educators, consumer representatives,
and interpreters between consumers and producers. At a time of intense competition and rapid technological change, home economists allowed corporate
managers to ensure that consumers had ways to make sense of a dizzying array
of new products and entirely new product categories. Home economists' educational role continued as they developed recipes, pamphlets, posters, films,
and filmstrips for use by home economics colleagues in high school and college classrooms, much like work done during the interwar period.[53] Through
all of these decades, home economists helped corporations in the push and
pull of responding to perceived shifts in demand and generating new trends.

At the same time, the conflict between "sales" and "service" that home
economists had confronted in the 1930s gave way by the 1950s to an increased
acceptance of selling as a part of the job. During the war, HEIB members' embrace of corporate goals brought them into bitter conflict with their educator
colleagues in the AHEA over price controls and grade labeling, which the larger
organization supported.[54] After the war, business home economists still saw
themselves as mediators, with service and education important parts of their
work, but with a different balance. Vocational adviser Genevieve Callahan's
1924 guide encouraged young home economics graduates to teach for a year
or two before looking for a business job. Such experience would help a home
economist organize her knowledge and "gain poise" in front of public audiences, but it would also help her "keep her balance and to keep from becoming
too commercial in her point of view when she does enter the business field." No

such warning appeared in the revised 1942 version of Callahan's guide. Teaching is listed as a possible "indirect route" to a business career, more for the sake of establishing contacts with local businesses than developing objectivity. Marguerite Zapoleon's 1956 vocational manual, *The College Girl Looks Ahead to Her Career Opportunities*, advised that home economists working in business "need some qualities of teachers," but it emphasized that they must be "aggressive enough to promote products in many ways."[55] These two later guides reflected the view of a newer generation of home economists who were not at all connected to the Progressive Era reform movements that influenced their predecessors and who understood their work in less idealistic terms, more explicitly adopting the profit-making orientation of their employers. As increasing numbers of HEIB members took jobs in advertising, the distinction between the two types of work—once a source of major conflict within the profession—diminished, then dissolved. "Everything done by the home economist in business can be considered a selling function," a 1959 article in *Sales Management* explained, "since the final objective of all her activities is to make more satisfied customers by insuring that the product is right and that the customer knows how to use it."[56] Although many aspects of business home economists' work on the job remained the same, home economists' understandings of how it fit into the American political economy changed. Home economists' more direct orientation toward the bottom line seemed to satisfy business managers in the short term, but the gradual erosion of their identity as educators cost home economists a major source of their value to corporate employers in the longer term.

Embracing the bottom line brought returns to many home economics directors whose employers promoted them to management positions. Mary B. Horton began her career as a bacteriologist with the Sheffield Farms Company, a division of the National Dairy Products Corporation. After serving in this role for a number of years, she earned a master's degree in home economics from New York University and initiated a consumer education program at Sheffield Farms. Appointed director of National Dairy's Sealtest Consumer Service in 1947, she was elected to the board of Sheffield Farms in 1949 and eventually promoted to vice president of the large dairy conglomerate. At General Foods Corporation, Ellen-Ann Dunham was made vice president in 1958 after more than twenty-five years in the Consumer Service Department. In 1966, Mercedes Bates, director of the Betty Crocker Kitchens at General Mills, became a corporate vice president—and the first woman officer in the history of the company. Salaries for these positions could be as high as $10,000 a year or more in 1957 for a director of a large consumer service or home economics department.[57] Although home economists in business tended to earn more than their counterparts in teaching, these instances of highly paid home economists in corporate leadership positions proved exceptional.

Many women expressed contentment with the relatively high salary and glamorous image that went along with the job, whether or not they were promoted to top management. "We've got a status and a salary pattern of our own," one anonymous business home economist told *Cosmopolitan* magazine in 1965. "Let the men go gray worrying about who'll get the next key to the executive washroom."[58] Other women found it hard to break out of the niches they had carved out and to advance to higher levels inside their respective firms. New home economics directors with larger departments managed groups of women who performed a series of specialized tasks. Whereas one-woman home economics departments had once conducted product testing, written recipes or instruction manuals, and given public demonstrations, now each of those duties was delegated to individual women who served the company more as technicians than as generalists with an integrated identity as mediators. Compared to their interwar predecessors, staff home economists in the 1950s, with their specialized roles, had less responsibility and less ability to know all perspectives. Even as home economists' opportunities for employment in business expanded and their relationship to the profit-making goals of their corporate employers became more explicit, their contributions to the corporate bottom line remained ambiguous, and their value was not always measurable in quantitative terms. Lacking the education in business or management skills for which successful corporate employees were judged, home economists' gendered, mediating role remained as intangible and invisible as it had been in the interwar years. As some of the only women with management-level jobs, home economists faced an almost impossible challenge of becoming legitimate business managers.

Thus, while home economists' work in business acquired a sort of glamour and cachet in the 1950s, their contributions to their firms were constantly disguised, devalued, or diminished. A 1948 General Foods publication described its Consumer Service Department as a "career girl's paradise" and declared it a "must" in the company's operations. However, the department was not an "operating group" that made decisions about products but rather a source of "special knowledge" supporting the actual (mostly male) decision makers. Women in the Consumer Service Department must "turn themselves into quite amazing combinations of bird-dogs, analysts, diplomats, coordinators and salesmen," explained Ella B. Myers, who once directed the company's advertising. "And they must do it all by suggestion and argument, not by order." She advised women in business not to behave like "free-wheeling individualists" but to work as a team and relinquish the need for personal credit. Urging them not to act like mothers who "always know best," Myers cautioned: "Being the greatest mothers in the world—in business—can mean being the greatest nuisances in the world." Home economists' turf in these corporations remained subject to threat from male managers who were uncomfortable with women in positions of authority and who tended to belittle women's contributions to the work of the firm.[59]

The vulnerability of home economics as "women's work" and the "softer" side of selling in these companies was reinforced by home economists' continued minimizing or disguising of their contributions to the enterprises that employed them. Satenig St. Marie's experience at the J. C. Penney Company in the 1960s provides a case in point. Initially hired as an educational consultant in the Consumer Services Department at Penney's in 1959, St. Marie was the "only woman on the professional level." Male managers "didn't know why I was there, but they tolerated me," she later recalled. When her original supervisor was promoted to another part of the company, a twenty-two-year-old male college graduate (thirteen years younger than St. Marie) was hired over her as the new director of the Consumer Services Department. After he moved on, Penney's gave St. Marie a chance to run the department, without the salary or the title. In this capacity she transformed the department's focus from developing curriculum materials for sewing classes to a broader consumer education program. St. Marie was eventually promoted to vice president, remaining with the company until her retirement in 1987. Indirectly, she believed that she benefited from the woman's movement and the consumer's movement, but St. Marie attributed her personal success at Penney's to her ability to negotiate the company's political hierarchies.

> As a woman in the company, I knew that I could never become the CEO, or even the President, but I knew which men were in the pipeline (because I developed my own grapevine) and planted my ideas with them. If I succeeded, they took full credit for it as their program that was in the best interest of the company, and I had the satisfaction of meeting my objective, which was to help educators, who in turn helped families in their communities. In my opinion, this is real power. To achieve it, you must have political skills and you must be willing to let others take credit for your ideas. You win some and you lose some, but professionally, it is stimulating and, at times, fun.

This survival strategy was identical to the one described by business home economists in the 1920s, and it placed them in a weak position when company managers evaluated their contributions in the context of new priorities.[60]

Even as they expanded their niche in business after World War II, home economists continued to confront some of the old challenges they had faced since the early 1920s as they sought to reconcile their professional identity with their value to their employers. While the HEIB Section and the AHEA provided home economists with a community (albeit an often conflicted one), these networks proved relatively weak in bolstering individual women in their efforts to navigate their careers in fast-changing commercial firms. At the same time, the 1950s and 1960s saw the emergence of new techniques with which firms could understand products and consumers, techniques that required the specialized knowledge not of the home economist but of other experts. Two developments inside consumer products firms posed particular challenges for home economists: the emergence of food technology and engineering, and the rise of modern marketing and market research.

Expertise under Fire

In a 1952 speech to sales associates in the gas industry, General Mills' home economics director, Marjorie Child Husted, questioned whether utility companies were getting the "full value of [their] investment in home service." Top management executives expected too little of home economists, Husted asserted, although they devoted substantial resources to including them in company operations. She urged managers to take home economists seriously as businesswomen, to demand more from them but to also listen to their ideas and give them room to build broader, more effective programs of customer service. "We must realize that home economists are professionally trained just as are engineers or chemists or lawyers," Husted explained. "And just as some professionally trained men have special attitudes that make them fit into business successfully, so some home economics trained women have a special flair for fitting into business — and can contribute a great deal to it." Like all important corporate employees, home economists needed continuing on-the-job training in sales and business techniques as well as support from executives. At General Mills, Husted boasted, the chairman of the board recognized the home economist as "one of the dynamos of great potential power." Utilities, in contrast, had "just made a start in home service," and Husted encouraged her audience of sales managers to take home economists "into partnership" and "build that success story."[61] Husted's lament suggested that many home economists in business were failing to reach their full potential in the postwar era, largely due to limited expectations on the part of employers. Twelve years later, in 1964, Helen Wolcott, HEIB national chairman and director of home economics and consumer service at Pillsbury, encouraged her home economics colleagues to assert themselves against corporate employers' narrow conceptions of their abilities and responsibilities. "Home economists must understand," she said, "that the service they supply to their own companies and to consumers must go beyond how-to's of product information. In coming years . . . home economists must guide the development of new products by realizing the potential practical applications of new technical knowledge."[62] Together, Husted and Wolcott pinpointed a common problem for business home economists in the 1950s and 1960s: although home economists saw their departments become more firmly rooted inside private firms and even expand in size, male corporate managers tended not to involve them in decision-making processes as much as the home economists desired. Too often, women in the field were consulted only at the end of the product development process when a new item was already being launched. Home economists' professional identity as mediators of consumption was gradually undermined by a series of developments simultaneously under way inside these firms.

In the postwar years, business home economists confronted challenges to their authority that stemmed in large part from the same sources as their success in the corporate world. In the interwar period, the idea that women professionals had special abilities to communicate with and educate women homemakers, and to represent them inside the firm, had supported home economists' claim to unique expert authority and provided them the basis for a certain level of job security. "One of the things I particularly like about my job is that I know that I don't need to worry for fear some smart young man will come along and take it away from me," explained one home economics consultant in the 1930s. "There are no smart young men who have the training or the experience or the backgrounds or the psychological aptitudes necessary for the work. Nor do any of the smart young men seem to have the slightest desire to acquire these qualifications. They seem to feel that this is women's work—and so far they have made no efforts to crash in on it."[63] Yet, while a threat from outside the field may not have felt imminent, the undefined nature of home economics work made it unstable at the outset and business home economists constantly had to justify their existence in their firms. Beginning in the 1950s, as the boundaries between men's and women's work shifted, home economists' mediating role (already intangible) became increasingly vulnerable to new, predominantly male fields of expertise. The emergence of food engineering, the transformation of marketing as a business management strategy, and the rise of market research began to erode the niches of expertise that home economists had carved out for themselves around consumer goods and homemaker preferences. Business home economists were forced to define and defend their contributions in new terms. Soon, with the proliferation of "smart young men" who had acquired specialized knowledge in these newer fields, being a woman provided less of a guarantee to unique authority and job security, and university home economics training came to be perceived as less valuable to managers concerned with remaining on the cutting edge.

Home economists became marginalized in their relationships to products, especially foods. The emergence of new ways of studying foods—"food technology" and "food engineering"—undercut home economists' expertise in the area of food and nutrition, replacing it with an academic discipline dominated by men. During World War II, food chemists and biochemists developed ways to meet emergency nutritional needs by enriching bread and flour with vitamins and minerals. In peacetime, enrichment and fortification became major selling points as managers of food-processing firms were attracted to the possibilities of manipulating the content and form of value-added food products. Many food companies established new research and development departments staffed by experts trained in new scientific fields. "Those weren't women who were put in the research department," home economist Ada Bessie Swann observed when appliance manufacturers started hiring food chemists and biochemists to collaborate on the development of new appliances during the war. "Here is an opportunity for our food economists to find work in the home equipment field."[64] Home economists were divided on the issue of whether to endorse the practice of enriched flour and bread. Many, including Jeanne Paris at Swift and Company, remained uncomfortable with "food additives." More important, home economists in the food industry found themselves overshadowed by these technical advances. Starting in the late 1950s and early 1960s, as food-manufacturing firms increased hiring of "food engineers" and "food technologists," home economists lost their claim to unique access to the latest developments in nutritional sciences. The new experts in food additives and enrichment were men. The very terms *food engineer* and *food technologist* signified that this codification of knowledge about food manufacturing was built around masculine professions. Home economists' relationship to products therefore became more limited to recipe development and testing.[65] By the early 1970s, home economists at Procter & Gamble devoted an estimated 80 percent of their time to writing recipes. Although this activity continued to be an important way that companies interpreted their products to consumers, it represented a considerable narrowing of responsibility when compared, for example, to the wide range of product development and testing duties that P&G's Eleanor Ahern had performed in the interwar period.[66]

At the same time, the developing field of marketing emerged to compete with home economists' claims to represent "the woman's viewpoint." As managers of consumer products firms looked for ways to take advantage of economic prosperity and expand their markets in the postwar years, they embraced new kinds of expertise to enhance their ability to identify and communicate with potential customers. Marketing became a major corporate force in the 1950s, as meeting consumer needs and shaping consumer demand became the basis for heightened competition. Summarizing a common assumption of the day, management guru Peter F. Drucker declared in 1954 that the purpose of every business enterprise was to "create a customer." A new occupational structure in marketing emerged with men in the key positions. With so many more new products to promote, the responsibilities of product sales managers broadened to encompass sales promotion, packaging, product planning, and market research as well as advertising. Sales managers of the prewar period became vice presidents in charge of sales, with higher status and stronger voices in company decision making. Successful marketing managers became some of the best-paid staff members, with career paths that led to top management positions and seats on corporate boards of directors.[67] Over time, such marketing executives were increasingly likely to have graduated from one of the nation's schools of business administration, where the field of marketing emerged as a specialization in its own right. Drawing on the pioneering work of academic social scientists who developed general principles and methods for analyzing markets and establishing marketing plans, business schools expanded their marketing programs. Beginning in the late 1940s, individuals such as Wroe Alderson and Reavis Cox at the University of Pennsylvania's Wharton School proposed theories of marketing that challenged neoclassical explanations of markets as the simple interactions of supply and demand. Arguing that only a systems-theoretical analysis of marketing could explain the rich heterogeneity of consumers' interactions with producers, Alderson and others created mathematical models to support a "professional, scientific apparatus" to analyze consumer tastes, determine the size of a sales force, and use the media to spread marketing messages. Increasingly, company leaders relied on these types of quantitative methods, including systems theory and operations research, to develop more purposeful approaches to decision making about market practice.[68] With consumer desires now cast as something to be "sorted out," rather than something fixed but mysterious (requiring home economists to reveal them by representing "typical" consumers), business leaders relied on these new kinds of expertise to determine the perspectives of potential buyers.

In addition, an emerging generation of marketing professionals developed new kinds of social scientific techniques and quantitative tools to study consumer behavior and analyze markets. To target potential customers effectively with the most appropriate products, many of these firms turned to market research, either establishing market research departments in-house or hiring consultants such as the Market Research Corporation of America (formed in 1939) on a project-by-project basis. Market research experts used a range of new techniques to examine groups of consumers, or "market segments," and to identify the characteristic buying practices that they shared, frequently establishing consumption patterns of various groups on the basis of age, income, and region. With refined information about what social groups purchased certain products, manufacturers made decisions about how to differentiate their products—through style, design, function, quality, and special features—from those of their competitors. In 1952, Sears, Roebuck & Company turned to "product planning consultants" Nowland & Schladermundt for advice on how to establish "direct communication" with consumers to determine promising product characteristics for the future. By the late 1950s, business schools offered courses to introduce students to market research techniques. At the same time, Ernst Dichter and Paul Lazarsfeld pioneered motivation research, shifting the focus on understanding not so much *who* consumers were but *why* they made the purchasing choices they did. By 1970, psychometric techniques for measuring tastes and econometric methods for segmenting markets became the mainstays of the marketing field. Analyzing and predicting social behavior outside the firm and "the composition of demand" became, in the words of historian Steven Sass, a "policy science much like finance."[69] New ways of knowing consumers led to a new paradigm for understanding consumers in increasingly complex terms.

The arrival of new marketing techniques in consumer products firms had mixed meanings for and diverse effects on home economists working in business. Insofar as these techniques triggered a rediscovery of women as consumers, the renewed attention to marketing initially gave male managers new reasons to value home economists' contributions to their firms. Echoing business leaders of the 1920s, managers in the 1950s invoked once again the established wisdom that 85 percent of consumer goods were purchased by women, and they hired more experts of all kinds to get closer to what one business writer called "that enigmatic and glittering prize, the female consumer."[70]

When home economists could help companies position themselves in closer proximity to this "prize," their role as mediator—both reviewing products from the point of view of consumers and promoting products to female buyers—remained important. Manufacturers of foods, fabrics, appliances, and other products used in the home had long relied on home economists "for guidance in developing new products and new uses for old ones," observed a 1959 article in *Sales Management*. Now these companies found that the home economist's status as part "sociologist" and part "teacher," along with her "creative temperament" and education in the natural sciences, made her especially useful in helping consumers understand and appreciate "the increasing complexity of many new products." Manufacturers experienced "more need than ever for the tips and information that enable the homemaker to use products and equipment to best advantage." These were the reasons, the trade article indicated, why firms hired home economists in unprecedented numbers in the 1950s.[71]

Male managers' emphasis on new methods of marketing and market research presented significant challenges to home economists' corporate roles, however. Whereas home economists' strength had depended on their ability to make connections between product engineering, marketing, and analysis of consumer use of products, now they competed with a new array of specialized experts in each of these areas. Home economists, once guardians of unique knowledge about consumers, now constituted just one of many groups of experts—including advertising agents, economists, sociologists, and marketing counselors—whom corporations enlisted to help them accelerate their pursuit of American homemakers. A young generation of male graduates from the nation's engineering and business schools were entering the corporate world with command over a new set of tools with which to understand and communicate with consumers. All of these new techniques made home economists' approach to understanding consumers seem unscientific and old-fashioned. After all, home economists had channeled their scientific research agenda in the direction of studying household goods from the user's perspective and had done relatively little to study consumer behavior in any systematic way. Now backed by enhanced social scientific methods, mediating between the firm and the consumer was cast in terms that were predominantly masculine and quantitative, rather than feminine and intuitive. Home economists came to be seen as technicians, useful for some purposes but less suited to the analytical or creative work of marketing. In this capacity, they were understood as important contributors, but now only as members of a large team of other more valued professionals, and with authority over a much smaller part of the whole.[72]

In addition, new approaches to marketing and market research led managers in the consumer products industries to question the concept of the "average" consumer, conceived by managers and home economists for decades as a white, middle-class woman who was largely demographically identical to most home economists. Whereas many male managers assumed a national, unified market of female middle-class consumers in the interwar period, new statistical surveys conducted in the 1950s revealed a market that was segmented by age, income, education, lifestyle, and class. Men, not only women, were recognized as consumers. Through the lenses of consumer surveys, corporate leaders discovered that consumer attitudes were changing along with social structure. Ongoing market research efforts placed the characterization of the "average" homemaker and consumer in constant flux. "Mrs. Consumer," whom many corporate managers claimed to know and understand with the help of home economists before World War II, seemed elusive and complex once again. As portrayed in the business press, the postwar consumer-homemaker was not only more discriminating than ever before but far more likely to be working full-time outside the home. Management experts such as Peter Drucker characterized young families in early 1960s as new kinds of consumers who were dealing with changing social realities.[73] As "Mrs. Consumer" came to be seen as a multiple rather than a single identity, home economists' claim to represent "her" as a unified construct slowly lost credibility.

Furthermore, market research provided a way for corporate managers to access consumers directly, without assistance from women mediators. By the mid-1960s, many food and appliance companies used "concept testing," interviews with "focus groups" of homemakers, and consumer panels to get feedback about prototype product models and determine which of its many product ideas in development to bring to market. In 1965 Swift added a Consumer Research Center to its exhibit *Food for Life* on display at the Museum of Science and Industry in Chicago, using the center to both pretest products and publicize its consumer research program.[74] As these new methods of market research took hold, home economists no longer played the role they once did in the larger process of developing products and marketing plans. Corporate managers began to relegate home economists to narrower, more circumscribed realms of customer relations and evaluation of finished products. "In business it is not uncommon for home economists to be called in to assist in marketing research today," Helen Canoyer, Cornell University's dean of home economics, reported in 1958. "Unfortunately, they are seldom viewed as essential to the initial formulation of the problem but are usually looked to for service contributions—such as testing a range or a recipe."[75] With home economists' relationship to food products reduced to product testing and recipe development, and their participation in marketing curtailed, home economists' mediating role became significantly diminished in the 1950s and 1960s—even as this narrower role also became more firmly institutionalized in many consumer products companies.

Just as home economists had to share the stage of knowing consumers with other professionals, they also faced competition from new methods used by consumer products firms to deliver messages to potential buyers. Television, in particular, made it possible for companies to communicate instantly and directly with consumers. This new medium diminished the importance of face-to-face contact with the nation's homemakers through the types of live demonstrations that home economists had presented on behalf of their employers since before World War I. In projecting their corporate identities through television advertisements, most firms chose not real home economists but women actors and glamorous women such as Adelaide Hawley Cumming, who portrayed General Mills' Betty Crocker on television beginning in 1950. As one observer explained, "The girl who bakes a cake for television stays behind the scenes. The face on camera is that of a professional model."[76] In fact home economists often scripted these televised segments. For "how-to-do-it commercials" that aired twice weekly in conjunction with the Kraft Television Theater, Marye Dahnke and her team at Kraft's headquarters in Chicago outlined demonstrations for featured products, documented step-by-step instructions through photographs, and then sent them to New York as the guidelines for filming by professional actors or models.[77] As food manufacturers replaced live cooking demonstrations with televised commercials and print versions of demonstrations in publications such as the *Betty Crocker Picture Cookbook* (1950), home economists were removed from the limelight. With some exceptions, new media made the corporation-sponsored "cooking school," in which home economists' personality work had been central, a thing of the past. While home economists were relegated to the discrete tasks of preparing food to be photographed, developing recipes, and corresponding with consumers, television advertisements and recipes on package labels made home economists increasingly invisible and abstract, as well as more disembodied and disconnected from the sophisticated spectacles of promotion in the postwar period.

The ultimate disembodiment of home economists' work came with corporations' increased reliance on images of fictional home economists, created by advertising agencies, to promote the idea that the companies were in touch with the daily lives of homemakers. General Mills had introduced Betty Crocker in the early 1920s and other firms had followed suit, but not until the 1940s did food manufacturers throw their weight behind these iconographic home economists by using pictorial images of the imaginary women they created aggressively on their packaging and promotional literature.[78] In projecting their professional identity, home economists had always played a balancing act between their collective image as scientific experts and average homemakers. Before and during the war, Kraft home economics director Marye Dahnke wore a pale colored dress rather than a white uniform for demonstrations, explaining that "a dress of this kind . . . is more in line . . . with what the average homemaker would wear when at work in her own kitchen[; it] gives an audience of homemakers the reassuring feeling that the demonstrator is just a practical woman like themselves engaged in making a good dish rather than a scientist using a laboratory technique."[79] This balance became more important to home economists and their employers as the conditions of domestic life and gender roles changed in the 1950s, but as the dual identity of homemaker and scientific expert became more difficult to maintain, corporate managers turned to the ad agencies for help. Motivation researcher and psychologist Ernest Dichter encouraged his clients in the food industry to seek a balance between creativity and the scientific expertise of the home economist. At his suggestion, General Mills altered the image of Betty Crocker in the early 1950s. Many other firms joined in this trend. General Foods introduced Frances Barton for the first time in 1948, and Swift brought its 1946 version of Martha Logan back to the drawing board in 1957 and again in 1970. In general, these new identities portrayed home economists as younger, more feminine, and less scientific. Under the control of advertising agencies, home economists' public identities could be changed and updated based on consumer surveys and other social scientific data. This process could take place rapidly, certainly more quickly than home economists could change themselves, and updated images could be easily disseminated throughout the expanding world of commercial media. Reduced to a series of advertising images that undermined their identities as scientific experts, business home economists lost many of the real and symbolic functions they had performed in the interwar years.[80]

All of these changes—the development of food engineering and new techniques in knowing and communicating with consumers—created a growing disjuncture between business home economists' desire to participate in corporate decision making and the responsibilities business managers gave them. As home economists' duties in consumer products firms narrowed, they also experienced a growing split between their professional identity and the value their employers ascribed to them. Many corporate managers were uncertain about what home economists were doing there at all. A 1965 survey of employers and potential employers of home economists in business in the

Swift & Company introduced the first image of its fictitious Martha Logan after extensive consumer research in 1946 (left) but replaced it in 1957 with a younger, less domestic yet maternal figure (center). Logan became more youthful still in what company literature called "the 1970 look." (Chicago History Museum)

Twin Cities found that only seven of twenty-two current employers, and only one of the twenty-four potential employers, had a "clear professional view of the home economist." The business managers surveyed registered confusion about the work home economists performed and how it related to the overall operation of a firm.[81]

While corporate managers could create ideal images of home economists on the advice of marketing and advertising consultants, business home economists faced the more difficult challenge of reinventing their professional identity to keep up with changing times. The HEIB Section's ongoing efforts to adjust the home economics curriculum and to provide continuing education were not able to turn the tide.[82] Although many colleges and universities had altered their curricula to help prepare home economists to work in business, women graduates continued to report that home economics programs did not fully prepare them for business jobs.[83] Some ambitious home economists obtained additional training in business management or communications, but they, too, complained that they were "constrained by the limits of the normal home economics position and pioneered in adapting their training and experience to new jobs in marketing and management, sometimes in new areas."[84] By the 1960s, cultivating interest in home economics work among company executives was a twofold problem: many companies had no home economics division at all, but many others advertised the presence of a home economist in the firm when they did not actually employ anyone with this type of training. The HEIB Section continued to combat the practice, "injurious to qualified home economists," of companies hiring unqualified individuals to assume home economics positions.[85] In spite of numerous initiatives, however, home economists failed to surmount the identity problem they confronted inside corporate firms.

The HEIB leadership's plea in 1967 that each member "refer to herself as a home economist" in interviews and publications was a telling admission of defeat.[86] By this time, as part of an ongoing struggle to demonstrate their worth to corporate employers, many women members in the field had stopped calling themselves "home economists," assuming newly preferred corporate titles such as "consumer service director," "consumer relations manager," or "consumer affairs specialist." These new titles clarified the roles that many women trained in home economics now performed in the business world and reflected the reality that many women with college degrees in the field found success in newly emerging corporate consumer affairs departments. At the same time, the trend signaled that the title *home economist* was fast losing its cachet and significance for both women trained in home economics and their corporate employers. The new nomenclature posed a specific threat to the HEIB organization, which, in the early 1970s, experienced its first decline in membership (although these numbers did rise after that to stabilize at around 3,000 members by the end of the decade).[87]

The problems of marginalization that Marjorie Child Husted identified in the early 1950s persisted into the 1970s. When the HEIB Section hired management consultant Robert W. Strain in 1970 to evaluate business managers' perceptions of home economists, Strain found that many firms did not use home economists to the fullest capacity and failed to use them both as "technicians" and "managers." Some firms were replacing home economists with women who were not trained with college degrees in the field. "Business management as a whole is not sold yet on the necessity of college preparation for the fulfillment of required duties," Strain reported. Many of his informants complained that home economists' attitudes lacked "resilience." One anonymous respondent said, "One must be able to roll with the punches without losing one's sense of rightness. One's position should be supported vigorously with facts, evidence, and persuasive argument; but one should support with equal vigor the decision of management if it should decide differently, and not lose a sense of balance in the process." The survey's characterization of business home economists as rigid and inflexible suggests that a significant number of women took critical stands on corporate decisions but failed to command respect from male colleagues for their contributions. Another survey confirmed that although business home economists wanted to participate in management and corporate planning, most corporate leaders preferred to limit their involvement to publicity and promotion activities.[88] Even as home economists employed in the consumer products and services industries transformed their identity in the postwar years from reformers to businesswomen, these surveys indicate both that home economists in business were not merely passive corporate agents and that they had limited power and influence over their employers.

The hardest blows came when many companies severely reduced or simply shut down the operations staffed by home economists—regardless of what they were called. Recalling the late 1960s and early 1970s, Philadelphia HEIB member Helen Fritz reported, "Many jobs in the home economics business field were threatened—some company departments were reduced or closed." The energy crisis had severe consequences for home economics work in utility companies, and firms in all industries felt the impact as America's postwar economic expansion came to a halt. By the late 1970s, the General Foods Consumer Center had a total staff of twenty home economists, down from sixty in 1955.[89] In the context of these new realities and with the rise of corporate diversification in the late 1960s, epitomized by the movement toward conglomerates of unrelated industries, home economists' mediating role became difficult if not impossible to justify, based as it was on constructs regarding the nature of business and consumers that were decades out of date.[90] Home economists were no longer regarded by business as their critical link to the mysterious female consumer.

Conclusion

In the decades after World War II, changes at the U.S. Department of Agriculture and in the consumer products industries eroded the institutional settings within which home economists had carved out a mediating role for themselves in the 1920s and 1930s. The Bureau of Human Nutrition and Home Economics continued to be a place where high-ranking women scientists could work in the 1940s. Two decades later, however, as officials in the USDA directed their attention away from the modernization of farm homes and the social problems associated with American agriculture, they abolished the bureau that had afforded home economists such an important platform from which to launch a research program devoted to consumer goods from the user's perspective.

Inside consumer products firms, home economists maintained their foothold through the postwar boom in consumer goods. The extensive proliferation of new products in this period allowed a number of highly visible women to establish particularly secure places within large food companies as well as with a number of other consumer products manufacturers. However, home economists' identity as consumer experts in these institutions became displaced by the arrival of new groups of male professionals. Food engineering and other new technical specialties further pushed aside home economists' knowledge of consumer products. The development of marketing as a business management tool and the rise of the new paradigm of market segmentation created a context in which home economists' claims to represent "the woman's viewpoint" lost much of their significance to corporate executives seeking to refine ways of both understanding and controlling consumer demand. While these changes exposed the extent to which the concept of the consumer as a white, middle-class woman was a cultural construct of an earlier era, they also left home economists in a vulnerable, defensive position in which they repeatedly sought to redefine and justify their worth to company management. Although they continued to shape consumer culture in important ways, home economists' loss of authority pointed to the reality that the intangible work of correlating production with consumption had always been a risky professional strategy. Finally, by the early 1970s, it proved untenable, as changes in business were matched by even greater upheavals in American social and political life, and home economists witnessed further erosion of their professional identity as consumer representatives, advocates, and educators.

8

Identity Crisis and Confusion:
Home Economics and Social Change, 1950–1975

As home economists' institutional bases in the public and private sectors eroded in the decades after World War II, the rise of second-wave feminism and the women's liberation movement in the 1960s placed home economists' field under harsh public scrutiny and criticism. Betty Friedan's landmark book *The Feminine Mystique* (1963) catalyzed this critique. Railing against the status quo of middle-class women trapped in suburbia, Friedan's best seller proposed a new definition of womanhood that looked beyond their roles as wives, mothers, and homemakers. Friedan aimed her critique largely at the media, suggesting that women were encouraged to stay at home in part so they could consume products for sale. While Friedan did not reject domesticity altogether, she urged women to find "creative work of [their] own" outside the home. By articulating skepticism about the rewards of domesticity for women, Friedan's book profoundly changed the cultural landscape in which home economics work was received.[1]

By the late 1960s, self-described radical feminists launched more aggressive attacks on the broad, social structures and middle-class values that they claimed confined women to the home. Their activism took the national culture by storm, dislodging many cultural norms and hitting home economists perhaps hardest of all. Through political action, such as a dramatic protest against the Miss America pageant in 1968, former child television actress Robin Morgan and her fellow activists worked to rupture the equation of women as homemakers in a direct assault on both home economics and home economists' claims to represent women; they even blamed home economists for the unequal relationships between the sexes. Speaking to the annual meeting of American Home Economics Association (AHEA) in Denver in June 1972, Morgan declared that she was "addressing the enemy." The homemaker, after all, was anathema to her, and she accused home economists of using their "immense power, psychological and economic," to prepare women for the miserable life of a housewife. Morgan invited home economists to change their image and, in the process, women's lives. "Quit your jobs," she commanded, asking them to abandon requirements that high school girls study home economics, or at least demand that it be required of high school boys. Morgan challenged her audience to "tell people the truth" about "the oppressions of women," including the despair of the homemaker who is "drinking herself to death in suburbia." She urged home economists to acknowledge their own "oppression as women" and join her crusade. "You run the risk of being obsolete. Those institutions that home economics has been hooked into are dying, and they are dying even without the feminist revolution." The nuclear family is crumbling. "It's your choice whether you're going to crumble with that system and stand in the way while history rolls over you or whether you're going to move with it. I hope that you will join us—but we're going to win in any event."[2]

At least a decade before Friedan and Morgan arrived on the scene, however, home economists' technical and educational function within American consumer society began to lose its relevance in the context of a broad series of social and cultural transformations. First came changes within American homes and within the middle class itself. Elements of the modern kitchen—gas or electric cooking ranges and refrigerators or mass-produced packaged foods— became the norm in most American households after World War II, and, by the 1960s, these products had become defining characteristics of the nation's standard of living. The values of economy, efficiency, health, nutrition, sanitation, and control became so embedded in notions of middle-class—and American national—identity that there was less need for a specific profession to "sell" the idea of modern living, and its principles and practices. Home economists' messages about cleanliness and efficiency, revolutionary at the end of the nineteenth century, became normalized by the late twentieth century as a new generation of women, members of an established middle class, grew accustomed to managing modern consumption in the very ways that home economists had been encouraging and educating consumers about for decades. Home economists' very success in promoting these new innovations as part of a middle-class value system meant that a younger generation of women required less instruction from experts about what to buy and how to use their new consumer purchases. At the same time, the middle class itself was changing as a rising proportion of homemakers in this cohort were choosing to work outside of the home.[3]

Challenges to the profession intensified as members of the baby boomer generation coming of age in the 1950s, 1960s, and 1970s began to question the middle-class norms of consumption with which home economists had become so closely identified. Two additional social movements emerged: consumerism and civil rights. While the rise of a new consumer movement in the 1950s gave home economists an opportunity to join in efforts to protect the rights of consumers, home economists' emphasis on educating consumers about economy and efficiency did not have as much to offer to a society trying to manage problems of abundance. Similarly, as participants in the emerging civil rights and environmental movements worked to address such social issues as inequality and pollution, most leading home economics advocates took a backseat in the calls for change (despite the origin of home economics as a social reform movement). In fact, as representatives of middle-class values with a stake in women's role in the home, home economists, to many observers, came to be seen as part—and even the source—of the problem. Similarly, a strong identity as middle-class women limited their ability to address issues related to the role of working-class or ethnic Americans in the consumer economy. This failure to remain in the progressive vanguard undermined home economists' credibility as consumer representatives and eventually brought them under direct fire from newer voices claiming to speak for women in the battles for consumers' and women's rights. Faced with these challenges, home economists turned inward, choosing to fight old battles and focus on a collective professional identity, eventually being overtaken by events that would redefine the consumer and the professional woman.

In a Turmoil

"Home economics today is in a turmoil," signaled Anna M. Creekmore, associate professor of home economics at Michigan State University, to an audience of home economics college administrators in 1968. "There seems to be among us in the field a frantic search for identity and status, a general confusion about what we are doing, an embarrassing sense of guilt about our 'image,' and, among the dedicated professionals, a deep questioning of home economics and its reason for being in today's world." Creekmore echoed a concern voiced by the editor of *What's New in Home Economics* in 1967, who argued that home economics had become "somewhat staid. . . . We don't prepare for the future enough in our work; we don't attract some of the bright young girls we should. We need to be a little more adventurous."[4] As I have already described, in the decades following World War II, home economists lost their power base within the agricultural establishment of the federal government. At the same time, home economists in business became marginalized by new specializations. By the late 1960s, as the internal critiques above suggest, home economics professors and teachers found that they were also losing ground in the field's original and one remaining stronghold: education.

As early as the 1950s, home economists began to identify problems of maintaining their turf within colleges and universities. Women deans and professors in home economics found themselves under siege, facing sexual discrimination by male colleagues and declining enrollments as increasing numbers of young women found educational opportunities elsewhere. In 1959, on the occasion of the AHEA's fiftieth anniversary, the organization's leaders prioritized assessing the profession's purpose in late-twentieth-century America. In a series of conferences and workshops, home economics educators and administrators met to clarify the boundaries and unifying concepts within home economics as an academic discipline. As an umbrella for a wide array of different subdisciplines ranging from interior design to child development to nutrition, home economics had become a very incoherent field. AHEA members had difficulty agreeing where the field began and ended. This confusion left home economists vulnerable to criticism from male administrators on the nation's campuses. In the words of one observer, home economics was a "job with a 1,000 titles," a term which suggested that home economists could literally do anything. But it was not a far stretch of the imagination to think that anyone else could do them as well. Such a broad definition was certainly no asset in an age of increasing job specialization. Just as the term *home economics* became irrelevant to women trained in home economics who worked in business and to their employers, it was also losing its significance in the larger society and was well on its way to becoming a pejorative term.[5]

The dramatic decline of the home economics movement in three historic areas of strength—government, business, and education—created challenges within the AHEA and the larger community of women trained in home economics. Members turned largely inward and backward when debating the future of their field. This internal focus left them unprepared for the significant social and political changes that impacted their collective professional identity. Beginning in the late 1950s, as a new consumer movement, a civil rights movement, and feminism all gained momentum, home economists as a group were so preoccupied with their "frantic search for identity and status" that they lacked a secure, clear basis of authority from which to participate in the major transformations that these initiatives brought about in both the public and private lives of American families.

Home economists' weakened position on college campuses and their preoccupation with surviving and clarifying the boundaries of their field put them in a relatively passive position as a third-wave consumer movement emerged in the late 1950s and early 1960s. Postwar affluence, a new kind of interest-group politics, and a renewed commitment to Keynesian economics—which emphasized consumer demand as the key to a nation's economy—created a movement that put pressure on elected leaders to step in and legislate on behalf of consumers. President John F. Kennedy's declaration of a Consumers Bill of Rights in 1962 built on ideas forged in the New Deal, but it marked a decisive shift in the place of consumption in American political culture. Over the next decade, leading activists such as Ralph Nader, who exposed the dangers of American automobiles in his landmark book *Unsafe at Any Speed* (1965), won passage of dozens of federal laws and regulations against unsafe products, misleading labeling and advertising, discriminatory banks and credit agencies, and other impediments to consumer well-being.[6] These activists created a new discourse about consumption that defined consumers as a political body in need of protection and representation by political advocates and highly technical experts.

Although home economists' identity as cultural mediators and their historical ties to Herbert Hoover and his faith in the mutuality of interests between industry and consumers were at odds with this new consumer discourse, the new consumer movement presented women in the field with opportunities to share their knowledge of consumer goods and consumer issues. After all, when President Kennedy created a twelve-member Consumers' Advisory Council, he chose Helen G. Canoyer, dean of home economics at Cornell University, to chair it. Canoyer joined Cornell in 1953, having earned a Ph.D. from the University of Minnesota's School of Business Administration, served as a professor of marketing and economics there for several years, and coauthored important textbooks on the economics of consumption. Canoyer's committee included Richard Morse, head of the Department of Family Economics at Kansas State University, as well as veteran 1930s labor activists such as Persia Campbell and Caroline Ware.[7] Although Canoyer and others urged home economists to get involved in consumer activism and many of her colleagues in the field served on state consumer councils, the relative lack of leadership from the home economics group as a whole signaled that theirs was a small voice in the growing public outcry in favor of government protection of the rights of consumers.[8] After Kennedy's assassination, Canoyer's committee succeeded in encouraging President Lyndon Johnson to appoint the nation's first presidential special assistant for consumer affairs. But Johnson chose veteran labor activist Esther Peterson to serve in this capacity, and later replaced her with actress Betty Furness. Furness drew on her high visibility as a representative for Westinghouse on television to call attention to consumer needs, but no similarly positioned home economist took as dramatic and public a stand on consumer protection. Nader and his cohort relied on other groups of male experts, notably quality-standards and safety-standards engineers, to evaluate the quality and safety of manufactured goods.[9] While the need for expertise on consumer products expanded dramatically during this era, professionals such as the engineering team at Consumers' Research ascended to this role, not home economists in government, business, or education.

Rather than functioning as a springboard for home economists to regain their public voice, the consumer movement served to boil up many of the old internal debates that paralyzed the AHEA and prevented its members from assuming leading roles in the campaign for increased legislation to protect consumers. Divisions over consumer issues in the 1930s between the organization's reform and business contingents were followed by a controversy in the mid-1940s over the AHEA's role in supporting grade-labeling legislation, which met bitter opposition from the Home Economics in Business (HEIB) Section. Although the AHEA membership voted to grant authority to its Legislative Committee to draft policy recommendations, HEIB members argued that the organization should abandon legislative work altogether.[10] The issue remained unresolved until the 1950s, when the new consumerism sparked discussions once more over using the organization to lobby for legislative action. While business home economists worked toward more secure and definite places inside corporations and recognition by male managers, many made the case that their utility to employers stemmed from their ability to combat the very consumer activism that other AHEA members wanted to promote. While some AHEA members joined the call for increased protective legislation and improved packaging and labeling practices, a powerful minority of HEIB members rose to the defense of corporations and the free enterprise system with which HEIB members were so strongly identified. By 1963 the organization resolved not to register as a lobbyist and continued instead to devote its limited political resources to seek funding for vocational education and what was left of home economics research at the U.S. Department of Agriculture—the bread-and-butter government funding issues with which the AHEA had been preoccupied for decades. Despite activism in some areas (the AHEA resolved that state home economics associations should work to establish state consumer councils and encourage members to serve on them, and in the late 1960s and early 1970s, the AHEA's Legislative Committee joined the chorus of critics in favor of increased regulation of the consumer products industries) divisions within the membership kept the AHEA on the margins of consumer activism.[11]

In the meantime, AHEA members maintained common ground through agreement that education, rather than legislative action, should be the central concern of all home economists. Most women in the field remained wedded to the notion that consumers, not business or government institutions, were responsible for their actions in the marketplace. "None of these [legislative] measures can protect the consumer from herself," wrote the editor of *What's New in Home Economics* in 1966. "She still must use judgment, whether buying or borrowing, caring for her children or feeding her family. And to make these decisions, she needs information." Echoing this rallying cry throughout the 1960s, many home economists continued to emphasize what Gwen J. Bymers called the "dual aspect of the consumer problem, the buyer and the seller's side of the counter." Bymers, an associate professor in the Department of Household Economics and Management at Cornell, objected to a sole focus on consumer protection and emphasized the need for broad consumer education.[12]

Yet even as home economists embraced their roles as educators, they struggled with how to teach about consumption in ways that made a difference for Americans at this moment of social change. As civil rights leaders joined the critiques of consumer advocates to highlight the ways that American consumption patterns reflected the economic inequality throughout the nation, the shortcomings of home economics' emphasis on middle-class consumers became ever more apparent. When President Johnson's Committee on Consumer Interests examined consumer education programs and looked for ways to expose larger numbers of students to "the fundamentals of buying, budgeting, and borrowing," it found a dire need for more knowledge in this area.[13] These findings, along with books such as Michael Harrington's *The Other America* (1962) and David Caplovitz's *The Poor Pay More* (1963) that helped to spark Johnson's War on Poverty, led Helen Canoyer and other home economists to call for members to reach out beyond a middle-class audience and focus more on the needs of workers in the nation's cities. While Doris E. Hanson, assistant dean in the School of Home Economics at Purdue University, raised the question of "which family to serve," the AHEA sponsored workshops on "working with low-income families" and a growing contingent of women in the field turned their attention to the needs of the nation's aging population. An important report on home economics in higher education by consultants Earl McGrath and Jack T. Johnson, published in 1968, called for home economics to play a more active role in the solution of social problems. McGrath and Johnson outlined an ambitious plan for revising the basic ideals and goals of home economics to emphasize "family service," and to reorganize education in the field of home economics to meet the needs of the "whole of American society," especially the urban populations.[14] In response, home economists gradually shifted their focus on the needs of a broader population, but their influence as educators diminished. A study of high school curricula in the early 1970s found that home economics lagged significantly behind a handful of other disciplines (such as business education and social studies) in providing coverage of consumer-education topics.[15]

While home economists' failure to assume a clear, leading educational role in the larger consumer movement ultimately left the American public confused about the identity and utility of this professional group, it put business home economists into an especially tight bind. Even as they worked to position themselves as a defense for business against "consumerism," few corporations relied on them in this capacity.[16] "An industrialist accuses home economists in business of failing consumers as well as their company managements by 'yes woman' tactics," explained the editor of *What's New in Home Economics* in 1967.[17] Yet the dominant public perception was that business home economists represented business and not consumers. "Have you *really* been working for [the consumer] for years?" Anna Fisher Rush, household equipment editor of *McCall's* and chair of the HEIB Section and the AHEA Consumer Interests Committee, asked her colleagues in 1965. Home economists did not use the consumer movement as an impetus to bring home economics to the forefront, she argued. "What has happened to our lines of communication with the American homemaker?" inquired Rush. "Have we failed in this business of educating consumers to cope with the bewildering abundance of our age? . . . Are others usurping our role as the spokesman for the consumer? And how long can we survive as a profession if we sit on our hands, and minds, while others assume the role of filling the present-day popular need for consumer information?"[18] One of the final blows to home economists' identity as consumer representatives came in 1969 when President Richard Nixon chose home economist Willie Mae Rogers, director of the Good Housekeeping Institute, to head his Consumer Affairs board. Critics argued that Rogers and the magazine publisher's testing bureau were too identified with business interests to represent consumer needs, and instead Nixon appointed Virginia Knauer, a Republican politician.[19] Even this conservative administration, which sought limited protection for consumers, understood the work of protecting consumers as political work and chose to move forward without home economists in the mix.

In the meantime, home economists' response to rise of feminism was more defensive than strategic. After the publication of Friedan's *The Feminine Mystique*, a group of professional women in their forties and fifties brought pressure on government to grant women equal opportunity in American economic and political life. As a group of political activists worked to establish equality for women in the workplace, the AHEA allied with business and professional women to support the work of the Federal Commission on the Status of Women, and the idea (voiced in 1962 by the National Federation of Business and Professional Women) of establishing state commissions in each of the fifty states. But when the National Organization for Women formed in 1966, vowing to support "the right of each woman to rise as high as she could in a competitive, free-market economy, unconstrained by legal barrier or biological accident," home economists remained disengaged for the most part.[20] Although the *Journal of Home Economics* acknowledged the economic realities of women's growing place in the public workplace and generated considerable discussion about the increasing numbers of families where women worked outside of the home, the publication was largely silent on the issue of women's rights until the early 1970s. As a growing social movement turned its attention to an attack on domesticity itself, the pages of the *Journal of Home Economics* suggest that home economists—who based their field on the notion that domestic consumption was women's special area of expertise—were largely oblivious to the rising contemporary call for women's liberation.[21]

Reacting to both feminist cries against domesticity and attacks from male administrators, many college home economics programs took steps to eliminate the word *home* from their names, adopting up to thirty different nomenclatures by the 1980s. The first call for name changing at schools of home economics came in 1960, and within four years ten institutions had dropped the name. Pennsylvania State University's program took on the new title of College of Human Development in 1967 and the one at Cornell University renamed itself the College of Human Ecology by 1969. Although the AHEA membership explored the idea of renaming the organization along similar lines, there was considerable lack of agreement, and the organization voted in 1969 not to change its name. Mercedes Bates, a HEIB member and AHEA president-elect, was among the women who opposed the name change. "After all," she argued, "a new dress doesn't change a woman's personality, and I don't think a new name is going to change our image. It seems to me that it's most important that we work within the framework of home economics as we know it to update our thinking and to project a forward looking image, and that we use the fifty years of effort that has gone into establishing us as one of the major disciplines."[22] Bates's assessment was apt: as we have seen, home economists had difficulty keeping up with the times, and those issues had something, but not everything, to do with the name. Although many of the more prominent schools changed their name, most did not, perpetuating confusion about home economics all the more.

In response to Robin Morgan's screed at the 1972 annual meeting, AHEA president Marjorie East, who endorsed the Equal Rights Amendment and believed that Morgan's speech was "good for the association," formed a "women's role" committee to explore how home economists viewed women's changing roles and to address "whether we see ourselves as part of the problem rather than the solution." When the committee met in the fall of 1972, its members confronted the disjuncture between how home economists saw themselves in the world and how the American public perceived them. Many committee members were shocked at Morgan's critique because, as East indicated, home economists had been "teaching dual roles for years." Susan F. Weis, a professor of home economics education at Pennsylvania State University, noted that "we teach one lifestyle and we ourselves practice another lifestyle." Most Americans knew only one home economist, their high school home economics teacher. Indeed, as critics in these years attacked high school home economics courses for being too limited and narrow, home economics had become subject to ridicule. "We must put part of the blame on ourselves," explained East. College teachers have "let high school teachers leave our colleges still better trained in foods and clothing than in child development, consumer education, decision-making, nutrition, and financial management."[23] Overall, the committee signaled that home economists as a group had not been keeping up with the major transformations spawned by the feminist movement. "We've really had our heads in the sand and haven't been listening," noted Virginia Trotter of the University of Nebraska. The discussions begun in this committee revealed some of the fundamental contradictions in the home economics field, and they generated further introspection and reconsideration of the assumptions about women in the home that were embedded in home economics.[24] Having been behind the curve on nearly every aspect of important social change since World War II, by the early 1970s, home economists could agree on little other than that their field had an image problem. After three decades of changes in technology, government, industry, and society as a whole, this concern over the image of the profession—while legitimate—signified a movement more concerned with internal issues than with facing the enormous transformations that had altered or demolished the foundation of their century-old movement.

Image Problem

In the early 1970s, to combat this "image problem," the AHEA commissioned Daniel Yankelovich Incorporated, a public relations firm, to conduct a study of public perception of the field. Yankelovich's team interviewed employers and potential employers of home economists in government and business, as well as home economics teachers, professors, and administrators. The Yankelovich report, completed in 1974, concluded that those in business, government, and higher education saw home economists in contradictory ways. While some individuals viewed home economists as skilled and active contributors to individual enterprises, others expressed uncertainty about the contribution of home economists to the goals of their institutions. Yankelovich's major claim was that home economics suffered from "a fractionated series of unrelated identities."[25]

The Yankelovich report revealed that by the 1970s home economists were no longer recognized as consumer experts or consumer representatives. The study identified "nutrition" and "consumer problems" as the top two areas of specialization within home economics, but it concluded that the field encompassed such a diverse range of subdisciplines "that there is no known and understood focus upon which a clear identity for home economics can rest." Although the report found that there were a number of standout individuals who made solid contributions to their employers through their subspecialties, the skills and expertise of these women were not named or understood as part of home economics. The groups surveyed tended to see home economists as "task-oriented performer[s]" rather than as contributors "at the level of knowledge and abstraction (and therefore broad helpfulness) which characterizes the professional approach." Home economists were perceived primarily as technicians or teachers, not creative professionals or researchers. Most dramatic, the report provided no indication that respondents saw home economists as representing either women or consumers. In sharp contrast to the rhetoric and reputation of home economists and their employers during the interwar period, the report was devoid of any suggestion that home economists spoke for an average homemaker or typical consumer. Instead, the research implied that home economists comprised a large, diverse group and that the public held "disjointed impressions" of their cultural and social identity. Opinions (or stereotypes) of practitioners in the field ranged from "bright, better-educated, more liberal, outgoing" and "intelligent, bright, aware, aggressive," to "not overly creative nor motivated, nice girls who want a safe berth" or "dull, conservative, not outgoing, domesticated, rural."[26]

Anthropologist Hermann K. Bleibtreu expressed similar perceptions in far stronger terms in a 1973 speech to the Home Economists in Business Section of the AHEA. Warning his audience of increased competition from other professions, he urged them to "come out from under your bushel and let your light shine." Home economists needed to show that they could "do things that nobody else can," he continued. "You have got to shake your image of out-of-date, home town, farm kids who are unwilling to upset the status quo but are willing to be subjugated and used." Home economists' expert contributions to corporate manufacturing were too narrowly technical, Bleibtreu argued, and he encouraged them to learn more about human behavior, social sciences, and other newer specialties related to their field that would place them in a better position to solve "People Problems." Discounting the value of the home economist's identity as a surrogate "little woman," "a woman and a 'homemaker' who represents all women and all homemakers," he encouraged home economists to become "independent professionals" with integrity who exercise power to "promote the general good" inside corporations. "Given your numbers nationally and the skills and education that many of you have . . . you should be able to develop into a quite formidable force. As it is, I don't believe that you are such a force."[27] These two independent pronouncements on the field pointed to the lack of a consistent public image for home economics and the overall weakness of the profession in the early 1970s. Reflecting the attitudes of people inside and outside of the discipline, Yankelovich and Bleibtreu signaled the passing of the historical moment in which home economists had served as important players in shaping a culture of consumption in the United States.

Conclusion

Just as Yankelovich failed to find a coherent identity in home economics, home economists were unable to formulate a consistent message about consumption in postwar America, creating openings for others—consumer protection agencies, governmental and nongovernmental, as well as social scientists—to take the leading role on consumer issues in the 1960s and beyond. Beginning in the late 1950s, the rise of a new, third-wave consumer movement politicized consumption in terms that forced many home economists to take sides in a national debate about advertising, product quality, and the government's responsibility to protect the rights and interests of consumers. By the early 1960s, as the call for civil rights gained momentum, many consumer activists looked for ways to address the inequality in American consumption patterns across racial and class divides. At the same time, a new feminist movement spurned female association with the domestic sphere and dealt a crowning blow to home economists' claims to represent American women. By raising questions about who consumers were—what they needed from business, government, and other institutions, as well as who should represent consumers—and about middle-class women's identity and place in society, these three important political currents disrupted the set of intertwined social and economic structures and cultural values that had allowed home economists to carve out a professional niche as mediators of consumption. Although economic abundance and the explosion of new products for the household had made the homemaker's job "more complex and more critical" and (potentially, at least) in need of more help from more trained home economists, public relations consultant Philip Lesly observed in 1967 that the home economics profession was "decreasing in public appreciation. Its image still smacks of eggbeaters and clothing dummies. Experts on education give it less attention in their planning and scheduling. And far too few capable girls are entering the field." Critiques like that of Lesly—who blamed home economists for talking primarily to themselves and to those who already "underst[oo]d them"—revealed that home economists were tied to an organization and an educational movement no longer in touch with the needs and interests of a growing segment of the population, and certainly no longer at the forefront of social, economic, or political change.[28]

Epilogue

Last summer my eleven-year-old son, a passionate gardener and avid early-twenty-first-century "foodie," wanted to learn to can fruits and vegetables. He was preparing to submit a number of projects for the local 4-H fair. The fair's premium book stipulated that all entries had to follow the guidelines of the U.S. Department of Agriculture (USDA) for safe water-bath canning. From researching the history of home economics, I knew that the required canning methods were pioneered by Louise Stanley and her colleagues at the Bureau of Home Economics decades ago. I had never done any canning myself, however, and after a couple of phone calls I learned that although both of my son's grandmothers had had some experience with it, neither of them was in a position to teach it to me or my son. How did we figure it out? We went to the local grocery store to buy some jars and found an entire display there featuring other canning equipment and a video screen where two women described the steps in preserving various foods. We bought some jars and some pectin for making jelly. At home we called the pectin company's "jamline" to get some guidance on how to adjust our recipe for this particular product, and we looked at the jar manufacturer's website for an overview of methods of water-bath canning. I realized we had come full circle, and that the legacy of home economics was still firmly planted in our consumer culture. When we wanted to learn a household task that our mothers or grandmothers were not able to teach us, we turned to the experts who had perfected not only canning but the idea of domestic expertise itself!

In these contemporary approaches to how-to instruction, however, the term *home economist* never came up. The function that home economists have been performing for more than a century remains key to our experiences as consumers, but the professional identity has disappeared. Indeed, efforts to reposition the discipline ultimately led to its renaming in the late twentieth century. In 1994, "home economics" was replaced by "family and consumer science," as a dominant group of members chose to change the name of the American

Home Economics Association (AHEA) to the American Association of Family and Consumer Sciences (AAFCS). With this new nomenclature, the organization cast aside an identity carefully selected by the founders of the field, members of a growing women's profession that was christened "home economics" (after much discussion and debate) 100 years earlier. This renaming signaled a formal break from the field's association with domesticity, highlighting instead issues of "family" and "consumption." Ironically, these were the very same subjects that the first generation of reform-minded home economists wanted their newly emerging field to embrace before the movement became entrenched in government and business institutions focusing on nutrition and consumer products. The choice to rename the AHEA marked the culmination of almost fifty years of introspection about the purpose of home economics (the name change itself being the result of more than thirty years of debate and discussion within the group). The split between home economists in education (represented by the educator-dominated AHEA) and those in business (represented by the Home Economics in Business [HEIB] Section within the AHEA)—two groups whose competing goals had underpinned debate within the field for decades—eventually became formal when a group of businesswomen left the "mother organization," soon creating the Consumer Trends Forum International in 1998. While many women educated in schools that had offered formal home economics programs joined this new organization, literature produced by the new group is devoid of any mention of the terms *home economics* or *home economist*. As late as 2010, the AAFCS, the former AHEA, maintained a membership of almost 6,000 (which, despite the break with the HEIB Section, included a new business group).[1] But these name changes—reflecting as they did the formal abandonment of the original vocabulary of the home economics movement—further underscored that the era had passed when home economics was seen as a force for social change and as a unique niche for professional women in the sciences.

In the 1920s and 1930s, home economists succeeded in finding a series of professional niches in government and business that allowed them to play a key role in interpreting new household technologies to an American public in transition from rural to urban and suburban, from home*maker* (i.e., someone who manufactured some portion of finished goods such as clothing and food in the home) to domestic consumer. Responding to cultural ideas that *women* and *consumers* were synonymous, male managers in government and business turned to home economists as stand-ins for the supposed "average" consumer. Efforts to expand mass production and distribution of household goods during this period created a need for technical know-how to adjust production and consumption and respond to the needs of an emerging consumer class. These circumstances gave home economists opportunities to perform the technical and cultural work, undergirding major socioeconomic and cultural transformation. At the Bureau of Home Economics, women such as Ruth O'Brien and Hildegarde Kneeland developed subspecialties in evaluating textile quality and surveying consumer behavior. Inside corporate manufacturers of processed foods and appliances, Eleanor Ahern at Procter & Gamble and her home economics colleagues played important roles in the development and promotion of new products including Crisco, processed cheese, and other packaged foods. At a time when these domestic goods—as well as kitchen utensils, appliances, and household cleansers—were new and the contours of middle-class identity were being redefined, home economists had a stable, collective identity as "ideal" modern, white, middle-class women, representatives and experts who guided many homemakers through these dramatic changes in the home. By promoting and interpreting both products *and ideas*—and helping to package manufactured goods and central utilities in terms of the principles of modern living that they espoused—home economists in government and business linked American consumer culture and middle-class values.

Although virtually irrelevant and invisible in the early twenty-first century, home economists served as a leading group of experts shaping modern American consumer society as it emerged a century earlier. Beginning around 1900, home economists studied manufactured and agricultural goods from the perspective of users and potential users. They served as important consumer experts during a critical chapter in the formation of a national culture of consumption. Especially during the interwar period, home economists' work—testing, describing, and teaching about new products—became part of how government agencies and corporations did business, helping producers adjust their goods to demand while also paving the way for acceptance of these new goods as educators of and interpreters to an emerging consumer class. In this capacity, home economists in education, government, and business sought to both represent and improve the lot of consumers. From within schools and universities across the nation, home economists promoted a culture of rational consumption and the idea that technological progress would improve social conditions. Inside the Bureau of Home Economics, where researchers sought to create an information clearinghouse about consumer products and consumer behavior, bureau chief Louise Stanley advocated continually on behalf of consumers' interests, working, for example, to persuade manufacturers and retailers to standardize products and labeling for the benefit of consumers. As a first generation of home economists found vocational opportunities in consumer products industries and utility companies, they attempted to advocate for consumers' interests from within corporate business enterprises.

Ultimately, given home economists' limited ability to overcome other more powerful forces emerging with the onset of an American consumer society, they were not successful in blending reform and professionalization strategies to shape and improve manufacturing and retail practices on behalf of consumers. Educational efforts to convince homemakers to resist the persuasive power of advertising and consume rationally were drowned out in the cacophony of mass marketing and advertising that came to define America's consumer culture. While the creation of a government agency, the Bureau of Home Economics, helped raise the field to prominence during the interwar years, its location within the USDA left it vulnerable to changing political priorities that always favored farm production over consumption and dramatically limited how much of Stanley's ambitious agenda could be realized. Within business, home economists who had imagined themselves capable of acting as a consumer conscience inside industry and commerce found themselves unable to overcome the profit-making imperatives—and the inherently irrational operations—of consumer capitalism.

Disagreements throughout the twentieth century among home economists in education, government, and business provide lenses through which we can view this formative period in the development of American consumer culture. Conflicts between home economics educators and their colleagues in business ultimately gave way to an accommodation to corporate imperatives. Especially when a product was new (and when corporate managers were still bound by assumptions that consumers were primarily female), home economists played a key role in helping corporations gain the confidence of American teachers and homemakers. When viewed closely, home economists' participation in these commercial enterprises emerges as part of the dynamic way in which manufacturers of processed and packaged foods and gas and electrical appliances achieved a powerful influence in American life. All of this suggests that home economists helped both government and business deliver more convincing messages to consumers. Yet, as Louise Stanley and Ruth O'Brien discovered in their many frustrated efforts to persuade manufacturers and retailers to give consumers accurate information about their products, the willingness of home economists to help government and business promote their messages was not always reciprocated by companies less willing to embrace home economists' defense of consumer interests.

While home economists' identifiable role in American consumer culture has all but disappeared from ordinary individuals' experiences in the twenty-first century, their legacy as mediators in the historical development of American consumer society persists today, especially with regard to the notion of professional and scientific expertise. Consumption in the United States remains intricately bound up with experts of all kinds whose work shapes the products we buy and the cultural terms through which we understand most goods and services. Even as the political economy of consumption shifted in the late twentieth century away from an emphasis on need for information—from labeling to how-to instruction—toward a focus on the protection of consumers' rights, the consumer economy still relies on the assumption that consumers can be represented by experts of all kinds. Industrial manufacturers, regulatory agencies, and consumer advocacy groups all rely on experts to develop and test consumer goods and instruct potential consumers in how to choose, maintain, and operate them. Consumers look to expert-generated product information to determine whether a product is safe or of good quality and value. When new products are introduced, experts emerge to perform the work of both technical instruction and cultural adaptation. To cite one example, with the rise in importance of "green living," a new group of experts readily interpreted the shades of better lightbulbs, household fabrics, and appliances according to this new standard, a standard with political and cultural, as well as environmental and economic, overtones. Consumers turn to labels and reports (some by government, some by businesses, and some by private, independent organizations) to gather information about products before they buy; the very sort of information that Stanley, O'Brien, and their fellow home economists fought for in the 1920s. A new actor that rose to prominence in the 1980s was the charismatic celebrity unaligned with home economists or any other professional group. Martha Stewart and her fellow "domestic celebrities," in television programs, books, magazines, and websites, attest to the continued importance of independent experts and commercial mass-media organizations in facilitating technological and cultural change in the consumer products and services industries. And in areas of manufacturing, techniques and strategies for balancing production and consumption have become far more refined and sophisticated since the heyday of home economics in business. The huge investment of labor and capital needed to release a new consumer product, and fast-changing processes of manufacturing and communicating with consumers (most recently via electronic social media) creates a continued demand for experts from various fields.[2] Where once some businesses relied more narrowly on a small number of home economists to inform production decisions and communicate with consumers, today this role is performed by dozens or even hundreds of specialists working in multiple disciplines.

Another example of home economists' lasting impact is the close relationship that continues to exist between middle-class identity and American consumer culture. Class status was tied to consumption long before the rise of modern consumer culture in the early twentieth century, and ways of demonstrating class status through consumption (conspicuous or otherwise) continue to evolve. But the presence of a large group of home economists working in government and business at a time when many of the parameters of middle-class consumer culture took form gave a special power to the values they espoused. Efficiency, sanitation, health, and economy remain associated with many of the goods available for sale, the advertising and marketing campaigns that promote them, the expectations Americans bring to the products they purchase, and the assumptions many individuals make about their identities and responsibilities as consumers. Smooth surfaces that are easy to clean, food that is kept at constant cold temperatures, and healthy meals now seem so normal and natural that it is easy to assume that their prevalence in our cultural discourse was inevitable rather than the result of a cultural transformation requiring the work of many individual mediators. To a great degree, Americans today tap into values once enshrined in a home economics curriculum to express a national identity and assert a standard of living that is distinct not only from Third World cultures but also from the cultures of other industrialized nations. At the same time, middle-class Americans also use health and nutrition as class identifiers, and contemporary policy makers point to the public health challenges of reforming a society stratified in terms of knowledge of nutritious food and the practicalities of getting healthy meals on the tables of all of the nation's families.[3] Even as luxury consumption exerts a cultural pull for many, middle-class culture still celebrates consumers who make sensible, controlled choices in the marketplace, resisting pure pleasure, impulse purchases, and cheap or shoddy goods.

Although gendered expertise of the type home economists once commanded is no longer central to product development and promotion, the experiences of women in the field who found vocational opportunities as consumer experts throughout the early and mid-twentieth century shed light on the ongoing but more complicated significance of gender in American consumer culture today. By constructing an ideal of the female consumer to which government leaders and company managers could subscribe, home economists contributed to the cultural construction of consumption as a white, middle-class, and feminine activity. They facilitated communication in ways that reinforced norms of proper feminine behavior and popular assumptions that consumption defined a women's relationship to domestic technology. This construction had contradictory implications. On the one hand, by proclaiming consumption as a legitimate activity for women, home economists made it a respectable enterprise. On the other hand, by feminizing consumption, they also marginalized both it and, by extension, their own expertise. Home economists' role as mediators of consumption helped obscure the more complex realities of their own activities as both consumers and producers, and their own role as pioneers for women in the sciences, government, and business. Confusion about women's relationship to consumption and the workplace continues to shape the division of labor in the public and private spheres today.

In our current era, when women play prominent roles in the sciences, government, and industry and when the importance of thrift, health, nutrition, sanitation, and expertise is both assumed and entwined with the culture in complex ways, it is easy to lose sight of the dramatic cultural changes that took place over the twentieth century, solidifying a place for consumption within middle-class identity. Yet these changes were not the result of abstract forces but the work of countless mediators, prominent among them the now nearly forgotten home economist, who helped shape our current cultural, political, and economic landscape. While Ellen Swallow Richards and the pioneers of home economics who gathered in Lake Placid more than 100 years ago might not have been able to envision what the United States would become over the next century, they would likely recognize many of the issues they sought to put on the nation's agenda as central features of today's consumer economy.

Notes

Abbreviations

AAAPSS	*Annals of the American Academy of Political and Social Science*
AAFCS Records	American Association of Family and Consumer Sciences Records, Collection Number 6578, Division of Rare and Manuscript Collections, Cornell University, Ithaca, New York (formerly American Home Economics Association Archives located in Alexandria, Virginia)
AE	*Agricultural Engineering*
AES Circular	*Agricultural Experiment Station Circular*
AFJ	*American Food Journal*
AFM Papers	Agnes Fay Morgan Papers, Berkeley, California
AHS Papers	Anna Howard Shaw Papers (Series X of the Mary Earhart Dillon Collection), Schlesinger Library, Radcliffe Institute for Advanced Study, Harvard University, Cambridge, Massachusetts
AKM	*American Kitchen Magazine*
AMB Papers	Amelia Muir Baldwin Papers, Schlesinger Library, Radcliffe Institute for Advanced Study, Harvard University, Cambridge, Massachusetts
AWNY Records	Advertising Women of New York Records, Schlesinger Library, Radcliffe Institute for Advanced Study, Harvard University, Cambridge, Massachusetts
BNRC	*Bulletin of the National Research Council*
BVI Records	Bureau of Vocational Information Records, Schlesinger Library, Radcliffe Institute for Advanced Study, Harvard University, Cambridge, Massachusetts
CF Papers	Christine Isobel (MacGaffey) Frederick Papers, Schlesinger Library, Radcliffe Institute for Advanced Study, Harvard University, Cambridge, Massachusetts
CG	*Country Gentleman*
CPC	Cookery Pamphlet Collection, Schlesinger Library, Radcliffe Institute for Advanced Study, Harvard University, Cambridge, Massachusetts
CRB	*Consumers' Research Bulletin*
CRGB	*Consumers' Research General Bulletin*
CSM	*Christian Science Monitor*
EM	*Electrical Merchandising*
ERN	*Electric Refrigeration News*
ESR	*Extension Service Review*
FE	*Food Engineering*
FHE	*Forecast for Home Economists*
FT	*Food Technology*

GH	*Good Housekeeping*
GHI Archives	Good Housekeeping Institute Archives, New York, New York
HBR	*Harvard Business Review*
HE	*Home Economist*
HEAFJ	*Home Economist and the American Food Journal*
HEIB Records	Home Economics in Business Section Records, Westerville, Ohio (now located in Schlesinger Library, Harvard University, Cambridge, Massachusetts)
HFRC	The Henry Ford Research Center, Dearborn, Michigan
HLM	*Housewives League Magazine*
IR	*Ice and Refrigeration*
IW	*Independent Woman*
IWPR Records	Institute of Women's Professional Relations Records, Schlesinger Library, Radcliffe Institute for Advanced Study, Harvard University, Cambridge, Massachusetts
JER Papers	James Earl Russell Papers, Special Collections, Teachers College, Columbia University, New York, New York
JHE	*Journal of Home Economics*
KC Archives	Kellogg Company Archives, Battle Creek, Michigan
KF Archives	Kraft Foods Archives, Morton Grove, Illinois
LPC	Lake Placid Conference on Home Economics
MCH Papers	Marjorie Child Husted Papers, Schlesinger Library, Radcliffe Institute for Advanced Study, Harvard University, Cambridge, Massachusetts
MSI	Museum of Science and Industry, Chicago, Illinois
MTM	*Melliand Textile Monthly*
NAL	National Agricultural Library, Beltsville, Maryland
NAWIV	*Notable American Women*, vol. 4, Records, Schlesinger Library, Radcliffe Institute for Advanced Study, Harvard University, Cambridge, Massachusetts
NB	*Nation's Business*
NBBVI	*News-Bulletin of the Bureau of Vocational Information*
NBS	National Bureau of Standards
NELA Bulletin	*National Electric Light Association Bulletin*
NELA Proceedings	*National Electric Light Association Proceedings*
NH	*Nation's Health*
NYSCHE Records	New York State College of Home Economics Records, Collection No. 23/2/749, Division of Rare and Manuscript Collections, Cornell University, Ithaca, New York
NYT	*New York Times*
P&G Archive	Procter & Gamble Archive, Cincinnati, Ohio
PCC	Product Cookbook Collection, National Museum of American History, Smithsonian Institution Archives Center, Washington, D.C.
PF	*Progressive Farmer*
PGCN	*Peoples Gas Club News*
PGLCCL	Peoples Gas, Light, and Coke Company Library, Chicago, Illinois
PHE	*Practical Home Economics*
PI	*Printer's Ink*
PIM	*Printer's Ink Monthly*
RCBHE	*Report of the Chief of the Bureau of Home Economics*

RCBHNHE	*Report of the Chief of the Bureau of Human Nutrition and Home Economics, Agricultural Research Administration*
RE	*Refrigerating Engineering*
RF Papers	Rockefeller Foundation Papers, Rockefeller Archive Center, North Tarrytown, New York
RG 16	Records of the Secretary of the United States Department of Agriculture, National Archives, Washington, D.C.
RG 69	Records of the Works Progress Administration, National Archives, Washington, D.C.
RG 176	Records of the Bureau of Home Economics and Human Nutrition, National Archives, Washington, D.C.
RW	*Refrigerating World*
Sears Archives	Sears, Roebuck and Company Archives, History Factory, Chantilly, Virginia
SM	*Sales Management*
Swift Records	Swift & Company Records, Chicago History Museum, Chicago, Illinois
TC	Special Collections, Teachers College, Columbia University, New York, New York
TT	*Timely Topics*
TW	*Textile World*
UCSC	Special Collections, University of Chicago
UMICH	University of Michigan Alumni Office, Ann Arbor, Michigan
USDA Bulletin	*United States Department of Agriculture Bulletin*
USDA Circular	*United States Department of Agriculture Circular*
USDA FB	*United States Department of Agriculture Farmers' Bulletin*
USDA Leaflet	*United States Department of Agriculture Leaflet*
USDA MP	*United States Department of Agriculture Miscellaneous Publication*
USDA OESB	*United States Department of Agriculture Office of Experiment Station Bulletin*
USDA TB	*United States Department of Agriculture Technical Bulletin*
USDA YA	*United States Department of Agriculture Yearbook of Agriculture*
USDPH Bulletin	*United States Department of Public Health Bulletin*
USFA Records	United States Food Administration Records, Hoover Institution Library and Archives, Stanford University, Palo Alto, California
WEIU Records	Records of the Women's Educational and Industrial Union, Schlesinger Library, Radcliffe Institute for Advanced Study, Harvard University, Cambridge, Massachusetts
WHC	*Woman's Home Companion*
WNIHE	*What's New in Home Economics*
WOA Papers	Wilbur Olin Atwater Papers, Special Collections and Archives, Wesleyan University Library, Middletown, Connecticut
WP	*Washington Post*
WWE	*Women's Work and Education*

Introduction

1. On the chronological development of home economics and the AHEA, see Bevier and Usher, *The Home Economics Movement*; Bevier, *Home Economics in Education*; Hunt, *The Life of Ellen H. Richards*; Craig, *The History of Home Economics*; Baldwin, *The AHEA Saga*; and

Pundt, *AHEA*. For more contextualized accounts from within the field, see Brown, *Philosophical Studies in Home Economics*; East, *Home Economics*, and "The Role of Home Economics in the Consumer Movement"; and Vincenti, "A History of the Philosophy of Home Economics."

2. Feminist scholarship of the 1970s emphasized home economics as concerned with the private sphere only. See, for example, Ehrenreich and English, *For Her Own Good*; and Matthews, *"Just a Housewife."* These works, like many published before the 1990s, generally portrayed home economists as either passive victims or corrupt accomplices in the rise of American consumer capitalism. Wright, *Moralism and the Model Home*, 156, downplays home economists' "ideals" and reform goals, arguing that they were "never made specific in their writings or their actions." For an excellent historiographical analysis of women and consumption, see Dirks, "Righteous Goods," 15–31.

3. Cohen, *A Consumers' Republic*; McGovern, *Sold American*; Glickman, *Buying Power*. For examples of works that present women's relationship to consumption in more complicated terms, see Peiss, *Hope in a Jar*; de Grazia, *The Sex of Things*; Scanlon, *Inarticulate Longings*; Alison Clarke, *Tupperware*; Nickles, "Object Lessons"; and Parr, *Domestic Goods*. On women as participants in American business history, see Yeager, *Women in Business*; Kwolek-Folland, *Engendering Business* and *Incorporating Women*; and Gamber, *The Female Economy*.

4. In the 1990s, scholars began to recognize the importance of home economics as a twentieth-century social and cultural movement and to address many of its complexities. For examples of this revisionist approach, see Stage and Vincenti, *Rethinking Home Economics*; Jones, *Mama Learned Us to Work*; Leavitt, *From Catherine Beecher to Martha Stewart*; and Elias, *Stir It Up*.

5. Although Melvil Dewey classified "home economics" under "useful arts" in the Dewey Decimal System, home economists objected because this emphasized the home as a center of production rather than of consumption. See Shapiro, *Perfection Salad*, 177–78; and Ellen H. Richards, "Ten Years of the Lake Placid Conference, Its History and Aims," in LPC, *Proceedings of the Tenth Annual Conference*, 20–21.

Historians of housework have written much about home economists' efforts to increase the efficiency of household production and management, but home economists' concerns for women's roles as consumers have been relatively overlooked. On home economists and housework, see Matthews, *"Just a Housewife"*; and Palmer, *Domesticity and Dirt*. On home economists' shift in emphasis from production to consumption, see Strasser, *Never Done*; and Cowan, *More Work for Mother*. Studies that address home economists' relationship to consumption tend to emphasize their promotion of the single-family home and to devote little attention to their broader agenda regarding consumption. See, for example, Wright, *Moralism and the Model Home*; and Hayden, *The Grand Domestic Revolution*. For more recent works that explore a range of cultural values promoted by home economists in relation to consumption, see Leavitt, *From Catherine Beecher to Martha Stewart*, 40–72; and Elias, *Stir It Up*.

6. Fritschner, "The Rise and Fall of Home Economics," provides the most comprehensive look at the development of home economics programs at land-grant colleges in the early twentieth century. See also Rossiter, *Women Scientists in America: Struggles and Strategies to 1940*, 199–203; and histories of individual colleges and universities, including Rose, Stocks, and Whittier, *A Growing College*; Dye, *History of the Department of Home Economics, University of Chicago*; and Eppright and Ferguson, *A Century of Home Economics at Iowa State University*.

7. Fritschner, "The Rise and Fall of Home Economics," 83–89. Fritschner indicates that the Smith-Hughes Act of 1917 set curriculum guidelines: about a quarter of the courses were in home economics, another quarter in science, a tenth in education, and almost half in general, nonvocational subjects.

8. On male discomfort with the world of consumption, see Carlson, "Artifacts and Frames of Meaning." On the efforts of corporate elites to dominate the "irrational" aspects of consumer culture, see Lears, *Fables of Abundance*. On corporate attempts to control distribution, see Chandler, *The Visible Hand*; Tedlow, *New and Improved*; Strasser, *Satisfaction Guaranteed*; and McGovern, *Sold American*.

9. Slater, *Consumer Culture and Modernity*.

10. Faith M. McAuley, "The 'Science' of Consumption," *JHE* 12 (July 1920): 317–18. A later *Journal of Home Economics* editorial labeled home economics "the science of ultimate consumption." See "Editorial," *JHE* 19 (April 1927): 46.

11. Cowan, "The Consumption Junction"; Oldenziel, "Man the Maker, Woman the Consumer"; Oudshoorn and Pinch, *How Users Matter*.

12. Cohen, *A Consumers' Republic*.

13. McGovern, *Sold American*.

14. Bowers, *The Country Life Movement in America*; Danbom, *The Resisted Revolution*; Daniel, *Breaking the Land*; Neth, *Preserving the Family Farm*; Jellison, *Entitled to Power*; Kolko, *The Triumph of Conservatism*; Kline, "Ideology and Social Surveys."

15. Glickman, *Buying Power*. See also Jacobs, *Pocketbook Politics*. More scholarly work is needed on home economists' political activities. Cohen argues that the American Home Economics Association was among the many women's organizations that fostered consciousness of citizens' identities as consumers. See Cohen, *A Consumers' Republic*, 7–9, 33–34. See also McGovern, *Sold American*, 189–90; East, "The Role of Home Economics in the Consumer Movement"; and Pundt, *AHEA*.

16. Swiencicki, "Consuming Brotherhood." On the ideology of separate spheres, see Kerber, "Separate Spheres, Female Worlds, Woman's Place." On the gendered construction of consumers as women, see Douglas, *The Feminization of American Culture*, 44–79; Marchand, *Advertising the American Dream*, 69, 162; Schudson, *Advertising, the Uneasy Persuasion*, 60–61, 178–208; Ewen, *Captains of Consciousness*, 159–76; Charles McGovern, "Consumption and Citizenship in the United States, 1900–1940," in Strasser, McGovern, and Judt, *Getting and Spending*, 45–46; Dirks, "Righteous Goods"; Scanlon, *Inarticulate Longings*; White, "Sentimental Heresies"; Steven Lubar, "Men/Women/Production/Consumption," in Horowitz and Mohun, *His and Hers*, 7–37. On the continual struggle for a hegemonic ideology of female consumption, see Smulyan, *Selling Radio*, 4.

17. Gilman, *Women and Economics*; Lane, *To "Herland" and Beyond*; Cott, *The Grounding of Modern Feminism*, 145–74.

18. Skocpol, *Protecting Soldiers and Mothers*; Koven and Michel, *Mothers of a New World*; Ladd-Taylor, *Mother-Work*; Sealander, *As Minority Becomes Majority*; Cott, *The Grounding of Modern Feminism*; Paula Baker, "The Domestication of Politics"; Sklar, "Historical Foundations of Women's Power"; Boris, *Home to Work*.

19. Leach, *Land of Desire*, 10–12. There is a large body of literature on American consumer culture in the twentieth century. See Lears, *Fables of Abundance*; Fox and Lears, *The Culture of Consumption*; Cohen, *A Consumers' Republic*; Cross, *An All-Consuming Century*; Susman, *Culture as History*; Daniel Horowitz, *The Morality of Spending*; Marchand, *Advertising the American Dream*; Schudson, *Advertising, the Uneasy Persuasion*; Strasser, *Satisfaction Guaranteed*; Tedlow, *New and Improved*; and Smulyan, *Selling Radio*.

20. On professional translators in the emerging consumer culture, see Marchand, *Advertising the American Dream*; and Horowitz and Mohun, *His and Hers*, 1–3; Lubar, "Men/Women/Production/Consumption," 28–30; and Blaszczyk, *Imagining Consumers*, 12–13. On the distinction between "users" and "consumers," see Parr, *Domestic Goods*.

21. "Report of Round Table Discussion Held Wednesday Morning, June 25, 1931," AAFCS

Records; Margaret Sawyer, "The Responsibility of Home Economics in the Field of Nutrition," *JHE* 16 (May 1924): 246–50.

22. Some historians have dismissed home economists and other professionals as mere "servants of power" who had false consciousness and "sold out" to consumer capitalism. See, for example, Levenstein, *Revolution at the Table*; Ewen, *Captains of Consciousness*; Ehrenreich and English, *For Her Own Good*; Matthews, *"Just a Housewife"*; and Baritz, *Servants of Power*.

23. Ronald R. Kline, "Agents of Modernity: Home Economists and Rural Electrification, 1925–1950," in Stage and Vincenti, *Rethinking Home Economics*, 237–52; Mark Rose, *Cities of Light and Heat*.

24. Zunz, *Why the American Century?*, xi–xii.

25. On the hardening of the boundaries between production and consumption in early-twentieth-century America, see Lubar, "Men/Women/Production/Consumption"; Oldenziel, *Making Technology Masculine*; and Leach, *Land of Desire*, 147.

26. Cowan, "The Consumption Junction." In addition to Cowan, a number of scholars have made the case for exploring the relationship between production and consumption, a richer understanding of women as technological actors, of users' perspectives on all types of technology, and of the work and technological know-how involved in consumption. See McGaw, "Women and the History of American Technology" and "No Passive Victims"; Lubar, "Men/Women/Production/Consumption"; and Lerman, Mohun, and Oldenziel, "The Shoulders We Stand on and the View from Here," 28–30. For examples of other works that explore the linkages between production and consumption, and mediators between them, see Horowitz and Mohun, *His and Hers*; Kline, "Agents of Modernity"; Blaszczyk, *Imagining Consumers*; Mark Rose, *Cities of Light and Heat*; Smulyan, *Selling Radio*; Parr, *Domestic Goods*; Nickles, "Object Lessons"; Carlson, "Artifacts and Frames of Meaning"; and Oldenziel, "Man the Maker, Woman the Consumer."

27. On the importance of interpreting scientific knowledge and its relationship to economic and social change, see Aitken, *Syntony and Spark*, epilogue. On "how-to" instruction, see Corn, "Educating the Enthusiast." On technical education, see Lerman, "From 'Useful Knowledge' to 'Habits of Industry.'"

28. On the debate about the social construction of technology, see Bijker, Hughes, and Pinch, *The Social Construction of Technological Systems*; Bijker and Law, *Shaping Technology/Building Society*; and Bijker, *Of Bicycles, Bakelite, and Bulbs*. On the shift in home economists' attention away from the working class and toward the middle class, see Levenstein, *Revolution at the Table*; and Shapiro, *Perfection Salad*. On the tensions between old and new notions of consumption, see Daniel Horowitz, *The Morality of Spending*. On the importance of education, information, and consumption to the formation of middle-class culture, see Radway, *A Feeling for Books*; Rubin, "Information, Please!" and *The Making of Middlebrow Culture*; Ohmann, *Selling Culture*, esp. chap. 7; and Nickles, "Object Lessons."

29. Wiebe, *The Search for Order*; Moskowitz, *The Standard of Living*; Chatriot, Chessel, and Hilton, *The Expert Consumer*.

30. On women's active roles in shaping consumer culture, see Peiss, *Hope in a Jar*; Gamber, *The Female Economy*; Dirks, "Righteous Goods"; de Grazia, *The Sex of Things*; Horowitz and Mohun, *His and Hers*; Scanlon, *Inarticulate Longings*; and Parr, *Domestic Goods*.

31. Brumberg and Tomes, "Women in the Professions"; Antler, *The Educated Woman and Professionalization*; Muncy, *Creating a Female Dominion in American Reform*; Walkowitz, "The Making of a Feminine Professional Identity"; Melosh, *"The Physician's Hand"*; Garrison, *Apostles of Culture*; Fitzpatrick, *Endless Crusade*.

32. Translating or instructional work in science has often been delegated to women and

ignored until recently by historians as part of the production of scientific knowledge. See Kohlstedt, "In from the Periphery." On women in public health, see Tomes, *The Gospel of Germs*; and Toon, "Managing the Conduct of the Individual Life." On home economics as a career opportunity for women scientists, see Rossiter, *Women Scientists in America: Struggles and Strategies to 1940*, 199–203.

33. Muncy, *Creating a Female Dominion in American Reform*, xiii–xiv.

34. Layton, *The Revolt of the Engineers*; Friedson, *Profession of Medicine*; Noble, *America by Design*; Bledstein, *The Culture of Professionalism*; Wiebe, *The Search for Order*, chap. 5; Baritz, *Servants of Power*.

35. Melosh, "*The Physician's Hand*," chap. 1; Brumberg and Tomes, "Women in the Professions"; Cott, *The Grounding of Modern Feminism*, chap. 7; Ginzberg, *Women and the Work of Benevolence*; Kunzel, *Fallen Women, Problem Girls*; Muncy, *Creating a Female Dominion in American Reform*; Garrison, *Apostles of Culture*; Walkowitz, "The Making of a Feminine Professional Identity." Oldenziel, *Making Technology Masculine*, analyzes the masculine construction of the professionalization process in the case of engineering.

36. "Studying these borderlands," as historian Steven Lubar has written, "can cast light on the big questions of consumption and production in a way that studying either side on its own never can." See Lubar, "Men/Women/Production/Consumption," 20. On the role of technological systems of production in the history of technology, see Hughes, *Networks of Power*.

Chapter 1

1. Woolman and McGowan, *Textiles* (1913), 370–71.

2. James, James, and Boyer, *Notable American Women, 1607–1950*, 3:663–65; Leonard, *Woman's Who's Who of America*, 904; Mary Schenck Woolman, "Chapters from the Lives of Leaders: A Bird's Eye View of the Home Economics Movement as It Develops," *HE* 6 (January 1928): 15–16; Rury, *Education and Women's Work*, 153–55; Woolman, *The Making of a Trade School*.

3. Cremin, Shannon, and Townsend, *A History of Teachers College Columbia University*, 64; Andrews, "The School of Household Arts, Teachers College, Columbia," 79.

4. Woolman, "Clothing Information Bureau"; "Conference on Clothing Specialists," *JHE* 13 (March 1921).

5. Women's Education Association, *Domestic Art*; Richards, *Domestic Economy as a Factor in Public Education*.

6. Strasser, *Never Done*; Cowan, *More Work for Mother*; Daniel Horowitz, *The Morality of Spending*, 67–70; Nancy Tomes, "Spreading the Germ Theory: Sanitary Science and Home Economics, 1880–1930," in Stage and Vincenti, *Rethinking Home Economics*, 34–54; Strasser, *Satisfaction Guaranteed*; Leach, *Land of Desire*; Marchand, *Advertising the American Dream*; Lears, *Fables of Abundance*; Schudson, *Advertising, the Uneasy Persuasion*.

7. James, James, and Boyer, *Notable American Women, 1607–1950*, 3:143–46; Hunt, *The Life of Ellen H. Richards*; Robert Clarke, *Ellen Swallow*; Richards, *The Chemistry of Cooking and Cleaning*; Richards, *Food Materials and Their Adulterations*; Richards, *Air, Water, and Food from a Sanitary Standpoint*; Richards, *Sanitation in Daily Life*; Rossiter, *Women Scientists in America: Struggles and Strategies to 1940*, 68–70.

8. Shapiro, *Perfection Salad*, 171; Levenstein, *Revolution at the Table*, chap. 4; James, James, and Boyer, *Notable American Women, 1607–1950*, 3:144–45; Richards, "The Story of the New England Kitchen."

9. Ellen Richards, "The Social Significance of the Home Economics Movement," *JHE* 3 (April 1911): 124. See also Daniel Horowitz, *The Morality of Spending*, 78–84.

10. On Progressive Era reformers, see Wiebe, *The Search for Order*, 196–223; Lustig, *Corporate Liberalism*; Trachtenberg, *The Incorporation of America*; Boyer, *Urban Masses and Moral Order in America*; Rodgers, "In Search of Progressivism"; Haber, *Efficiency and Uplift*; Graham, *Managing on Her Own*; Taylor, *Principles of Scientific Management*; Tichi, *Shifting Gears*; Banta, *Taylored Lives*; and Jordan, *Machine-Age Ideology*.

11. Ellen H. Richards, "Housekeeping in the Twentieth Century," *AKM* (March 1900): 205. See also LPC, *Proceedings of the Sixth Annual Conference*, 31; and Ellen H. Richards, "Ten Years of the Lake Placid Conference on Home Economics, Its History and Aims," in LPC, *Proceedings of the Tenth Annual Conference*, 24.

12. Tomes, "Spreading the Germ Theory," 39–40; Stage, "From Domestic Science to Social Housekeeping," 224; Richards, *The Cost of Living*; Richards, *The Cost of Food*. Williams, "Healthier Homes through Education," provides the most thorough account of the Lake Placid conferences. See also "Announcement: The American Home Economics Association and the Journal of Home Economics," *JHE* 1 (February 1909): 1; Stage, "Ellen Richards"; Weigley, "It Might Have Been Euthenics"; Ehrenreich and English, *For Her Own Good*, 155–56; Wright, *Moralism and the Model Home*, 154; and Shapiro, *Perfection Salad*, 176–77, 181–82, 213.

13. On middle-class formation in this period, see Daniel Horowitz, *The Morality of Spending*, 67–108; Radway, *A Feeling for Books*; Moskowitz, *The Standard of Living*; and Grier, *Culture and Comfort*.

14. LPC, *Proceedings of the First, Second, and Third Conferences*, 6. See also Abel, *Successful Family Life on the Moderate Income*. On Richards's focus on the middle class, see Shapiro, *Perfection Salad*, 171; Daniel Horowitz, *The Morality of Spending*, 78–84; and Levenstein, *Revolution at the Table*.

15. Sklar, "Historical Foundations of Women's Power," 60–61. There is an extensive body of historical literature on women and reform in the nineteenth century. See Leach, *True Love and Perfect Union*; Ryan, *Cradle of the Middle Class*; Ginzberg, *Women and the Work of Benevolence*; and Boylan, *The Origins of Women's Activism*.

16. See membership lists, LPC; Young, *Pure Food*; Muncy, *Creating a Female Dominion in American Reform*, 59; Deutsch, *Women and the City*; Scott, *Natural Allies*.

17. Hunt, "Woman's Public Work for the Home," in LPC, *Proceedings of the Ninth Annual Conference*, 12, 15. See also Stage, "Ellen Richards" and "From Domestic Science to Social Housekeeping."

18. Veblen, *The Theory of the Leisure Class*; Gilman, *Women and Economics*. On women and theories of consumption, see Dirks, "Righteous Goods," 157–214. On the marginalists, see Livingston, *Pragmatism and the Political Economy of Cultural Revolution*; Leach, *Land of Desire*, 231–44; Daniel Horowitz, *The Morality of Spending*, 30–49; Devine, "The Economic Function of Woman," *AAAPSS* 5:3 (1895): 361–76; and Storrs, *Civilizing Capitalism*, 3–4. For discussions of Devine among home economists, see LPC, *Proceedings of the Fourth Annual Conference*, 55.

19. Hunt, *Revaluations* and *Home Problems from a New Standpoint*; and Dirks, "Righteous Goods." On Hunt, see Dye, *History of the Department of Home Economics, University of Chicago*, 13–14; and Leonard, *Woman's Who's Who of America*, 415; East, "The Role of Home Economics in the Consumer Movement," 276; Wright, *Moralism and the Model Home*, 160. On Talbot, see Talbot, *More than Lore*; James, James, and Boyer, *Notable American Women, 1607–1950*, 3:423–24; Leonard, *Woman's Who's Who of America*, 800; Tomes, "Spreading the Germ Theory," 35; and Fitzpatrick, *Endless Crusade*, 30–32, 84–86. On Smith, see Leonard, *Woman's Who's Who of America*, 763; *HLM* (April 1913): 31; "The Square Deal in Ithaca," *HLM*

(June 1913): 25–26; "How the Turkeys Jumped the Middlemen," *HLM* (November 1913): 11–4; and "National Headquarters Opened," *HLM* 5:2 (February 1915): 3–10. For other examples of home economists' support of the National Consumers' Leagues, see Breckinridge and Talbot, *The Modern Household*, 41–43; Woolman and McGowan, *Textiles* (1913), 371–77; Woolman and McGowan, *Textiles* (1926), 507–12; and Richards, "The Social Significance of the Home Economics Movement," 117.

20. Hunt, "Household Adjustment to Technical Development."

21. A search for the LPC members in John Leonard's biographical directory, *Woman's Who's Who of America* (1914), the only one that registered information about women's views on the "woman question," revealed listings of fifty-one of the more than 350 individuals listed in the conference proceedings. On Richards, see Hunt, *The Life of Ellen H. Richards*, 91; and James, James, and Boyer, *Notable American Women, 1607–1950*, 3:143. On Dewey, see "Annie Godfrey Dewey," *JHE* 15 (July 1923): 359. Isabel Bevier insisted in a 1929 interview that she was not a feminist. See Helen Hayes Peffer, "[Isabel Bevier] 68 Years Young," *IW* 8 (1929): 487, 527–28, cited in Rossiter, *Women Scientists in America: Struggles and Strategies to 1940*, 355n44.

22. Henrietta Goodrich, "Suggestions for a Professional School of Home and Social Economics," LPC, *Proceedings of the First, Second and Third Conferences*, 26.

23. Ellsworth, "Theodore Roosevelt's Country Life Commission"; Danbom, *The Resisted Revolution*; Bowers, *The Country Life Movement in America*; Hempstead, "Agricultural Change and the Rural Problem"; Kline, "Ideology and Social Surveys."

24. On home economists' scientific training, see Rossiter, *Women Scientists in America: Struggles and Strategies to 1940*, 60, 64, 65–70; Rossiter, "Mendel the Mentor"; and Fritschner, "The Rise and Fall of Home Economics," 83–89. On home economists' faith in technological progress, see Kline, "Ideology and Social Surveys." On Abel, see *Woman's Who's Who in America*, s.v. "Abel, Mary Hinman"; and Hayden, *The Grand Domestic Revolution*, 151–62. On Bevier, see Moores, *Fields of Rich Toil*, 176–204, esp. 180; Rossiter, *Women Scientists in America: Struggles and Strategies to 1940*, 70n43; Leonard, *Woman's Who's Who of America*, 34–35; Bane, *The Story of Isabel Bevier*; Bevier, "Chapters from the Lives of Leaders," *HE* (May 1928): 117, 136, 140; and James, James, and Boyer, *Notable American Women, 1607–1950*, 1:141–42. On Elliott, see Tomes, *The Gospel of Germs*, 142–43, 144, 151, 244.

25. On Kingsbury, see James, James, and Boyer, *Notable American Women, 1607–1950*, 2:335–36. See also Dorothy Ross, "Development of the Social Sciences"; Stage, "From Domestic Science to Social Housekeeping," 224; and Berlage, "The Establishment of an Applied Social Science."

26. Toepfer, "James Earl Russell and the Rise of Teachers College," 181–91; Shapiro, *Perfection Salad*, 47–126; Bevier and Usher, *The Home Economics Movement*; Betters, *The Bureau of Home Economics*, 6–7.

27. Cremin, *The Transformation of the School*, viii–ix; Westbrook, *John Dewey and American Democracy*, 93–111, 189; Rury, *Education and Women's Work*, 136–37, chap. 4; Kantor and Tyack, *Work, Youth, and Schooling*. On manual training in the 1870s and 1880s, see Lerman, "From 'Useful Knowledge' to 'Habits of Industry.'" On Snedden, see Rury, *Education and Women's Work*, 158; Drost, *David Snedden and Education for Social Efficiency*; and Kliebard, *The Struggle for the American Curriculum*, chap. 4. On home economists' alliance with vocational educators, see Rima Apple, "Liberal Arts or Vocational Training? Home Economics Education for Girls," in Stage and Vincenti, *Rethinking Home Economics*, 79–95; and Palmer, *Domesticity and Dirt*, 89–110.

28. Goodrich, "Suggestions for a Professional School of Home and Social Economics," 26–27, 30; Williams, "Healthier Homes through Education," 57–84.

29. Hunt, *Revaluations*; Annie Dewey, "The Tyranny of Things," LPC, *Proceedings of the Eighth Annual Conference*, 57–60.

30. LPC, *Proceedings of the Sixth Annual Conference*, 31; Stage, "Ellen Richards."

31. Helen Kinne, "Women and Machinery," LPC, *Proceedings of the Eighth Annual Conference*, 89; Goodrich, "Suggestions for a Professional School of Home and Social Economics," 34–35.

32. LPC, *Proceedings of the First, Second and Third Conferences*, 5. See also Stage, "Ellen Richards." On Dewey and the feminization of the library profession, see Garrison, *Apostles of Culture*, chaps. 10–15.

33. Goodrich, "Suggestions for a Professional School of Home and Social Economics," 33, 36; Pundt, *AHEA*, xiv, 2–6; Gladys Branegan, "Our Heritage and Its Challenge," *JHE* 34 (September 1942): 416.

34. Helen Horowitz, *Alma Mater*.

35. Betters, *The Bureau of Home Economics*, 10; True, *A History of Agricultural Extension Work in the United States*; Rasmussen, *Taking the University to the People*. On home economics extension in various states, see Babbitt, "The Productive Farm Woman"; Schweider, "Education and Change in the Lives of Iowa Farm Women"; Elbert, "Women and Farming," 245–64; Sturges, "'How're You Gonna Keep 'Em Down on the Farm?'"; Jensen, "Canning Comes to New Mexico," and "Crossing Ethnic Barriers in the Southwest"; Neth, *Preserving the Family Farm*; Jellison, *Entitled to Power*; Carmen Harris, "Grace under Pressure," in Stage and Vincenti, *Rethinking Home Economics*, 203–28; and Jones, *Mama Learned Us to Work*, 107–69.

36. Rasmussen, *Taking the University to the People*, 86–87; Palmer, *Domesticity and Dirt*, 89–110; Betters, *The Bureau of Home Economics*, 5; Eppright and Ferguson, *A Century of Home Economics at Iowa State University*, 76; Bix, "Equipped for Life"; Fritschner, "The Rise and Fall of Home Economics," 79–89, 103–26, 229–45, 276–93; Rury, *Education and Women's Work*, 147; Kyrk, "Home Economics."

37. Fritschner, "The Rise and Fall of Home Economics" and "Women's Work and Women's Education."

38. Cremin, Shannon, and Townsend, *A History of Teachers College Columbia University*, 64, 89, 119–20; Toepfer, "James Earl Russell and the Rise of Teachers College," 181–91; Andrews, "The School of Household Arts, Teachers College, Columbia"; Maurice A. Bigelow to James Earl Russell, June 25, 1917, Folder 172, RG 6, JER Papers.

39. Gordon, *Gender and Higher Education in the Progressive Era*, chap. 3; Fitzpatrick, *Endless Crusade*, 29–34, 71–91; Muncy, *Creating a Female Dominion in American Reform*, chap. 3; Dye, *History of the Department of Home Economics, University of Chicago*, 14–18, 21, 23–26, 58–59, 118–32, 154, 168, 172–76; Sicherman and Green, *Notable American Women: The Modern Period*, 637–38; Katherine Blunt, "What Is Graduate Work in Home Economics?," *JHE* 15 (April 1923): 186–90; Collins, "Domestic Sciences."

40. Dorothy Ross, "Development of the Social Sciences," 114–21; Veysey, *The Emergence of the American University*, 98–113; Eppright and Ferguson, *A Century of Home Economics at Iowa State University*, 19, 23, 25, 26–27, 33–34, 38.

41. Beecher, *A Treatise on Domestic Economy*, 185–95. On relationships between production and consumption in nineteenth-century American households, see Boydston, *Home and Work*; Cowan, *More Work for Mother*; Strasser, *Never Done*; and Caroline L. Hunt, "Report of Standing Committee on Home Economics in Higher Education," in LPC, *Proceedings of the Sixth Annual Conference*, 39.

42. On rural America at this time, see Barron, *Mixed Harvest*. On the relationship between professionals and middle-class culture, see Radway, *A Feeling for Books*; Bledstein, *The Cul-*

ture of Professionalism; and Ohmann, *Selling Culture*. There are many institutional histories of state home economics colleges, but historians need a better demographic analysis of the students who attended them and how this population changed over time. See, for example, Rose, Stocks, and Whittier, *A Growing College*; Eppright and Ferguson, *A Century of Home Economics at Iowa State University*; and Dye, *History of the Department of Home Economics, University of Chicago*.

43. Charlotte M. Gibbs, "Problems in University Work in Textiles," *Proceedings of the Ninth Lake Placid Conference on Home Economics*, 29–30; Leonard, *Woman's Who's Who of America*, 323–24.

44. Dorothy Ross, "Development of the Social Sciences"; Geiger, *To Advance Knowledge*; Veysey, *The Emergence of the American University*, 121–79; Oleson and Voss, *The Organization of Knowledge in Modern America*; Rossiter, *Women Scientists in America: Struggles and Strategies to 1940*, 199–203; Fritschner, "The Rise and Fall of Home Economics," 83–89; Berlage, "The Establishment of an Applied Social Science"; Faith M. McAuley, "The 'Science' of Consumption," *JHE* 12 (July 1920): 317–18.

45. Bevier, "The Development of Home Economics," *GH* (October 1910): 465; Bane, *The Story of Isabel Bevier*, 125. See also Daniel Horowitz, *The Morality of Spending*, 78–84.

46. Quoted in Eppright and Ferguson, *A Century of Home Economics at Iowa State University*, 82.

47. Terrill, *Household Management*, 6, 13–14; Kinne and Cooley, *Foods and Household Management*, 326–37.

48. LPC, *Proceedings of the Ninth Annual Conference*, 8–9; Dye, *History of the Department of Home Economics, University of Chicago*, 15–21, 160–66; East, "The Role of Home Economics in the Consumer Movement," 275–76; Frances L. Swain, "Our Professional Debt to Marion Talbot," *JHE* 41 (April 1949): 185–86; Stage, "From Domestic Science to Social Housekeeping," 222; Breckinridge and Talbot, *The Modern Household*.

49. Shapiro, *Perfection Salad*; Bevier and Usher, *The Home Economics Movement*, part 1, 44–51; Bevier, *Home Economics in Education*, 134–40; Levenstein, *Revolution at the Table*, chap. 12; Bane, *The Story of Isabel Bevier*, 39; C. F. Langworthy, "For the Homemaker: Food Selection for Rational and Economical Living," *JHE* 8 (June 1916): 316; Eppright and Ferguson, *A Century of Home Economics at Iowa State University*, 51–52; Goldstein, "Home Economics"; Kinne and Cooley, *Foods and Household Management*; Rossiter, *Women Scientists in America: Struggles and Strategies to 1940*, 200–203; Mary Barber, *History of the American Dietetic Association*.

50. Eppright and Ferguson, *A Century of Home Economics at Iowa State University*, 27–35; Richards and Talbot, *Home Sanitation*. On other domestic reformers, see Wright, *Moralism and the Modern Home*; Clifford Clark, *The American Family Home*, 103–92; and Boris, *Art and Labor*.

51. Tomes, "Spreading the Germ Theory," 39. See also Tomes, *The Gospel of Germs*, 139–54, 196–204, 243–45; Elliott, *Household Bacteriology*; and Hoy, *Chasing Dirt*.

52. Watson, *Textiles and Clothing*, 166–68; Woolman and McGowan, *Textiles* (1913), 266, 274. See also Iva L. Brandt, "A Course in Textile Shopping," *JHE* 11 (December 1919): 540; Kinne and Cooley, *Shelter and Clothing*, part 2; Gamber, *The Female Economy*, chap. 4; Eppright and Ferguson, *A Century of Home Economics at Iowa State University*; and Cremin, Shannon, and Townsend, *A History of Teachers College Columbia University*; and Connelly, "The Transformation of the Sewing Machine and Home Sewing in America," chap. 5.

53. Woolman and McGowan, *Textiles* (1913), 274–75, 346–55, 358–59, chap. 16. On dress reform, see Whitney, *The Economics of Dress*; Gamber, *The Female Economy*, 109–11; and Steele, *Fashion and Eroticism*, 145–50, 161–72.

54. Goodrich, "Suggestions for a Professional School of Home and Social Economics," 34–35; Kinne, "Women and Machinery," 89.

55. *Teachers College Curriculum* (1915–16), TC.

56. Cremin, Shannon, and Townsend, *A History of Teachers College Columbia University*, 93–94; Toepfer, "James Earl Russell and the Rise of Teachers College," 236–39; Eppright and Ferguson, *A Century of Home Economics at Iowa State University*, 78, 80–81.

57. Hoffecker, *Beneath Thy Guiding Hand*; Eppright and Ferguson, *A Century of Home Economics at Iowa State University*, 48–51, 105–6; Bix, "Equipped for Life."

58. Quoted in Bane, *The Story of Isabel Bevier*, 49–50.

59. "Lecture Notes on Applied Art, 1920," Folder 18, Box 1, AMB Papers. See also Eppright and Ferguson, *A Century of Home Economics at Iowa State University*, 98–101, 107; Goldstein and Goldstein, *Art in Everyday Life*; Jennings, *Cheap and Tasteful Dwellings*.

60. Flora Rose to Marcia Grimes, August 23, 1917, Student File, Class of 1917, NYSCHE Records.

61. Rose, Stocks, and Whittier, *A Growing College*, 61. See also Levenstein, *Revolution at the Table*, chap. 11; Rossiter, *Women Scientists in America: Struggles and Strategies to 1940*, 120–21; Jellison, *Entitled to Power*, 22–24; Babbitt, "Producers and Consumers," 260–92, 299–300.

62. Quoted in Hoover, *An American Epic*, 35. See also ibid., chaps. 4, 5, 8, and 14; Nash, *The Life of Herbert Hoover*, 41–44, 152–62, 227–62; Hoover, *The Memoirs of Herbert Hoover*, 240–80; Mullendore, *History of the United States Food Administration*; Dixon, *The Food Front in World War I*; Dawley, *Struggles for Justice*, 164–65, 195–96; and Jordan, *Machine-Age Ideology*, 33–90.

63. Quoted in Nash, *The Life of Herbert Hoover*, 153. See also ibid., 44, 156–62; Hoover, *An American Epic*, 122; and Guerrier, *An Independent Woman*, 97–106.

64. Reference to the "great army" quoted in Nash, *The Life of Herbert Hoover*, 153. On the pledge campaign, see ibid., 40–44; Levenstein, *Revolution at the Table*, 138; Report, July 6, 1917, Folder: "First Home Card," Box 2, 5-H, USFA Records; and Hoover, *An American Epic*, 57.

65. Frank, "Housewives, Socialists and the Politics of Food"; Jacobs, *Pocketbook Politics*, 54–66; Babbitt, "Producers and Consumers," 262–87.

66. Ray Lyman Wilbur to Herbert C. Hoover, October 31, 1917, Folder 8, Box 1, 5-H, USFA Records; Robinson and Edwards, *The Memoirs of Ray Lyman Wilbur*, 262.

67. "Food Administration Invites Every Woman to Register and Sign Pledge," June 17, 1917, Folder 9, Box 1, 5-H, USFA Records.

68. Hoover, untitled speech, 1917, nos. 470–79, Speeches and Articles, 1917–18, Subseries C: Writings and Speeches, M-133, AHS Papers; Tarbell, *All in the Day's Work*, 36, 319–22; Minutes of Meeting of July 10, 1917, Folder 9, Box 1, 5-H, USFA Records; Rossiter, *Women Scientists in America: Struggles and Strategies to 1940*, 120–21; Breen, *Uncle Sam at Home*, chaps. 7, 8; Emily Newell Blair, "First Aides to Uncle Sam," *IW* (September 1938): 277; Blair, *The Woman's Committee, United States Council of National Defense*, 56–63.

69. Abby Marlatt, Sarah Field Splint, Martha Van Rensselaer, Flora Rose, Alice Peloubet Norton, and Mary Schenck Woolman all went on record in Leonard's biographical dictionary as favoring suffrage. See Leonard, *Woman's Who's Who of America*. Rossiter, however, suggests that home economists' heritage was more conservative than that of many suffragists. See Rossiter, *Women Scientists in America: Struggles and Strategies to 1940*, 121.

70. Sullivan, "In Pursuit of Legitimacy."

71. Minutes of Meeting of July 10, 1917; "Conference on Home Economics Called by Mr. Hoover, June 2, 1917," Folder: "Advisory Committee on Home Economics," Box 3, 5-H, USFA Records. See also Levenstein, *Revolution at the Table*, 139.

72. Elliot Rose, "The Nutritional Sciences and the United States War Food Administration"; Levenstein, *Revolution at the Table*, chap. 11; Rossiter, *Women Scientists in America: Struggles and Strategies to 1940* and "Mendel the Mentor."

73. Herbert Hoover, speech to Prospective State Food Administrators, Chevy Chase Club, July 10, 1917, Public Statements File, Hoover Papers, quoted in Nash, *The Life of Herbert Hoover*, 43. See also Jordan, *Machine-Age Ideology*, 110–28.

74. Mullendore, *History of the United States Food Administration*, 100–101; Babbitt, "Producers and Consumers"; Jellison, *Entitled to Power*, 23.

75. Elliot Rose, "The Nutritional Sciences and the United States War Food Administration"; Folder: "Advisory Committee on Home Economics," Box 3, 5-H, USFA Records. The composition of the home economics advisory committee shifted over time and also included Sarah Louise Arnold (Simmons), Jennie Snow (director of home economics at the Chicago Public Schools) and Elizabeth Sprague (University of Kansas). See "Home Economics Workers in Washington, D.C.," *JHE* 9 (August 1917): 391; Rossiter, *Women Scientists in America: Struggles and Strategies to 1940*, 120–21.

76. Nash, *The Life of Herbert Hoover*, 156–60; Blunt, Sprague, and Powdermaker, *Food and the War*; Dye, *History of the Department of Home Economics, University of Chicago*, 42, 334–45; Elliot Rose, "The Nutritional Sciences and the United States War Food Administration," 49–54.

77. Rose, *Everyday Foods in War Time*, 33, 71. See also Blunt, Swain, and Powdermaker, *Food Guide for War Service at Home*, 55–57; Levenstein, *Revolution at the Table*; and Shapiro, *Perfection Salad*.

78. Hill, *Economical War-Time Cook Book*, 6–7, 11, 22–34; Mary Swartz Rose, *Everyday Foods in War Time*, appendix.

79. Blunt, Swain, and Powdermaker, *Food Guide for War Service at Home*, 55–57. See also Elliot Rose, "The Nutritional Sciences and the United States War Food Administration," 47–48, 50; Hamin, "Tables Turned, Palates Curbed"; Hayes, "Vitamins"; and Levenstein, *Revolution at the Table*, 138–51.

80. Strasser, *Never Done*, 22–23; Ola Powell, *Successful Canning and Preserving*, 5–6; Tomes, *The Gospel of Germs*, 149–50, 170; Minutes of Meeting, July 10, 1917; Alice Ross, "Home Canning"; Babbitt, "Producers and Consumers," 268–71.

81. Eagles, Pye, and Taylor, *Mary Swartz Rose*, 87–90; Rasmussen, *Taking the University to the People*, 88–90; Clark and Munford, *Adventures of a Home Economist*, 112–13.

82. "Editorial," *JHE* 9 (May 1917): 236.

83. "Minutes of the First Meeting of Advisory Committee on Home Economics," June 17, 1917, Folder: Advisory Committee on Home Economics, Box 3, 5-H, USFA Records; Mary Swartz Rose, *Everyday Foods in War Time*, 71; Strasser, *Waste and Want*, 153–55; U.S. Department of Agriculture, Food Thrift Series; "A Clothing Information Bureau," *JHE* 12 (July 1920): 325–26; Woolman, "Clothing Information Bureau." On Norton, see Dye, *History of the Department of Home Economics, University of Chicago*, 168; James, James, and Boyer, *Notable American Women, 1607–1950*, 2:637–38; and Betters, *The Bureau of Home Economics*, 31–40. See also Ruth O'Brien, "Bureau of Home Economics and Human Nutrition Celebrates a Quarter Century of Service," *JHE* 40 (June 1948): 294.

84. Nash, *The Life of Herbert Hoover*, 40–44; Levenstein, *Revolution at the Table*, 138; Report, July 6, 1917, Folder: "First Home Card," Box 2, 5-H, USFA Records; Hoover, *An American Epic*, 57.

85. Robinson and Edwards, *The Memoirs of Ray Lyman Wilbur*, 263–65; Nash, *The Life of Herbert Hoover*, 155–56, 249.

86. Hoover, *An American Epic*, 60–62; Nash, *The Life of Herbert Hoover*, 155–56, 227–51; Minutes of Advisory Committee on Home Economics, February 8, 1918, Folder: Advisory Committee on Home Economics, Box 3, 5-H, USFA Records.

87. Nash, *The Life of Herbert Hoover*, 249–50; Hoover, *An American Epic*, 60–62; Rossiter, *Women Scientists in America: Struggles and Strategies to 1940*, 121; Levenstein, *Revolution at the Table*, 139–41.

88. Bane, *The Story of Isabel Bevier*, 143.

89. Eagles, Pye, and Taylor, *Mary Swartz Rose*, 88–90. See also "Statement of War Service," Folder 708B, Box 41, RG 6, JER Papers.

90. Rose, Stocks, and Whittier, *A Growing College*, 62; Bane, *The Story of Isabel Bevier*, 65; Levenstein, *Revolution at the Table*, 137–46.

91. "Minutes of First Meeting of the Advisory Committee on Home Economics," July 17, 1917; Adams, *Women Professional Workers*, 129. On the role of experts in middle-class culture, see Radway, *A Feeling for Books*.

92. Mullendore, *History of the United States Food Administration*, 100–101; Babbitt, "Producers and Consumers"; Jellison, *Entitled to Power*, 23–24; Rasmussen, *Taking the University to the People*, 70–71, 74–75, 76; Rose, Stocks, and Whittier, *A Growing College*, 60–62; Danbom, *The Resisted Revolution*, 104.

93. Quoted in Eppright and Ferguson, *A Century of Home Economics*, 75; and Bane, *The Story of Isabel Bevier*, 63, 65. See also Bane, *The Story of Isabel Bevier*, 61–66, 140; Lynn K. Nyhart, "Home Economists in the Hospital, 1900–1930," in Stage and Vincenti, *Rethinking Home Economics*, 135–39.

94. William Powell, *Pillsbury's Best*; Middleton, "Made School Lunch, Rose to Success," *Forbes* (29 June 1918): 205–6; Martha Jane Phillips, "Home Economics in Business," File 131, Series 2, BVI Records.

95. Rasmussen, *Taking the University to the People*, 86–87; Palmer, *Domesticity and Dirt*, 89–110; Eppright and Ferguson, *A Century of Home Economics at Iowa State University*, 130–252; Bix, "Equipped for Life"; Cremin, Shannon, and Townsend, *A History of Teachers College Columbia University*, 64, 89, 119–20; Toepfer, "James Earl Russell and the Rise of Teachers College," 181–91; Fritschner, "The Rise and Fall of Home Economics," 103–26, 229–45, 276–93; Kyrk, "Home Economics"; Dye, *History of the Department of Home Economics, University of Chicago*, 43–93.

Chapter 2

1. Louise Stanley, "The Housekeeper, a Consumer and a Producer," *AFJ* 18 (December 1923): 580; Theodore Tiller, "Woman Chief of New U.S. Economic Bureau to Teach Nation How to Save and Spend," *New York Evening Telegram* (September 16, 1923); Williams, "Healthier Homes through Education," 51–52; Finneran, "Louise Stanley," 16–20; Rossiter, *Women Scientists in America: Struggles and Strategies to 1940*, 229, 233; American Home Economics Association, *Home Economists*, 48; Dye, *History of the Department of Home Economics, University of Chicago*, 195–96; "Louise Stanley," *JHE* 46 (September 1954): 454; Sicherman and Green, *Notable American Women: The Modern Period*, 657–59; "Biographical Notes from the History of Nutrition: Louise Stanley—June 8, 1883–July 15, 1954," *Journal of the American Dietetic Association* 47 (October 1965): 344; Rossiter, "Mendel the Mentor."

2. Betters, *The Bureau of Home Economics*, 41–43.

3. H. E. Brennan to Minna Denton, February 9, 1921, Folder: Home Economics Conference Suggestions, Box 989, Entry 17, RG 16.

4. Betters, *The Bureau of Home Economics*, 21–40; Levenstein, *Revolution at the Table*,

chaps. 4 and 9; Stanley, "The Housekeeper, a Consumer and a Producer." Atwater later served as the editor of the *Journal of Home Economics* and chaired the Women's Joint Congressional Committee in 1926–28. See "Atwater, Helen Woodard," *The National Cyclopedia of American Biography* (1963), 358–59; James, James, and Boyer, *Notable American Women, 1607–1950*, 1:66–67; Leonard, *Woman's Who's Who of America*, 59; and Box 13, WOA Papers. On Hunt, see *Revaluations*, 42; *Who Was Who in America* 1:607; and Leonard, *Woman's Who's Who of America* (1914), 415.

5. Dye, *History of the Department of Home Economics, University of Chicago*, 217; Gladys Baker, "Women in the U.S. Department of Agriculture," 195; Betters, *The Bureau of Home Economics*, 33–34; *Who Was Who in America* 3, s.v. "Denton, Minna Caroline"; *American Men of Science* (1937), s.v. "Denton, Minna Caroline"; Betters, *The Bureau of Home Economics*, 30–40; C. F. Langworthy, "The Office of Home Economics: Some Results of the Work Carried on during the Fiscal Year, 1918–1919," *JHE* 11 (December 1919): 519–32.

6. Henry Wallace to C. W. Pugsley, July 20, 1922, Folder: Home Economics, Box 902, Entry 17, RG 16; Pugsley, "Home Economics and United States Department of Agriculture," address before the General Session, American Home Economics Association, Corvallis, Ore., August 2, 1922, General Imprint Collection, NAL; Baker et al., *Century of Service*, 101–2, 107–8, 112–13, 118–22; Kunze, "The Bureau of Agricultural Economics' Outlook Program."

7. Cott, *The Grounding of Modern Feminism*, 86–99; General Federation of Women's Clubs to Secretary Edwin Meredith, December 18, 1920, Folder: Home Economics, Box 754, Entry 17, RG 16.

8. Isabel Bevier to C. W. Pugsley, December 19, 1922; C. W. Pugsley to Isabel Bevier, December 27, 1922; C. W. Pugsley to Secretary Wallace, December 27, 1922; and Henry Wallace to C. W. Pugsley, July 20, 1922, all in Folder: Home Economics, Box 902, Entry 17, RG 16. See also Baker et al., *Century of Service*, 103; Jellison, *Entitled to Power*; and Neth, *Preserving the Family Farm*.

9. Muncy, *Creating a Female Dominion in American Reform*; Ladd-Taylor, *Mother-Work*; Sealander, *As Minority Becomes Majority*; Cott, *The Grounding of Modern Feminism*; Paula Baker, "The Domestication of Politics"; Sklar, "Historical Foundations of Women's Power"; Stage, "Ellen Richards"; Boris, *Home to Work*.

10. Betters, "A Bureau of Domestic Science Proposed in 1898," *JHE* 22 (May 1930): 378–80.

11. The USDA included the Bureau of Animal Industry, the Bureau of Plant Industry, the Bureau of Chemistry, the Bureau of Soils, the Bureau of Entomology, the Bureau of Biological Survey, the Bureau of Public Roads, and the Bureau of Agricultural Economics. See *USDA YA* (1923): ii.

12. On Ball, see Baker et al., *Century of Service*, 100, 102–4, 113, 224, 442, 453, 461. Ball sent his query to Isabel Bevier, Louise Stanley, Anna E. Richardson (Iowa State College), Jessie Whitacre (Agricultural College of Utah), Mary Matthews (Purdue University), Helen B. Thompson (Kansas State Agricultural College), Ruth Wheeler (State University of Iowa), Alice Blood (Simmons College), Edna White (Merrill-Palmer School), and Ruth Wardall (University of Illinois). See E. W. Ball to Madam, April 14, 1923, Folder: Home Economics Conference Suggestions, Box 989, Entry 17, RG 16.

13. Mary L. Matthews to E. W. Ball, May 5, 1923 (original emphasis); and Isabel Bevier to E. D. Ball, May 26, 1923, both in Folder: Home Economics Conference Suggestions, Box 989, Entry 17, RG 16.

14. Edna White to E. W. Ball, June 1, 1923; and Jessie Whitacre to E. W. Ball, May 10, 1923, both in Folder: Home Economics Conference Suggestions, Box 989, Entry 17, RG 16; Katherine Blunt, "What Is Graduate Work in Home Economics?," *JHE* 15 (April 1923): 186–90.

15. Ruth Wardall to E. W. Ball, May 10, 1923; and Edna White to E. W. Ball, June 1, 1923,

both in Folder: Home Economics Conference Suggestions, Box 989, Entry 17, RG 16. On War-dall, see Moores, *Fields of Rich Toil*, 199.

16. Minna Denton to Dr. Ball, n.d., Folder: Home Economics Conference Suggestions, Box 989, Entry 17, RG 16; Minna C. Denton, "List of Work of Government Research Laboratories and Offices Which Deal with Subject Matter of Interest to Home Economics Teachers and Students," Partial Report to the Committee on Research Information of the American Home Economics Association, June 1921, unpublished manuscript, General Imprint Collection, NAL.

17. Alice Blood to E. W. Ball, June 2, 1923; Ruth Wardall to E. W. Ball, May 10, 1923; Anna E. Richardson to E. W. Ball, May 16, 1923; and Edna White to E. W. Ball, June 1, 1923, all in Folder: Home Economics Conference Suggestions, Box 989, Entry 17, RG 16. On Richardson, see Eppright and Ferguson, *A Century of Home Economics at Iowa State University*, 88–90; and *JHE* 23 (June 1931): 517–31.

18. Louise Stanley to E. W. Ball and attached report titled "The Field of Research Which Should Be Covered by the Bureau of Home Economics," May 29, 1923, Folder: Home Economics Conference Suggestions, Box 989, Entry 17, RG 16.

19. Ruby Green Smith to E. W. Ball, June 20, 1923, Folder: Home Economics Conference Suggestions, Box 989, Entry 17, RG 16; Ruby Green Smith to Home Bureau Managers and Home Bureau Presidents of New York State, July 3, 1923; "Home Economics, 6-12-23"; and "Dr. Stanley Discusses New Bureau of Home Economics," September 24, 1923, all in Folder: Home Economics, Box 989, Entry 17, RG 16; Betters, *The Bureau of Home Economics*, 42; "Bureau of Home Economics," *JHE* 15 (December 1923): 708; Louise Stanley, "The New Bureau of Home Economics," *WHC* (February 1924): 29, 106.

20. On Wardall, see Moores, *Fields of Rich Toil*, 199; and Ruth Wardall to E. W. Ball, June 22, 1923, AAFCS Records.

21. On Bevier, see Moores, *Fields of Rich Toil*, 186–92; and Isabel Bevier to E. D. Ball, May 26, 1923. On Stanley, see Louise Stanley, "A First-Year Course in Home Economics for Southern Agricultural Schools," *USDA Bulletin*, no. 540 (1917); Baker et al., *Century of Service*, 106; Gladys Baker, "Women in the U.S. Department of Agriculture," 196–98; and E. D. Ball to Louise Stanley, June 22, 1923, Folder: Home Economics Conference Suggestions, Box 989, Entry 17, RG 16.

22. Louise Stanley to Secretary Wallace, October 4, 1923; and Louise Stanley to Secretary Wallace, November 1, 1923, both in Folder: Home Economics, Box 989; and Jamison to Pugsley, August 2, 1922, Folder: Home Economics, Box 902, all in Entry 17, RG 16; Watkins, "Political Activism and Community-Building among Alliance and Grange Women in Western Washington"; Stanley, "The New Bureau of Home Economics," 106.

23. Muncy, *Creating a Female Dominion in American Reform*.

24. Seely, *Building the American Highway System*.

25. Pugsley to Wallace, July 21, 1922; and Pugsley to Wallace, August 3, 1922, both in Folder: 1922 — Home Economics, Box 902, Entry 17, RG 16; Louise Stanley to Secretary Wallace, October 5, 1923, Folder: Home Economics, Box 989, Entry 17, RG 16. On Langworthy and respiration calorimetry, see "Charles Ford Langworthy, 1864–1932," *JHE* 24 (May 1932): 442–44; Betters, *The Bureau of Home Economics*, 43; Levenstein, *Revolution at the Table*, 73–75; and Hamin, "Tables Turned, Palates Curbed."

26. Louise Stanley to Ball, July 24, 1923, Folder: Home Economics Conference Suggestions, Folder: Home Economics, Box 989, Entry 17, RG 16; "Dr. Stanley Discusses New Bureau of Home Economics," September 24, 1923, in Folder: Home Economics, Box 989, Entry 17, RG 16; Ruth O'Brien, "Bureau of Human Nutrition and Home Economics Celebrates a Quarter Century of Service," *JHE* 40 (June 1948): 294; Gladys Baker, "Women in the U.S. Depart-

ment of Agriculture," 195–99; Rossiter, *Women Scientists in America: Struggles and Strategies to 1940*, 229; Betters, *The Bureau of Home Economics*, 67–68. On McLaughlin, see Dye, *History of the Department of Home Economics, University of Chicago*, 241. On Munsell, see *American Men of Science* (1933); and Howes, *American Women, 1935–1940*. On King, see Dye, *History of the Department of Home Economics, University of Chicago*, 327–28; and Eppright and Ferguson, *A Century of Home Economics at Iowa State University*, 188.

27. *RCBHE* (1926): 2.

28. Louise Stanley to Ball, July 19, 1923, Folder: Home Economics; and Louise Stanley to Ball, n.d., Folder: Home Economics—Conference, both in Box 989, Entry 17, RG 16. On Kneeland, see "Kneeland," Folder: Kneeland, H., Box 550, RG 176; *American Men of Science* (1933); and Howes, *American Women, 1935–1940*; Kneeland, "The Field of Research in Economics of the Home," *JHE* 17 (January 1925): 15–19; "Bureau of Home Economics," *JHE* 16 (April 1924): 229–30.

29. Louise Stanley, "Plans for the Bureau of Home Economics," *JHE* 15 (December 1923): 679–83; Stanley, "The New Bureau of Home Economics"; Kline, "Ideology and Social Surveys," 367–77; Betters, *The Bureau of Home Economics*, 34–36.

30. Eppright and Ferguson, *A Century of Home Economics at Iowa State University*, 124, 218; Ruth O'Brien, "The Value of Textile Chemistry to the Home Economics Student," *JHE* 9 (April 1917): 171–74; and Kathleen M'Laughlin, "Sidelines Stressed for Girl Chemists," *NYT* (April 16, 1939): 25; Worner, "Opportunities for Women Chemists in Washington," 585; O'Brien to Clarice Louisba Scott, January 18, 1927; and Ruth O'Brien to Sybil Smith, February 26, 1927, both in Folder: S, Box 705, RG 176; Ellen McGowan to Emma Hirth, September 8, 1921, File 300, Series 2, BVI Records; Adelaide Handy, "Streamlined Garb Tested for Women in War Plants," *NYT* (March 30, 1941); "Ruth O'Brien, Expert on Textiles, U.S. Aide," *WP* (March 13, 1976): E:6. See also "Miss Ruth O'Brien Appointed Assistant Chief, Bureau of Human Nutrition and Home Economics"; "Personal Information about Ruth O'Brien," 1956; and "Notes about Ruth O'Brien," all in AAFCS Records; "Twelfth Annual Meeting of AHEA," *JHE* 11 (September 1919): 412; Ruth O'Brien, "Textile Committee Report," *JHE* 16 (September 1924): 502–3; "Textile Section," *JHE* 15 (October 1923): 550–52; Pundt, *AHEA*, 30, 41–42; Ruth O'Brien and Lydia Jacobson, "The Discoloration of Cotton Fabrics in Laundering," *JHE* 15 (February 1923): 59–64; Ruth O'Brien and Mary Louise Price, "Effect of Bleaching on Tensile Strength of Cotton Fabrics," *JHE* 14 (June 1922): 262–66, and *JHE* 14 (August 1922): 382–88.

31. Memorandum from Ruth O'Brien to Mr. Jump, July 28, 1928, Folder: Personnel and Business Administration, 1923–28, Box 544, RG 176.

32. "Names and Operating Titles of the Scientific Staff of the Bureau of Home Economics, 4/16/25," Folder: Laura McLaughlin, Box 600, RG 176; E. W. Ball, "List of Workers in the Bureau of Home Economics," April 28, 1924, Folder: Dr. E. D. Ball, Box 583, RG 176; "List of Technical Workers in the Department of Agriculture and Outline of Department Functions," *USDA MP*, no. 233 (1935).

33. "Dr. Stanley Discusses New Bureau of Home Economics," in Folder: Home Economics, Box 989, Entry 17, RG 16; O'Brien, "Bureau of Human Nutrition and Home Economics Celebrates a Quarter Century of Service"; Gladys Baker, "Women in the U.S. Department of Agriculture," 195–99.

34. E. W. Ball to Louise Stanley, June 22, 1923, Folder: Home Economics Conference Suggestions, Box 989, Entry 17, RG 16; Betters, *The Bureau of Home Economics*, 41–42; "The New Chief of the New Bureau," *JHE* 15 (September 1923): 494–95; "Dr. Stanley Discusses New Bureau of Home Economics," in Folder: Home Economics, Box 989, Entry 17, RG 16.

35. Betters, *The Bureau of Home Economics*, 86; Louise Stanley to E. D. Ball, July 19, 1923.

36. *RCBHE* (1929): 2; *RCBHE* (1930); *RCBHE* (1931); *RCBHE* (1932); *RCBHE* (1933); *RCBHE*

(1934); *Report of the Secretary of Agriculture*, 1935–40; Betters, *The Bureau of Home Economics*, 73–76; Helen Atwater and Marjorie Heseltine, "The Home Economist in Public Service," *WWE* 11:1 (February 1940): 1–5; Worner, "Opportunities for Women Chemists in Washington," 584; Rossiter, *Women Scientists in America: Struggles and Strategies to 1940*, 228–29.

37. Stanley, "New Horizons in the Professional Training of Home Economists"; Louise Stanley, "Chapters from the Lives of Leaders: What Are the Opportunities in Research in Home Economics?," *HE* 6 (February 1928): 35–36, 47–48.

38. Louise Stanley to Walter J. Greenleaf, January 9, 1932, Folder: Interior: Education, Office of—1924–32, Box 565, RG 176.

39. Rossiter, *Women Scientists in America: Struggles and Strategies to 1940*, 201–3; *RCBHE* (1926): 2; *RCBHE* (1927): 2; Louise Stanley, "Canning Fruits and Vegetables at Home," *USDA FB*, no. 1471 (1926; revised 1931, 1933).

40. *RCBHE* (1929): 1.

41. McGovern, *Sold American*, 164–66; Kellogg, "Gauging the Nation"; Cochrane, *Measures for Progress*. See also Betters, *The Bureau of Home Economics*, 37; Minna C. Denton, "List of Work of Government Research Laboratories and Offices Which Deal with Subject Matter of Interest to Home Economics Teachers and Students," Partial Report to the Committee on Research Information of the American Home Economics Association, June 1921, unpublished manuscript, General Imprint Collection, NAL; and Hazel Blair, "She Works for Farm Women," *CG* 89 (February 23, 1924): 11, 41.

42. Louise Stanley to Walter J. Greenleaf, January 9, 1932.

43. *RCBHE* (1925): 2; *RCBHE* (1926): 1.

44. University research by home economists merits further historical investigation. See Bix, "Equipped for Life"; Eppright and Ferguson, *A Century of Home Economics at Iowa State University*; and Rose, Stocks, and Whittier, *A Growing College*.

45. Galambos, "The Emerging Organizational Synthesis in Modern American History" and "Technology, Political Economy, and Professionalization"; Hawley, *Great War and the Search for a Modern Order* and "Herbert Hoover, the Commerce Secretariat, and the Vision of the Associative State."

46. Wilbur O. Atwater, "The Chemical Composition of American Food Materials," *USDA OES B*, no. 28 (1906); "New Bureau of Home Economics Prepares a Helpful Chart," *AFJ* 18 (November 1923): 532; *RCBHE* (1927): 2; Charlotte Chatfield, "Proximate Composition of Beef," *USDA Circular*, no. 389 (1926); *RCBHE* (1928): 2; Charlotte Chatfield and Laura I. McLaughlin, "Proximate Composition of Fresh Fruits," *USDA Circular*, no. 50 (1928); *RCBHE* (1930): 3; Betters, *The Bureau of Home Economics*, 44–45; *RCBHE* (1938): 9.

47. Ruth Van Deman, "Bureau of Home Economics," *Childhood Education* 5 (1929): 357; Folder: Munsell, Box 725, RG 176; *RCBHE* (1926): 3; *RCBHE* (1927): 3; Hazel Munsell to Miss Schmidt, December 8, 1928, Folder: Munsell, Hazel E., Box 550, RG 176; Betters, *The Bureau of Home Economics*, 45–46; "Vitamins in Food Materials," *USDA Circular*, no. 84 (1929); Esther Peterson Daniel and Hazel E. Munsell, "Vitamin Content of Foods: A Summary of the Chemistry of Vitamins, Units of Measurement, Quantitative Aspects in Human Nutrition, and Occurrence in Foods," *USDA MP*, no. 275 (1937); *RCBHE* (1937): 2–3; *RCBHE* (1938): 3; Levenstein, *Revolution at the Table*, 149.

48. *RCBHE* (1938): 10; Ruth O'Brien, "The Program of Textile Research in the Bureau of Home Economics," *JHE* 22 (April 1930): 281–87; Hounshell and Smith, *Science and Corporate Strategy*, 161–68; Matthews, *The Textile Fibres*; Woolman and McGowan, *Textiles* (1926); Denny, *Fabrics and How to Know Them*; Ruth O'Brien to Elizabeth Weirick, July 25, 1924, Folder: Sears, Roebuck & Co., Box 701, RG 176.

49. Ruth O'Brien, "Textile Buying Problems of the Consumer," Rough Draft of Talk to Be

Given at Kansas Farm and Home Week, February 6, 1930, AAFCS Records; O'Brien, "The Program of Textile Research."

50. *JHE* 17 (December 1925): 677; Margaret S. Furry, "Textile Research in the Bureau of Home Economics," *JHE* 22 (October 1930): 841; Betters, *The Bureau of Home Economics*, 51; Ruth O'Brien to Frank Whittemore, March 24, 1928, Folder: "W," Box 702, RG 176. Other division staff members included Margaret Bostian (Hays), Bess Marie Viemont Morrison, Margaret Smith Furry, Mary Aleen Davis, and Esther C. Peterson.

51. Margaret B. Hays, "A Controlled Humidity Room for Testing Textiles," *JHE* 23 (July 1931): 662–68; Agnes Fay Morgan to R. W. Hodgson, November 10, 1943, Folder: Hodgson, R. W., Box 1, AFM Papers.

52. Ruth O'Brien, Esther C. Peterson, and Ruby K. Worner, "Bibliography on the Relation of Clothing to Health," *USDA MP*, no. 62 (1929); O'Brien, "The Program of Textile Research," 286–87.

53. "A Bureau Devoted Exclusively to the Scientific Study of the Homemaker's Problems," March 28, 1925, Folder: Historical Records, Box 597, RG 176; Louise Stanley, "The U.S.D.A. Bureau of Home Economics Contribution toward a Better Farm Homes Program," *AE* 7 (April 1926): 137; "Names and Operating Titles of the Scientific Staff of the Bureau of Home Economics, 4/16/25," Folder: Laura McLaughlin, Box 600, RG 176. On Gray, see *Woman Citizen* (September 20, 1924); Howes, *American Women, 1935–1940*; C. Rowena Schmidt to Louise Stanley, Folder, Stanley, L. 1923–29, Box 551, RG 176. On Wood, see James, James, and Boyer, *Notable American Women, 1607–1950*, 644–45; Hutchison, "American Housing, Gender, and the Better Homes Movement," 72–73; Wright, *Moralism and the Model Home*, 135, 317n49; Hayden, *The Grand Domestic Revolution*, 273; and Calder, *Financing the American Dream*, 212–13.

54. Ruth O'Brien to Hogan-Spencer-Whitley Co., March 10, 1926, Folder: Washing Machine Exhibit, Box 719, RG 176; *RCBHE* (1925): 2; *RCBHE* (1934): 1; *RCBHE* (1935): 10–12; *RCBHE* (1938): 15.

55. *RCBHE* (1927): 3–4; Van Deman, "Bureau of Home Economics," 357.

56. Finneran, "Louise Stanley," 25–29. Publications issued by the USDA included "Home Canning of Fruits and Vegetables," *USDA FB*, no. 1211 (1921; revised 1923); Louise Stanley, "Canning Fruits and Vegetables at Home," *USDA FB*, no. 1471 (1926; revised 1931, 1932, 1933); and Louise Stanley and Mabel Stienbarger, "Home Canning of Fruits, Vegetables, and Meats," *USDA FB*, no. 1762 (1936; revised 1938, 1941, 1942). See also *RCBHE* (1930): 6; *RCBHE* (1931): 7; *RCBHE* (1933): 7; and Louise Stanley to Jean Simpson, March 25, 1933, and Ruth Van Deman to Ann Batchelder, September 17, 1936, both in Folder: *Ladies' Home Journal*, Box 206, RG 176.

57. Harold L. Lang and Anna H. Whittelsey, "Removal of Stains from Clothing and Other Textiles," *USDA FB*, no. 861 (1917); Lydia Ray Balderston, "Home Laundering," *USDA FB*, no. 1099 (1920); Laura I. Baldt, "Selection and Care of Clothing," *USDA FB*, no. 1089 (1920); "Methods and Equipment for Home Laundering," *USDA FB*, no. 1497 (1926; revised 1929, 1937, 1940); *RCBHE* (1925): 17–18; "Stain Removal from Fabrics, Home Methods," *USDA FB*, no. 1474 (1926); Lloyd E. Jackson, "Dry Cleaning and Dyeing of Fabrics of Fur," *JHE* 16 (December 1924); Betters, *The Bureau of Home Economics*, 51–52.

58. Bannister, *Sociology and Scientism*; Bulmer, Bales, and Sklar, *The Social Survey in Historical Perspective*; Converse, *Survey Research*; Harrison and Eaton, *Bibliography of Social Surveys*; Louise O. Bercaw, "Rural Standards of Living: A Selected Bibliography," *USDA MP*, no. 116 (1931).

59. *American Men of Science* (1933); Howes, *American Women, 1935–1940*; Kneeland, "The Field of Research in Economics of the Home," 16–17.

60. Elna H. Wharton to F. M. Russell, February 25, 1924, Box 600, RG 176; Betters, *The Bureau of Home Economics*, 56–64.

61. *Household Management and Kitchens*, chap. 1; Betters, *The Bureau of Home Economics*, 62–64; *RCBHE* (1927): 7–8; *RCBHE* (1926): 8–9.

62. Cowan, *More Work for Mother*, 178, 189, 199; Kline, "Ideology and Social Surveys"; Hildegarde Kneeland, "Women on Farms Average 63 Hours' Work Weekly in Survey of 700 Homes," *USDA YA* (1928): 620–22.

63. *RCBHE* (1929): 9; Kneeland, "Is the Modern Housewife a Lady of Leisure?," 301; Hayden, *The Grand Domestic Revolution*, 182–227, 267–77; *RCBHE* (June 1927): 7–8; Betters, *The Bureau of Home Economics*, 63–64; Boydston, *Home and Work*.

64. Betters, *The Bureau of Home Economics*, 35–36; Ellis L. Kirkpatrick, "Standard of Life in a Typical Section of Diversified Farming," *Cornell University Agricultural Experiment Station Bulletin*, no. 423 (July 1923); Ellis L. Kirkpatrick, Helen W. Atwater, and Ilena M. Bailey, "Family Living in Farm Homes: An Economic Study of 402 Farm Families in Livingston, N.Y.," *USDA Bulletin*, no. 1214 (1924); Kline, "Ideology and Social Surveys"; Daniel Horowitz, *The Morality of Spending*.

65. On Williams, see *The National Cyclopedia of American Biography* (1966), 265–66. On the debate about social survey methods, see Martin Bulmer, "The Decline of the Social Survey Movement and the Rise of American Empirical Sociology," in Bulmer, Bales, and Sklar, *The Social Survey in Historical Perspective*; and Bannister, *Sociology and Scientism*.

66. Louise Stanley to E. W. Allen, February 18, 1925, and attached staff list, Folder: Stanley, L., 1924–31, Box 551, RG 176; Carl Arlsberg to W. A. Jump, March 21, 1924; Louise Stanley to Mr. Jump, March 24, 1924, Folder: Personnel and Business Administration, 1923–28, Box 544, RG 176; Box 728, RG 176; Edith Hawley, "Diet in Town and Country Compared in General Survey," *USDA YA* (1930): 226–27; Betters, *The Bureau of Home Economics*, 61; *RCBHE* (1925): 12–13; *RCBHE* (1926): 6; "Dietary Scales and Standards for Measuring a Family's Nutritive Needs," *USDA TB*, no. 8 (1927); "A Short Method of Calculating Energy, Protein, Calcium, Phosphorous, and Iron in the Diet," *USDA TB*, no. 105 (1929); Hawley, *Economics of Food Consumption*. On Hawley, see *American Men of Science* (1933); and Howes, *American Women, 1935–1940*.

67. "Notes about Hazel K. Stiebeling," AAFCS Records; Rothe, *Current Biography 1950*, 548–50; Yost, *American Women of Science*, 158–76; Ware and Braukman, *Notable American Women: Completing the Twentieth Century*, 614–15; Krieghbaum, "Servants of the People"; Levenstein, *Paradox of Plenty*, 55, 58, 63, 65, 76.

68. Dye, *History of the Department of Home Economics, University of Chicago*, 244; "Day Monroe, May 24, 1937," Folder: Monroe, Day, 1935–37, Box 559, RG 176.

69. *USDA YA* (1931): 79–80.

70. Betters, *The Bureau of Home Economics*, 58–59.

71. Duncan and Shelton, *Revolution in United States Government Statistics*. See also U.S. National Resources Committee, Industrial Committee, *Consumer Expenditures in the United States*, *Consumer Incomes in the United States*, and *Family Expenditures in the United States*. On Williams, see *The National Cyclopedia of American Biography* (1966), 265–66. See also Kneeland et al., "Plans for a Study of the Consumption of Goods and Services by American Families," *Journal of the American Statistical Association* (March 1936); Berolzheimer, "A Nation of Consumers"; *RCBHE* (1934): 3–4; *RCBHE* (1936): 6–7; *RCBHE* (1937): 6–8; *RCBHE* (1938): 5–8; *RCBHE* (1939): 4–9; "Consumer Purchases Study: Family Income and Expenditures, Pacific Region," *USDA MP*, no. 339; *USDA MP*, no. 345; *USDA MP*, no. 356; and *USDA MP*, no. 370 (1939).

72. *RCBHE* (1926): 1.

73. See, for example, "Reindeer Recipes," *USDA Leaflet*, no. 48 (1929); Elizabeth F. Whiteman and Ellen K. Keyt, "Soybeans for the Table," *USDA Leaflet*, no. 166 (1938); and Elizabeth F. Whiteman and Fanny W. Yeatman, "Honey and Some of Its Uses," *USDA Leaflet*, no. 113 (1936).

74. Betters, *The Bureau of Home Economics*, 47; Florence B. King, H. P. Morris, and E. F. Whiteman, "Some Methods and Apparatus Used in Measuring the Quality of Eggs for Cake Making," *Cereal Chemistry* 13 (January 1936): 37–49.

75. *RCBHE* (1926): 4; *RCBHE* (1928): 4; *RCBHE* (1930): 5; *RCBHE* (1931): 3–4; *RCBHE* (1932): 3; *RCBHE* (1933): 4–5; *RCBHE* (1934): 8–9; Betters, *The Bureau of Home Economics*, 47–48; "Shrinkage (Loss of Weight) and Heat Penetration during the Roasting of Lamb and Mutton as Influenced by Carcass Grade, Ripening Period, and Cooking Method," *USDA TB*, no. 440 (1934); Lucy M. Alexander and Fanny Walker Yeatman, "Cooking Beef According to the Cut," *USDA Leaflet*, no. 17 (1927; revised 1928); Lucy Alexander, "Meat Cooking Need Not Be Guesswork if Thermometer Is Used," *USDA YA* (1927): 441–42.

76. *RCBHE* (1931): 2–3; *RCBHE* (1937): 5; Florence B. King, "Obtaining a Panel for Judging Flavor in Foods," *Food Research* 2:3 (1937): 207–19.

77. Furry, "Textile Research in the Bureau of Home Economics." See also M. S. Eisenhower and A. P. Chew, "The USDA: Its Structure and Functions," *USDA MP*, no. 88 (1934): 129; and Arthur M. Hyde, "The Producer Considers Consumption," *JHE* 25 (February 1933): 91–95.

78. Edna L. Clark, "Cotton in Farm Women's Garb Partly Replaced by Silk and Rayon," *USDA YA* (1927): 224–25; "The Changing Uses of Textile Fibers in Clothing and Household Articles," *USDA MP*, no. 31 (1928).

79. Ruth O'Brien, "Cotton Fabrics Again in Fashion's Favor for Women's Summer Wear," *USDA YA* (1928): 233–35; Eisenhower and Chew, "The USDA."

80. Mary A. Lindsley, "Opportunities for the Home Economics Trained Woman in Hotel Work," *PHE* 7 (November 1929): 322, 346–47; Louise Stanley to Dr. A. F. Woods, August 15, 1932, Folder: Scientific Work, Division of, 1926–32, Box 543, RG 176; Ruth O'Brien to Louise Stanley, January 2, 1929, Folder: Stanley, L. 1924–31, Box 551, RG 176; Ruth O'Brien, "Sheets Wear Chiefly at Shoulder Height, Durability Tests Show," *USDA YA* (1930): 474–75; Betters, *The Bureau of Home Economics*, 53–54.

81. *RCBHE* (1927): 8; Ruth O'Brien, "Cotton Trade Feels Changes of Styles in Women's Clothing," *USDA YA* (1927): 232–34; Esther C. Peterson, "Cotton Fabric Finish May Be Restored by Right Laundering," *USDA YA* (1927): 219–21; K. M. Downey and R. E. Elmquist, "Cotton Fabrics as Affected by Variations in Pressure and in Length of Exposure during Ironing," *USDA TB*, no. 517 (1928).

82. Betters, *The Bureau of Home Economics*, 51–52; Esther C. Peterson and Tobias Dantzig, "Fabrics' Stiffness Is Measurable by Device Made for the Purpose," *USDA YA* (1928): 279–80; Peterson and Dantzig, "Stiffness in Fabrics Produced by Different Starches and Starch Mixtures and a Quantitative Method for Evaluating Stiffness," *USDA TB*, no. 108 (1929); Louise Stanley to Anna Steese Richardson, January 25, 1928, Box 12; and Ruth O'Brien to Mr. Jump, July 28, 1928, both in Folder: Personnel and Business Administration, 1923–28, Box 544, RG 176; Margaret S. Furry, "Stiffness Produced in Fabrics by Different Starches and Sizing Mixtures," *JHE* 25 (February 1933): 143–49; Margaret S. Furry, "Dasheen Starch Found Suitable for Sizing and Finishing," *TW* (April 2, 1932); Margaret S. Furry, "Evaluating Starches for Sizing and Finishing," *Melliand Textile Monthly* 6 (September 1932).

83. O'Brien, "The Program of Textile Research"; Handy, "Streamlined Garb Tested for Women in War Plants."

84. "Publications of the Bureau of Home Economics, U.S. Department of Agriculture, July, 1923–January, 1930"; *RCBHE* (1929): 1–2; Betters, *The Bureau of Home Economics*, 11; Kline, "Ideology and Social Surveys," 367.

Chapter 3

1. F. J. Schlink to Ruth O'Brien, December 22, 1927; Ruth O'Brien to F. J. Schlink, January 13, 1928; F. J. Schlink to Ruth O'Brien, January 14, 1928; Ruth O'Brien to F. J. Schlink, February 4, 1928; F. J. Schlink to Ruth O'Brien, February 23, 1928; Ruth O'Brien to Hazel Kyrk, April 4, 1928; Hazel Kyrk to Ruth O'Brien, May 2, 1928; Ruth O'Brien to Helen Canon, April 5, 1928; Ruth O'Brien to Ruth Wardall, April 5, 1928; Ruth O'Brien to Benjamin Andrews, April 5, 1928; Benjamin Andrews to Ruth O'Brien, April 16, 1928; and Helen Canon to Ruth O'Brien, April 18, 1928, all in Folder: S, Box 705, RG 176.

2. Charles W. Pugsley, "Home Economics and United States Department of Agriculture," speech to American Home Economics Association Annual Meeting, August 1922, quoted in Betters, *The Bureau of Home Economics*, 41. Stanley quoted in Theodore Tiller, "Woman Chief of New U.S. Economic Bureau to Teach Nation How to Save and Spend," *New York Evening Telegram* (September 16, 1923).

3. *RCBHE* (1929): 2.

4. *RCBHE* (1935): 1.

5. For arguments that USDA extension agents encouraged consumption, see Babbitt, "The Productive Farm Woman"; and Jellison, *Entitled to Power*, chaps. 2 and 3. For a more complex picture, see Jones, *Mama Learned Us to Work*, 14–22, 107–38.

6. Ruth Van Deman, "Books and Literature," *JHE* 15 (December 1923): 717–18.

7. *RCBHE* (1929): 2.

8. Hutchison, "American Housing, Gender, and the Better Homes Movement," 62–63, 97–98, 173; Clements, *Hoover, Conservation, and Consumerism*; Louise Stanley, "The U.S.D.A. Bureau of Home Economics Contribution toward a Better Farm Homes Program," *AE* 7 (April 1926): 137–38.

9. Cohen, *A Consumers' Republic*, chap. 1; Campbell, *Consumer Representation in the New Deal*; Donohue, *Freedom from Want*, chaps. 6, 7; McGovern, *Sold American*, 221–60.

10. Hazel Blair, "She Works for Farm Women," *CG* 89 (February 23, 1924): 11, 41.

11. *RCBHE* (1927): 10–11; "Publications of the Bureau of Home Economics, U.S. Department of Agriculture, July, 1923–January, 1930," Folder: Lists, Box 602, RG 176; Ruth Van Deman, "Talk at Extension Meeting," April 14, 1923, Box 519, RG 176; Smulyan, "Radio Advertising to Women in Twenties America," 306–7; Van Deman and Yeatman, *Aunt Sammy's Radio Recipes Revised*; Josephine Hemphill, "Broadcasting Home Economics from the Department of Agriculture," *JHE* 19 (May 1927): 275–78; *RCBHE* (1933): 13.

12. Ruth O'Brien to Hogan-Spencer-Whitley Co., March 10, 1926, Folder: Washing Machine Exhibit, Box 719, RG 176; *RCBHE* (1925): 2.

13. Elna H. Wharton to F. M. Russell, February 25, 1924, Folder: F. M. Russell, Box 600; Folder: *Ladies' Home Journal*, Box 206; and Folder: General Foods, Box 53, all in RG 176.

14. This evidence runs counter to the arguments of Dolores Hayden (*The Grand Domestic Revolution*) and Gwendolyn Wright (*Moralism and the Modern Home*), who maintain that home economists were primarily motivated by the desire to promote single-family living.

15. Ruth O'Brien to Louise Stanley, September 27, 1924, Folder: Ruth O'Brien, Box 600, RG 176; Cott, *The Grounding of Modern Feminism*, 163–74; Ruth O'Brien and Maude Campbell, "Present Trends in Home Sewing," *USDA MP*, no. 4 (1927); Connelly, "The Transformation of

the Sewing Machine and Home Sewing in America," chap. 5; Gamber, *The Female Economy*, chap. 4.

16. Ruth O'Brien, "The Program of Textile Research in the Bureau of Home Economics," *JHE* 22 (April 1930): 282–83; Ruth O'Brien, "Textile Buying Problems of the Consumer," Rough Draft of Talk to Be Given at Kansas Farm and Home Week, February 6, 1930, AAFCS Records; "Selection of Cotton Fabrics," *USDA FB*, no. 1449 (1926).

17. "Division of Textiles, U.S. Bureau of Home Economics," n.d., Folder: Stanley, L., 1924–31, Box 551; and "Lists and Bibliographies Available from the Division of Textiles and Clothing," Folder: Bibliography on Hygiene and Clothing, c. 1927, Box 708, both in RG 176; *RCBHE* (1927): 9; *RCBHE* (1928): 5. See also, for example, "Fitting Dresses and Blouses," *USDA FB*, no. 1530; "Window Curtaining," *USDA FB*, no. 1633; and "Stain Removal from Fabrics: Home Methods," *USDA FB*, no. 1474 (1926).

18. *RCBHE* (1934): 10–11; *RCBHE*. (1935): 13; "Present Guides for Household Buying," *MP*, no. 193 (1934). For examples of the bureau's quality guides, see Bess M. Viemont and Margaret B. Hays, "Quality Guides in Buying Household Blankets," *USDA Leaflet*, no. 111 (1935); Clarice L. Scott, "Quality Guides in Buying Women's Coats," *USDA Leaflet*, no. 117 (1936); Bess Morrison Viemont, Margaret B. Hays, and Ruth O'Brien, "Guides for Buying Sheets, Blankets, Bath Towels," *USDA FB*, no. 1765 (1936); and Clarice L. Scott, "Women's Dresses and Slips—A Buying Guide," *USDA FB*, no. 1851 (1940).

19. Campbell, *Consumer Representation in the New Deal*, 194–261; Cohen, *A Consumers' Republic*, 19, 28–30; *RCBHE* (1934): 13; *RCBHE* (1936): 2; Donohue, *Freedom from Want*, chap. 7; Box 554, RG 176.

20. Louise Stanley to Jean Simpson, March 16, 1933, Folder: *Ladies' Home Journal*, Box 206, RG 176; Hazel K. Stiebeling and Medora M. Ward, "Diets at Four Levels of Nutritive Content and Cost," *USDA Circular*, no. 296 (1933); *RCBHE* (1933); *RCBHE* (1934).

21. Letters to the bureau merit further study. They can be found in the bureau's general records organized alphabetically by author throughout RG 176. See also Betters, *The Bureau of Home Economics*, 67.

22. M. L. Manning to Fanny Walker Yeatman, November 19, 1926; Fanny Walker Yeatman to M. L. Manning, June 3, 1924; M. L. Manning to Fanny Walker Yeatman, June 29, 1926; Fanny Walker Yeatman to M. L. Manning, June 30, 1926; M. L. Manning to Fanny Walker Yeatman, July 5, 1926; and F. W. Yeatman to M. L. Manning, June 7, 1928, all in Folder: Yeatman, F. W., Box 725, RG 176.

23. Edna McCulley to Ruth Van Deman, December 2, 1935, Folder: Elizabeth McCormick Memorial Fund–McCz, Box 215, RG 176.

24. Mary Maloney to BHE, November 3, 1937, Folder: Mainea-Mamz, Box 219, RG 176; Rex quoted in Report from W. R. M. Warton to P. B. Dunbar, September 8, 1930, U.S. Department of Agriculture, RG 16, cited in Smulyan, "Radio Advertising to Women in Twenties America," 307; Mrs. Joe Malano, April 1, 1937, Folder: Mainea-Mamz, Box 219; and Mrs. Charles I. Salter to USDA, January 13, 1927, Folder: S., Box 705, both in RG 176.

25. Helen Atwater, "Guides to the Efficient Choice of Household Goods," *International Congress for Scientific Management* (London, 1935), Box 13, WOA Papers.

26. McGovern, *Sold American*.

27. H. E. Brennan to Minna Denton, February 9, 1921, Folder: Home Economics Conference Suggestions, Box 989, Entry 17, RG 16; Anita Newcomb McGee to the Bureau of Home Economics, October 10, 1936, Box 216; and Ruth Van Deman, "The Consumer Emerges," August 22, 1935, Folder: Van Deman, 1935–37, Box 561, both in RG 176.

28. Finneran, "Louise Stanley," 50–54; Levenstein, *Paradox of Plenty*, 54–55; Gladys Baker,

"Women of the U.S. Department of Agriculture," 179; "Bureau of Home Economics," *JHE* 26 (1934): 630–31; Stiebeling and Ward, "Diets at Four Levels of Nutritive Content and Cost."

29. Eleanor Loeb, "Consumer Defense," *PHE* (October 1930): 292, 309; "Reasons for Acting Academic or How to Remain a Bureau Chief," *CRGB* 2:2 (January 1933): 9; F. J. Schlink, "The Responsibility of the Home Economist as a Consumer," *PHE* (September 1930): 261–62; McGovern, *Sold American*, 163–85, 248–53; Glickman, "The Strike in the Temple of Consumption," 99–128; Donohue, *Freedom from Want*, 184.

30. Hazel Kyrk, "The Selection of Problems for Home Economics Research," *JHE* 25 (October 1933): 686; Kyrk, "Home Economics," 429.

31. Ruth O'Brien, "Problems the Homemaker Meets at the Dry Goods Counter," Radio Talk—WRC, February 14, 1930, and Irma Gross to Alice Edwards, September 4, 1927, AAFCS Records.

32. E. H. Bradley to Mr. Cronin, October 19, 1922, Folder: Home Economics, Box 902: 1922, Entry 17, RG 16; Baker et al., *Century of Service*, 111; Daniel, *Breaking the Land*, 16–18.

33. Ella Burns Myers to Lucy M. Alexander, May 26, 1931; Lucy M. Alexander to Ella Burns Myers, June 3, 1931; and Ella Burns Myers to Lucy M. Alexander, June 20, 1931, all in Folder: General Foods, Box 53, RG 176; General Foods Consumer Service Department, *General Foods Cook Book*.

34. Sidney Musher to F. W. Yeatman, November 13, 1928; F. W. Yeatman to Sidney Musher, November 26, 1928, Folder: Yeatman, F. W., Box 735, RG 176. See also Boston Woven Hose and Rubber Company to Fanny Walker Yeatman, April 8, 1930, Folder: Yeatman, F. W., Box 725, RG 176.

35. Hawley, "Herbert Hoover, the Commerce Secretariat, and the Vision of the Associative State"; William Barber, *From New Era to New Deal*; Alchon, *The Invisible Hand of Planning*; Seely, *Building the American Highway System*, 119–21; Layton, *The Revolt of the Engineers*, 201–4; Cochrane, *Measures for Progress*, 138–229; Kellogg, "Gauging the Nation," 243–44; Hutchison, "American Housing, Gender, and the Better Homes Movement," 27–29; McGovern, *Sold American*, 164–70. The entire May 1928 issue of the *Annals of the Academy of Political and Social Science* was devoted to standardization.

36. Pundt, *AHEA*, 24, 30, 37, 41–42, 46, 58–59, 66, 71–72, 84, 96, 103, 124, 129, 217–18; East, "The Role of Home Economics in the Consumer Movement"; "Cooperation with the Division of Simplified Practice," n.d.; and Ruth O'Brien to Mathilde C. Hader, January 28, 1929, both in AAFCS Records.

37. "Accuracy of Household Measuring Cups," May 2, 1924; and "Annual Report, Minna Denton, 1923–24," both in Folder: Denton, M. C., Box 583, RG 176. See also P. G. Agnew to Ruth Van Deman et al., December 23, 1924; P. G. Agnew to W. C. Coye, December 23, 1924; and Ruth Van Deman to P. G. Agnew, December 29, 1924, all in Folder: Greta Gray, Box 599, RG 176.

38. Stanley, "The Development of Better Farm Homes," *AE* 7 (April 1926): 130.

39. Committee on Commercial Standardization and Simplication Files, 1927–31, AAFCS Records; Folder: Commerce—National Bureau of Standards, 1923–30, Box 563, RG 176.

40. Louise Stanley to Lita Bane, August 12, 1933, Folder: *Ladies' Home Journal*, Box 206, RG 176; Campbell, *Consumer Representation in the New Deal*, 40–41; Ware, *Beyond Suffrage*, 51–52, 53, 92–96; Lizabeth Cohen, "The New Deal State and the Making of Citizen Consumers," in Strasser, McGovern, and Judt, *Getting and Spending*, 117–19; Donohue, *Freedom from Want*, 225–43.

41. *RCBHE* (1935): 1.

42. Campbell, *Consumer Representation in the New Deal*, 49–53; *RCBHE* (1934): 10; "The

Consumer and the NRA," *JHE* 26 (January 1934): 30–32; "The Consumer and the New Deal," *JHE* 26 (February 1934): 102–3.

43. Rosamond Cook, "Standardization or Taking the Guesswork out of Buying," *JHE* 20 (March 1928): 164–66; Jessie V. Coles, "The Use of Standardization by Consumers in Buying," *JHE* 23 (October 1931): 932–33; Coles, *The Standardization of Consumers' Goods*; Committee on Standardization of Consumers' Goods, "When You Buy a Refrigerator."

44. O'Brien, "Can the Federal Bureaus Help the Household Buyer?"; O'Brien and Hartley, "Selection," 3.

45. O'Brien, "The Program of Textile Research," 282–83; Betters, *The Bureau of Home Economics*, 69.

46. Pundt, *AHEA*, 30, 41–42, 51, 66, 212; Miriam Birdseye, "Some Suggestions from the Textile Section," *JHE* 11 (September 1919): 388–92; "Twelfth Annual Meeting of AHEA," *JHE* 11 (September 1919): 412; "Recent Work of the Committee on the Standardization of Textiles," *JHE* 12 (March 1920): 101–9; "Textile Section," *JHE* 15 (October 1923): 550–52; Ruth O'Brien, "Textile Committee Report," *JHE* 16 (September 1924): 502–3.

47. O'Brien and Hartley, "Selection."

48. Alice L. Edwards to R. M. Hudson, September 8, 1927; and Ruth O'Brien to Dr. Stanley and Miss Edwards, November 21, 1927, both in AAFCS Records.

49. Mary A. Lindsley, "Opportunities for the Home Economics Trained Woman in Hotel Work," *PHE* 7 (November 1929): 322, 346–47; Louise Stanley to Dr. A. F. Woods, August 15, 1932, Folder: Scientific Work, Division of, 1926–32, Box 543, RG 176; Ruth O'Brien to Stanley, January 2, 1929, Folder: Stanley, L. 1924–31, Box 551, RG 176; Ruth O'Brien, "Sheets Wear Chiefly at Shoulder Height, Durability Tests Show," *USDA YA* (1930): 474–75; Betters, *The Bureau of Home Economics*, 53–54; O'Brien and Hartley, "Selection," 29–30; P. G. Agnew, "Technical Standards for Consumer Goods—A 'Five-Year Plan'?," *ASA Bulletin* 63 (July 1931). See also Pundt, *AHEA*, 212; Ruth O'Brien to Marie Sellers, February 21, 1925, Folder: S, Box 705, RG 176; "Textile Section," *JHE* 17 (January 1925): 39–40; and Ruth O'Brien, "Textile Standardization: An S.O.S. from the Textile Section," *JHE* 19 (September 1927): 519–21.

50. Agnew, "Technical Standards for Consumer Goods"; "Quality Standards for the Consumer," *JHE* 23 (October 1931): 971–72.

51. Boorstin, *The Americans*, 97–100; Kidwell and Christman, *Suiting Everyone*, 103–8.

52. Mary Schenck Woolman to Ruth O'Brien, April 4, 1925; and Elizabeth Weirick to Ruth O'Brien, n.d., both in Folder: W, Box 702, RG 176.

53. Ruth O'Brien, "An Annotated List of Literature References on Garment Sizes and Body Measurements," *USDA MP*, no. 78 (1930); Ruth O'Brien to W. L. Ware, December 11, 1925; Ruth O'Brien to A. M. Helinich, May 31, 1929; and Ruth O'Brien to Janet Stevens Wilcox, November 27, 1925, all in Folder: Anthropometry, Box 708, RG 176.

54. I. J. Fairchild to Division of Trade Standards' File, March 8, 1932, Folder: Commerce—NBS—1932, Box 563, RG 176; Ruth O'Brien to A. M. Helinich, May 31, 1929, Folder: Anthropometry, Box 708, RG 176; Roy Cheney to Alice Edwards, March 28, 1929, AAFCS Records.

55. *RCBHE* (1937): 12–13; "Personal Information about Ruth O'Brien," 1956, AAFCS Records; "Asks Propaganda for Boys' Styles," *NYT* (July 13, 1939); Ruth O'Brien and Meyer A. Girshick, "Children's Body Measurements for Sizing Garments and Patterns: A Proposed Standard System Based on Height and Girth of Hips," *USDA MP*, no. 365 (1939); Ruth O'Brien, Meyer A. Girshick, and Eleanor P. Hunt, "Body Measurements of American Boys and Girls for Garment and Pattern Construction: A Comprehensive Report of Measuring Procedures and Statistical Analysis of Data on 147,000 American Children," *USDA MP*, no. 366 (1941); Ruth O'Brien and William C. Shelton, "Women's Measurements for Garment and Pattern Con-

struction," *USDA MP*, no. 454 (1941); Finneran, "Louise Stanley," 61; Kidwell and Christman, *Suiting Everyone*, 109–11; Patricia Wen, "Size Often an Immeasurable Problem," *Boston Globe* (December 23, 1998): A1, A14–15.

56. Cravens, "Child-Saving in the Age of Professionalism"; Cott, *The Grounding of Modern Feminism*, 91–92, 167–71; Berlage, "The Establishment of an Applied Social Science," 204–9; Ellen Miller, "Clothing Your Child," *Catholic Woman Magazine* (April 1927), offprint in Folder: Children's Clothing, Box 709, RG 176; M. West, "Child Care: The Preschool Age," *Children's Bureau Publication*, no. 30 (1922); E. D. Reid, "Why Children Are Cross," *Hygeia* 3 (1925): 384–6; Iva I. Sell, "Clothes for the Pre-school Child," *JHE* 20 (July 1928): 477–80; Ruth O'Brien, Esther C. Peterson, and Ruby K. Worner, "Bibliography on the Relation of Clothing to Health," *USDA MP*, no. 62 (1929): 33–45; Mary A. Davis, "Children's Rompers," *USDA Leaflet*, no. 11 (1927); Ruth O'Brien, "Sun Suits for Children," *USDA Leaflet*, no. 24 (1928); Ruth O'Brien, "New Developments in Designing Children's Clothing," *JHE* 21 (October 1929): 748–49.

57. Grace C. Dimelow to Ruth O'Brien, June 14, 1928; Ruth O'Brien to Grace C. Dimelow, June 14, 1928; Ruth O'Brien to Malcolm S. Black, August 7, 1929; and "The Butterick Publishing Company Takes Pleasure in Announcing . . . ," n.d., all in Folder: Butterick Publishing Co., Box 703, RG 176; Dickson, "Patterns for Garments," 125–27; Finneran, "Louise Stanley," 49–50; "Rompers and Children's Patterns," *JHE* 23 (December 1931): 1180; *JHE* 23 (August 1931): 801.

58. Kathleen Paul Jones to Bureau of Home Economics, February 11, 1932, AAFCS Records; Ruth O'Brien to Louise Stanley, March 9, 1931, Folder: Stanley, L., 1924–31, Box 551, RG 176.

59. Leone Anne Heuer to Ruth O'Brien, July 31, 1930, Folder: S, Box 701; Leone Anne Heuer to Ruth O'Brien, July 2, 1931; Leone Anne Heuer to Clarice Scott, July 2, 1931; Leone Anne Heuer to Clarice Scott, August 3, 1931; Clarice Scott to Leone Anne Heuer, August 13, 1931; Leone Anne Heuer to Clarice Scott, August 17, 1931; and Clarice Scott to Theodore Uehling, January 4, 1932, all in Folder: Clarice Scott, Box 724, RG 176.

60. Miller, "Clothing Your Child"; "The Merchant to the Child," *Fortune* 4 (November 1931): 71; Winifred Davenport, "Self-Help Clothes," *Parents* (November 1933): 29.

61. Anderson, *Refrigeration in America*, 86–96, 103–19; C. W. Hutt to American Public Health Association, August 10, 1926; and Louise Stanley to C. W. Hutt, September 23, 1926, both in Folder: Refrigeration Studies, Box 726, RG 176.

62. Cowan, *More Work for Mother*, 128–43; Nye, *Electrifying America*, 275–76, 356; Nickles, "'Preserving Women'"; Tedlow, *New and Improved*, 305–28; Lupton and Miller, *The Bathroom, the Kitchen, and the Aesthetics of Waste*, 60–63; Anderson, *Refrigeration in America*; Strasser, *Never Done*, 19–22; Olney, *Buy Now, Pay Later*, 113–44, 159n37.

63. Tomes, "The Private Side of Public Health," and *The Gospel of Germs*, 147; Minna Denton, "The Household Refrigerator," *JHE* 8 (1916): 660–63; Angus D. McLay, "Electro-Mechanical Refrigeration," *NELA Bulletin* 11 (1924): 155; "A Homemade Milk Refrigerator," *USDPH Bulletin*, no. 102 (1919); "The Application of Refrigeration to the Handling of Milk," *USDA FB*, no. 98 (1914); "Memo—April 13, 1927," Folder: BHE—C—1924–32, Box 532; and J. I. Lauritzen to Edna P. Amidon, October 3, 1927, Folder: Refrigeration 2, Box 726, both in RG 176.

64. Madge J. Reese, "Farm Home Conveniences," *USDA FB*, no. 927 (1918; revised 1928); Greta Gray, "Convenient Kitchens," *USDA FB*, no. 1513 (1926); "Care of Food in the Home," *USDA FB*, no. 1374 (1923; revised 1926); Samuel Clark to Louise Stanley, April 13, 1927, Folder: BHE—C—1924–32, Box 532, RG 176.

65. C. W. Hutt to American Public Health Association, August 10, 1926; and Louise Stanley to C. W. Hutt, September 23, 1926, both in Folder: Refrigeration Studies, Box 726, RG 176;

Louise Stanley, "Research on Home Refrigerators," *RE* 16 (August 1928): 41–44; G. E. Miller, "Electric Refrigeration for the Home," *JHE* 18 (June 1926): 303–7.

66. Marchand, *Advertising the American Dream*, 269–72; Borden, *The Economic Effects of Advertising*, 403–21.

67. E. W. Lloyd, "Selling and Servicing Domestic Refrigerating Machines," *NELA Proceedings* 82 (1925): 510.

68. *Proceedings of the Sixth Annual Convention of the National Association of Ice Industries* (1923), 180–94; "Food in the House Refrigerator," *NH* 6 (1924): 595–97; Victoria Carlsson, "Food Changes in an Ice Refrigerator and an Electrically Controlled Refrigerator: A Comparative Study," *NH* 8 (1926): 233–36; "Columbia University Refrigerator Tests," *RE* 12 (June 1926): 440; Jean Broadhurst and Victoria Carlsson, "Keeping Food in the Home Refrigerator in the Light of Recent Research," *GH* 83 (July 1926): 96–97, 205; E. H. Parfitt, "The Home Refrigerator," *AES Circular*, no. 124 (1925); Ruth Jordan, "Factors in the Management of the Ice Cooled Refrigerator in the Home," *Indiana Agricultural Experiment Station Bulletin*, no. 316 (1926); Lisa Mae Robinson, "Safeguarded by Your Refrigerator: Mary Engle Pennington's Struggle with the National Association of Ice Industries," in Stage and Vincenti, *Rethinking Home Economics*, 253–70, and "Regulating What We Eat"; Mary Pennington, "Increasing Influence of Household Refrigeration Bureau," *IR* 72 (May 1927): 432–44; "Household Refrigeration Bureau Report," *IR* 73 (November 1927): 337–39.

69. W. D. McElhinny to Bureau of Home Economics, December 1, 1926, Folder: Refrigeration (Old Material), Box 726, RG 176; G. E. Miller to Samuel Clark, August 31, 1925, Folder: BHE—C—1924-32, Box 532, RG 176; Lloyd, "Selling and Servicing Domestic Refrigerating Machines," 510–12; "Report of Refrigeration Committee," *NELA Proceedings* 83 (1926): 280.

70. "Bureau of Home Economics Household Refrigeration Project," March 28, 1927, Folder: Stanley, L., 1923–29; and Samuel Clark to Louise Stanley, June 5, 1926, Folder: Stanley, L., 1924–31, both in Box 551, RG 176; *RCBHE* (1927): 4; C. W. Hutt to American Public Health Association, August 10, 1926; and Louise Stanley to C. W. Hutt, September 23, 1926, both in Folder: Refrigeration Studies, Box 726, RG 176.

71. Louise Stanley to Dr. A. F. Woods, August 15, 1932, Folder: Scientific Work, Division of, 1926–32, Box 543, RG 176; U.S. Department of Agriculture, Office of the Secretary, "Agreement Relative to the Study of Refrigeration for Use in the Home"; Louise Stanley to Kelvinator Corporation, October 10, 1925; and Leslie Smith to Louise Stanley, June 29, 1927, all in Folder: Refrigeration (Old Material), Box 726, RG 176; "Study of Refrigeration in Homes Inaugurated," *NELA Bulletin* 14 (October 1927): 654; Finneran, "Louise Stanley," 32. The American Gas Association was notably absent from the cooperative project. The AGA's lack of participation might have been due to its failure to promote gas refrigeration as vigorously as the electrical industry promoted electric refrigeration. Although some consumers expressed interest in the relative advantages of noiseless gas refrigeration, the primary goal of the bureau's home economists was to promote food preservation, and specific machines only secondarily. See Cowan, *More Work for Mother*, 128–43.

72. Louise Stanley to Samuel Clark, November 2, 1926, Folder: BHE—C—1924-32, Box 532, RG 176; Stanley, "Studies in Household Refrigeration"; Mary Pennington, "Testing of Household Refrigerators," *IR* 72 (June 1927): 515–17; *Proceedings of the 10th Annual Convention of the National Association of Ice Industries* (November 1927), 124.

73. Louise Stanley to Reuben E. Ottenheimer, November 28, 1927, Folder: Refrigeration (Old Material), Box 726, RG 176; "New York Section," *RE* 13 (April 1927): 319; *Proceedings of the 10th Annual Convention of the National Association of Ice Industries* (November 1927), 124; "Household Refrigerators," *Proceedings of the 6th Annual Convention of the National Association of Ice Industries* (November 1923), 159; Stanley, "Research on Home Refrigerators," 41.

74. Louise Stanley to Samuel Clark, April 18, 1927, Folder: BHE — C — 1924–32, Box 532, RG 176; Samuel Clark to Louise Stanley, June 24, 1927, Folder: Stanley, L., 1923–29, Box 551, RG 176; Lucile Reynolds to Louise Stanley, July 11, 1927; and Lucile Reynolds to Louise Stanley, August 3, 1927, both in Folder: Lucile Reynolds, Box 600, RG 176; "Study of Refrigeration in Homes Inaugurated"; Stanley to Mr. O. C. Small, November 26, 1927; Dye, *History of the Department of Home Economics, University of Chicago*, 251; and Student File, Class of 1930, NYSCHE Records. On the questionnaire, see Folder: Refrigeration Questionnaire, Box 726, RG 176; "Household Refrigeration Summary Report for the Period of Oct. 15–Nov. 15, 1927"; and Lucile Reynolds to Louise Stanley, December 10, 1927, both in Folder: Lucile Reynolds, Box 600, RG 17; Mary Sherman, "A Census of Home Equipment," *CG* 90:21 (May 23, 1925): 19–20; Mary Sherman, "Housekeeping on 40,000 Farms," *CG* 92 (May 1927): 26, 28, 88–89; Lucile Reynolds to E. P. Allen, January 17, 1928, Folder: Refrigeration, Box 726, RG 176.

75. Elise Glatz Cooper to Lucile Reynolds, December 2, 1927; Untitled poem; and Margaret Thomas to Lucile Reynolds, January 25, 1928, all in Folder: Refrigeration, Box 726, RG 176.

76. "Reasons Given by Homemakers for Their Choice in Refrigerators," attached to letter from Louise Stanley to Elizabeth MacDonald, May 7, 1930, Folder: Frigidaire, Box 53, RG 176.

77. "Study of Refrigeration in Homes Inaugurated"; "Refrigeration Project Laboratory Tests: October 7, 1927 — Mildred Porter," Folder: Refrigeration (Old Material), Box 726, RG 176; Mildred Porter to Katherine G. Cornell, May 3, 1928, Folder 1, Box 64, RG 176; "Temperature and Ice Consumption in an Ice Cooled Refrigerator as Affected by Room Temperature," *RE* 18 (October 1929): 93–96; Mildred Porter, "Refrigerator Economy Is Not Increased by Blanketing the Ice," *USDA YA* (1930): 453–54. Although Porter initially designed her investigations to compare three pairs of identical cabinets — one of each pair ice-cooled and the other mechanically cooled — her conclusions did more to clarify questions about ice refrigeration than to illuminate the relative advantages of the two systems or — despite widely publicized contemporary incidents of lethal poisoning from household refrigeration — about the safety of household refrigeration coolants. Mildred Porter, "Report on Refrigeration Project: Laboratory Tests, October 17, 1927," Folder: Stanley, L., 1923–29, Box 551; Louise Stanley to Mr. O. C. Small, November 26, 1927, Folder: Refrigeration (Old Material), Box 726; and Mildred Porter to Katherine Cornell, November 29, 1927, Folder: Kaa-Kelv, Box 64, all in RG 176; Mildred Porter, "A Test of Five Household Refrigerators," *IR* 78 (January 1930): 49–50. On safety issues, see A. H. Kegle, W. D. McNally, and A. S. Pope, "Methyl Chloride Poisoning from Domestic Refrigerators," *Journal of the American Medical Association* 9 (1929): 353–58; "Abstracts," *JHE* 21 (December 1929): 951; Hounshell and Smith, *Science and Corporate Strategy*, 155–56; and Tarr and Tebeau, "Managing Danger in the Home Environment."

78. Lucile Reynolds to Dr. Fellers, January 7, 1928, Folder: Refrigeration, Box 726; and Anna Pabst to Louise Stanley, March 9, 1929, Folder: BHE L–R 1927–32, Box 533, both in RG 176; Anna Pabst, "Milk in the Household Refrigerator," *IR* 76 (January 1929): 14–15; Anna Pabst, "Meat Keeping in Home Refrigerators Studies in Varying Conditions," *USDA YA* (1931): 369–70.

79. "Household Refrigeration Charts 1–6," Folder: HE — Louise Stanley — 1924–31, Box 551, RG 176; Louise Stanley to C. C. Callahan, September 4, 1930, Folder: Kaa-Kelv, Box 64, RG 176. These charts were also reprinted in *ERN* (September 25, 1929).

80. Mary Pennington, "Household Refrigeration Bureau Report," *IR* 75 (December 1928): 428; Leslie Smith to Louise Stanley, October 21, 1929, Folder: HE — Louise Stanley — 1924–31, Box 551, RG 176; Kingsley, *Home Service Work for the Ice Industry*, 108–16; "Teaching the Public Food and Temperature Facts: Report of Activities, National Food Preservation Program, 1929," Folder: Refrigeration (2), Box 536, RG 176; "Plan Presented at NELA Convention," *ERN* (June 5, 1929): 1, 5; "Kelvinator Issues Literature on Food Preservation Drive,"

ERN (August 14, 1929): 5; "U. S. Dept. of Agriculture Charts Show Proper Food Temperatures," *ERN* (September 25, 1929); "Columbia University Graduates Grading Essays in National Food Preservation Contest: Prizes Awarded to Winners in Essay Contest," *ERN* (December 18, 1929): 1, 8; "Extract from Mrs. Cornell's Communication," January 3, 1928, Folder: Refrigeration; and Louise Stanley to Lucile Reynolds, June 21, 1928, Folder: Refrigeration 2, both in Box 726, RG 176.

81. "Why Set Danger Point at 50 Degrees F," *IR* 77 (July 1929): 7–8; "Temperature and Moisture," *IR* 78 (March 1930): 200; "Ice Refrigerator Men Argue Merit of 50 Degree Standard," *ERN* (July 3, 1929): 1, 10–11.

82. Louise Stanley, "Household Refrigerators," *RW* 68 (June 1933): 9–11; Tobey, *Technology as Freedom*; Field, "'Electricity for All'"; Nickles, "'Preserving Women'"; Mary Pennington to Louise Stanley, March 10, 1933, Folder: Mary Pennington, Box 255, RG 176.

83. Richard B. Lambert to Lucile Reynolds, May 6, 1928; Lucile Reynolds to Richard B. Lambert, May 12, 1928, Folder: Refrigeration, Box 726, RG 176.

84. Leslie Smith to Louise Stanley, August 18, 1928; Louise Stanley to Leslie Smith, 28 September 1928; and Louise Stanley to Leslie Smith, September 28, 1928, all in Folder: Refrigeration Studies, Box 726, RG 176.

85. Lucile Reynolds to Florence Clauss, February 3, 1928; Florence Clauss to Lucile Reynolds, February 3, 1928; Florence Clauss, "Luxury Appeal Too Limited: Sell Every Day Uses," *EM* 39 (March 1928): 76–79.

86. "New York Section," *RE* 13 (April 1927): 319; Stanley, "Research on Home Refrigerators," 41.

87. Florence Clauss to Louise Stanley, January 30, 1928; and Louise Stanley to Florence Clauss, February 1, 1928, both in Folder: Refrigeration, Box 726, RG 176; Clauss, "Luxury Appeal Too Limited."

88. P. G. Agnew to Ruth Van Deman et al., December 23, 1924; P. G. Agnew to W. C. Coye, December 23, 1924; and Ruth Van Deman to P. G. Agnew, December 29, 1924, all in Folder: Greta Gray, Box 599, RG 176; Alice Edwards to Committee on Cooperation with Division of Simplified Practice, May 9, 1927; Alice Edwards to P. G. Agnew, June 9, 1927; and Alice Edwards to P. G. Agnew, June 14, 1927, all in AAFCS Records; Stanley, "Studies in Household Refrigeration"; Pennington, "Testing of Household Refrigerators"; *Proceedings of the Tenth Annual Convention of the National Association of Ice Industries* (November 1927), 124; "Conference on Simplification of Dimensions of Ice Cuts," *IR* 74 (June 1928): 528; "Simplification of Ice Cuts," *IR* 75 (August 1928): 133–34; R. L. Lockwood to Louise Stanley, June 21, 1928, Folder: Refrigeration Studies, Box 726, RG 176.

89. Faith M. Williams, "Standard Specifications for Household Buying Are Being Developed," *USDA YA* (1931): 488–89; Mary E. Pennington, "Grading Refrigerators," *RW* 64 (July 1929): 21–22; O'Brien and Hartley, "Selection," 29; Louise Stanley to Eloise Davison, June 13, 1934, Folder: Electric Home and Farm Authority, Box 571, RG 176.

90. Stanley, "Household Refrigerators"; Tobey, *Technology as Freedom*; Field, "'Electricity for All'"; Nickles, "'Preserving Women'"; Mary Pennington to Louise Stanley, March 10, 1933, Folder: Mary Pennington, Box 255, RG 176; Pennington, "Grading Refrigerators"; Editorial, "What Kind of Refrigerator Is Wanted?," *JHE* 21 (September 1929): 667–69.

91. Stanley, "Household Refrigerators"; Louise Stanley to Jeannette Eaton, May 13, 1933, Folder: Pictorial Review, Box 259; Mary Pennington to Louise Stanley, March 29, 1933; and Mary Pennington to Louise Stanley, April 20, 1933, all in Folder: Mary Pennington, Box 255, RG 176.

92. Field, "'Electricity for All'"; *RCBHE* (1935): 10–11; Nickles, "'Preserving Women,'" 725–26.

93. Williams, "Standard Specifications for Household Buying Are Being Developed"; Pennington, "Grading Refrigerators"; O'Brien and Hartley, "Selection," 29; Louise Stanley to Eloise Davison, June 13, 1934, Folder: Electric Home and Farm Authority, Box 571, RG 176.

94. "The Household Refrigerator: Points to Look for in Selecting," Bureau of Home Economics, 1940, typescript, General Imprints Collection, NAL.

95. Nickles, "'Preserving Women.'"

Chapter 4

1. *HEIB Membership Directory* (1935), AAFCS Records. The best contemporary account of the jobs available for home economists in these companies is Woodhouse, *Business Opportunities for the Home Economist*. Woodhouse does not mention names of individual women or firms. See also Marjorie Heseltine, "Home Economics Women in Business," *HEAFJ* 6 (March 1928): 66, 80; "Home Economics in Business," *HE* 5 (December 1927): 208–9, 220, 222–24; "Home Economics Goes into Business," *NBBVI* (January 1, 1923): 1–5; Winifred Stuart Gibbs, "The Sales and Advertising Value of the Home Economics Woman," *PIM* 13 (September 1926): 31–32, 142–47; Eloise Davison, "Home Economics Invades Business," *IW* 10 (March 1931): 106–7, 127–28; and Edith M. Barber, "Home Economics—A Widening Field," *IW* 11 (August 1932): 2–3.

Brief historical discussions of home economists in business after 1920 can be found in Rossiter, *Women Scientists in America: Struggles and Strategies to 1940*, 258–59; Strasser, *Never Done*, 212; and Levenstein, *Revolution at the Table*, 156–58, 198. Pundt, *AHEA*, and Sowinski, *A Forward Force*, both provide a general chronology of the establishment of the HEIB Section. See also *HEIB Membership Directories* (1927–40), and the newsletter *Timely Topics*, both in AAFCS Records.

2. Charles Dillon, *Experiment 63*, January 1936, typescript; and Lillian B. Storms to Edna T. Amidon, August 17, 1936, AAFCS Records. On Dillon, see *Who Was Who among North American Authors*, 432; and *Who Was Who in America* 2:156. See also "Chicago HEWIBS Hold Opening Meeting," *WNIHE* (October 1936): 3.

3. On similar struggles by other groups, see Muncy, *Creating a Female Dominion in America Reform*; Layton, *The Revolt of the Engineers*; and Noble, *America by Design*.

4. Both Shapiro, *Perfection Salad*, and Hess and Hess, *The Taste of America*, present more simplistic interpretations of home economists' relationship with business, arguing that home economists simply "sold out" to corporate interests.

5. Anna Burdick to Louise Stanley, October 21, 1930, Folder: Federal Board for Vocational Education, 1929–32, Box 564, RG 176; Frederick, *Selling Mrs. Consumer*; "Mrs. Consumer Speaks Her Mind: How Women Look at Your Store," Folder 10, Box 1, CF Papers; "New Books," *JHE* 21 (November 1929): 856–57.

6. Matthews, *"Just a Housewife,"* 170. See also ibid., 168–71. Hayden, *The Grand Domestic Revolution*, 285. On Frederick's early career, see ibid., 214–19; Stage, "Ellen Richards," 32; and Rutherford, *Selling Mrs. Consumer*, 46–85. Stuart Ewen describes Frederick as "the leading spokeswoman of home economics," although he notes her ties to the advertising profession. See Ewen, *Captains of Consciousness*, 97. For Barbara Ehrenreich and Deirdre English, Christine Frederick was the vehicle through which "the domestic science leaders themselves . . . passed the banner of 'right living' on to the manufacturers of appliances, soups, convenience foods, and household aids." See Ehrenreich and English, *For Her Own Good*, 180. Susan Strasser was one of the first historians to explicitly distinguish between Christine Frederick and home economists as a group, arguing that Frederick's writing was influential for many but not all home economists. See Strasser, *Never Done*, 246–50, 256–57. More

recently, Janice Rutherford's biography of Frederick, *Selling Mrs. Consumer*, confirms that Frederick was not a home economist and explores the similarities and differences between the style and content of her teachings and those of home economists.

7. Dorothy Dignam recalled that a member of the press gave "birth to the phrase" on the occasion of Frederick's 1920 speech to the National Convention of Associated Advertising Clubs of the World. See Dignam, "Career Chronology of Mrs. Christine Frederick," 1962, Box 1, Folder 3, AWNY Records. On advertising women's use of the "women's viewpoint," see Dirks, "Advertisements for Themselves"; and Scanlon, *Inarticulate Longings*, chap. 6.

8. Janice Rutherford characterizes Frederick as relatively independent from all professional groups. See Rutherford, *Selling Mrs. Consumer*, 20–22, 69. See also Sicherman and Green, *Notable American Women: The Modern Period*, 249–50. On her work with the Advertising Women of New York, see Rutherford, *Selling Mrs. Consumer*, 67–71, 128–30.

9. Graham, *Managing on Her Own*.

10. Warren I. Susman, "'Personality' and the Making of Twentieth-Century Culture," in Susman, *Culture as History*, 171–85. See also Fox, "The Culture of Liberal Protestant Progressivism."

11. Mary E. Keown to Edna N. White, May 18, 1920, Folder: History, HEIB Records. On Keown, see "Mary Keown Will Be Missed," *ESR* 21 (October 1950): 175; and Sallie Hill, "The Home," *PF* 61 (January 1946): 35, 40. See also Sowinski, *A Forward Force*, 1; Mary Keown, "A Summary of Three Years Work of the Home Economics in Business Section," 1924, Folder: History, HEIB Records; and Mary E. Keown, "Winning Support of the Home Economics Leaders to Teach Electric Laundering," *EM* 29 (April 1923): 3256–57.

12. Marie Sellers, "Into Orbit 1923," June 23, 1962, speech, Folder: 1962 Convention Program—Old Slides, HEIB; Edna White to Mary Keown, May 21, 1920, Folder: History, HEIB; "History, Home Economics Women in Business Dept., American Home Economics Association," c. 1934; and Bess M. Rowe to Verna McCallum, January 3, 1959, Folder: Home Economics in Business—National, all in HEIB Records.

13. On other women in business in this period, see Cott, *The Grounding of Modern Feminism*, 215–39; Alpern, "In the Beginning"; Yeager, *Women in Business*; Kwolek-Folland, *Incorporating Women*, chap. 4, and *Engendering Business*; and Peiss, "Making Faces" and *Hope in a Jar*. See also contemporary discussions in *Independent Woman*, the journal of the Business and Professional Women's Club.

14. "Petition Presented at Swampscott," Folder: History, HEIB Records; also reprinted in Sowinski, *A Forward Force*, appendix, 81.

15. Mary Keown, "A Summary of Three Years Work of the Home Economics in Business Section," 1924, Folder: History, HEIB Records.

16. "Report of Round Table Discussion Held Wednesday Morning, June 25, 1931," AASCF Records. See also Mary Keown, "A Summary of Three Years Work of the Home Economics in Business Section," 1924, Folder: History, HEIB Records; and Mary Keown, "Home Economics in Business," *JHE* 16 (August 1924): 457–58.

17. Mary Reed Hartson, "The Home Economics 'Business Woman,'" *AFJ* 18 (August 1923): 370; Elsie Stark, "Why I Entered the Commercial World," *HEAFJ* 6 (October 1928): 288; Marie Sellers, "Into Orbit 1923," June 23, 1962, speech, Folder: 1962 Convention Program—Old Slides, HEIB Records.

18. Lindman, "Early Leaders in Home Economics in Business," 1962, Folder: 1962 Convention—Program—Old Slides, HEIB Records; "The Business Section at Work and Play," *TT* (February 1929): 7.

19. Wiebe, *The Search for Order*, 147; Allen, *Only Yesterday*; Leuchtenberg, *The Perils of Prosperity*.

20. Pundt, *AHEA*, 24, 31, 56.

21. "How to Co-operate with Home Demonstration Agents," *PI* (May 21, 1925): 104, 108.

22. Pundt, *AHEA*, 35.

23. *JHE* 14 (November 1922): 565–68; "Corvallis Meeting," Folder: History, HEIB Records; Martha Jane Phillips, "Home Economics in Business," File 131, Series 2, BVI Records.

24. "Home Economists and the Business World," Proceedings of the 1922 Annual Meeting, *JHE* 14 (November 1922): 523–24.

25. Edna White to Mary Keown, May 21, 1920; Sowinski, *A Forward Force*, 1; Mary Keown, "A Summary of Three Years Work of the Home Economics in Business Section," 1924, Folder: History, HEIB Records; Pundt, *AHEA*, 6, 8, 30.

26. "Home Economics in Business," *JHE* 14 (February 1922): 100–101; Pundt, *AHEA*, 38–39; Sowinski, *A Forward Force*, 1–2.

27. Mary Keown, "To the Women Interested in the Home Economics in Business Section of the American Home Economics Association," February 8, 1924, 1–3, Folder: History, HEIB Records; "Home Economics in Business Group Committee Report," *JHE* 16 (March 1924): 166–67. Although the committee discussed "plans for development standards for such work in business organizations," it did not really outline any such guidelines. See also Bess Rowe, "Report of the Committee Appointed to Present a Plan for Establishing Standards of Home Economics Work in Business," New Orleans, 1923, reprinted in Sowinksi, *A Forward Force*, appendix; and Pundt, *AHEA*, 51.

28. Marie Sellers, "Home Economics Goes into Business," speech to the New York State Home Economics Association, April 18, 1927, Chronological File: 1927, HEIB Records.

29. Keown, "Home Economics in Business"; Mary Keown, "A Summary of Three Years Work of the Home Economics in Business Section," 1924, Folder: History, HEIB Records; Jean K. Rich, "The Food Manufacturer and the Trained Woman," *AFJ* 18 (April 1923): 176; Gibbs, "The Sales and Advertising Value of the Home Economics Woman," 31.

30. Margaret Justin, "Greetings to the Members of the Business Section of the AHEA," *TT* (May 1929): 3. See also Lita Bane, "Greetings from the National President," *TT* (June 1928): 1, HEIB Records.

31. Margaret McCabe, a member of the class of 1930, later complained about Cornell professors' failure to introduce her adequately to possible business careers. McCabe recalled "the failure of the College to prepare or rather acquaint the student with the opportunites [*sic*] in the business world. . . . If you wanted to teach or to be a Home Demonstration Agent, then the professors understood you, but if you had any other ideas . . . Heaven help you, there was no understanding, no comprehension and no preparation for such a student." She further remembered "the way H.E.I.B. was used as a political tool in N.Y. and controlled the H.Ec. jobs. . . . Yet, we never even heard of H.E.I.B. when I was in school." Margaret McCabe to Esther Stocks, October 21, 1950, Student File, Class of 1930, NYSCHE Records.

32. Pundt, *AHEA*, 139.

33. "Membership List," Chronological File: 1925, HEIB Records. Also reproduced as "Membership List, Approved through February 14, 1924," in Sowinski, *A Forward Force*, appendix.

34. On Alice Bradley, see Mabel C. Bradley and Elizabeth H. Bradley, "Alice Bradley— Pioneer," *JHE* 39 (March 1947); and Alice Bradley, "Chapters from the Lives of Leaders: What Is Expected of the Home Economics Woman in Business," *HEAFJ* 6 (March 1928): 53. On Donham, see S. Agnes Donham, "Chapters from the Lives of Leaders: How I Found the Path That Led to Income Management," *HE* 5 (December 1927): 203–5; "S. Agnes Donham," in American Home Economists Association, *Home Economists*, 56–57; and "S. Agnes Donham,"

JHE 51 (October 1959): 729. On Johnson, see Anna M. Cooley, "In Memoriam, Helen Louise Johnson," *JHE* 18 (May 1926): 272–73. See also Eloise Davison, "Home Economics Invades Business," *IW* 10 (March 1931): 106.

35. On the reform zeal of extension agents in the 1920s, see Jones, *Mama Learned Us to Work*, 111. On scientific training, see Fritschner, "The Rise and Fall of Home Economics," 83–89.

36. "Membership List." A 1927 survey of seventy-seven home economists in business confirms this general impression of the educational background of home economists in business. See Laura V. Clark, "A Study of Occupations, Other than Homemaking, Open to Women Trained in Home Economics," *Vocational Education News Notes* (March 1926): 15–18, File 127, Series 2, BVI Records.

37. On Wessling, see "Questionnaire for Chemists," January 1920, File 272, Series 2, BVI Records. On Keown, see "Mary Keown Will Be Missed"; and Hill, "The Home." On Sawyer, see Margaret Sawyer, "The Responsibility of Home Economics in the Field of Nutrition," *JHE* 16 (May 1924): 249–50; Margaret Sawyer, "American Home Economics Association and the Health Program," *JHE* 16 (December 1924): 683; Margaret Sawyer, "The Educational Department," *Wellville Post* (June 1925): 6; and "Once upon a Time: A History of the Consumer Service Department, 1924–1949," 1, KF Archives.

38. Marian G. Burts to Esther Stocks, November 1, 1940, Student File, Class of 1937, NYSCHE Records; *TT* (February 1928): 3; *TT* (October 1928): 11, AASCF Records. On general trends, see Cott, *The Grounding of Modern Feminism*, 182–83, 197–99; on the struggle of home demonstration agents to combine marriage and career, see Jones, *Mama Learned Us to Work*, 124–38.

39. "Department of Home Economics in Business. Presented by Miss Chinn, Chairman," 1934, Folder: Reports, Correspondence, 1934–51, HEIB Records.

40. Sowinski, *A Forward Force*, 87–89; *HEIB Membership Directories* (1927–40), AASCF Records.

41. "Electrical Women Form Organization," *EM* 34 (December 1925): 5766; "Electrical Women's Round Table Has First Birthday," *EM* 36 (November 1926): 132; Marie Sellers to Verna McCallum, n.d., Folder: HEIB—National, HEIB Records; Isabel Nelson Young to Chairman, November 17, 1938, Folder: Reports, Correspondence, 1934–51, HEIB Records.

42. On Davison, see Ronald R. Kline, "Agents of Modernity: Home Economists and Rural Electrification, 1925–1950," in Stage and Vincenti, *Rethinking Home Economics*, 241. See also chaps. 3 and 6. On Heseltine, see "Marjorie M. Heseltine," *JHE* 60 (January 1968): 4; and *Who's Who of American Women* (1961). On Floyd, see *TT* (October 1928): 12, AAFCS Records.

43. At age fourteen, Lindman took her first job, as a cut-glass designer. Educated at State Teachers College in West Chester, Pennsylvania, and at Cornell University, Lindman received her B.S. in 1919 from Teachers College Columbia University. *TT* (October 1928): 15, AAFCS Records; Fredrika D. Borchard, "Much Praised Navy Cook Book Just On," *CSM* (October 31, 1946): 4; Obituary, *NYT* (September 3, 1963): 33; Ina Lindman, "Early Leaders in Home Economics in Business," 1962, Folder: 1962 Convention—Program—Old Slides, HEIB Records.

44. Schiffman, "An Outline of Opportunities in Home Economics"; Callahan, *Preparation for the Business Field of Home Economics* (1934), 18; Callahan, *Preparation for the Business Field of Home Economics* (1942), 18; Laura V. Clark, "Study of Occupations." 12 On "prizes of the field," see Maule, *She Strives to Conquer*, 259–60.

45. Cott, *The Grounding of Modern Feminism*, 225–26.

46. Hartson, "The Home Economics 'Business Woman'"; S. Agnes Donham, "The Educational Value of Business Organizations," speech to the annual meeting of the AHEA, 1922,

File 131, Series 2, BVI Records; *JHE* 14 (November 1922): 566–67; Mary O'Leary, "Preparation for Business Home Economists as Contrasted with Preparation for Teaching," 2, AAFCS Records.

47. Hutchison, "American Housing, Gender, and the Better Homes Movement," 45.

48. *JHE* 14 (February 1922): 100–101; Rich, "The Food Manufacturer and the Trained Woman," 176. On educational advertising and selling, see Marchand, *Advertising the American Dream*, 8–9; and Toon, "Managing the Conduct of the Individual Life."

49. Martha Jane Phillips, "Home Economics in Business," File 131, Series 2, BVI Records.

50. "Report of Round Table Discussion Held Wednesday Morning, June 25, 1931," AAFCS Records; Mary E. Keown, "The Home Economics Worker in the Food Industry," *AFJ* 17 (November 1922): 24; Martha Jane Phillips, "Home Economics in Business," File 131, Series 2, BVI Records. On "voice of the public," see Marie Sellers, "Into Orbit 1923," June 23, 1962, speech, Folder: 1962 Convention Program—Old Slides, HEIB Records.

51. "Report of Round Table Discussion Held Wednesday Morning, June 25, 1931," AAFCS Records.

52. "Report of Committee on Making the Consumer Tie-Up," 1926, Chronological File: 1926, HEIB Records.

53. Keown, "The Home Economics Worker in the Food Industry," 24.

54. Ruth O'Brien to Lenore Sater, February 12, 1929, Folder: "O'Brien, R.," Box 551, RG 176.

55. See Marjorie Heseltine to Alice Edwards, October 27, 1928, Folder: HEIB, 1924–30; and Janette Kelley, "Home Economics Business Field in New England," speech to the Home Economics Women in Business Section, January 21, 1938, Chronological File: 1938, both in HEIB Records. On advertising women, see Dirks, "Advertisements for Themselves"; Scanlon, *Inarticulate Longings*, chap. 6; Marchand, *Advertising the American Dream*, 33–35; and Ewen, *Captains of Consciousness*.

56. Martha Jane Phillips, "Home Economics in Business," File 131, Series 2, BVI Records.

57. Hounshell and Smith, *Science and Corporate Strategy*, chap. 15; Noble, *America by Design*.

58. *JHE* 14 (November 1922): 566–67; Gibbs, "The Sales and Advertising Value of the Home Economics Woman," 147.

59. Martha Jane Phillips, "Home Economics in Business," File 131, Series 2, BVI Records; O'Leary, "Preparation for Business in Home Economics as Contrasted with Preparation for Teaching," 2, AAFCS Records.

60. *JHE* 16 (August 1924): 457–58.

61. "The Woman in the Industry," *EM* 39 (June 1928): 90–92. See also "Report of Round Table Discussion Held Wednesday Morning, June 25, 1931," AAFCS Records; Sawyer, "The Responsibility of Home Economics in the Field of Nutrition."

62. Marye Dahnke, "A Business Career in Home Economics," *Forecast* (April 1937): 192; "Report of Round Table Discussion Held Wednesday Morning, June 25, 1931," AAFCS Records; Woodhouse, *Business Opportunities for the Home Economist*, 118; Zunz, *Making America Corporate*.

63. O'Leary, "Preparation for Business in Home Economics as Contrasted with Preparation for Teaching," AAFCS Records, 7–8; Callahan, *Preparation for the Business Field of Home Economics* (1942), 19.

64. Hochschild, *The Managed Heart*; Kolm, "Women's Labor Aloft."

65. "Business Changes," *TT* (October 1928): 15; Louise Fitzgerald, "Home Economics Workers in Dairy Councils," *AFJ* 17 (December 1922): 23. See also Maule, *Careers for the Home Economist*, 151–58.

66. Dahnke, "A Business Career in Home Economics," 192.

67. "History, Home Economics Women in Business Department, American Home Economics Association," 1934–35, Folder: 1934, HEIB Records; "Home Service at University of Chicago Convention," *PGCN* (August 16, 1923): 259, PGLCC Library. For incomplete runs of *Timely Topics* newsletters, see HEIB and AAFCS Records. On the title origins and its content, see *TT* (October 1928): 5, AAFCS Records; and Alice Edwards to Florence LaGanke Harris, December 5, 1929, Folder: HEIB, 1924–30, HEIB Records. See also *TT* (November 1927): 3–4; and *TT* (February 1928): 5, both in AAFCS Records; *TT* (June 1928): 6; and *TT* (July 1930): 18, HEIB Records.

68. HEIB historian Jeanne Paris Sowinski referred to the issue of membership standards as a "nagging problem." See Sowinski, *A Forward Force*, 8. On "orgies," see Lita Bane to Katherine Blunt, October 7, 1927, Folder: HEIB, 1924–30, HEIB Records. On male engineers' debates over membership criteria, see Layton, *The Revolt of the Engineers*, 88–93.

69. Katharine Blunt to Lita Bane, October 4, 1927, Folder: HEIB, 1924–30; "Report of Committee on 'The Next Step in Standardization,'" Home Economics in Business Section, July 2, 1926; and Barbara Reid Robson, "Discussion Following Presentation of Report on 'The Next Step in Standardization,'" 6, both in Chronological File: 1926, all in HEIB Records. See also Lita Bane to Katherine Blunt, November 30, 1927, Folder: HEIB, 1924–30, HEIB Records; and Marjorie Heseltine, "The Chairman's Report," *TT* (October 1928): 3, AAFCS Records.

70. Florence LaGanke Harris, "Report of 1930–1931 Activities of Home Economics in Business Department," 3, HEIB Reports, 1928–29; and "Department of Home Economics in Business. Presented by Miss Chinn, Chairman," 1934, Folder: Reports, Correspondence, 1934–51, both in HEIB Records. See also Florence La Ganke Harris to Margaret Justin, October 24, 1929, Folder: HEIB, 1924–30; Helen W. Atwater to Margaret Justin, September 26, 1929, HEIB, 1924–30; "Report of the Chairman for Year 1930–1931," 3–4, Folder: HEIB Reports, 1928–39; Aubyn Chinn to Helen Atwater, May 15, 1928, Folder: HEIB, 1924–30; "Revisions of Standards Report," 1927, Folder: HEIB, 1924–30; *TT* (November 1927); *TT* (October 1928); and Mary Barber to Lita Bane, August 9, 1927, Folder: HEIB, 1924–30, all in HEIB Records.

71. Dorothy Shank to the Chairmen of Local Groups, March 25, 1938, Folder: HEIB Reports, 1928–39, HEIB Records.

72. "Report of Committee on 'The Next Step in Standardization,'" Home Economics in Business Section, July 2, 1926, Chronological File: 1926, HEIB Records.

73. The committee included Ina Lindman, Helen Downing, R. Leone Rutledge, and Barbara Reid Robson. See "Report of Committee on Making the Consumer Tie-Up," 1926, Chronological File: 1926, HEIB Records.

74. Marjorie Heseltine, "The Chairman's Report," *TT* (October 1928): 3, AAFCS Records. See also Barbara Reid Robson, "Discussion Following Presentation of Report on 'The Next Step in Standardization,'" Chronological File: 1926, HEIB Records.

75. Florence LaGanke Harris, "Report of 1930–1931 Activities of Home Economics in Business Department," 3, HEIB Reports, 1928–29; and "Department of Home Economics in Business: Presented by Miss Chinn, Chairman," 1934, Folder: Reports, Correspondence, 1934–51, both in HEIB Records.

76. Harriet Howe, "Specific Needs in Business Consumer Cooperation," speech to the HEIB midyear meeting, January 19, 1940, File: 1940, HEIB Records; Pundt, *AHEA*, 140–76. On consumer politics in the New Deal era, see Cohen, *A Consumers' Republic*, chap. 1; Glickman, "The Strike in the Temple of Consumption"; and McGovern, *Sold American*, 221–60.

77. Florence LaGanke Harris, "Preliminary Report Given at General Association Meeting," 1932, Folder: Reports, Correspondence, 1934–51, Box 1; and Aubyn Chinn Wentworth to Ethel J. Russell, March 14, 1959, Folder: Home Economists in Business—National, both in HEIB Records.

78. Dewey Palmer, "Are Home Economists Helping the Ultimate Consumer?," AAFCS Records. On the changing relationship between Consumers' Research and home economists, see McGovern, *Sold American*, 189–90, 202–3.

79. Frances Zuill to Helen Atwater, October 10, 1932, AAFCS Records.

80. Cora M. Winchell to Alice Edwards, October 20, 1932; Marie Dye to Alice Edwards, November 1, 1932; and Lucy Gillett to Alice Edwards, October 25, 1932, all in AAFCS Records. Ruth L. Kelly, of Denton, Texas, and national chair of the Student Clubs Department of the AHEA, was "entirely in favor of its publication." See Ruth L. Kelly to Alice Edwards, November 5, 1932, AAFCS Records.

81. Lucy Gillett to A. Edwards, October 25, 1932; Cora M. Winchell to Alice Edwards, October 20, 1932; Marie Dye to Alice Edwards, November 1, 1932; and Margaret Whittemore to Alice Edwards, October 21, 1932, all in AAFCS Records.

82. Dewey Palmer to Helen Atwater, November 25, 1932, AAFCS Records; *CRGB* 3:2 (January 1934): 24; "What Home Economists Work At," *CRGB* 2:2 (January 1933): 5; "When Teachers Tell Pupils How to Buy," *CRGB* 2:2 (January 1933): 10–11.

83. Edith Tolton Raye to Frances Zuill, April 10, 1934, Folder: Reports, Correspondence, 1934–51, HEIB Records. Anna Steese Richardson, associate editor of *Woman's Home Companion*, reported in 1935 that 6 million women in America had been exposed to propaganda against advertising by women's clubs, including the AHEA, where, she reported, she "met the bitterest antagonism to advertising. Time and again I felt as if I were beating my bear hands against this stone wall of prejudice." Quoted in *CRGB* (June 1935): 24.

84. Mathilde C. Hader to Alice Edwards, June 6, 1934, AAFCS Records. On Hader, see *JHE* 22 (January 1930): 84; Hader, "Attempt to Aid Consumers in Norway," *JHE* 19 (April 1927): 185–88; "Effect of Electricity on the Life of Women in Norway," *JHE* 21 (April 1929): 248–53; "Specialism, Coordination, and Education for Homemaking," *JHE* 22 (January 1930): 26–28; "Consumers' Research and the Home Economist," *JHE* 22 (April 1930): 292–95; "Conference on Employer-Employee Relationships in the Home," *JHE* 23 (July 1931): 640–42; and "The Berlin Housing Exhibit," *JHE* 23 (December 1931): 1134–35.

85. Mathilde C. Hader to Alice Edwards, June 6, 1934, AAFCS Records.

86. Marion F. Breck to Mathilde Hader, July 16, 1934, Folder: Reports, Correspondence, 1934–51, HEIB Records; Marion F. Breck to Kathryn Van Aken Burns, May 16, 1935, AAFCS Records.

87. Executive Committee Minutes and Correspondence, 1934, AAFCS Records.

88. Marjorie East, "The Role of Home Economics in the Consumer Movement," 280; Kathryn Van Aken Burns to Beatrice G. Trudelle, October 6, 1936, Folder: Reports, Correspondence, 1934–51, HEIB Records.

89. Mary Barber, "The Responsibility of a Home Economics Woman in Business to the American Home Economics Association," 1938, Chronological File: 1939, HEIB Records.

90. Marietta Eichelberger, "Report of Research Survey Committed of Home Economics Women in Business Department, American Home Economics Association," Folder: HEIB Reports, 1928–39, HEIB Records.

91. "Business Meeting, January 14, 1939," 4–5, Chronological File: 1939, HEIB Records.

92. Woodhouse, *Business Opportunities for the Home Economist*, 1–15; Harriet Howe, "Specific Needs in Business Consumer Cooperation," speech to the HEIB midyear meeting, January 19, 1940, File: 1940, HEIB Records. On Howe, see Lisa Mae Robinson, "Safeguarded by Your Refrigerator: Mary Engle Pennington's Struggle with the National Association of Ice Industries," in Stage and Vincenti, *Rethinking Home Economics*, 269.

93. Janette Kelley, "Home Economics Business Field in New England," Mid-Year Meeting Report, 1938, Chronological File: 1938, HEIB Records.

Chapter 5

1. Marye Dahnke, "A Business Career in Home Economics," *Forecast* (April 1937): 165–66.

2. Dahnke, "Home Economics in the Cheese Business," *AFJ* 5 (April 1927): 121–23.

3. *Who's Who of American Women* (1958), 301; Dahnke, "A Business Career in Home Economics," 166; "Heads Home Economics Department," *Cheesekraft* 5 (July–August 1925): 5; Marye Dahnke, "Our Home Economics Department," *Cheesekraft* 6 (January 1926): 13–14; Marye Dahnke, "Our New Kitchen," *Cheesekraft* 5 (Summer 1926): 8; and "To Please a Nation's Tastes," *Kraftsman* 2 (August–September 1944), all in KF Archives; Kraft-Phenix Cheese, *Cheese and Ways to Serve It*.

4. Eloise Davison, "Home Economics Invades Business," *IW* 10 (March 1931): 106; "Report of Round Table Discussion Held Wednesday Morning, June 25, 1931," AAFCS Records; "MIRRO Celebrates 50 Years of Home Economics Consumer Service," 1977, Folder: Company Histories, HEIB Records.

5. Woodhouse, *Business Opportunities for the Home Economist* is the best survey of corporate jobs held by home economists in the interwar period. Woodhouse began this study in 1929 under the aegis of the Institute of Women's Professional Relations, and finished it almost a decade later with funding from the Works Progress Administration. Unfortunately, the book does not mention specific names, and the repositories for both of these institutions contain little primary material relating to the extensive survey. See IWPR Records; "Report of Progress on a Study of Home Economics Trained Women in Business," June 14, 1932, AAFCS Records; Folder: CS-3836/99000, Box 84: Connecticut, Entry 31, PC-37, Statistical Projects, 1935–38, RG 69; Folder 4279, Box 361, Series 200S, RF Papers. On Woodhouse, see "Chase Woodhouse, Ex-representative from Connecticut," *NYT* (December 13, 1984); Cott, *The Grounding of Modern Feminism*, 163–64, 238, 354n40; and Rossiter, *Women Scientists in America: Struggles and Strategies to 1940*, 264–66, 387n33.

6. Strasser, *Satisfaction Guaranteed*, 253–60; Levenstein, *Revolution at the Table*; Chandler, *The Visible Hand*, 494–95.

7. Cowdrey's Salad Cream, *Choice Salad Receipts from Miss Parloa's New Cook-Book*, CPC. Many of these early "product cookbooks" were anonymously authored. See *Bi-carbonate of Soda* (Penn's Salt Manufacturing Co., 1876) and *Ayer's Home Economics* (Dr. J. C. Ayer, c. 1882), both in Recipe Collection, HFRC.

8. Weigley, *Sarah Tyson Rorer*, 25, 41–42, 53–59, 71–75, 104–5, 116–17, 96–97, 127, 128–29, 141–42, 157, 158–60, 188–89; Shapiro, *Perfection Salad*, 191–216.

9. Shapiro, *Perfection Salad*, 195; Harland, *The Story of Canning and Recipes*; Farmer, *Rumford Recipe Book*, Box 3, Recipe Collection, HFRC; Wilson, *Rumford Southern Recipes*, and Maddocks, *Rumford Recipes*, CPC; *Miss Parloa's Cook Book* (Minneapolis: Washburn-Crosby, 1880); and Mary J. Lincoln, ed., *Pure Food Cook Book: Wholesome Economical Recipes* (N. K. Fairbank, 1903), both in PCC; Johnson, *The Enterprising Housekeeper*. On Marion Harland, see Matthews, *"Just a Housewife,"* 166–68; and Smith, "Marion Harland." On baking powders, see Adams, *Women Professional Workers*, 128; and Ethelyn Middleton, "Made School Lunch, Rose to Success," *Forbes* (29 June 1918): 205–6.

10. Chandler, *The Visible Hand*, 289–99, 348–50; "Food Mergers—What Has Happened and Why," *Business Week* (September 14, 1929): 29, 32, cited in Levenstein, *Revolution at the Table*, 150–52.

11. Schudson, *Advertising, the Uneasy Persuasion*, 14–43. See also Strasser, *Satisfaction Guaranteed*; Tedlow, *New and Improved*; and Drucker, *Management*.

12. Sass, *The Pragmatic Imagination*, 156, 173–74, 216–18; Leach, *Land of Desire*, 362; Cruickshank, *A Delicate Experiment*; special issue on marketing in *AAAPSS* 209 (May 1940);

Converse, *Survey Research*; Sally Clarke, "Consumer Negotiations"; Zunz, *Why the American Century?*, 59–62, 94–103; Sally Clarke, "Consumers, Information, and Marketing Efficiency at General Motors"; Roland Marchand, "Customer Research as Public Relations: General Motors in the 1930s," in Strasser, McGovern, and Judt, *Getting and Spending*, 85–110.

13. McGovern, *Sold American*, 36–48; Charles McGovern, "Consumption and Citizenship in the United States, 1900–1940," in Strasser, McGovern, and Judt, *Getting and Spending*, 45; Marchand, *Advertising the American Dream*, 33–35, 66–69; Cott, *The Grounding of Modern Feminism*, 172; Scanlon, *Inarticulate Longings*, chap. 6, esp. 171–72; "Woman, the 85 Per Cent Buyer—In Electrical Stores, Too?," *EM* 31 (January 1924): 4047; Winifred Stuart Gibbs, "The Sales and Advertising Value of the Home Economics Woman," *PIM* 13 (September 1926): 31–32, 142–47; Curti, "The Changing Concept of Human Nature in the Literature of American Advertising"; Schudson, *Advertising, the Uneasy Persuasion*, chap. 6, 60–61; Ewen, *Captains of Consciousness*; Dirks, "Advertisements for Themselves."

14. *BNRC* (March 1920): 119; *BNRC* (December 1921); "Editorial: Importance of the Biochemist in the Food Industry," *AFJ* 16 (July 1921): 18; Mowery and Rosenberg, *Technology and the Pursuit of Economic Growth*, 62–66.

15. These firms included the Glass Container Association of America, the National Canners Association, Fleischmann Yeast, H. J. Heinz, Swift, Corning Glass Works, National Biscuit Company, and Kansas Flour Mills. See "Funds Available in 1920 in the United States of America for the Encouragement of Scientific Research," *BNRC* (March 1921). In 1923, the Container Club, Edible Gelatin Manufacturers of America, Laundryowners National Association, and Stove Founders' Research Association were among the trade associations sponsoring fellowships at the Mellon Institute of Industrial Research. See Thackray, "University-Industry Connections and Chemical Research," 219–24; and Hounshell and Smith, *Science and Corporate Strategy*, 287, 290–93.

16. Ina S. Lindman, "Industrial Fellowships," *TT* (October 1928): 6–7, 13, AAFCS Records. On women researchers at the Mellon Institute in the early 1920s, see Beatrice Doerschuk, "Industrial Chemistry," October 4, 1921 Interview, File 277, Series 2, BVI Records; Alice Lucille Wakefield, "Questionnaire for Chemists," File 273, Series 2, BVI Records; and W. A. Hamor to Florence Jackson, November 22, 1923, Folder 117, Box 11, Series B-8, WEIU Records. On the Mellon Institute, see also Weidlein and Hamor, *Science in Action*; and Servos, "Engineers, Businessmen, and the Academy." On corporations' need for access to the "newer nutrition," see Levenstein, *Revolution at the Table*, chap. 12.

17. On the origins of public relations in this era, see Tedlow, *Keeping the Corporate Image*. On women in public relations, see Donato, "Keepers of the Corporate Image." On missionaries, see Callahan, *Preparation for the Business Field of Home Economics* (1934), 8; and Florence Clauss, "Missionaries," *EM* 41 (March 1929): 82–85.

18. Quoted in Leach, *Land of Desire*, 113. See also 146–50.

19. Kolko, *The Triumph of Conservatism*, 103, 108–9; Young, *Pure Food*; Strasser, *Satisfaction Guaranteed*, 253, 60; Levenstein, *Revolution at the Table*, 49–50; Chandler, *The Visible Hand*, 494–95.

20. Lulu Graves, "Food in Its Relation to Health," *AFJ* 16 (June 1921): 6–8; Gibbs, "The Sales and Advertising Value of the Home Economics Woman," 142.

21. Edwards, *Contested Terrain*, 90–97; Daniel Nelson, *Managers and Workers*; Kwolek-Folland, "Gender, Self, and Work in the Life Insurance Industry," 173–74.

22. In 1927, Marie Sellers estimated that only 50 of about 70,000 food manufacturers employed trained home economists. See Marie Sellers, "Home Economics Goes into Business," speech to the New York State Home Economics Association, April 18–19, 1927, Chronological File: 1927, HEIB Records.

23. Schisgall, *Eyes on Tomorrow*, 27–42; Lief, *"It Floats,"* 144, 293; Advertising Age, *Procter & Gamble*, 19.

24. *BNRC* (December 1921): 66; Schisgall, *Eyes on Tomorrow*, 87–98, 105–6; Lief, *"It Floats,"* 146–47; Procter & Gamble, *Into a Second Century with Procter & Gamble*, 37–38, 45–46.

25. Eleanor Ahern, "A Short History of the Home Economics Department" (1958), 2, P&G Archive; Strasser, *Satisfaction Guaranteed*, 9–12; Lief, *"It Floats,"* 103–8; *Tested Crisco Recipes*; Neil, *The Story of Crisco*; Hill, *The Whys of Cooking*.

26. B. B. George to R. F. Rogan, March 9, 1922, P&G Archive. On Rogan, see Obituary, *Cincinnati Post–Times Star* (October 30, 1965); and Obituary, *Cincinnati Enquirer* (October 30, 1965).

27. P. W. Hanna, "Knowing before We Go Ahead," *System* 40 (August 1921): 168–69; Marjorie Heseltine, "Home Economics Women in Business," *HEAFJ* 6 (March 1928): 80; "Home Economics Goes into Business," *NBBVI* (January 1, 1923): 4.

28. Corinne Tetedoux to J. P. Darnall, April 24, 1922; R. F. Rogan to R. R. Deupree, October 14, 1922, P&G Archive. The 1922 Cincinnati City Directory lists Darnall as a "clerk" at P&G, but by the time he retired sometime before World War II he was an "advertising executive." See Obituary, *Cincinnati Times Star* (July 8, 1952).

29. Rogan to Darnall, May 6, 1922; B. B. George to R. F. Rogan, May 16, 1922, Rogan to Darnall, May 29, 1922; P&G Archive.

30. J. P. Darnall to Calumet Baking Powder Company, J. P. Darnall to Armour & Company, J. P. Darnall to Igleheart Bros., J. P. Darnall to Swift & Company, J. P. Darnall to Royal Baking Powder Company, June 6, 1922; and J. P. Darnall to Merrell-Soule Sales Corp., June 8, 1922, all in P&G Archive.

31. W. H. Sizemore to J. P. Darnall, June 8, 1922, P&G Archive.

32. Austin S. Igleheart to J. P. Darnall, June 20, 1922, P&G Archive; "MIRRO Celebrates 50 Years of Home Economics Consumer Service," 1977, Folder: Company Histories, HEIB Records.

33. Ruth Watson to J. P. Darnall, June 12, 1922, P&G Archive. See also Ruth Watson, "A Woman's Advice Necessary in Marketing of Food Products," *AFJ* 17 (November 1922): 25–26.

34. Robert G. Soule to J. P. Darnall, June 10, 1922, P&G Archive; F. C. Soule, "How Home Economics Work Helped Food Manufacturer," *AFJ* 17 (January 1922): 22–23. On Hartson, see also "Builders of the American Food Industries," *AFJ* 16 (February 1921): 16; and Gibbs, "The Sales and Advertising Value of the Home Economics Woman," 142.

35. Mary Keown to Winifred Stuart Gibbs, November 3, 1922, Folder: 1923, HEIB Records. See also "List of Home Economics Women in Business," n.d., File 131, Series 2, BVI Records.

36. Levenstein, *Revolution at the Table*, 103, 111; *Biographical Cyclopaedia of American Women*, 161; *Who Was Who in America* 1:450–51; *Who Was Who among North American Authors*, 583; Gibbs, *Lessons in Proper Feeding for the Whole Family*, and *The Minimum Cost of Living*; "Editorial Comment," *AFJ* 6 (February 1928); *PHE* 17 (March 1922): 38; *PHE* 17 (June 1922): 43; *AFJ* 20 (January 1925): 52; "Scientific Cooperation with Food Manufacturers," *AFJ* 17 (May 1922): 17; *AFJ* 17 (June 1922): 27.

37. R. K. Brodie, "Policy and Purpose of the Home Economics Dept.," April 1, 1924; R. F. Rogan to R. R. Deupree, October 14, 1922; R. F. Rogan to J. P. Darnall, October 17, 1922; J. P. Darnall to R. F. Rogan, October 19, 1922; J. P. Darnall to Mr. Ficken, November 29, 1922; and R. F. Rogan to R. R. Deupree, December 1, 1922, all in P&G Archive; Schisgall, *Eyes on Tomorrow*, 136.

38. R. K. Brodie to A. K. Schoepf, June 5, 1924, P&G Archive.

39. "Research Laboratories in Industrial Research Establishments of the United States of America," *BNRC* (December 1921): 66; Wesson, "Some Phases of Progress in Vegetable Oil

Production"; "Food Problems," October 8, 1923; R. B. Kidd to A. K. Schoepf, February 1, 1922, P&G Archive.

40. *Who's Who of American Women* (1958), 23; Eleanor Ahern, "A Short History of the Home Economics Department" (1958), 1, P&G Archive; American Dietetic Association, *Recipes for Institutions; University of Chicago Alumni Directory* (1913): 228, UCSC.

41. A. K. Schoepf to R. F. Rogan, July 24, 1924, P&G Archive. The Home Economics Department seems to have had little to do with a significant component of Blackman's advertising strategy for P&G: the use of daytime radio broadcasting to women which, beginning in 1923, featured well-known home economist Ida Bailey Allen reading recipes, discussing Crisco, and giving instructions on domestic matters. See Lief, *"It Floats,"* 151–52, 172–74, 176–80; and Smulyan, "Radio Advertising to Women in Twenties America," 308.

42. Eleanor Ahern, "A Short History of the Home Economics Department" (1958), 2–3, P&G Archive; Splint, *The Art of Cooking and Serving*, PCC; "Food Manufacturers Issue a Unique Book," *AFJ* 21 (August 1926): 374.

43. Eleanor Ahern, "A Short History of the Home Economics Department" (1958), 3–4, P&G Archive. See also Carter, *Cooking Hints and Tested Recipes*, PCC; advertisement, *WHC* (October 1929): 44–45; "Supplementary Reading on Pastries—Cakes—Frying," *AFJ* 21 (February 1926).

On Betty Crocker, see Shapiro, *Something from the Oven*, 180–84; Marling, *As Seen on TV*, 206; and Nichaman, "Betty Crocker."

44. For example, see "Suggestions to Teachers Regarding Sources of Material," *HEAFJ* 6 (September 1928): 253–66.

45. Norman Lewis, "Too Many Recipe Booklets? Not According to the Facts and Figures Disclosed by This Investigation," *PI* (April 9, 1925): 105–6.

46. For a theoretical discussion of making laboratories public, see Latour, "Give Me a Laboratory and I Will Raise the World."

47. Corn, "Hands-On Literacy"; Corn, "Educating the Enthusiast"; Lubar, "Representation and Power."

48. Eleanor Ahern, "A Short History of the Home Economics Department" (1958), 7, P&G Archive; Lief, *"It Floats,"* 153–54; Advertising Age, *Procter & Gamble*, 18, 146–47; Schisgall, *Eyes on Tomorrow*, 105–8.

49. Eleanor Ahern, "A Short History of the Home Economics Department" (1958), 4–5, P&G Archive. Ahern did not specify when this event took place, but it most likely coincided with the development of Crisco's improved emulsifying properties, for which P&G received a series of patents between 1934 and 1938. See Procter & Gamble, *Into a Second Century with Procter & Gamble*, 19; Lief, *"It Floats,"* 183–84; and Schisgall, *Eyes on Tomorrow*, 136–38.

50. Lief, *"It Floats,"* 153, 163–64; Schisgall, *Eyes on Tomorrow*, 139.

51. "The New Science of Homemaking," *AFJ* 21 (August 1926): 386; Procter & Gamble, *What a Doctor Knows about a Woman's Charm*. On cleanliness as a theme in advertising, see Vinikas, *Soft Soap, Hard Sell*; Marchand, *Advertising the American Dream*, 56, 162, 210–12, 218–19, 246; Hoy, *Chasing Dirt*; and Tomes, *The Gospel of Germs*.

52. Procter & Gamble, *Into a Second Century with Procter & Gamble*, 29–31.

53. *Food and Health Education* 5 (May 1927): 79.

54. Dorothy E. Shank, "A Glimpse into an Ideal Commercial Research Kitchen and Its Work," *AFJ* 5 (December 1927): 410–12; Dorothy E. Shank, "Operating a Research Kitchen," *American Gas Journal* 128 (March 1928): 64–66.

55. "MIRRO Celebrates 50 Years of Home Economics Consumer Service," 1977, Folder: Company Histories, HEIB Records; "Home Economics in Business," *HE* 5 (December 1927): 220.

56. Margaret Mitchell, "Home Economists in the Equipment Field," 1937 speech, Folder: 1930s minutes, HEIB Records.

57. Ibid.

58. Regina Lee Blaszczyk, "'Where Mrs. Homemaker Is Never Forgotten': Lucy Maltby and Home Economics at Corning Glass Works, 1929–1965," in Stage and Vincenti, *Rethinking Home Economics*, 163–80; Blaszczyk, *Imagining Consumers*, 208–48, 259–70.

59. See the table in chapter 4; Woodhouse, *Business Opportunities for the Home Economist*, 105–28; Grace L. Pennock, "Selling through a Woman's Eyes," *EM* 50 (October 1933): 38–39, and "The Relationship between Engineering and Home Economics," *AE* 14 (November 1933): 299–301, 308.

60. "Elizabeth S. Weirick Remembered," *Tower News* (April 16, 1976), Merchandise Development and Testing Laboratories Collection, Sears Archives; Weirick, "Experiences in the Field of Merchandise Control"; *University of Chicago Alumni Directory* (1910): 123; and *University of Chicago Alumni Directory* (1913): 145, both in UCSC; Dye, *History of the Department of Home Economics, University of Chicago*; Malone, *Dictionary of American Biography*, 417; *The National Cyclopedia of American Biography* (1916), 40; *Who Was Who in America* 1:790.

61. Strasser, *Satisfaction Guaranteed*, 203–51; Emmet and Jeuck, *Catalogues and Counters*; Elizabeth Weirick, "A Textile Laboratory Inside," *JHE* 17 (December 1925): 718–20. See also Virginia Pearson, "Interview with A. V. H. Mory," June 23, 1946, typescript; Virginia Pearson, "Sears Merchandise Testing and Development Laboratory," July 3, 1946, typescript; and A. V. H. Mory, "The Beginnings of Our Testing Laboratories," July 17, 1918, typescript, all in Sears Archives.

62. Virginia Pearson, "Interview with A. V. H. Mory," June 23, 1946, typescript; Virginia Pearson, "Sears Merchandise Testing and Development Laboratory," July 3, 1946, typescript; Virginia Pearson, "A History of the Laboratory as I Remember It," February 1974, typescript; Elizabeth Weirick, "What Sears, Roebuck and Co. Are Doing to Give Their Customers the Best of Materials Obtainable and to Improve Their Service to These Customers," paper presented to a Joint Meeting of the American Chemical Society and the American Institute of Chemical Engineers, Purdue University, November 30, 1932, 3–4; and Elizabeth Weirick, "Control of Merchandise through Laboratory Inspection," address to the Industrial Management Society, Chicago, January 11, 1940, all in Sears Archives. See also Ellen McGowan to Emma Hirth, September 8, 1921, File 300, Series 2, BVI Records; "Sears Clinic Boon to Dollar Stretchers," *TT* (March 1933), AAFCS Records; Sears, Roebuck and Company, *Sears, Roebuck and Co. at the Century of Progress*, 14–16; and Weirick, "Experiences in the Field of Merchandise Control."

63. Additional female members of Weirick's staff included Eleanor L. Fisher, Laura Pratt, Mary Antrim Linsley, and Abbie Claire Dennen. See *TT* (June 1933): 8; *HEIB Membership Directories* (1925–40), AAFCS Records; A. V. H. Mory to Beatrice R. Harron, April 23, 1919; and Ellen McGowan to Emma Hirth, September 8, 1921, File 300, Series 2, BVI Records. See also Virginia Pearson, "A History of the Laboratory as I Remember It," February 1974, typescript, Sears Archives; and Weirick, "Experiences in the Field of Merchandise Control."

64. "Report of Round Table Discussion Held Wednesday Morning, June 25, 1931," 2, AAFCS Records; *HEIB Membership Directories* (1925–40), AAFCS Records; Ruth O'Brien to Elizabeth Weirick, July 25, 1924, Folder: "Sears, Roebuck & Co.," Box 701, RG 176.

65. Virginia Pearson, "Sears Merchandise Testing and Development Laboratory," July 3, 1946, typescript, 2–5, Sears Archives.

66. Elizabeth Weirick, "What Sears, Roebuck and Co. Are Doing to Give Their Customers the Best of Materials Obtainable and to Improve Their Service to These Customers," 3–6, 8–12, Sears Archives.

67. John Black, "Sears, Roebuck Laboratory: A Factor in Textile Development," *TW* 80:7 (August 1931): 598–99; Elizabeth Weirick, "What Sears, Roebuck and Co. Are Doing to Give Their Customers the Best of Materials Obtainable and to Improve Their Service to These Customers," 12–20, Sears Archives.

68. Elizabeth Weirick, "What Sears, Roebuck and Co. Are Doing to Give Their Customers the Best of Materials Obtainable and to Improve Their Service to These Customers," 20–23, Sears Archives.

69. Ibid., 25.

70. "Consumer Education," undated typescript; and "Facts," (1936), Folder: Reports (2), Box: Merchandise Development and Testing Laboratory (MDTL), both in Sears Archives. On corporate uses of consumer activists' rhetoric, see McGovern, *Sold American*, 315–16.

71. Elizabeth Weirick, "What Sears, Roebuck and Co. Are Doing to Give Their Customers the Best of Materials Obtainable and to Improve Their Service to These Customers," 26, Sears Archives; "Sears Clinic Boon to Dollar Stretchers"; "Consumers' Shopping Guide," *JHE* 28 (1936): 712. See also "Consumer Education"; *Sears Clinic of Household Science* (1932); "New Trail Blazed by 'Consumer Guide,'" *Daily News-Graphic* (July 31, 1936): 17, 20; "Scientific Buying Is Goal of Sears Roebuck Guide," *Industrial Standardization* (October 1936): 259; and "Sears-Roebuck Issues New Shopping Guide," *National Consumer News* (October 10, 1936): 5, 12, all in Box: MDTL, Sears Archives.

72. Virginia Pearson, "A History of the Laboratory as I Remember It," February 1974, typescript, Sears Archives.

73. Quoted in Virginia Pearson, "Sears Merchandise Testing and Development Laboratory," July 3, 1946, typescript, 2, Sears Archives.

74. Article in *CRB* (December 1935), cited in *Facts* (1936), a Sears publication for salespeople about Consumers' Research, Box MDTL, Reports (2), Sears Archives.

75. On testing laboratories in department stores, see Benson, *Counter Cultures*, 106–7; and Ephraim Freedman, "The Testing of Merchandise by Department Stores," *JHE* 22 (September 1930): 732–35.

76. Sellers, "Home Economics Goes into Business," speech to the New York State Home Economics Association, April 18–19, 1927, Chronological File: 1927, HEIB Records.

77. Rosilyn Bloch Frank, "A Survey of Household Experiment Stations in the City of New York," May 20, 1921, File 126, Series 2, BVI Records; "Testing House Is a Real Home," *EM* 28 (December 1922): 111.

78. Mott, *A History of American Magazines*, 134–37.

79. "Good Housekeeping Institute," *GH* (August 1912): 278–81; *GH* 100 (May 1935): 8; Mott, *A History of American Magazines*, 137–39. On the origins of agricultural experiment stations, see Ferleger, "Uplifting American Agriculture," 6; Carstensen, "The Genesis of an Agricultural Experiment Station"; and Charles Rosenberg, "Science, Technology, and Economic Growth."

80. Mott, *A History of American Magazines*, 133, 137–38; Helen Louise Johnson, "More Varied Diet Needed for Rural Homes," *AFJ* 16 (December 1921): 13; Weigley, *Sarah Tyson Rorer*, 89–90; "In Memoriam, Helen Louise Johnson," *JHE* 18 (May 1926): 272–3; Leonard, *Woman's Who's Who of America*, 435; Katharine Fisher, "Housekeeping Emerges from the Eighties," *GH* 100 (1935): 226; "The Good Housekeeping Institute," *GH* 57 (October 1913); Helen Louise Johnson, "What Home Economics Has Done for Mary," *Harper's Bazaar* 45 (August–September 1911): 366, 412; "Portrait," *Harper's Bazaar* 46 (November 1912): 547. On Peyser and Bradt, see *GH* 54 (September 1912): 422; and "Good Housekeeping Institute: A Little Story of Its Growth and Service," *GH* 54 (August 1912): 278–81. Peyser later applied her experience at *Good Housekeeping* and other magazines to her book *Cheating the Junk Pile*

(1922). From 1927 to 1931, she was listed as a member of the HEIB Section of the AHEA and employed as a journalist at *House and Garden*.

81. Mott, *A History of American Magazines*, 138. On Wiley, see Young, *Pure Food*; Coppin, "James Wilson and Harvey Wiley"; Levenstein, *Revolution at the Table*, 159; Dr. Walter Eddy, "At Your Service: The Story of the Good Housekeeping Bureau," *GH* 100 (May 1935): 92, 268–70; Harvey Wiley, "Our Opportunities in an Unbounded Field," *GH* 54 (May 1912): 593a–593k; Arthur Wallace Dunn, "Dr. Wiley and His Work," *GH* 54 (May 1912): 593l–o; and Mott, *A History of American Magazines*, 133.

82. On Fisher's work at GHI, see Herbert R. Mayes, "Town Hall," *GH* (April 1953): 16–17; Obituary, *NYT* (March 17, 1958): 29; "Product Use and Development," unpublished brochure, c. 1941, 23, GHI Archives; and "Good Housekeeping Institute in Its New Home," *EM* 41 (March 1929): 92–93.

83. *The Story of Good Housekeeping Institute* (1923), 15, 17–19; *The Story of Good Housekeeping Institute* (1929), 11.

84. *The Story of Good Housekeeping Institute* (1923), 18, 23; *The Story of Good Housekeeping Institute* (1929), 10, 13–15; "The Woman in Industry," *EM* 39 (June 1928): 92.

85. *The Story of Good Housekeeping Institute* (1923), 13, 22–23, 29; *The Story of Good Housekeeping Institute* (1929), 13–15, 18, 20; "The Woman in Industry."

86. *The Story of Good Housekeeping Institute* (1923), 13, 18, 28, 29; *The Story of Good Housekeeping Institute* (1929), 10.

87. *The Story of Good Housekeeping Institute* (1923), 26–29. These reports remain unavailable to researchers today. Those from the 1920s and 1930s have been destroyed; more contemporary ones are closed, following institute policy.

88. McGovern, *Sold American*, 187–217; Glickman, "The Strike in the Temple of Consumption."

89. *The Story of Good Housekeeping Institute* (1923), 16, 26–28.

90. McGovern, *Sold American*, 316–21.

91. Gibbs, "The Sales and Advertising Value of the Home Economics Woman," 147.

92. Marchand, *Advertising the American Dream*, 285–333; Wise, *Willis R. Whitney, General Electric, and the Origins of U.S. Industrial Research*, 282–301; Hounshell and Smith, *Science and Corporate Strategy*, 287; McGovern, *Sold American*, 315–16; Weiner, *From Working Girl to Working Mother*; Marian Fedder to Flora Rose, February 14, 1932; and Marion Bretsch to Miss Fitchen, May 20, 1932, both in Student File, Class of 1931, NYSCHE Records; "Report of Public Relations Committee, Home Economics Women in Business Department, American Home Economics Association," 1937, Chronological File: 1937, HEIB Records.

93. Anonymous interviewee quoted in Woodhouse, *Business Opportunities for the Home Economist*, 14–15.

94. Anonymous interviewee quoted in Woodhouse, *Business Opportunities for the Home Economist*, 38–39.

95. Speech to HEIB meeting, January 1, 1924, quoted in Sowinski, *A Forward Force*, 3.

Chapter 6

1. Eloise Davison, "Home Economics Invades Business," *IW* 10 (March 1931): 127; Ada Bessie Swann, "Home Economics Work with Electric and Gas Utility Companies," *HEAFJ* 6 (November 1928): 317–18; "How New Jersey Electric Company Uses the 'Home Electrical' Section of 'Electrical Merchandising' to Reach the Women's Clubs," *EM* 29 (February 1923): 3094; "Building Up the Home Service Department by Radio," *EM* 35 (February 1926): 6091–92; Ada Bessie Swann, "What of the Future of Home Economics in Utilities?," 1927 speech,

Folder: "Speeches, Annual Meetings, Etc.," AAFCS Records; *EM* 53 (June 1935): 36–37; "Helping 3,000,000 Women to Choose and to Use Electrical Equipment," *EM* 57 (May 1937): 13; "Companion Home Service Center," *WHC* 62 (November 1935): 98–99.

2. Florence R. Clauss, "Home Service—A Major Activity," *EM* (April 1930): 44; [American Gas Association], *Home Service* (1930); Jessie McQueen, "In Home Service," *JHE* 33 (October 1941): 579. Although only nine (or less than 10 percent) of the original members of the Home Economics in Business (HEIB) Section of the American Home Economics Association (AHEA) worked for utility companies in 1925, by 1940 the number had increased to slightly more than 100 women, or 17 percent of the total membership. (See the table in chapter 4.) This group tended to include only directors or assistant directors of home service departments, but the expansion of representation within the HEIB membership corresponded to a growth in the number of home service departments in utilities and the total number of women they employed. See also "Positions for Women at the New York Edison Company," March 31, 1917, File 101, Series 2, BVI Records.

3. Hughes, *Networks of Power*, 214–26; Forty, *Objects of Desire*, 183–93; Nye, *Electrifying America*, 238–380.

4. McCraw, *TVA and the Power Fight*; Thelen, *The New Citizenship*. Nye, *Image Worlds*, 135–47; Wilkes, "Power and Pedagogy"; "Public Relations for the Contractor-Dealer," *EM* 35 (April 1926): 6235.

5. Strasser, *Never Done*, 67–84; Cowan, *More Work for Mother*, 89–99, 155; Kyvig, *Daily Life in the United States*; Nye, *Electrifying America*, 264–65; Mark Rose, *Cities of Light and Heat*, 65–169; Busch, "Cooking Competition." On fear and resistance, see also Kline, *Consumers and the Country*; and Gooday, *Domesticating Electricity*.

6. C. E. Greenwood, "Merchandising Electrical Appliances through Utilities," in Dameron, *Merchandising Electrical Appliances*, 92.

7. Lawrence Wray, "Design for Selling," *EM* 52 (October 1934): 2–3, 52; Meikle, *Twentieth-Century Limited*; Forty, *Objects of Desire*; Buddensieg, *Industriekultur*; Lupton and Miller, *The Bathroom, the Kitchen, and the Aesthetics of Waste*; Lurito, "The Message Was Electric"; Marchand, *Advertising the American Dream*, 235–84; Nye, *Electrifying America*, 259–83.

8. Katherine A. Fisher, "Home Service Activity Is Selling Higher Standards of Living," *EM* 42 (November 1929): 95.

9. Ada Bessie Swann, "Five Years of Home Service," *EM* 46 (July 1931): 27; Ada Bessie Swann, "The Home Service Program of the NELA," *NELA Bulletin* 18 (August 1931): 535; National Electric Light Association, *Home Service*. Several historians have noted the importance of home economists in utility companies. See Nye, *Electrifying America*, 250–53, 386; Rossiter, *Women Scientists in America: Struggles and Strategies to 1940*, 258–59; Ronald R. Kline, "Agents of Modernity: Home Economists and Rural Electrification, 1925–1950," in Stage and Vincenti, *Rethinking Home Economics*, 237–52; Mark Rose, *Cities of Light and Heat*; Lisa Mae Robinson, "Safeguarded by Your Refrigerator: Mary Engle Pennington's Struggle with the National Association of Ice Industries," in Stage and Vincenti, *Rethinking Home Economics*, 253–70; Sicilia, "Selling Power," 509–17; Busch, "Cooking Competition," 242–44; and James C. Williams, "Getting Housewives the Electric Message: Gender and Energy Marketing in the Early Twentieth Century," in Horowitz and Mohun, *His and Hers*, 95–114.

10. Baritz, *Servants of Power*; Noble, *America by Design*.

11. Nye, *Electrifying America*; Hughes, *Networks of Power*, 223–24; Nye, *Image Worlds*, 157; Mark Rose, *Cities of Light and Heat*, 65–89.

12. W. A. Bayard, "What Crowder's Order Means to You," *EM* 20 (July 1918): 26–27; Clara Zillessen, "Exit Bridget!," *EM* 18 (October 1917): 209.

13. Nye, *Electrifying America*, 168–81; Chandler, *The Visible Hand*.

14. "Who Sells Electrical Appliances in 1926?," *EM* 35 (January 1926): 6052; Dameron, *Merchandising Electrical Appliances*, 74–75; Lawrence Wray, "But There's Another New York," *EM* 59 (March 1938): 6–7, 64–65; "Washington's Newest 'New Deal': The Electric Institute," *EM* 51 (May 1934): 56–58; "$1,000,000 in 10 Months," *EM* 54 (July 1935): 12–13; *EM* 54 (December 1935): 14.

15. The journal's predecessor, *Selling Juice*, was launched in 1905, renamed *Selling Electricity* in 1907, and then *Electrical Merchandising* in 1916 when it was purchased by the McGraw Publishing Company. See "How Times Have Changed," *EM* 51 (May 1934): 36–37, 62.

16. Nye, *Image Worlds*, 122–24; Strasser, *Never Done*, 76–78; Hughes, *Networks of Power*, 214–26; Platt, *The Electric City*.

17. "To Cash in on the 'Kitchen Movies,'" *EM* 17 (February 1917): 59; Earnest A. Dench, "How the Electrical Dealer Can Use Movie Slides to Advantage," *EM* 19 (January 1918): 44; "Our Responsibility to 'Service,'" *EM* 36 (December 1926): 125.

18. Frank B. Rae Jr., "Why Shouldn't Service Pay?," *EM* 26 (December 1921): 287–89. See also "Store Demonstrations When Sale Is Made Save Servicing Charges Afterward," *EM* 31 (April 1924): 4232–33.

19. Florence R. Clauss, "When Is a Washer Well Sold?," *EM* 38 (October 1927): 84–86; L. C. Spake, "Helping Dealers Sell Electric Ranges," *EM* 21 (June 1919): 297–98; Jay J. Keith, "'Home Appliances—Nothing Else,'" *EM* 21 (June 1919): 294–95; "Electric Waffles While You Pay Your Electricity Bill," *EM* 26 (November 1921): 255; "What Demonstrating Can Do," *EM* 26 (December 1921): 320.

20. *EM* 17 (June 1917): 290; "The New Spirit in Merchandising—An Editorial," *EM* (February 1917): 50–51; "New York Has New Demonstration Kitchen-Laundry—'At Your Service,'" *EM* 31 (February 1924): 4130; Nye, *Image Worlds*, 128–31.

21. Lidda Kay, "Is Your Store Popular with Women?," *EM* 24 (October 1920): 201–2.

22. Elizabeth Durkee Kohlwey, "The 'Feminine Touch' and a Woman's Ideas on Store Arrangement," *EM* 23 (June 1920): 312; "Get Local Women in on the Job," *EM* 30 (October 1923): 3662; Keith, "'Home Appliances—Nothing Else'"; "'Electrabode' Aims to Please the Ladies, Says Mosley," *EM* 30 (July 1923): 3494; "An Electrical 'House of Service' Where Women Like to Buy," *EM* 28 (December 1922): 100; "Make Your Store Inviting to Women," *EM* 30 (July 1923): 3496.

23. "An Electrical 'House of Service' Where Women Like to Buy"; "Between 3,000 and 4,000 New Retail Electrical Stores Have Been Opened within the Past Twelve Months," *EM* 23 (May 1920): 219; "Some Live Ideas Employed by a Lighting Company in Opening New Electric Store in a Community Where the Municipality Sells the Electricity," *EM* 18 (December 1917): 300; *EM* 21 (June 1919): 295; Benson, *Counter Cultures*, 83–101; Leach, "Transformations in a Culture of Consumption"; Leach, *Land of Desire*; Lawrence, "Geographical Space, Social Space, and the Realm of the Department Store."

24. "What to Tell 'Em in the Home Electric," *EM* 28 (December 1922): 94–97; Nye, *Electrifying America*, 20, 265–67, 356–59, 309; Mark Rose, *Cities of Light and Heat*, 83–86, 163.

25. "Editorial," *EM* 17 (March 1917): 129. See also *"Reason*: Angel-Food Cake," *EM* 36 (October 1926): 101.

26. "A 'Cooking Bee' Always Brings the Women Out," *EM* 30 (July 1923): 3497. See also "Making It Easy for You to Put on an Electric Range Demonstration," *EM* 30 (August 1923): 3565; "Interesting the Ladies in Electric Cooking," *EM* 20 (October 1918): 174; Preston S. Arkwright, "We Cannot WISH for LOAD . . . and Get It," *EM* 48 (July 1932): 26; Busch, "Cooking Competition," 242–44; Sicilia, "Selling Power," 509–17.

27. "Should the Salesman Be a Housework Expert?," *EM* 28 (November 1922): 108.

28. Frank B. Rae Jr., "Buying Tomorrow's Good-Will with Today's Dollars," *EM* 21 (March

1919): 115–17. See also Tom J. Casey, "Common Sense Merchandising," *EM* 26 (July 1921): 30–33; Clotilde Grunsky, "Always with a Smile!," *EM* 31 (March 1924): 4148–49, 4172; Grunsky, "The Value of a Smile," *EM* 31 (March 1924); and "Prospects from Club Women," *EM* 56 (October 1936): 18.

29. "Women in the Industry," *EM* 35 (February 1926): 6118.

30. "Where the Wives Can Help," *EM* 30 (November 1923): 3770; Earl E. Whittehorne, "Sanders Imports a 'Lady Moses' to Lead the House-Maid Home Again," *EM* 21 (January 1919): 18–19; "We Must Enlist the Aid of Women," *EM* 30 (November 1923): 3738–39; "The Women's Clubs—A Ready Made 'Home Electrical' Audience," *EM* 26 (July 1921): 35; "Get the Women's Clubs to Hold an Electrical Show," *EM* 26 (August 1921): 96; "'Have Women Wait on Women,' Says Ohio Dealer," *EM* 28 (December 1922): 110; Mrs. M. V. Martin, "Woman's Viewpoint a Valuable Asset in Selling," *EM* 32 (August 1924): 4527–28; Earl E. Whittehorne, "Women in Business," *EM* 26 (October 1921): 191–94; "This Woman Dealer Sets a Fast Pace Selling Lighting Fixtures to Women," *EM* 25 (January 1921): 8–9; "Co-operating to Develop Retail Distribution and Consumer Demand," *EM* 19 (February 1918): 77–79; Clara H. Zillessen, "What It Means to Be an Appliance Saleswoman Today," *EM* 23 (May 1920): 248–49; "Getting More Women Customers," *EM* 33 (May 1925): 5269; "The Saleswoman on the Outside Selling Job," *EM* 34 (December 1925): 5724; Williams, "Getting Housewives the Electric Message." On Sheridan, see "Women in Business," *EM* 28 (October 1922): 191–94; and "Women in the Industry," *Electragist* (November 1923): 24–26.

31. "Woman, the 75 Per Cent Buyer—In Electrical Stores, Too?," *EM* 31 (January 1924): 4047.

32. Bayard, "What Crowder's Order Means to You."

33. Callahan, *Preparation for the Business Field of Home Economics* (1934), 8; Florence Clauss, "Missionaries," *EM* 41 (March 1929): 82–85.

34. "Building Up the Home Service Department by Radio," *EM* 35 (February 1926): 6091.

35. Ada Bessie Swann, "What of the Future of Home Economics in Utilities?," 1927 speech, AAFCS Records; Swann, "Home Economics Work with Electric and Gas Utility Companies."

36. "Finding New Channels to Reach 120,000,000 People with the Electrical Story," *EM* 27 (January 1922): 87, 98, 99; Mrs. C. B. Tate Jr., "The Field of Women in Public Relations," *NELA Bulletin* 9 (April 1922): 249–50; H. T. Sands, "Address of Chairman Insull Presented at the Atlantic City Convention," *NELA Bulletin* 9 (July 1922): 438–40; H. T. Sands, "Meeting of Women's Public Information Committee of Middle West Utilities Company," *NELA Bulletin* 9 (October 1922): 602–3; May S. Fletemeyer, "Women and Public Utilities," *NELA Bulletin* 11 (November 1924): 692; "The Women's Committee—A Statement," *NELA Bulletin* 12 (July 1925): 454; Martin J. Insull, "The Women's Committee's First Ten Years," *NELA Proceedings* 88 (1931): 128–33. On public relations in this period, see Tedlow, *Keeping the Corporate Image*; and Donato, "Keepers of the Corporate Image." On similar gendered divisions of labor in other American industries, see Kwolek-Folland, "Gender, Self, and Work in the Life Insurance Industry"; and Leidner, "Selling Hamburgers and Selling Insurance."

37. Swann, "The Home Service Program of the NELA"; Swann, "Home Economics Work with Electric and Gas Utility Companies"; Ada Bessie Swann, "What of the Future of Home Economics in Utilities?," 1927 speech, AAFCS Records; "Home Service Committee Names Personnel," *EM* 44 (November 1930): 75; "Appointment of Jessie McQueen as Home Service Counselor," *Natural Gas* (August 1929); "Mrs. Peterson's Convention Story," *PGCN* (November 2, 1925): 5; "News from Our Home Service Department," *PGCN* (September 1, 1925): 7; and Jessie McQueen to Joseph A. Conforti, July 31, 1930, all in PGLCC Library; [American Gas Association], *Home Service* (1925); "Home Service Directors to Meet in Chicago," *EM* 43 (March 1930): 88; Florence R. Clauss, "Home Service—A Major Activity"; Swann, "Five Years

of Home Service"; Ada Bessie Swann, "Home Service of the Future Is a Community Service," *EM* 43 (June 1930): 90–92.

38. National Electric Light Association, *Home Service*; [American Gas Association], *Home Service* (1930).

39. "Sell More Appliances to Homes!," *EM* 35 (June 1926): 6306; Catherine Warren, "A Challenge to Women," *CG* 90:1 (3 January 1925): 19, 2; *Who Was Who in America*, 1:1117; Wilkes, "Power and Pedagogy," 93–96; "Clubwoman Stays in Utilities Pay," *Washington Star* (October 4, 1928); Mary Sherman, "A Census of Home Equipment," *CG* 90 (May 23, 1925): 19–20; Mary Sherman, "Housekeeping on 40,000 Farms," *CG* 92 (May 1927): 26, 28, 88–89.

40. Eppright and Ferguson, *A Century of Home Economics at Iowa State University*, 90, 110, 117, 134, 136, 166, 332, 353; Bix, "Equipped for Life"; Logie, *Careers in the Making*, 145–51; Arthur Bartlett, "Field Marshall Female," *This Week* (November 16, 1941); Eloise Davison, "Twentieth Century Homemaking," *NELA Bulletin* 14 (September 1927): 578–79.

41. Isabell Davie, "Iowa College to Pioneer Short Course in Electrical Equipment," *NELA Bulletin* 14 (February 1927): 111, 127; *EM* 37 (March 1927): 128; Isabell Davie, "Women from Fifteen States Attend Pioneer Course in Electrical Equipment Economics at Iowa University," *NELA Bulletin* 14 (April 1927): 239–42; Robert F. Pack, "The Rise of an Industry," *NELA Bulletin* 14 (July 1927): 404.

42. *TT* (November 1927): 6; "Short Course in Electrical Household Equipment at Columbia University," *NELA Bulletin* 15 (June 1928): 346; "Three Weeks' Course on Electricity and Household Electrical Equipment," 1929, Folder: Davison, E., Box 611, RG 176; "Oklahoma A&M College to Hold Short Course in Electrical Household Equipment," *NELA Bulletin* 15 (February 1928): 94; William Stokes, "Course in Electrical Household Equipment at Purdue University," *NELA Bulletin* 16 (May 1929): 309; Kline, "Agents of Modernity," 241.

43. Ruth B. Comstock, "A College and a Utility Cooperate on Home Lighting," *EM* 62 (December 1939): 14–15; Marian Fedder to Flora Rose, February 14, 1932, Student File, Class of 1931, NYSCHE Records; [American Gas Association], *Home Service* (1930), 10–11; "Home Economics and the Manufacturer: A Unique Three Day School Program," *PHE* 7 (May 1929): 135.

44. Clauss, "Home Service—A Major Activity," 46; "The Growing Importance of Home Service," *EM* 42 (September 1929): 110–11.

45. Strasser, "'The Smile That Pays'"; Spears, "'All Things to All Men.'"

46. Florence Clauss, "She Finds the Prospects, He Makes the Sales," *EM* 39 (May 1928): 90–92; [American Gas Association], *Home Service* (1930), 6. On the sexual division of labor in the workforce, see Kessler-Harris, *Out to Work*, 128, 139–42, 157–58, 203–4, 230–34.

47. National Electric Light Association, *Home Service*, 23–26; Swann, "Home Economics Work with Electric and Gas Utility Companies," 318.

48. Clara H. Zillessen, "Home Service . . . The Dorothy Dix of the Appliance Business," *EM* 45 (June 1931): 55.

49. Florence Freer, "Home Service . . . Opens the Door," *EM* 47 (June 1932): 44–45.

50. S. T. Henry, "Saving the Sale: Home Service Department Functions as Super-Saleswoman . . . But Never Takes an Order," *EM* 46 (September 1931): 52–53; Zillessen, "Home Service . . . The Dorothy Dix of the Appliance Business"; Kane, *Dear Dorothy Dix*. On "soothing over distraught feelings," see Ada Bessie Swann, quoted in "Making the Consumer Tie-Up," Chronological File: 1926, HEIB Records.

51. Quoted in Ada Bessie Swann, "What of the Future of Home Economics in Utilities?," 1927 speech, AAFCS Records.

52. Swann, "Home Service of the Future Is a Community Service," 91; Swann, "The Home Service Program of the NELA," 535; "Philadelphia's First 'Home Electric,'" *EM* 30 (December

1923): 3797; "Encouraging Social Contacts with Women's Clubs," *EM* 33 (March 1925): 5162; "Meet Mrs. Mitchell of Our Courtesy Department," *EM* 38 (July 1927): 102–3; "7,000 Joiners," *EM* 52 (September 1934): 58–59; "The Electrical Arts Club of Dallas," *EM* 44 (August 1930): 47; "They Call It Leisure House," *EM* 61 (May 1939): 26.

53. On the "emotional labor" of airline stewardesses, see Hochschild, *The Managed Heart*. Suzanne Kolm's term *personality work* aptly fits home economists, who frequently used the term *personality* in describing their jobs. See Kolm, "Women's Labor Aloft." See also Alison Clarke, *Tupperware*; Biggart, *Charismatic Capitalism*; and Leidner, "Selling Hamburgers and Selling Insurance," 157.

54. Warren I. Susman, "'Personality' and the Making of Twentieth-Century Culture," in Susman, *Culture as History*, 277–78, 280.

55. Bayard, "What Crowder's Order Means to You."

56. Swann, "Home Economics Work with Electric and Gas Utility Companies." See also Florence Freer, "Home Service—Its Functions and Accomplishments," *NELA Bulletin* 19 (December 1932): 733; and "Neighborly," *EM* 41 (February 1929): 62–63.

57. *PGCN* 10 (March 15, 1922): 65, PGLCC Library; Gibbs, "The Sales and Advertising Value of Home Economics Woman," *PIM* 13 (September 26, 1926): 144.

58. "Mrs. Anna J. Peterson," n.d.; *PGCN* 10 (March 15, 1922): 74; and "Adult Cooking Demonstrations," Folder 4, Box 1-C, 1922–57, all in PGLCC Library.

59. "How to Conduct a Cooking School," *EM* 34 (August 1925): 5461; Busch, "Cooking Competition," 242–44; Sicilia, "Selling Power," 509–17; J. V. Purcell to Department Superintendents, March 6, 1922, PGLCC Library; *PGCN* 10:6 (March 15, 1922); Frederick, *Selling Mrs. Consumer*, 281–82.

60. "Cooking Class for Gas Company Girls," 1922, typescript; "A Real Home Cooking Class," *PGCN* (October 2, 1922): 254; *PGCN* (May 1, 1922): 119; *PGCN* (June 1, 1922): 147; "Canning Day in Our Home Service Department," *PGCN* (June 1, 1923): 167; and "Home Service Prepares Canning Exhibit," *PGCN* (August 15, 1924): 4, all in PGLCC Library.

61. Smulyan, "Radio Advertising to Women in Twenties America," 300; "Mrs. Peterson Broadcasts the Story of Home Service," *PGCN* (December 15, 1922): 323; "Our Home Service Department," *PGCN* (May 16, 1923): 150; "Radio Tea Audience Fills Our Big Auditorium," *PGCN* (June 15, 1923): 180; and "Our Home Service Department," *PGCN* (July 16, 1923): 219, all in PGLCC Library. See also "Building Up the Home Service Department by Radio," *EM* 35 (February 1926): 6091–92; Jane Stern and Michael Stern, "Neighbors," *New Yorker* (April 15, 1991): 78–93.

62. "New Broadcasting Installation in Mrs. Petersen's [*sic*] Office," *PGCN* (July 15, 1924): 10; "News from Our Home Service Department," *PGCN* (January 16, 1924): 4; "Home Canning Grows in Popularity," *PGCN* (July 1, 1925): 5; "New Clubs and Picnic Sponsored by Home Service," *PGCN* (August 1, 1925): 9; "Home Service and the Young Idea," *PGCN* (September 15, 1925): 5–6; "Miss Chambers Broadcasts Daily," *PGCN* (December 1, 1925): 5; "Woman's Hour New Home Service Feature," *PGCN* (January 16, 1926): 5; and "What to Eat to Keep Fit, Told by Mrs. Peterson," *Chicago Evening American* (February 1, 1926), all in PGLCC Library.

63. "Thousands of 'Fans' in Throng at Home Service Radio Tea," *PGCN* (January 2, 1924): 6; Rice, *Seventy-Five Years of Gas Service in Chicago*, 51; "Record Crowd of Women Throngs Home Service Auditorium," *PGCN* (March 1, 1924): 10; "Our Home Service Department," *PGCN* (March 1, 1923): 67; "Opening Dates, Branch Home Service Auditoriums," undated typescript; "Our Home Service Department," *PGCN* (November 15, 1923): 355; "Important Events in Our Company History for the Year of 1924," *PGCN* (January 2, 1925): 9; and "New Irving Park Store Opens," *PGCN* (October 1, 1926): 3, all in PGLCC. I thank Michael Conzen

and Rachel Neuman for assistance in researching these neighborhoods. See *Local Community Fact Book of Metropolitan Chicago for 1980.*

64. "Our Home Service Department," *PGCN* (June 1, 1923): 167; "Gas Company Model Kitchen on Wheels," *PGCN* (October 16, 1922): 265; "Our Home Service Department," *PGCN* (May 16, 1923): 150; and "Motor Kitchen Starts Summer Program," *PGCN* (June 1, 1924): 11, all in PGLCC Library.

65. "Our Home Service Department," *PGCN* (March 1, 1924): 10; and "'Radio Pals' Swamp Mrs. Peterson with Letters Telling How They 'Listen In' on Radio Every Day," *PGCN* (April 15, 1924): 8, all in PGLCC Library; Peterson and Badenoch, *Mrs. Peterson's Simplified Cooking*; Camille Stagg Jilke, "Quick, Easy Foods Nothing New," *Chicago Sun-Times* (October 20, 1972).

66. Gibbs, "The Sales and Advertising Value of the Home Economics Woman," 144; Wilkes, "Power and Pedagogy," 76–77.

67. "Anna J. Peterson Defines Personality," *PGCN* (February 16, 1925): 3–4, PGLCC Library.

68. "Miss Alice Bradley Draws Large Summer Crowd," *PGCN* (July 15, 1925): 10, PGLCC Library.

69. "Mrs. Peterson Is Hostess to Northwest Side Merchants," *PGCN* (December 1, 1923): 367, PGLCC Library.

70. "Miss Fox Comes from Beloit to Train," *PGCN* (March 16, 1925): 4; "Mrs. Peterson Helps Inaugural of Beloit Home Service," *PGCN* (August 15, 1925): 9; and "Mrs. Peterson at Convention," *PGCN* (October 15, 1925): 9, all in PGLCC Library. See also "Meet Mrs. Mitchell of Our Courtesy Department," *EM* 38 (July 1927): 102–3.

71. S. T. Henry, "Saving the Sale," *EM* 46 (September 1931): 52–53. See also Shirley Virginia Carter, "A Housewife's Slant of Selling Electrical Things," *EM* 28 (December 1922): 70–71.

72. Florence Clauss, "How Can We Sell More Ranges?," *EM* 40 (October 1928): 60–62; Busch, "Cooking Competition," 224–25.

73. "How to Conduct a Cooking School," *EM* 34 (August 1925): 5461–62. See also "Butte, Mont., Holds Successful Electric-Range Cooking School," *EM* 33 (January 1925): 5053.

74. Cowan, *More Work for Mother*. My findings runs counter to scholars who argue that home economists forced their priorities about food onto a malleable, unsuspecting public. See Shapiro, *Perfection Salad*; Hess and Hess, *The Taste of America*; and Ehrenreich and English, *For Her Own Good*.

75. Fisher, "Home Service Activity Is Selling Higher Standards of Living," 95; Elsie Hinkley, "Report of Subcommittee on Trends in Home Service," in [American Gas Association], *Home Service* (1930), 6; George Leibman, "Home Economics as a Phase of Customer Relations," *NELA Bulletin* 15 (August 1928): 493–501; Florence Clauss, "Making Friends," *EM* 41 (June 1929): 76–77, 113; "Biggest, Best," *EM* 45 (February 1931): 49. See also "Some Questions We Answer," *PGCN* (July 1, 1922): 176; and "Tuning In with Home Service," *PGCN* (February 1, 1924): 3, both in PGLCC Library.

76. "The Growing Importance of Home Service," *EM* 42 (September 1929): 110–11.

77. Florence R. Clauss, "When Is a Washer Well Sold?"; "New York Has New Demonstration Kitchen-Laundry—'At Your Service,'" *EM* 31 (February 1924): 4130.

78. Florence Freer, "Organize Laundry Demonstrations," *EM* 47 (February 1932): 54; "362 Women Asked of Home Service," *EM* 47 (April 1932): 56–57; Isabell Davie, "Help from Home Service," *EM* 53 (March 1935): 13–15, 68–69.

79. Dorothy Blake, "Why Women Buy Electrical Goods," *EM* 23 (June 1920): 292–93. See also Ethel Rose Peyser, "What She Wants to Know," *EM* 26 (October 1921): 189–90; and Peyser, *Cheating the Junk-Pile* (1922).

80. "Not All Women Are Sound-Proof to Technical Talk," *EM* 24 (December 1920): 318;

Gerald Stedman, "The Buyer Is Not Dumb," *EM* 56 (September 1936): 2–3, 47; "The Too-Expert Expert," *EM* 56 (July 1936): 24; "No Expert Demonstrators," *EM* 50 (December 1933): 28.

81. Camilla Ryneers, "Keep Up with Your Customers on Housekeeping Methods," *EM* 39 (March 1928): 92–93.

82. Clauss, "Making Friends," 113. See also "The Electrical Arts Club of Dallas," *EM* 44 (August 1930): 47; and "Teaching Women to Service Their Own Appliances," *EM* 32 (December 1924): 4788.

83. "The Stuff That Lamps Are Made Of," *EM* 29 (January 1923): 3036–37. See also Nye, *Image Worlds*, 116–23; "Good Light Lightens Labor," *EM* 23 (June 1920): 11; and Cox, "Plain and Fancy," 49–51.

84. Helen A. Smith to Beatrice Doerschuk, January 17, 1924; and Helen A. Smith to Beatrice Doerschuk, January 30, 1924, both in File 117, Series 2, BVI Records. See also Helen Smith to Myra Robinson, May 29, 1928, Class of 1928, NYSCHE Records; "Women in Engineering," *NBBVI* (March 1, 1924): 39; and newspaper clippings and *Midwest Engineer* (August 1952), UMICH. On home economics as a path for scientifically trained women to advance in higher education, see Rossiter, *Women Scientists in America: Struggles and Strategies to 1940*, 110.

85. Florence R. Clauss, "Home Service for Dealers," *EM* 47 (March 1932): 44; "Selling Lamp Shade Materials in the Lamp Department," *EM* 35 (February 1926): 6124; "Lamp Shade Classes Promote Better Lighting," *EM* 38 (October 1927): 88–89; Sears, Roebuck and Company, *1927 Spring-Fall Catalog*, 327; L. C. Spake, "Buying Hunches from the Fixture Market," *EM* 23 (March 1920): 122–23; and "Teaches Women to Make Own Lamp Shades," *EM* 19 (April 1918): 207; Maril, *American Lighting*, 134–39; *NELA Bulletin* 16 (March 1929): 176; and Florence R. Clauss, "Home Lighting Progress," *EM* 41 (April 1929): 70. On handmade goods and consumer culture in the late nineteenth century, see Bercaw, "Solid Objects/Mutable Meanings"; and Elizabeth Nelson, *Market Sentiments*.

86. "Lamp Shade Classes Promote Better Lighting," 89.

87. Laing, *Lighting*, 67–68.

88. Luckiesh and Moss, "The New Science of Seeing"; Luckiesh and Moss, *Lighting for Seeing*; "35,000 I.E.S. Lamps in 1938," *EM* 60 (December 1938): 19. See also Nye, *Electrifying America*, 363–66; Sicilia, "Selling Power," 493–509; Rossell, "Compelling Vision"; "The New Edison Lighting Institute," *EM* 33 (March 1925): 5172–73; "Home Lighting Course at Edison Lighting Institute," *EM* 35 (May 1926): 6299; "Westinghouse to Open Lighting Institute," *EM* 41 (May 1929): 107–8; "*Electrical Merchandising* Plans a Model Store for the Westinghouse Lighting Institute," *EM* 42 (July 1929): 85–88; "There *Is* No Cashier in This Central Station Store," *EM* 42 (December 1929): 67–69; Luckiesh and Moss, *The Science of Seeing*, 322–27; and Frank B. Rae Jr., "Does Sight Saving Menace Merchandising?," *EM* 53 (February 1935): 25, 30–31.

89. "Pleasure versus Appliances," *EM* 54 (August 1935): 32; "Demonstrating Better Light—Better Sight," *EM* 50 (September 1933): 48.

90. "Lighting Trends Discussed at Forum of 200 Lighting Advisers," *EM* 59 (March 1938): 64–65.

91. Clauss, "Home Service—A Major Activity."

92. "Home Service and Merchandise Sales," *EM* 43 (April 1930): 76.

93. David Nye argues that the electrical industry "was virtually immune to the Depression," while Roland Marchand characterized advertising during the Depression as distinctly "loud, cluttered, undignified, and direct." See Nye, *Electrifying America*, 348; and Marchand, *Advertising the American Dream*, 300. On the shift in refrigerator production and marketing,

see Nickles, "Object Lessons" and "'Preserving Women'"; Tedlow, *New and Improved*; and Robinson, "Safeguarded by Your Refrigerator."

94. "Is Home Service a Commercial Activity?," *EM* 40 (July 1928): 71; Hinkley, "Report of Subcommittee on Trends in Home Service."

95. Zillessen, "Home Service . . . The Dorothy Dix of the Appliance Business." See also Clauss, "Home Service—A Major Activity"; June Thatcher to Esther Stocks, January 5, 1938; and Dorothy Foley to Esther Stocks, June 11, 1937, both in Student File, Class of 1936, NYSCHE Records.

96. Clotilde Grunsky, "Women Are Indispensable," *EM* 58 (September 1937): 15–16; Laurence Wray, "Cold Figures on Home Service," *EM* 53 (April 1935): 11, 34; "The Dollar and Cent Value of Home Service," *EM* 64 (August 1940): 50, 92. See also Laurence Wray, "Educating Boston," *EM* 42 (December 1929): 59; Isabell Davie, "Home Service Sells Refrigeration," *EM* 53 (May 1935): 11–15, 51; and Mark Rose, *Cities of Light and Heat*, 162–63.

97. McQueen quoted in Marie Sellers, "HEWIB Report from the Middle Atlantic States, January 21, 1938," Chronological File: 1938, HEIB Records. Howe quoted in *Proceedings of the Nineteenth Annual Convention of the National Association of Ice Industries* (1936), 163–76, and Robinson, "Safeguarded by Your Refrigerator," 269.

98. Swann, "The Home Service Program of the NELA"; "Come off the Pedestal, Home Economists," *EM* 56 (December 1936): 10.

99. Interview, Home Economics Study, Institute for Women's Professional Relations, September 1935, Folder 4279, Box 361, Series 200S, RF Papers.

100. Beatrice C. Jackson to Flora Rose, March 20, 1941, Student File, Class of 1929, NYSCHE Records.

Chapter 7

1. Jessie McQueen, "The Same Job—With a Flag to Carry," *JHE* 34 (September 1942): 443; Pundt, *AHEA*, 142–85.

2. Marling, *As Seen on TV*; May, *Homeward Bound*; Rossiter, *Women Scientists in America: Before Affirmative Action*; Oldenziel and Zachmann, *Cold War Kitchen*, 1–29; Haddow, *Pavilions of Plenty*; Galison and Hevly, *Big Science*; Hughes and Hughes, *Systems, Experts, and Computers*; Leslie, *The Cold War and American Science*.

3. *RCBHE* (1940): 18–19; *RCBHE* (1942): 2–3, 8; *RCBHNHE* (1943): 8; *RCBHNHE* (1944): 8–9; *RCBHNHE* (1945): 9–10.

4. Bess V. Morrison, "Cotton Utilization Studies in the Bureau of Home Economics," *JHE* 33 (October 1941): 585–86; *RCBHE* (1940): 12–14; *RCBHE* (1941): 13–14; *RCBHE* (1942): 8; *RCBHNHE* (1943): 10; *RCBHNHE* (1944): 9–10; Ruth O'Brien, "Cotton Fabric Research in the BHE," *JHE* 32 (September 1940): 443–47; "Streamlined Garb Tested for Women in War Plants," *NYT* (March 30, 1941) 2:4; *RCBHE* (1942): 7; *RCBHNHE* (1943): 10.

5. *RCBHE* (1942): 1, 2, 6, 9, 10–11; Pundt, *AHEA*, 160–62, 169–70.

6. Bentley, *Eating for Victory*, 24–29; Levenstein, *Paradox of Plenty*, 65–66, chap. 5; "Home Economics in the Defense Program," *JHE* 33 (April 1941): 248; "Home Economists and National Defense," *JHE* 33 (February 1941): 108–9; Helen S. Mitchell, "The National Nutrition Outlook," *JHE* 33 (October 1941): 537–40; Eloise Davison, "The Home Economist and Defense," *JHE* 34 (February 1942): 97; Pundt, *AHEA*, 142–85; Finneran, "Louise Stanley," chaps. 4, 5; "Health and Welfare in the Defense Program," *JHE* 33 (April 1941): 248–50; "Nutrition in the Defense Program," *JHE* 33 (April 1941): 250–51; Baker et al., *Century of Service*, 324–25; Hazel Stiebeling, "The National Research Council's Committee on Food Habits," *JHE* 33 (October 1941): 541–43; Rothe, *Current Biography 1950*, 548–50; *RCBHE* (June 1942): 3.

7. Ruth O'Brien, "BHNHE Celebrates a Quarter Century of Service," *JHE* 40 (June 1948): 296.

8. "Reorganized Bureau," *JHE* 35 (April 1943): 230–31; "Bureau of Human Nutrition and Home Economics," *JHE* 35 (May 1943): 269–70; Pundt, *AHEA*, 168–69, 175.

9. "Report of the Advisory Committee on BHNHE," *JHE* 38 (September 1946): 451; Pundt, *AHEA*, 174–75.

10. Krieghbaum, "Servants of the People"; "Hazel K. Stiebeling"; Yost, *American Women of Science*, 158–76; Ware and Braukman, *Notable American Women: Completing the Twentieth Century*, 614–15.

11. Pundt, *AHEA*, 198–99; Rossiter, *Women Scientists in America: Before Affirmative Action*, 173; "Report of the Advisory Committee on the Bureau of Human Nutrition and Home Economics," *JHE* 40 (September 1948): 396; Ruth O'Brien and Georgian Adams, "RMA Home Economics Research," *JHE* 40 (March 1948): 120–22; "Report of the Advisory Committee on the Bureau of Human Nutrition and Home Economics," *JHE* 41 (September 1949): 391–92; O'Brien, "BHNHE Celebrates a Quarter Century of Service"; Emily C. Davis, "The BHNHE Reporting," *JHE* 44 (November 1952): 721.

12. Rasmussen and Baker, *The Department of Agriculture*, 77.

13. *JHE* 45 (December 1953): 704; "Ruth O'Brien, Expert on Textiles, U.S. Aide," *WP* (March 13, 1976): E:6; Pundt, *AHEA*, 229–30.

14. *The Bureau of Human Nutrition and Home Economics*, 13–15; Peet and Sater Thye, *Household Equipment*; Lenore Sater Thye, "A Step-Saving U Kitchen," *USDA Home and Garden Bulletin*, no. 14 (1951).

15. Rasmussen and Baker, *The Department of Agriculture*, 48; Baker et al., *Century of Service*, 374–81; "U.S. Department of Agriculture Reorganization Plans," *JHE* 45 (December 1953): 704; "Redirection of Research in USDA Home Economics Programs," *JHE* 47 (April 1955): 232; "Report of the Advisory Committee on Human Nutrition and Home Economics Research," *JHE* 47 (September 1955): 515; "USDA Announces Changes in Home Economics Research Branches," *JHE* 47 (November 1955): 652; Pundt, *AHEA*, 253.

16. "Report of the Advisory Committee on Human Nutrition and Home Economics," *JHE* 48 (September 1956): 548–49; "Federal Research Related to Home Economics," *JHE* 48 (September 1956): 547–48; "Federal Research Related to Home Economics," *JHE* 49 (September 1957): 562–63; Pundt, *AHEA*, 274, 288–89, 299, 306, 310.

17. Emily C. Davis, "Reporting News of Home Economics Research of the Agricultural Research Service, USDA," *JHE* 50 (October 1958): 653.

18. Pundt, *AHEA*, 297; "Changes for USDA Home Economics Unit," *JHE* 54 (January 1962): 8.

19. Rossiter, *Women Scientists in America: Before Affirmative Action*, 174, 284; Pundt, *AHEA*, 337; "Research in Clothing and Housing in USDA to Be Phased Out," *JHE* 57 (March 1965): 172; "Excerpts from AHEA Statement Supporting Continuation of Clothing and Housing Research in the U.S. Department of Agriculture," *JHE* 57 (June 1965): 457; "Report on USDA Research Funding," *JHE* 58 (January 1966): 4; "Hazel K. Stiebeling Retires from the USDA," *JHE* 55 (September 1963): 545; *JHE* 56 (January 1964): 68.

20. Rossiter, *Women Scientists in America: Before Affirmative Action*, 284.

21. Rasmussen and Baker, *The Department of Agriculture*, 49–50.

22. Rossiter, *Women Scientists in America: Before Affirmative Action*, 165–85.

23. Pundt, *AHEA*, 343; "Consumers All," *USDA YA* (1962).

24. Levenstein, *Paradox of Plenty*, 78; McGrath and Johnson, *The Changing Mission of Home Economics*; Virginia B. Vincenti, "Home Economics Moves into the Twenty-First Cen-

tury," in Stage and Vincenti, *Rethinking Home Economics*, 313; Rossiter, *Women Scientists in America: Before Affirmative Action*, 177–80.

25. On General Mills, see Box: "Defense: Civilian Services," Imprint Collection, SL; General Foods Corporation, *How to Bake by the Ration Book*. On the food industry's use of advertising during World War II, see Levenstein, *Paradox of Plenty*, 74–76; and Bentley, *Eating for Victory*.

26. Marie Sellers, "Prospects for the 1942 Graduate in Business Home Economics," *JHE* 34 (June 1942): 362; Jessie McQueen, "Gearing Household Equipment Programs to the Present Defense Needs," *JHE* 33 (October 1941): 579; McQueen, "The Same Job—With a Flag to Carry"; Callahan, *Preparation for the Business Field of Home Economics* (1942), 11; Maule, *Careers for the Home Economist*, 132–33, 147–50; Ada Bessie Swann, "Household Equipment in Wartime: What to Expect When the War Ends and in the Future after the War," speech to the Home Economics Women in Business, June 5, 1943, Folder: 1943, HEIB Records.

27. Margaret Mitchell, "Adjustment of Home Economics Departments in the Equipment Field to Wartime Conditions," Folder: 1942, HEIB Records; "Help in Teaching Nutrition," Westinghouse advertisement, *JHE* 37 (April 1945): 13; "The Homemaker and the War Is Theme of Westinghouse Exhibit at Museum of Science and Industry in Chicago," August 22, 1942; "Supplementary Information on Westinghouse Exhibit at Museum of Science and Industry," n.d.; Westinghouse Electric and Manufacturing Company, *The ABC's of Eating for Health*, MSI.

28. Mary I. Barber, "Feeding the New Army," *Quartermaster Review* (July–August 1941), KC Archives; File: Mary Barber, Folder: 42 "Home Economists, B–F," Box 22, *NAWIV*; Hall of Fame Nominations, 1982, HEIB Records.

29. Fredrika D. Borchard, "Much Praised Navy Cook Book Just On," *CSM* (October 31, 1946): 4; Obituary, *NYT* (September 3, 1963): 33; Ina S. Lindman, "Early Leaders in Home Economics in Business," Folder: 1962 Convention—Program—Old Slides, HEIB Records; Ina S. Lindman, "Training for Home Economics in Business," *JHE* 38 (April 1946): 207.

30. Grace C. Dimelow to Lydia Humphreys, June 21, 1946, Student File, Class of 1920, NYSCHE Records; Sowinksi, *A Forward Force*, 31–33; Jessie McQueen, "Home Service in War Time," June 22, 1942, speech, HEIB Records.

31. On the consumer products industries in postwar America, see Goldstein, *Do It Yourself*; Nickles, "Object Lessons"; Hounshell and Smith, *Science and Corporate Strategy*; Blaszczyk, *Imagining Consumers*; Susan Strasser, "The Convenience Is Out of This World: The Garbage Disposer and American Culture," in Strasser, McGovern, and Judt, *Getting and Spending*, 263–80; Alison Clarke, *Tupperware*; Meikle, *American Plastic*; Strasser, *Never Done*, chap. 14; Cowan, *More Work for Mother*, chap. 7; and Lifshey, *The Housewares Story*. On food production and consumption in this period, see Levenstein, *Paradox of Plenty*, chap. 7; Erika Endrijonas, "Processed Foods from Scratch: Cooking for a Family in the 1950s," in Inness, *Kitchen Culture in America*, 157–73"; Christopher Holmes Smith, "Freeze Frames: Frozen Foods and Memories of the Postwar American Family," in Inness, *Kitchen Culture in America*, 175–209; Marling, *As Seen on TV*, chap. 6; and Shapiro, *Something from the Oven*.

32. Bradley and Bradley, "Alice Bradley," 149; Maule, *Executive Careers for Women*, 40–45. See also Rossiter, *Women Scientists in America: Before Affirmative Action*, 256–76; Frances M. Fuller and Mary B. Batchelder, "Opportunities for Women at the Administrative Level," *HBR* 31 (January 1953): 111–28; Knowles, "Harvard-Radcliffe Program in Business Administration"; and Kwolek-Folland, *Incorporating Women*, chap. 5.

33. Sowinski, *A Forward Force*, 37, 45; Helen Robertson, "Home Economics in Business Department, American Home Economics Association," March 14, 1958, Folder: 1958; and

Home Economics in Business Directories, 1940–55, both in HEIB Records; Josephine Hemphill, "Home Economics Unlimited," *JHE* 47 (November 1955): 655; Zapoleon, *The College Girl Looks Ahead to Her Career Opportunities*, 122; Joan Lutz Dater, "The Home Economist . . . Liaison with the Consumer," *Aerosol Age* (June 1967): 40, 110.

34. Katharine Fisher, "Wanted: More Home Economists for Business," *JHE* 39 (June 1947): 326.

35. Maule, *Careers for the Home Economist*, 143–44, 147–48; Esther Stocks to Margaret McCabe, January 23, 1951, Student File, Class of 1930, NYSCHE Records.

36. "Home Economics Paves the Way," *WNIHE* (January 1966): 48. See *WNIHE* (February 1968): 87.

37. "Vocational Guidance Project," *JHE* 36 (February 1944): 87–88; "A Look Back . . . 60 Years of HEIB," Slide Presentation Given at the 1984 Annual Meeting, HEIB Records; Lindman, "Training for Home Economics in Business"; "HEIB's Teach Techniques," *JHE* 39 (May 1947): 290–91; "Home Economics in Business Department," *JHE* 40 (February 1948): 94; Mary E. Hawkins, "Trainees Finish Course," *JHE* 41 (November 1949): 525–26; "Graduate Program Offered for HEIB's," *JHE* 44 (May 1952): 363–64.

38. Notebooks of HEIB Minutes, June 24, 1951 through June 20, 1959, HEIB Records; American Home Economics Association, *Career Opportunities in Home Economics in Business*.

39. Pundt, *AHEA*, 222, 241. See also Solomon, *In the Company of Educated Women*, chap. 12, esp. 63; and Rossiter, *Women Scientists in America: Before Affirmative Action*, 167.

40. Fisher, "Wanted: More Home Economists for Business," 325; "Report of the Public Relations Committee to the HEIB," 1948, Folder: 1948, HEIB Records; Pundt, *AHEA*, 212.

41. "A Home Economics Career in Business," *WNIHE* (September 1964): 105–7; Marling, *As Seen on TV*, 206; Nichaman, "Betty Crocker"; Shapiro, *Something from the Oven*, 180–96; Sowinski, *A Forward Force*, 34; Helen Fritz, "Philadelphia HEIBs: 57th Anniversary," February 27, 1983, typescript, 2–4, Folder: Local Group Histories, HEIB Records.

42. Leone Ann Heuer, "Fabric Forecast," *JHE* 54 (February 1946): 74–78; Jules LaBarthe Jr., "Fabric Facts versus New Names," *JHE* 44 (June 1952): 419–22; M. Lelyn Branin, "The Coal You Wear," *WNIHE* (November 1946): 60–61, 144, 146; Hounshell and Smith, *Science and Corporate Strategy*, chap. 18; Hardin, "Industry Structure and the Marketing of Synthetic Fibers"; American Chemical Society, *Chemistry in the Economy*, chap. 4.

43. Alexis Sommaripa, "Teachers of Home Economics—A World with You," *FHE* (October 1941), quoted in Maule, *Careers for the Home Economist*, 182–83. See also Maule, *Careers for the Home Economist*, 190–92. See "The Wonders Women Work in Marketing," *SM* (October 2, 1959): 33–36; and Joseph B. Quig, "The Consumer Looks at 1953 Fabrics," *JHE* 45 (November 1953): 643–47.

44. Harper W. Boyd Jr. and Sidney J. Levy, "New Dimension in Consumer Analysis," *HBR* 41 (November 1963): 131–34; Joyce Champion, "Laundry Is Really the Care and Understanding of Fabrics," *WHIHE* (March 1966); Strasser, *Never Done*, 267–72; Cowan, *More Work for Mother*.

45. *JHE* 46 (November 1954): 692; Anne Lyng, "Laundry Aids and Their Effects on Textiles and Laundry Equipment," *WNIHE* (October 1964): 70–71; "Consumer Education: A New Direction," *Moonbeams* (March 1970): 10–12, P&G Archive; "The Wonders Women Work in Marketing"; "A Home Economics Career in Business," *WNIHE* (February 1965): 88.

46. Dorothy Siegert Lyle to Rosemary Archibald, March 2, 1982, Rosemary Archibald Notebook, HEIB Records; Lyle, *Focus on Fabrics*.

47. Notebooks of HEIB Minutes, June 24, 1951–June 20, 1959, HEIB Records.

48. "Women's Work Eased by Home Economists," *Food Field Reporter* (April 24, 1961): 1,

7; Strasser, *Never Done*, chap. 14; Nichaman, "Betty Crocker"; Marling, *As Seen on TV*, 219–20; "The Fabulous Market for Food," *Fortune* (October 1953): 135, 137; Levenstein, *Revolution at the Table*, 202–3; "The Wonders Women Work in Marketing"; Endrijonas, "Processed Foods from Scratch"; Smith, "Freeze Frames"; May, *Homeward Bound*, 75–77.

49. "I Remember When . . . ," *GF News* (May 1950): 6–7, KF Archives.

50. Ferguson, *General Foods Corporation*; "Once upon a Time: A History of the Consumer Service Department, 1924–1949"; "GF Alert to Consumer Problems," *GF Newsletter* 1 (April 1940): 1, 4; and "The Proof of the Pudding: GF's Consumer Service Department," *GF Newsletter* 5 (August 1944), all in KF Archives.

51. "Service behind Every Package," Consumer Service Department typed manuscript, December 1955; and "The Story of General Foods Kitchens and How They Serve the Home Kitchen!" (1958), both in KF Archives; T. C. Taylor, "Sharp Consumer-Contact Program Sees Future Business: General Foods Has Restyled Its Kitchen Department to Give It a Broader Marketing Role," *FE* 30 (December 1958): 44–46.

52. Sellers quoted in "I Remember When . . ."; "Service behind Every Package"; "Come into Our Kitchens," *GF News* 19 (September 1958); and "Advice and Consent," *GF News* (February 1960): 8–10, both in KF Archives.

53. "HEIBs Discuss How to Prepare the Most Useful Teaching Aids," *WNIHE* (October 1966): 30, 107–9.

54. Helen Robertson to Ethel Russell, October 15, 1959, Folder: HEIB National—1960s—History, HEIB Records; Pundt, *AHEA*, 177–78.

55. Callahan, *Preparation for the Business Field of Home Economics* (1934), 8; Callahan, *Preparation for the Business Field of Home Economics* (1942), 8–9, 22; Zapoleon, *The College Girl Looks Ahead to Her Career Opportunities*, 117, 122.

56. "The Wonders Women Work in Marketing."

57. Rossiter, *Women Scientists in America: Before Affirmative Action*, 274; Maule, *Executive Careers for Women*, 42–43, 44. On Dunham, see Hall of Fame Nominations, 1989, HEIB Records; and Student File, Class of 1932; and Oral Interview of Ellen-Ann Dunham, August 26, 1964, both in NYSCHE Records. On Bates, see Pundt, *AHEA*, 346.

58. Joan Younger, "Home Economists: Today's New Glamour Girls," *Cosmopolitan* (April 1965): 12.

59. "Serving the Consumer," *GF Newsletter* 9 (September 1948): 1, 6–9, KF Archives.

60. Satenig St. Marie, "Reminiscences," in Stage and Vincenti, *Rethinking Home Economics*, 197–300.

61. Marjorie Child Husted, "A Critical Evaluation of Modern Home Service," speech to the Mid-West Regional Gas Sales Conference, Chicago, April 23, 1952, typescript, Box 2, MCH Papers. Also quoted in Rossiter, *Women Scientists in America: Before Affirmative Action*, 274–75.

62. Paraphrased in "A Home Economics Career in Business," *WNIHE* (September 1964): 107; *WNIHE* (November 1967): 47. See also Jeanne Paris Sowinski, author's interview, December 1998.

63. Anonymous woman quoted in Maule, *She Strives to Conquer*, 261.

64. Ada Bessie Swann, "Household Equipment in Wartime: What to Expect When the War Ends and in the Future after the War," speech to the Home Economics Women in Business, June 5, 1943, Folder: 1943, HEIB Records.

65. On the rise of food technology and food science, see Bentley, *Eating for Victory*; Levenstein, *Paradox of Plenty*, chap. 7; N. W. Desrosier, "Education of a Food Technologist," *FT* 12 (February 1958): 10–12; "What Is a Food Technologist?," *FT* 13 (January 1959): 9–10; H. A. Bullis, "New Product Development Key to Success at General Mills," *FE* 30 (January 1958):

53–56. On correlations between engineering and masculinity, see Oldenziel, *Making Technology Masculine.*

66. "The P&G Test Kitchens," *Moonbeams* (May/June 1972): 3–7, P&G Archive.

67. Drucker, *The Practice of Management*, quoted in Boyd and Levy, "New Dimension in Consumer Analysis," 129; "The Marketing Man: Rising Star in the Corporate Firmament," *SM* (July 21, 1961): 67–72; "Marketing Dominates View from Above," *SM* (June 7, 1963): 20.

68. Sass, *The Pragmatic Imagination*, 308–9; "Operations Research in Marketing," *HBR* (January–February 1967): 30–38, 40, 42, 44, 187–88; "The Marketing Revolution," report on the proceedings of National Conference of the American Marketing Association, December 1955, Folder: Correspondence, 1956, Box: Merchandise Development and Testing Laboratory/Meeting Files/Publications, Sears Archive.

69. Cohen, *A Consumers' Republic*, 292–344; Nowland & Schladermundt, "Product Planning Studies, to Ascertain Preferences of Consumers," July 30, 1952, typescript report for Sears, Roebuck & Company, Sears Archive; Daniel Horowitz, "The Emigré as Celebrant of American Consumer Culture: George Katona and Ernst Dichter," in Strasser, McGovern, and Judt, *Getting and Spending*, 149–66; Marling, *As Seen on TV*, 212–13; Nickles, "Object Lessons"; Zunz, *Why the American Century?*, 103–6; Sass, *The Pragmatic Imagination*, 319–20.

70. *Fortune* magazine writer Gilbert Burck, quoted in Maule, *Executive Careers for Women*, 29.

71. "The Wonders Women Work in Marketing."

72. Maule, *Executive Careers for Women*, 29.

73. Tedlow, *New and Improved*, xxi–xxiii, 6; Nickles, "Object Lessons"; Cohen, *A Consumers' Republic*, 292–344; Zunz, *Why the American Century?*, 94–103; Peter F. Drucker, "Meet Tomorrow's Customer: Changes in Buying Habits Will Offer New Sales Opportunities," *NB* 51 (June 1963): 102–5.

74. Cameron Day, "Consumer Testing: Mighty Power behind the Product," *SM* (July 2, 1965): 20–22; Roland Marchand, "Customer Research as Public Relations: General Motors in the 1930s," in Strasser, McGovern, and Judt, *Getting and Spending*, 85–110. On Swift, see *Progress* (November–December 1965): 5; *Progress* (January–February 1967): 8; and "Testing Consumer Tastes," *National Provisioner* (December 17, 1966), all in Swift Records. On Kraft, see "The Curtain Rises on the New Kraft Kitchens," *Kraftsman* 20 (March–April 1962): 6, KF Archives.

75. Helen G. Canoyer, "Home Economics in Marketing Research," *JHE* 50 (June 1958): 419–20.

76. Younger, "Home Economists"; Shapiro, *Something from the Oven*, 191–92.

77. "The Consumer Be Served," *Kraftsman* 11 (November–December 1953): 18–19; and "Meet the Kraft Home Economist," *Kraftsman* 22 (March–April 1964): 27, both in KF Archives.

78. Nichaman, "Betty Crocker"; "Once upon a Time: A History of the Consumer Service Department, 1924–1949," KF Archives.

79. Maule, *Careers for the Home Economist*, 153.

80. Marling, *As Seen on TV*, 212–13; McCann-Erickson Inc., "Martha Logan Picture Study," January 1955, Folder 2, Box 2, Swift Records.

81. Louise A. Stedman and Paul S. Anderson, "Employer Acceptance of the Mature Home Economist," *JHE* 57 (December 1965): 767–72.

82. Callahan, *Preparation for the Business Field of Home Economics* (1942), 18–19; HEIB Preconvention Program, June 16–17, 1949, Folder: 1949; Elizabeth Sweeney Herbert, Notes on September 16, 1949, HEIB meeting, Folder: 1950; *HEIB National News Notes* (April 1970); and Helen Fritz, "Philadelphia HEIBs: 57th Anniversary," February 27, 1983, typescript, 2–4, Folder: Local Group Histories, all in HEIB Records.

83. Editorial, *WNIHE* (November 1965): 6. See also Gladys A. Baird, "College Preparation for Home Economists in Business," *WNIHE* (November 1965): 8, 10–11, 17.

84. Helen Fritz, "Philadelphia HEIBs: 57th Anniversary," February 27, 1983, typescript, 2–4, Folder: Local Group Histories, HEIB Records.

85. Minutes of the HEIB Advisory Committee Meeting, June 19, 1953; *HEIB National News Notes* (October 1960); HEIB Annual Report, April 26, 1961, Folder: 1961; and Minutes of the HEIB Annual Business Meeting, June 25, 1972, Folder: 1972, all in HEIB Records; Sowinksi, *A Forward Force*, 57.

86. HEIB Suggestions for Implementing Program of Work, 1966–67, Folder: 1967, HEIB Records.

87. Sowinski, *A Forward Force*, 55–61.

88. Robert W. Strain, "Business Values the Home Economist," *JHE* 62 (January 1970): 49–53; "HEIBs Speak Out," *JHE* 65 (1973): 32, cited and discussed in Rossiter, *Women Scientists in America: Before Affirmative Action*, 484n81.

89. Helen Fritz, "Philadelphia HEIBs: 57th Anniversary," February 27, 1983, typescript, 2–4, Folder: Local Group Histories, HEIB Records; "Service behind Every Package"; "General Foods Consumer Center," c. 1977, KF Archives.

90. Sicilia, "Distant Proximity," 270.

Chapter 8

1. On Friedan and her impact, see Daniel Horowitz, *Betty Friedan and the Making of "The Feminine Mystique"*; and Shapiro, *Something from the Oven*, 231–47.

2. Rosalind Rosenberg, *Divided Lives*, 192–95; "What Robin Morgan Said at Denver," *JHE* 65 (January 1973): 13.

3. Epstein and Goode, *The Other Half*; Marling, *As Seen on TV*; Meyerowitz, *Not June Cleaver*.

4. "The Concept Basic to Home Economics," *JHE* 60 (February 1968): 93. See also "Editorial," *WHIHE* (February 1967): 8.

5. Rossiter, *Women Scientists in America: Before Affirmative Action*, 165–85; Pundt, *AHEA*, 297–373; Virginia B. Vincenti, "Home Economics Moves into the 21st Century," in Stage and Vincenti, *Rethinking Home Economics*, 301–5; Margaret W. Rossiter, "The Men Move In," in Stage and Vincenti, *Rethinking Home Economics*, 110–14.

6. Cohen, *A Consumers' Republic*, 345–97; Daniel Horowitz, *The Anxieties of Affluence*, 162–202.

7. Rose, Stocks, and Whittier, *A Growing College*, 275–79; Canoyer, "The Consumer Advisory Council," *JHE* 55 (March 1963): 160–62; Pundt, *AHEA*, 315; Canoyer, "For the Consumer: What Breakthroughs?," *JHE* 58 (September 1966): 523–27; Canoyer and Vaile, *Income and Consumption* and *Economics of Income and Consumption*; *Who's Who in the East*.

8. Canoyer, "The Consumer Advisory Council"; Anna Fisher Rush, "Consumer Programs: Role of Home Economists," *WNIHE* (October 1965): 27, 19, 83–84; Esther Peterson, "Consumer Representation in the White House," in Angevine, *Consumer Activists*; William H. Marshall, "Home Economists and Legislation Affecting Families," *JHE* 59 (October 1967): 641–42; "Larger Issues," *JHE* 59 (October 1967): 620.

9. On Furness, see Cohen, *A Consumers' Republic*, 349. On safety and standards engineering, see Mohun, "Use, Misuse, and Abuse," and "Product Safety and the Law." On Nader, see *The Ralph Nader Reader*; and Cohen, *A Consumers' Republic*, 354–55.

10. Pundt, *AHEA*, 177–79. See also the JHE forum itself published in late 1944; Ada Bessie Swann, "Household Equipment in Wartime: What to Expect When the War Ends and in

the Future after the War," speech to the Home Economics Women in Business, June 5, 1943, Folder: 1943, HEIB Records; "Should the AHEA Abandon Legislative Work?," *JHE* 36 (November 1944): 562–67; Helen Robertson to Ethel Russell, October 15, 1959, Folder: HEIB National—1960s History," HEIB Records.

11. Pundt, *AHEA*, 297–373, esp. 322, 328.

12. Editorial, *WNIHE* (October 1966): 8; Bymers, "Consumer Education and the Home Economist," *JHE* 55 (May 1963): 329.

13. Quoted in Rush, "Consumer Programs," 27.

14. McGrath and Johnson, *The Changing Mission of Home Economics*; Earl McGrath, "Mission of Home Economics," *JHE* 60 (February 1968): 85–92. On the issues of poverty in the United States at this time, see Daniel Horowitz, *The Anxieties of Affluence*, 129–61.

15. Elizabeth Duncan Koontz, "The Extension Worker and the Changing Role of Women," *JHE* 63 (November 1971): 588–90; Canoyer, "For the Consumer"; Thomas M. Brooks, "Consumer Education: Can We Improve Our Score?," *JHE* 65 (September 1973): 33–35; Nancy Harries, "An Active Role for Home Economists in Consumer Affairs," *JHE* 63 (January 1971): 24–29.

16. Philip Lesly, "Home Economics Is Losing Out in the Space Age," *WNIHE* (March 1967): 25–26; "Suggestions for Local Group Implementation, HEIB 1968–69 Program of Work," Folder 1968–69; HEIB Section report, 1970–71, Folder: 1971, HEIB Records.

17. "Are We Meeting Our Responsibilities?," *WNIHE* (March 1967): 18.

18. Rush, "Consumer Programs."

19. *NYT* (February 20, 2007).

20. On Friedan's critique, see Daniel Horowitz, *The Anxieties of Affluence*, 120–27. See also Rosenberg, *Divided Lives*, 180–219; and Pundt, *AHEA*, 326.

21. The *Journal of Home Economics* published one of its first articles advocating for second-wave feminism in 1968. See Francena L. Miller, "Womanpower: A Prime Resource," *JHE* 60 (November 1968): 693–96. For an example of later discussions, see "Today's Frontiers: Tomorrow's Realities," *JHE* 63 (September 1971): 407–8.

22. Rossiter, *Women Scientists in America: Before Affirmative Action*, 180–83; Rose, Stocks, and Whittier, *A Growing College*, 527; Pundt, *AHEA*, 317; Patricia Durey Murphy, "What's in a Name?," *JHE* 59 (November 1967): 702–7; *HEIB National News Notes* (April 1970).

23. No one has critically examined the content of high school home economics courses over the course of the twentieth century, and the extent to which it varied and became watered down by the 1950s is not clear. On the early twentieth century, see Rury, *Education and Women's Work*.

24. "The Women's Role Committee Speaks Out," *JHE* 65 (January 1973): 10–15.

25. Daniel Yankelovich Inc., *Home Economist Image Study: A Qualitative Investigation*, May 1974, AAFCS Records; Vincenti, "Home Economics Moves into the 21st Century," 301–3; Virginia B. Vincenti, "Chronology of Events and Movements Which Have Defined and Shaped Home Economics," in Stage and Vincenti, *Rethinking Home Economics*, 328; "New Directions," *JHE* (1959); "New Directions II," *JHE* (1975).

26. Yankelovich, *Home Economics Image Study*.

27. Bleibtreu, speech to the HEIB annual meeting, 1973, Folder: 1973, HEIB Records.

28. Lesly, "Home Economics Is Losing Out in the Space Age." See also Lynwood Schrader, "Consider the Economics in Home Economics," *WNIHE* (October 1967): 92, 96; and Pundt, *AHEA*, 297–373, esp. 316.

Epilogue

1. Carolyn Jackson to author, October 19, 2011.
2. Chatriot, Chessel, and Hilton, *The Expert Consumer*, 1–18; McGovern, *Sold American*, 369.
3. Jennifer Grossman, "Food for Thought (and for Credit)," *NYT* (September 2, 2003).

Bibliography

Manuscript Collections

Ann Arbor, Michigan
 University of Michigan Alumni Office
Battle Creek, Michigan
 Kellogg Company Archives
Beltsville, Maryland
 National Agricultural Library
Berkeley, California
 Agnes Fay Morgan Papers
Cambridge, Massachusetts
 Schlesinger Library, Radcliffe Institute for Advanced Study, Harvard University
  Advertising Women of New York Records
  Amelia Muir Baldwin Papers
  Bureau of Vocational Information Records
  Cookery Pamphlet Collection
  Adelaide Hawley Cumming Papers
  Christine Isobel (MacGaffey) Frederick Papers
  Home Economists in Business Records
  Marjorie Child Husted Papers
  Imprint Collection
  Institute of Women's Professional Relations Records
  Notable American Women, vol. 4, Records
  Records of the Women's Educational and Industrial Union
  Anna Howard Shaw Papers (Series X of the Mary Earhart Dillon Collection)
Chantilly, Virginia
 History Factory
  Sears, Roebuck and Company Archives
Chicago, Illinois
 Chicago History Museum
  Swift & Company Records
 Museum of Science and Industry
 Peoples Gas, Light, and Coke Company Library
 Special Collections, University of Chicago
Cincinnati, Ohio
 Procter & Gamble Archive
Dearborn, Michigan
 The Henry Ford Research Center
Ithaca, New York
 Division of Rare and Manuscript Collections, Cornell University

American Association of Family and Consumer Sciences Records, Collection
Number 6578 (formerly American Home Economics Association Archives
located in Alexandria, Virginia)
New York State College of Home Economics Records, Collection Number 23/2/749
Middletown, Connecticut
Special Collections and Archives, Wesleyan University Library
Wilbur Olin Atwater Papers
Morton Grove, Illinois
Kraft/General Foods Archives
New York, New York
Good Housekeeping Institute Archives
Special Collections, Teachers College, Columbia University
James Earl Russell Papers
North Tarrytown, New York
Rockefeller Archive Center
Rockefeller Foundation Papers
Palo Alto, California
Hoover Institution Library and Archives, Stanford University
U.S. Food Administration Records
Washington, D.C.
National Archives
Record Group 16, Records of the Secretary of the U.S. Department of Agriculture
Record Group 69, Records of the Works Progress Administration
Record Group 176, Records of the Bureau of Home Economics and Human Nutrition
National Museum of American History, Smithsonian Institution Archives Center
Product Cookbook Collection
Trade Catalog Collection
Warshaw Collection of Advertising Ephemera
Westerville, Ohio
Home Economics in Business Section Records (now located in Schlesinger Library,
Harvard University, Cambridge, Massachusetts)

Periodicals, Trade Journals, and Government Serials

Agricultural Engineering
Agricultural Experiment Station Circular
American Food Journal
American Kitchen Magazine
Annals of the American Academy of Political and Social Science
Boston Globe
Bulletin of the National Research Council
Business Week
Catholic Woman Magazine
Cereal Chemistry
Cheesekraft
Chicago Evening American
Chicago Sun-Times
Childhood Education
Children's Bureau Publications

Christian Science Monitor
Cincinnati Enquirer
Cincinnati Post–Times Star
Cincinnati Times Star
Consumers' Research Bulletin
Consumers' Research General Bulletin
Cosmopolitan
Country Gentleman
Daily News-Graphic
Delineator
Electragist
Electrical Merchandising
Electric Refrigeration News
Extension Service Review
Food and Health Education
Food Engineering
Food Research
Food Technology
Forbes
Forecast
Forecast for Home Economists
Fortune
GF News
GF Newsletter
Good Housekeeping
Harper's Bazaar
Harvard Business Review
HEIB National News Notes
Home Economist
Home Economist and the American Food Journal
Housewives League Magazine
Hygeia
Ice and Refrigeration
Independent Woman
Indiana Agricultural Experiment Station Bulletin
Industrial Standardization
Journal of Home Economics
Journal of the American Dietetic Association
Journal of the American Medical Association
Journal of the American Statistical Association
Kraftsman
Melliand Textile Monthly
Moonbeams
National Association of Ice Industries Proceedings
National Consumer News
National Electric Light Association Bulletin
National Electric Light Association Proceedings
National Provisioner
Nation's Business

Nation's Health
Natural Gas
NELA Bulletin
NELA Proceedings
News-Bulletin of the Bureau of Vocational Information
New Yorker
New York Evening Telegram
New York Times
Parents
Peoples Gas Club News
Practical Home Economics
Printer's Ink
Printer's Ink Monthly
Progress
Progressive Farmer
Quartermaster Review
Refrigerating Engineering
Refrigerating World
Report of the Chief of the Bureau of Home Economics
Report of the Chief of the Bureau of Human Nutrition and Home Economics, Agricultural
    Research Administration
Report of the Secretary of Agriculture
Sales Management
System
Textile World
This Week
Timely Topics
Tower News
United States Department of Agriculture Bulletin
United States Department of Agriculture Circular
United States Department of Agriculture Farmers' Bulletin
United States Department of Agriculture Leaflet
United States Department of Agriculture Miscellaneous Publication
United States Department of Agriculture Office of Experiment Station Bulletin
United States Department of Agriculture Technical Bulletin
United States Department of Agriculture Yearbook of Agriculture
United States Department of Public Health Bulletin
Vocational Education News Notes
Washington Post
Washington Star
What's New in Home Economics
Woman Citizen
Woman's Home Companion
Women's Work and Education

Books and Articles

Abel, Mary Hinman. *Successful Family Life on the Moderate Income*. New York: J. B. Lippincott, 1921.

Adams, Elizabeth Kemper. *Women Professional Workers: A Study Made for the Women's Educational and Industrial Union*. New York: Macmillan, 1921.

Advertising Age. *Procter & Gamble: The House That Ivory Built*. Lincolnwood, Ill.: NTC Business, 1988.

Aitken, Hugh. *Syntony and Spark: The Origins of Radio*. New York: John Wiley & Sons, 1976.

Alchon, Guy. *The Invisible Hand of Planning: Capitalism, Social Science, and the State in the 1920s*. Princeton, N.J.: Princeton University Press, 1985.

Allen, Frederick Lewis. *Only Yesterday: An Informal History of the 1920s*. New York: Harper and Brothers, 1931.

Alpern, Sara. "In the Beginning: A History of Women in Management." In *Women in Management: Trends, Issues and Challenges in Managerial Diversity*, vol. 4, *Women and Work*, edited by Ellen A. Fagenson, 19–51. Newbury Park, Calif.: Sage, 1993.

[American Chemical Society]. *Chemistry in the Economy*. Washington, D.C.: American Chemical Society, 1973.

[American Dietetic Association]. *Recipes for Institutions*. New York: Macmillan, 1922.

[American Gas Association]. *Home Service: Its Aims, Activities, and Achievements*. New York: American Gas Association, 1925.

———. *Home Service: Report of the 1930 Committee*. New York: American Gas Association, 1930.

[American Home Economics Association]. *Career Opportunities in Home Economics in Business*. Washington, D.C.: American Home Economics Association, 1954.

———. *Home Economists: Portraits and Brief Biographies of the Men and Women Prominent in the Home Economics Movement in the United States*. Baltimore: American Home Economics Association, 1929.

American Men of Science: A Biographical Directory. 5th ed. New York: Science, 1933. 6th ed. New York: Science, 1937.

Anderson, Oscar E. *Refrigeration in America: A History of a New Technology and Its Impact*. Princeton, N.J.: Princeton University Press, 1953.

———. *Health of a Nation: Harvey Wiley and the Fight for Pure Food*. Chicago: University of Chicago Press, 1958.

Andrews, Benjamin. *Economics of the Household*. New York: Macmillan, 1923.

———. "The School of Household Arts, Teachers College, Columbia." In *Equipment for Teaching Domestic Science*, edited by Helen Kinne, 74–81. New York: Teachers College, Columbia University, 1910.

Angevine, Erma, ed. *Consumer Activists: They Made a Difference—A History of Consumer Action Related by Leaders in the Consumer Movement*. Mount Vernon, N.Y.: National Consumers Committee for Research and Education, Consumers Union Foundation, 1982.

Antler, Joyce. *The Educated Woman and Professionalization: The Struggle for a New Feminine Identity, 1890–1920*. New York: Garland, 1980.

Appadurai, Arjun. *The Social Life of Things: Commodities in Cultural Perspective*. Cambridge: Cambridge University Press, 1986.

Apple, Rima D. "'They Need It Now': Science, Advertising and Vitamins, 1925–1940." *Journal of Popular Culture* 22:3 (1988): 65–88.

Babbitt, Kathleen R. "The Productive Farm Woman and the Extension Home Economist in New York State, 1920–1940." *Agricultural History* 67 (1993): 83–101.

Baker, Gladys L. "Women in the U.S. Department of Agriculture." *Agricultural History* 50 (1976): 190–201.

Baker, Gladys L., Wayne D. Rasmussen, Vivien Wiser, and Jane M. Porter. *Century of Service:*

The First 100 Years of the United States Department of Agriculture. Washington, D.C.: U.S. Department of Agriculture, 1963.

Baker, Paula. "The Domestication of Politics: Women and Political Society, 1780–1920." *American Historical Review* 89 (1984): 620–47.

Baldwin, Keturah E. *The AHEA Saga: A Brief History of the Origin and Development of the American Home Economics Association and a Glimpse at the Grass Roots from Which It Grew*. Washington, D.C.: American Home Economics Association, 1949.

Bane, Lita. *The Story of Isabel Bevier*. Peoria, Ill.: Charles A. Bennett, 1955.

Bannister, Robert C. *Sociology and Scientism: The American Quest for Objectivity, 1880–1940*. Chapel Hill: University of North Carolina Press, 1987.

Banta, Martha. *Taylored Lives: Narrative Productions in the Age of Taylor, Veblen, and Ford*. Chicago: University of Chicago Press, 1993.

Barber, Mary I., ed. *History of the American Dietetic Association, 1917–1959*. Philadelphia: J. P. Lippincott, 1959.

Barber, William J. *From New Era to New Deal: Herbert Hoover, the Economists, and American Economic Policy, 1921–1933*. Cambridge: Cambridge University Press, 1985.

Baritz, Loren. *Servants of Power: A History of the Use of Social Science in American History*. Middletown, Conn.: Wesleyan University Press, 1960.

Barron, Hal S. *Mixed Harvest: The Second Great Transformation in the Rural North, 1870–1930*. Chapel Hill: University of North Carolina Press, 1997.

Becker, Jane S. *Selling Tradition: Appalachia and the Construction of an American Folk, 1930–1940*. Chapel Hill: University of North Carolina Press, 1998.

Beecher, Catharine E. *A Treatise on Domestic Economy: For the Use of Young Ladies at Home, and at School*. Boston: Marsh, Capen, Lyon, & Webb, 1841.

Benson, Susan Porter. *Counter Cultures: Saleswomen, Managers, and Customers in American Department Stores, 1890–1940*. Urbana: University of Illinois Press, 1986.

Bentley, Amy. *Eating for Victory: Food Rationing and the Politics of Domesticity*. Urbana: University of Illinois Press, 1998.

Bercaw, Nancy. "Solid Objects/Mutable Meanings: Fancywork and the Construction of Bourgeois Culture, 1840–1880." *Winterthur Portfolio* 26 (Winter 1991): 231–47.

Berlage, Nancy K. "The Establishment of an Applied Social Science: Home Economists, Science, and Reform at Cornell University, 1870–1900." In *Gender and American Social Science: The Formative Years*, edited by Helene Silverberg, 185–231. Princeton, N.J.: Princeton University Press, 1998.

Betters, Paul Vernon. *The Bureau of Home Economics: Its History, Activities and Organization*. Washington, D.C.: Brookings Institution, 1930.

Bevier, Isabel. *Home Economics in Education*. Philadelphia: J. B. Lippincott, 1924.

Bevier, Isabel, and Suzanne Usher. *The Home Economics Movement*. Boston: Whitcomb and Barrows, 1906.

Biggart, Nicole Woolsey. *Charismatic Capitalism: Direct Selling Organizations in America*. Chicago: University of Chicago Press, 1989.

Bijker, Wiebe E. *Of Bicycles, Bakelite, and Bulbs: Toward a Theory of Sociotechnical Change*. Cambridge: MIT Press, 1995.

Bijker, Wiebe E., Thomas P. Hughes, and Trevor Pinch, eds. *The Social Construction of Technological Systems*. Cambridge: MIT Press, 1987.

Bijker, Wiebe E., and John Law, eds. *Shaping Technology/Building Society: Studies in Sociotechnical Change*. Cambridge: MIT Press, 1992.

Biographical Cyclopaedia of American Women. Vol. 1. New York: Halvord, 1924.

Bix, Amy Sue. "Equipped for Life: Gendered Technical Training and Consumerism in Home Economics, 1920–1980." *Technology and Culture* 43:4 (October 2002): 728–54.

Blair, Emily Newell. *The Woman's Committee, United States Council of National Defense: An Interpretive Report.* Washington, D.C.: U.S. Government Printing Office, 1920.

Blair, Karen J. *The Clubwoman as Feminist: True Womanhood Redefined, 1868–1914.* New York: Holmes and Meier, 1980.

Blaszczyk, Regina Lee. *Imagining Consumers: Design and Innovation from Wedgwood to Corning.* Baltimore: Johns Hopkins University Press, 2000.

Bledstein, Burton. *The Culture of Professionalism: The Middle Class and the Development of Higher Education in America.* New York: W. W. Norton, 1976.

Blumin, Stuart M. *The Emergence of the Middle Class: Social Experience in the American City, 1760–1900.* Cambridge: Cambridge University Press, 1989.

Blunt, Katherine, Elizabeth Sprague, and Florence Powdermaker. *Food and the War.* Boston: Houghton Mifflin, 1918.

Blunt, Katherine, Frances Swain, and Florence Powdermaker. *Food Guide for War Service at Home.* New York: Charles Scribner's Sons, 1918.

Boorstin, Daniel J. *The Americans: The Democratic Experience.* New York: Random House, 1973.

Borden, Neil H. *The Economic Effects of Advertising.* Chicago: Richard D. Irwin, 1942.

Boris, Eileen. *Art and Labor: Ruskin, Morris, and the Craftsman Ideal in America.* Philadelphia: Temple University Press, 1986.

———. *Home to Work: Motherhood and the Politics of Industrial Homework in the United States.* New York: Cambridge University Press, 1994.

Bowers, William. *The Country Life Movement in America, 1900–1920.* Port Washington, N.Y.: Kennikat, 1974.

Boydston, Jeanne. *Home and Work: Housework, Wages, and the Ideology of Labor in the Early Republic.* New York: Oxford University Press, 1990.

Boyer, Paul S. *Urban Masses and Moral Order in America, 1820–1920.* Cambridge: Harvard University Press, 1978.

Boylan, Anne M. *The Origins of Women's Activism: New York and Boston, 1797–1840.* Chapel Hill: University of North Carolina Press, 2002.

Bradley, Alice. *Electric Refrigerator Menus and Recipes.* Cleveland: General Electric, 1927.

Breckinridge, Sophonisba, and Marion Talbot. *The Modern Household.* Boston: Whitcomb and Barrows, 1912.

Breen, William J. *Uncle Sam at Home: Civilian Mobilization, Wartime Federalism, and the Council of National Defense, 1917–1919.* Westport, Conn.: Greenwood, 1984.

Brown, JoAnne. *The Definition of a Profession: The Authority of Metaphor in the History of a Profession, 1890–1930.* Princeton, N.J.: Princeton University Press, 1992.

Brown, Marjorie M. *Philosophical Studies in Home Economics.* Vols. 1 and 2. East Lansing: Michigan State University College of Human Ecology, 1985, 1993.

Brumberg, Joan Jacobs, and Nancy Tomes. "Women in the Professions: A Research Agenda for American Historians." *Reviews in American History* 10 (1982): 275–96.

Buddensieg, Tilmann. *Industriekultur: Peter Behrens and the AEG, 1907–1914.* Cambridge: MIT Press, 1984.

Bulmer, Martin, Kevin Bales, and Kathryn Kish Sklar, eds. *The Social Survey in Historical Perspective, 1880–1940.* Cambridge: Cambridge University Press, 1991.

[Bureau of Human Nutrition and Home Economics]. *The Bureau of Human Nutrition and Home Economics: What It Is . . . What It Does.* Washington, D.C.: U.S. Government Printing Office, 1953.

Busch, Jane. "Cooking Competition: Technology on the Domestic Market in the 1930s." *Technology and Culture* 24 (1983): 222–45.

Calder, Lendol. *Financing the American Dream: A Cultural History of Consumer Credit.* Princeton, N.J.: Princeton University Press, 1999.

Callahan, Genevieve. *Preparation for the Business Field of Home Economics.* San Francisco: Home Economics in Business Group of the San Francisco Bay Region, 1934.

———. *Preparation for the Business Field of Home Economics.* Washington, D.C.: American Home Economics Association, 1942.

Campbell, Persia. *Consumer Representation in the New Deal.* New York: Columbia University Press, 1940.

Canoyer, Helen G., and Robert S. Vaile. *Economics of Income and Consumption.* New York: Ronald, 1951.

———. *Income and Consumption.* New York: Henry Holt, 1938.

Carstensen, Vernon. "The Genesis of an Agricultural Experiment Station." *Agricultural History* 34 (1960): 19–20.

Carter, Winifred S. *Cooking Hints and Tested Recipes.* Cincinnati: Procter & Gamble, 1937.

Chandler, Alfred D., Jr. *The Visible Hand: The Managerial Revolution in American Business.* Cambridge: Harvard University Press, 1977.

Chase, Stuart, and Frederick J. Schlink. *Your Money's Worth: A Study in the Wastes of the Consumer's Dollar.* New York: Macmillan, 1926.

Chatriot, Alain, Marie-Emmanuelle Chessel, and Matthew Hilton, eds. *The Expert Consumer: Associations and Professionals in Consumer Society.* Aldershot, U.K.: Ashgate, 2006.

Clark, Ava Milam, and J. Kenneth Munford. *Adventures of a Home Economist.* Corvallis: Oregon State University Press, 1969.

Clark, Clifford Edward, Jr. *The American Family Home, 1800–1960.* Chapel Hill: University of North Carolina Press, 1986.

Clarke, Alison J. *Tupperware: The Promise of Plastic in 1950s America.* Washington, D.C.: Smithsonian Institution Press, 1999.

Clarke, Robert. *Ellen Swallow: The Woman Who Founded Ecology.* Chicago: Follett, 1973.

Clarke, Sally. "Consumers, Information, and Marketing Efficiency at GM, 1921–1940." *Business and Economic History* 25 (Fall 1996): 186–95.

———. "Consumer Negotiations." *Business and Economic History* 26 (Fall 1997): 101–21.

Clements, Kendrick A. *Hoover, Conservation, and Consumerism: Engineering the Good Life.* Lawrence: University Press of Kansas, 2000.

Cochrane, Rexmond C. *Measures for Progress: A History of the National Bureau of Standards.* Washington, D.C.: U.S. Department of Commerce, 1966.

Cohen, Lizabeth. *A Consumers' Republic: The Politics of Mass Consumption in Postwar America.* New York: Alfred A. Knopf, 2003.

Coles, Jessie V. *The Standardization of Consumers' Goods.* New York: Ronald, 1932.

Collins, Nina. "Domestic Sciences at Bradley Polytechnic Institute and the University of Chicago." *Journal of the Illinois State Historical Society* 95:3 (2002): 275–99.

Committee on Standardization of Consumers' Goods. "When You Buy a Refrigerator." *Consumer Purchasing Leaflet,* no. 3. 2d ed. Washington, D.C.: American Home Economics Association, 1935.

Converse, Jean M. *Survey Research: Roots and Emergence, 1890–1960.* Berkeley: University of California Press, 1987.

Copeland, Melvin T. *And Mark an Era: The Story of the Harvard Business School.* Boston: Little, Brown, 1958.

Coppin, Clayton. "James Wilson and Harvey Wiley: The Dilemma of Bureaucratic Entrepreneurship." *Agricultural History* 64 (Spring 1990): 167–81.

Corn, Joseph J. "Educating the Enthusiast: Print and the Popularization of Technical Knowledge." In *Possible Dreams: Enthusiasm for Technology in America*, edited by John L. Wright, 18–33. Dearborn, Mich.: Henry Ford Museum and Greenfield Village, 1992.

Cott, Nancy F. *The Bonds of Womanhood: "Woman's Sphere" in New England, 1780–1835.* New Haven, Conn.: Yale University Press, 1977.

———. *The Grounding of Modern Feminism.* New Haven, Conn.: Yale University Press, 1987.

———. "What's in a Name? The Limits of 'Social Feminism,' or Expanding the Vocabulary of Women's History." *Journal of American History* 76 (December 1989): 809–29.

Cowan, Ruth Schwartz. "The Consumption Junction: A Proposal for Research Strategies in the Sociology of Technology." In *The Social Construction of Technological Systems*, edited by Wiebe E. Bijker, Thomas P. Hughes, and Trevor J. Pinch, 261–80. Cambridge: MIT Press, 1987.

———. *More Work for Mother: The Ironies of Household Technology from the Open Hearth to the Microwave.* New York: Basic Books, 1983.

[Cowdrey's Salad Cream]. *Choice Salad Receipts from Miss Parloa's New Cook-Book.* Boston: Cowdrey's Salad Cream, n.d.

Cox, Henry Bartholomew. "Plain and Fancy: Incandescence Becomes a Household Word!" *Nineteenth Century* (Autumn 1980): 49–51.

Craig, Hazel Thompson. *The History of Home Economics*, edited by Blanche Margaret Stover. New York: Practical Home Economics, 1945.

Cravens, Hamilton. "Child-Saving in the Age of Professionalism, 1915–1930." In *American Childhood: A Research Guide and Historical Handbook*, edited by Joseph M. Hawes and N. Ray Hiner, 415–88. Westport, Conn.: Greenwood, 1985.

———. "Establishing the Science of Nutrition at the USDA: Ellen Swallow Richards and Her Allies." *Agricultural History* 64 (Spring 1990): 122–33.

———. "History of the Social Sciences." In *Historical Writing on American Science: Perspectives and Prospects*, edited by Sally Gregory Kohlstedt and Margaret W. Rossiter, 183–287. Baltimore: Johns Hopkins University Press, 1986.

Cremin, Lawrence A. *The Transformation of the School: Progressivism in American Education, 1876–1957.* New York: Alfred A. Knopf, 1962.

Cremin, Lawrence A., David A. Shannon, and Mary Evelyn Townsend. *A History of Teachers College Columbia University.* New York: Columbia University Press, 1954.

Cross, Gary. *An All-Consuming Century: Why Commercialism Won in Modern America.* New York: Columbia University Press, 2000.

Cruickshank, Jeffrey L. *A Delicate Experiment: The Harvard Business School, 1908–1945.* Boston: Harvard Business School Press, 1987.

Cummings, Richard Osborn. *The American and His Food: A History of Food Habits in the United States.* Chicago: University of Chicago Press, 1940.

Curti, Merle. "The Changing Concept of Human Nature in the Literature of American Advertising." *Business History Review* 41 (Winter 1967): 335–57.

Dameron, Kenneth, ed. *Merchandising Electrical Appliances.* New York: Electrical Merchandising Joint Committee, 1933.

Danbom, David. *The Resisted Revolution: Urban America and the Industrialization of Agriculture, 1900–1930.* Ames: Iowa State University Press, 1979.

Daniel, Pete. *Breaking the Land: The Transformation of Cotton, Tobacco, and Rice Cultures since 1880.* Urbana: University of Illinois Press, 1985.

Davidson, J. Brownlee, Herbert M. Hamlin, and Paul C. Taff. *A Study of the Extension Service in Agriculture and Home Economics in Iowa*. Ames, Iowa: Collegiate, 1933.

Davis, Allen F. *Spearheads for Reform: Social Settlements and the Progressive Movement, 1890–1914*. New York: Oxford University Press, 1967.

Dawley, Alan. *Struggles for Justice: Social Responsibility and the Liberal State*. Cambridge: Belknap, 1991.

de Grazia, Victoria, with Ellen Furlough. *The Sex of Things: Gender and Consumption in Historical Perspective*. Berkeley: University of California Press, 1996.

Denny, Grace. *Fabrics and How to Know Them*. N.p., 1923.

Deutsch, Sarah. *Women and the City: Gender, Space, and Power in Boston, 1870–1940*. Oxford: Oxford University Press, 2000.

Devine, Edward T. "The Economic Function of Woman." *Annals of the American Academy of Political and Social Science* 5:3 (1895): 361–76.

Dixon, Maxcy Robson. *The Food Front in World War I*. Washington, D.C.: American Council of Public Affairs, 1944.

Donato, Katharine M. "Keepers of the Corporate Image: Women in Public Relations." In *Job Queues, Gender Queues: Explaining Women's Inroads into Male Occupations*, edited by Barbara F. Reskin and Patricia A. Roos, 129–43. Philadelphia: Temple University Press, 1990.

Donham, S. Agnes. *Marketing and Housework Manual*. Boston: Little, Brown, 1917. Rev. ed., 1925, 1930, 1937.

———. *Spending the Family Income*. Boston: Little, Brown, 1921. Rev. ed., 1931, 1933, 1941.

Donohue, Kathleen G. *Freedom from Want: American Liberalism and the Idea of the Consumer*. Baltimore: Johns Hopkins University Press, 2003.

Douglas, Ann. *The Feminization of American Culture*. New York: Knopf, 1977.

Drost, Walter E. *David Snedden and Education for Social Efficiency*. Madison: University of Wisconsin Press, 1967.

Drucker, Peter. *Management: Tasks, Responsibilities, Practices*. New York: Harper & Row, 1974.

———. *The Practice of Management*. New York: Harper & Brothers, 1954.

Duncan, Joseph A., and William C. Shelton. *Revolution in United States Government Statistics, 1926–1976*. Washington, D.C.: U.S. Department of Commerce, Office of Statistical Policy and Standards, 1978.

Dye, Marie. *History of the Department of Home Economics, University of Chicago*. Chicago: Home Economics Alumni Association, 1972.

Eagles, Juanita Archibald, Orrea Florence Pye, and Clara Mae Taylor. *Mary Swartz Rose, 1874–1941: Pioneer in Nutrition*. New York: Teachers College Press, 1979.

East, Marjorie. *Caroline Hunt, Philosopher for Home Economics*. University Park, Pa.: Division of Occupational and Vocational Studies, College of Education, Pennsylvania State University, 1982.

———. *Home Economics: Past, Present, and Future*. Boston: Allyn and Bacon, 1980.

———. "The Role of Home Economics in the Consumer Movement." In *Consumer Activists: They Made a Difference—A History of Consumer Action Related by Leaders in the Consumer Movement*, edited by Erma Angevine, National Consumers Committee for Research and Education, 274–87. Mount Vernon, N.Y.: Consumers Union Foundation, 1982.

Edwards, Richard. *Contested Terrain: The Transformation of the Workplace in the Twentieth Century*. New York: Basic Books, 1979.

Ehrenreich, Barbara, and Deirdre English. *For Her Own Good: 150 Years of Expert Advice to Women*. Garden City, N.Y.: Anchor, 1978.

Elbert, Sarah. "Women and Farming: Changing Structures, Changing Roles." In *Women and Farming: Changing Roles, Changing Structures*, edited by Wava B. Haney and Jane B. Knowles, 245–64. Boulder, Colo.: Westview, 1988.

Elias, Megan. *Stir It Up: Home Economics in American Culture*. Philadelphia: University of Pennsylvania Press, 2010.

Elliott, S. Maria. *Household Bacteriology*. Chicago: American School of Home Economics, 1907.

Ellsworth, Clayton S. "Theodore Roosevelt's Country Life Commission." *Agricultural History* 34 (October 1960): 155–72.

Emmett, Boris, and John E. Jeuck. *Catalogues and Counters: A History of Sears, Roebuck and Company*. Chicago: University of Chicago Press, 1950.

Eppright, Ercel Sherman, and Elizabeth Storm Ferguson. *A Century of Home Economics at Iowa State University: A Proud Past, a Lively Present, a Future Promise*. Ames: Iowa State University Home Economics Alumni Association, 1971.

Epstein, Cynthia Fuchs, and William Josiah Goode. *The Other Half: Roads to Women's Equality*. Englewood Cliffs, N.J.: Prentice-Hall, 1971.

Ewen, Stuart. *Captains of Consciousness: Advertising and the Social Roots of the Consumer Culture*. New York: McGraw-Hill, 1976.

Farmer, Fannie Merritt. *Rumford Recipe Book*. Providence, R.I.: Rumford, 1913.

Ferguson, James L. *General Foods Corporation: A Chronicle of Consumer Satisfaction*. New York: Newcomen Society of the United States, 1985.

Ferleger, Lou. "Uplifting American Agriculture: Experiment Station Scientists and the Office of Experiment Stations in the Early Years after the Hatch Act." *Agricultural History* 64 (Spring 1990): 5–23.

Field, Gregory H. " 'Electricity for All': The Electric Home and Farm Authority and the Politics of Mass Consumption." *Business History Review* (Spring 1990): 32–60.

Fitzpatrick, Ellen. *Endless Crusade: Women Social Scientists and Progressive Reform*. New York: Oxford University Press, 1990.

Forty, Adrian. *Objects of Desire: Design and Society from Wedgwood to IBM*. New York: Pantheon, 1986.

Fox, Richard Wightman. "The Culture of Liberal Protestant Progressivism, 1875–1925." *Journal of Interdisciplinary History* 23:3 (Winter 1993): 639–60.

Fox, Richard Wightman, and T. J. Jackson Lears, eds. *The Culture of Consumption: Critical Essays in American History, 1875–1940*. New York: Pantheon, 1983.

Frank, Dana. "Housewives, Socialists and the Politics of Food: The 1917 New York Cost-of-Living Protests." *Feminist Studies* 11 (Summer 1985): 255–85.

Frederick, Christine. *Selling Mrs. Consumer*. New York: Business Bourse, 1929.

Friedson, Eliot. *Profession of Medicine: A Study of the Sociology of Applied Knowledge*. New York: Harper and Row, 1970.

Frigidaire Experimental Kitchen. *Frigidaire Recipes*. Dayton, Ohio: Frigidaire, 1928.

Fritschner, Linda Marie. "Women's Work and Women's Education: The Case of Home Economics, 1870–1920." *Sociology of Work and Occupations* 4 (May 1977): 209–34.

Galambos, Louis. "The Emerging Organizational Synthesis in Modern American History." *Business History Review* 44 (Autumn 1970): 278–90.

———. "Presidential Address: What Makes Us Think We Can Put Business Back into American History." *Business and Economic History*, 2d ser., 20 (1991): 1–11.

———. "Technology, Political Economy, and Professionalization." *Business History Review* 57 (Winter 1983): 47–93.

Galison, Peter, and Bruce Hevly, eds. *Big Science: The Growth of Large-Scale Research*. Stanford, Calif.: Stanford University Press, 1992.

Gamber, Wendy. *The Female Economy: The Millinery and Dressmaking Trades, 1860–1930*. Urbana: University of Illinois Press, 1997.

Garrison, Dee. *Apostles of Culture: The Public Librarian and American Society, 1876–1920*. New York: Free Press, 1979.

Geiger, Roger L. *To Advance Knowledge: The Growth of American Research Universities, 1900–1940*. New York: Oxford University Press, 1986.

Gelber, Steven M. *Hobbies: Leisure and the Culture of Work in America*. New York: Columbia University Press, 1999.

General Foods Consumer Service Department. *General Foods Cook Book*. New York: General Foods Corporation, 1932.

General Foods Corporation. *How to Bake by the Ration Book*. New York: General Foods Corporation, 1943.

Gibbs, Winifred Stuart. *Lessons in Proper Feeding for the Whole Family*. New York: New York Association for Improving the Condition of the Poor, 1909. Rev. ed., 1911, 1912.

———. *The Minimum Cost of Living: A Study of Families of Limited Income in New York City*. New York: Macmillan, 1917.

Gilman, Charlotte Perkins. *Women and Economics: A Study of the Economic Relation between Men and Women as a Factor in Social Evolution*. Edited by Carl Degler. New York: Harper & Row, 1966. Reprint of 1898 edition.

Ginzberg, Lori D. *Women and the Work of Benevolence: Morality, Politics and Class in the Nineteenth-Century United States*. New Haven, Conn.: Yale University Press, 1990.

Glickman, Lawrence B. *Buying Power: A History of Consumer Activism in America*. Chicago: University of Chicago Press, 2009.

———. *A Living Wage: American Workers and the Making of Consumer Society*. Ithaca, N.Y.: Cornell University Press, 1997.

———. "The Strike in the Temple of Consumption: Consumer Activism and Twentieth-Century American Political Culture." *Journal of American History* 88 (June 2001): 99–128.

Goldstein, Carolyn M. *Do It Yourself: Home Improvement in 20th-Century America*. Washington, D.C.: National Building Museum; New York: Princeton Architectural Press, 1998.

———. "Home Economics." In *The Oxford Encyclopedia of Food and Drink in America*, vol. 1, edited by Andrew F. Smith, 677–85. New York: Oxford University Press, 2004.

Goldstein, Harriett, and Vetta Goldstein. *Art in Everyday Life*. New York: Macmillan, 1925.

Gooday, Graeme. *Domesticating Electricity: Technology, Uncertainty and Gender, 1880–1914*. London: Pickering & Chatto, 2008.

[Good Housekeeping Institute]. *Household Engineering*. New York: Good Housekeeping Institute, 1918.

———. *The Story of Good Housekeeping Institute*. New York: Good Housekeeping Institute, 1923.

———. *The Story of Good Housekeeping Institute*. New York: International Magazine Company, 1929.

Gordon, Lynn D. *Gender and Higher Education in the Progressive Era*. New Haven, Conn.: Yale University Press, 1990.

Graham, Laurel. *Managing on Her Own: Dr. Lillian Gilbreth and Women's Work in the Interwar Era*. Norcross, Ga.: Engineering and Management, 1998.

Gray, Greta. *House and Home*. Philadelphia: J. B. Lippincott, 1923.

Gray, James. *Business without Boundary: The Story of General Mills*. Minneapolis: University of Minnesota Press, 1954.

Grier, Katherine C. *Culture and Comfort: Parlor Making and Middle-Class Identity, 1850–1930*. Washington, D.C.: Smithsonian Institution Press, 1997.

Guerrier, Edith. *An Independent Woman: The Autobiography of Edith Guerrier*. Amherst: University of Massachusetts Press, 1992.

Haber, Samuel. *Efficiency and Uplift: Scientific Management in the Progressive Era, 1890–1920*. Chicago: University of Chicago Press, 1964.

Hackett, Bruce, and Loren Lotsenhiser. "The Unity of Self and Object." *Western Folklore* 44 (1985): 317–24.

Haddow, Robert. *Pavilions of Plenty: Exhibiting American Culture Abroad in the 1950s*. Washington, D.C.: Smithsonian Institution Press, 1997.

Hardin, Amy L. "Industry Structure and the Marketing of Synthetic Fibers." *Business and Economic History*, 2d ser., 19 (1990): 213–22.

Harding, T. Swann. *Two Blades of Grass: A History of Scientific Development at the United States Department of Agriculture*. Norman: University of Oklahoma Press, 1947.

Harland, Marion. *The Story of Canning and Recipes*. Washington, D.C.: National Canners Association, 1910.

Harrison, Shelby M., and Allen Hendershott Eaton. *Bibliography of Social Surveys*. New York: Russell Sage Foundation, 1930.

Hawley, Edith. *Economics of Food Consumption*. New York: McGraw-Hill, 1932.

Hawley, Ellis. *The Great War and the Search for a Modern Order: A History of the American People and Their Institutions, 1917–1935*. New York: St. Martin's, 1979.

———. "Herbert Hoover, the Commerce Secretariat, and the Vision of the Associative State." *Journal of American History* 61 (June 1974): 116–40.

Hayden, Dolores. *The Grand Domestic Revolution: A History of Feminist Designs for American Homes, Neighborhoods, and Cities*. Cambridge: MIT Press, 1981.

Hayes, Joanne Lamb. "Vitamins." In *The Oxford Encyclopedia of Food and Drink in America*, vol. 2, edited by Andrew F. Smith, 589–90. New York: Oxford University Press, 2004.

Helly, Dorothy O., and Susan M. Reverby, eds. *Gendered Domains: Rethinking Public and Private in Women's History*. Ithaca, N.Y.: Cornell University Press, 1992.

Hess, John L., and Karen Hess. *The Taste of America*. New York: Penguin, 1977.

Hill, Janet McKenzie. *Economical War-Time Cook Book*. New York: George Sully, 1918.

———. *The Whys of Cooking*. Cincinnati: Procter & Gamble, 1916.

Hochschild, Arlie Russell. *The Managed Heart: Commercialization of Human Feeling*. Berkeley: University of California Press, 1983.

Hoffecker, Carol. *Beneath Thy Guiding Hand: A History of Women at the University of Delaware*. Newark: University of Delaware Press, 1994.

Hoffschwelle, Mary S. "The Science of Domesticity: Home Economics at George Peabody College for Teachers, 1914–1939." *Journal of Southern History* 57 (November 1991): 659–80.

Hoover, Herbert. *An American Epic*. Vol. 2. Chicago: Henry Regnery, 1960.

———. *The Memoirs of Herbert Hoover: Years of Adventure, 1874–1920*. New York: Macmillan, 1951.

Horowitz, Daniel. *The Anxieties of Affluence: Critiques of American Consumer Culture, 1939–1979*. Amherst: University of Massachusetts Press, 2004.

———. *Betty Friedan and the Making of "The Feminine Mystique."* Amherst: University of Massachusetts Press, 1998.

———. *The Morality of Spending: Attitudes toward the Consumer Society in America, 1875–1940*. Baltimore: Johns Hopkins University Press, 1985.

Horowitz, Helen Lefkowitz. *Alma Mater: Design and Experience in the Women's Colleges from Their Nineteenth-Century Beginnings to the 1930s*. New York: Alfred A. Knopf, 1984.

Horowitz, Roger, and Arwen Mohun, eds. *His and Hers: Gender, Consumption, and Technology*. Charlottesville: University of Virginia Press, 1998.

Hounshell, David A. *From the American System to Mass Production, 1800–1932: The Development of Manufacturing Technology in the United States*. Baltimore: Johns Hopkins University Press, 1984.

Hounshell, David A., and John Kenly Smith Jr. *Science and Corporate Strategy: DuPont R&D, 1902–1980*. New York: Cambridge University Press, 1988.

Household Management and Kitchens: Research Report of the President's Conference on Home Building and Home Ownership. Vol. 9. Washington, D.C.: U.S. Government Printing Office, 1932.

Howes, Durward, ed. *American Women, 1935–1940: A Composite Biographical Dictionary*. Detroit: Gale Research, 1981.

Hoy, Suellen. *Chasing Dirt: The Pursuit of American Cleanliness*. New York: Oxford University Press, 1995.

Hughes, Thomas P. *Networks of Power: Electrification in Western Society*. Baltimore: Johns Hopkins University Press, 1983.

Hughes, Thomas P., and Agatha C. Hughes. *Systems, Experts, and Computers: The Systems Approach in Management and Engineering, World War II and After*. Cambridge: MIT Press, 2000.

Hull, Harry Blair. *Household Refrigeration*. Chicago: Nickerson & Collins, 1924.

Hummer, Patricia M. *Decade of Elusive Promise: Professional Women in the United States, 1920–1930*. Ann Arbor, Mich.: UMI Research Press, 1979.

Hunt, Caroline L. *Home Problems from a New Standpoint*. Boston: Whitcomb and Barrows, 1908.

———. "Household Adjustment to Technical Development." *Studies in Social Christianity*, in Josiah Strong, ed., *The Gospel of the Kingdom* 4:4 (April 1912): 60–63.

———. *The Life of Ellen H. Richards, 1842–1911*. Boston: Whitcomb and Barrows, 1912.

———. *Revaluations: With a Brief Account of the Author's Life*. Baltimore: Waverly, 1929.

Inness, Sherrie. *Dinner Roles: American Women and Culinary Culture*. Iowa City: University of Iowa Press, 2001.

———, ed. *Kitchen Culture in America: Popular Representations of Food, Gender, and Race*. Philadelphia: University of Pennsylvania Press, 2001.

Institute of Home Economics. *Home Economics Research in the U.S. Department of Agriculture*. Washington, D.C.: U.S. Government Printing Office, 1958.

Jacobs, Meg. "'How about Some Meat?' The Office of Price Administration, Consumption Politics, and State Building from the Bottom Up, 1941–1946." *Journal of American History* 84 (December 1997): 910–41.

———. *Pocketbook Politics: Economic Citizenship in Twentieth-Century America*. Princeton, N.J.: Princeton University Press, 2005.

James, Edward T., Janet Wilson James, and Paul S. Boyer, eds. *Notable American Women, 1607–1950*. Vols. 1–3. Cambridge: Belknap, 1971.

Jellison, Katherine. *Entitled to Power: Farm Women and Technology, 1913–1963*. Chapel Hill: University of North Carolina Press, 1993.

Jennings, Jan. *Cheap and Tasteful Dwellings: Design Competitions and the Convenient Interior, 1979–1909*. Knoxville: University of Tennessee Press, 2005.

Jensen, Joan. "Canning Comes to New Mexico: Women and the Agricultural Extension Service, 1914–1919." *New Mexico Historical Review* 57 (1982): 361–86.

———. "Crossing Ethnic Barriers in the Southwest: Women's Agricultural Extension Education, 1914–1940." *Agricultural History* 60 (Spring 1986): 169–81.

Johnson, Helen Louise. *The Enterprising Housekeeper*. Philadelphia: Enterprise Manufacturing, 1896.

Jones, Lu Ann. *Mama Learned Us to Work: Farm Women in the New South*. Chapel Hill: University of North Carolina Press, 2002.

Jordan, John M. *Machine-Age Ideology: Social Engineering and American Liberalism, 1911–1939*. Chapel Hill: University of North Carolina Press, 1994.

Kamminga, Harmke, and Andrew Cunningham, eds. *The Science and Culture of Nutrition*. Amsterdam: Rodopi for the Wellcome Institute Series in the History of Medicine, 1995.

Kane, Harnett T. *Dear Dorothy Dix: The Story of a Compassionate Woman*. Garden City, N.Y.: Doubleday, 1952.

Kantor, Harvey, and David B. Tyack, eds. *Work, Youth, and Schooling: Historical Perspectives on Vocationalism in American Education*. Stanford, Calif.: Stanford University Press, 1982.

[Kelvinator Corporation]. *Cooking with Cold*. Cleveland: Kelvinator Corporation, 1932.

Kennedy, David M. *Over Here: The First World War and American Society*. New York: Oxford University Press, 1980.

Kerber, Linda K. "Separate Spheres, Female Worlds, Woman's Place: The Rhetoric of Women's History." *Journal of American History* 75 (June 1988): 9–39.

Kessler-Harris, Alice. *Out to Work: A History of Wage-Earning Women in the United States*. New York: Oxford University Press, 1982.

Kidwell, Claudia, and Margaret C. Christman. *Suiting Everyone: The Democratization of Clothing in America*. Washington, D.C.: Smithsonian Institution Press, 1974.

Kingsley, Margaret. *Home Service Work for the Ice Industry*. Chicago: Nickerson & Collins, 1931.

Kinne, Helen, ed. *Equipment for Teaching Domestic Science*. New York: Teachers College Columbia University, 1910.

Kinne, Helen, and Anna M. Cooley. *Foods and Household Management*. New York: Macmillan, 1916.

———. *Shelter and Clothing: A Textbook of the Household Arts*. New York: Macmillan, 1920.

Kliebard, Herbert M. *The Struggle for the American Curriculum, 1893–1958*. Boston: Routledge and Kenan Paul, 1986.

Kline, Ronald R. *Consumers and the Country: Technology and Social Change in Rural America*. Baltimore: Johns Hopkins University Press, 2000.

———. "Ideology and Social Surveys: Reinterpreting the Effects of 'Labor-Saving' Technology on American Farm Women." *Technology and Culture* 38 (April 1997): 355–85.

Kneeland, Hildegarde. "Homemaking in This Modern Age." *Journal of the AAUW* 27 (January 1934): 74–79.

———. "Is the Modern Housewife a Lady of Leisure?" *Survey Graphic* 62 (June 1, 1929): 301–10.

Knowles, Jane. "Harvard-Radcliffe Program in Business Administration: Training for Business." *Radcliffe Quarterly* 73 (December 1987): 27–29.

Kohlstedt, Sally Gregory. "In from the Periphery: American Women in Science, 1830–1880." *Signs: Journal of Women in Culture and Society* 4 (Autumn 1978): 81–96.

Kolko, Gabriel. *The Triumph of Conservatism: A Reinterpretation of American History, 1900–1916*. New York: Macmillan, 1963.

Koven, Seth, and Sonya Michel, eds. *Mothers of a New World: Maternalist Politics and the Origins of Welfare States*. New York: Routledge, 1993.

Kraft/Phenix Cheese. *Cheese and Ways to Serve It*. Chicago: Kraft-Phenix Cheese, 1933.

Krieghbaum, Hiller. "Servants of the People, Part Four: At the Bureau of Home Economics." *Survey Graphic* 27 (February 1938): 116.

Kunze, Joel. "The Bureau of Agricultural Economics' Outlook Program in the 1920s as a Pedagogical Device." *Agricultural History* 64 (1990): 252–61.

Kunzel, Regina G. *Fallen Women, Problem Girls: Unmarried Mothers and the Professionalization of Social Work, 1890–1945*. New Haven, Conn.: Yale University Press, 1993.

Kwolek-Folland, Angel. *Engendering Business: Men and Women in the Corporation*. Baltimore: Johns Hopkins University Press, 1994.

———. "Gender, Self, and Work in the Life Insurance Industry." In *Work Engendered: Toward a New History of American Labor*, edited by Ava Baron, 168–90. Ithaca, N.Y.: Cornell University Press, 1991.

———. *Incorporating Women: A History of Women and Business in the United States*. New York: Twayne, 1998.

Kyrk, Hazel. "Home Economics." In *Encyclopaedia of the Social Sciences*, edited by Edwin R. A. Seligman and Alvin Johnson, 7:427–31. New York: Macmillan, 1932.

Kyvig, David E. *Daily Life in the United States, 1920–1939: Decades of Promise and Pain*. Westport, Conn.: Greenwood, 2001.

Ladd-Taylor, Molly. *Mother-Work: Women, Child Welfare, and the State, 1890–1930*. Urbana: University of Illinois Press, 1994.

———. *Raising a Baby the Government Way: Mothers' Letters to the Children's Bureau, 1915–32*. New Brunswick, N.J.: Rutgers University Press, 1986.

Laing, Alistair. *Lighting*. London: Victoria and Albert Museum, 1982.

Lake Placid Conference on Home Economics. *Proceedings of the First, Second and Third Conferences*. Lake Placid, N.Y., 1901.

———. *Proceedings of the Fourth Annual Conference*. Lake Placid, N.Y., 1902.

———. *Proceedings of the Fifth Annual Conference*. Boston, Mass., 1903.

———. *Proceedings of the Sixth Annual Conference*. Lake Placid, N.Y., 1904.

———. *Proceedings of the Seventh Annual Conference*. Lake Placid, N.Y., 1905.

———. *Proceedings of the Eighth Annual Conference*. Lake Placid, N.Y., 1906.

———. *Proceedings of the Ninth Annual Conference*. Lake Placid, N.Y., 1907.

———. *Proceedings of the Tenth Annual Conference*. Lake Placid, N.Y., 1908.

Lane, Ann J. *To "Herland" and Beyond: The Life and Work of Charlotte Perkins Gilman*. Charlottesville: University of Virginia Press, 1990.

Latour, Bruno. "Give Me a Laboratory and I Will Raise the World." In *Science Observed: Perspectives on the Social Study of Science*, edited by Karin D. Knorr-Cetina and Michael Mulkay, 141–70. London: Sage, 1983.

Lawrence, Jeanne Catherine. "Geographical Space, Social Space, and the Realm of the Department Store." *Urban History* 19 (April 1992): 64–83.

Layton, Edwin T., Jr. *The Revolt of the Engineers: Social Responsibility and the American Engineering Profession*. Cleveland: Case Western University Press, 1971.

———. "Veblen and the Engineers." *American Quarterly* 14 (Spring 1962): 64–72.

Leach, William. *Land of Desire: Merchants, Power, and the Rise of a New American Culture*. New York: Pantheon, 1993.

———. "Transformations in a Culture of Consumption: Women and Department Stores, 1870–1920." *Journal of American History* 71 (1984): 319–42.

————. *True Love and Perfect Union: The Feminist Reform of Sex and Society*. New York: Basic Books, 1980.

Lears, T. J. Jackson. *Fables of Abundance: A Cultural History of Advertising in America*. New York: Basic Books, 1994.

————. *No Place of Grace: Antimodernism and the Transformation of American Culture, 1880–1920*. New York: Pantheon, 1981.

Leavitt, Judith A. *American Women Managers and Administrators: A Selective Biographical Dictionary of Twentieth-Century Leaders in Business, Education, and Government*. Westport, Conn.: Greenwood, 1985.

Leavitt, Sarah A. *From Catherine Beecher to Martha Stewart: A Cultural History of Domestic Advice*. Chapel Hill: University of North Carolina Press, 2002.

Leidner, Robin. "Selling Hamburgers and Selling Insurance: Gender, Work, and Identity in Interactive Service Jobs." *Gender and Society* 5 (June 1991): 154–77.

Lemons, J. Stanley. *The Woman Citizen: Social Feminism in the 1920s*. Urbana: University of Illinois Press, 1973.

Leonard, John. *Woman's Who's Who of America*. New York: American Commonwealth, 1914. Reprint, Detroit: Gale Research, 1976.

Lerman, Nina E., Arwen Palmer Mohun, and Ruth Oldenziel. "The Shoulders We Stand on and the View from Here: Historiography and Directions for Research." In *Gender Analysis and the History of Technology*, special issue, *Technology and Culture* 38 (January 1997): 9–30.

Leslie, Stuart W. *The Cold War and American Science: The Military-Industrial-Academic Complex at MIT and Stanford*. New York: Columbia University Press, 1993.

Leuchtenberg, William E. *The Perils of Prosperity, 1914–1932*. Chicago: University of Chicago Press, 1958.

Levenstein, Harvey. *Paradox of Plenty: A Social History of Eating in Modern America*. New York: Oxford University Press, 1993.

————. *Revolution at the Table: The Transformation of the American Diet*. New York: Oxford University Press, 1988.

Lief, Alfred. *"It Floats": The Story of Procter & Gamble*. New York: Rinehart, 1958.

Lifshey, Earl. *The Housewares Story: A History of the American Housewares Industry*. Chicago: National Housewares Manufacturers Association, 1973.

Livingston, James. *Pragmatism and the Political Economy of Cultural Revolution, 1850–1940*. Chapel Hill: University of North Carolina Press, 1994.

Logie, Iona Robertson, ed. *Careers in the Making*. New York: Harper and Brothers, 1942.

Lubar, Steven. "Representation and Power." *Technology and Culture* 36S (April 1995): S54–S81.

Luckiesh, Matthew, and Frank K. Moss. *Lighting for Seeing*. Cleveland: General Electric, 1931.

————. "The New Science of Seeing." *Transactions of the Illuminating Engineering Society* 25 (1930): 15–49.

————. *The Science of Seeing*. New York: D. Van Nostrand, 1937.

Lupton, Ellen, and J. Abbott Miller. *The Bathroom, the Kitchen, and the Aesthetics of Waste: A Process of Elimination*. Cambridge: MIT List Visual Arts Center, 1992.

Lurito, Pamela W. "The Message Was Electric." *IEEE Spectrum* (September 1984): 84–95.

Lustig, R. Jeffrey. *Corporate Liberalism: The Origins of Modern American Political Theory, 1890–1920*. Berkeley: University of California Press, 1982.

Lyle, Dorothy Siegert. *Focus on Fabrics*. Silver Spring, Md.: National Institute of Drycleaning, 1958. Rev. ed., 1964, 1967.

Maddocks, Mildred. *The Consumer's Viewpoint*. New York: Good Housekeeping Institute, 1920.

———. *Rumford Recipes*. Providence, R.I.: Rumford, 1911.

Malone, Dumas, ed. *Dictionary of American Biography*. Vol. 6. New York: Charles Scribner's Sons, 1933.

Marchand, Roland. *Advertising the American Dream: Making Way for Modernity, 1920–1940*. Berkeley: University of California Press, 1985.

Maril, Nadja. *American Lighting, 1840–1940*. Westchester, Pa.: Schiffer, 1989.

Marling, Karal Ann. *As Seen on TV: The Visual Culture of Everyday Life in the 1950s*. Cambridge: Harvard University Press, 1994.

Matthews, Glenna. *"Just a Housewife": The Rise and Fall of Domesticity in America*. New York: Oxford University Press, 1987.

Matthews, J. Merritt. *The Textile Fibres: Their Physical, Microscopical and Chemical Properties*. 3d ed. New York: J. Wiley & Sons, 1916.

Maule, Frances. *Careers for the Home Economist: Fields Which Offer Openings to the Girl with Modern Training in the Homemaking Arts*. New York: Funk and Wagnalls, 1943.

———. *Executive Careers for Women*. New York: Harper & Brothers, 1957.

———. *She Strives to Conquer: Business Behavior, Opportunities and Job Requirements for Women*. New York: Funk and Wagnalls, 1936.

May, Elaine Tyler. *Homeward Bound: American Families in the Cold War Era*. New York: Basic Books, 1988.

McCraw, Thomas K. *TVA and the Power Fight, 1933–1939*. Philadelphia: Lippincott, 1971.

McGaw, Judith A. "No Passive Victims, No Separate Spheres: A Feminist Perspective on Technology's History." In *In Context: History and the History of Technology, Essays in Honor of Melvin Kranzberg*, edited by Stephen H. Cutcliffe and Robert C. Post, 172–91. Bethlehem, Pa.: Lehigh University Press, 1989.

———. "Women and the History of American Technology." *Signs* 7 (1982): 798–828.

McGovern, Charles F. *Sold American: Consumption and Citizenship, 1890–1945*. Chapel Hill: University of North Carolina Press, 2006.

McGrath, Earl J., and Jack T. Johnson. *The Changing Mission of Home Economics: A Report on Home Economics in the Land-Grant Colleges and State Universities*. New York: Teachers College Press, 1968.

Meikle, Jeffrey L. *American Plastic: A Cultural History*. New Brunswick, N.J.: Rutgers University Press, 1995.

———. *Twentieth-Century Limited: Industrial Design in America, 1925–1939*. Philadelphia: Temple University Press, 1979.

Melosh, Barbara. *"The Physician's Hand": Work Culture and Conflict in American Nursing*. Philadelphia: Temple University Press, 1982.

Meyerowitz, Joanne Jay, ed. *Not June Cleaver: Women and Gender in Postwar America, 1945–1960*. Philadelphia, Pa.: Temple University Press, 1994.

Moores, Richard Gordon. *Fields of Rich Toil: The Development of the University of Illinois, College of Agriculture*. Urbana: University of Illinois Press, 1970.

Morantz-Sanchez, Regina. *Sympathy and Science: Women Physicians in American Medicine*. New York: Oxford University Press, 1985.

Moskowitz, Marina. *The Standard of Living: The Measure of the Middle Class in Modern America*. Baltimore: Johns Hopkins University Press, 2004.

Mott, Frank Luther. *A History of American Magazines*. Vol. 5. Cambridge: Harvard University Press, 1968.

Mowery, David, and Nathan Rosenberg. *Technology and the Pursuit of Economic Growth*. Cambridge: Cambridge University Press, 1989.

Mullendore, William. *History of the United States Food Administration, 1917–1919*. Stanford, Calif.: Stanford University Press, 1941.

Muncy, Robyn. *Creating a Female Dominion in American Reform, 1890–1935*. New York: Oxford University Press, 1991.

Musson, Albert Edward, and Eric Robinson. *Science and Technology in the Industrial Revolution*. Manchester, U.K.: Manchester University Press, 1969.

Nader, Ralph. *The Ralph Nader Reader*. New York: Seven Stories Press, 2000.

Nash, George H. *The Life of Herbert Hoover: Master of Emergencies, 1917–1918*. New York: W. W. Norton, 1996.

The National Cyclopedia of American Biography. Vol. 15. New York: James T. White, 1916. Vol. 46. New York: James T. White, 1963. Vol. 49. New York: James T. White, 1966.

[National Electric Light Association]. *Home Service: Helpful Suggestions for Organizing and Operating Home Service Departments*. New York: National Electric Light Association, 1930.

Neil, Marion Harris. *The Story of Crisco*. Cincinnati: Procter & Gamble, 1913.

Nelson, Daniel. *Managers and Workers: Origins of the New Factory System in the United States, 1880–1920*. Madison: University of Wisconsin Press, 1975.

Nelson, Elizabeth White. *Market Sentiments: Middle-Class Market Culture in Nineteenth-Century America*. Washington, D.C.: Smithsonian Institution Press, 2004.

Nerad, Maresi. *The Academic Kitchen: A Social History of Gender Stratification at the University of California, Berkeley*. Albany: State University of New York Press, 1999.

Neth, Mary. *Preserving the Family Farm: Women, Community, and the Foundations of Agribusiness in the Midwest, 1900–1940*. Baltimore: Johns Hopkins University Press, 1995.

Nickles, Shelley. "'Preserving Women': Refrigerator Design as Social Process in the 1930s." *Technology and Culture* 43:4 (October 2002): 693–727.

Noble, David F. *America by Design: Science, Technology, and the Rise of Corporate Capitalism*. Oxford: Oxford University Press, 1977. Nye, David. *Electrifying America: Social Meanings of a New Technology, 1880–1940*. Cambridge: MIT Press, 1990.

———. *Image Worlds: Corporate Identities at General Electric, 1880–1930*. Cambridge: MIT Press, 1985.

O'Brien, Ruth. "Can the Federal Bureaus Help the Household Buyer?" In *Problems of the Household Buyer: Proceedings of a Conference Organized by the Department of Home Economics at the University of Chicago*. Ann Arbor, Mich.: Edwards Brothers, 1927.

O'Brien, Ruth, and Olive Hartley. "Selection: An Analysis of Consumers' Facilities for Judging Merchandise." Excerpt from the Report of the Subcommittee on Purchasing Procedures of the Committee on Household Management of the President's Conference on Home Building and Home Ownership, 1931.

Ohmann, Richard. *Selling Culture: Magazines, Markets, and Class at the Turn of the Century*. London: Verso, 1996.

Oldenziel, Ruth. *Making Technology Masculine: Men, Women, and Modern Machines in America, 1870–1945*. Amsterdam: University of Amsterdam Press, 1999.

———. "Man the Maker, Woman the Consumer: The Consumption Junction Revisited." In *Feminism in Twentieth-Century Science, Technology, and Medicine*, edited by Angela N. H. Creager, Elizabeth A. Lunbeck, and Londa Shiebinger, 128–48. Chicago: University of Chicago Press, 2001.

Oldenziel, Ruth, and Karin Zachmann, eds. *Cold War Kitchen: Americanization, Technology, and European Users*. Cambridge: MIT Press, 2009.

Oleson, Alexandra, and John Voss, eds. *The Organization of Knowledge in Modern America, 1860–1920*. Baltimore: Johns Hopkins University Press, 1979.

Olney, Martha L. *Buy Now, Pay Later: Advertising, Credit, and Consumer Durables in the 1920s*. Chapel Hill: University of North Carolina Press, 1991.

Oudshoorn, Nelly E. J., and Trevor J. Pinch, eds. *How Users Matter: The Co-Construction of Users and Technology*. Cambridge: MIT Press, 2003.

Palmer, Phyllis. *Domesticity and Dirt: Housewives and Domestic Servants in the United States, 1920–1945*. Philadelphia: Temple University Press, 1989.

Parr, Joy. *Domestic Goods: The Material, the Moral, and the Economic in the Postwar Years*. Toronto: University of Toronto Press, 1999.

Patten, Simon N. *The New Basis of Civilization*. New York: Macmillan, 1907.

Peet, Louise Jenison, and Lenore E. Sater Thye. *Household Equipment*. New York: John Wiley & Sons, 1934. 2d ed., 1940. 3d ed., 1946. 4th ed., 1955. 5th ed., 1961.

Peiss, Kathy. *Hope in a Jar: The Making of America's Beauty Culture*. New York: Metropolitan, 1998.

———. "Making Faces: The Cosmetics Industry and the Cultural Construction of Gender, 1890–1930." *Genders* 7:1 (Spring 1990): 143–69.

Percival, Caroline. *Martha Van Rensselaer*. Ithaca, N.Y.: Alumni Association of the College of Home Economics at Cornell University, 1957.

Peterson, Anna J., and Nena W. Badenoch. *Mrs. Peterson's Simplified Cooking*. Home Service Edition. Public Service Gas Company. Chicago: American School of Home Economics, 1924.

Peyser, Ethel Rose. *Cheating the Junk-Pile: The Purchase and Maintenance of Household Equipments*. New York: E. P. Dutton, 1922. 2d ed., 1930.

Platt, Harold L. *The Electric City: Energy and the Growth of the Chicago Area, 1880–1930*. Chicago: University of Chicago Press, 1991.

Poovey, Mary. *Uneven Developments: The Ideological Work of Gender in Mid-Victorian England*. Chicago: University of Chicago Press, 1988.

Powell, Ola. *Successful Canning and Preserving*. Philadelphia: J. B. Lippincott, 1917.

Powell, William J. *Pillsbury's Best: A Company History from 1869*. Minneapolis: Pillsbury, 1985.

[Procter & Gamble]. *Into a Second Century with Procter & Gamble*. Cincinnati: Procter & Gamble, 1944.

———. *What a Doctor Knows about a Woman's Charm*. Cincinnati: Procter & Gamble, 1927.

Pundt, Helen. *AHEA: A History of Excellence*. Washington, D.C.: American Home Economics Association, 1980.

Radway, Janice. *A Feeling for Books: The Book-of-the-Month Club, Literary Taste, and Middle-Class Desire*. Chapel Hill: University of North Carolina Press, 1998.

Rasmussen, Wayne D. *Taking the University to the People: Seventy-Five Years of Cooperative Extension*. Ames: Iowa State University Press, 1989.

———, ed. *Readings in the History of American Agriculture*. Urbana: University of Illinois Press, 1960.

Rasmussen, Wayne D., and Gladys L. Baker. *The Department of Agriculture*. New York: Praeger, 1972.

Rice, Wallace. *Seventy-Five Years of Gas Service in Chicago*. Chicago: Peoples Gas, Light, and Coke, 1925.

Richards, Ellen H. *Air, Water, and Food from a Sanitary Standpoint*. New York: Wiley, 1900.

———. *The Chemistry of Cooking and Cleaning: A Manual for Housekeepers*. Boston: Estes & Lauriat, 1882.

———. *The Cost of Food: A Study in Dietaries*. New York: Wiley, 1901.

———. *The Cost of Living as Modified by Sanitary Science*. New York: J. Wiley & Sons, 1899.

———. *The Cost of Shelter*. New York: J. Wiley & Sons, 1905.

———. *Domestic Economy as a Factor in Public Education*. New York:New York College for the Training of Teachers, 1889.

———. *Food Materials and Their Adulterations*. Boston: Estes & Lauriat, 1886.

———. *Sanitation in Daily Life*. Boston: Whitcomb and Barrows, 1919.

———. "The Story of the New England Kitchen." In *Rumford Kitchen Leaflets*, no. 17. Boston: Richards, 1893.

Richards, Ellen H., and Marion Talbot. *Home Sanitation: A Manual for Housekeepers*. Boston: Ticknor, 1887.

Robinson, Lisa Mae. "Regulating What We Eat: Mary Engle Pennington and the Food Research Laboratory." *Agricultural History* 64 (Spring 1990): 143–53.

Robinson, Edgar Eugene, and Paul Carroll Edwards, eds., *The Memoirs of Ray Lyman Wilbur, 1875–1949*. Stanford, Calif.: Stanford University Press, 1960.

Rodgers, Daniel. "In Search of Progressivism." *Reviews in American History* 10 (1982): 113–32.

Rose, Flora, Esther H. Stocks, and Michael W. Whittier. *A Growing College: Home Economics at Cornell University*. Ithaca: New York State College of Human Ecology, 1969.

Rose, Mark H. *Cities of Light and Heat: Domesticating Gas and Electricity in Urban America*. University Park: Pennsylvania State University Press, 1995.

Rose, Mary Swartz. *Everyday Foods in War Time*. New York: Macmillan, 1917.

Rosenberg, Charles. "Science, Technology, and Economic Growth: The Case of the Agricultural Experiment Station Scientists, 1875–1914." In *No Other Gods: On Science and American Social Thought*, 153–72. Baltimore: Johns Hopkins University Press, 1976.

Rosenberg, Rosalind. *Beyond Separate Spheres: Intellectual Roots of Modern Feminism*. New Haven, Conn.: Yale University Press, 1982.

———. *Divided Lives: American Women in the Twentieth Century*. New York: Hill and Wang, 1992.

Ross, Alice. "Home Canning." In *The Oxford Encyclopedia of Food and Drink in America*, vol. 1, edited by Andrew F. Smith, 185. New York: Oxford University Press, 2004.

Ross, Dorothy. "Development of the Social Sciences." In *The Organization of Knowledge in Modern America, 1860–1920*, edited by Alexandra Oleson and John Voss, 107–39. Baltimore: Johns Hopkins University Press, 1979.

———. *The Origins of American Social Science*. New York: Cambridge University Press, 1991.

Rossiter, Margaret W. "Mendel the Mentor: Yale Women Doctorates in Biochemistry, 1898–1937." *Journal of Chemical Education* 71:3 (March 1994): 215–19.

———. *Women Scientists in America: Before Affirmation Action, 1940–1972*. Baltimore: Johns Hopkins University Press, 1995.

———. *Women Scientists in America: Struggles and Strategies to 1940*. Baltimore: Johns Hopkins University Press, 1982.

———. "'Women's Work' in Science, 1880–1910." *Isis* 71 (1980): 381–98.

Rothe, Anna, ed. *Current Biography 1950*. New York: H. W. Wilson, 1950.

Rubin, Joan Shelley. "Information Please! Culture and Expertise in the Interwar Period." *American Quarterly* 35 (Winter 1983): 499–517.

———. *The Making of Middlebrow Culture*. Chapel Hill: University of North Carolina Press, 1992.

Rury, John. *Education and Women's Work: Female Schooling and the Division of Labor in Urban America, 1870–1930*. Albany: State University of New York Press, 1991.

Rutherford, Janice Williams. *Selling Mrs. Consumer: Christine Frederick and the Rise of Household Efficiency*. Athens: University of Georgia Press, 2003.

Ryan, Mary. *Cradle of the Middle Class: The Family in Oneida County, New York, 1790–1865*. Cambridge: Cambridge University Press, 1985.

Rydell, Robert W. *All the World's a Fair: Visions of Empire at American International Expositions, 1876–1916*. Chicago: University of Chicago Press, 1984.

Sass, Steven A. *The Pragmatic Imagination: A History of the Wharton School, 1881–1981*. Philadelphia: University of Pennsylvania Press, 1982.

Scanlon, Jennifer. *Inarticulate Longings: The "Ladies' Home Journal," Gender, and the Promises of Consumer Culture*. New York: Routledge, 1995.

Schiffman, Ruth Yeomans. "An Outline of Opportunities in Home Economics." In *Careers for Women: New Ideas, New Methods, New Opportunities*, 2d ed., edited by Catherine Filene, 318–20. Boston: Houghton Mifflin, 1934.

Schisgall, Oscar. *Eyes on Tomorrow: The Evolution of Procter & Gamble*. Chicago: J. G. Ferguson, 1981.

Schudson, Michael. *Advertising, the Uneasy Persuasion: Its Dubious Impact on American Society*. New York: Basic Books, 1984.

Schweider, Dorothy. "Education and Change in the Lives of Iowa Farm Women, 1900–1940." *Agricultural History* 60 (Spring 1986): 200–215.

Scott, Anne Firor. *Natural Allies: Woman's Associations in American History*. Urbana: University of Illinois Press, 1991.

Sealander, Judith. *As Minority Becomes Majority: Federal Reaction to the Phenomenon of Women in the Work Force, 1920–1965*. Westport, Conn.: Greenwood, 1983.

[Sears, Roebuck and Company]. *1927 Spring–Fall Catalog*. Chicago: Sears, Roebuck, 1927.

———. *Sears, Roebuck and Co. at the Century of Progress*. Chicago: Sears, Roebuck, 1933.

Seely, Bruce E. *Building the American Highway System: Engineers as Policy Makers*. Philadelphia: Temple University Press, 1987.

Servos, John W. "Engineers, Businessmen, and the Academy: The Beginnings of Sponsored Research at the University of Michigan." *Technology and Culture* 37 (October 1996): 721–62.

Shapiro, Laura. *Perfection Salad: Women and Cooking at the Turn of the Century*. New York: Farrar, Straus, Giroux, 1986.

———. *Something from the Oven: Reinventing Dinner in 1950s America*. New York: Viking Penguin, 2004.

Sherman, Henry, and Sybil Smith. *The Vitamins*. 2d ed. Washington, D.C.: American Chemical Society, 1931.

Sicherman, Barbara, and Carol Hurd Green, eds. *Notable American Women: The Modern Period*. Cambridge: Belknap, 1980.

Sicilia, David B. "Distant Proximity: Writing the History of American Business since 1945." *Business and Economic History* 26 (Fall 1997): 270.

Silverberg, Helene, ed. *Gender and American Social Science: The Formative Years*. Princeton, N.J.: Princeton University Press, 1998.

Sklar, Kathryn Kish. *Catharine Beecher: A Study in American Domesticity*. New York: Norton, 1976.

———. "Historical Foundations of Women's Power in the Creation of the American Welfare State, 1830–1930." In *Mothers of a New World: Maternalist Politics and the Origins of Welfare States*, edited by Seth Koven and Sonya Michel, 43–93. New York: Routledge, 1993.

Skocpol, Theda. *Protecting Soldiers and Mothers: The Political Origins of Social Policy in the United States*. Cambridge: Harvard University Press, 1992.

Slater, Don. *Consumer Culture and Modernity*. Cambridge, U.K.: Polity Press, 1997.

Smulyan, Susan. "Radio Advertising to Women in Twenties America: 'A Latchkey to Every Home.'" *Historical Journal of Film, Radio and Television* 13:3 (1993): 299–314.

———. *Selling Radio: The Commercialization of American Broadcasting*. Washington, D.C.: Smithsonian Institution, 1994.

Solomon, Barbara Miller. *In the Company of Educated Women: A History of Women and Higher Education in America*. New Haven, Conn.: Yale University Press, 1985.

[Sowinski, Jeanne Paris]. *A Forward Force . . . Home Economists in Business*. Vienna, Va.: Home Economists in Business, 1983.

Spears, Timothy B. "'All Things to All Men': The Commercial Traveler and the Rise of Modern Salesmanship." *American Quarterly* 45 (1993): 524–57.

Splint, Sarah Field. *The Art of Cooking and Serving*. Cincinnati: Procter & Gamble, 1927.

Stage, Sarah. "Ellen Richards and the Social Significance of the Home Economics Movement." In *Rethinking Home Economics*, edited by Sarah Stage and Virginia B. Vincenti, 17–33. Ithaca, N.Y.: Cornell University Press, 1997.

———. "From Domestic Science to Social Housekeeping: The Career of Ellen Richards." In *Power and Responsibility: Case Studies in American Leadership*, edited by David M. Kennedy and Michael E. Parrish, 211–28. San Diego: Harcourt Brace Jovanovich, 1986.

Stage, Sarah, and Virginia B. Vincenti, eds. *Rethinking Home Economics: Women and the History of a Profession*. Ithaca, N.Y.: Cornell University Press, 1997.

Stanley, Louise. "New Horizons in the Professional Training of Home Economists." *Survey* (July 1, 1928): 290–91.

Steele, Valerie. *Fashion and Eroticism: Ideals of Feminine Beauty from the Victorian Era to the Jazz Age*. New York: Oxford University Press, 1985.

Storrs, Landon. *Civilizing Capitalism: The National Consumers' League, Women's Activism, and Labor Standards in the New Deal Era*. Chapel Hill: University of North Carolina Press, 2000.

Strasser, Susan. *Never Done: A History of American Housework*. New York: Pantheon, 1982.

———. *Satisfaction Guaranteed: The Making of the American Mass Market*. New York: Pantheon, 1989.

———. "'The Smile That Pays': The Culture of Traveling Salesmen, 1880–1920." In *The Mythmaking Frame of Mind: Social Imagination and American Culture*, edited by James Gilbert et al., 155–77. Belmont, Calif.: Wadsworth, 1993.

———. *Waste and Want: A Social History of Trash*. New York: Metropolitan, 1999.

Strasser, Susan, Charles McGovern, and Matthias Judt, eds. *Getting and Spending: European and American Consumer Societies in the Twentieth Century*. Cambridge: Cambridge University Press, 1998.

Sturges, Cynthia. "'How're You Gonna Keep 'Em Down on the Farm?' Rural Women and the Urban Model in Utah." *Agricultural History* 60 (Spring 1986): 182–99.

Sullivan, Joan. "In Pursuit of Legitimacy: Home Economists and the Hoover Apron in World War I." *Dress* 26 (1999): 31–46.

Susman, Warren I. *Culture as History: The Transformation of American Society in the Twentieth Century*. New York: Pantheon, 1984.

Swiencicki, Mark A. "Consuming Brotherhood: Men's Culture, Style and Recreation as Consumer Culture, 1880–1930." *Journal of Social History* 31:4 (Summer 1998): 773–808.

Talbot, Marion. *More than Lore: Reminiscences of Marion Talbot*. Chicago: University of Chicago Press, 1936.

Tarbell, Ida M. *All in the Day's Work: An Autobiography*. New York: Macmillan, 1939.

Tarr, Joel A., and Mark Tebeau. "Managing Danger in the Home Environment, 1900–1940." *Journal of Social History* (Summer 1996): 797–816.

Taylor, Frederick Winslow. *Principles of Scientific Management*. New York: Harper and Brothers, 1915.

Tedlow, Richard. *Keeping the Corporate Image: Public Relations and Business, 1900–1950*. Greenwich, Conn.: JAI Press, 1979.

———. *New and Improved: The Story of Mass Marketing in America*. New York: Basic Books, 1990.

Terrill, Bertha. *Household Management*. Chicago: American School of Housekeeping, 1905. Rev. ed., 1907.

Tested Crisco Recipes. Cincinnati: Procter and Gamble, 1912.

Thackray, Arnold. "University-Industry Connections and Chemical Research: An Historical Perspective." In *University-Industry Relationships: Selected Studies*, edited by the National Science Board, 193–233. Washington, D.C.: U.S. Government Printing Office, 1983.

Thelen, David. *The New Citizenship: Origins of Progressivism in Wisconsin, 1885–1900*. Columbia: University of Missouri Press, 1972.

Tichi, Cecelia. *Shifting Gears: Technology, Literature, Culture in Modernist America*. Chapel Hill: University of North Carolina Press, 1987.

Tobey, Ronald. *Technology as Freedom: The New Deal and the Electrical Modernization of the American Home*. Berkeley: University of California Press, 1996.

Tomes, Nancy. *The Gospel of Germs: Men, Women, and Science in American Life*. Cambridge: Harvard University Press, 1998.

———. "The Private Side of Public Health: Sanitary Science, Domestic Hygiene, and the Germ Theory, 1870–1900." *Bulletin of the History of Medicine* 64 (1990): 509–39.

Trachtenberg, Alan. *The Incorporation of America: Culture and Society in the Gilded Age*. New York: Hill and Wang, 1982.

True, Alfred Charles. *A History of Agricultural Extension Work in the United States, 1785–1923*. Washington, D.C.: U.S. Government Printing Office, 1928.

U.S. Department of Agriculture. *Food Thrift Series*. Washington, D.C.: U.S. Government Printing Office, 1917.

U.S. National Resources Committee, Industrial Committee. *Consumer Expenditures in the United States: Estimates for 1935–1936*. Washington, D.C.: U.S. Government Printing Office, 1939.

———. *Consumer Incomes in the United States: Their Distribution in 1935–1936*. Washington, D.C.: U.S. Government Printing Office, 1938.

———. *Family Expenditures in the United States*. Washington, D.C.: U.S. Government Printing Office, 1941.

Vail, Mary Beals. *Approved Methods for Home Laundering*. Cincinnati: Procter & Gamble, 1906. Rev. ed., 1918.

Van Deman, Ruth, and Fanny Walker Yeatman. *Aunt Sammy's Radio Recipes Revised*. Washington, D.C.: U.S. Government Printing Office, 1931.

Vanek, Joann. "Household Technology and Social Status: Rising Standards of Living and Status and Residence Differences." *Technology and Culture* 19:3 (July 1978): 361–75.

Veblen, Thorstein. *The Theory of the Leisure Class: An Economic Study in the Evolution of Institutions*. New York: Macmillan, 1899.

Veysey, Laurence R. *The Emergence of the American University*. Chicago: University of Chicago Press, 1965.

Vinikas, Vincent. *Soft Soap, Hard Sell: American Hygiene in an Age of Advertisement*. Ames: Iowa State University Press, 1992.

Vulte, Hermann T. *Household Chemistry for the Use of Students in Household Arts*. Easton, Pa.: Chemical, 1915, 1917, 1920.

Vulte, Hermann T., and Sadie Vanderbilt. *Food Industries: An Elementary Text-Book on the Production and Manufacture of Staple Foods*. Easton, Pa. .: Chemical, 1914. 2d ed., 1916; 3d ed., 1920.

Walkowitz, Daniel. "The Making of a Feminine Professional Identity: Social Workers in the 1920s." *American Historical Review* 95 (October 1990): 1051–75.

Waller-Zuckerman, Mary Ellen. "Marketing the Women's Journals, 1873–1900." *Business and Economic History*, 2d ser., 18 (1989): 99–108.

Walsh, Margaret. "The Democratization of Fashion: The Emergence of the Women's Dress Pattern Industry." *Journal of American History* 66 (1979): 299–319.

Ware, Susan. *Beyond Suffrage: Women in the New Deal*. Cambridge: Harvard University Press, 1981.

Ware, Susan, and Stacy Braukman, eds. *Notable American Women: Completing the Twentieth Century*. Cambridge: Belknap, 2004.

Watson, Kate Heintz. *Textiles and Clothing*. Chicago: American School of Home Economics, 1907.

Weidlein, Edward R., and William A. Hamor. *Science in Action*. New York: McGraw-Hill, 1931.

Weigley, Emma Seifrit. "It Might Have Been Euthenics: The Lake Placid Conferences and the Home Economics Movement." *American Quarterly* 26 (March 1974): 79–96.

———. *Sarah Tyson Rorer: The Nation's Instructress in Dietetics and Cookery*. Philadelphia: American Philosophical Society, 1977.

Weimann, Jeanne Madeline. *The Fair Women: The Story of the Woman's Building, World's Columbian Exposition, Chicago, 1893*. Chicago: Academy Chicago, 1981.

———. "A Temple to Woman's Genius: The Woman's Building of 1893." *Chicago History* 6 (April 1977): 23–33.

Weiner, Lynn Y. *From Working Girl to Working Mother: The Female Labor Force in the United States, 1820–1980*. Chapel Hill: University of North Carolina Press, 1985.

Weirick, Elizabeth S. "Experiences in the Field of Merchandise Control." *Journal of Chemical Education* 16 (December 1939): 585–87.

Wesson, David. "Some Phases of Progress in Vegetable Oil Production." In *Twenty-Five Years of Chemical Engineering Progress*, edited by Sidney Kirkpatrick, 226–33. New York: American Institute of Chemical Engineers, 1933.

Westbrook, Robert B. *John Dewey and American Democracy*. Ithaca, N.Y.: Cornell University Press, 1991.

———. "Tribune of the Technostructure: The Popular Economics of Stuart Chase." *American Quarterly* 32 (1980): 387–408.

[Westinghouse Electric and Manufacturing Company]. *The ABC's of Eating for Health*. Mansfield, Ohio: Westinghouse, 1942.

White, Elizabeth Alice. "Sentimental Heresies: Rethinking *The Feminization of American Culture*." *Intellectual History Newsletter* 15 (1993): 23–31.

[White Enamel Refrigerator Company]. *Housewives' Favorite Recipes*. St. Paul, Minn.: White Enamel Refrigerator, 1916.

Whitney, Belle Armstrong. *The Economics of Dress*. Battle Creek, Mich.: Good Health, 1907.

Who's Who in the East. 6th ed. Chicago: A. N. Marquis, 1957.

Who's Who of American Women. 1st ed. Chicago: A. N. Marquis, 1958. 2d ed. Chicago: A. N. Marquis, 1961.

Who Was Who among North American Authors, 1921–1939. Reprint, Detroit: Gale Research, 1976.

Who Was Who in America, 1897–1942. Vol. 1. Chicago: A. N. Marquis, 1943. Reprint, 1968. Vol. 2. Chicago: A. N. Marquis, 1950. Vol. 3. Chicago: A. N. Marquis, 1960.

Wiebe, Robert H. *The Search for Order, 1877–1920*. New York: Hill and Wang, 1967.

Wilson, Mary. *Rumford Southern Recipes*. Providence, R.I.: Rumford, n.d.

Wilson, Richard Guy, Dianne Pilgrim, and Dickran Tashjian. *The Machine Age in America, 1918–1941*. New York: Brooklyn Museum, 1986.

Wise, George. *Willis R. Whitney, General Electric, and the Origins of U.S. Industrial Research*. New York: Columbia University Press, 1985.

Wolfe, Allis Rosenberg. "Women, Consumerism, and the National Consumers' League in the Progressive Era, 1900–1923." *Journal of Labor History* 16 (Summer 1975): 378–98.

Women's Education Association. *Domestic Art: Explanatory Leaflet of Exhibit under the Direction of the Committee on Public Schools of the Women's Education Association, Mechanic Arts High School, Boston, June 13–23, 1896*. Boston: Women's Education Association, 1896.

Wood, Edith Elmer. *The Housing of the Unskilled Wage Earner: America's Next Problem*. New York: Macmillan, 1919.

Woodhouse, Chase Going. *Business Opportunities for the Home Economist*. New York: McGraw-Hill, 1938.

Woolman, Mary Schenck. "Clothing Information Bureau: What a Clothing Bureau Can Do, How to Organize It." Boston: Clothing Information Bureau, Women's City Club of Boston, n.d. Widener Library, Harvard University.

———. *The Making of a Trade School*. Boston: Whitcomb and Barrows, 1910.

Woolman, Mary Schenck, and Ellen Beers McGowan. *Textiles: A Handbook for the Student and the Consumer*. New York: Macmillan, 1913. Rev. ed., 1926.

Worner, Ruby K. "Opportunities for Women Chemists in Washington." *Journal of Chemical Education* 16 (1939): 583–85.

Wright, Gwendolyn. *Moralism and the Model Home: Domestic Architecture and Cultural Conflict in Chicago, 1873–1913*. Chicago: University of Chicago Press, 1980.

Yeager, Mary A., ed. *Women in Business*. Cheltenham, U.K.: Edward Elgar, 1999.

Yost, Edna. *American Women of Science*. Philadelphia: Frederick A. Stokes, 1943.

Young, James Harvey. "Food and Drug Regulation under the USDA, 1906–1940." *Agricultural History* 64 (Spring 1990): 134–42.

———. *Pure Food: Securing the Federal Food and Drugs Act of 1906*. Princeton, N.J.: Princeton University Press, 1989.

Zapoleon, Marguerite Wykoff. *The College Girl Looks ahead to Her Career Opportunities*. New York: Harper & Brothers, 1956.

Zunz, Olivier. *Making America Corporate: 1870–1920*. Chicago: University of Chicago Press, 1990.

———. *Why the American Century?* Chicago: University of Chicago Press, 1998.

Dissertations, Theses, Papers, and Unpublished Manuscripts

Babbitt, Kathleen R. "Producers and Consumers: Women of the Countryside and Cooperative Extension Service Home Economists, New York State, 1870–1935." Ph.D. diss., SUNY Binghamton, 1995.

Berolzheimer, Alan Roy. "A Nation of Consumers: Mass Consumption, Middle-Class Standards of Living, and American National Identity, 1910–1950." Ph.D. diss., University of Virginia, 1996.

Connelly, Marguerite. "The Transformation of the Sewing Machine and Home Sewing in America, 1850–1929." Ph.D. diss., University of Delaware, 1994.

Corn, Joseph. "Hands-On Literacy: Forty Years of Automotive Texts." Paper presented to the International Communication Association Annual Meeting, San Francisco, May 26, 1989.

Dickson, Carol Anne. "Patterns for Garments: A History of the Paper Garment Pattern Industry in America to 1976." Ph.D. diss., Ohio State University, 1979.

Dirks, Jacqueline K. "Advertisements for Themselves: Professional Advertising Women and the 'Woman's Viewpoint.'" Paper presented at the Ninth Berkshire Conference on the History of Women, Vassar College, Poughkeepsie, N.Y., June 12, 1993.

———. "Righteous Goods: Women's Production, Reform Publicity and the National Consumers' League, 1891–1919." Ph.D. diss., Yale University, 1994.

Finneran, Helen T. "Louise Stanley: A Study of the Career of a Home Economist, Scientist, and Administrator, 1923–53." Master's thesis, American University, 1965.

Fritschner, Linda Marie. "The Rise and Fall of Home Economics." Ph.D. diss., University of California, Davis, 1973.

Hamin, Mark T. "Tables Turned, Palates Curbed: Energy, Economy, and Equilibrium in American Nutritional Science, 1880–1930." Ph.D. diss., University of Pennsylvania, 1999.

Hempstead, Katherine. "Agricultural Change and the Rural Problem: Farm Women and the Country Life Movement." Ph.D. diss., University of Pennsylvania, 1992.

Hutchison, Janet Anne. "American Housing, Gender, and the Better Homes Movement, 1922–1935." Ph.D. diss., University of Delaware, 1990.

Kellogg, Nelson Robert. "Gauging the Nation: Samuel Wesley Stratton and the Invention of the National Bureau of Standards." Ph.D. diss., Johns Hopkins University, 1992.

Kolm, Suzanne Lee. "Women's Labor Aloft: A Cultural History of Airline Flight Attendants in the United States, 1930–1978." Ph.D. diss., Brown University, 1995.

Lerman, Nina E. "From 'Useful Knowledge' to 'Habits of Industry'": Gender, Race, and Class in Nineteenth-Century Technical Education." Ph.D. diss., University of Pennsylvania, 1993.

McCleary, Ann Elizabeth. "Home Demonstration and Domestic Reform in Rural Virginia, 1900–1940." Ph.D. diss., Brown University, 1996.

Mohun, Arwen. "Use, Misuse, and Abuse: Product Liability and Risk in Postwar America." Paper delivered at the Society for the History of Technology Annual Meeting, Amsterdam, the Netherlands, 2004.

———. "Product Safety and the Law: Making an American Risk Society, 1945–1990." Paper delivered at the Organization of American Historians Annual Meeting, Washington, D.C., 2006.

Nichaman, Shira. "Betty Crocker: America's First Lady of Food." Master's thesis, George Washington University, 1994.

Nickles, Shelley Kaplan. "Object Lessons: Designers, Consumers, and the Household Appliance Industry, 1920–1965." Ph.D. diss., University of Virginia, 1998.

Rose, Elliott Francis. "The Nutritional Sciences and the United States War Food Administration, 1917–1918." Master's thesis, University of California, Davis, 1966.

Rossell, Edward Graham Daves. "Compelling Vision: From Electric Light to Illuminating Engineering, 1880–1940." Ph.D. diss., University of California at Berkeley, 1998.

Sicilia, David. "Selling Power: Marketing and Monopoly at Boston Edison, 1886–1929."
    Ph.D. diss., Brandeis University, 1991.
Smith, Karen Manners. "Marion Harland: The Making of a Household Word." Ph.D. diss.,
    University of Massachusetts, 1990.
Toepfer, Kenneth Harold. "James Earl Russell and the Rise of Teachers College, 1897–1915."
    Ph.D. diss., Columbia University, 1966.
Toon, Elizabeth. "Managing the Conduct of the Individual Life: Public Health Education
    and American Public Health, 1910–1940." Ph.D. diss., University of Pennsylvania, 1998.
Vincenti, Virginia B. "A History of the Philosophy of Home Economics: A Thesis in Home
    Economics Education." Ph.D. diss., Pennsylvania State University, 1981.
Wilkes, James David. "Power and Pedagogy: The National Electric Light Association and
    Public Education, 1919–1928." Ph.D. diss., University of Tennessee, 1973.
Williams, Elizabeth. "Healthier Homes through Education: The Lake Placid Home Econo-
    mists and Progressive Educational Reform, 1899–1908." Master's thesis, University of
    Wisconsin, Madison, 1988.

Index

Abel, Mary Hinman, 32, 33, 51, 70–71

Addams, Jane, 28, 30, 37

Advertisers and advertising: and women consumers, 8–9; and business communication with consumers, 10, 160, 180–81, 198, 276; and rational consumption, 41, 101; and retail environments, 41, 198; home economics research on, 68, 101; and consumer education, 107, 110, 160, 166–68; and home economists representing consumers, 112, 114, 298, 300; and refrigeration, 125, 127, 132–33; and Frederick, 141–42; business home economists distinguished from women in, 156, 158–59, 160, 168; and advertising materials in home economics education, 169–70; and business home economists, 176–77, 189, 197, 266; and "truth in advertising," 178, 181, 182, 203; and food industry, 179–80, 183–87, 191, 204, 209; and Procter & Gamble, 183–86, 188–89, 192, 193, 342 (n. 41); and product testing, 201, 203, 204, 205; and utility companies, 209, 212, 228, 232; and household equipment manufacturers, 211; and television, 244, 276; and World War II, 253; and fictional home economists, 276–78; and consumer movements, 286; propaganda against, 338 (n. 83)

Advertising Women of New York, 141

Aging population, 288

Agricultural Adjustment Administration (AAA), 105, 107

Agricultural extension service: and curricula on consumption, 3, 4; expansion of, 7, 66; and role of home economists, 17, 36, 42, 52, 59, 64, 73, 78, 139, 145, 151, 152, 155; and business home economists,

54, 146, 147, 165; and home economics education, 73, 80; and home economics research, 96; and consumer education, 106–7, 230; and textiles and clothing, 121; and utility companies, 220. *See also* Home demonstrations

Agricultural Research Administration (ARA), 247

Agricultural Research Center, 247

Agricultural Research Service (ARS), 250–51

Agriculture: modernization of, 3, 7, 31–32, 52, 63, 65, 101, 252; marketing of agricultural crops, 4, 66, 108, 244, 250, 252; and professionalism of home economists, 16, 74–78; and World War I food conservation program, 57; depression in sales of products, 65, 92, 93; and production/consumption relationship, 80, 92, 96; public policy on, 244

Ahern, Eleanor, 154, 189–93, 205, 260, 272, 297, 342 (n. 49)

Alderson, Wroe, 272

Alexander, Lucy, 112

Allen, Ida Bailey, 106, 342 (n. 41)

Allen, Olive, 189–90

Aluminum Goods Manufacturing Company, 194

American Association for Labor Legislation, 30

American Association of Family and Consumer Science (AAFCS), 296

American Association of Textile Chemists and Colorists, 83

American Association of University Women, 73, 84, 89, 109

American Balsa Wood Company, 125

American Chemical Society, 83, 197

American Country Life Association, 73

American Dietetic Association, 154, 189

American Engineering Standards Committee (AESC), 98, 109

American Farm Bureau Association, 73

American Farm Bureau Federation (AFBF), 73

American Food Journal, 149, 188, 190

American Gas Association (AGA), 219, 241, 242, 329 (n. 71)

American Grocery Manufacturer's Association, 154

American Home Economic Association (AHEA): mission of, 1, 35; lobbying of, 14; lack of code of ethics, 16; and home economics education, 35, 36, 60; and World War I food conservation program, 53; and Stanley, 62; and home economics research, 65, 66, 250–52, 287; and Bureau of Home Economics, 73, 99, 109; and standardization, 89, 113, 114, 115, 117–18, 131, 287; and Grace Dodge Hotel, 94; Committee on Standardization of Measuring Cups, 113–14; and New Deal, 115; and commercial exhibitors, 147, 167, 170, 171; Education Section, 148; Institutional Economics Section, 148; Textiles Section, 148; Standards Committee, 148–49; growth of, 150; reform goals of, 150; and consumer capitalism, 166; and consumer education, 166, 168, 288; and consumer advocacy, 169; and World War II programs, 242, 248, 249; Committee on Federal Research Related to Home Economics, 250, 252–53; and public relations, 260; and feminist movement, 282, 290; and professional identity, 285, 287, 290; divisions within, 287, 296, 298; renaming of, 295–96; and citizens' identities as consumers, 307 (n. 15). *See also* Home Economics in Business Section

American Institute of Chemical Engineers, 197

American Library Association, 35

American Red Cross, 151, 242, 256

American Society for Testing Materials, 83

American Society of Refrigeration Engineers, 130

American Standards Association (ASA), 86, 109, 113, 114, 119, 131–32, 166

American Stove Company, 193

American Washing Machine Manufacturers Association, 143, 151

Andrews, Benjamin, 98

Antitrust legislation, 182, 213

Applecroft Experimental Station, 141, 142

Arlsberg, Carl, 90

Armour & Company, 60, 185, 196

Arts and crafts movement, 38–39

Associationalism, 100

Association of Collegiate Alumnae, 28

Atwater, Helen, 65, 167

Atwater, Wilbur Olin, 26, 32–33, 64–65, 75, 82

Auchter, Eugene C., 247, 248

Baby boomer generation, 20, 283–84

Bacteriology, 37, 42, 55, 124, 127, 129, 181, 255

Badenoch, Nena, 226, 228

Bailey, Ilena, 76

Bailey, Liberty Hyde, 32

Baldwin, Amelia Muir, 45

Ball, Elmer W., 67–71, 317 (n. 12)

Ball Brothers Company, 154, 162

Bane, Lita, 58

Barber, Mary I., 145, 146, 154, 170–71, 255–56, 260

Barkley Misbranding Bill, 117–18

Barnes, Virginia Kraft, 143

Bates, Mercedes, 290

Bayard, W. A., 218

Beecher, Catherine, 27

Better Light–Better Sight (campaign), 234–36

Betty Crocker: and home economists as mediators for corporations, 18; as popular icon, 190, 276–77; and World War II, 254; portrayals of, 276, 277

Bevier, Isabel, 32, 34, 45, 53, 58–60, 66, 68, 71, 73, 311 (n. 21), 317 (n. 12)

Bigelow, William Frederick, 202

Binghamton Gas Works, 151

Bird's Eye, 263

Blackman Company, 183, 184–85, 189–90, 342 (n. 41)

Blair, Emily Newell, 115

Blair, Wes, 188–89, 192

Blake, Dorothy, 231

Bleibtreu, Hermann K., 292–93
Blood, Alice, 69–70, 317 (n. 12)
Blunt, Katherine, 37, 53, 68, 148
Booher, Lela E., 108
Borden's, 156, 160
Boston Woven Hose and Rubber Company, 146, 154
Bradley, Alice, 150, 151
Bradt, Cecelia, 202
Breck, Marion, 169–70
Breckinridge, Sophonisba, 37, 41
Brennan, H. E., 64, 65, 69, 74, 95, 108
Brodie, Renton K., 188, 189
Brooklyn Edison Company, 240
Brooks, Mildred, 186–87
Budgeting: and home economics education, 1, 40, 41, 43, 45; and women consumers, 8; and consumer education, 22, 23, 24, 27, 31, 106, 140, 223, 236, 246, 247, 288; and middle-class standard of living, 27–28, 31; and consumer products, 79, 80; and home economists' research, 80, 84, 87, 90–91, 99, 126; Frederick on, 140
Burdick, Anna, 139, 140, 142
Bureau of Domestic Science, proposals for, 67
Bureau of Home Economics (BHE): and home economists' employment, 4–5, 6, 7, 8, 15, 16, 139; Stanley's leadership of, 4–5, 17, 31, 62–64, 70, 71, 73–78, 79, 84, 96–97, 103, 133–34, 248–49, 297, 298; research agenda of, 9, 17, 18, 63–64, 65, 66, 67–70, 73, 74–77, 79–80, 84, 96, 101–2, 103, 109–10, 139, 243, 244, 248, 249; and home economists' user-oriented approach, 12, 17–18, 78–92, 96, 101, 116, 252, 297; and home economists as mediators, 17; refrigeration investigations, 18, 115–16, 123–27, 129–33, 329 (n. 71), 330 (n. 77); creation of, 62, 63, 65, 66, 298; mission of, 63, 67–68, 70, 71, 101–2; and private sphere/public sphere, 67; divisions of, 71, 297; and consumer education, 100, 102, 104–9, 110, 111, 133; communications network of, 103–9, 110, 116, 133; and information on brand-name goods, 108–9, 116, 117, 130, 133; critics of, 109–10; and representation of consumers, 111–16, 123, 134–35; and standardization, 113–14, 115,

119, 134; and business home economists, 158, 178; and cooperation between business and government institutions, 182; and World War II, 244–45; legacy of, 252
Bureau of Human Nutrition and Home Economics (BHNHE): renaming of, 243, 247; and nutrition research, 247–50, 251, 253; and budget cuts, 248, 249–53, 280
Burns, Kathryn Van Aken, 170
Business Bourse publishing firm, 141
Business home economists: as corporate employees, 10, 11, 14, 16, 18, 19, 136, 139, 140, 142, 177, 205–6, 257, 258, 266–70, 274, 277–80, 287, 298, 332 (n. 4); and consumer service, 13, 155–60, 163, 171, 172, 182, 194, 208, 209, 211–13, 218, 220–31, 232, 236–40, 265, 269, 346 (n. 2); professional ideals of, 18, 137–39, 142, 149, 155, 156, 158, 159, 163, 172–73, 176, 207, 258, 259, 269, 277; opportunities for, 136, 149, 164, 172, 177, 220, 257–58, 265–66, 334 (n. 31), 339 (n. 5); and retail environments, 136, 152, 177, 182, 193, 195, 201, 205, 209, 212, 213, 215, 217, 227, 243; and Experiment 63 drama, 136–38, 172; and consumer movements, 137, 166, 171, 198, 206, 268, 289; role of, 137–38, 244, 285; and production/consumption relationship, 138, 142, 146, 149, 161–62, 172, 173; and Frederick, 139–42; as sellouts, 140, 332 (n. 4); and publishing industry, 141; as consumer representatives, 141, 157–58, 207, 279, 281, 284, 289, 298; and consumer education, 142, 146, 147, 156, 157, 176, 178, 181, 182, 198, 199, 222, 257, 265, 266, 268, 281, 289; legitimacy of, 143, 145–50, 155, 156, 158, 163, 164, 170–71, 172, 176; and food industry, 145, 147, 148, 150, 152, 174, 176, 177–78, 193, 209, 243, 254, 262–65, 269, 271–72, 276, 281, 340 (n. 22); and textiles and clothing, 147, 148, 159, 193, 209, 260–62, 265; and utility companies, 150, 152, 154, 157, 160–61, 194, 208, 209, 212, 215, 218–26, 236, 260, 262, 346 (n. 2); educational background of, 151, 152, 159, 335 (n. 36); salaries of, 154–55, 164, 196, 266–67; and "right living," 156; and access to "the woman's viewpoint," 156, 157, 158, 160,

203, 215, 218, 272, 273–74, 281, 296; and
science, 156, 159–60, 163, 172; as translators between consumers and producers,
160–61, 171, 181, 191, 192, 193, 208, 243,
257; and diplomacy metaphor, 161–62,
172, 173, 181; and "personality work,"
162–63, 212, 224–25, 229, 276, 350 (n. 53);
criticism of, 166–72; influence of, 177–78;
and scientific cookery, 189; and gender
ideology, 199–200, 206–7, 267–74, 277,
279–80, 281; and ethics, 239–40; and
World War II, 253–54, 257; and nutrition, 254–57, 271; marginalization of,
284. *See also* Home Economics in Business Section
Business institutions: and home economists' research, 4, 69, 96; home economists' relationship with, 9, 16, 18, 61,
298; communication with consumers, 10;
and home economists' user-oriented approach, 12, 80, 274; and professionalism
of home economists, 15–16; government
regulation of, 176. *See also* Corporations;
Manufacturers
Butterick Publishing Company, 121, 257
Bymers, Gwen J., 288

Cable Act of 1922, 66
Callahan, Genevieve, 155, 265–66
Calumet Baking Powder, 185, 186
Calvin, Henrietta, 51
Campbell, Persia, 286
Canon, Helen, 98
Canoyer, Helen G., 275, 286, 288
Caplovitz, David, 288
Carlson, Gudrun, 187
Carrigan, Jack, 215
Carter, Winifred S., 190
Central Committee on the Standardization
of Textile Fabrics, 113, 117–18
Central Hudson Gas and Electric Corpora-
tion, 238
Chambers, Ruth, 226
Charity Organization Society, 33
Chase, Stuart, 107
Chatfield, Charlotte, 82
Chautauquas, 33
Chicago World's Columbian Exposition
(1893), 25, 32, 210

Child care centers, and World War II, 242
Children's Bureau, 59, 66, 69–70, 74, 99,
154, 246
Children's clothing, 120–21, 123
"Child study" movement, 120, 123
Child welfare reformers, 15
Chinn, Aubyn, 166
Chittick, James, 196
Chloupek, Gene, 194
Citizenship: and rational consumption, 17,
19, 39, 45, 102, 133; and education, 34; for
married women, 66; and consumption,
101–11; and corporate citizenship, 177
Civil rights movement, 284, 285, 288, 293
Clark, Laura, 155
Clark, Samuel C., 75, 127
Class status, and consumption, 300. *See
also* Elite women; Low-income families;
Middle class; Working-class families;
Working-class women
Clauss, Florence, 217, 221, 230, 236
Clothing Information Bureau, 22
Cohen, Lizabeth, 2, 7, 14, 105, 307 (n. 15)
Cold War, 8, 243
Collier, Allen C., 183
Commercial hospitality, 182
Commission for the Relief of Belgium
(CRB), 47
Conference on Home Building and Home
Ownership (1931), 118, 198–99
Connecticut Agricultural Experiment Sta-
tion, 108
Constantine, Dorothy, 190
Consumer activism: and top-down gov-
ernment reforms, 7; forms of, 8; and
O'Brien, 76; home economists pro-
moting, 286, 287; and economic in-
equality, 293. *See also* Consumer
movements
Consumer Advisory Board (CAB), 105, 115
Consumer Affairs, 289
"The Consumer and the New Economic
Order" meeting (1934), 168
Consumer behavior: home economists' re-
search on, 4, 64, 65, 69, 78, 79, 86–92, 96,
98–99, 102, 183, 245, 297; home economists' reforming of, 17
Consumer capitalism: and Frankfurt
school, 1; development of, 2, 4, 5, 6, 10;

role of state in relation to, 6; home economics' role in, 10, 11, 100, 134, 140, 145,
306 (n. 2), 308 (n. 22); and role of women
consumers, 27; critiques of, 98, 107, 110;
and American Home Economic Association, 166; and business home economists, 176, 298
Consumer culture: women consumer's role
in, 1–2, 29, 300; home economists' role
in, 2, 10, 13, 14, 27, 203, 234, 281, 288, 295,
297, 298–99, 300; and middle class, 2,
10, 13, 14, 27, 203, 288, 297, 300; development of, 2, 10, 298; and business home
economists, 178, 241; and gender ideology, 300
Consumer education: and home economists, 3, 4, 7, 8, 11, 12, 13; and budgeting, 22, 23, 24, 27, 31, 106, 140, 223, 236,
246, 247, 288; and home management,
51, 59, 71, 108, 201; and Bureau of Home
Economics, 100, 102, 104–9, 110, 111, 133;
and food science, 105, 106, 110, 177; and
nutrition, 106, 108–9, 110, 230, 241, 254,
255, 351 (n. 74); and household appliances, 106–7, 217; and home economists'
representing consumers, 111–16, 265; and
women's clubs and organizations, 115,
199, 208; and business home economists,
142, 146, 147, 156, 157, 176, 178, 181, 182,
198, 199, 222, 257, 265, 266, 268, 281, 289;
and utility companies, 208, 212, 221, 223,
225–28, 240, 241, 254–55; and consumer
movements, 284, 287–88, 289; and home
economics education, 289; and expert
role, 299
Consumer movements: as challenge to
home economists, 5, 19, 253, 284, 285–87,
293; and "purchaser consumer" paradigm, 7; and consumer consciousness,
14, 299; and business home economists,
137, 166, 171, 198, 206, 268, 289; and
product testing, 205; and consumer education, 284, 287–88, 289; and lobby for
legislative action, 287. *See also* Consumer
activism
Consumer needs: and corporate capitalism,
9; and science of consumption, 12; and
manufacturers, 12, 17–18; and household
equipment manufacturers, 18, 194; diver-

sity of, 111; and New Deal, 114–15; home
economists' role in defining, 135, 193,
203, 205; and marketing, 272
Consumer products: and rational consumption, 3, 40, 45; home economists'
research on, 4–5, 64, 69, 78, 79, 80,
81–86, 97, 101, 102, 109–10, 243, 245, 297;
home economists as guides to, 5, 6, 8, 9,
11, 20; home economists as mediators
with engineers on, 5, 6–7, 9, 10–11, 12,
15, 80, 100, 111, 193, 198; and business
home economists, 5, 139, 157, 173, 174,
176, 177, 205–6, 207, 265, 271, 280–81;
quality of, 8, 30–31, 78, 92, 96, 105, 108,
157, 199; creating demand for, 10; standard specifications for, 12, 18, 69, 78, 86,
89, 92, 99, 101–2, 109, 112–16, 134, 157,
166, 298; development strategies, 14, 181,
183, 193–200, 207, 209, 299; scientific research defining physical qualities of, 17;
and consumer education, 107, 265, 297;
Frederick on, 140; and business communication with consumers, 180, 299–300;
corporate research on, 181; and Cold
War, 243; growth in, 243, 257, 281, 294;
and World War II, 244–45; prototypes
of, 275. *See also* Product testing
Consumer Purchases Study (CPS), 91–92,
249
Consumer research programs, 275
Consumers: home economists as representatives of, 3, 4, 7, 8, 10, 100, 111–16,
133, 138, 265, 292; as political actors, 7;
corporations' relationship to, 16, 25, 79,
110; home economists' constructing of
models of, 18; business tools for understanding, 19; home economists as advocates of, 99–100, 134, 169, 281; identity of,
114, 300; business home economists as
representatives of, 141, 157–58, 207, 279,
281, 284, 289, 298; diversity of, 158, 293–
94; and motivation research, 273
Consumers' Advisory Council, 253, 286
Consumers Bill of Rights (1962), 286
Consumers' Counsel Division of the Agricultural Adjustment Administration, 105,
107
Consumer society: origins of, 2, 10, 17; role
of home economists in, 3, 6, 8, 9, 11, 142,

297, 299; and women's identity, 3, 8, 13, 22; role of state in, 7; and technological change, 7, 308 (n. 26); role of home-makers in, 31

Consumers' Research, 109, 110, 138, 139, 166–68, 169, 171, 199, 205, 287

Consumer surveys, 12–13, 275, 277

Consumer Trends Forum International, 296

Consumption: historical studies of, 2; science of, 5, 12–13, 26, 32, 38–39, 59, 63, 81, 95, 97, 101, 111, 133–34, 177, 203; home economists' role in state policies on, 7–8; home economists' influence in discourses of, 20, 23, 50, 96, 300–301; moral potential of, 29, 30; and home economics education, 38; and World War I food conservation programs, 46–58; economics of, 70, 71, 75–76, 86–92, 98; and home economists' expert role, 74–78, 293, 299; home economists' research on, 75–76, 78, 79; lack of federal policy on, 100; and citizenship, 101–11; cultural language about, 107, 243, 286, 293, 297; politicization of, 114, 166, 168, 286, 293, 299; and World War II rationing programs, 242, 245; and economic inequality, 288, 293; and class status, 300. *See also* Mass consumption; Production/consumption relationship; Rational consumption

Container Club, 340 (n. 15)

Continuous-process machinery, 179

Cooke, Morris, 209

Cooley, Anna, 41

Coons, Callie Mae, 250

Cooperative living, 88–89

Corning Glass Works, 154, 195, 340 (n. 15)

Corn Products Refining Company, 225

Corporate capitalism: predominance of, 2, 3; and consumer needs, 9; fine-tuning of, 10; home economists' autonomy from, 15; and business home economists, 139, 156, 173, 241

Corporations: and consumer capitalism, 10; and home economists as mediators with homemakers, 12, 177; relationship to consumers, 16, 25, 79, 110; and World War I food conservation program, 60; and corporate citizenship, 177; and home economics departments, 177, 180, 181–83,

206, 243, 278–79. *See also* Business home economists

Cost-benefit analyses: and homemakers, 17, 39–40; and marketplace reform, 99, 111; and rational consumption, 104, 134

Cost-of-living studies, 70, 90, 91

Cotton Textile Institute, 95

Country life movement, 32

Cowan, Ruth Schwartz, 12, 230, 308 (n. 26)

Cox, Reavis, 272

Creekmore, Anna M., 284

Creel, George, 48

Crisco shortening, 183, 184, 188–92, 297, 342 (nn. 41, 49)

Crissey, Lucille, 196

Cumming, Adelaide Hawley, 276

Dahnke, Marye, 136, 154, 161, 163, 174, 176–78, 260, 276–77

Dallas Electrical Arts Club, 223

Dallas Power and Light Company, 223

Daniel Yankelovich Incorporated, 291–92, 293

Darnall, John P., 184–85, 187–88, 341 (n. 28)

Dash Home Laundry Institute, 261

Daughters of the American Revolution, 73

Davison, Eloise, 154, 220

Delineator, 150, 156

Delineator Home Institute, 200

Dennen, Abbie Claire, 343 (n. 63)

Denton, Minna C., 64, 65, 69, 71, 79, 113

Department stores, 213, 216

Detroit Edison, 217

Deupree, Richard Redwood, 184

Devine, Edward T., 29

Dewey, Annie Godfrey, 26, 31, 35

Dewey, John, 34

Dewey, Melvil, 26, 35, 306 (n. 5)

Dichter, Ernst, 273, 277

Dignam, Dorothy, 333 (n. 7)

Dillon, Charles, 136

Dimelow, Grace, 121, 257

Division of Simplified Practice (DSP), 113, 114, 131

Dix, Dorothy, 223

Domestic science, 1, 3, 23, 27–29, 32–34, 37, 42, 178–79, 184–85

Domestic sphere. *See* Private sphere/public sphere

Donham, S. Agnes, 147, 150–51, 159–60
Downing, Helen, 337 (n. 73)
Dreft, 192
Drucker, Peter F., 272, 275
Dunham, Ellen-Ann, 262, 266
DuPont, 260–61
Dye, Marie, 167

East, Marjorie, 291
Eating habits: reform of, 23, 24, 25, 27, 28, 32, 48; and urban cooking schools, 33; and rational consumption, 40–42; improvement of, 242, 245–46; home economists' research on, 246; and convenience foods, 262
Economics, of consumption, 70, 71, 75–76, 77, 86–92, 98
Edible Gelatin Manufacturers of America, 340 (n. 15)
Edison Electric Institute, 209
Edwards, Alice, 169
Ehrenreich, Barbara, 332 (n. 6)
Eichelberger, Marietta, 171
Eisenhower, Dwight D., 250
Electrical Merchandising, 213, 214, 216, 217, 221, 230, 237
Electrical Women's Round Table, 154, 208
Electric Home and Farm Authority (EHFA), 130, 132, 154, 220
Electronic social media, 299
Elite women: and production/consumption relationship, 29–30, 38; and household appliances, 34
Elliott, S. Maria, 33, 42
Ellwood, Vera B., 232
Emmons, Harriet Cole, 143
English, Deirdre, 332 (n. 6)
Environmental movement, 284, 299
Equal Rights Amendment, 291
Equal Suffrage League, 31
Evaporated Milk Association, 171
Ewen, Stuart, 332 (n. 6)
Experiment 63 (drama), 136–37
Expert role: and consumer society, 3; and diversity of experts, 10, 13, 299–300; cultural power of, 13; and home economists' collective authority as experts, 15–16, 24, 51, 58, 59, 60–61, 74–78, 96, 97, 103, 270–71, 281; and nutrition, 17, 253, 271; in fed-

eral bureaucracy, 18; and contraction of home economists' influence, 19, 292; and surveys, 25–26; and social conditions, 26; in democracy, 52; and home economists as consumer experts, 63–64, 65, 86, 99, 101, 107, 115, 116, 133, 139, 182, 183, 187, 191, 203, 272, 281, 295, 297, 300–301; and business home economists, 141, 178, 269–80, 293
Extension Service Review, 151

Fair-trade legislation, 182
Family and consumer science, as academic field, 295–96
Family research, 251
Farmer, Fannie, 179, 189, 224
Farmers' Alliance, 73
Farmer's institutes, 33
Farmer's Wife (magazine), 143, 150
Farquhar, Helen P., 226–27
Federal Board for Vocational Education, 36, 71, 139
Federal Commission on the Status of Women, 290
Federal Emergency Relief Administration, 154
Federal Trade commission, 198, 205
Federated American Engineering Societies, 112
Female consumers. *See* Women consumers
Feminist historians, on home economics, 1, 306 (n. 2)
Feminist movement: as challenge to home economists, 5, 19, 282–83, 285, 289–91, 293; and private sphere/public sphere, 66, 293
Feminized service professions, 14
Fisher, Eleanor L., 343 (n. 63)
Fisher, Katharine, 160–61, 202–4, 205, 258, 259, 260
Fitzgerald, Louise, 147, 162, 187
Fleischmann Yeast, 340 (n. 15)
Floyd, Myrtle, 154
Food industry: and World War I food conservation programs, 47; and business home economists, 145, 147, 148, 150, 152, 174, 176, 177–78, 193, 209, 243, 254, 262–65, 269, 271–72, 276, 281, 340 (n. 22); and recipes and cookbooks, 178–79, 184,

186, 188, 189, 190–91, 225, 254, 262–64,
265, 271–72, 275–76, 339 (n. 7); demand
for home economics in, 178–83; modernization of, 179; and advertising, 179–80,
183–87, 191, 204, 209; and home economists as translators to consumers, 181;
and home economics departments, 181,
183–88, 193, 243, 260, 262; and product
testing, 181, 184–87, 194, 204, 275–76;
and public goodwill, 181–82; and utility
companies, 219
Food products: home economists' as instructors for, 5; packaged, 6, 24, 95, 257,
297, 298; and middle class, 13; food value
of homemade versus commercially prepared, 93, 264; and consumer education,
105; and home economists representing consumers, 112, 265; and standardization, 114; and business home economists, 173, 174, 177, 263; convenience,
257, 262–65; frozen, 263; and food technology and engineering, 269, 271, 277,
281; and food additives, 271
Food science: and food preparation methods, 33, 41, 60, 70, 85, 89, 92, 103, 110,
177, 192, 225–26, 228–30, 244, 255, 263;
and home economics education, 41,
51–52; and food preservation methods,
42, 51, 53–55, 57, 85, 103, 106, 124–27,
129, 134–35, 194, 245, 255, 295; home
economists' research on, 64, 68, 70, 75,
81–82, 85, 90, 91–92, 95, 245, 246, 247–
48, 249; and production/consumption
relationship, 92; food utilization studies,
92–93; and rational consumption, 101;
and consumer education, 105, 106, 110,
177; and refrigeration, 124–27, 129, 133;
and food distribution, 252
Foreign Agriculture Service, 246
Frances Barton, 277
Frankfurt school, 1
Frederick, Christine, 139–42, 225, 332 (n. 6)
Frederick, J. George, 141
Freeman, Orville L., 251
Freer, Florence, 240
Friedan, Betty, 282, 283, 289
Frigidaire Corporation, 126, 130
Fritschner, Linda Marie, 306 (n. 7)
Fritz, Helen, 280

Frysinger, Grace, 148
Furness, Betty, 286–87
Furry, Margaret S., 94

Garland School of Homemaking (Boston),
45
Gendered division of labor: and consumer
society, 9; and professionalism of home
economists, 14–15, 19; and vocational
education, 34; and utility companies,
221–23, 236–40; and private sphere/
public sphere, 301
Gender ideology: and home economists, 6,
8, 9; and consumption as female, 14; and
negotiations, 161; and business home
economists, 199–200, 206–7, 267–74,
277, 279–80, 281; and utility companies,
213–19; and "gender containment," 243–
44; and higher education, 259; and consumer culture, 300. *See also* Elite women;
Middle-class: women of; Rural women;
Women consumers
General Committee on Standardization,
113, 118
General Electric, 213, 232, 234–35, 237
General Federation of Women's Clubs, 28,
51, 66, 73, 129, 199, 220
General Foods, 254, 262–65, 266, 267–68,
277, 280
General Mills, 18, 150, 154, 190, 254, 260,
269–70, 276–77
General Motors, 180
George, Benjamin B., 184, 185
Georgia Power Company, 238
Gibbs, Charlotte M., 39
Gibbs, Winifred Stuart, 149, 160, 188, 206
Gilbreth, Lillian, 142
Gillett, Lucy, 167–68
Gilman, Charlotte Perkins, 9, 29, 35, 88
Glass Container Association of America,
340 (n. 15)
Glickman, Lawrence, 2, 8
Good Housekeeping (magazine), 201–2, 204
Good Housekeeping Institute (GHI), 107,
160–61, 177, 201–5, 258, 260, 289
Good Housekeeping Seal of Approval, 202,
204
Good Luck Jar Rubber, 146
Goodrich, Henrietta, 31, 35

Gorman, Vivette, 226

Government institutions: home economists' relationship with, 3, 4, 9, 12, 14, 16, 61, 64, 139, 142, 151, 244, 298; communication with consumers, 10; and professionalism of home economists, 15; and consumer goods in marketplace, 16; and consumer needs, 17–18; and home economics education, 36; and utility companies, 219

Government regulations: and household equipment manufacturers, 18; and public health, 74; and corporations' use of home economics, 176, 178, 182, 198

Grange, 73

Gray, Greta, 84

Great Depression: and Bureau of Home Economics, 77, 91, 105–6, 245; and Home Economics in Business Section, 150, 164; and food industry, 191; and product testing, 197, 198; and business home economists, 206, 238; and utility companies, 212, 241

Great Society, 252

Green living, 299

Hader, Mathilde C., 169, 170

Hamor, William A., 181

Hanson, Doris E., 288

Harland, Marion, 179

Harrington, Michael, 288

Harris, Florence LaGanke, 166

Hart, Mary Irene, 186, 194

Hartley, Olive, 118

Hartson, Mary Reed, 145, 156, 187

Hatcher, Eugenia, 265

Hawley, Edith, 90

Hayden, Dolores, 140, 324 (n. 14)

Health-for-Victory (campaign), 255

Hearst, William Randolph, 202

Hearst International Magazine building, 202

Heath, Ruth, 194

Heseltine, Marjorie, 154, 158–59, 165

Heuer, Leone Anne, 121, 199

Higher education: and home economists' research agenda, 3–4, 64, 73, 252, 253; emergence of, 17; and home economists' teaching specialty, 17, 21–22, 36–38, 152; women attaining degrees, 28; and home economics curricula, 36, 38–45, 59, 60–61, 67, 74, 151, 152, 167, 220, 239, 240, 258–59, 271, 278, 285, 288, 290, 313 (n. 42); and nutrition education, 37–38, 39, 41; and economics, 41. *See also* Land-grant agricultural colleges

Hill, A. Elizabeth, 83

Hill, Janet McKenzie, 33, 54, 179, 184

Hills Brothers Foods, 154

H. J. Heinz, 340 (n. 15)

Hochschild, Arlie, 162

Holland, Dorothy, 260

Home decoration, 45, 84

Home demonstrations: and public relations, 5; and modernization of agriculture, 7; and business communication with consumers, 10; high attendance at, 13; and home economists, 18, 36, 38, 63, 103; and World War I food conservation program, 52, 53, 55, 59; and nutrition, 66; and ties to industry, 111; and business home economists, 146, 156, 181; and Procter & Gamble, 184

Home economics: development of, 1, 7, 16–17, 26–28, 30–32, 35; reform goals of, 1, 11, 12, 15, 16, 24, 25, 30–31, 46, 52, 60, 62, 74, 78, 221, 240, 241, 284, 287, 296, 306 (n. 2); stereotypical image of, 2, 110, 284, 291–93, 294; marginalization of, 5, 284–91; as social and cultural movement, 11, 30–31, 251, 306 (n. 4); as academic discipline, 36–45, 70, 71, 285, 290–91, 295; as research field, 63–64, 67–68, 74; as term, 71, 285, 295, 296; internal critiques of, 284–85, 287, 298; in Dewey Decimal System, 306 (n. 5)

Home Economics in Business (HEIB) Section: professional identity of, 18, 292–93; creation of, 138, 143, 145–50, 172, 176, 334 (nn. 27, 31); and Frederick, 141; membership standards of, 148, 164–65, 337 (n. 68); profile of members, 150–55; and advertising industry, 158–59, 160, 266; and consumer education, 159, 166, 289; structure and activities of, 163–66; and code of practice, 165–66; criticism of, 166–72; members of, 177, 197, 206, 257, 262, 269, 279, 346 (n. 2); and utility com-

panies, 219, 240; and military mobilization, 255; and career counseling, 258–60;
and continuing education, 278; and corporate hiring, 278–80; and standards,
287; renaming of, 296. *See also* Business
home economists

Home economists: professional goals of,
2–3, 4, 5–6, 9, 14–16, 17, 26, 35, 36–38,
46, 51, 59–60, 62, 63, 68, 69, 73, 74–78,
79, 110, 137–39, 250; as consumer educators, 3, 4, 7, 11, 12, 13, 68; and rational
consumption, 3, 4, 306 (n. 5); research
agenda of, 3–4, 9, 17, 63–64, 68, 71; and
access to "the woman's viewpoint," 4, 13,
19, 79, 99, 101, 112, 130, 141, 159, 180, 296,
333 (n. 7); secondary relationship with
market, 10–11; social goals of, 11; construction of ideal consumers, 13; teaching specialty within higher education,
17, 21–22, 36–38, 152; and parameters of
"right living," 27, 34, 41, 113; and vocational education, 34; professional identity of, 285, 287, 290, 292, 295–96. *See
also* Business home economists
—as mediators: and consumer products, 5,
6–7, 9, 10–11, 12, 15, 80, 100, 111, 193, 198;
and household goods, 9, 12; and brokering class, 10–11; and facilitating negotiations, 11; and production/consumption
relationship, 11, 12, 16, 25, 181, 243, 294,
308 (n. 26), 309 (n. 36); and exchange of
information, 11–12; and technological
change, 11–12, 14, 19, 218, 232, 241, 296,
297; and translating between consumers
and producers, 12, 80, 81, 97, 157, 158,
160, 208, 221, 241, 252, 265, 273–76, 286;
and middle class, 13; and professionalism of home economists, 15–16; and representation of consumers, 111–16, 292;
and business home economists, 163, 193,
265, 267, 270–71, 280; challenges to, 244,
280, 301; legacy of, 299–301

Homemakers: shift from production to
consumption, 1, 3, 6, 296, 306 (n. 5),
308 (n. 26); home economists' relationship with, 3, 4, 9, 12, 16, 30, 31, 188, 203,
242, 270, 271, 273–74, 277, 282–83, 289,
292, 293, 298; consulting spouses on decisions, 8, 215; and rational consump-

tion, 17, 39, 45, 62–63, 104, 110–11; home
economists' instructions for household
goods, 18; and quality of consumer products, 30; role in consumer society, 31; and
vocational education, 34; and home economics education, 36; and World War I
food conservation program, 48, 49, 51,
57; and home economists' research, 68,
70, 79, 81, 87; and Bureau of Home Economics, 79, 97, 101, 106, 107, 116, 117; and
production/consumption relationship,
87; and household tasks, 88–89; and
standardization, 116; and refrigeration,
127, 130; and business home economists,
157, 158, 176, 208, 264, 270, 271; and consumer education, 208; identity of, 244;
"focus groups" of, 275

Homemaker Testing Service, 265

Home management: and industrialization,
3; and home economics education, 37,
40–41, 44, 45, 53; and production/con-
sumption relationship, 38; and consumer
education, 51, 59, 71, 108, 201; home
economists' research on, 65, 87, 126, 127,
248, 250; as public concern, 67; and science of consumption, 81; and business
home economists, 148, 181; and mass-
circulation magazines, 201. *See also*
Budgeting

Homeowners, and middle class, 13

Home service departments: and consumer
products industry, 5; of utility companies, 13, 194, 208, 209, 211–13, 218, 219,
220–31, 232, 236–40, 254–55, 258, 260,
262, 269, 346 (n. 2); origins of, 81

Hoover, Herbert: and World War I food conservation program, 4, 46–49, 51–52, 55,
57–60; home economists' alliance with,
8, 18, 51–52, 60, 80, 102, 107, 114, 118,
242, 286; as advocate of efficiencies, 100;
presidency of, 105–6, 198; and cooperation between government and industry,
112, 146; and standardization, 112–13

Hoover, Jessie, 158

Horton, Mary B., 266

Household appliances: purchase of, 6;
and middle class, 13; home economists'
demonstrations of, 19, 214, 223, 225; and
utility companies, 24, 44, 210, 211, 214–

17; quality of, 30; and rational consumption, 44, 101; home economists' research on, 84, 86, 244, 245, 250, 252; and household tasks, 88; and consumer education, 106–7, 217; and standardization, 114, 245; and New Deal, 130; and business home economists, 173, 177, 190, 191, 193, 261, 262, 265, 298; and product testing, 198, 202–4; and retail environments, 213; and home economics education, 220; utilitarian and aesthetic dimensions of, 229–36; innovations in, 257

Household equipment and goods: and rational consumption, 3, 39–40; home economists' as instructors for, 5; state advocacy for purchasing, 7; and home economists as mediators, 9, 12; and refrigeration, 18, 115–16, 123–27, 129–33; and rational consumption, 44; quality of, 62; home economists as experts of, 63–64; home economists' research on, 65, 69, 74, 77, 81, 84, 85, 97, 101, 103, 244, 250; and home economists representing consumers, 112, 114; simplification of, 112–13; standardization of, 112–16; and home economics education, 220; and rural areas, 249. *See also* Product testing

Household equipment manufacturers: and consumer needs, 18, 194; home economists' employment with, 136; and business home economists, 148, 152, 195, 209; and home economics departments, 177, 183, 193–95, 255; and recipes and cookbooks, 193–94; and utility companies, 211; and World War II, 254–55

Household management. *See* Home management

Household Refrigeration Bureau, 125

Houser, T. V., 200

Housework: and industrialization, 3; and home economics education, 34; energy studies on, 75, 88; economic value of, 88, 89; tasks constituting, 88, 217; simplifying, 224; time necessary for, 230; and labor-saving devices, 236; efficiency of, 306 (n. 5)

Housing: and women's organizations, 28; and American Home Economics Association, 71, 77; home economists' research

on, 84, 89, 104, 249, 250, 251–52; and single-family living, 84, 104, 306 (n. 5), 324 (n. 14); and business home economists, 156

Howe, Eleanor, 238

Howe, Frederick, 105

Howe, Harriet, 171–72

Howes, Ethel Puffer, 84, 88

Hull House, 30, 37

Hunt, Caroline, 28–31, 32, 34–35, 51, 65, 82

Husted, Marjorie Child, 154, 260, 269–70, 279

Idaho Power Company, 238

Igleheart, Austin S., 186

Igleheart Brothers, 185, 186

Igleheart Milling Company, 194

Immigrants, 25, 33, 48

Industrialization: and consumption decisions, 3; of home, 6–7; value associated with, 25, 27; critiques of, 26; and vocational education, 34

Industrial Revolution, 8

Institute for the American Home, 251

Institute for the Coordination of Women's Interests, 84

Institute of American Meat Packers, 150, 187

Institute of Home Economics, 251

Institute of Women's Professional Relations, 339 (n. 5)

Insull, Martin, 218–19

Interwar period: and home economists' research, 4, 79, 89, 96, 97, 100, 102–3, 110, 246; home economists' influence during, 14, 15, 16, 18, 292, 297, 298; and rational consumption, 101; and science of consumption, 111, 134; and business home economists, 138, 155, 159, 163, 164, 176, 195, 208, 265, 267, 270, 277, 339 (n. 5); and Frederick, 141; and business communication with consumers, 180; and mass-circulation magazines, 201; and utility companies, 209–12, 213, 214; and Bureau of Home Economics, 252; and sales and marketing campaigns, 275

Ivory Soap, 183, 192

Jackson, Beatrice C., 240

J. C. Penney Company, 268

Jell-O gelatin products, 262, 264

Jewish women, and World War I food conservation program, 48

Johnson, Helen Louise, 51, 148, 150, 151, 179, 201–2

Johnson, Hugh, 115

Johnson, Jack T., 253, 288

Johnson, Lyndon B., 286, 288; Committee on Consumer Interests, 288

Jones, Kathleen Paul, 121

Journal of Home Economics, 56, 71, 76, 87, 166–68, 171, 253, 290

Justin, Margaret, 14, 149

Kansas Flour Mills, 340 (n. 15)

Kelley, Florence, 30

Kelley, Janette, 172, 188

Kellogg Company, 145, 146, 150, 154, 170, 255–56

Kelly, Ruth L., 338 (n. 80)

Kennedy, John F., 253, 286

Keown, Mary E., 143, 149, 151, 157, 158, 160

Keynesian economics, 286

Kiene, Julia, 255

King, Florence B., 75, 92–93

Kingsbury, Susan, 33

Kingsley, Margaret, 238

Kinne, Helen, 41

Kitchens on Wheels, 228

Kline, Ronald, 11

Knauer, Virginia, 289

Kneeland, Hildegarde, 75–76, 87–88, 89, 90–92, 95, 297

Knight, Dorothy, 151–52

Kolm, Suzanne, 162, 350 (n. 53)

Kraft Cheese Company, 136, 154, 161, 174, 176, 260, 276–77

Kyrk, Hazel, 41, 75–76, 87, 90, 98, 109–10

Labor management, and welfare capitalism, 182, 183

Labor theory of value, 29

Ladies' Home Journal, 125, 140, 141, 143, 150

Lake Placid conferences (1899–1907): and Richards, 26–28; and budgeting, 27–28; and women's education, 28–29; and economic power of women's consumption, 30; and home as site for social change, 31; and quality of consumer products, 31;

and women's suffrage, 31, 311 (n. 21); and nutrition science, 32; and scientific study of social conditions, 33; and educational programs, 33–35, 60; and home economics development, 35, 179, 201

Land-grant agricultural colleges: expansion of, 7; and women's education, 28; and domestic science, 33, 34; and home economics education, 36, 38, 44, 103; and agricultural extension agencies, 52; and World War I food conservation program, 53; and home economics research, 96, 253

Langworthy, Charles Ford, 32, 65, 75

Lathrop, Julia, 69–70, 74

Laundryowners National Association, 340 (n. 15)

Law of marginal utility, 29

Lazarsfeld, Paul, 273

Leach, William, 10

League of Advertising Women, 159

League of Women Voters, 73, 109

Leiby, Cora Irene, 207

Leisure House, 223

Leonard, John, 31, 311 (n. 21), 314 (n. 69)

Lesly, Philip, 294

Levenstein, Harvey, 253

Lever Brothers, 172, 191

Libby, McNeill and Libby, 152

Librarians, professional organization of, 35

Lilienthal, David, 209

Lincoln, Mary J., 33, 179

Lindman, Ina S., 146, 154, 162, 256–57, 335 (n. 43), 337 (n. 73)

Lindsley, Mary, 94

Linsley, Mary Antrim, 343 (n. 63)

Loeb, Eleanor, 109

Lord, Isabel Ely, 51

Low-income families: and home economists' research on household appliances, 84; and food products, 105; home economists working with, 288. *See also* Working-class families; Working-class women

Lubar, Steven, 309 (n. 36)

Luckiesh, Matthew, 234, 235

Luxury: as corrupting influence, 35; and middle-class consumer culture, 300

Lyle, Dorothy Siegert, 262
Lynd, Robert, 89, 115
Lyng, Anne, 261

MacLeod, Sarah, 143
Malano, Mrs. Joe, 107
Maloney, Mary, 106
Maltby, Lucy, 154, 195
Manhattan Trade School for Girls, 22, 33
Manning, M. L., 106
Manual Training High School (Providence, R.I.), 33
Manufacturers: and consumer needs, 12, 17–18; and product development strategies, 14; home economists' employment with, 15, 16, 17, 18, 19, 136; and rational consumption, 45; and home economists' research, 69, 79, 86, 95, 103; and textiles and clothing, 76, 117, 118, 119, 120–21, 123; and Bureau of Home Economics, 110, 111; and home economists representing consumers, 112, 126, 134, 203–4, 297, 298; and grading systems, 117, 118, 131; and refrigeration industry, 123–27, 129–33; and Frederick, 141
Marchand, Roland, 125, 352 (n. 93)
Marketing. *See* Sales and marketing campaigns
Marketplace: reform of, 99, 100, 104; and rational consumption, 101, 116; and standardization, 113, 115
Market research, development of, 12, 19, 244, 271, 273–75, 281
Market Research Corporation of America, 273
Marlatt, Abby, 33, 51, 314 (n. 69)
Martha Logan, 277
Mason, John, 55
Mason, Lucy Randolph, 30
Mass-circulation magazines: and expert role, 13, 59; advertising in, 24; educational articles in, 33; and World War I food conservation program, 53, 59; and home economists' research, 85, 103; and consumer education, 107; and business home economists, 147, 150, 152, 155, 156, 157; and product testing, 200–205; and utility companies, 219, 220; and home economics departments, 243

Mass consumption, political economy of, 8, 100
Mass production, 6, 179, 296–97
Matthews, Glenna, 140
Matthews, J. Merritt, 196
Matthews, Mary, 67–68, 317 (n. 12)
Maule, Frances, 257
May, Elaine Tyler, 243
Maytag, 261
McAuley, Faith M., 5, 39
McCabe, Margaret, 334 (n. 31)
McCall's, 289
McCann-Erickson advertising agency, 68
McCulley, Edna, 106
McElhinny, W. D., 126
McGee, Anita Newcomb, 108
McGovern, Charles, 2, 7
McGowan, Ellen Beers, 21, 43
McGrath, Earl J., 253, 288
McLaughlin, Laura Ida, 75
McLean, Beth Bailey, 260
McNutt, Paul, 246
McQueen, Jessie, 219, 238, 242
Mediation. *See* Home economists: as mediators
Mellon Institute of Industrial Research, 181, 340 (n. 15)
Meloney, Marie, 156
Mendel, Lafayette B., 62
Men's identity, and consumer society, 3, 8
Merrell-Soule Sales Corporation, 185, 187
Merrill-Palmer School (Detroit), 68
Middle class: and consumer culture, 2, 10, 13, 14, 27, 203, 288, 297, 300; role of consumption in, 2, 45, 59; and standard of living, 3, 27–28, 31, 32, 35, 102, 211, 283, 300; consumer products for, 5, 79; and home economists as mediators, 13; values of, 17, 25, 27, 35, 100, 206, 236, 283–84; identity of, 34, 45, 59, 100, 102, 133, 135, 191, 283, 297, 300, 301; and World War I food conservation program, 58; and refrigeration, 124, 125, 133; and utility companies, 209, 211, 216, 227, 232; social change in, 283–84
—women of: and production/consumption relationship, 1, 22, 23–24, 28, 29–30, 38, 40, 293, 308 (n. 26); and nineteenth-century ideas about morality, 2; and gen-

der ideology of consumers, 8; and Lake Placid conferences, 26, 27–28, 30, 35; and home economists' expert role, 59, 60–61; rural women as, 67; and Bureau of Home Economics, 73–74, 99, 102, 111, 297; and business home economists, 157, 158, 177, 275, 281; and food industry, 191; and utility companies, 213, 215, 225, 241

Military-industrial complex, 243

Milwaukee Electric Railway and Light Company, 232

Miss America pageant, 282

Mitchell, Margaret, 194–95, 255

Modernity, and business home economists, 147

Modern kitchen, defining elements of, 6, 191

Modern Priscilla, 143, 200

Monroe, Day, 90, 91, 140

Montgomery Ward, 158

Morality: nineteenth-century ideas about, 2, 25, 27; moral potential of consumption, 29, 30, 39, 43, 52, 67; and women as producers, 30; and rational consumption, 43, 52; and Frederick, 140; and stereotypical images of women, 222

Morgan, Robin, 282–83, 291

Morse, Richard, 286

Mory, A. V. H., 196, 197, 200

Moskowitz, Marina, 13

Mosley, F. M., 215

Moss, Frank, 234, 235

Mullaney, Bernard J., 228

Muncy, Robyn, 15, 74

Munsell, Hazel E., 75, 82

Myers, Ella B., 267–68

Nader, Ralph, 286, 287

National Association for Ice Industries (NAII), 125, 126, 130, 238

National Association of Manufacturers, 34

National Biscuit Company, 340 (n. 15)

National Bureau of Standards, 18, 69, 78–79, 113–14, 119, 131, 245

National Canners Association, 179, 340 (n. 15)

National Congress of Mothers, 73

National Congress of Parents and Teachers, 109

National Consumer-Retailer Council, 166

National Consumers' Leagues, 30, 65

National Council of Women, 73

National Dairy Council, 147, 150, 162, 187

National Education Association, 33

National Electric Light Association (NELA), 161, 209, 218, 219–20, 222, 237, 241

National Emergency Council, 105

National Federation of Business and Professional Women, 290

National Home Service Conference (1930), 219

National Housewives' League, 30

National Institute of Cleaning and Drying, 261–62

National Nutrition Conference, 246

National Organization for Women, 290

National Recovery Administration (NRA), 105, 115

National Research Council (NRC), 246, 254; Committee on Food and Nutrition, 246; Committee on Food Habits, 246

National Resources Planning Board, 91

National Retail Institute, 140

National Society for the Promotion of Industrial Education, 34

Nearing, Scott, 41

Neil, Marion Harris, 184

Nelson, Donald, 200

New Deal: regulatory role of, 7; and consumer product initiatives, 8; and production/consumption relationship, 91, 100; and rational consumption, 100, 102, 107; and planned economy, 100, 114; and consumer education, 105; and Bureau of Home Economics, 106, 107–8; and consumer needs, 114–15; and standardization, 119; and utilities, 130; and politicization of consumption, 168, 286; antitrust legislation of, 213

New England Kitchen, 25, 32

New England Women's Press Association, 28

The New Science of Seeing, 234

Newspapers: educational articles in, 33; and Bureau of Home Economics, 106, 107; and business home economists, 150, 152, 155; and product testing, 200–205

New York Association for Improving the Condition of the Poor, 167

New York City Economics Association, 159

New York Tribune Institute, 200

Nixon, Richard, 289

Norge, 237

Normal schools, and women's education, 28

North American Dye Corporation, 147, 159

Northern States Power Company, 239

Northwestern Yeast Company, 151, 187

Norton, Alice Peloubet, 31, 37, 56–57, 314 (n. 69)

Nowland & Schladermundt, 273

Nutrition and nutritional science: home economists' training in, 4, 17, 32–33, 51, 181; and Richards, 24–25; and higher education, 37–38, 39, 41; and rational consumption, 40, 41, 60; advances in, 51, 75, 82, 178; and World War I food conservation programs, 53–55, 60; home economists' research on, 64–65, 68, 75, 82, 84, 90, 92, 97, 102, 245–50, 251, 253; and home demonstrations, 66; and home economists' user-oriented approach, 96; and consumer education, 106, 108–9, 110, 230, 241, 254, 255, 351 (n. 74); and World War II, 242, 246, 254, 255–57; and business home economists, 254–57, 271

Nye, David, 124, 352 (n. 93)

O'Brien, Ruth: and home economics research, 75, 76, 83–84, 93, 94, 95, 110, 249, 250; and consumer behavior, 76, 98, 99; and standards, 86, 115, 116, 117–21, 123, 197, 249, 297, 298, 299; and production/consumption relationship, 104–5; and consumer education, 111; and Consumer Advisory Board, 115; and grading systems, 116–17; and World War II, 245; retirement of, 252

Office of Experiment Stations, 82

Office of Home Economics (OHE), 55–56, 64–65, 68, 71, 75–78, 79, 85–86, 89, 97, 124

Office of Price Administration (OPA), 92, 245

Office of War Information, 47–48

O'Leary, Mary, 156, 160, 162

Organized labor, and vocational education, 34

Oxydol, 192

Pabst, Anna, 127

Palmer, Dewey H., 166–68, 170

Parent-Teachers Association, 73

Paris Sowinski, Jeanne, 260, 271, 337 (n. 68)

Patten, Simon Nelson, 29

Pearson, Virginia, 196–97, 200

Pennington, Mary Engle, 125–26, 130, 131–32, 238

Peoples Gas, Light, and Coke Company of Chicago, 224–29

Peoples Gas Club News, 225

Peterson, Anna J., 224–26, 228–29

Peterson, Esther, 286

Peyser, Ethel Rose, 202, 344–45 (n. 80)

Philadelphia Cooking School, 178–79, 201

Philadelphia Electric Company, 217, 260

Philadelphia Textile School, 196

Philanthropy, 47

Phillips, Martha Jane, 147, 157, 159, 160

Pictorial Review, 147

Pillsbury, 60, 260, 270

Pompeian Corporation, 112

Poole, Grace Morrison, 115

Porter, Mildred B., 127, 131, 330 (n. 77)

Positivist sociology, 87, 89

Postum Cereal Company, 145, 151, 154, 162

Poverty, 33, 252, 288

Pratt, Laura, 343 (n. 63)

Pratt Institute of Household Science and Arts, 195

Printer's Ink, 141, 147

Priscilla Proving Plant, 200

Private enterprises, home economists' relationship with, 3, 4

Private sphere/public sphere: and home economics, 1, 67, 142, 306 (n. 2); and home products, 8; and influence of home economists, 9, 14, 15; and women's education, 28–29; and feminist movement, 66, 293; and Frederick, 140; and business home economists, 141, 241; and utility companies, 221; and "gender containment," 243–44; and culture of domesticity, 258, 293, 296; and gendered division of labor, 301

Recommended daily allowances, and healthy diet, 246

Red Cross, 59

Refrigeration industry: and Bureau of Home Economics, 18, 115–16, 123–27, 129–33, 329 (n. 71), 330 (n. 77); and consumer education, 125, 126–27; and grading system, 131–32; standardization of, 131–32, 134; and product testing, 203; and sales and merchandising, 237

Research Foundation for the American Home, 251

Retail environments: home economists' influence on, 2, 5, 14, 18, 76, 79, 111, 134, 298; and business communication with consumers, 10, 24, 243; and home economists as mediators, 11; and home economics education, 41; and advertising, 41, 198; and World War I food conservation programs, 47; and home economists' research, 111; and standardization, 117, 118, 119, 121, 123, 166, 297; and business home economists, 136, 152, 177, 182, 193, 195, 201, 205, 209, 212, 213, 215, 217, 227, 243; and Frederick, 142; and business strategies, 183–84; and home economics departments, 193, 196–200, 206; and public goodwill, 199; and household appliances, 213; and luxury market, 216

Rex, Mrs. Harold B., 106–7

Reynolds, Lucile W., 127

Rich, Jean K., 149, 157

Richards, Ellen Swallow: and professional goals, 2–3, 26; and consumption, 21, 27; sanitary science, 23, 24–25, 28, 32, 33, 42; and surveys, 25–26, 32; and expert role, 26, 35; opposition to women's suffrage, 31; and food science, 41; and Stanley, 62; legacy of, 301

Richardson, Anna E., 70, 317 (n. 12)

Richardson, Anna Steese, 338 (n. 83)

Robson, Barbara Reid, 337 (n. 73)

Rochester Gas and Electric Corporation, 233–34, 261

Rogan, Ralph, 184, 185, 188

Rogers, Willie Mae, 260, 289

Roosevelt, Eleanor, 106

Roosevelt, Franklin D., 100, 105, 114, 246

Roosevelt, Theodore, 32

Rorer, Sarah Tyson, 178–79, 201

Rose, Flora, 31, 46, 53, 58, 240, 314 (n. 69)

Rose, Mark, 11, 212

Rose, Mary Swartz, 37, 53, 54, 55–56, 58, 90

Rossiter, Margaret, 252, 314 (n. 69)

Rowe, Bess, 143, 147–48

Royal Baking Powder Company, 145, 149, 157, 185, 186–87

Rumford Company, 179, 225

Rumford Kitchen exhibit, 25, 32

Rumsey, Mary Harriman, 115

Rural areas: drain of population from, 32; and demonstration work in home economics, 36, 59, 63; and land-grant colleges, 38; and World War I food conservation program, 48–49, 52, 57; and middle-class standards, 87; and standard of living, 89, 91, 99; and refrigeration, 127; and income, spending, and saving studies, 245; and household equipment, 249; and migration to urban areas, 252

Rural women: as consumers, 7, 24, 27, 66; and household products, 64; and women's clubs and organizations, 65; as farmers' wives and business partners, 66; and production/consumption relationship, 66, 88, 181; and Bureau of Home Economics, 66–67, 73, 74, 252; and home economics education, 71; and textiles and clothing, 104

Rush, Anna Fisher, 289

Russell, James Earl, 34, 37

Rutherford, Janice, 333 (nn. 6, 8)

Rutledge, R. Leone, 337 (n. 73)

Sabin, Mary, 40

St. Marie, Satenig, 268

Sales and marketing campaigns: and business communication with consumers, 10, 180, 190, 272–73; and business home economists, 176–77, 236–40, 257, 265, 266, 271, 272–74; and consumer education, 182; and utility companies, 211, 212, 221–23, 236–40, 254; and demonstrations, 214–17, 223; and household appliances, 214–18, 237; and World War II, 253, 254; and marketing specialty, 272–75; and consumer culture, 300

Sales Management, 274

provement in, 87, 102; and rural areas, 89, 91, 99; home economists' research on, 89, 91, 102

Stanley, Louise: leadership of Bureau of Home Economics, 4–5, 17, 31, 62–64, 70, 71, 73–78, 79, 84, 96–97, 103, 133–34, 248–49, 297, 298; and standards, 86, 101–2, 114, 115–16, 297, 298, 299; and production/consumption relationship, 92; household equipment studies, 95; and consumer behavior, 99; and consumer education, 108–9, 110; and consumer needs, 111; and Consumer Advisory Board, 115; and refrigeration industry, 123, 124–27, 129–32; and Frederick, 139; and food science, 247, 295; and Ball, 317 (n. 12)

Stark, Elsie, 145, 260

Stewart, Martha, 299

Stiebeling, Hazel K., 90, 91, 108–9, 246, 248–49, 251

Stock market crash of 1929, 105, 238

Stone, Ursula, 90

Stove Founders' Association, 340 (n. 15)

Strain, Robert W., 279

Strasser, Susan, 332 (n. 6)

Susman, Warren, 142

Swann, Ada Bessie, 208, 211, 219, 220, 222, 224, 237, 239, 271

Swans Down Cake Flour, 186, 254, 262

Sweeney, Mary, 70, 147

Swiencicki, Mark, 8

Swift and Company, 150, 185, 260, 271, 275, 277, 340 (n. 15)

Systems theory, 243, 272

Table Talk (magazine), 179, 201

Talbot, Marion, 30, 31, 32, 37, 41

Tampa Electric Company, 223

Taylor, Alonzo, 90

Teachers College at Columbia University, 34, 36–37

Technical education, and home economists, 5

Technological change: role of home economists in, 5, 6–7, 26; and consumer society, 7, 308 (n. 26); and home economists as mediators, 11–12, 14, 19, 218, 232, 241, 296, 297; consumers' adapta-

tion to, 16, 24, 26, 35, 111; social impact of, 25–26, 33; and consumer decisions, 64; and home economists' research, 84, 88; and refrigeration, 124–27, 132; and utility companies, 212, 214, 216, 218, 229; and Cold War, 243; and expert role, 299

Tennessee Valley Authority, 132, 220

Terhune, Mary Virginia Hawes, 179

Terrill, Bertha, 40

Tetedoux, Corinne, 184–85, 189

Textile Fiber Products Identification Act (1960), 118, 261

Textiles and clothing: home economists' research on, 18, 65, 68, 75, 76, 77, 81, 82–84, 86, 93–94, 96, 97, 103, 244, 249, 250, 251–52; and rational consumption, 21, 22–23, 42–43, 83, 101; and instruction of working-class women, 21–22; quality of, 30, 297; and higher education, 37, 39, 42–43; standardization of, 76, 86, 113–14, 115, 116–21, 123, 134, 197; home laundering and stain removal, 86, 103, 104, 105, 107, 192, 231, 260; and production/consumption relationship, 92, 93–94, 104; and consumer education, 104–5, 107, 199; and home economists representing consumers, 112, 134–35; sizes of, 118–19; children's, 120–21, 123; and business home economists, 147, 148, 159, 193, 209, 260–62, 265; and home economics departments, 177; and product testing, 195–98; and World War II, 245; and product innovations, 257

Thompson, Helen B., 70, 317 (n. 12)

Thompson, J. Walter, 184

Thorson, Valentine, 239

Thrift Leaflets, 65

Thye, Lenore Sater, 249, 252

Timely Topics, 162, 164

Tomes, Nancy, 42

Trotter, Virginia, 291

True, Alfred C., 26

Twentieth Century Club, 28

Union Gas Company, 254

United Fruit Company, 154, 256

United Nations, 246

U.S. Department of Agriculture (USDA): and modernization, 3, 7, 31–32, 52, 63, 65, 101,

252; and home economists' knowledge of consumers, 4; promotion of agricultural production, 16; and management of overproduction, 19; and World War I food conservation program, 53; and home economists' research, 64–65, 93, 253, 284, 287; Bureau of Agricultural Economics, 66, 89, 92, 249, 317 (n. 11); and agricultural depression, 92; Bureau of Animal Industry, 92, 317 (n. 11); and standard of living in rural areas, 99; quality grades of, 105, 116–17; information on brand-name goods, 108–9, 116; and standardization, 119; Bureau of Chemistry, 125, 317 (n. 11); home economists employed by, 151, 252; expansion of, 244–48; Bureau of Agricultural Chemistry and Engineering, Division of Protein and Nutrition Research, 247; changes in, 248–53, 280, 298; school lunch program of, 249; budget cuts to, 249–53; political priorities of, 298; Bureau of Biological Survey, 317 (n. 11); Bureau of Entomology, 317 (n. 11); Bureau of Plant Industry, 317 (n. 11); Bureau of Public Roads, 317 (n. 11); Bureau of Soils, 317 (n. 11). *See also* Agricultural extension service; Bureau of Home Economics; Bureau of Human Nutrition and Home Economics; U.S. Department of Interior

U.S. Department of Commerce, 116–17

U.S. Department of Interior: Office of Education, 36, 78, 246; Bureau of Education, 53

U.S. Department of Labor, 66, 67; Bureau of Labor Statistics (BLS), 91, 245

U.S. Extension Service, 146

U.S. Food Administration (USFA): food conservation campaigns, 4, 17, 22, 23, 46–60, 62, 176; home economists working with, 50–60; Advisory Committee on Nutrition, 51, 53; Advisory Committee on Home Economics, 51, 59, 315 (n. 75); and reform, 52

U.S. Laboratory of Food Inspection, 196

U.S. Public Health Service, 124, 246

U.S. Supreme Court, 115

U.S. Treasury Department, Division of Savings, 56

University of Chicago, 5, 36–37

Urban areas: critiques of, 26; and school curricula, 34; and standard of living, 89; and refrigeration, 127, 133; and business home economists, 152; and utility companies, 212; and household appliances, 213; and income, spending, and saving studies, 245; migration to, 252

Urban working poor, living conditions of, 87

Utility companies: home economists' employment with, 5, 11, 15, 16, 136, 280; public relations campaigns of, 5, 19, 209, 214, 216, 218, 219, 221, 224, 228–29, 237, 240, 241; home service departments of, 13, 194, 208, 209, 211–13, 218, 219, 220–31, 232, 236–40, 254–55, 258, 260, 262, 269, 346 (n. 2); and home economists as mediators, 18–19, 297, 298; and modern plumbing, 24; and household appliances, 24, 44, 210, 211, 214–17; and refrigeration, 124, 125, 126, 133; and business home economists, 150, 152, 154, 157, 160–61, 194, 208, 209, 212, 215, 218–26, 236, 260, 262, 346 (n. 2); home economics departments of, 208, 211, 213–14, 243; and consumer education, 208, 212, 221, 223, 225–28, 240, 241, 254–55; and balancing energy load through domestic consumption, 209; and sales and marketing campaigns, 211, 212, 221–23, 236–40, 254; and demonstrations, 214–17, 223, 225–30, 254–55, 258; and cooking classes, 225–26, 228–30, 231; and recipes and cookbooks, 228, 239; and utilitarian and aesthetic dimensions of household appliances, 229–36; and home lighting, 233–36, 241

Van Deman, Ruth, 108

Van Rensselaer, Martha, 31, 32, 34, 42, 46, 53, 121, 150, 314 (n. 69)

Veblen, Thorstein, 29, 35, 41

Vitamins, 54–55, 75, 82, 85, 230, 246, 255, 271

Vocational education, 34, 35, 36, 71, 73, 139

Vulte, Hermann, 37

Waldo, Richard H., 201

Wallace, Henry C., 62, 63, 65–66, 67, 69, 73, 109

living, 89; and Children's Bureau, 99; and utility companies, 227

Working-class women: and work skills, 21–22; and middle-class women's power as consumers, 30; and utility companies, 225; home economists' relationship with, 284

Works Progress Administration (WPA), 91, 119, 339 (n. 5)

World War I: and food conservation, 4, 5, 8, 17, 22, 23, 46–60, 62, 65, 102, 103, 176, 179, 242; and expert role, 13; and rational consumption, 17, 46, 55–60; and home economists as textile specialists, 22

World War II: and home economists' role in home front, 5, 19, 242–46; and rationing, 242–43, 244, 245, 254; and business home economists, 253–54, 257

Wright, Gwendolyn, 324 (n. 14)

W. W. Gossard Company, 207

Yeatman, Fanny Walker, 106, 112

Zapoleon, Marguerite, 266

Zillessen, Clara, 217

Zuill, Frances, 167, 168

Zunz, Olivier, 11